"This is a very welcome collection of studies that in part sketches Dennis Duling's intellectual journey. Significantly, it makes an important contribution to Matthean studies in general and social-science approaches to Matthew in particular. Dennis Duling's work is always engaging, always stimulating, and always insightful."

—WARREN CARTER
author of *Matthew: Storyteller, Interpreter, and Evangelist*

"This is a wonderful resource not only on a variety of aspects of the Gospel of Matthew in social-science perspective, but also on the development of a scholar who has focused his attention over the years on the world behind and inside of the first Gospel."

—CAROLYN OSIEK
coauthor of *A Woman's Place*

"Dennis Duling's *A Marginal Scribe* is to date the most thorough, methodologically consistent, and nuanced application of social-science models to the Gospel of Matthew. Engaging the best of scholarship on Matthew and a breathtaking range of social-science theory, Duling demonstrates the heuristic value of carefully constructed models: such models as 'the marginal man' and 'limited egalitarianism' allow the reader to see Matthew in a new light. *A Marginal Scribe* is not only a serious work of Matthaean scholarship but a model of how to think within explicitly designed social-science frames."

—JOHN S. KLOPPENBORG
author of *Excavating Q*

"This important book draws together and integrates Dennis Duling's impressive work over twenty years, fruitfully combining social-scientific and traditional approaches to Matthew and the Matthaean community. Duling investigates Matthew's social world and meaning by such means as small-group theory, marginality theory, and scholarship on ancient scribalism. Matthew is thereby firmly anchored within the structures of an advanced agrarian empire. Future work simply cannot ignore this book."

—DOUGLAS E. OAKMAN
coauthor of *Palestine in the Time of Jesus*

"This is a learned and sage account by a knowledgable veteran of a vast range of groundbreaking exegetical research over the past several decades. Partly an instructive overview of social-scientific criticism, its inception and method, and partly a clear description of various heuristic models useful to exegetical analysis, this work in its entirety delivers a fresh illumination of the Gospel of Matthew at every turn. Duling deftly shows how tested social scientific models clarify the meaning and social import of key or controverted Matthean passages. The volume is a 'must-read' for both biblical hermeneutes in general and Matthean scholars in particular. For students and scholars alike, it constitutes a solid point of departure for reflection on method, models, matrices, Matthew, and marginals."

—JOHN H. ELLIOTT
author of *Conflict, Community, and Honor*

"Dennis C. Duling is without peer in the application of social-scientific methods to the Gospel of Matthew. In this volume, comprising updated previous studies and new material, he shares the fruits of his work over the past two decades. Duling's mastery of his subject is evident throughout as he sheds much needed light on the Gospel text, the evangelist and his readers, and the first-century Mediterranean world in which they lived."

—DAVID C. SIM
editor of *Matthew and His Christian Contemporaries*

"Duling employs social-scientific models, the most prominent being Gerhard Lenski's macrosocial model of social stratification, to cast light on a number of Matthean passages related to the author's community, its factions, its ethnicity, and its leadership. The result is a rich, fruitful, seasoned, refined body of research that enables us to see better the writing's author and his community. To this end, Duling especially and carefully defines marginality theory and applies it to various passages leading his readers to a reasonable conclusion: 'Matthew' was a marginal scribe. This book adds significantly not only to the scholarly literature on Matthew but also to the usefulness of thoughtful social-scientific inquiry."

—STUART L. LOVE
author of *Jesus and Marginal Women*

"Duling's *A Marginal Scribe* is a tightly integrated collection of essays using social-scientific perspectives of major importance for the study of Matthew's Gospel. Working with a profound grasp of the history and nature of social-scientific interpretation, and exemplary in the courtesy he affords other scholars, Duling offers penetrating understandings of important dimensions of Matthew that have already impacted heavily on Matthean scholarship and will continue to do so for many years to come."

—PHILIP F. ESLER
author of *Sex, Wives, and Warriors*

A Marginal Scribe

MATRIX
The Bible in Mediterranean Context

EDITORIAL BOARD

John H. Elliott   John S. Kloppenborg
Anselm Hagedorn   Douglas E. Oakman
K. C. Hanson   Gary Stansell

•

PREVIOUSLY PUBLISHED VOLUMES

Richard L. Rohrbaugh
The New Testament and Social-Science Criticism

Markus Cromhout
Jesus and Identity

Pieter F. Craffert
The Life of a Galilean Shaman

Douglas E. Oakman
Jesus and the Peasants

Stuart L. Love
Jesus and the Marginal Women

Eric C. Stewart
Gathered around Jesus

A Marginal Scribe

*Studies of the Gospel of Matthew in
Social-Scientific Perspective*

DENNIS C. DULING

CASCADE Books • Eugene, Oregon

A MARGINAL SCRIBE
Studies of the Gospel of Matthew in Social-Scientific Perspective

Matrix: The Bible in Its Mediterranean Context 7

Copyright © 2012 Dennis C. Duling. All rights reserved. Except for brief quotations in critical publications or reviews, no part of this book may be reproduced in any manner without prior written permission from the publisher. Write: Permissions, Wipf and Stock Publishers, 199 W. 8th Ave., Suite 3, Eugene, OR 97401.

Cascade Books
An Imprint of Wipf and Stock Publishers
199 W. 8th Ave., Suite 3
Eugene, OR 97401

www.wipfandstock.com

ISBN 13: 978-1-60608-085-6

Cataloging-in-Publication data:

Duling, Dennis C.

    A marginal scribe : studies of the gospel of Matthew in social-scientific perspective / Dennis C. Duling.

    Matrix: The Bible in Its Mediterranean Context 7

    xxii + 386 p.; 23 cm. Includes bibliographical references and index.

    ISBN 13: 978-1-60608-085-6

    1. Bible. N.T. Gospel of Matthew—Social-scientific criticism. 2. Bible. N.T. Gospel of Matthew—Criticism, interpretation, etc. I. Title. II. Series

BS2575.2 D79 2012

Manufactured in the U.S.A.

To Clio Alice

and

the Context Group

"[T]here is virtually nothing that cannot be conceptualized and analyzed by non-mathematical models—religion and ideology, economic institutions and ideas, the state and politics, simple descriptions and development sequences. The familiar fear of a priorism is misplaced: any hypothesis can be modified, adjusted or discarded when necessary. Without one, however, there can be no explanation; there can be only reportage and crude taxonomy, antiquarianism in its narrowest sense."

—Moses Finley, *Ancient History*, 66

Contents

List of Figures | *ix*
Acknowledgments | *xi*
List of Abbreviations | *xv*
Introduction | 1

1 The Emergence of Social-Scientific Criticism in New Testament Study | 8
2 The Gospel of Matthew and Social-Scientific Criticism | 36
3 The Gospel of Matthew and Social-Scientific Models | 62
4 Matthew's Plurisignificant "Son of David" in Social-Scientific Perspective: Kinship, Kingship, Magic, and Miracle | 91
5 Matthew and Marginality | 120
6 "Egalitarian" Ideology, Leadership, and Factional Conflict in the Gospel of Matthew | 145
7 The Matthean Brotherhood and Marginal Scribal Leadership | 179
8 Matthew 18:15–17: Conflict, Confrontation, and Conflict Resolution in a "Fictive" Kin Association | 212
9 Matthew as a Marginal Scribe in an Advanced Agrarian Society | 245
10 Ethnicity, Ethnocentrism, and the Matthean *Ethnos* | 288
11 A Marginal Scribe: Putting It All Together | 329

Permissions | 339
Bibliography | 341

Figures

Chart 1.1: Outline of Bryan Wilson's Seven Sect Subtypes | 26

Table 2.1: Labeling in Jesus' Trial (Matthew) | 42

Chart 3.1: A Simplified Macroscopic-Microscopic Continuum (Ritzer) | 66

Model 3.1: The Dynamics of Distribution Systems (Lenski) | 68

Model 3.2: An Advanced Agrarian Society (Lenski) | 70

Model 3.3: The Roman Orders: Strata Structure and Its Effects (Alföldy) | 72

Model 3.4: The Preindustrial City (Sjøberg; Rohrbaugh) | 77

Model 3.5: The Core/Periphery Structure of Empire (Motyl) | 79

Model 3.6: Societies Representing the Three Phases of History (Kautsky) | 82

Chart 4.1: Son of David and Related References | 94

Model 4.1: Social Stratification in First-Century Palestinian Society | 97

Chart 4.2: Social Stratification of Persons and Groups in the Gospel of Matthew | 98

Model 4.2: Primary and Secondary Groups | 105

Chart 4.3: Son of David, Compassion, Mercy, and Healing | 109

Model 4.3: Challenge and Response in an Agonistic Honor/Shame Society | 114

Chart 4.4: Challenge and Response in the Temple | 115

Outline 5.1: Lower Social Strata in the Gospel of Matthew | 132–33

Model 5.1: Task Allocation Models: Hierarchical vs. Non-hierarchical Groups (Herbst) | 137

Chart 5.1: Groups (Turner Compared with Herbst) | 138
Chart 6.1: Clustered Status Designations in the New Testament | 158
Model 6.1: Leader Emergence (Aubrey and Ellis) | 172
Model 6.2: Task Allocation Models (= Model 5.1) | 175
Model 6.3: A Grid/Group Model (Douglas and Malina) | 176
Chart 7.1: Matthew 28:5, 7+8 and Matthew 28:10+16 | 197
Chart 7.2: Matthew 8:18–22 and Luke 9:57–60 | 200
Chart 7.3: Scribes Contrasted with Peasants and Artisans in Ben Sira | 206
Chart 8.1: Matthew 18:15–22 and Its Lukan Parallels | 213
Chart 9.1: A Fictional Distributive System for the Roman Empire | 248
Model 9.1: The Overlap between Vertical and Marginal Ranking | 250
Chart 9.2: Duling and Billson Marginality Categories Compared | 251
Model 9.2: A Venn Diagram of Culturally Marginal Persons and Groups | 254
Model 9.3: Marginality and Four Degrees of Acculturation (Berry) | 256
Model 9.4: Degree of Cultural and Psychological Change as a Function of Phases and Varieties of Acculturation (Berry) | 257
Model 9.5: Four "Directions" of Marginality (Weisberger) | 259
Chart 9.3: Economic and Religious Grids for Ranking Ancient Judeans (Cohen) | 261
Outline 9.1: Twenty-Two References to *Grammateus* Categorized | 272
Table 9.1: Marginal Status and Marginality Consciousness (Germani) | 286
Model 9.6: Menches' Network: Lines of Correspondence between Menches, the Village Scribe, and His Superiors and Subordinates (Verhoogt) | 287
Model 10.1: A Socio-Cultural Model of Ethnicity (Duling) | 295

Acknowledgments

A BOOK BASED ON ARTICLES written over a period of over two decades is indebted to many people. Unfortunately, I must be selective. Those most responsible for laying critical foundations were J. Arthur Baird of the College of Wooster, Floyd V. Filson of McCormick Theological Seminary, and Norman Perrin, my graduate professor at the University of Chicago Divinity School. The latter two institutions supported me heavily with grants and fellowships, as did Canisius College, Buffalo, New York, and for these I am deeply grateful. Moreover, Canisius has always given me research and technological services (my thanks to the library and Estelle Siener!). In the period these chapters were first written as articles I benefited from conversations with colleagues in the Religious Studies and Theology Department at Canisius. I note particularly Benjamin Fiore, S.J., now President of Campion College, University of Regina, Saskatchewan, Canada; Paula McNutt, now New Senior Vice-President for Academic Affairs and Dean at Carroll College in Helena, Montana; Trevor Watt, emeritus; Timothy Wadkins; Christopher Lee; and recently, Rebecca Krawiec and Jonathan Lawrence.

A very special thanks goes to the National Endowment for the Humanities. My interest in the social sciences as interpretative tools emerged in a Summer Seminar under the direction of Wayne Meeks at Yale University in 1979, continued in a NEH Summer Seminar on Josephus with Louis Feldman at Yeshiva University in 1983, and developed during a 1984-1985 NEH Fellowship culminating in a visit to the Middle East and Greece and a semester's research at Heidelberg University where I was privileged to have weekly conversations with Gerd Theissen.

I am indebted to many colleagues in professional societies, especially the Society of Biblical Literature. I note Matthew scholars Jack Dean Kingsbury, John Kampen, Elaine Wainwright, Andries van Aarde, Andrew Overman, Anthony Saldarini (whose premature death was a great loss to us all), and Warren Carter, who encouraged my work on marginality. Scholars in the Matthew Section responded to some of the early versions of chapters in this book. Very influential in my thinking was the SBL Social-Scientific Criticism of the New Testament Section, initially chaired by Bruce Malina and John Pilch, then by Douglas Oakman and Philip Esler (who shared that job with me), and lastly by Dietmar Neufeld and Richard DeMaris. Also, from 1993–2004 I participated in the Catholic Biblical Association's Task Force on the Social Sciences and Biblical Interpretation convened by Bruce Malina. I owe a word of appreciation to the Eastern Great Lakes Biblical Society, which provided a continual context for colleagues to make constructive criticism. It was in this context that David Fiensy first introduced me to Gerhard Lenski's model of social stratification. I thank two members of the *Studiorum Novi Testamenti Societas*: David Sim, who invited me to present my work to the Matthew Seminar at Montreal, Canada; and Vernon Robbins, who did the same at the Socio-Rhetorical section of *SNTS* when it met in Bonn, Germany.

In 1986 Robert Funk invited me to join the Jesus Seminar where I got to know scholars (some already mentioned) in a satellite group, "Social Facets," which eventually became the Context Group in 1989. In the early days this group included John Elliott (chair), Bruce Malina, John Pilch, Richard Rohrbaugh, Jerome Neyrey, Paul Hollenbach, Vernon Robbins, Josephine M. Ford, Carolyn Osiek, Douglas Oakman, and myself. We were very soon joined by K. C. Hanson, Philip Esler, Gary Stansell, David Bossman, Scott Bartchy, Halvor Moxnes, Stuart Love, Wolfgang Stegemann, Andries van Aarde, Mauro Pesce, Eugene Botha, David Rhoads, Dietmar Neufeld, Richard DeMaris, Mark McVann, and John Kloppenborg, its current chair, and eventually also by Santiago Guijarro, Ernest van Eck, Steven Muir, Ritva Williams, Zeba Crooke, Alicia Batten, and Giovanni Battista Bazzana. The Context Group has attracted younger scholars, including Eric Stuart, Jason Lamoreaux, Marcus Kromhaut, and Coleman Baker. Other scholars have joined in from time to time, including David Aune, Marcus

Acknowledgments

Borg, Kathleen Corley, William Herzog, Raymond Hobbs, Chris Seeman, Christian Strecker, Johan Strijdom, Edward Wilson, Jonathan Draper, and Lucretia Yaghjian. (My apologies if I missed anyone). It is absolutely amazing that most members of the Context Group have been together some twenty-five years. I marvel that in that time span they have heard and commented on every chapter in this book but chapter 3 (their influence is there, also) and the Conclusion. A hearty thanks! I am immeasurably indebted to three scholars active in the above societies, John Elliott, Douglas Oakman, and Stuart Love, who read and offered detailed criticisms and comments on the penultimate version of this book. They are colleague-friends without measure. I am also deeply indebted to the sharp, professional eyes of Wipf and Stock typographer Kristen Bareman and copy editor Jacob Martin. Of course, I alone am responsible for its form and content.

This book is dedicated, first, to my beautiful granddaughter, Clio Alice Granville, who came along too late to be a dedicatee in my previous publications, and, second, to my colleagues in the Context Group, some of whose names appear above. I shall say more about some of them in chapters 1 and 2.

Finally, as always, I owe everything to the love of my life for over fifty years, Gretchen (Smith) Duling, whose qualities of affectionate love, inner and outer beauty, infinite patience, and robust humor are my great pleasures, whose leadership skills and devotion to community are truly amazing, and whose scholarship, initiative, and perseverance are a continual source of inspiration.

Abbreviations

Ancient Texts

1QM	War Scroll (DSS)
1QS	Community Rule (DSS)
2 Clem	2 Clement
4QMMT	Miqtzât Maasëh ha-Torâh
4QpPs^a	Qumran *pesher* on the Psalms
1QpHab	Qumran *pesher* on Habakkuk
Aer.	Hippocrates, *De aera, aquis, locis*
Ant.	Josephus, *Antiquitates Judaicae* (*Antiquities of the Judeans*)
'Arak	'Arakin
b.	Babylonian Talmud (*Babli*)
B	Vaticanus, Biblical manuscript in the Vatican
Bek.	Bekorot
BJ	Josephus, *Bellum Judaicum* (*Judean War*)
Mo'ed	Mo'ed Qaṭan
CII (CIJ)	*Corpus Inscriptionum Iudaicarum* (Frey, ed., 1936–1952)
CD	Damascus Document (Cairo Geniza); fragments found at Qumran (DSS)
Decal.	Philo, *Decalogue*
De. Inv.	Cicero, *De Inventione*
Demai	Demai
Did.	Didachē
Diog. L.	Diogenes Laertius, *The Lives and Opinions of Eminent Philosophers*
Diss.	Epictetus, *Discourses*
DSS	Dead Sea Scrolls
Ad. Haer.	Epiphanius, *Adversus Haereses* (*Against Heresies*)

Geogr.	Strabo, *Geographica*
Gorg.	Plato, *Gorgias*
Gosp. Eb.	Gospel of the Ebionites
Gosp. Thom.	Gospel of Thomas (NHC)
Hec. Ab.	Hecataeus of Abdera
Hdt.	Herodotus, *Histories*
Inst. Ora.	Quintilian, *Institutio Oratoria*
LXX	Septuagint
m.	Mishnah
Mak.	Makkoth
NHC	Nag Hammadi Corpus
Phae.	Plato, *Phaedrus*
NH	Pliny, *Naturalis historia*
Physio.	Pseudo-Aristotle, *Physiognomics*
P.Oxy	Oxyrhynchus Papyri
Prog.	Theon, *Progymnasmata* (2, n. 61)
Rhet. Her.	*Rhetorica ad Herennium*
Rhet.	Aristotle, *Rhetoric*
Q	A reconstructed Synoptic Gospel source (German *Quelle*, "source")
Resp.	Plato, *Respublica* (*Republic*)
S	Sinaiticus, Biblical manuscript discovered at Mt. Sinai
Sif.	*Sifra*, a Midrashic commentary on Leviticus
Sir	Ben Sira or Sirach or Ecclesiasticus
Soph.	Plato, *Sophist*
Special M	A reconstructed Synoptic Gospel source unique to the Gospel of Matthew
t.	Tosefta
T 12 Patr.	Testaments of the Twelve Patriarchs
Theaet.	Plato, *Theaetetus*
TPsJ	Targum Pseudo-Jonathan
y.	Jerusalem Talmud (*Yerushalmi*)
Yoma	Yoma

Periodicals, Serials

AA	*American Anthropologist*
ABR	*Australian Biblical Review*

Abbreviations xvii

AFJC	*Anales de la Funcación Joaquin Costa*
AE	*American Ethnologist*
AES	*Archives Européennes de Sociologie*
AHR	*The American Historical Review*
AJS	*American Journal of Sociology*
AnBib	*Analecta Biblica*
AppPsych	*Applied Psychology: An International Review*
ARA	*Annual Review of Anthropology*
ARS	*Annual Review of Sociology*
ASR	*American Sociological Review*
BA	*Biblical Archaeologist*
BAT	*Biblical Archaeology Today. Proceedings of the International Congress on Archaeology*
Bib	*Biblica*
BibInt	*Biblical Interpretation*
BJRL	*Bulletin of the John Rylands University Library of Manchester*
BJSoc	*British Journal of Sociology*
BMCR	*Bryn Mawr Classical Review*
BR	*Biblical Research*
BJS	*Brown Judaic Studies*
BSac	*Bibliotheca Sacra*
BTB	*Biblical Theology Bulletin*
BTF	*Bangalore Theological Forum*
BZ	*Biblische Zeitschrift*
CA	*Current Anthropology*
CBQ	*Catholic Biblical Quarterly*
CBR	*Currents in Biblical Research*
ChrCent	*Christian Century*
CI	*Critical Inquiry*
CommViat	*Communio Viatorum*
Conc	*Concilium*
CR	*The Classical Review*
CSSH	*Comparative Studies in Society and History*
CurBS	*Currents in Research: Biblical Studies*
EDCC	*Economic Development and Cultural Change*
EGLBSP	*Eastern Great Lakes Biblical Society Proceedings*

EGLMBSP	Eastern Great Lakes and Midwest Biblical Society Proceedings
Eirene	Eirene
ERS	Ethnic and Racial Studies
Exp	The Expositor
FJT	Finnish Journal of Theology (Teologinen Aikakauskirja, Teologisk Tidskrift)
Forum	Forum
GOS	Group and Organizational Studies
GU	Guardian Unlimited
HAR	Hebrew Annual Review
Hist	Historia
HistAnth	History and Anthropology
HistTh	History and Theory
HR	History of Religions
HTR	Harvard Theological Review
HTS	Hervormde Teologiese Studies
HUCA	Hebrew Union College Annual
HumRelat	Human Relations
Hyst	Hystos
IESS	International Encyclopedia of the Social Sciences
Int	Interpretation
IRMS	International Review of Modern Sociology
ISBE	International Standard Bible Encyclopedia
Iss	Issues
JAAR	Journal of the American Academy of Religion
JBL	Journal of Biblical Literature
JCCP	Journal of Cross-Cultural Psychology
JCR	Journal of Conflict Resolution
JECS	Journal of Early Christian Studies
JPR	Journal of Peace Research
JQR	Jewish Quarterly Review
JR	Journal of Religion
JRH	Journal of Religious History
JRS	Journal of Religious Studies
JSHJ	Journal for the Study of the Historical Jesus
JSJ	Journal for the Study of Judaism in the Persian, Hellenistic, and Roman Periods

JSNT	Journal for the Study of the New Testament
JSNTSup	Journal for the Study of the New Testament Supplements
JSP	Journal for the Study of the Pseudepigrapha
JSSR	Journal for the Scientific Study of Religion
JTS	Journal of Theological Studies
Kairos	Kairos
List	Listening. Journal of Religion and Culture
Miss	Missiology
Narr	Narrative
NovT	Novum Testamentum
NovTSup	Novum Testamentum Supplements
NTS	New Testament Studies
PASS	Publication of the American Sociological Society
PRS	Perspectives in Religious Studies
PsyBull	Psychological Bulletin
Relig	Religion
RestQ	Restoration Quarterly
RevQ	Revue de Qumran
RHPR	Revue d'Histoire et de Philosophie Religieuses
RSR	Religious Studies Review
SC	Scrittura e civiltà
SE	Studia Evangelica
SEÅ	Svensk exegetisk årsbok
Semeia	Semeia
SJT	Scottish Journal of Theology
SNTSU	Studien zum Neuen Testament und Seiner Umwelt
SocForces	Social Forces
SociolAn	Sociological Analysis
SociolForum	Sociological Forum
SociolPers	Sociological Perspectives
SociolRelig	Sociology of Religion
SociolTheor	Sociological Theory
SP	Sacra Pagina
SSH	Social Science History
Theol	Theology
TheorSoc	Theory and Society
TLZ	Theologische Literatur Zeitung

TS	*Theological Studies*
ThTo	*Theology Today*
TU	*Texte und Unterzuchungen*
TynBul	*Tyndale Bulletin*
TZT	*Tübinger Zeitschrift für Theologie*
VE	*Vox Evangelica*
ZNW	*Zeitschrift für die Neutestamentliche Wissenschaft und die Kunde der Alteren Kirche*

Reference Works

ABD	*The Anchor Bible Dictionary*. 6 vols. Edited by David Noel Freedman. New York: Doubleday, 1992
ANRW	*Aufstieg und Niedergang der römischen Welt: Geschichte und Kultur Roms im Spiegel der neueren Forschung*. Edited by Hildegard Temporini and Wolfgang Haase. List of volumes and those in preparation online: http://www.bu.edu/ict/anrw/pub/index.html. Berlin: de Gruyter, 1972–
BDAG	Walter Bauer, Frederick W. Danker, W. F. Arndt, and F. W. Gingrich. *Greek-English Lexicon of the New Testament and Other Early Christian Literature*. 3rd ed. Chicago: University of Chicago Press, 2000
CDB	John J. Pilch. *The Cultural Dictionary of the Bible*. Collegeville, MN: Liturgical, 1999
CII	*Corpus Inscriptionum Iudaicarum*. Edited by J. B. Frey. 2 vols. Rome and Paris. Vol. 1 republished as *Corpus of Jewish Inscriptions: Jewish Inscriptions from the Third Century B.C. to the Seventh Century A.D*. New York: Ktav, 1936
DSS	*Dictionary of the Social Sciences*. Edited by J. Gould and W. L. Kolb. New York: Free Press, 1964
ECA	*Encyclopedia of Cultural Anthropology*. Edited by David Levinson and Melvin Ember. Sponsored by Human Relations file at Yale University. 4 vols. New York: Holt, 1996
HSP	*The Handbook of Social Psychology*. 2nd ed. Edited by Gardner Lindzey and Elliott Aronson. Oxford: Addison-Wesley, 1968

Abbreviations

IDB	*The Interpreter's Dictionary of the Bible.* 4 vols. Edited by George Arthur Buttrick. Nashville; Abingdon, 1962
IBDSup	*The Interpreter's Dictionary of the Bible Supplement.* Edited by Keith Crim. Nashville: Abingdon, 1976
LSJ	Henry George Liddell, Robert Scott, and Henry Stuart Jones. *A Greek-English Lexicon.* 9th ed. Oxford: Clarendon, 1996
OTP	*The Old Testament Pseudepigrapha.* Edited by James H. Charlesworth. 2 vols. Garden City, NY: Doubleday, 1983
PW	*Paulys Realencyclopädie der classischen Altertumswissenschaft: neue Bearbeitung.* Edited by August Pauly, Georg Wissowa, Wilhelm Kroll, Kurt Witte, Karl Mittelhaus, Konrat Ziegler. 18 vols. Stuttgart: Metzler, 1894–1980
SSNTI	*The Social Sciences and New Testament Interpretation.* Edited by Richard L. Rohrbaugh. Peabody, MA: Hendrickson, 1996
TDNT	*Theological Dictionary of the New Testament.* Edited by Gerhard Kittel and Gerhard Friedrich. Translated by Geoffrey W. Bromiley. 10 vols. Grand Rapids: Eerdmans, 1964–76

Miscellaneous

AAR	American Academy of Religion
BASTARDS	Bay Area Seminar for Theology and Related Disciplines
CBA	Catholic Biblical Association
EGLBS	Eastern Great Lakes Biblical Society
LCL	Loeb Classical Library
NRSV	New Revised Standard Version
RSV	Revised Standard Version
SBL	Society of Biblical Literature
SNTS	*Studiorum Novi Testamenti Societas*
SSCNT	Social-Scientific Criticism of the New Testament Section, SBL

Introduction

THE STUDIES IN THIS book were written over many years. In a period when New Testament Christology was very popular and tended to focus on New Testament titles of honor, some of these studies grew out of a 1970 dissertation on the Son of David title in the Hebrew Bible, the literature of the Second Temple, some rabbinic and pseudepigraphical texts, and the New Testament. In 1972 I presented the results of the dissertation at a general session of the *Studiorum Novi Testamenti Societas* at Claremont, California, and summarized them in an article in *New Testament Studies*.[1] It was a natural move to shift research to Son of David redaction in the Gospel of Matthew,[2] and then to related magical traditions about Solomon, David's literal son.[3] The methods of this early Davidic and Solomonic research were historical, tradition-historical, and redaction critical, not social-scientific. In my book *Jesus Christ Through History*,[4] however, I wrote a chapter on the Chicago School highlighting Shailer Mathews, well known for his social context studies in the history of New Testament study. This chapter piqued my old interest in the social context of the Christ Movements generated in my graduate school days at the University of Chicago Divinity School where Mathews had taught, and led me to apply for and receive a National Endowment for the Humanities (NEH) Summer Seminar in 1979 on "The Social World of Early Christianity" led by Wayne Meeks at Yale University. There I rethought the whole Davidic/Solomonic complex through the lenses of sociology and anthropology.[5]

1. Duling, "The Promises to David."
2. Duling, "The Therapeutic Son of David."
3. Duling, "Solomon, Exorcism, and the Son of David."
4. Duling, *Jesus Christ Through History*, 211–17.
5. Duling, "Behold?" (unpublished).

The same year while teaching at Canisius College I became active in the Eastern Great Lakes Biblical Society, a regional section of the Society of Biblical Literature, the Catholic Biblical Association, and the American Schools of Oriental Research. In that society I gave a paper on Solomon the following year.[6] The work on the Solomonic material continued with writing the Introduction and Commentary on *The Testament of Solomon* for *The Old Testament Pseudepigrapha* edited by James H. Charlesworth in 1983.[7] In that year I was fortunate to join a second NEH Summer Seminar, this one led by Louis Feldman at Yeshiva University. This led to a Seminar paper on the redaction of Solomon legends in Josephus' writings, which was presented at the Society of Biblical Literature and then published.[8] The following year my Eastern Great Lakes Biblical Society Presidential Address focused on Solomonic traditions.[9] My last studies of the Solomon legend were articles that summarized modern *Testament of Solomon* research.[10]

Having whetted my appetite for social contexts and the social-scientific dimensions of ancient magic in the Meeks seminar, I applied for and received a NEH Fellowship to study social history with Gerd Theissen at the University of Heidelberg, Germany, in 1984–1985. In Heidelberg's Theologisches Seminar I presented my first paper that combined redaction criticism on Matthew with the social sciences.[11] In revised form I presented it again at the Society of Biblical Literature in 1985, my respondent being Bruce Malina.[12] When Robert Funk invited me to join the newly formed Jesus Seminar in 1986, I accepted, especially pleased to learn that the Seminar also had a "Social Facets" satellite group led by John Elliott of the University of San Francisco. That group included a number of scholars exploring the social sciences (Bruce Malina, Creighton University; Jerome Neyrey, Jesuit School of Theology in Cambridge; John Pilch, Marquette University; Richard Rohrbaugh, Lewis and Clark University; and Douglas

6. Duling, "The *Testament of Solomon* and New Testament Demonology."
7. Duling, *The Testament of Solomon*.
8. Duling, "The Eleazar Miracle."
9. Duling, "The Legend of Solomon."
10. Duling, "The Testament of Solomon"; "Solomon, Testament of."
11. Duling, "Sociological Reflections."
12. Duling, "Insights from Sociology."

Oakman, Pacific Lutheran University). In this transitional period I gave historical Jesus papers at the Jesus Seminar (related to the Gospel of Matthew),[13] but also participated in the Social Facets group discussions and edited Social Facets articles for Funk's journal *Forum*.[14] When the Social Facets group parted ways with the Jesus Seminar in 1989, I chose to remain with Social Facets, renamed "The Context Group." The group met every year, most often in Portland, Oregon.[15] Meanwhile I started and chaired a social-scientific criticism section at the regional Eastern Great Lakes Biblical Society and in that society I continued to present papers.[16]

The next two decades I participated in several meetings of the social sciences group directed by Bruce Malina at the Catholic Biblical Association, gave social-scientific papers on Matthew and the social sciences at the *Studiorum Novi Testamenti Societas* (Montreal; Bonn),[17] and more such papers at international Social Context meetings in Canada, Europe, and Africa.[18] I was also active in the Matthew Section of the Society of Biblical Literature and some papers in this book were presented there.[19] As a member of the Steering Committee of the Social-Scientific Criticism of the New Testament (SSCNT) section of the Society of Biblical Literature and then a co-chair and program organizer from 2000 to 2006, first with Douglas Oakman of Pacific Lutheran University, subsequently with Philip Esler, then of St. Andrews University, I helped organize programs inviting several

13. E.g., Duling, "Binding and Loosing"; "Against Oaths."

14. For further discussion of Social Facets and the Context Group, see chap. 1 below.

15. http://www.contextgroup.org/. It also met several times near Philadelphia and recently in Lewiston, New York, near Buffalo.

16. Duling, "The Testament of Solomon"; "Matthew and the Problem of Authority"; "The Legend of Solomon"; "Recent Research"; "Matthew's Plurisignificant Son of David"; "Matthew and Marginality"; "Response to Shawn Kelley"; "Recruitment"; "Social-Science Reflections"; "Review: *Portraits of Paul*"; "Dots and Lines"; "Review of *Reconstructing*"; "Ethnicity and Paul's Self-Identification."

17. E.g., Duling, "Matthew as a Marginal Scribe"; "Ethnicity, Ethnocentrism, and the Matthean *Ethnos*."

18. Spain twice (Rafael Aguirre; Santiago Guijarro Oporto); Scotland (Philip F. Esler); Germany (Gerd Theissen; Wolfgang Stegemann); the Czech Republic (Raymond Hobbs); South Africa (Andries van Aarde).

19. Duling, "Matthew and Marginality"; "Egalitarian Ideology"; "Matthew 18:15–17"; "Matthew as a Marginal Scribe."

scholars from fields in the social sciences. These included anthropologist James C. Scott of Yale University, macrotheorist of aristocratic empires John Kautsky of St. Louis University, Rabbinics specialist and feminist Tal Ilan then of Tel Aviv, who received a healthy SBL grant (the first of its kind), and social memory theorist Jeffrey Olick of the University of Virginia.

In summary, all the chapters in this book but chapters 3 and 11 were first presented and discussed in sessions at the Social Context Group, and all of those but chapters 1, 2, and 11 (written for this book) were presented and discussed at other academic society meetings, namely, the Eastern Great Lakes Biblical Society, the Society of Biblical Literature, and the *Studiorum Novi Testamenti Societas*. They were then published in one form or another in various academic journals, Context Group collections, Matthew collections, and memorial volumes for scholars. Research reviews from the 1990s considered some of their ideas as "cutting edge" approaches to Matthew[20] and several scholars have built on or extended these ideas.[21]

The following chapters will include a number of social-scientific models and theories, especially those presented in chapter 3. Most prominent is Gerhard Lenski's macrosocial model of social stratification in an "advanced agrarian society," sometimes coordinated with John Kautsky's model of a commercialistic aristocratic empire, Géza Alföldy's model of social stratification in Roman society, and Gideon (and Andrée) Sjøberg's work on the preindustrial city.[22] I was first introduced to the Lenski model in a paper given by David Fiensy of Kentucky Christian University at the 1989 Spring meeting of the Eastern Great Lakes Biblical Society.[23] I began to think about my previous redaction critical and social-historical work on Matthew with this social-scientific model in mind. Curiously, the following Fall

20. Anderson, "Life on the Mississippi"; Senior, "Matthean Scholarship" (Matthew group SBL); "Directions."

21. Arlandson, *Women*; Vledder, *Conflict*; Carter, "Matthew and the Margins"; *Matthew and the Margins*; *Matthew and Empire*; Wainwright, "Only to the Lost Sheep"; "The Mary Magdalene Tradition"; Senior, "Between Two Worlds"; Love, *Jesus and Marginal Women*. See chap. 2 below.

22. Lenski, *Power and Privilege*; Lenski and Lenski, *Human Societies* (5th ed.; see Nolan for the 8th ed.); Alföldy, *Die römische Gesellschaft*; Kautsky, *The Politics of Aristocratic Empires*; Sjøberg, *The Preindustrial City*.

23. Fiensy's paper was based on his book *The Social History of Palestine*.

Introduction

the Social Facets group, still associated with the Jesus Seminar, met in Toronto and there I met Herman Waetjen, whose *A Reordering of Power: A Socio-Political Reading of Mark's Gospel*, just published, also drew on the Lenski model. In this period I read Anthony Saldarini's 1988 *Pharisees, Scribes, and Sadducees*[24] and Richard Horsley's 1989 *Sociology and the Jesus Movement* (which I reviewed in 1991), and discovered that both found the model useful.[25] The model also informed Saldarini's *Matthew's Christian-Jewish Community* in 1994, John Dominic Crossan's *The Birth of Christianity* in 1998, and Wolfgang and Ekkehard Stegemann's *The Jesus Movement: A Social History of Its First Century* (German 1995; English 1999).

My first experiment with the Lenski model was in the spring of 1991 in a Context Group paper on the Matthean infancy.[26] I then developed the model in a paper on the "Son of David" given at the first international meeting of the Context Group at Medina del Campo, Spain, in the following summer, published the following year.[27] Slightly reformulated, and under the influence of Fiensy, the Lenski model became important for understanding Herodian Palestine in my revision of Norman Perrin's *The New Testament: Proclamation and Parenesis, Myth and History* in 1994.[28] In the meantime, I discovered that my experimenting with the Lenski model in the Context Group was not accidental. Although I came to it by way of Fiensy's work, the "fountainhead" for this innovation in Biblical study turned out to be Marvin Chaney at the Graduate Theological Union in the San Francisco Bay area. Context member Richard Rohrbaugh who had studied at the Graduate Theological Union had already used the model in his 1978 dissertation under Chaney's influence[29] and others from the Bay Area knew or were using it: Elliott in his work on social-scientific criticism in 1986,[30] Antoinette Wire in her study of

24. Saldarini, *Pharisees*.
25. Horsley, *Sociology*; Duling, "Review of R. Horsley."
26. Duling, "The Matthean Infancy" (unpublished).
27. Duling, "Matthew's Son of David."
28. Perrin and Duling, *The New Testament*, 3rd ed., 56.
29. Rohrbaugh, *The Biblical Interpreter*, who used the model later in "The Social Location of the Marcan Audience."
30. Elliott, "Social-Scientific Criticism," 13–14.

Matthew in 1991,[31] and Stuart Love in his study of gender in the New Testament.[32] Chaney, Rohrbaugh, and I each gave papers based on the influence of Lenski and John Kautsky in a session of the Social-Scientific Criticism of the New Testament at the Society of Biblical Literature in 2000. Kautsky was our guest and informally responded.

Marginality theory is also prominent in this book. By 1990 the social-scientific term "marginality" had become common in North America, especially in relation to oppressed minorities and women. It had also entered the biblical scholars' lexicon and was a major concept in the work of my Canisius College colleague, Paula McNutt, a social-scientific critic of the Hebrew Scriptures, whose work I eventually reviewed at the Eastern Great Lakes Biblical Society.[33] Despite widespread usage of the concept, there appeared to be no *theoretical* discussion of marginality in the biblical field. Since part of social-scientific criticism is to define one's theoretical orientation "up front," I researched, wrote, and published a marginality paper exploring the work of several theorists in the social science literature,[34] combining marginality theory with macro- and microsociological views, all used as a heuristic lens for interpreting Matthew. I subsequently wrote two articles on Matthew as a marginal scribe, refining the language and conceptuality with four different kinds of marginality based on marginality theory in the sociological literature.[35] These studies influenced several articles and books on Matthew and marginality by other scholars.[36] In 1999 the Matthew Group of the Society of Biblical Literature at Boston devoted its whole session to marginality, and my 1993 paper on "Matthew and Marginality" was cited as foundational.

---

31. Wire, "Gender Roles"; see chap. 3 below.

32. Love, "Gender Roles"; *Jesus and Marginal Women*. See chap. 2 below.

33. McNutt, *Reconstructing*.

34. Duling, "Matthew and Marginality" and chap. 5 below. The main theorists were Park, "Human Migration"; "Personality"; Stonequist, *The Marginal Man*; Schermerhorn, "Marginal Man"; Germani, *Marginality*; Turner, *The Ritual Process*; *Dramas, Fields, and Metaphors*. Social-scientific clarification was aided later by sociologist Billson, "No Owner Soil" (see chaps. 9 and 11 below); on Park, see also Weisberger, "Marginality and Its Directions."

35. Duling, "The Matthean Brotherhood"; "Matthew as a Marginal Scribe." Social-scientific clarification was aided by Billson, "No Owner Soil." See chaps. 5, 7, and 9.

36. See chap. 2 below, where a number of them are cited.

Introduction 7

The last major chapter in this book (chapter 10) on ethnicity theory and modeling as it relates to Matthew has had some influence, as well.[37] I have continued exploring ethnicity in several articles about Paul and have since developed a second model.[38]

At the 2000 Social-Scientific Study of the New Testament session in the Society of Biblical Literature on the influence of Gerhard Lenski and John Kautsky, Professor Anne Wire of San Francisco Theological Seminary in the Graduate Theological Union arose and asked when I would be gathering my studies on the social-scientific criticism of Matthew together into a book that would make them easily accessible. This book (at last!) attempts to do that. I thank especially Dr. K. C. Hanson, editor in chief at Wipf and Stock and Cascade Books, for his encouragement to undertake it.[39] Others who have influenced my thinking on this subject are gratefully noted in the Acknowledgments.

---

37. See Cromhout, *Jesus and Identity*, 81–98; *Walking*.

38. Duling, "'Whatever Gain I Had'"; "2 Corinthians 11:22"; the new model is in "Ethnicity and Paul's Letter to the Romans."

39. See "Acknowledgments" in this book.

CHAPTER 1

The Emergence of Social-Scientific Criticism in New Testament Study

> Social-scientific criticism of the Bible is that phase of the exegetical task which analyzes the social and cultural dimensions of the text and of its environmental context through the utilization of the perspectives, theory, models, and research of the social sciences.
>
> —John H. Elliott, *What Is Social-Scientific Criticism?*, 7

John Elliott's definition of social-scientific criticism of the Bible in the above epigraph stresses the social sciences as tools to analyze social and cultural features of biblical texts. He defines social-scientific criticism further as "a component of the historical-critical method of exegesis" that complements the various other historical criticisms of biblical study.[1]

Inclusion of the social sciences among the methods of historical-critical research of the Bible has a long history that must be set within the larger context of the fascinating struggle between the fields of history and the social sciences in the modern era. This chapter looks at this historical drama and indicates how social-scientific criticism became increasingly accepted as an interpretative tool in biblical study. Combined with chapter 2, it presents a foundation for the rest of the studies in this book.

---

1. Elliott, *What Is Social-Scientific Criticism?* 9–35; *Home*, 1–20; Osiek, *What Are They Saying?*; Horrell, "The Origins and Revival."

The Larger Context: Historians and Social Theorists

Early eighteenth-century intellectuals who pioneered what became the social sciences took a keen interest in history, but it was usually history in the "grand" sense, mainly broad evolutionary history. Montesquieu (1689–1755) and Condorcet (1743–1794) believed that society had evolved from hunters, to herders, to farmers, to more politically "advanced" societies, a schema that still has relevance for cultural evolution.[2] August Comte (1798–1857) also had an evolutionary schema of Western civilization, but his stages correlated with the development of human beings from childhood ("theological") to youth ("metaphysical") to adulthood ("positivistic" or scientific).[3] He is credited with naming the scientific study of society "sociology."

Grand evolutionary theories also preoccupied two of the three most influential "classic" sociologists. Karl Marx (1818–1883) posited five major stages of social-economic organization prior to the rise of modern communism.[4] Max Weber (1864–1920) compared civilizations, theorized about the secularization of the West,[5] and even wrote social-historical studies of ancient Romans and Judeans.[6] Thus, he has been called a "historical sociologist." Finally, the "father of American anthropology," German-born Franz Boas (1858–1942) rejected comparative cross-cultural organismic/evolutionary theories as reductionistic and racist armchair anthropology. Boas emphasized fact-finding field work. He is often called a "historical particularist" because he was interested in the history of the individual cultures he studied. He also located anthropology in the humanities, not the natural sciences.[7]

---

2. Montesquieu, *The Spirit*, 1748 (hunters → pastoralists → politically organized societies); Condorcet, *Outline*, 1795 (hunters → herders → farmers → western societies). See preface and chap. 3 for Lenski's views of societal evolution.

3. Comte, *Course*, 6 vols., 1830–1842.

4. Marx, Preface to *A Contribution* (primitive communism → the slave system of ancient Greece and Rome → the feudal system of medieval Europe → modern capitalism → socialism).

5. Weber, *The Protestant Ethic*.

6. E.g., Weber, *Roman Agrarian History*; *Ancient Judaism* (originally separate articles, 1917–1919). In this book I use the term "Judeans" or "Israelites" (the Matthean term) rather than "Jews," and "Christ believers" rather than "Christians," except when citing or quoting other scholars' views. For the issues see, Elliott, "Jesus the Israelite"; Esler, *Conflict and Identity in Romans*, 67–68; Hanson and Oakman, *Palestine*, 11.

7. Boas, *Race*.

Some early historians took up social analysis, as well. In his *Democracy in America* (1835) Alexis de Tocqueville (1805–1859) commented (sometimes distastefully!) on the American "social character."[8] A few decades later Frederick Jackson Turner (1861–1932) argued that the individualistic, democratic "American" character was forged by openness to the western frontier ("frontier mentality").[9] Most influential of all, especially in Europe somewhat later, were the early leaders of the French *Annales* school,[10] Mark Bloch (1886–1944) and Lucien Febvre (1878–1956). They incorporated geography, economics, and cultural anthropology in their explanations of historical trends over long periods of time ("total history") and typified each epoch by a collective *mentalité*.[11]

These early representatives of cross-disciplinary interest were exceptional; most historians and social scientists went down separate paths. In the field of history Leopold von Ranke (1795–1886), the "father of modern historiography," saw the historian's primary task as simply gathering and correlating facts from primary sources, the goal being to describe "what really happened" without reference to *any* interpretative theory, social-scientific or otherwise.[12] In the social sciences, most theorists followed August Comte's view that sociology should not concern itself with particular historical events, but strive for general social "laws."[13] Especially important in this regard was Émile Durkheim (1858–1917), the third of the "classical" sociologists (besides Marx and Weber), who contrasted the historian's interest in interpreting unique, particular events in the past with the sociologist's focus on repeatable generalities of societies in the present.[14] Durkheim's views became foundational for the emergence of Structural Functionalism, the theory that the various parts of society function to maintain the whole social body in a state of balance, equilibrium, or health. This

---

8. Tocqueville, *Democracy* (original French 1835, 1840). He included Americans' love of money, their tendency to form associations, and their subordination of African Americans.

9. Turner, *The Frontier*.

10. Original journal title: *Annales d'histoire, economique et sociale*.

11. Burke, *The French Historical Revolution*.

12. "*Wie es eigentlich gewesen [ist]*" in von Ranke, *Geschichte*, 1824.

13. Comte, *Outline*.

14. Durkheim, *L'Année Sociologique* II, v.

theory, analogous to the physical organism's attempt to maintain homeostasis, was distinctly ahistorical.[15] It valued social harmony and stability over social conflict and change, and in that respect was socially conservative.[16] In the mid-twentieth century the most influential social theorists, sociologist Talcott Parsons (1902–1979) and anthropologists Bronislaw Malinowski (1884–1942) and Radcliffe-Brown (1881–1955), were ahistorical Structural Functionalists.[17]

This all too brief overview is meant to make a single, decisive point: although there were exceptions, most historians came to see their main task as describing and understanding particular persons and events in and through past time, and thus associated themselves with the humanities. Most sociologists and anthropologists, in contrast, tried to explain social relations and interconnections in collectivities at a single moment in time, usually the present, and thus associated themselves with the sciences—hence the name "social sciences."[18] This separation was still very much alive in the late twentieth century, as any organization of university fields and faculties shows. Social historian Peter Burke described the point well in 1980 and again in 1992:

> Sociologists [social theorists][19] and historians each see the mote in their neighbour's eye. Unfortunately, each group tends to perceive the other in terms of a rather crude stereotype. In Britain, at least, many historians still regard sociologists [social theorists] as people who state the obvious in a barbarous

---

15. For the view that Durkheim should *not* be considered ahistorical, see Bellah, "Durkheim and History."

16. The major alternative to consensus theory is conflict theory, which views social conflict as necessary for social change and reform; its main foundation is Marxist theory. See Horsley's view of Theissen in n. 84 below and a discussion of conflict theorist Dahrendorf in chap. 2 below (and n. 67).

17. The evolution of societal *structures* viewed *organically* in the work of Herbert Spencer had lost its influence; see Bohannan and Glazer, *High Points*, 3–28.

18. These contrasts are sometimes expressed as "diachronic" (through time) versus "synchronic" (a single point in time); ideographic (descriptive) versus nomothetic (law oriented); "understanding"/"interpreting" social arrangements versus "explaining" them. The philosophical distinction comes from Dilthey, who distinguished between *Verstehen* ("understanding") and *Erklären* ("explanation"), the human sciences and the natural sciences; cf. Makkreel, *Dilthey*.

19. Burke's first edition of *History and Social Theory* was 1980. In his second edition, 1992, he usually replaces "sociology" with "social theory"; this quotation is an exception, so I have put "social theory" in brackets.

and abstract jargon, lack any sense of place and time, squeeze individuals without mercy into rigid categories, and, to cap it all, describe these activities as "scientific." Sociologists [social theorists], for their part, have long viewed historians as amateurish, myopic fact-collectors and bean counters without system or method, the imprecision of their "data base" matched only by their incapacity to analyze it. In short, despite the increasing number of bilinguals, . . . sociologists [social theorists] and historians still do not speak the same language. Their dialogue, as the French historian Fernand Braudel once put it, is usually "a dialogue of the deaf."[20]

Burke noted that in the latter part of the twentieth century, "bilinguals" like himself were increasing. This comment can be easily illustrated by analyzing historical and social-scientific methods in this period,[21] and particularly by the emergence of new academic journals. The *International Review of Social History* was launched already in 1937, but many more interdisciplinary journals appeared after World War II: *Past and Present* in England (1952); *Comparative Studies in Society and History* (1957) and the *Journal of Social History* in the United States (1967); and *Geschichte und Gesellschaft* (*History and Society*) in Germany (1974). Journals such as these emphasized the benefits of combining history and social theory. Gordon Marshall wrote in *The Journal of Historical Sociology* (1988) these words:[22] "In my understanding of history and sociology, there can be no relationship between them because, in terms of their fundamental preoccupations, history and sociology are and always have been the same thing. Both seek to understand the puzzle of human agency and both seek to do so in terms of the process of social structuring. It is the task that commands the attention, and not the disciplines."[23]

A similar new cooperation was appearing between historians and anthropologists. Influential British social anthropologist E. E. Evans-Pritchard (1902–1973), realizing that small-scale, aboriginal,

20. Burke, *History and Social Theory*, 2–3.

21. Lipset, "History and Sociology"; Schulze, *Sociologie und Geschichtswissenschaft*.

22. *The Journal of Historical Sociology*; see also Marshall, "Historical Sociology," *A Dictionary of Sociology*.

23. *Journal of Historical Sociology*, http://www.wiley.com/bw/journal.asp?ref=0952-1909. See Wong and Savor, eds., *Twenty Years*; Abrams, *Historical Sociology*.

"history-less" societies, the main source for anthropological research, were disappearing, rejected the field's dominant ahistorical Structural Functionalism, located social anthropology in the humanities (as Boas had done), predicted that anthropology would move toward social and cultural history, and argued that there is no fundamental difference between what social anthropologists and historians do: study social life.[24] Even the *structural* anthropologist Claude Levi-Strauss (1908–2009), impressed by the *Annales* school, believed that historians and anthropologists share the same subject (social life), goal (understanding "man"), and method, differing primarily in complementary perspectives: "history organizes its data in relation to conscious expressions of social life, which anthropology proceeds by examining its unconscious foundations."[25] In 1954 the journal *Ethnohistory* came into existence, and in 1988 *History and Anthropology* sought "to address the intersection of anthropologically-informed history and historically-informed anthropology," thus rejecting the dominant ahistoricism.[26] American anthropologist Bernard Cohn captured the new cooperative mood in his essay on "Anthropologyland" and "Historyland":

> Historians and anthropologists have a common subject matter, "otherness"; one field constructs and studies "otherness" in space, the other in time. Both fields have a concern with text and context . . . Both forms of knowledge entail the act of translation. The goals of the accounts practitioners develop are understanding and explanation, rather than the construction of social laws and prediction . . . Both are dependent upon reporting their results in a literary form . . . Both have as central to their projects the study of change . . .[27]

In short, the original cooperation between social theorists and historians that had mostly dissolved reappeared once again.

24. Evans-Pritchard, *Social Anthropology*, based on a 1950 BBC program; see Bohannan and Glazer, *High Points*, 407–21. For Evans-Pritchard anthropology-as-science in quest of general laws was a nineteenth-century confusion.

25. *Structural Anthropology* 1,18 (*Anthropologie Structurale* 1. 24–5); the comment is cited in Johnson, *Claude Levi-Strauss*, 14. Levi-Strauss' chapter was titled "History and Anthropology."

26. "Aims and Scope" of *History and Anthropology*: http://www.tandf.co.uk/journals/titles/02757206.asp. A. F. C. Wallace, past president of the American Anthropological Association, concentrated on past communities (e.g., Wallace, *Death*) and wrote for this journal.

27. Cohn, "History and Anthropology," 198–99.

Historians and Social Scientists in New Testament Study: Social Stratification as a Case Study

Shifting cooperation and conflict between historians and social theorists sets the stage for understanding cooperation and conflict between historians and social theorists in studies of the ancient Mediterranean world and the New Testament.[28] I would like to illustrate this pendulum swing more specifically with a theme that will be central to studies of Matthew in this book: the social level of Jesus followers and Christ believers.[29]

Differences of opinion about the social level of the early Jesus and Christ movements already existed in the ancient world. Second-century Pliny the Younger thought that the Christ Movement included people of every social rank, including Roman citizens,[30] but third-century Celsus stated that its converts were "rogues, thieves, burglars, poisoners, despoilers of temples and tombs," "the foolish, dishonorable, . . . stupid, and . . . slaves, women, and little children."[31]

Differences of opinion about social stratification have persisted. In 1895 prominent Oxford historian and archaeologist William Ramsay (1851–1939) portrayed the Apostle Paul as a "missionary statesman," an aristocrat-friendly Roman citizen with the ability to move about freely among the elite strata in the courts and salons of the eastern Mediterranean.[32] However, Marxist interpreters developed a quite different picture. Marx's colleague Friedrich Engels (1820–1895), who had been taught by New Testament critic Bruno Bauer (1809–1882),[33] judged that "Christianity was originally a movement of oppressed people: it first appeared as a religion of slaves and freedmen, of poor people deprived of all rights, of peoples subjugated or dispersed by Rome."[34] Under Engels's influence, Rosa Luxemburg

---

28. For early Hebrew Bible works, see Gottwald, ed., *Social Scientific Criticism*.
29. Horrell, "The Origins and Revival."
30. Pliny the Elder, *Epistles*, X.96.9.
31. *Against Celsus* III.44, drawn from Celsus' *Logos* Alēthēs.
32. Ramsay, *St. Paul the Traveller*; see Gasque, *Sir William M. Ramsay*.
33. Engels, "Bruno Bauer and Early Christianity." Marx and Engels rejected Bauer's Hegelianism, but Engels thought that the skeptical Bauer had the best explanation of how the Christian "nonsense" became the religion of the Empire.
34. Engels, "On the History."

argued from passages in Acts that the earliest church was peopled with landless, impoverished, debt-ridden peasants who sold their remaining possessions and developed a sort of primitive communism.[35] Karl Kautsky held similar views, backing them up with Jesus' "revolutionary" pronouncements about blessing the poor and rebuking the rich.[36] For Marxist interpreters class conflict was inevitable and in that conflict Jesus and the first followers were from the "lower classes."

The Marxists were not alone. In 1908 Adolf Deissmann (1866–1937) argued that the Greek of the New Testament, known from recently discovered inscriptions and nonliterary Greek papyri, was the "common" (*koinē*) Greek spoken every day by the lower social strata.[37] By the mid-1920s several New Testament scholars were publishing books about social life in the early churches.[38] Form criticism of the New Testament was emerging in this period and this led Swiss scholar Oscar Cullmann to call for a "special branch of sociology, devoted to the study of the laws which govern the growth of popular [oral] traditions."[39] Meanwhile, Shirley Jackson Case of the "Chicago School" proposed a "social-historical method" in which "[t]he ultimate unit in history is not the document but the contemporary social order, of which the document may have been merely an incidental product" (1921).[40] In this vein Case's colleague Shailer Mathews (1863–1941) wrote about the revolutionary "social mind" of ancient Palestinians as rooted in social, political, and economic inequities; in that context Jesus, a poor man, admonished love of family and neighbor, renunciation of wealth, and giving to the poor

---

35. Luxemburg, *Socialism and the Churches*; see Boer, "On Christian Communism"; Acts 2:32–35; 2:44–45.

36. K. Kautsky, *Der Ursprung des Christentums*; J. H. Kautsky, *Karl Kautsky*.

37. Deissmann, *Light*, 144; see his Appendix XI, "Kautsky's 'Origin of Christianity.'" The preference for the term "social strata" over "social class" is because the latter is derived from Marxist analysis of modern industrial societies. See MacMullen, *Roman Social Relations*, via Meeks, *The First Urban Christians*; discussion by Rohrbaugh, "Methodological Considerations." See chap. 9 below.

38. Schumacher, *Die soziale Lage* (1924); Lohmeyer, *Soziale Fragen* (1925); Cadoux, *The Early Church* (1925).

39. Cullmann, "Les recéntes études" (1925) cited in Gager, "Shall We Marry Our Enemies?" 260; Schütz, "Introduction," 7; Tidball, "On Wooing a Crocodile."

40. Case, "The Historical Study of Religion," 4; see Schubert, "Shirley Jackson Case." For the Chicago School, see Arnold, *Near the Edge of Battle*; Baird, *History*, 305–30; Hynes, *Shirley Jackson Case*; Duling, *Jesus Christ Through History*, 211–17.

(1928).⁴¹ The "lower class" origins of the Jesus and Christ Movements gained further credibility from influential German sociologist Ernst Troeltsch who argued that authentic religious movements, or "sects," arise among the lower social strata (1912; English 1931).⁴² From another quarter, Michael Rostovtzeff's influential work on the social and economic history of the Romans (1926) described them in Marxist categories as composed of an oppressed, "proletarian" peasantry and an urban "bourgeoisie."⁴³

The influential proletarian hypothesis in New Testament study of the 1920s soon encountered opposition.⁴⁴ Some historical critics said that it was too general, especially for Paul's urban communities; that communism in Acts stressed consumption, not Marx's "means of production"; and that in any case Acts' romanticized image of the early Jerusalem community was not trustworthy for historical reconstruction. In 1933, influential Harvard historian and classicist A. D. Nock posed an alternative to Deissmann's view, namely, the Greek Old Testament, or Septuagint, was more important for New Testament vocabulary than the nonliterary papyri.⁴⁵ Floyd Filson produced an influential article on Paul's "house churches" in 1939, arguing that they were composed "more nearly of a cross section of society" than of the "lower classes."⁴⁶ Finally, theological giants in the 1920s and 1930s, Rudolf Bultmann and Karl Barth, held views unfavorable to the social sciences. Bultmann's existentialist hermeneutic was individualistic⁴⁷ and Barth's theology stressed that the "Wholly Other" God of the Bible cannot be subjected to human reason, thus the human sciences.⁴⁸ As the clouds of World War II gathered, discussion about the social level of the early followers of Jesus and Paul waned.

41. Mathews, *Jesus on Social Institutions*; see Duling, *Jesus Christ Through History*, 205–11.

42. "Churches of the disinherited," see Troeltsch, *The Social Teachings*, I, 44; Niebuhr, *The Social Sources*, 26–76.

43. Rostovtzeff, *The Social and Economic History*.

44. Weiss, *Der Erste Korintherbrief*, xvi, argued against the proletarian hypothesis.

45. Nock, "Vocabulary."

46. Filson, "Significance," 111.

47. Bultmann, *Jesus Christ and Mythology*; Theissen, "Zur Forschungsgeschichtlichen," 6–7, makes a similar critique of form criticism (see further below).

48. Scroggs, "The Sociological Interpretation," 165; Barth, *Epistle to the Romans*. Barth never rejected communism.

However, just as historians in general began to find insights from the social sciences after World War II, so also historians of antiquity and the Bible returned to social questions. Joachim Jeremias' influential *Jerusalem in the Time of Jesus: An Investigation into Economic and Social Conditions during the New Testament Period* (1962) was published.[49] In the 1970s Peter Brown, an influential social historian of the early church, was much influenced by anthropology and the *Annales* school of social history.[50] Important also was social historian Ramsay MacMullen, whose exploration of Roman social relations offered patterns of social stratification (1974).[51] T. F. Carney's argument that social-scientific models can help explain the ancient world (1975) did not at first attract much attention[52]—it would—but influential economic historian M. I. Finley's view that models are useful to interpret ancient economies did (1985).[53]

Thus, once again New Testament scholars began to analyze social structures and relations in their texts. In European and North American academic circles[54] the initial catalyst was New Zealander E. A. Judge, who published *The Social Pattern of the Christian Groups in the First Century* (1960).[55] However, in the postwar political climate of global politics dominated by Marxist Communism, the proletarian hypothesis dear to the earlier Marxists did not fare well, nor did Deissmann's views. Interpretation of 1 Cor 1:26–29 easily illustrates the mood. When Deissmann wrote about this passage, he concentrated on Paul's reference to the majority at Corinth, namely, the uneducated, powerless, weak, low, and despised "nobodies."[56] Judge, in contrast, elaborated on Paul's minority, namely, the wise, powerful, and nobly born—the patrons and leaders of Paul's urban house churches.[57] Judge wrote: "Far

49. Jeremias, *Jerusalem*.

50. Brown, "The Rise and Function of the Holy Man"; "Sorcery, Demons"; *The World of Late Antiquity*.

51. MacMullen, *Roman Social Relations*, included a lexicon of snobbery; see his recent *The Second Church*.

52. Carney, *The Shape of the Past*.

53. Finley, *Ancient History and Models*; see recently Manning and Morris, *The Ancient Economy*.

54. For Latin America, see comments below on liberation theology.

55. Judge, "The Social Pattern," reprinted in Scholer, *Social Distinctives*, 1–56.

56. Deissmann, *Light from the Ancient East*.

57. E.g., Gaius, Crispus, Stephanus, Fortunatus, Erastus, Aquila, Prisca, Phoebe.

from being a socially depressed group, then, if the Corinthians are at all typical, the Christians were dominated by a socially pretentious section of the population of the big cities ... The peasantry and persons in slavery on the land were the most underprivileged classes. *Christianity left them largely untouched.*"[58]

With some exceptions, something like a chorus of agreement arose. Wilhelm Wuellner concluded from the same passage that the Corinthian believers "came by and large from the fairly well-to-do *bourgeois* circles with a fair percentage also from upper class people as well as the very poor" (1973).[59] For Robert Grant the early church was largely "middle class" and in a hierarchically organized society it succeeded "from the top down" (1977).[60] Ronald Hock argued that Paul loathed his "tentmaking" trade, an attitude that would have been typical of the aristocratic distaste for working with one's hands (1978; 1980).[61] Abraham Malherbe studied the level of literary sophistication of New Testament Greek and concluded that its writers came from at least "the upper levels of secondary school education" (1983).[62] Judge heartily approved.[63] Finally, just as the old proletarian hypothesis had gained sociological support from Ernst Troeltsch, so the new analysis of Paul's letters received sociological support from a sociologist of new religions, Rodney Stark. To be sure, Stark accepted that early "Christianity" had emerged from a Palestinian rural "Jewish sect," but he also argued that it evolved quickly into a Greco-Roman, urbanized "Christian cult," and on the analogy that modern cults recruit predominantly from the middle and upper classes, so also did the ancient urban "Christian" cult (1986; 1987a; 1987b).[64] Malherbe was led to wonder whether a "New Consensus" might be emerging, one in which the social level of early Christ believers was "higher than

---

58. Judge, "The Social Pattern," 60; in Scholer, 44 (italics mine). See Kreissig, "Zur sozialen Zusammensetzung."

59. Wuellner, "The Sociological Implications," 666–72.

60. Grant, *Early Christianity and Society*, 11.

61. Hock, "Paul's Tentmaking"; *The Social Context*.

62. Malherbe, *Social Aspects*, 45.

63. Judge, "The Social Identity," in Scholer, 131.

64. Stark, "The Class Basis," 216–25; see his *The Rise of Christianity*, chap. 2, and the comments of White, "Sociological Analysis," 257–61.

Deissmann had thought" (1983).[65] Maybe Sir William Ramsay had not been totally wrong!

The "New Consensus"—if it ever really existed[66]—was never uniformly consensual. One reason was that it tended to find its main support in the urban communities of Paul, not in the rural atmosphere of the gospels. Also, doubt arose that Paul's social level was relatively high. In 1998 Justin Meggitt made a case from Paul's comments about labor and poverty that Paul was indeed very poor[67] and in 2006 Todd Still objected to Hock's theory that Paul loathed manual labor by noting that Hock had not taken seriously the value of work among Judeans or Paul's statements about work in 1 Thessalonians. For Still, the elitist image of Paul simply would not work.[68]

There have been mediating positions. Gerd Theissen concluded from his study of personal names in Paul's Corinthian correspondence (1982) that *both* Deissmann and Judge were correct: the majority was from the lower classes, but an influential minority was from the upper classes; indeed, this status difference was precisely what caused other conflicts at Corinth (2001; 2003).[69] Wayne Meeks, heeding Ramsay MacMullen's warning that the Marxist "class" concept was based on modern industrial economics and does not fit the "status" categories of ancient Greco-Roman society,[70] emphasized that in Pauline congregations there were multiple "statuses," although none represented the very top or very bottom.[71] Moreover, a person could be ranked high by one status indicator, such as wealth or education, and low by

---

65. Malherbe, *Social Aspects*, 31; Malherbe, 59, said that Deissmann "aimed too low."

66. Hochschild, *Geschichte*.

67. Meggitt, *Paul, Poverty*. Theissen, "The Social Structure," 72, rejected Meggitt's "homogenous mass" as unlikely—the Corinthian community was stratified and some were not poor—but he accepted that *most* "Christians" belonged to the "subdecurional" classes; see also Theissen, "Social Conflicts."

68. Still, "Did Paul Loathe Manual Labor?" 795.

69. Theissen, *Social Setting*, 106–10.

70. See above, n. 37.

71. Meeks, *The First Urban Christians*, 72–73; cf. MacMullen, *Roman Social Relations*; Gager, "Shall We Marry Our Enemies?" 262; Rohrbaugh, "Methodological Considerations."

another, such as birth or gender, a mixed ranking that caused "status dissonance" (1983).[72]

Most important, there was doubt about the supposed "New Consensus" in other quarters. In an important study on Jesus and the poor, Louise Schottroff and Wolfgang Stegemann did not accept it[73] and Robin Scroggs noted that it overvalued the historicity of Acts' view of Paul and focused on the issue of wealth without taking seriously the socio-cultural dynamics typically found in the Synoptic Gospels.[74] These last observations shared at least one point with the Marxists, namely, it is always necessary to keep in view the wider Christ Movements, including those in the gospels and Acts. With that in view I take up critical study of the gospels in relation to the social sciences.

Form Criticism, the Historical Jesus, and the Social Sciences

The historical critical method that dominated gospel research and the quest for the historical Jesus in the mid-twentieth century was form criticism. As practiced by Rudolf Bultmann, it categorized the speech and action forms of "the Jesus tradition" of the Synoptic Gospels and attempted to trace their evolutionary sequence from simple to more complex forms as they were transmitted orally in various contexts or "life settings" (*Sitze im Leben*) in the early churches.[75] Recall that in the 1920s Oscar Cullmann had called for a *sociology* of oral tradition.[76] Klaus Berger thought that form criticism's *Sitz im Leben* ("setting in life") was a step in that direction.[77] However, Berger's Heidelberg colleague Gerd Theissen objected that Bultmann's "life settings" were not so much social as they were ecclesiastical (preaching, teaching, liturgy, missionary propaganda). Most important, Bultmann's attempt

---

72. On "status dissonance" ("status discrepancy") as a contrast with "status crystallization" ("status congruence") see Lenski, "Status Crystallization," and Barnett, "Introduction," 177–81; the concept is used by Meeks, *First Urban Christians*, 73, and Theissen, "Social Structure of Pauline Communities," 67. See further Lipset, "History and Sociology," in Lipset, *Revolution and Counterrevolution*, 7–8. I make further comments about status dissonance in chap. 9 below (see n. 10).

73. Schottroff and Stegemann, *Jesus and the Hope of the Poor*.

74. Scroggs, "Sociological Interpretation," 170.

75. Bultmann, *Geschichte*.

76. See above on interests in the 1920s.

77. Berger, "Wissenssoziologie und Exegese," 125.

to isolate the earliest forms of Jesus' teachings by contrasting them with contemporary Judean teachings and the evangelists' interpretations (the eventual "Criterion of Dissimilarity") was wrongheaded. A convincing "sociological" approach required continuity, not discontinuity, with Jesus' "Jewish" context and so Theissen developed new, "historical plausibility" criteria to explore that continuity, such as the "local color" of certain stories, implied references in the gospels to key historical events, and *written* traditions about Jesus that date as early as the 40s.[78] One of Theissen's results: Jesus did not spring from the "lower class," but from the "marginal middle class," and, like the Cynic philosophers of his day, *voluntarily chose* his poor, homeless, vagabond, prophetic lifestyle.[79] This corresponded with Theissen's thesis that Jesus' started a peace movement that experimented with love and reconciliation ("love your neighbor," "love your enemy"). Thus, said Theissen, Jesus not only tried to divert, transfer, project, transform, and symbolize aggressive conflict, but ultimately to *overcome and contain it.*

Theissen's sociological theory of the voluntary "wandering charismatic" prophet of peace became very influential in Jesus research.[80] Yet, it too found criticism. Wolfgang Stegemann agreed with Theissen's continuity-with-"Judaism" emphasis, but rejected his view that Jesus emerged from the "marginal middle class" and voluntarily chose his poor, vagabond lifestyle; rather, Jesus was forced to live that way by "bitter necessity" brought on by oppressive socioeconomic conditions in Palestine.[81] Richard Horsley not only agreed; he drew on the widespread social-historical opinion that there was nothing equivalent to a "middle class" in the ancient world. Jesus could not therefore have been "middle class."[82] Rather, argued Horsley, Jesus emerged from the lower strata and developed a radical social program, the revitalization of Galilean villages, which was supported by the rural poor (the "have-nots") who suffered under the oppressive yoke of most native

78. Theissen and Merz, *Historical Jesus*, 115–21; Theissen, *Gospels in Context, passim;* Theissen and Winter, *Quest for the Plausible Jesus.*

79. Theissen, *Sociology*, 114.

80. E.g., Crossan, *Historical Jesus.*

81. Stegemann, "Vagabond Radicalism," argued that Theissen's key texts (e.g., Mark 10:28–30; QMt 10:8–10; Luke 5:20, 28; 12:33; 14:33; 18:22) were redactional, not historical Jesus material.

82. Horsley, *Bandits; Sociology;* cf. Christ, "Grundfragen."

aristocrats ("the haves").[83] Jesus did not try to overcome or contain social conflict, as Theissen thought, but rather *provoked* it![84]

All this looks rather different from the "New Consensus" based primarily on Paul's writings. One can even hear echoes, however faintly, of Marxist theory in the debates about Jesus' social status. Other social historians joined in the discussion, such as Sean Freyne,[85] and social-scientific critics such as K. C. Hanson and Douglas Oakman.[86] Even "Regionalist" archaeologists such as Eric Meyers and James Strange offered their opinions of Jesus' social status in relation to the extent of the "Hellenization" and economic development of Lower Galilee.[87] Did Jesus assimilate to, or rebel from, Hellenistic cultural influences? Was this traveling artisan really poverty stricken, from the lower social strata? These debates continue to the present.[88] Again, they are often interlocked with the question whether the Jesus Movement was a sect, a category that, as we shall see, eventually became central to the interpretation of the Matthean community. This point deserves further comment.

The Sect Model

The study of "sect" has been central to the history-versus-social sciences debate and very important for the study of the New Testament and the Gospel of Matthew in particular, especially in relation to our case study, social stratification. Sociologist Ernst Troeltsch, drawing on Max Weber's contrast between "church" and "sect,"[89] defined "sect"

---

83. Horsley, *Jesus*. See Wallace, "Revitalization Movements"; Duling, "Readers Guide: Millennialism"; "Millennialism."

84. For Horsley, Theissen's Structural Functionalism was too conservative and thus he should have used more Conflict Theory (based primarily on Dahrendorf's *Class and Class Conflict*). See Duling, "Review of R. Horsley" (n. 16 above) and see chap. 2 below (and n. 67) for observations about Dahrendorf.

85. Freyne, *Galilee*.

86. Hanson, "Galilean Fishing Economy"; Hanson and Oakman, *Palestine*; Duling, "The Jesus Movement" (= "Die Jesusbewegung").

87. See, e.g., Edwards and McCollogh, eds., *Archaeology and the Galilee*; Horsley, *Galilee*; Reed, *Archaeology*.

88. Questions were debated in 2009 SBL sessions about Jesus, archeology, economics, and social models related to Galilee.

89. Weber, "Über einige Kategorien"; cf. *Economy and* Society, 56, 476, 1164; Swatos, "Weber or Troeltsch?"

as an egalitarian, perfectionistic, totalistic, voluntary, intimate fellowship of love that focuses on inward experience and sets itself against the church, the state, and the world; it is non-conforming and non-accommodating, thus radical and revolutionary, often anticipating the millennium, and is usually led by a prophet.[90] He held that "sects" have their origins in, and recruit from, the "lower classes."[91]

Ernst Troeltsch's view of "sect" became central to New Testament study. Often sects were correlated with millennial movements and in the 1970s John Gager carried this analysis further. Gager was a member of a new social history group in the Society of Biblical Literature (see below), but asserted in *Kingdom and Community* (1975) that he did not want to produce a *social history* (of early "Christianity"), but rather to concentrate on *sociological theory*.[92] One of his theories was Peter Berger's and Thomas Luckman's influential "social construction of reality," that is, that what people take for granted as "objective reality" is in fact their social group's subjective perception of that reality.[93] Gager also drew on anthropological analyses. One of them was I. C. Jarvie's four-point cross-cultural model of millenarian (millennial) movements: 1) the promise of heaven on earth—soon; 2) the overthrow or reversal of the present social order; 3) a terrific release of emotional energy; and 4) the brief life span of the movement.[94] Gager added a fifth point from Max Weber, "the central role of a messianic, prophetic, or *charismatic* leader."[95] For Gager the Palestinian Jesus Movement fit this millenarian model and it explained why the Christ Movement(s) expanded rapidly when the millennial bliss

---

90. Steeman, "Church, Sect, Mysticism, Denomination"; Swatos, "Weber or Troeltsch?"; Elliott, "The Jewish Messianic Movement"; "Phases."

91. Troeltsch, *The Social Teachings* I, 44, and Niebuhr, *The Social Sources*, 26–76, viewed sects as "churches of the disinherited" (above, n. 42). See Duling, "Small Groups."

92. Gager, *Kingdom and Community*, 10.

93. Berger and Luckman, *The Social Construction*, 19. The concept had been used previously by Meeks, "Man from Heaven," 70–72.

94. Gager, *Kingdom and Community*, 20–21; Jarvie, *The Revolution in Anthropology*, 51; Gager also cites studies by Peter Worsley, Kennelm Burridge, A. F. C. Wallace, Norman Cohn, Yonina Talman, Sylvia Thrupp, Victor Turner and for the Greco-Roman period, S. R. Isenberg; see Duling, "Reader's Guide: Millennialism"; "Millennialism."

95. Gager, *Kingdom and Community*, 21. "Charisma" and "charismatic leader" are derived from Weber, *Economy and Society*, 241.

Jesus promised did not materialize.[96] Although Gager was more interested in the *consciousness* of being deprived ("relative deprivation" theory[97]) than real socio-economic deprivation, he did agree with Troeltsch that the Jesus Movement—in effect, a millennial "sect"—was drawn largely from the lower social strata.

John Gager's book generated strong reactions. A common complaint was historical, that is, his millennial social-scientific model was too simplistic, too deductive, too general, too lacking in attention to historical detail.[98] Most historians of ancient millennial literature preferred "close comparisons" from the immediate environment (mainly Judean millennial groups), not "distant comparisons" from other cultures, for example, Melanesian cargo cults of the South Pacific.[99] Even social historian Richard Horsley was cautious. He allowed for the possibility of distant comparisons in theory, but doubted that appropriate ones could be found.[100] Others charged that Gager's Weber-based notion of "charismatic leadership" evolving into "institution building" ("routinization of charisma") and Ernst Troeltsch's "sect"/"church" contrast were simply too Western and too Christian.[101] Ironically, the same critique was made of his supposed "distant" comparisons—they were said to be influenced by Christianity.[102] The old historians-versus-social theorists debate was still very much alive!

In response Gager reasserted that he was not engaging in "social description" (social history), but rather "sociological explanation."[103] The criticism that his Weber/Troeltsch sect model was too Christian

---

96. In millennial groups the "cognitive dissonance" is produced by unfulfilled promises and leads to modifying hopes, but also to intensified group behavior (e.g., launching a mission); see Festinger, *A Theory*; *When Prophecy Fails*.

97. Aberle, "A Note."

98. J. Z. Smith, "Too Much Kingdom"; Holmberg, *Sociology*.

99. E.g., Collins, *The Apocalyptic Imagination*, 205–6; Holmberg, *Sociology*, 79–81; Rowland, "Reading," 79–81; Trompf, *Cargo Cults*, was also doubtful. Hellholm, "The Problem," 27, and *Apocalypticism* offers a more social-contextual definition of apocalypticism; see Duling, "Reader's Guide: Millennialism" and "Millennialism."

100. Horsley, *Sociology*, 7, also had in mind Gager's use of cargo cults.

101. Wilson, *Magic*; Holmberg, *Sociology*, chap. 4; for a critique of the Weber category, see Malina, "Jesus as Charismatic Leader?"; and Seland, "Jesus as Faction Leader." Elliott proposed a compromise, "Jewish Messianic Movement"; "Phases."

102. Smith, "Too Much Kingdom," 127–28; Holmberg, *Sociology*, 80; Wilson, *Magic*, 1.

103. Gager, "Social Description."

was a little odd since a number of modern *Jewish* scholars had used it to help explain ancient *Judean* millennialism.[104] Derek Tidball wrote that the historical critics were being too cautious.[105] For a number of New Testament scholars the sect analysis of sociologist Bryan Wilson came to the rescue. Wilson had developed a typology of "sect" types based on third world societies that, although not totally uninfluenced by Christianity, were essentially non-Western and non-Christian.[106] His typology subdivided sect into seven deviant "responses to the world" (the accepted social order) and needs to be outlined here (Chart 1.1).

Especially relevant for biblical material were Wilson's conversionist, revolutionist, and reformist subtypes. Robin Scroggs had already used Wilson's analysis for his view that Jesus appealed to the poor and "riffraff" and that the early Christ Movement was a "lower class" sect engaged in agrarian protest.[107] Other scholars took up Wilson's broader, cross-cultural analysis: John Elliott for the 1 Peter community (1981),[108] Robert Jewett for the 1 Thessalonians congregation (1986),[109] Philip Esler for Luke-Acts (1987),[110] Anthony Saldarini for the Pharisees (1988),[111] Margaret MacDonald for Pauline and Deutero-Pauline communities (1988),[112] Wayne Meeks (1989) and Philip Esler (1994b) for Paul's communities,[113] and Esler for the Gospel of John (1994a).[114] I should add in response to the criticism that

---

104. Isenberg, "Millenarism"; Schiffman, "Jewish Sectarianism"; Sharot, *Messianism*, 18–19; Baumgarten, "Ancient Jewish Sectarianism."

105. Tidball, *Introduction*.

106. Wilson, *Magic and the Millennium*; "An analysis of Sect Development." For critical analyses of the use of Wilson in New Testament study, see Craffert, "An Exercise"; Luomanen, "The 'Sociology of Sectarianism'"; Jokiranta, "Learning from Sectarian Responses," is critical, but also more positive.

107. Scroggs, "Early Christianity," 171.

108. Elliott, *Home*, using Wilson's "conversionist sect."

109. Jewett, *The Thessalonian Correspondence*, 1986, focused on Sharot's analysis, but also cited Wilson.

110. Esler, *Community and Gospel*.

111. Saldarini, *Pharisees*, 72, 286–87; Cohen, *From the Maccabees to the Mishna*, 124–73, 241, argued that the Pharisees were not a sect in Wilson's terms.

112. MacDonald, *Pauline Churches*.

113. Meeks, "'Since Then,'" used Wilson in a more sociological vein; Esler, "Sectarianism."

114. Esler, "Introverted Sectarianism."

Chart 1.1 Outline of Bryan Wilson's Seven Sect Subtypes

Subtype	Description	Response to "the world"
Acceptance of "the world"	Accepts beliefs, norms, values, goals of dominant society as plausible	God accepts it
1. Conversionist	The world is corrupt because men are corrupt. Salvation requires *transformation of the self*, a change of heart. The believer knows that (s)he is saved now.	God will change us
2. Revolutionist	Only *transformation of the world*, of the natural and social orders, will do. Believers may participate in the process. Hope is in a new dispensation. Salvation is imminent.	God will overturn it
3. Introversionist	The world is irredeemably evil. Salvation requires withdrawing from it. Can be individual, but usually leads to a separated community preoccupied with its own holiness. A *transformed set of relationships*. Community perceived as the source and seat of salvation.	God calls us to abandon it
4. Reformist	Changing the world gradually for the better is the means to salvation. Closer to "acceptance," but requires supernatural aid, or divine inspiration. "Social reform" with a "religious" orientation.	God calls us to amend it
5. Utopian	Reconstruct the world according to divinely given principles. Establish a new social organization in which evil will be gradually eliminated. Less radical than the revolutionist response, but more than the reformist response. More active and constructive than introversionist response.	God calls us to reconstruct it
6. Manipulationist	It is possible to cope with the world by a *transformed set of relationships*. One must learn the right means, the correct techniques. Salvation is a present possibility. It can be health, wealth, longevity, happiness, status, success.	God calls us to change perception
7. Thaumaturgical	Salvation comes through supernatural help, a special, local dispensation. Its operation is magical: healing, miracles, oracles, etc., are the means.	God will grant particular dispensations and particular miracles

millennialism is Christian that anthropologists have found evidence for it in "distant," *non*-Christian cultures, namely, early Latin America, Africa, and China.[115]

Other scholars have attempted to update and refine their definitions of "sect." Michael White defined it as a "deviant or separatist movement within a cohesive and religiously defined dominant culture," although it shares that culture's worldview.[116] Joseph Blenkinsopp offered an appealing view that captured the parent-child metaphor: "A sect is not only a minority, and not only characterized by opposition to norms accepted by the parent-body, but also claims in a more or less exclusive way to be what the parent-body claims to be. Whether such a group formally severs itself, or is excommunicated, will depend largely on the degree of self-definition attained by the parent-body and the level of tolerance obtaining within it."[117]

However one defined or described "sect," it became clear that, as Wayne Meeks put it, Christianity's beginning as a millennial messianic "Jewish" sect had become "a commonplace in modern scholarship" (1986).[118] Given Troeltsch's and others' correlation of "sect" and "lower class," this conclusion has decisive implications about the social stratification for some early Christ Movements that at least counterbalance the supposed "New Consensus." Indeed, it has some echoes from Deissmann and the Marxist proletarian hypothesis.

I have gone into the millennial sect discussion briefly for four reasons: its integral connection to the old—and not so old—history-versus-social sciences debate; its widespread influence as a model in New Testament studies; its relation to social stratification in the early Christ Movements, particularly with regard to the lower social strata, taken up in subsequent studies about the Palestinian peasantry; and, most important, its impact on Matthean studies.

---

115. Duling, "Readers Guide: Millennialism"; "Millennialism"; Hellholm, passim, for Latin America.
116. White, "Shifting Sectarian Boundaries," 14.
117. Blenkinsopp, "Interpretation," 1–2.
118. Meeks, *The Moral World*, 98–102.

The Social-Sciences and Four Academic Associations

Methodological ferment as a result of renewed contact with the social sciences in New Testament studies after World War II is very clear from its growing presence in four academic associations.[119] A brief survey is in order.

In 1972 several scholars of the Society of Biblical Literature met to begin exploring the "social description" of early Christianity.[120] After three years Jonathan Z. Smith proposed that the group devote itself to the following working agenda:

1. description of *social facts* in the early Christian materials;
2. a *social history* of early Christianity or its phases;
3. analysis of the *social organization* of early Christianity;
4. interpreting early Christianity as a *"social world"* that offered meaning and a plausibility structure for believers.[121]

In 1977, this group was renamed "The Social World of Early Christianity Seminar,"[122] in 1983 the "Social History of Early Christianity Consultation," and recently the "Social History of Formative Christianity and Judaism." As these titles suggest, the focus is "social description," "social world," and "social history"—historical research informed by social facts and analysis of groups in understanding two interrelated movements, "Formative Judaism and Christianity," and the way they constructed and maintained their ideologies and practices.

As already noted, John Gager shifted his interest from social *history* to social *theory*. This contrast in method was illustrated at a 1981 SBL session on 1 Peter. David Balch stressed the 1 Peter community's assimilation to Greco-Roman society and used a "social description" (social history) approach.[123] In contrast, John Elliott emphasized

---

119. Oakman, "After Ten Years"; Esler, "The Context Group Project"; Elliott, "From Social Description to Social-Scientific Criticism"; Pilch, *Social Scientific Models*, 1–4. See also Horrell, "Origins and Revival of Interest."

120. Elliott, ibid. In the following year they were formally constituted as a working group.

121. Smith, "Social Description" [italics mine].

122. It examined the work of Gerd Theissen; see Schütz, "Steps Toward a Sociology."

123. Balch, *Let Wives Be Submissive*.

the community's conflict with Greco-Roman society and preferred as a method "sociological exegesis" (what became social-scientific criticism). Following Scroggs, he used Bryan Wilson's sect model.[124] Underlying this difference in method and result was—again!—the classic tension between historians and social theorists.

In 1981 the social history section now had almost a decade's track record. Nonetheless, in 1983 a second SBL Consultation appeared that followed the social theory approach. Its first session took up Elliott's previously discussed 1 Peter study (1981),[125] Bruce Malina's new "insights from cultural anthropology" book (1981),[126] and Thomas Carney's book (outside the field) showing the usefulness of social-scientific models for interpreting/explaining the ancient world (1975).[127] The following year this group was renamed "Social Sciences and New Testament Interpretation," and then, at the urging of Malina, it became in 1996 "Social-Scientific Criticism of the New Testament."[128] Social historian Michael White, following Norman Gottwald's lead,[129] urged a compromise between the two factions when he called for "balanced, mutual interaction of critical historical and sociological issues,"[130] but both groups continue to operate independently, sometimes with overlapping agendas.[131]

In addition to the new social-scientific group in the SBL, three others must be mentioned. In various Catholic Biblical Association (CBA) Seminars and Task Forces Bruce Malina had developed a cultural anthropological approach using models, or "social scenarios."[132] In 1977 a paper he presented in Wayne Meeks's National Endowment for the Humanities Summer Seminar on the social history of early

124. Elliott, *Home*; also "1 Peter"; "From Social Description," 28; see Horrell, *Between Conformity and Resistance*.
125. Elliott, *Home*.
126. Malina, *New Testament World*; see his "Social Sciences."
127. Carney, *Shape of the Past*.
128. Elliott, *What Is Social-Scientific Criticism?*
129. See n. 138 for the BASTARDS.
130. White, "Sociological Analysis," 262; Gottwald, *Tribes*.
131. Recent program units for the SBL are, "Social History of Formative Christianity and Judaism" and "Social Scientific Criticism of the New Testament," as well as "Social Sciences and the Interpretation of the Hebrew Scriptures."
132. Pilch, "Recollections"; private communication, "Birth and *Vorgeschichte* of the Context Group."

Christianity was presented again in the CBA's Healing Task Force.[133] He then sponsored a "Continuing Seminar" in the CBA called "The Sociological Approach to the New Testament," which became a continuing "Task Force" in 1981.[134] Elliott, who had given a social-scientific paper at the CBA in 1979,[135] now joined forces with Malina to orient the new CBA Task Force to the social sciences. It continues to the present, reorganized under new leadership in 2009.[136]

A third group, the European-based New Testament society *Studiorum Novi Testamenti Societas (SNTS)*, has members who have had strong interest in the social sciences,[137] some of whom are also Social Context members.

Finally, a group emerged outside these three professional societies.[138] In 1986 Elliott, who participated in both the SBL and CBA groups and was also a co-convener of a small group of biblical scholars interested in the social sciences in the San Francisco Bay area,[139] was asked by Robert Funk and Burton Mack to chair a "Social Facets" satellite group of the Jesus Seminar being formed at the University of Redlands, California. This group met along with the Jesus Seminar for three years, but in 1989 constituted itself separately as the Social Context Group with Elliott remaining as its chair. A number of its members were active in the SBL and CBA, as well as the *SNTS*. This group has become increasingly international, with meetings in Spain, Scotland, Germany, the Czech Republic, Russia, and South Africa.

---

133. Pilch, *Social Scientific Models*, 2–3.

134. Other members included John Pilch, Dennis Hamm, and John Elliott and eventually Jerome Neyrey, Walter Taylor, Douglas Oakman, and myself.

135. Elliott, "Method," which became the Introduction to *Home*; see Elliott, "On Wooing Crocodiles," 9.

136. Its 2009 agenda was a retrospective view of the group from its inception to the present.

137. E.g., Gerd Theissen; Ronald Piper; Sean Freyne; Torrey Seland; Petri Luomanen; Jutta Jokiranta; David DeSilva; Carolyn Osiek; and Vernon Robbins, who for some years convened a section on Socio-Rhetorical Criticism.

138. Oakman, "After Ten Years"; Esler, "The Context Group Project."

139. Formed in the 1970s the group took the name the "Bay Area Seminar for Theology and Related Disciplines" (BASTARDS). The other co-convener was Norman Gottwald, *Tribes of Yahweh*; "Revisiting the Tribes of Yahweh."

It meets yearly and is currently chaired by John Kloppenborg of the University of Toronto.[140]

In summary, from the 1970s to the present, many New Testament scholars in North America, Europe, and South Africa have learned from the social sciences.[141] Their work has become prominent in various professional societies. If one adds to their number scholars using the social sciences, but not active in these three societies (for example, biblical scholars who use the analysis of Marx, especially liberation theologians in Latin America);[142] social-scientific Hebrew Bible scholars;[143] social-scientific dissertations; and various other SBL and CBA groups that now incorporate the social sciences, it is clear that the social sciences, virtually ignored in mid-twentieth century New Testament criticism, are back! One finds the social sciences in at least two interrelated forms: social history and social-scientific criticism. In 2005 Norman Gottwald wrote, "One can now speak of an ongoing sub-discipline of social critical biblical study that is building on agreed upon practices and protocols within the framework of a community of discourse."[144]

To set the stage for the way in which the recent wave of interest in the social sciences has influenced the interpretation of the Gospel of Matthew in the next chapter, I turn to examples of interest in the social sciences in non-Matthean gospels.

The Social Sciences and Whole Gospel Criticism

Social-scientific study of whole gospels lagged behind its use in the interpretation of Jesus, Paul, and certain other New Testament

---

140. It has also met near Philadelphia; near Buffalo, New York; and near Cedar Rapids, Iowa.

141. My own participation has been in the Matthew section and Social-Scientific Criticism of the New Testament section of the Society of Biblical Literature, the Eastern Great Lakes Biblical Society, the Catholic Biblical Association, *Studiorum Novi Testamenti Societas*, and the Context Group since its inception in 1986; see the Preface. The chapters in this book have benefitted from comments by members of these groups.

142. Gutierrez, Boff, Segundo, Sobrino, Bonino, particularly Sobrino's *Jesus the Liberator*. For Marxist interpretation of the gospels, see below.

143. E.g., Gottwald, *Social Scientific Criticism*.

144. Gottwald, "Revisiting the Tribes of Yahweh."

books. That is not surprising. After World War II the main method for interpreting the gospels as a whole was redaction criticism, which sought to analyze the evangelists' omission, inclusion, elaboration, and placement of traditions and sources, and their free composition of new material. This is essentially a literary critical method.[145] Gerd Theissen pointed out the major flaw of this approach: its focus on the evangelists' individual literary creativity did not stimulate interest in, or analysis of, everyday social life.[146] Yet, interpreters interested in the social sciences could not dispense with redaction criticism. Not only did the gospels contain detailed resource material useful for social analysis, as researchers of the Jesus traditions knew; and not only did Marxist literary critics point out that literature mirrors the ideological and contextual perspectives of writers, whether upper class ("reactionary") or lower class ("progressive");[147] redaction critics themselves usually offered hypotheses about "the community" in which or for which a gospel was originally written.[148] Thus, those interested in everyday social life could indeed gain insights from redaction criticism, despite its "flaw." Social-scientific critic Philip Esler undertook such an analysis of the Lukan writings, calling his method "socio-redaction criticism" (1987).[149]

There are excellent examples of the combination of redaction criticism and the social sciences in non-Matthean gospels. The "apocalyptic" flavor of Markan redaction suggested the millennial sect model.[150] Markan antiestablishment and poverty themes led to Marxist analysis.[151] Luke-Acts' focus on church and spirit lent itself

145. Perrin, *What Is Redaction Criticism?* For the language "Composition Criticism" in relation to Matthew, see Tobin, "The Legacy of William Thompson," 3, in Aune, *The Gospel of Matthew in Current Study*.

146. Theissen, "Zur Forschungsgeschichtlichen Einordnung," 6–7. The Chicago School leveled the same critique at then current literary criticism.

147. Eagleton, *Marxism and Literary Criticism*.

148. Stanton, "Origin and Purpose of Matthew's Gospel"; Harrington, "Sociological Concepts and the Early Church." See Runesson, "Rethinking Early Jewish-Christian Religions" for further references.

149. Esler, *Community and Gospel in Luke-Acts*, 67–70; in line with Elliott, Stanton, "Matthew's Gospel and the Damascus Document," 85, says that sociological insights "complement redaction critical and literary critical approaches."

150. Kee, *Community*; Mack, *Myth*. Cf. Mark 13.

151. Belo, *Materialist Reading*; Myers, *Binding the Strong Man*. See Mark 10:21; 12:42–43.

to sect analysis[152] and its emphasis on wealth and poverty suggested economic and anthropological analyses.[153]

As for explicit experiments in social-scientific model-building, the first joint publication of the Context Group, *The Social World of Luke-Acts* (1991), was programmatic and illustrates the broad range of interest.[154] It is worth listing the contributions. Bruce Malina's initial study proposed constructing ancient Mediterranean social "scenarios" —models of typical social attitudes and arrangements—as a way to bridge the tremendous linguistic and cultural gaps between the ancient Mediterranean world and the present-day West.[155] He teamed with Jerome Neyrey to interpret Luke-Acts through what were considered to be Mediterranean core values: "honor and shame,"[156] "dyadic (significant, other-directed) personalities" typical of "collectivistic" or group-centered societies,[157] and deviance and "labeling theory."[158] Richard Rohrbaugh examined Luke-Acts' references to towns/cities using a model of the "preindustrial city";[159] Douglas Oakman its image of the "countryside" through peasant studies;[160] John Pilch its "health care system";[161] John Elliott its household and temple contrast;[162] and Halvor Moxnes its "patron-client relations."[163] Neyrey also looked at Luke-Acts' symbolism,[164] Vernon Robbins its "implied" author's social

152. Esler, *Community and Gospel*, 67–70; cf. Acts 2.

153. Moxnes, *Economy*, 24–25; Luke 16:14. Moxnes said that redaction criticism "does not play an important part in this study," but he frequently examined Lukan redaction, claiming that it "... points to [the author's] intentions" and that it is "transparent" for Luke's own time."

154. Neyrey, ed., *Social World*. Redaction was sometimes assumed.

155. Malina, "Reading Theory Perspective," based on Halliday, *Language as Social Semiotic*.

156. Malina and Neyrey, "Honor and Shame in Luke-Acts"; for this theme in the Gospel of Matthew, see chap. 3 below.

157. Malina and Neyrey, "First-Century Personality."

158. Malina and Neyrey, "Conflict in Luke-Acts"; for deviance and labeling in the Gospel of Matthew, see chap. 3 below.

159. Rohrbaugh, "The Pre-industrial City"; Sjøberg, *The Preindustrial City*; see Model 3.4 in chap. 3 below.

160. Oakman, "The Countryside."

161. Pilch, "Sickness and Healing."

162. Elliott, "Temple versus Household."

163. Moxnes, "Patron-Client Relations."

164. Neyrey, "The Symbolic Universe."

location,[165] Mark McVann its ritual as "status transformation,"[166] and Neyrey the social significance of its references to meals and table fellowship.[167] I add that one year later, Malina and Rohrbaugh broke new ground with a social-scientific "scenario" commentary on all three Synoptic Gospels (1992).[168] Finally, the Gospel of John's otherworldly language and community, once explored by Wayne Meeks in terms of the sect category,[169] suggested to Esler the "introversionist" sect subtype of Bryan Wilson (1994)[170] and to Bruce Malina and Richard Rohrbaugh the sociolinguistic theories of "antilanguage" and "antisociety" by Michael A. K. Halliday (1998).[171]

These non-Matthean gospel examples suggest that by the late 1980s and early 1990s, scholars who were interested in gospel criticism and were informed by the social sciences were finally catching up with earlier Jesus and Paul research on social stratification and sect. Although redaction criticism had been deficient in offering detailed social-contextual analyses, the predominantly literary methods could not be ignored.

Summary

This chapter began by examining in a general way the historical relationship between history and the social sciences beginning in the Enlightenment. In an age when it was thought possible to master scientific knowledge, historians were fascinated by the social dimensions of human behavior and social scientists were attracted to historical evolution of societal types. As the fields developed and matured, however, they parted company. Historians found a home in the humanities, attempted to describe the causal relations among past facts, and sought to avoid theory where possible. Social scientists tried to reason more like natural scientists, at first attempting general "laws" of group

165. Robbins, "The Social Location."
166. McVann, "Rituals of Status Transformation."
167. Neyrey, "Ceremonies."
168. Malina and Rohrbaugh, *Social-Science Commentary on the Synoptic Gospels.*
169. Meeks, "The Man from Heaven."
170. Esler, "Introverted Sectarianism"; cf. Berger, *Exegese*, 218–41.
171. Malina and Rohrbaugh, *Social Science Commentary on the Gospel of John*; see Halliday, "Anti-Languages."

behavior, but eventually, as this approach softened, moved under the influence of Durkheim to an abstract, essentially ahistorical explanatory Structural Functionalism. Such ahistoricism came to dominate much sociology and anthropology by the mid-twentieth century. There were exceptions to this split: on the one hand the social histories of Max Weber, on the other the work of the French *Annales* school in attempting to understand "mentalities" in whole historical epochs. After World War II, however, historians and social scientists increasingly reestablished friendly cooperation and a number of cross-disciplinary journals relating sociology and anthropology to history appeared.

The relationship of the social sciences to the historical study of the Bible followed a similar course. There was a great attraction to understand social contexts of biblical peoples in the early part of the twentieth century, in part influenced by Marxist theory, in part stimulated by the Chicago School and Deissmann's work. This interest peaked in the 1920s. In the wake of critical views of Marx, as well as Neo-orthodox theology and doubts about the historicity of key New Testament texts, interest in social sciences as an interpretative historical tool waned. After World War II, however, there was a renewed interest in social contexts, although with much less influence of Marxist theory. The earliest phase concentrated on the historical Jesus and Pauline communities, but eventually the contexts of the gospels also came into play. In these developments, the agendas of social historians and social-scientific critics often overlapped, but the two groups remain separate to this day. With this background in mind, I turn to the subject of chapter 2: the social sciences and the Gospel of Matthew.

CHAPTER 2

The Gospel of Matthew and Social-Scientific Criticism

OUR FIRST CHAPTER SURVEYED the historical drama that illustrates the tension and interplay between the fields of history and the social sciences, the larger stage of the story portraying how the social sciences became increasingly accepted and used as an interpretative tool in historical-critical biblical study. Although most study of the complete gospels was relatively late to adopt social-scientific criticism—the earliest studies concentrated rather on the historical Jesus, Paul, and the early churches—by the late 1980s a number of gospel critics began to mine the social sciences for theories and models to help understand or explain these narrative genres. This chapter narrows the discussion to the appearance of social-scientific criticism as a major tool for interpreting one of those gospels, the Gospel of Matthew.

Before turning to this story, a brief word needs to be said about three historical problems if only because solving them would contribute much to understanding social constructs, relations, and conflicts in the gospel. These problems are the gospel's author, its time of composition, and its place of composition.[1]

Author, Time, Place

There is a second-century CE Papias tradition that Jesus' disciple "Matthew" (who in this gospel alone is identified as a Galilean toll collector in Matt 9:9; 10:3) put together the "sayings" (*logia*) of Jesus

---

1. For detail, see Duling, *The New Testament*, chap. 9; "Gospel according to Matthew," Intro.; "The Gospel of Matthew."

in the "Hebrew dialect" (*Hebraiois dialectō*), in which each had to "translate" (*hermēneusen*) them (Papias in Eus. *HE* 3.39.16).[2] In the late second century Irenaeus of Lyons added that the gospel was written when Peter and Paul were in Rome (presumably before the Gospel of Mark), which by modern calculations would have been in the late 50s or early 60s (Ire. *Haer* 3.1.1). By the late fourth century Jerome deduced that this gospel in the "Hebrew dialect" was written in Judea for "the Jews" (Preface to his *Commentary on Matthew*) and had to be "translated" into Greek (Jer. *Vir. Ill.* 3).

Most modern historical critics do not accept these traditions without question. First, although the gospel does contain many of Jesus' sayings (and speeches), it is not simply a collection of them. Second, if Papias (in Eusebius) meant that the gospel was composed in the "Hebrew (or Aramaic) language" and had to be "translated"—the usual interpretation by both ancient and modern scholars[3]—his statement does not correspond with the modern view that the gospel was originally written in Greek. Third, the author certainly knew about the destruction of Jerusalem in 70 CE (Matt 22:7; cf. 22:41; 24:15–16); therefore, the gospel must have been written after 70 CE, not in the 50s or early 60s, when Peter and Paul were in Rome. Fourth, this later dating (after 70 CE) corresponds with the Two Source Theory that the writer of the Gospel of Matthew used the Gospel of Mark, usually dated about 70 CE, as a source. Fifth, and finally, Jesus' main opponents, the Pharisees, who sought to gain authority and control of the Judeans after the war with Rome, were the writer's main opponents, as well, and this fact helps explain the multiplication and intensification of anti-Pharisee passages in the gospel. Although no position is airtight, these issues, when combined with the probability that Ignatius of Antioch cited a phrase written by the Matthean author (Matt 3:15 in Ig. *Smyr* 1.1; cf. also Ig. *Phil* 3:1 [Matt 15:13]) in 110 CE,[4]

---

2. Since Papias' comment follows a similar comment about "Mark," it is usual to assume that it refers not simply to a *person* named "Matthew," but also to his *composition*.

3. This view of Papias' meaning is not universal. *Hebraiois dialectō* could mean in "Hebrew style" (see, e.g., Gundry, *Matthew*, xxi–xxii), in which case *hērmēneusen* would mean not "translated," but "interpreted," a suggestion that removes the problem that the gospel was not translated into Greek from a Semitic language.

4. Possible references to the Gospel of Matthew in 1 Pet 2:12 (Matt 5:16) and 3:14 (Matt 5:10) would, if 1 Peter were dated to the late first century, push this date

favor a date of composition between 70 and 110 CE, and most critics settle for about 80–90 CE. All this corresponds with the thesis that superscriptions (titles) to all four gospels, which begin with the formula "according to," are thought to have been inserted into gospel manuscripts to distinguish them according to second-century CE opinion. In short, their authors, never identified within the gospels themselves, are anonymous.

To know the place of composition would be extremely important for both social-historical criticism and social-scientific criticism. Jerome's Judean location faces a host of alternative locations in modern criticism. Terms in the gospel about cities and wealth,[5] and especially the gospel's Semitic Greek and focus on the Torah, suggest to scholars that it was written in an urban area where both Judeans and Greeks lived, thus in some key eastern Mediterranean city. Various scholars' options have been listed by John Meier, W. D. Davies and Dale Allison, and Warren Carter, among others.[6] By way of summary, I offer the Davies-Allison list and add to it a few scholars and locations (italicized).

Jerusalem:	A. *Plummer*,[7] M. Albertz, W. C. Allen, A. Schlatter, T. H. Robinson, J. Schiewind, W. Michaelis, A. Wikenhauser, M. Hengel (tentatively)
Caesarea Maritima:	B. T. Viviano
Galilee to Greater Syria	A. Segal, (A. Saldarini)[8]
Sepphoris	J. A. Overman (tentatively), *A. Gale*[9]
Phoenicia (Tyre or Sidon):	G. D. Kilpatrick, H. B. Green, (A. Saldarini),[10] L. M. White[11]

---

back a generation. However, the references in this case may be oral tradition.

5. Kingsbury, "The Verb *Akolouthein*"; *Matthew as Story*, 125.

6. Meier, "Antioch"; Davies and Allison, *Gospel* I, 138-39; Carter, *Matthew*, 24.

7. Plummer, *An Exegetical Commentary*, xxxiii.

8. Segal, "Matthew's Jewish Voice," 26-30; Saldarini, *Matthew's Jewish-Christian Community*, 26 ("somewhere in Syria or Coele Syria").

9. Overman, *Matthew's Gospel*, 159 n. 20, gives a slight preference for Sepphoris over Tiberias; Gale, *Redefining Ancient Borders*, 41–63.

10. See n. 8 above.

11. White, "Crisis Management," 241 (the mixed environment of "the Syro-

Alexandria, Egypt:	S. G. F. Brandon, S. van Tilborg
East of the Jordan River (Pella):	R. T. Herford, H. J. Schoeps, *W. Marxsen*, H. D. Slingerland, G. Theissen[12]
An unknown city in Syria:	F. V. Filson, P. Bonnard, G. Strecker, W. Marxsen, D. Hill, N. Perrin, L. Goppelt, M. D. Goulder, E. Lohse, E. Schweizer, G. Künzel, S. Freyne
Edessa in Syria	B. W. Bacon (tentatively), R. E. Osborne
Antioch in Syria	J. Weiss, B. H. Street, M. S. Enslin, A. H. McNeile, R. H. Fuller, R. E. Brown, R. H. Gundry, J. P. Meier, J. Zumstein, U. Luz (with reservations), *W. Carter*[13]

The variety of proposed locations illustrates the problem. Jerusalem fits Jerome's traditional Judea location, but if modern dating after the Roman destruction of Jerusalem in 70 CE is correct, it would not have been a likely city for a heavily Judean gospel to have been written in Greek. The tendency to hunt for a city or town in Galilee, Phoenicia, or southern Syria corresponds to the recent tendency to think of the gospel as "Christian *Jewish*" rather than "Jewish *Christian*" (see below). Arguments have been marshaled for other Palestinian cities, especially in Galilee, such as Caesarea Maritima (the "Roman capital" of Palestine), Sepphoris, or Tiberias, or cities further north in Syro-Phoenicia on the Mediterranean coast, such as Tyre and Sidon. An internal geographical reference to Galilee and Judea as "beyond [west of] the Jordan" (Matt 19:1; 4:15) suggests some city east of the Jordan (Pella?). Other cities in Syria have been suggested, such as Edessa. Among them, Antioch has attracted most scholars. It had a large Judean population, was important for the Gentile mission, was not that far from Palestine, and, as noted, Ignatius of Antioch was well acquainted with the gospel and probably even cited it. There are close connections between the gospel and the *Didachē*, often thought to

---

Phoenician region" in the Canaanite Woman story is "a symbol of its [the Matthean community's] own situation." The addition of "Syro" here is broader than Phoenicia.

12. Theissen, *Gospels*, 17, 249–51.
13. Carter, *Matthew*, 24-25.

have been written in Antioch, although its provenance is also much debated.¹⁴ The model disciple in the gospel, Peter, was influential at Antioch (Gal 2:11–14). Those who argue for a particular location can point out the weaknesses of alternative positions, but they also recognize, as Davies and Allison put it, that "[w]e shall never know beyond a reasonable doubt where the autograph of Matthew was completed."¹⁵ I have generally accepted the Davies and Allison reasoning, which is consistent with those of Meier, Carter, and others that Antioch is as good an "educated guess" as any.¹⁶

In short, conclusions about the gospel's precise place of composition are, unfortunately, uncertain, but Antioch is possible. The usual dating 80–90 CE is plausible, and, although the author is unknown, one can say much more about him by internal analysis, as I shall indicate especially in chapter 9.

Social-Scientific Studies of the Gospel of Matthew

I begin with a study that was not a social-scientific work—it was literary-critical, feminist, and theological—but, as its title states, it implied a social dimension. This study was Amy-Jill Levine's *The Social and Ethnic Dimensions of Matthean Salvation History: Go Nowhere Among the Gentiles* (1988).¹⁷ Jesus' mission command to the disciples in Matt 10:5–6 (cf. 15:24), "Go nowhere among the Gentiles," but only to "the lost sheep of the house of Israel," is in tension with his post-resurrection mission command to go to and baptize "all nations" ["Gentiles"; "peoples"] (28:19).¹⁸ A widespread redaction critical interpretation is that these two passages are related as a sequential "salvation history" schema in which Judean ethnic exclusivism in the first passage is su-

---

14. Draper, "Torah and Troublesome Apostles"; Jefford, "The Milieu of Matthew." See chap. 6, n. 85.

15. Davies and Allison, *The Gospel* I, 139.

16. Ibid., 146–47; Meier, "Antioch" and "Summary"; Carter, *Matthew*, 24; see Duling, *The New Testament*, chap. 9; "The Gospel according to Matthew," Intro.; "The Gospel of Matthew."

17. "Ethnicity" was in the title, but did not lead to a discussion of ethnicity theory.

18. See chap. 10 below for a discussion of *ethnē* and the problem of its translation "Gentiles," "nations," or "peoples."

perseded by a universalist perspective in the second. Levine argued that this "ethnic" interpretation of salvation history sets "Jew" against "Gentile" in a way that is actually anti-Jewish. Most important, it slides by the key *social* emphasis in the first passage: the disciples should go to "the *lost sheep* of the house of Israel" (Matt 10:6). Who are the lost sheep? For Levine they are what she calls the "marginalized" from among the Israelite crowds who follow and accept Jesus, and thus are "Jewish."[19] However, when Jesus' promises have been fulfilled to Israel, this social message is extended to the Gentiles (Matt 28:19). In short, the ethnic conflict that is so pronounced in the period of Jesus—"Jew" versus "Gentile"—is superseded by a *social* gospel: it is Jesus' message in behalf of the powerless against the powerful that is extended to all—"Jew" *and* "Gentile." Levine's feminist parallel was that Jesus' egalitarian Kingdom supersedes the patriarchalism of the elite "Jewish" rulers.[20]

That same year (1988) the first significant book interpreting the Gospel of Matthew *social-scientifically* appeared, that is, *Calling Jesus Names: The Social Value of Labels in Matthew* by Bruce Malina and Jerome Neyrey.[21] Its claim to use redaction criticism recalls Philip Esler's "socio-redaction criticism," but its strong suit was really the social sciences.[22] Theologians and New Testament scholars had often written about "Christology from above" or "Christology from below." Malina and Neyrey shifted to "Christology from the side," that is, Jesus as seen by his contemporaries—friends and especially enemies. They analyzed two passages or "text segments." The first was the Pharisees' charge that Jesus exorcized demons by the power of Beelzeboul, the

---

19. For a more social-scientific analysis of marginality, see chaps. 5, 7, and 9 below.

20. A critique that Levine did not fully carry out the salvation-historical shift is found in Donaldson, "Review."

21. Malina and Neyrey, *Calling Jesus Names*.

22. Graham Stanton, "Matthew's Christology," 100, n. 3, viewed the book positively but commented that its authors "make hardly any use of redaction criticism." There is a certain cogency to the remark, since they are not redaction critics. Yet, in their interpretation of the Jesus' trial they often referred to the Matthean writer's "compositional changes" and "characteristics," and claimed that their "use of social science models falls within the accepted 'historical' concerns of form and redaction criticism . . ." (142). See following note.

Prince of Demons (plus Jesus' implied counteraccusation in Q).[23] This charge was interpreted as an ancient Mediterranean example of "witchcraft accusation" typical of central African witchcraft societies.[24] In Matthew the accusation illustrates the attempt of a group to expel one perceived as a disguised deceiver or evil agent threatening group purity, that is, an accusation that Jesus is a "witch." From the perspective of modern deviance and labeling theory, it is an example of "deviance labeling," or negative name-calling, which is used by the Pharisees to rid themselves of a successful rival.[25]

Malina and Neyrey's second "text segment" was the Matthean version of Jesus' trial, a longer section that required that they carry out deviance and labeling theory in greater detail. The authors postulated four typical phases of the "labeling process":

Table 2.1 Labeling in Jesus' Trial (Matthew)

Labeling Process	Jesus' Trial in Matthew
1) negative labeling	the high court condemns Jesus as a blasphemer deserving death[a]
2) garnering popular support and legitimacy by disseminating the label	witnesses testify to Jesus' anti-temple prediction;[b] the people call for his death
3) establishing that the person has been consistently deviant	acts and sayings of Jesus lead up to the charges
4) reinforcing the accusation/label by "status degradation rituals"	Jesus is scourged, stripped, spit upon, struck, slapped, mocked as king, and crucified[c]

a. Matt 26:65–66.

b. Matt 26:60–63; in Matt 24:2 such a prediction is made, so the witnesses are not "false."

c. Matt 27:26–44; Malina and Neyrey, *Calling Jesus Names*, 81.

---

23. Malina and Neyrey initially focused on reconstructed Q/Matt (12:22, 25, 27–28, 30) because it contains the counteraccusation missing from Mark 3:22 (6–7); oddly, this reconstruction does not include Matt 12:24 (= Luke 11:15//Mark 3:22), the Beelzeboul accusation itself; however, it is taken up later in their more extensive analysis (*Calling Jesus Names*, 58–65).

24. Douglas, *Witchcraft Confessions*; also Evans-Pritchard, *Witchcraft*; Nahman Ben-Yehuda, *Deviance and Moral Boundaries*.

25. See further, Becker, *Outsiders*; Erickson, *Wayward Puritans*; Pfuhl, *Images of Deviance*.

Understanding the trial as a process of deviance labeling shows how those in power use a social phenomenon to condemn and execute Jesus. Of course, Jesus is also labeled positively in the gospel ("prominence labeling"), first by "his friends"— his disciples who follow, confess, and worship him—but also by the Matthean writer who emphasizes Jesus' royal pedigree, teachings, labels (titles) of honor, fulfillment of Scripture, and resurrection (a "status *elevation* ritual").[26] Clearly, *Calling Jesus Names* presented a fresh, new approach to social attitudes and relations in the gospel.

Malina and Neyrey's study, the first published book of social-scientific criticism on the Gospel of Matthew, highlighted *social theory*. In 1989, a year later, a conference on *social history*, "The Social History of the Matthean Community in Roman Syria," took place in Dallas, Texas. Four scholars in the conference's resulting book edited by David Balch (1991)[27] also drew heavily on the social-scientific *theory*. Not surprisingly, perhaps, three of them used sect analysis. Rodney Stark, the only professional sociologist in the book, sought to explain how an obscure "revitalization movement" from the Palestinian countryside conquered the mighty Roman Empire;[28] he found his answer in the sociological theory that a social revolution is generated by a social crisis, in this instance the squalid living conditions of Greco-Roman cities such as Antioch, the location usually proposed for the Matthean gospel's composition.[29] As already noted, this specialist in modern sects and cults[30] argued that the rural Jesus *sect* evolved into an urban *cult* and, like modern cults, recruited largely from the higher social strata;[31] it also offered what pagan cults did not, a community in which believers are required to love God, each other, and even outsiders.[32] It

---

26. Ibid., chap. 4.

27. Balch, ed., *Social History*.

28. Stark, "Antioch"; see Wallace, "Revitalization Movements"; Duling, "Readers' Guide: Millennialism"; "Millennialism."

29. Stark drew on Stambaugh, *The Ancient Roman City*, but did not discuss Sjøberg's *The Preindustrial City*. For a critique, see Coleman, "1998," 141–43.

30. Stark, *A Theory of Religion*; Stark and Bainbridge, "Of Churches"; "Networks of Faith."

31. Hence, Stark's support of the "New Consensus" noted in chap. 1 above.

32 Stark, "The Class Basis"; "How New Religions Succeed"; "Epidemics"; *The Rise of Christianity*; see Duling, "Small Group Research"; "Recruitment."

is clear that the sect-to-cult model was having important implications for social stratification in relation to the Gospel of Matthew.

Two other contributors illustrate the increasing importance of sect analysis. Drawing on four of Bryan Wilson's sect subtypes (see Chart 1.1), Anthony Saldarini proposed that the Matthean group was, like the original Jesus Movement group, a reformist "Jewish" sect, but that it had become less "revolutionist" (millennial) and "thaumaturgical" (healing), and more "conversionist" (open to both Judeans and non-Judeans).[33] He wed this complex model with social deviance theory and recent studies of ancient Greco-Roman "voluntary associations."[34] Result: the Matthean reformist/conversionist sect was also a "*deviant* voluntary association" that sought societal change ("alienative deviance") and addressed internal group needs ("expressive deviance").

A third contributor, Michael White, accepted the "deviant Jewish sect" hypothesis,[35] but shifted emphasis to the gospel's internally inconsistent social roles, norms, and behaviors, arguing that they pointed to a community in crisis, as Stark had maintained. After surveying social and political crises of the late first century, White settled on the crisis that occurred when Herod Agrippa II's territories were incorporated into the Roman province of Syria in 93 CE as the gospel's time of composition, a plausible place being an unknown Syrophoenician city.[36]

The most social-scientific contribution in Balch's social history collection—social-scientific in the sense of being indebted to cross-cultural "distant comparisons" and generalized models—was Anne Wire's "Gender Roles in a Scribal Community." Against the backdrop of Gerhard Lenski's macromodel of an advanced agrarian society (see further, below and chapter 3) and Gideon Sjøberg's preindustrial city model,[37] Wire examined clan-based "scribal communities" of the

---

33. Saldarini, "The Gospel of Matthew," 58–59.

34. For my view of the Matthean community as a voluntary association, see chap. 8.

35. White, "Crisis Management," 213–14.

36. Ibid., 232, 236.

37. Lenski, *Power and Privilege*; Lenski and Lenski, *Human Societies* (cf. Nolan, *Human Societies*); Sjøberg, *The Preindustrial City*. Lenski and Sjøberg were important also for Rohrbaugh, "The Pre-industrial City"; Wire, "Gender Roles"; and Love,

ancient Chinese Qing Dynasty and isolated five general features of such communities: "(1) They reinterpret in writing a revered literary tradition (2) in such a way as to teach concrete ritual and ethical behavior (3) which can assure the proper fulfillment of set roles within a community of identification (4) sanctioned by adequate rewards and punishments (5) in order to reassert right order in a situation where it is perceived to be under some threat."[38] For Wire the Qumran covenanters and Pharisees share these features and they, in turn, are "close comparisons" with the Matthean community.[39] The latter, however, was distinctive in being (1) a socially mixed group that (2) criticized patriarchalism and (3) cared for "marginal" persons, particularly women.[40]

An influential social-historical book on Matthew from this period also drew on Wilson's sect model, namely, J. Andrew Overman's *Matthew's Gospel and Formative Judaism: The Social World of the Matthean Community* (1990). Overman tracked "Jewish" sectarian movements from the fall of the First Temple (587 BCE) to the fall of the Second Temple (70 CE)[41] and argued that in the following period "Matthean Judaism," a localized "Jewish" sect striving for power, came into conflict with a "coalition of [Jewish] sects" led by Pharisees and scribes, that is, what Jacob Neusner called "formative Judaism."[42] This sectarian struggle would help explain the Matthean gospel's many controversies about purity, leadership roles, group boundaries, discipline, authority, Torah interpretation, and the like.

A number of articles and books on Matthew and the social sciences followed. Graham Stanton, a Redaction Critic who came to believe that Matthew's Gospel was "particularly well-suited to careful use of sociological insights,"[43] made a "close comparison" with the

---

Jesus and Marginal Women. For both models, see Duling, "Empire." I have used Lenski extensively in this book; see esp. chap. 3. For Rohrbaugh's model based on that of Sjøberg, see chap. 3, Model 3.4.

38. Wire, "Gender Roles," 91.

39. Ibid., 184; on "distant" and "close" comparisons, see Esler, *Community and Gospel,* 9–12.

40. See chaps. 5, 7, and 9 for marginality theory.

41. See Simon, *Jewish Sects*; Blenkinsopp, "Interpretation"; Schiffman, "Jewish Sectarianism"; *Sectarian Law.*

42. Neusner, "Formation"; also Cohen, "The Significance of Yavneh."

43. Stanton, "Matthew's Gospel," 85.

Damascus Document from the Dead Sea Scrolls,⁴⁴ observing that both documents betrayed a beleaguered, threatened, highly disciplined, sharp-boundaried group led by a "charismatic leader." In short, it was a "sect" that had *already* separated from its "parent-body";⁴⁵ thus, the disciples in the gospel were urged to have a "higher righteousness" than the Pharisees who were blind guides and who persecuted church leaders.⁴⁶ For Stanton the "church" was clearly being distinguished from the "synagogue." Thus, the Matthean sect had already separated from "Judaism"; it was *extra muros*, "outside the walls"; it was a "new people" with a "new self-identification."⁴⁷ The "parting of the ways" between "Judaism" and "Christianity" had taken place.⁴⁸

In *Matthew's Christian-Jewish Community* (1994) Anthony Saldarini presented the reverse view. Expanding his "deviant voluntary association/sect" hypothesis with Wilson's sect analysis and other theories,⁴⁹ Saldarini argued that from a sociological perspective deviant sects always remain *within* the boundaries of their parent communities, in this case Israel. Thus, the Matthean sect had not separated; it was still "Jewish," not "Christian," as Stanton claimed.⁵⁰ The "parting of the ways" between "Judaism" and "Christianity" had *not* fully taken place. In agreement with Overman, then, the Matthean community was "Christian-*Jewish*," not "Jewish-*Christian*."

Work on Matthew related to the social sciences must include two books by Warren Carter, namely, *Matthew and the Margins: A Sociopolitical and Religious Reading* (2000) and *Matthew and Empire: Initial Explorations* (2001). By way of background, recall that some social historians were concerned that social-scientific critics were too ahistorical. From the opposite direction came some Literary and

---

44. Ibid., 88–89, seems to have (mis)understood "distant comparison" as modern theory.

45. For the parent/child metaphor taken from Troeltsch, see Blenkinsopp, "Interpretation," 1–2; White, "Shifting Sectarian Boundaries," 14. Their views are noted above.

46. Matt 15:14; 23; 15:13; 16:17, 19, 24, 26.

47. Stanton, *Gospel*, 113–45; see also his "Revisiting Matthew's Communities."

48. See further, Dunn, *Jews and Christians*; Wilson, *Related Strangers*; Stanton, ibid., chap. 7.

49. Social psychology, resource mobilization, and sociology of knowledge.

50. Stanton, "Origin and Purpose," 1914–16.

Reader-Response Critics who viewed them as too historical. Well acquainted with the latter perspective, Carter argued from two influential literary critics, Wilhelm Iser and especially Peter Rabinowitz, that readers (and hearers) deduced from the gospel narrative (Literary Criticism's "implied reader") must be correlated with hypothetical *real* readers (and hearers) whom the *real* author expected would read his text. The reason is that these readers, the ancient Mediterranean contemporaries of the author, shared with the Matthean author the same general "social-historical environment," "sociohistorical experience," "cultural conventions," or "sociohistorical context."[51] In these studies Carter built on some of my research on social stratification[52] and marginal persons,[53] along with the work of Jung Young Lee,[54] to show that the gospel writer legitimates a marginal way of life: living between two competing worlds ("in betweenness") in tension with the "normative scheme," yet having chosen this way of life voluntarily.[55]

More indebted to explicit social-scientific theory and modeling was Jerome Neyrey's *Honor and Shame in the Gospel of Matthew* (1998).[56] Neyrey defined honor, a "core value" in the Mediterranean world, as follows: "the generalized term which refers to the worth or value of persons both in their own eyes and in the eyes of their village or neighborhood."[57] He demonstrated that honor was bestowed on, or *ascribed* to, Jesus, but that Jesus also *acquired* honor. The key innovation of Neyrey's study was the correlation of Mediterranean "honor and shame" with ancient Greco-Roman "praise and blame": to praise is to honor, to blame is to shame. The ability to praise and

---

51. Carter *Households and Discipleship*, 19-20, 34-39; *Matthew: Storyteller, Interpreter, Evangelist*; "Matthew 4:18-22," 58-61; see Iser, *The Act of Reading*; Rabinowitz, "Whirl Without End," 85.

52. *Matthew and the Margins*, 17-21, draws directly on Arlandson's model of social stratification, but Arlandson, *Women*, 20-24, n. 28, states: "I base my discussion on his [Duling's])." All three of us depend on Lenski's macrosociology; see chap. 3.

53. Carter used my views of marginality in "Matthew and the Margins" at the 1997 Catholic Biblical Association (Seattle, WA) and in *Matthew and the Margins* (pp. 43-49 and footnotes).

54. Lee, *Marginality*; on Lee, see also chap. 9 and nn. 100-103.

55. For more analysis, see chaps. 5, 7, and 9.

56. Neyrey, *Honor and Shame*.

57. Ibid., 15; for its centrality see Aristotle, *Nicomachean Ethics* 4.3.9-12.

blame was a rhetorical skill that ancient students learned from secondary school handbooks, the *Progymnasmata*,[58] the eighth exercise of which concentrated on the *encomium*, a speech of praise typically spoken at public ceremonies and memorials. Neyrey surmised that it would have been known to educated Judeans such as the author of the Gospel of Matthew.[59] Thus, in a manner *similar to* the *encomium*[60] the Matthean writer glorified the character and virtuous life of his hero Jesus with warm and enthusiastic honor/praise, stressing typical virtues: 1) his noble origin; 2) his birth marked by dreams, signs, portents, or celestial phenomena, and his nurture, education, and training (mostly ignored, except for Jesus' trade); 3) his courage, wisdom, magnanimity, deeds of body (absent), fortune, and power; and 4) his noble death (despite his shameful crucifixion, Jesus displays courage and piety and his death is voluntary; it benefits others and is victorious). Finally, building on K. C. Hanson's study of the beatitudes, Neyrey interpreted the Sermon on the Mount as Jesus' turning the honor/shame cultural norm upside down: "How honorable are the poor in spirit . . ."[61]

Two more social-scientific approaches to the gospel need to be mentioned. In his study of conflict in the Matthean miracle stories of Matthew 8–9 (1997),[62] Evert-Jan Vledder first surveys exegetical treatments of conflict in the gospel that he deems "inadequate"[63] because they are not well grounded in conflict theory. He then takes up the social-scientific conflict theories of Louis Coser and particularly Ralf Dahrendorf.[64] Dahrendorf believed that theories of social consensus

---

58. Neyrey, ibid., 78–83; Theon, *Progymnasmata*. Rhetorical conventions are derived from Aristotle, *Rhetoric*; Cicero *De Inventione*; Quintilian *Institutio Oratoria*; the *Rhetorica ad Herennium*.

59. E.g., Ben Sira 44–50.

60. Neyrey never argued that the gospel fit an *encomium* genre precisely.

61. Neyrey, chap. 8, "Honoring the Dishonored"; see Hanson, "How Honorable! How Shameful!"

62. Vledder, *Conflict*, 45–53; see Duling, "Review of Evert-Jan Vledder"; Malina, "Review of Evert-Jan Vledder."

63. Theissen, *The Miracle Stories*; Luz, *Das Evangelium nach Matthäus*; Patte, *The Gospel according to Matthew*; Saldarini, "The Gospel of Matthew," and Stanton, "Matthew's Gospel and the Damascus Document."

64. Coser, *Functions*; Dahrendorf, "Toward a Theory of Social Conflict"; *Class and Class Conflict*; Kriesberg, *The Sociology of Social Conflicts*. Dahrendorf's conflict

(for example, Structural Functionalism) needed to be countered by theories of social conflict rooted in Marx. However, Marx did not foresee certain capitalist developments such as the growth of a large middle class, the legalization of collective bargaining, and the strike, factors that mitigate the necessity of a class revolution. In Dahrendorf's revision of Marx, conflict should be seen as a never-ending spiral of tension between two "imperatively coordinated associations," the one consisting of dominant, organized "interest groups" whose power is *legitimate*—backed by legal authority and force—and who seek to preserve the status quo, the other consisting of subjected, unorganized "quasi-groups" who oppose their rulers, attempt to organize, and seek to change the status quo. Using this revised Marxism and Lenski's model of hierarchical stratification in an advanced agrarian society,[65] Vledder interprets conflict in the gospel as that between a small, elite ruling class and their retainers who want to preserve the status quo, on the one hand, and the masses, that is, peasants, expendables, and artisans who want social change, on the other. Locating the gospel in a mainly urban area in Galilee or Syria, and drawing on my stratification studies, he distributes the groups of the gospel into Lenski-inspired social strata and considers the Matthean community as a "voluntarily marginalized" community[66] that is not yet totally separated from "formative Judaism." Vledder views conflict between social strata—upper "haves" and lower "have-nots"—as a context in which to read the miracle stories of Matthew 8–9. For example, the leper from the "crowds" (a "quasi-group"), who represents the "unclean and degraded" social stratum, is told by Jesus to report to the priest who represents the elite ruler stratum with power and authority (an "interest group") (Matt 8:2–4). Again, when the servant of a centurion who is a military representative of Rome with authority (an unclean Gentile) is healed (Matt 8:5–13), Jesus not only crosses social/religious boundaries voluntarily by helping him, the Gentile himself becomes a "voluntary marginal."[67] In another example Jesus crosses boundaries when

---

theory countered structural functionalism's conservatism with a revised version of Marx; Horsley, *Sociology*, used Dahrendorf's views in his critique that Theissen's understanding of the Jesus Movement was too conservative (chap. 1, nn. 16 and 84).

65. Dahrendorf's analysis is not limited to capitalist societies.
66. See chaps. 5, 7, and 9; on "formative Judaism" see the views of Overman above.
67. See chap. 5 for voluntary and involuntary marginality.

he touches Peter's sick mother-in-law (Matt 8:14–15). These healing stories illustrate fulfillment of Isaiah's prophecy, "He took our infirmities and bore our diseases" (Matt 8:17),[68] which is also evidence of the healer/exorcist's divine authority, an implied contrast with the authority of earthly powers.

Finally, I note Stuart Love's recent book about Jesus and marginal women (2009),[69] an excellent example of Esler's "socio-redaction criticism." Love's landscape includes four interrelated "social domains" commonly analyzed in social-scientific criticism of the New Testament[70] and three kinds of marginality taken from my work,[71] but his key model is Lenski's hierarchically stratified advanced agrarian society and most especially the male-dominated household within it. To these he adds models that deal with private and public space, folk healing in non-Western societies, honor and shame, and purity, all of which aid in interpreting four stories about women: the healing of the hemorrhaging woman and restoration of a girl to life (Matt 9:9–26),[72] the healing of the Canaanite woman's daughter (Matt 15:21–28),[73] the anonymous woman who anoints Jesus,[74] and the women at Jesus' cross and tomb.[75] Love's main thesis is that the Matthean writer is resisting the tendency of his relatively wealthy, urban community to assimilate Jesus' teaching to the social and gender stratification characteristic of the Mediterranean world. Thus, Jesus is interpreted as calling his community back to Jesus' "unconventional vision of the new surrogate family of God."[76]

One should not leave the discussion of social-scientific criticism of Matthew without a brief comment about Marxism.[77] "Liberation

---

68. Matt 8:17 is a "formula quotation" (a literary "aside") from Isa 53:4 in Hebrew.

69. Love, *Jesus and Marginal Women*.

70. Kinship, politics, economics, and religion; Love, *Jesus and Marginal Women*, 97–102. See further, Malina, *Christian Origins*, 86; Hanson and Oakman, *Palestine*, 3.

71. Structural, cultural, and ideological marginality (Love, ibid., 7–11); see chap. 9.

72. Love, ibid., chap.5.

73. Ibid., chap.6.

74. Matt 26:1–16; Love, ibid., chap.7.

75. Matt 27:55–21; Love, ibid., chap.8.

76. Ibid., 21.

77. For Marxist biblical criticism, see Boer, "Twenty-Five Years"; also "On Christian Communism."

theologians" in Latin America used Jesus' concern for the poor as a theological foundation to organize local "base communities" that sought to achieve social justice for the poor by redistribution of wealth.[78] Many Roman Catholic officials in Latin America were initially supportive because of its biblical theme, the "preferential option for the poor,"[79] but official Rome came to reject liberation theology because its focus on class struggle was believed to have Marxist overtones.[80] With respect to Matthew in particular, Richard Horsley's *The Liberation of Christmas: The Infancy Narratives in Social Context* touches on Marxism insofar as it, like Vledder's *Conflict in the Miracle Stories*, drew on Dahrendorf's revisionist Marxist views about socio-economic conflict.[81] It should be noted that, although Gerhard Lenski was critical of the success of Marxism in socialist societies—he was not a Marxist as such[82]—his ecological-evolutionary macromodel is indebted to scholars who have been so influenced.[83] He has been influential among scholars of the Matthean Gospel including Anthony Saldarini, Ann Wire, Stuart Love, Evert-Jan Vledder, and myself. Yet, in contrast to interpretations of the Gospel of Mark,[84] there exists no explicit, thoroughgoing Marxist or Neo-Marxist interpretation of Matthew. That is probably unfortunate since the gospel is recognized on all fronts as being pervaded with religious, political, and economic conflict (Matt 28:19–20).

---

78. E.g., Gutiérrez, *A Theology of Liberation*; Sobrino, *Jesus the Liberator*.

79. Gutiérrez's theology was central to the Medellin and the Puebla Conferences (1968; 1979) and defined the "Preferential Option for the Poor." For Protestant views, see Stegemann and Schottroff's *Jesus and the Hope of the Poor* and Herzog's *Parables as Subversive Speech*.

80. Led by Cardinal Ratzinger, now Pope Benedict XVI, liberation theology was condemned by the Vatican in 1984 and 1986.

81. Horsley, *Liberation*; Dahrendorf, "Toward a Theory of Social Conflict"; *Class and Class Conflict*; cf. also Horsley's *Sociology*; Vledder, *Conflict*.

82. Lenski, "Marxist Experiments in Destratification"; Barnett, "Introduction," 165–66.

83. Archaeologist V. Gordon Childe and anthropologist Walter Goldschmidt, strong influences on Lenski, are often considered to have had Marxist inclinations; see chap. 3, n. 18.

84. For Belo, *A Materialist Reading*, Mark's narrative is a fundamental challenge to the theology of bourgeois Christianity; see also Myers, *Binding the Strong Man*.

Summary

This chapter narrows the field to the way in which social-scientific criticism became one of the major tools for interpreting the Gospel of Matthew beginning in the late 1980s. After a brief comment about the author, date, and place of composition of the gospel, it takes up Amy-Jill Levine's historical, redactional, and feminist 1988 view that Jesus' command to the disciples not to go to the Gentiles, but only to the "lost sheep of the House of Israel" (Matt 10:5–6, cf. 15:24), an *ethnic* command, by the end of the gospel became an *ethical* command to extend the care for the "lost sheep" to all "marginal" peoples (Matt 28:19), including women. That same year the first social-scientific critical book on Matthew by Bruce Malina and Jerome Neyrey stressed the idea that deviance and labeling theory is a profitable way to interpret two text segments in the gospel. The first was the Matthean opponents' charge that Jesus was in league with the ruler of demons (9:34; 12:24), a "witchcraft accusation." This was seen as negative labeling. It was extended to become a labeling process in the accusations, mocking, and death sentence during Jesus' trial. In 1989 a conference on Matthew in Dallas, Texas, produced papers (edited and published two years later by David Balch) that stressed social-historical methods, but included a few scholars who emphasized social-scientific *theories*: revitalization movements and sect/cult theory (Rodney Stark), sect and deviance theory (Anthony Saldarini, seconded by Michael White), and agrarian macrosociology and preindustrial city life (Antoinette Wire). Meanwhile, in 1990 Andrew Overman analyzed the Matthean community as a sect in the context of Judean sectarianism. Graham Stanton agreed with the sect hypothesis, but argued that the Matthean community was no longer "Jewish": the child had separated from its parent Israel. Anthony Saldarini objected that according to deviance theory the child does not separate, and then developed the thesis that the Matthean community was a "deviant voluntary association/sect." Warren Carter interpreted the gospel with the help of my theories of social stratification and marginality (along with Jung Young Lee's revision of marginality), and, like Saldarini (and myself), saw potential value in interpreting the Matthean community as a voluntary association. For Jerome Neyrey a Mediterranean "honor and shame" model was an appropriate lens for interpreting ancient Greco-Roman

The Gospel of Matthew and Social-Scientific Criticism 53

rhetoric "praise and blame." Evert-Jan Vledder extended my suggestions about conflict between the upper and lower strata in an advanced agrarian society (via Lenski and Fiensy) by correlating them with Ralf Dahrendorf's theory that social conflict arises between competing "imperatively coordinated associations," one preserving the status quo (the elite and their retainers), the other challenging it (the peasants, artisans, and expendables), all as a backdrop for understanding the Matthean miracle stories in Matthew 8–9. Finally, Stuart Love showed how the Matthean writer resists assimilating Jesus' teaching to the hierarchical social and gender norms of Mediterranean society.

Clearly, social-scientific interpretation of the Gospel of Matthew had arrived!

Addendum 1: The Challenge of Postmodernism to Historiography and Social-Scientific Criticism[85]

In his *Historiography in the Twentieth Century: From Scientific Objectivity to the Postmodern Challenge* (1997), Georg Iggers includes a chapter called "The Revival of Narrative" in which he discusses literary theorists in France and North America who have called for the surrender of rational inquiry and realistic historical reconstruction, as well as the removal of the distinctions between fact and fiction, and history and poetry.[86] In a subsequent chapter titled "The 'Linguistic Turn': The End of History as a Scholarly Discipline?" Iggers includes Foucault's stress on the text rather than the author's intention,[87] Clifford Geertz's view of culture as a text,[88] and 1930s–1960s New Criticism.[89] Iggers takes the postmodern challenge to historiography very seriously, especially its unmasking of covert power and its warnings about utopianism and progress. However, he thinks that going in this direction too far is a return to anti-Enlightenment conservative and Romantic thought, which leads to Nietzsche, Heidegger, and

---

85. This section was originally the introduction to "Matthew 18:15–17." See chap. 8.

86. Lawrence Stone, Roland Barthes, Paul De Man, Hayden White, Dominick La Capra, Jacques Derrida.

87. Foucault, "What Is an Author?"

88. Geertz, "Deep Play," 448–53; "Thick Description," 9–10.

89. Ransom, *The New Criticism*.

the radical right of the 1920s and 1930s.[90] He is willing to admit the postmodernist stress on the limitations of rationality, but he observes that practicing historians do not abandon rationality and the reality of concrete history. He acknowledges that "grand narratives" of great persons and key events must give way to history on the margins, that is, the history of everyday life (*microhistoria* and "cultural history"), but he does not think that historians need totally abandon broad historical structures and transformations.[91] Important for this book, "[m]*icrohistoria* does not reject the social sciences in toto, but stresses the methodological need of testing their constructs against reality on a small scale."[92] With regard to the "linguistic turn," he agrees with Carroll Smith-Rosenberg that "while linguistic differences structure society, social differences structure language."[93] Thus, the historian cannot obtain "objectivity," but (s)he can obtain plausibility based on rational strategies. In short, the intent of a good deal of the new social and cultural history has not been to repudiate the Enlightenment heritage, for all its weaknesses, but to engage in a critical reconstruction of it. "The alternative to an albeit chastened Enlightenment is barbarism."[94]

Iggers' reflections about historiography direct attention to the "revival of narrative," which has also been important to much biblical study. Terry Eagleton observes that in the history of literary theory there has been a progression from author (Romanticism and the nineteenth century) to text (New Criticism) to reader (Reader-Response Criticism).[95] It is not an accident that studies of narrative often develop an "author-text-reader" model.[96]

Many biblical critics and Matthean scholars in particular have joined in some or all of these moves.[97] Warren Carter has participated

90. Bambach, *Heidegger's Roots*.
91. Iggers, *Historiography*, 104.
92. Ibid., 110.
93. Ibid., 133.
94. Ibid., 147.
95. Eagleton, *Literary Theory*, 74.
96. Booth, *The Rhetoric of Fiction*; Chatman, *Story and Discourse*.
97 E.g., Kingsbury, *Matthew as Story*; Edwards, "Reading Matthew"; Anderson, *Matthew's Narrative Web*, 25–36; Bauer and Powell, *Treasures New and Old*; cp. Rhoads, Michie, Dewey, *Mark as Story*.

in them,[98] but he—similar to Iggers, I think—has chosen to hold on to a serious place for concrete history.[99] Carter draws on literary critic Wilhelm Iser's view that the *hypothetical* "implied reader" should be seen in relation to an equally hypothetical *actual* reader external to the text.[100] Carter goes further and follows Peter Rabinowitz's modification of Iser by stressing the "intended reader," or "authorial audience," that is, the hypothetical persons whom the real author hoped would read the text.[101] "The intended reader . . . is not reducible to textual features but can be determined only by an examination of the interrelation between the text and the context in which the work was produced. The intended reader, in other words, is a *contextualized* implied reader, and studies of reading that start here have the potential to open up new questions of history, culture, and ideology."[102] In short, while the world of the literary text may not correspond *precisely* to the "real world," there is a measure of correspondence with it; and while the text may not provide a precisely accurate view of its intended readers, it does offer a generalized view of them.

Warren Carter's narratological method based on Iser and Rabinowitz is important for Matthean studies because, among other things, he is concerned about "joining the authorial audience."[103] This position allows modern readers to become more "considerate" by means of historical research, social-historical research, and social-scientific modeling.[104] Not surprisingly, then, Carter speculates about the probable historical context of the First Evangelist, uses social-historical data in his interpretation, and explores important sociological and anthropological models related to the Matthean group. As noted above, some of these models are derived from my work.[105]

---

98. Carter, *Households and Discipleship*; *Matthew: Storyteller, Interpreter, Evangelist*; "Matthew 4:18–22"; *Matthew and the Margins*. Carter's views are sketched above.

99. In his more recent work, Carter has focused on "empire studies," a distinctly historical theme. See chap. 3.

100. Carter, *Households and Discipleship*, 34–39; see Iser, *The Act of Reading*.

101. Rabinowitz, "Truth in Fiction"; *Before Reading*; "Whirl Without End"; *Authorizing Readers*.

102. Rabinowitz, "Whirl Without End," 85.

103. Carter, *Matthew: Storyteller, Interpreter, Evangelist*, 4–6.

104. Ibid., 18–43.

105. See above, nn. 55, 56.

Addendum 2: The Challenge to Social-Scientific Criticism in Louise Lawrence's Critique of Mediterranean Anthropology

Some biblical historians have been critical of high levels of generalization found in the studies of some social-scientific critics.[106] One of those is Louise Lawrence in her book *An Ethnography of the Gospel of Matthew* (2003).[107] Lawrence says that she desires to further the cause of the use of anthropological insights in New Testament interpretation,[108] but she offers a sharp critique of social-scientific criticism as practiced in the Context Group. Since she focuses on interpretation of the Gospel of Matthew, she deserves a place in this chapter.

As background, culture critic Edward Said once argued that Western scholars have developed a romanticized, ethnocentric stereotype of the Middle East and Middle Easterners, especially Arabs, which he labeled "Orientalism" (1978).[109] Anthropologist Michael Herzfeld, inspired by Said, argued that in the wake of the disappearance of small-scale societies, anthropologists Julian Pitt-Rivers, J. G. Peristiany, and others created a new, exotic cultural area to investigate, "the Mediterranean,"[110] and analyzed it like a small-scale society, that is, as a self-contained, unified area with a common set of "core values," especially "honor and shame." On the analogy of Edward Said's "Orientalism," Herzfeld named this approach "Mediterraneanism," and argued that it obscured the variety and richness of local, individual Mediterranean communities and cultures. He reoriented what Said believed to be Western ethnocentric characterizations of the East to what he, Herzfeld, believed to be Northern European ethnocentric characterizations of the South.[111] João de Pina-Cabral agreed.[112]

Louise Lawrence transfers Herzfeld's critique of "Mediterraneanism" to the work of New Testament scholars who use Mediterranean

106. E.g., Downing, "'Honor' among Exegetes."
107. Lawrence, *Ethnography*.
108. Ibid., 5–6.
109. Said, *Orientalism*.
110. Pitt-Rivers, *The People of the Sierra*; *The Fate of Shechem*; "Honor"; Pitt-Rivers, ed., *Mediterranean Countrymen*; Peristiany, ed., *Honour and Shame*; Peristiany and Pitt-Rivers, *Honour and Grace*.
111. Herzfeld, "Honour and Shame"; "Of Horns and History"; "'As in Your Own House'"; "Excuses for Everything."
112. Pina-Cabral, "The Mediterranean."

anthropology, particularly those whom she thinks are members of the "Context Group."[113] She highlights Malina's notion of Mediterranean pivotal or core values, particularly "honor and shame,"[114] but also his characterization of Mediterranean society as having scarce material and human resources (a "limited good society") and dominant males who are family-centered, anti-introspective, other-directed ("dyadic"), competitive, and combative ("agonistic")—men who defend challenges to their honor, especially with regard to the women in their households. For Lawrence, this complex corresponds to what Pitt-Rivers called "honor *precedence*," but ignores what he called "honor *virtue*," the honor associated with the individual conscience, glorifying an omniscient deity, and grace. More to the point, echoing Herzfeld, Lawrence argues that it is a static stereotype about Mediterraneans that obscures their variety and individuality. It is an "outdated view of culture."[115] Lawrence draws further inspiration from Russian literary critic/linguist Mikhail Bakhtin who argued that language does not have fixed meanings, as she considers "honor-and-shame" discourse to have, but is multilayered, used differently in different social contexts, and is sometimes self-contradictory.[116] It is characterized by individual, variant linguistic "voices" ("heteroglossia") that are surprising, ever-changing, open-ended, even dialoguing competitively with each other ("dialogism"). Thus, language, particularly in the modern novel, cannot be reduced to univocal cultural meanings such as "honor/shame." The appropriate method for studying Mediterranean cultures is not "Mediterranean anthropology," then, but ethnography, and in the case of Matthew, "literary ethnography."[117] Lawrence wants to analyze local communities and marginal perspectives without generalized, abstract models.[118]

113. See also Lawrence, "For Truly, I tell you," who again generalizes about her version of "The Context Group." Lawrence analyzes studies by Robbins, deSilva, Laniak, Campbell, and Neyrey. While Robbins was a charter member of Social Facets Seminar in 1986 and on its Steering Committee from 1987-89, and while he has occasionally published with Contexters, only Neyrey in this list has been a regular Context Group member, and other Context Group scholars are barely noticed.

114. Malina, *The New Testament World*.

115. Lawrence, *Ethnography*, 25. Her subtitle is *A Critical Assessment of the Use of the Honour and Shame Model in New Testament Studies*.

116. Green, *Mikhail Bakhtin and Biblical Scholarship*.

117. Lawrence, *Ethnography*, 40.

118. Ibid., 21. Compare the "cookie cutter" critique of models at the beginning of chap. 3 below.

Lawrence next turns to Jerome Neyrey's *Honor and Shame in the Gospel of Matthew* sketched above. She admits that his paralleling ancient Mediterranean praise/blame rhetoric with honor/shame is "the most impressive" of the several scholars she evaluates.[119] However, it is also subject to the Said-inspired, Herzfeld/Pina-Cabral critique of "Mediterraneanism": it interprets Matthean passages with a static, abstract, generalized, *a priori*, ethnocentric honor/shame model that fails to take account of the individual variations, nuances, and competing meanings of Matthean language (Bakhtin's heteroglossia and dialogism). In short, it does not take seriously the Matthean gospel's "literary ethnography." For example, the Matthean political leaders in need of public recognition of honor fit the model, but Herod's anxieties (Matt 2:3, 17; 14:3–5) and Pilate's vacillation at Jesus' trial (Matt 27:11–26), examples of fluidity of power and individual introspective reflection, do not.[120] Similarly, the antitheses (Matt 5:17–48), Sabbath controversies (Matt 12:1–14), and commandment breaking (Matt 15:1–20) do not exhibit agonistic "challenge-and-riposte" between Jesus and his opponents.[121] The peasant's "limited good" comes from a modern Mexican rural mindset (note: a distant comparison) that does not fit Matthew's ancient urban context. The beatitudes, the king settling accounts, the rich young man, the laborers in the vineyard parable, and compassion for the least of the brethren show that God's grace trumps society's "limited good" in Matthew's world.[122] And so it goes: individualistic, non-gendered, introspective attitudes, choices, and actions, not to mention divine mandates, in the Matthean text do not conform to the dyadic, collectivistic personalities of the honor/shame model, as conceived by Neyrey. For Lawrence, Neyrey's view of Matthew's Jesus as a "counter-cultural" response to Mediterranean core values implies a static culture that did not exist. Moreover, his view that the gospel's praise of Jesus comes closest to the ancient *encomium* is not convincing since the *encomium* was a genre learned in the education of Greco-Roman elites, and that does not fit either the education of this writer or his writing.

119. Ibid.

120. Ibid., 117–29.

121. See also Lawrence, "For truly, I tell you," 695–99.

122. Beatitudes: Matt 5:1–12; the king settling accounts: Matt 18:23–35; rich young man: Matt 19:16–26; laborers in the vineyard parable: Matt 10:1–16; compassion for the least of the brethren: Matt 25:31–46.

Lawrence's study is ambitious and she has made some important observations about culture, certain trends in anthropology, agonistic honor precedence and honor virtue, Bakhtin's potential for New Testament studies, and Herzfeld's and Pina-Calbral's anti-Mediterraneanist critique.[123] I add that her stance corresponds to postmodern tendencies in anthropology that stress the dynamic, ambivalent "dialogical self" or "multidimensional self" in contrast to more static, "essentialist" unitary versions of the self that are said to reflect and internalize culture. Her literary ethnographical approach is a clear warning against unwarranted generalization in interpreting the New Testament and the Gospel of Matthew. Indeed, I shall often in this book highlight the tension between generalization and historical particularity.

Nonetheless, Lawrence's view of both Mediterranean anthropology and those who use it in New Testament research is ironically a monochromatic caricature. As Zeba Crook has pointed out, Pitt-Rivers' "Mediterranean" was never a static, one-dimensional cultural area to which stereotyped Mediterranean personalities must conform; it was a field of study with heuristic potential.[124] Moreover, it is clear that recent anthropologists are defending Pitt-Rivers. Dionigi Albera's sketch of Mediterranean anthropology reports that Pitt-Rivers' views have been caricatured, and that Pitt-Rivers considered the Mediterranean as a unity only for the purposes of comparison.[125] Paul Sant Cassia totally agrees.[126] He adds that for Pitt-Rivers honor "is not only the internalization of the values of society in the individual but the externalization of his self-image in the world."[127] The critique that southern Mediterraneans easily spot northern ethnocentric stereotypes of them[128] is a generalization that does not take account of the fact that some Mediterraneanists are from the South.[129]

---

123. Crook, "Method and Models," 90. I am much indebted to Crook's critique for parts of this section.

124. Ibid. See Pitt-Rivers, *The Fate of Shechem*, ix.

125. Albera, "The Mediterranean," 217–18, 222.

126. Sant Cassia, "Review Article."

127. Pitt-Rivers, "Honor," 504, cited by Crook, "Method and Models," 93b.

128. E.g., Pina-Cabral, "The Mediterranean."

129. Albera, "The Mediterranean," 223–26.

Lawrence's judgment that Mediterranean anthropology is "outdated" is, I think, premature. It is true that Mediterranean anthropology passed through a crisis of confidence in the 1980s and 1990s, but there are clear signs of a renaissance in a new form and with new emphases.[130] Dionigi Albera states that there is a renewal of Mediterranean studies in a context of globalization that takes account of the anti-Mediterraneanist critique.[131] Christian Bromberger calls for a new perception of space and softer language and conceptuality about the Mediterranean, such as "heterogeneous blocs," "a system of complementary differences . . . in a well-meaning co-existence," a "loose unity of family resemblances," and of "polythetic notions, [and] differences."[132] Dionigi Albera and Anton Blok agree that Julian Pitt-Rivers' Mediterranean is not an "*object* of study," but a "*field* of study," and they accept his perspective.[133] Peregrine Horden and Nicholas Purcel represent a new breed of Mediterranean-oriented social historians who admit that there is no turning back from critiques undergirded by postmodernism and "the linguistic turn,"[134] but their massive study of the Mediterranean Sea area, which they call a "new thalassology,"[135] assembles ethnographic and historical materials showing that honor and shame in the Mediterranean has been central down through the centuries. They stress the "history *of*" the Mediterranean in the sense of geography and "indispensable frameworks," not "history *in*" the Mediterranean in the sense that Mediterraneans share particular cultural or psychological traits.[136] They conclude, "Area studies, in many ways the creation of cultural anthropology and long suspect in that discipline, now flourishes again."[137] I add that Mikhail Bakhtin's insights about heteroglossia and diologism, so significant for literature,

---

130. Albera, Blok, and Bromberger, eds., *L'anthropologie de la Mediterranee*; see Sant Cassia, "Review Article."

131. Albera, "Anthropology of the Mediterranean."

132. Bromberger, "Towards an Anthropology of the Mediterranean."

133. Sant Cassia, "Review Article," 92.

134. I discuss this issue further in chap. 7 below.

135. It goes beyond Fernand Braudel's classic topographical, ecological, environmental orientation, a materialism favored by Boissevain; see Braudel, *The Mediterranean*; Boissevain, "Towards a Social Anthropology," 84a.

136. Horden and Purcell, *The Corrupting Sea*; "Four Years of Corruption," 357.

137. Horden and Purcell, "The Mediterranean and 'the New Histology,'" 3.

especially the modern novel, are less applicable to ancient literature, which often lacks character development.

Finally, Lawrence's critique of the Context Group is also, again ironically, a monochromatic caricature. Context Group members use many different theories and models and operate at many different levels of abstraction depending on their subject matter and the aims of their studies. Malina did operate at a high level of abstraction, but he also emphasized "abduction," that is, the back-and-forth interplay of models and primary sources. Models must be constantly "tested for fit."[138] They are heuristic and adjustable lenses that, as Crook says, initially derive from observations about conventional behavior.[139] It needs to be said that the aim of social-scientific criticism is to understand and explain the Bible not simply "in" and "in front of," but also "behind" the text; its main orientation is that modern Mediterranean cultures provide *better* clues for interpreting biblical texts than modern, Western individualistic cultures. Adapting Bakhtin's insights in order to understand interactions between changing gospel characters and modern readers is an intriguing hermeneutical agenda, but it better suits the individualism of modern literary critical approaches to the gospels, especially reader-response criticism, as in Barnet's Bakhktin-based study of Matthew.[140] At the same time it is possible to use models and postulate cultural tendencies and inner connections without denying the existence of individual variables, "countercultural" impulses, or the grace of God.[141]

---

138. Malina, "Interpretation." "Abduction," a dialectic between deduction and induction, came from the logic of mathematician Charles Peirce.

139. Crook, "Method and Models," 92; cf. Carney, *The Shape of the Past*. I discuss models more fully in chap. 2.

140. See Barnet, *Not the Righteous but Sinners*, who draws on McCracken, "Character in the Boundary." For my acceptance of Carter's analysis, see chap. 6.

141. At the Society of Biblical Literature in 2010 Crook, "Manufacturing Orientalism," made a similar critique of Crossley's *Jesus in an Age of Terror*, which also caricatures the Context Group in terms of Said's Orientalism.

CHAPTER 3

Matthew and Social-Scientific Models[1]

THE TWO PREVIOUS CHAPTERS, one on the emergence of social-scientific criticism, the other on its hermeneutical significance for the Gospel of Matthew, often refer to social-scientific theories and models.[2] In the present chapter, I present a brief, general statement about models, and then I illustrate with several useful models that are helpful for interpreting the Gospel of Matthew.

Models and Model Building

From the perspective of cognitive psychology humans think by generalizing the information taken in from the external world and by distributing it into manageable categories, or "chunking."[3] Although we are conditioned by factors such as culture, ethnicity, and gender, we all compare, contrast, and synthesize. In empiricist terms we arrange the world we perceive into abstract categories.[4] For example, those who design supermarkets where we shop for food use food categories that we take for granted so that we can find what we want: meat, poultry, vegetables, fruits, canned food, dairy products, frozen foods, bulk foods, and the like. These generalizations have still further subcategories. Fruit can be categorized into apples, oranges, pears,

---

1. The first section of this chapter down to "Vertical Dimension Models" (p. 67) is revised from the introduction to Duling, "Matthew's Son of David in Social Scientific Perspective" (see chap. 4 below). The rest of this chapter is a revised version of Duling, "Empire."
2. Galt and Smith, *Models*, 24–27.
3. Malina, *The New Testament World* (1981 ed.), 16–18.
4. Kaplan and Kaplan, *Cognition and Environment*.

and so on. Refining even more, one can choose Mackintosh or Red Delicious apples, navel oranges, or tangerines. Similarly, vegetables can be subcategorized into, say, beans or lettuce, and for lettuce, further subcategories include iceberg, bib, or Romaine. Food can also be categorized "ethnically" and nationally, that is, Italian, Mexican, Mediterranean, Chinese, kosher (Jewish), and the like. Categories and subcategories—we classify. If one wants to be more scientific, Linnaeus' famous taxonomies illustrate the point—kingdom, phylum, class, order, family, genus, and species—with respect to plants and animals, all with appropriate Latin names.

By analogy, cognitive psychologists say that we filter the information we perceive from the "outside" world and formulate mental categories of it, that is, we form "cognitive maps," from the general to the specific.[5] We perpetually do this; we construct "models" of reality in our heads and then interpret, rearrange, and readjust them. We really have no choice about using such models since we can hold only so many things in our heads at once (plus or minus seven). We use them whether we are conscious of doing so or not. We can often consciously construct them if we would like to represent them, as we do when we draw a street map for a friend on a napkin.[6]

I shall now make four points about models.

First, models facilitate the categorization process by simplifying a complex mass of otherwise unmanageable information in order to better grasp it and understand it.[7] Some models are built to scale, like a model airplane, a globe of the world, a Spider Man or Barbie doll. These models are "isomorphic" models, from the Greek words for "same" or "equal" (*isos*) and "form" (*morphē*). Usually they are smaller, more manageable versions that represent some greater reality. Other models, however, select and highlight only *representative* aspects of something or someone, like a flow chart or a cartoon caricature. These models are "homomorphic" models, from the Greek "same" (*homo*) and "form" (*morphē*).

This book uses homomorphic models, that is, models that simplify more complex social arrangements. They are not "true" or "false"

---

5. Downs and Stea, *Maps in Minds*.
6. Carney, *Shape of the Past*, 5; Malina, *New Testament World* (1981), 16–24.
7. Elliott, "Social-Scientific Criticism," 5–6; Esler, *Modelling Early Christianity*, 4–8.

in the usual sense of the term; rather, they are simply ways of looking at social structures or relations. When their configuration changes over time, they can represent social change. They can be checked for their power to represent what they want to represent ("tested for fit"). If necessary, they can be modified if certain features need to be highlighted, or relationships change, or structures are better understood (modified for "fit").[8] When a model fits, it allows those who use it to see social realities that might have gone unnoticed if they were to focus on the masses of information that populate our environment. Homomorphic models focus on the forest, not the trees; the whole map, not just particular streets or highways or buildings.

Second, it is possible to look at simplified models themselves from various locations or perspectives, that is, to understand what they represent in different ways, just as a photographer can photograph an object from various perspectives. This is called "viewpoint." The terms "emic" and "etic" in the field of anthropology have been coined by Kenneth Pike from the linguistic terms "phonemic" and "phonetic" in the field of linguistics.[9] Emic refers to the conscious or unconscious models or information of "the natives" being observed, the information coming to the observer primarily from an informant. "Native models" are emic models. Native information is emic information. In contrast, etic models are the generalized, "universalized" models of an outside observer who has studied comparable models cross-culturally.[10] Conceptual, homomorphic models are etic models. They are "derived" by studying and comparing similar structures or relationships in many cultures. They are said to be "imposed" from the outside. They are tested to see if they fit descriptions from observers. When one studies social structures or relations and modifies the model to achieve a closer "fit," an etic model then becomes, once again, a "derived" etic model.[11]

Third, just as maps can represent various levels, from, say, a whole country to a village, or in contemporary computer terms, by

---

8. Malina, *The New Testament World* (1981).

9. Pike, "Emic and Etic Standpoints"; see Harris, "History and Significance"; Headland, Pike, and Harris, *Emics and Etics*. As related to modeling in social-scientific criticism, see Esler, *Modelling Early Christianity*, 4–8.

10. Galt and Smith, *Models*, 45–50.

11. Berry and Dasen, "Introduction," 17.

zooming out or in, and just as we can see the earth below from a jet plane at 30,000 feet, from a high hill or just looking down towards our feet—so models can be conceived and analyses made at various "levels of analysis" or "levels of abstraction." We can view a society further away, at a more general, abstract level, such as a political, economic, and social system of an empire or state—a "high level of abstraction"—or at a more particular, more concrete level, for example, regional or local social groupings—a "low level of abstraction." Analyses from these levels are termed "macrosocial" and "microsocial."

Often there is a criticism of model making that it is a "cookie cutter" approach to complex historical data, that is, it forces the data into a preconceived mold. Much of Lawrence's critique of social-scientific Criticism and the Context Group in Addendum 2 of the last chapter is of this sort. Again, it should be noted that models are not a form of absolute truth, but "heuristic," that is, they are ways of imagining complex information, and they can be adjusted when "fit" does not occur. The economic historian M. I. Finley put it this way:

> It is in the nature of models that they are subject to constant adjustment, correction, modification or outright replacement. Non-mathematical models have few if any limits to their usefulness: whereas cliometric models are restricted to quantitative data, there is virtually nothing that cannot be conceptualized and analyzed by non-mathematical models—religion and ideology, economic institutions and ideas, the state and politics, simple descriptions and development sequences. The familiar fear of *a priorism* is misplaced: any hypothesis can be modified, adjusted or discarded when necessary. Without one, however, there can be no explanation; there can be only reportage and crude taxonomy, antiquarianism in its narrowest sense.[12]

George Ritzer uses the studies of Georges Gurvich to develop a macroscopic-microscopic continuum of social levels, from "higher" to "lower" levels of abstraction,[13] imaginary points from which to conceive mental maps and engage in analysis.

---

12. Finley, *Ancient History*, 66.
13. Ritzer, *Contemporary Sociological Theory*, 309.

Chart 3.1 A Simplified Macroscopic-Microscopic Continuum (Ritzer)

Macroscopic
1. World systems
2. Societies
3. Organizations
4. Groups
5. Interaction
6. Individual thought and action
Microscopic

Fourth, and last, microsocial models can be either emic (natives' models), that is, occasionally people in a "native" group will develop their own classifications, or etic, that is, derived observers' models. Macrosocial models—the "big picture"—tend by their nature to be outside observers' etic models.

For historians who are willing to use social-scientific models as heuristic lenses for generalizing about social realities, the following point is important: "The higher the level of abstraction, the more the specific details of a historical situation tend to lose their focus. The lower the level of abstraction the more important such particularities become."[14]

Social-scientific theory and modeling are very important for interpreting the ancient Mediterranean world, especially because ancient mental maps, as stated previously, are quite different from modern ones. As already observed, modern interpreters often view ancient societies through the lenses of modern societies, a very natural tendency. To take an example, models of social and economic relations between the rich and the poor derived from the economies of modern industrial nations are anachronistic for interpreting the ancient world;[15] however, preindustrial agrarian, peasant societies—many in the present-day third world[16]—will prove useful for understanding and explaining such arrangements in Mediterranean antiquity.

14. Rohrbaugh, "Social Location of Thought," 25.

15. See the caution about Marxist categories such as "class" in the previous chapter.

16. I have constructed a hypothetical fictional system of Mediterranean status categories in chap. 9 below.

Vertical Dimension Models

Social Stratification in an Advanced Agrarian Society

In chapter 1, I mentioned macrosociologist Gerhard Lenski's ecological-evolutionary model of social stratification in an advanced agrarian society and its influence in understanding social stratification in the ancient Mediterranean and the Gospel of Matthew.[17] Here I shall sharpen that model.

Lenski holds the view that humans cooperate in order to survive; that cooperation requires a necessary division of labor in the production of resources; and that self or group interest leads to the quest for power, or carrying out one's individual or social will, even when opposed by others.[18] Those who gain *power* also possess much land, the only true sign of wealth, and gain control of the economic surplus for their own benefit, despite occasional nods to altruism (for example, concern for the poor). Those in power also grow in social *privilege*, although there are other necessary variables. Finally, both power and privilege yield *prestige*. A feedback loop shows how prestige feeds still greater power. In its simplest form, the dynamics of the distribution of valued resources based on *power, privilege, and prestige* looks like Model 3.1:[19]

---

17. Lenski, *Power and Privilege*, Preface ii, 49, 54–55, 81, 84, 158–159; Nolan and Lenski, *Human Societies*, 153–95; "Rethinking Macrosociological Theory," 163–71; "Societal Taxonomies," 10–13. See also Barnett, "Introduction."

18. Lenski, *Power and Privilege*; "Rethinking Macrosociological Theory"; "Societal Taxonomies." Lenski described his perspective as "materialist" in the tradition of archeologist V. Gordon Childe and anthropologist Walter Goldschmidt ("Societal Taxonomies," 10–13; see p. 51 and n. 83 above). Sociological theorist Jonathan Turner, who acknowledges that the single most important influence on him was Lenski (Turner, *Societal Stratification* [1984], 54–55, 81, 84, 158–59; Preface ii, 49), finds Lenski's synthesis to be especially attractive. Turner adds that the more complex the society, the more important are political power and material wealth for understanding the dynamics of the social system (ibid., 61–62).

19. Lenski, *Power and Privilege*, 43.

Model 3.1 The Dynamics of Distribution Systems (Lenski 1966: 45)

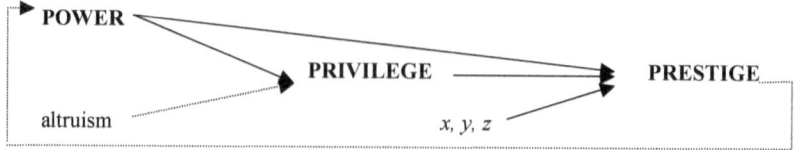

For Lenski, "variations in *subsistence technology* have been the most powerful single cause of variations in societal systems of stratification in the total universe of human societies, past and present."[20] Lenski traces these variations chronologically, a form of cultural evolution.

About 4,000 to 3,000 BCE "*simple* agrarian societies," which had developed beyond horticultural societies, underwent major advances produced not only by the invention of writing and the calendar, but especially by new technology, such as the wheel, harnessing of animals for work and land transportation, wind power, and most importantly, the plow, which made possible the cultivation of land and agricultural surplus. Technological advance was followed by increased productivity; expansion of the general population; the growth of cities; shortage of land; labor surpluses; increased division of labor and specialization; increased trade and rise of the merchant/trading groups; use of commodity money, facilitating exchange; the development of economic surplus controlled by an elite governing class; the need of the elite for professional armies; expanded wars of conquest to control land and resources; increased inequality between the urban, educated elite (the consumers) and the rural, uneducated peasants (the producers); slavery as the main means for heavy work; new ideologies; and the emergence of universal religions. Although kinship relations were still the chief integrating factor, as was already the case in horticultural societies, politics was becoming increasingly dominated by kings, empires, complex administration, and imperialism. Economic exchange was more and more based on agriculture and the development of trade, and interdependent with politics. Religion, locked in with kinship, politics, and economics, was characterized by

---

20. Lenski, "Rethinking Macrosociological Theory," 169; "Societal Taxonomies," 22–23. Lenski knew that subsistence technology had to be related to ecosystems; plow agriculture did not develop in the tropics!

large temple-state complexes and religious legitimation of the new social order, although religious ideology claimed the reverse, that is, that the deity was the true ruler, and the king his "tenant farmer." As for leisure and the arts, there were religious festivals, games, professional entertainers, monuments, and literatures. Recreation was often crude and violent. Most important for our purposes, all this meant that social stratification was marked by a sharp division between the tiny minority, the urban ruling elites at the top, who were able to extract the economic surplus from the masses of poor, and the vast majority, the rural peasants at the bottom, who were barely subsisting. In between were retainers of the elites, among whom were those who, unlike the masses, could read and write, namely, the scribes.

The shift from simple to "*advanced* agrarian societies" took place about 1200 BCE to 900 BCE when iron was increasingly used for everyday tools and implements (the early Iron Age). This advancement encouraged a number of technical innovations important for war and work, the most important of which was the *iron-tipped* plow. *Advanced* agrarian societies were increasingly characterized by famine, plague, poor sanitary conditions (especially in the cities), and corresponding high infant mortality rates; regional and local economic specialization (mining ores; grains; figs; olive oil); a stronger "command economy," that is, commanded by the politically powerful and urban elite, especially royal families, and strengthened by taxation; growth of commerce (traders and merchants); some weakening of kinship ties as the chief social integrating force; and a growth in the "expendable" stratum, which included people such as beggars, prostitutes, and the destitute. Exploitation of the peasant classes remained the rule. While "official" religions still legitimized political establishments, trans-local religions grew and there was an increasing tendency to separate religion from politics (priest-kings were rare). There was also a growth of magic and fatalism.

Thus, the *simple* agrarian society became in the second millennium BCE an *advanced agrarian society*.[21] Lenski's macromodel accents sharp vertical social stratification.

---

21. Lenski, *Human Societies*, 194.

Model 3.2 An Advanced Agrarian Society [Lenski]
(Nolan and Lenski 1999: 190 [see Lenski 1966: 284])

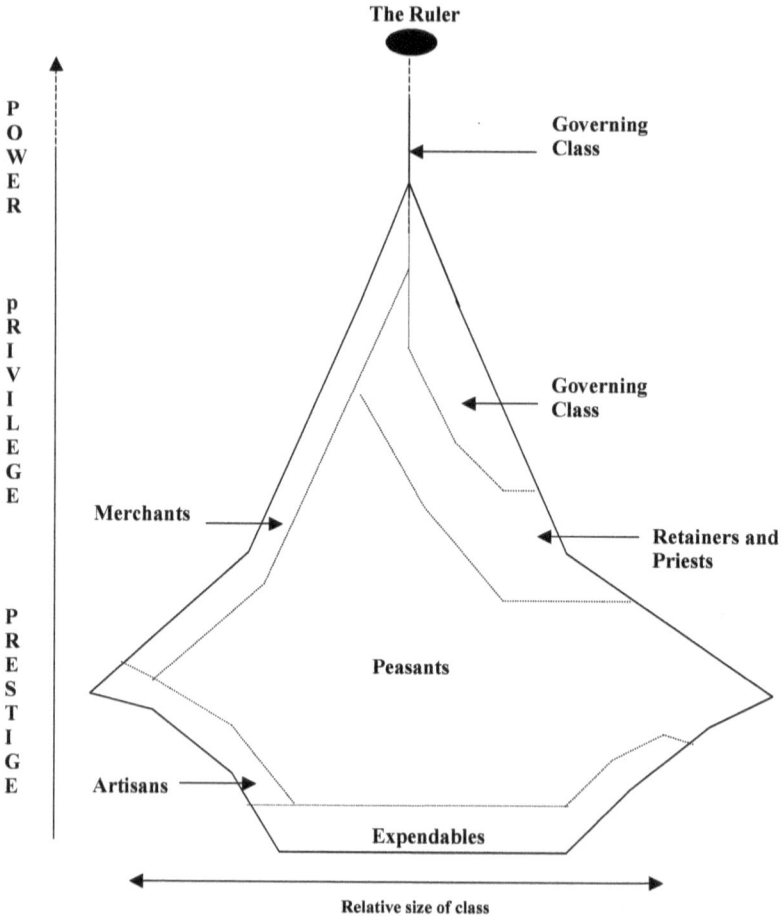

This model implies that those who successfully compete for control of the growing agricultural surplus gradually grow in political and economic power, privilege, and prestige, the three main bases for vertical social ranking. The highest social stratum consists of rulers; beneath them are other governing strata and their "retainers," that is, those who serve them. Still lower are merchants, peasants, and artisans. At the bottom are the "expendables," such as bandits and prostitutes. The dotted lines (added) illustrate the great gap between the upper stratum and the lower strata; the width line at the bottom hints at the relative size of the strata.

Lenski is well aware that his macromodel oversimplifies,[22] that is, that people actually rank each other in a variety of ways, such as family status, gender, ethnic group, and educational level. Lenski calls these various ways of ranking "class systems."[23] They are different ways of ranking status, or *ranking variables*. There are other variables such as the relative importance of each ranking system ("weight"), the social distance between the upper and the lower strata ("span"), and the relation of a particular ranking variable to the whole social system ("shape"). He calls all the status ranking variables taken together "the distributive system," and he constructs a model of a hypothetical Latin American society to illustrate it.[24]

Finally, it should be added that social ranking varies from time to time (a historical factor) and place to place (a local factor) and that variables such as self-identity and other-identity, that is, ranking *other* peoples, usually ethnocentrically, must be taken into consideration. It is also the case that when an individual perceives that his or her ranking in a society is relatively high in one class system and relatively low in another—for example, in actual versus fictive kin relations—"status dissonance" can result.[25] This is a recurring feature of marginal persons and communities.[26] To be complete an analyst would have to plot each of the ranking variables from each of these different perspectives, a daunting, if not impossible, task. Hence, there is a persistent tendency to retreat to the macromodel, as Lenski himself does, because of its simple heuristic potential and explanatory power.[27]

---

22. It is an etic, homomorphic model; see the above discussion.

23. Lenski, *Power and Privilege*, 75, 78; Rohrbaugh, "Methodological Considerations," 519–46.

24. Lenski, *Power and Privilege*, 82; see pp. 246–49 below for a revision of this "distribution system" for the Roman Empire.

25. For terminology of "status dissonance," see p. 20, n. 72 above, and chap. 9, n. 37 below.

26. See chap. 2, n. 56 above; chap. 5 below; and chap. 9, n. 37 below.

27. Turner, *Societal Stratification*, 61–62: Lenski's macromodel sometimes obscures his "class systems" analysis.

Roman Orders

Narrowing to the Mediterranean world, Lenski's most frequent example of vertical social stratification in an advanced agrarian society is the Roman Empire.[28] This focus is not surprising. Ramsay MacMullen emphasized that the key to Roman social relations was "verticality"[29] and T. F. Carney argued that antiquity was typified by *many* pyramids of power.[30] An especially potent example of this sort of ancient pyramidal social stratification at the macrosocial level is the analysis of Roman orders by social historian and epigrapher Géza Alföldy.[31]

Model 3.3 The Roman Orders: Strata Structure and Its Effects (Alföldy) (Alföldy, *The Social History of Rome*, 146, Alföldy's statistics added)

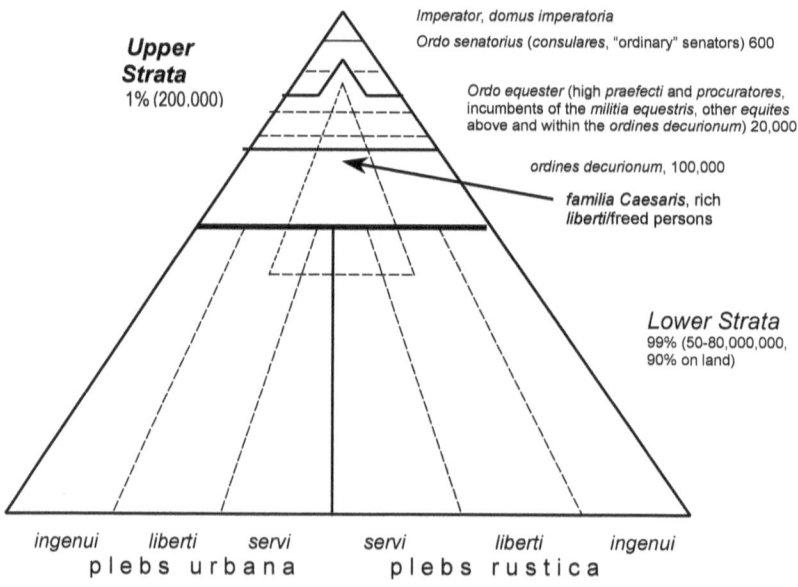

Alföldy's pyramid of social stratification does not reflect as well as Lenski's the unequal size of upper and lower strata, or the tremendous

---

28. Lenski, *Power and Privilege*; Lenski and Lenski, *Human Societies* (1987 ed.), 176, 178, 179, 182, 188, 189, 191.
29. MacMullen, *Roman Social Relations*.
30. Carney, *Shape of the Past*, 90.
31. Alföldy, *Social History of Rome*, 146.

gap between them.³² For example, the wealthiest documented fortune in the Roman Empire was 400,000,000 sesterces, while sixty-four poor Egyptian peasant families shared a single *aroura* (2,200 square meters). It also does not visually illustrate the unequal size of urban (*plebs urbana*) and rural (*plebs rustica*) sectors, for example, about 90 percent of the population was on the land.³³ It is nonetheless an excellent clarifying model of the Roman social status system. By way of historical background, Alföldy indicates that *economically* there was little difference between the Republic and the early empire; *politically*, however, there were new developments that radically altered the social system. Most important, the emperor and his household displaced the old patrician oligarchy at the top of the political/social pyramid. Senators, provincial legates, equestrians, and client kings increasingly served an emperor who had absolute power. A client king who received the emperor's title "friend of Caesar" with its attendant gifts and Roman citizenship received the greatest honor.³⁴

Alföldy emphasizes Roman *ordo*, or "orders,"³⁵ an emic political ranking category of the native distribution system. The Emperor himself conferred *ordo*. It was based not only on a recipient's political power, wealth, and social prestige, but also on his being a freeborn male of aristocratic heritage, a full citizen, and, if from the provinces, a person of favorable ethnicity.³⁶ Upward social mobility between orders was rare, but advancement *within* orders was possible on the basis of merit, skill, education, experience, legal expertise, and loyalty to the Emperor. Advancement was especially common in the military; indeed, it was the chief means of upward social mobility among the Romans.

Under Augustus the highest, or senatorial, order (*ordo senatorius*) became more uniform, restricted, and separate.³⁷ There were only

32. Ibid., 109.

33. See the urban/rural modifications of Lenski's macromodel in Fiensy, *Social History*, 17.

34. For the "friend of Caesar" type, see Braund, *Rome and the Friendly King*.

35. Alföldy, *Social History*, 106. Eventually there were basically two strata, the *honestiores*, or few at the top, and *humiliores* and *tenuiores*, or the many at the bottom.

36. E.g., not Greek, Asian, Cappadocian, Syrian, Judaean, and especially Egyptian. On ethnicity, see chap. 10 below.

37. Alföldy, *Social History*, 106.

600 senators[38] and being a senator required land-based wealth of at least 1,000,000 *sesterces*.[39] There was sharp internal stratification, yet some internal mobility.

The equestrian order (*ordo equester*) was larger, about 20,000,[40] and required assets of 400,000 *sesterces*. It was more loosely structured and had more offices. It was possible for provincials, citizens of other ethnic backgrounds, sons of freedpersons, and occasionally even a freedperson to enter this order on the basis of individual achievement, especially in the military. The most highly placed equestrians became members of the aristocracy.

A third order, the decurions (*ordo decurionum*), consisted of elites in each city of the empire, usually magistrates and wealthy members of the town council who supported public works as patrons.[41] High birth was not an absolute requirement. There were about 1,000 cities, each with about 100 or so decurions who had uniform functions: criminal law, administration, overseeing distribution of food, and public works. One could advance from vice-head of the community (*aedilis*) to head magistrate (*duumvir*). Decurions from large cities might advance to the equestrian order.

Another upper stratum group in the cities consisted of wealthy freedpersons (*liberti*) who owned land and engaged in trade, banking, and craft production. They often became benefactors. However, they did not usually move to the higher orders because of their servile origins.

The last upper-level group was the *familia Caesaris*, or the Emperor's slaves and freedpersons. Despite their power—some freedmen had freeborn wives—they could not join the senatorial order and only rarely entered the equestrian order.

With respect to the lower social strata, the boundaries were more fluid. The main division, again, was between urban and rural. In the cities they included professionals, administrators, small businessmen, shopkeepers, smiths, musicians, artists, actors, secretaries, philosophers, craftspersons, freedpersons, and slaves. Perhaps a third to a half

---

38. Seutonius, *Augustus* 39.2.

39. Earlier 400,000; cf. Dio, 54.17.3; 54.26.3f. (Alföldy 115). Actual wealth was much greater.

40. Alföldy, *Social History*, 122.

41. Ibid., 126.

Matthew and Social-Scientific Models

of urbanites consisted of slaves and many more had servile backgrounds. Freedpersons usually became clients of their former masters.

Lenski's model of vertical stratification has been widely used in biblical scholarship,[42] and has become increasingly common in studies of Matthew.[43] With the aid of Alföldy's discussion of Roman orders, David Fiensy "regionalized" the model for Herodian Palestine,[44] a modification I shall take up in detail in chapter 4.

Ancient Cities

Influenced by Max Weber,[45] sociologist Gideon Sjøberg of the University of Texas (Austin) and his spouse Andrée[46] construct from cross-cultural examples three types of society: simple "folk society," "preindustrial civilized society," and "industrial urban society." Like the Lenskis, they think that the main advances are brought about by

42. Rohrbaugh, *The Biblical Interpreter*; "The Social Location of the Marcan Audience." Rohrbaugh was influenced by Marvin Chaney, "Systematic Study of the Israelite Monarchy"; others who have used Lenski include Coote and Whitelam, "The Emergence of Israel," 113–14; Knight, "Political Rights and Powers," 115; Saldarini, *Pharisees*; Waetjen, *A Reordering of Power*; Elliott, "Social-Scientific Criticism," 13–14; Horsley, *Sociology*; Oakman, *Jesus and the Economic Questions*; "The Archeology of First-Century Galilee"; Fiensy, *Social History*; Seeman, "The Urbanization of Herodian Galilee"; Herzog, *Parables as Subversive Speech*, 53–66; Craffert, "Relationships"; Crossan, *The Birth of Christianity*; Stegemann and Stegemann, *The Jesus Movement*; McNutt, *Reconstructing*, 245; Carter, *Matthew and the Margins*, 18; 561 n. 86. See also Osiek, *What Are They Saying*, 39–43. There was a Social-Scientific Criticism of the New Testament session in the 2000 Society of Biblical Literature on Lenski and Kautsky. It featured papers by Chaney, Rohrbaugh, and myself (an early version of chap. 9). Kautsky was present and responded to the papers. See chap. 1 above. For Matthean scholarship, see the following note.

43. In addition to the studies in this book, see Saldarini, *Matthew's Christian-Jewish Community*; Love, "The Household"; "The Place of Women"; "Jesus Heals the Hemorrhaging Women"; *Jesus and Marginal Women*; Vledder, *Conflict in the Miracle Stories*; Wainwright, "Only to the Lost Sheep or to All the Nations"; Carter, *Households and Discipleship*; "Matthew and the Margins"; *Matthew and the Margins*; Senior, "The Gospel of Matthew in Current Study"; "Directions"; "Matthean Scholarship?"; "Between Two Worlds"; Neyrey, "Jesus, Gender, and the Gospel of Matthew," 52. For its importance for Matthean research, see Senior, ibid., and Anderson, "Life on the Mississippi," 169–218.

44. See Fiensy, *Social History*, 158.

45. See chap. 1 above.

46. Sjøberg, *Preindustrial City*; "Preindustrial City," 438–45; also Sjøberg and Sjøberg, "Preindustrial City."

technological innovation. They do not distinguish between advanced horticultural, simple agrarian, and advanced agrarian, as do the Lenskis, however, but consider them together under "preindustrial." Their book *The Preindustrial City* is ". . . a survey of the preindustrial civilized society with special emphasis upon the city, the hub of all major activity therein."[47]

The Sjøbergs offer rich descriptions of the daily life, politics, economics, and religion in ancient cities. Such cities were mostly small, approximately 5–10,000 people;[48] about 10 percent of the population lived in them. They were crowded and unsanitary. Autocratic kings ruled them with absolute authority, collected taxes, and maintained law and order. City bureaucracies were rigidly hierarchical and family/friendship-based. Their economies were underdeveloped and corruption was rampant. Guild-organized craftspersons minimized competition and controlled pricing.[49] Elite families controlled hierarchical religion. Educated males interpreted the religious norms that justified the social and religious order.

This paragraph only hints at the Sjøbergs' rich descriptions, but Richard Rohrbaugh's Sjøberg-based model of the preindustrial city illustrates the usefulness of their work.[50] In this model of a typical preindustrial city, elites live in the central city adjacent to temple, palace, and government buildings, while artisans, poor, and outcasts live on the periphery. Real, visible walls divide physical space, which replicates social boundaries that divide social space.[51]

The Sjøbergs also have their critics,[52] and they themselves say that their early work should have included more about gender and great literature.[53] Nonetheless, and most important here, their "preindustrial city" model offers a snapshot of social stratification in the cities of the Roman Empire.[54]

47. Sjøberg, *Preindustrial City*, 332.
48. Ibid., 323.
49. Ibid., 325–26.
50. Modified from Rohrbaugh, "Preindustrial City," 135.
51. Sjøberg, *Preindustrial City*, 324–28.
52. Adams, "Review of *The Preindustrial City*," 1105–7. One criticism is that their history is weak, a criticism that reflects the history-versus-social sciences story.
53. Sjøberg and Sjøberg, "Preindustrial City."
54. The Sjøbergs often mention the Roman Empire; see *Preindustrial City*, 44, 56–57, 69, 71–73.

Model 3.4 The Preindustrial City [Sjøberg; Rohrbaugh]
(after Rohrbaugh, "The Preindustrial City in Luke-Acts," 135)

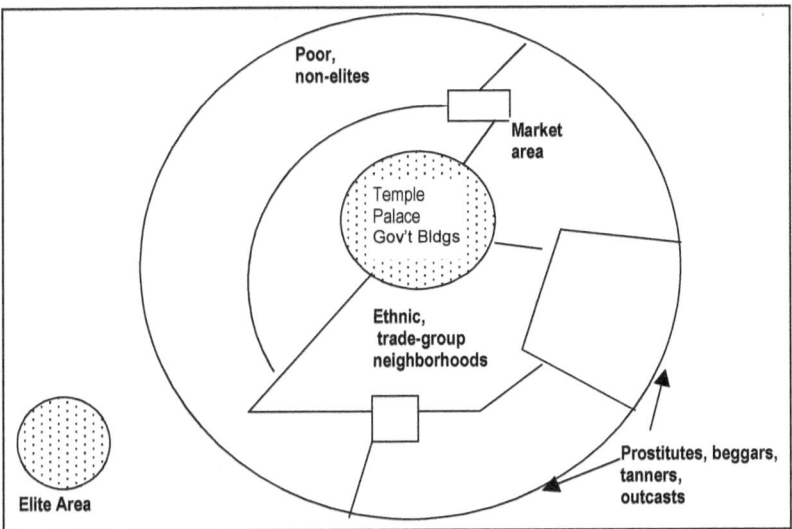

The Horizontal Dimension

The vertical dimension, social stratification in advanced agrarian societies, is useful for visualizing social ranking throughout the Roman Empire, and Roman orders provide a specific example. The vertical dimension can be supplemented with a horizontal dimension, shifting the focus in the direction of imperialism.

Imperial Control of Weaker Polities

Michael Doyle's view of empire is very helpful for understanding the expansion of the Roman Empire. He defines empire as "a relationship, formal or informal, in which one state controls the effective political sovereignty of another political society."[55] This definition emphasizes control.[56] In Doyle's language a "metropole," defined as "a center of great size or enormous population, spectacular wealth and resources or a large army,"[57] controls both the domestic and foreign politics of other

---

55. Doyle, *Empires*, 45.
56. Ibid., 24–30; see above under "Definitions."
57. Ibid., 128.

governments. It can do so because it has a strong, centralized governmental bureaucracy; a sense of community evoked by a belief among both elite and masses that its control is legitimate; and enough social differentiation to have many resources. For Doyle, a polity is weaker than a metropole not simply because of technology—well-organized armies often defeat their technological superiors—but because of less developed social organization. He describes several subtypes of weaker polities: 1) *"tribal"* (no centralized state, little stratification, strong communal village loyalties); 2) *"patrimonial"* (centralized state, some stratification, weak community loyalties); 3) *"feudal"* (disaggregated state, some social differentiation, common civilization, pyramidal loyalties); 4) *"fractionated"* (central state, thorough social differentiation, shared civilization, pyramidal loyalties); 5) *"settler"* (colonial government, differentiated society, community loyalty toward metropole). These can be used to analyze polities in the Roman Empire.

Another of Doyle's definitions distinguishes between empire, which is a polity, and imperialism, which is a policy:

> Empire . . . is a relationship, formal or informal, in which one state controls the effective political sovereignty of another political society. It can be achieved by force, by political collaboration, by economic, social, or cultural dependence. Imperialism is simply the process or policy of establishing or maintaining an empire.[58]

Doyle's perspective provides a heuristic lens for viewing the horizontal dimension of the Roman Empire, especially when expanded by Alexander Motyl.

Core/Periphery Model (A Rimless Wheel, Hub and Spokes)

Alexander Motyl adds to and structures Doyle's kind of analysis by defining and modeling interactions between "the core" (Doyle's "metropole") and multiple "peripheries" (Doyle's weaker polities); he also includes non-peripheries, those beyond empire control.[59] Motyl

---

58. Ibid., 45.

59. Motyl, *Imperial Ends*. Motyl builds on Galtung, "A Structural Theory of Imperialism," and several studies of Rein Taagepera, which for the Roman Empire period is best presented in "Size and Duration."

Matthew and Social-Scientific Models 79

defines "empire" as "a hierarchically organized political system with a hublike structure—a rimless wheel—within which a core elite and state dominate peripheral elites and societies by serving as intermediaries for their significant interactions and by channeling resource flows from the periphery to the core and back to the periphery."[60] Motyl presents his view of empire so defined with a simple etic, homomorphic model of a rimless wheel with hub-and-spokes.

Model 3.5 The Core/Periphery Structure of Empire (Rimless Wheel, Hub and Spokes)
(Motyl, *Imperial Ends*, 16)

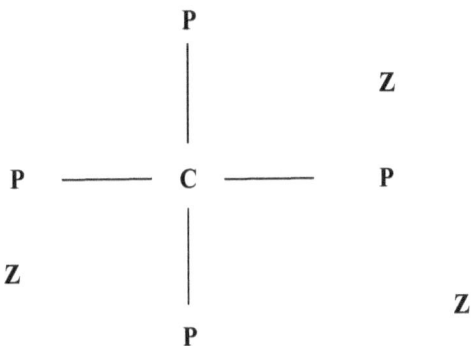

(legend: **C** = core; **P** = peripheries; **Z** = nonimperial polities)

For Motyl an empire must have at least two peripheries (P); otherwise, it would have no geographical boundaries. Spokes with no rim represent the flow back and forth between core and periphery. There are no significant political and economic links between or among the peripheral polities themselves, hence no rim. Likewise, there are no significant links between the various empire polities (P) and polities beyond or outside the empire (Z).[61] It needs to be added that Motyl also thinks of the "interaction structure" between core and periphery as *vertical*—the core not only controls but is (and considers itself) superior to peripheries—and to that extent his horizontal model can

---

60. Motyl, *Imperial Ends*, 4.
61. There can be economic triangular relationships such as occurred between England, the US, and Africa in the slave trade.

be easily correlated with the vertical models described above simply by raising the "C," thus creating a three-dimensional tent or pyramid.

Motyl also analyzes several empire subtypes, which represent variations in the model. For example, the length and number of spokes can differ. There can be a few short spokes ("tightly massed" and "territorially contiguous") called a *"continuous empire"* (e.g., the Hapsburg Empire, the Prussian Empire, the Napoleonic Empire, the Chinese Empire). There can be many long spokes representing distant, far-flung peripheries, called a *"discontinuous empire"* (e.g., the Spanish Empire, the Portuguese Empire, the British Empire). There can be a mixture, which Motyl calls a *"hybrid empire"* (e.g., the Third Reich). There can be different kinds of elite rule of peripheries, which he, like Doyle, describes as *formal* (much interference in local affairs) and *informal* (substantial local rule).

For Motyl empires are *political systems* that, as S. N. Eisenstadt put it, require maintaining a "very delicate balance" to survive.[62] Yet, they provide "the most massive and enduring form of government [people have ever] known prior to the modern period."[63] Why? They are able to channel resources, provide security, and promote the common defense. Yet, their hub-like structure encourages furthering dominance of the elite core over non-elite peripheries. There is little chance of successful rebellion because elites in peripheral regions benefit immensely from their relationship with core elites.

The Horizontal Dimension and the Roman Empire

Doyle stresses the generally accepted historical fact that most Roman expansion took place under the Republic; the goal of the emperors was to preserve what the senators had accomplished.[64] He goes on to say that Roman expansion can be analyzed from several perspectives. It had social and cultural roots in the core values of fidelity, honor, and religion. The economic need was for more land to support a growing population. It had a military machine with appropriate means of advancement. Land was confiscated by Roman farmer-soldiers and

---

62. Motyl, *Imperial Ends*, 21; Eisenstadt, *Decline of Empires*, 4.
63. Motyl, ibid., 23.
64. Ibid., 83.

booty was lucrative for the conquerors. Whole provinces became client states of their Roman patrons. Thus, using Doyle's categories, the metropole controlled weaker polities, which in the West were mainly tribal societies centered in villages and in the East mainly patrimonial monarchies and fractionated republics.

From Motyl's perspective the Roman Empire can be described as a "discontinuous empire" because it had many long spokes, mainly to Mediterranean coastal areas. Doyle thinks that the Roman pattern was *formal*, which he defines further as "rule by annexation and government by colonial governors supported by metropolitan troops and local collaborators."[65] It should be added that rule was more *informal* in certain senatorial provinces and native-ruled polities where client kings collaborated with the imperial powers. That would be the case in Palestine under Herod the Great where regional gubernatorial control directly responsible to Caesar was combined with local client king rule and ratified by the emperor's grant of the title "friend of Caesar." While for Motyl there are many peripheries that can establish boundaries, the outer boundaries under Rome remained fluid—less "geographically fixed" than in modern nation-states.

Alföldy's analysis of vertical social stratification also offers information about how the Roman order was extended to the provinces.[66] Important factors included new road networks, admission of provincials to the military, grants of citizenship to provincial elites, and new cities, the main location of imperial expansion.

The Peasantry

"Commercialized" Empires and Peasants

John Kautsky's macrosocial views are much indebted to Gerhard Lenski's and are sometimes correlated with Lenski's perspective in New Testament interpretation.[67] Kautsky develops three types of society in human history, although he does not think that they are necessarily sequential. He calls them "primitive societies," "traditional aristocratic

---

65. Doyle, *Empires*, 135.
66. See, e.g., Millar, *The Roman Empire*.
67. Kautsky, *The Politics*. Kautsky was a guest of the Society of Biblical Literature's Social-Scientific Criticism of the New Testament section in 2000. See chap. 1 above.

empires," and "modern societies." He offers a simplified model of his evolutionary scheme.[68]

Model 3.6 Societies Representing the Three Phases of History (Kautsky, *The Politics of Aristocratic Empires*, 27 [slightly adapted]; ▌ = Roman Empire)

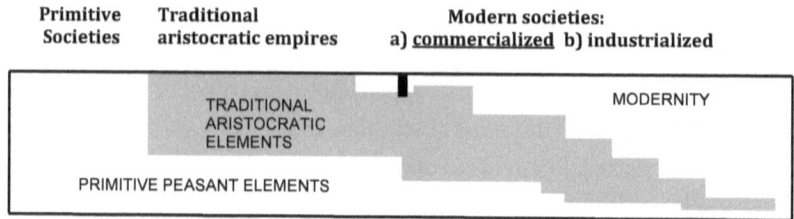

The key concepts in Kautsky's analysis are "aristocracy" and "aristocratic empire":

> An *aristocracy* . . . is a ruling class in an agrarian economy that does not engage in productive labor but lives wholly or primarily off the labor of peasants. Hence *aristocratic empires* must contain not only aristocrats but also peasants who, in turn, live in agrarian primitive societies. Because . . . it takes many peasants to support one aristocrat, this also implies that aristocratic empires are necessarily a good deal larger than primitive societies.[69]

Ancient Egypt, Mesopotamia, and early Medieval Europe, says Kautsky, are typical "*traditional* aristocratic empires." Empires in which aristocrats have given up some of their power to a class of merchants, financiers, and tax collectors, or have become merchants themselves, are called "*commercialized* empires." The Roman Empire belongs in this modified type,[70] although it still retains some "primitive peasant elements." What this commercialism means in the Roman Empire is succinctly summarized by Dominic Crossan:

> Put bluntly: in a traditional agrarian empire, the aristocracy takes the [agricultural] *surplus* [of the land] from the peasantry;

---

68. Kautsky, *The Politics*, 21–27.
69. Ibid., 24 (italics mine).
70. Ibid., 159–82.

in a commercializing agrarian empire, the aristocracy takes the *land* [itself] from the peasantry. The former devours the industry and productivity of the peasantry; the latter their very identity and dignity. Commercialization moves [... the peasant] in increasing numbers down the terrible slope from small freeholder to tenant farmer to day-laborer to beggar or bandit.[71]

K. C. Hanson and Douglas Oakman do not study the peasantry in the Gospel of Matthew as such, but they explore the peasantry in ancient Palestine, the scene of Jesus' life in Matthew, in a great deal of detail.[72] Since the gospel has much to say about the crowds around Jesus, I would like to briefly discuss peasant resistance to political domination.

Peasant Resistance

John Kautsky, whose analysis is indebted to that of Lenski, emphasizes that aristocrats claim reciprocity, but in reality exploit peasants. Here I mention three forms of peasant resistance relevant for the historical context of the Roman Empire and Matthew, namely, millennial movements, peasant revolts, and nonviolent resistance.[73]

MILLENNIAL MOVEMENTS

The term "millennialism," derived from the description of the 1,000-year reign of Christ and the martyrs in Revelation 20:4–8 (Latin *mille*, "1,000"), is the social-scientific term for what biblical scholars usually call "apocalypticism."[74] Millennial (or apocalyptic) movements view the present order as oppressive (natural or social), as being in crisis. Some causes are flood, drought, volcanic eruptions, *coup d'état*, military conquest, cultural oppression, and the like. A key theme is that this

---

71. Crossan, *The Birth of Christianity*, 157–58.
72. Hanson and Oakman, *Palestine*.
73. Crossan, *The Birth of Christianity*, 159; Kautsky, *The Politics*, 280–308.
74. Duling, "*BTB* Readers Guide: Millennialism" and "Millennialism," the social-scientific part of which is based mainly on: Wallace, "Revitalization Movements"; Talmon, "Millenarian Movements," "Millenarism"; Burridge, *New Heaven, New Earth*; and La Barre, "Materials for a History of Studies of Crisis Cults."

present order will soon end, usually by some cataclysmic event; it will be replaced by a new, perfect, blissful, and trouble-free world (*Endzeit*, "end time"), often believed to be a restoration of some perfect time and place, usually "of old" (*Urzeit*, "original time," "golden age"). This ideology can be so intense that those who believe it prepare for the new age or attempt to force its coming by radical political activity. Typically, a prophet or messiah emerges, sometimes preceded by a forerunner. This figure usually experiences altered states of consciousness; (s)he crystallizes common experiences and offers a new solution to social problems. (S)he attracts followers (Weber's "charismatic leader") who also have such experiences and either await the coming new order or attempt to bring it about by political activity (see further below). Such groups are usually loosely organized, and sometimes splinter. On rare occasions, they become organized with hierarchical leaders (Weber: "routinization of charisma"). If the movement is successful, the population at large adopts their views as normative. Cultural transformation occurs, eventually accompanied by doctrine, ritual, and a social program. This becomes the new social system.

Millennial ideology was very widespread in Judean circles of the Hellenistic and Roman periods.[75] In the canonical gospels, including the Gospel of Matthew, Jesus' central teaching is remembered as the "Rule/Kingdom/Empire of God/Heaven." Many New Testament scholars have seen Jesus' teaching as a form of millennialism.[76]

Peasant Rebellion

Millennialism sometimes becomes the ideology of peasant rebellion. In peasant rebellion, local elites—landlords, village leaders, local scribes—join forces with peasants in revolt, indeed often help lead it.[77] Whether against native ruling strata, foreign occupying powers, or both, peasant revolts do not usually succeed, mainly because their enemies are too powerful and well organized. Another reason is that

---

75. See Duling, "Kingdom of God/Heaven," 51; for Jesus, Allison, *Jesus of Nazareth* and Ehrman, *Jesus*.

76. For Matthean millennial sectarianism, see Sim, *The Gospel of Matthew and Christian Judaism*.

77. Linton, "Nativistic Movements," *passim*; Naquin, *Millenarian Rebellion in China*.

local elites benefit enormously as collaborators with imperial elites and therefore do not ordinarily join in alliances against them.

Stephen Dyson has studied various native revolts in the Roman period and isolated two patterns of resistance.[78] In the Western Empire, illustrated by revolts in Spain (197 BCE) and among the Nasamones (86 BCE) and Frisians (28 CE), conflict between Rome and tribal peoples centered mainly on payment of taxes in coin, a Roman policy that introduced an alien and distrusted monetary economy and fostered abuses by tax collectors. Also, Roman agricultural settlements, particularly in North Africa, led to loss of land and conflict between Roman agricultural and local pastoral economies. Strong pockets of resistance emerged especially in the mountainous buffer zones between Roman agricultural settlements and remote, more independent tribal communities. While Romanized native aristocracies supported the Roman occupation, native religions tended to perpetuate traditional values. When extremist religious rebels emerged, they were simply eliminated.

More familiar to scholars of Greco-Roman antiquity is the second pattern, which was typical of the Eastern Empire, especially in Greece and Judaea.[79] The primary factor that led to resistance in the East, says Dyson, was rapid acculturation (Hellenization and Romanization). As in the West, natives had to adjust to a "colonial" administrative structure that forced upon them taxes, governors, and soldier-farmers who confiscated their land. Rebellions usually occurred just when imperial powers had come to think that the major problems of conquest had been solved.[80] It is possible to see the Judean Rebellion against Rome in 66 CE in this light, and to envision that the Gospel of Matthew, written in the following generation, saw the rebellion as God's punishment of Israel.[81]

Daniel Little has highlighted two models of peasant rebellion, the class conflict model and the local politics model.[82] The class conflict model, which goes back to Karl Marx, stresses "the property sys-

78. Dyson, "Native Revolt Patterns."

79. Ibid.

80. E.g., Arminius, Batavian, Boudicca, the Pannonian-Dalmatian and Vercingetorix.

81. See Hanson and Oakman, *Palestine*; see Matt 22:7.

82. Little, "Local Politics and Class Conflict."

tem," that is, rural property arrangements determine class relations among landlords, tenants, laborers, and the imperial occupation. Peasants experience exploitation when the agricultural surplus is extracted by elites in the form of rents, interest, corvée labor, taxation, and tribute. They develop "class consciousness" and are motivated to collective political action whenever sufficient political resources and organization are present. Thus, "[r]ebellions and popular collective action are rational strategies of collective self-defense on the part of subordinate classes."[83]

Little recognizes that the class conflict model has great explanatory power, but he thinks that it usually operates at too general a level to take account of *local* politics, which becomes the basis for his second model. In China, for example, political resistance has taken a different form in wet-rice regions than it has in dry cropping areas. Also, it is necessary to take account of "non-class" factors: religion, inter-village conflict, kinship, and religious organizations. Little's critique is similar to that observed among various scholars in chapter 1 and chapter 2, Appendix 2: general modeling can obscure variables related to the local conditions, temporal changes, and varieties of ranking.[84] In short, the interpreter must be conscious of levels of abstraction and be aware of exceptions. This critique is also present in the following analysis.

Everyday Peasant Resistance

Political scientist James C. Scott has analyzed a peasant village, which he calls "Sedaka" (not its real name), in the "rice bowl" of Malaysia.[85] His procedure is to paint a social "landscape": background, middle ground, and foreground.

The *background* is postcolonial Malaysia's attempt to insure a self-sufficient supply of rice, raise the standard of living, and avoid civil strife, all by building an infrastructure, sponsoring peasant resettlement schemes, and introducing a second crop ("double cropping").

---

83. Ibid., 3; also Wolf, *Peasants*.

84. My hypothetical "distribution system" in the Roman Empire in chap. 9 is an exercise in varieties of ranking.

85. Scott, *Weapons of the Weak*; *Moral Economy of the Peasant*; *Domination and the Arts of Resistance*.

The *middle ground* is regional, namely, the Muda region of Kedah (NW Malaysia) from 1970 to 1980, which was the "beneficiary" of an irrigation program that included dams and canals; new high-yielding, fast-growing strains of rice; fertilizers; "double-cropping"; mechanization; credit bureaus; and milling and marketing opportunities. The program immediately increased Malaysian rice production about 250 percent and the region became a showpiece of Southeast Asia's "Green Revolution." Scott's *foreground* is the peasant village of Sedaka. Double-cropping was introduced in 1971 and harvest combines appeared in 1976. Scott describes the unintended effect of the Green Revolution in Sedaka:

> Before, large landowners rented land out to poorer tenants; now they rent increasingly to wealthy entrepreneurs [some Chinese] or farm their land themselves with machinery. Before, large farmers hired poorer neighbors to plough and harrow their fields with water buffalo; now they hire wealthy tractor owners to prepare their land. Before, larger farmers hired poorer neighbors to transplant their paddy; now many of them broadcast their own seed [scattered rice is more difficult to cultivate than rows]. Before, these same farmers hired the poor to reap and thresh their crop; now they hire wealthy combine owners for the same job. Before, well-to-do villagers had good reason to provide advance wages and give *zakat* payments to their work force; now, if they have a work force at all, they see no need to be as openhanded. Before, the village rich had good reason to build a reputation with lavish feasts; now many of them regard such large feasts as a waste of money. Taken together, these reversals call into question virtually every assumption that governed the social relations of production before double-cropping.[86]

In short, there had been inequities before, but also cooperation, reciprocity, and mutual interdependence rooted in kinship, neighborhood, and religion; with agricultural innovations, much of that vanished. Modern capitalistic developments served to disrupt the moral economy of the peasants.[87]

How did the peasants of Sedaka respond? In contrast to much of Southeast Asia, there was no peasant revolt. "There [were] no riots,

---

86. Scott, *Weapons of the Weak*, 179–80.
87. Ibid., 74.

no demonstrations, no arson, no organized social banditry, no open violence."[88] Rather, the peasants resorted to grumbling, foot-dragging, dissipation, false compliance, pilfering, petty theft, arson, sabotage, feigned ignorance, malicious gossip, slander, rumormongering, jokes, offhand comments, innuendoes, flight to another village, and a nostalgic appeal to the not-so-good "good old days."[89] They avoided thoroughly threshing every bundle of cut paddy, stuffed their pockets with rice at the end of the day, and left some bundles for family members to glean later. They threatened to go on strike. They engaged in nighttime petty theft of the rich. Occasionally, they murdered their farm animals. They told stories about famous "social bandits" of former times.[90]

Why did resistance take these seemingly placid forms? Scott offers a few explanations: the changes in Sedaka were gradual, the conditions of wealthier villagers did in fact improve,[91] poor people did not actually starve, two-thirds of land tenancies were still kinship-based, and village relations were in part still rooted in friendship, faction, patronage, and ritual.

Routine, everyday forms of peasant resistance such as those just described raise important theoretical issues. As Scott notes, Marxists like Antonio Gramsci explain such apparent proletarian passivity by the concept of "hegemony,"[92] that is, the ruled stratum accepts the ideology of the ruling stratum as natural, as a given ("the dominant ideology thesis"). This passivity corresponds to an institutionalized form of Marx's "false consciousness," which, Marx held, inhibits social change. Scott takes a different view. He thinks that Gramsci's generalized Marxist explanations do not sufficiently take into account the mediation of real-life class experience, which, as E. P. Thompson says, "gives a coloration to culture, to values, and to thought; it is by means of experience that the mode of production exerts a determining pressure upon other activities . . . ."[93] The interpreter needs to take

---

88. Ibid., 273.
89. Ibid., 280, xvi, xvii, 255–303.
90. Kheng, *Social Banditry and Rural Crime in Kedah, 1910–1929*.
91. Scott, *Weapons of the Weak*, 147.
92. Gramsci, *Selections*.
93. *Poverty of Theory and Other Essays*, 98.

into account the more subtle aspects of language and social relations, that is, proverbs, folksongs, history, customs, ritual, and religion. It is necessary to understand not only what is said publicly ("onstage"; the "partial transcript"), but also privately, among family, friends, and work-companions ("offstage"; the "full transcript"). Scott himself calls his method "phenomenology" and "ethnology";[94] it may be best understood as an example of what anthropologist Clifford Geertz calls "thick description" of culture.[95] For Scott, as for other critics, general theory should be counterbalanced by contextual specificity.[96]

It is impossible for scholars of ancient empires, thus the Roman Empire, to gain access to the "full transcript" of ancient peasants to the degree that Scott does. Nonetheless, it is possible to gain *some* insight into ancient transcripts by looking carefully at storytelling, labeling, symbols, and the like, and then to offer a reading with imperialist glasses. That reading can be a lens for understanding the peasant stratum of the Gospel of Matthew.[97]

Summarizing Conclusion

In this chapter I have presented several models that are important for the interpretation of the Gospel of Matthew. The first four are the most important for this book: hierarchical social arrangements in advanced agrarian societies (Gerhard and Jean Lenski); hierarchical Roman orders (Geza Alföldy); aristocratic empires (John Kautsky); and the preindustrial city (Gideon and Andrée Sjøberg). I have also included Roman imperial expansion (Michael Doyle; Alexander Motyl); millennial movements (A. F. C. Wallace; Yonina Talmon; Kenelm Burridge; Weston La Barre); peasant rebellion (Stephen Dyson; Daniel Little); and everyday peasant resistance (James C. Scott). These models, especially the first four, overlap, reinforce each other, and therefore can be combined in social-scientific criticism.

94. Scott, *Weapons of the Weak*, 46–47.

95. Geertz, "Thick Description." For Scott's admiration of Geertz, see Scott, *Weapons of the Weak*, 45, 138–40.

96. For certain similarities with some of Lawrence's critique of Mediterraneanism, see chap. 2 above.

97. Riches, "Matthew's Missionary Strategy."

They create a bridge to subsequent chapters, which will take up specific topics and exegete specific passages. Occasionally, I shall use other theories, for example, marginality and ethnicity, and models, especially small group models. The model or models will be developed, usually at the beginning of the chapters, and will be used as heuristic lenses to interpret specific passages, usually redactional, in the gospel.

CHAPTER 4

Matthew's Plurisignificant "Son of David" in Social-Scientific Perspective

Kinship, Kingship, Magic, and Miracle[1]

IT IS WELL KNOWN in gospel studies that the Gospel of Matthew has a number of references to Jesus as the "Son of David" that are greater than the number of what I take to be his source, the Gospel of Mark. The studies indicating this point are from the perspective of the Two-Source Theory and redaction criticism.[2] In this study, I seek to advance beyond this approach by interpreting the Matthean emphasis with insights derived from the social sciences. Using as heuristic devices some of the social-scientific models developed in chapter 3 and others, I want to obtain a sharper focus on the Matthean Son of David.

More specifically, I use three etic, homomorphic models, or outside observers' models, that summarize and simplify the complex data.[3] The first is Lenski's macrosocial model for social stratification in an advanced agrarian society discussed in the first three chapters, which in this chapter I shall elaborate at a "lower level of abstraction," that is, for the region of ancient Palestine. The second and third models in this chapter were not presented in chapter 3. They are a microsocial model

---

1. Discussed at the Social Sciences and the New Testament, Medina del Campo, Spain, 1991; published in *Biblical Theology Bulletin* 22/3 (1992): 99–116. This version contains some reorganization, minor changes, and a few additional bibliographical items.

2. Lövestam, "Die Davidssohnfrage"; Kingsbury, "The Title 'Son of David'"; Duling, "The Therapeutic Son of David"; Loader, "Son of David"; recently, Le Donne, *The Historiographical Jesus*, chap. 5 ("The Therapeutic Son of David").

3. For description of these terms and concepts, see chap. 3.

for analyzing small groups derived from networking anthropology, and a microsocial model for "challenge/response" in an advanced agrarian society that is also an "honor/shame society."[4] They will be modified in relation to concrete historical contexts proposed for the gospel, and thus become what are sometimes called "derived models." As such, they become the lenses for interpreting the Son of David text segments in the Gospel of Matthew, our "native informant."

Literary and Social-Historical Presuppositions about the Gospel

As a prelude, there is a measure of consensus in contemporary Matthean studies that the composition now called "According to Matthew" in New Testament manuscripts was written by an anonymous, Christ-believing Judean male living in a Mediterranean urban environment (Antioch in Syria?) about 80–90 CE. This was the postwar period when the Pharisees of the Academy at Yavneh were in the process of asserting their authority over competing Judean groups.[5] Another common critical conviction is that this writer was implicitly referring to himself when he wrote, "Therefore every scribe (Greek: *grammateus*) who has been trained for the kingdom of heaven is like a householder (*oikodespotēs*) of the household who brings out of his treasure (storage room) what is new and what is old" (Matt 13:52; cf. 23:34). I accept this virtual consensus,[6] but for convenience refer to the writer by his traditional name, "Matthew."

Initially, I want to emphasize two important points about this virtual consensus. First, approximately fifty-plus years separate the writing of the gospel (80–90 CE) from the time of the story about Jesus he portrays (ca. 30 CE). What took place in the interim was undoubtedly the most significant historical event of the first-century Mediterranean world: the wars between the Romans and the Judeans, 66–70 CE. These were climaxed by the catastrophic destruction of Jerusalem and the Temple in 70 CE and were followed by the eventual attempt of the

---

4. See further discussion below and see chap. 2.

5. Luz, *Matthew 1–7*, 49–76; Davies and Allison, *Matthew 1–7*; cf. Neusner, "Formation"; Overman, *Matthew's Gospel*.

6. Duling, *The New Testament*, 329–44; see chaps. 2, 7, and 9.

Matthew's Plurisignificant "Son of David"

Pharisees to reorganize Judeans everywhere under Pharisaic leadership. As redaction critics have demonstrated, these events have powerfully affected the way in which the story of Jesus was reported, and thus for understanding its nuances, as well as its writer, the learned scribe/scholar "Matthew." This chapter hopes to shed social-scientific light on this fact in relation to the concept of "Son of David."

"Plurisignification" and a Son of David Inventory

"Plurisignification" refers to word-signs with several possible meanings depending on the literary context.[7] The Hebrew or Aramaic "son of" signifies literal physical kinship relations, but can also refer to the "sons"/descendants of some remote ancestor, whether they were actual or mythical persons ("sons of Abraham"; "sons of Adam"); son of a fictive "father" ("my son") in a fictive kinship group ("pseudo-kinship"); son as metaphor ("son of man" = human being).[8] Thus, in the New Testament, "son of" in Greek, which derives from the Semitic languages, can signify: 1) direct kinship (Mark 10:46); 2) ancestral kinship (Acts 2:35); 3) fictive kinship (Acts 2:36); 4) a kinship metaphor in relation to qualities (Mark 3:17); 5) a kinship metaphor in relation to physical characteristics, as genus is to species ("Son of Man," i.e., a human being); and 6) a fictive-kinship metaphor in relation to the deity ("Son of God").

"Son of David" in Matthew is plurisignificant. "Emic data,"[9] that is, attestation of this formulation "Son of David" by the native writer of the gospel, ranges from references to David's literal son Solomon to Jesus as a distant descendant, and in several ways. Chart 4.1 contains the references to "Son of David" and related ideas in literary sequence.

---

7. Wheelwright, *The Burning Fountain*, 115–23; cf. Barthes, *S/Z*.

8. Pitt-Rivers, *Mediterranean Countrymen*; Elliott, "Temple Versus Household"; Neyrey, "Ancestors"; "Family"; "Fathers."

9. For a discussion of etic and emic, see chap. 3.

Chart 4.1 Son of David and Related References

(Legend: * = "Son of David" from Narrative Source; ** = doublet; + = "Son of David" added by Matthew; # = "Son of David" from Narrative Source *implied* by Matthew)

1:1	the "book" of the "origin" of Jesus Christ, "Son of David, Son of Abraham" introduces the genealogy of Jesus.
1:6	David, a key ancestor in the genealogy.
1:6	Solomon directly descended from David in the genealogy.
1:7	Solomon, the father of Rehoboam in the genealogy.
1:16	Jesus is the last son = descendant of Abraham and David.
1:17	David is explicitly stated as a dividing line between the first and second divisions of the 3 x 14 genealogy; 2/3 of the genealogy are his "sons."
1:20:+	Jesus' father Joseph is addressed by the dream-vision angel as "son of David."
6:29:	the lilies of the field are better clothed than Solomon in all his glory.
9:27: **	two blind men cry to Jesus: "Son of David, have mercy on me."
12:1–8:	the hungry David and those who were with him illegally ate the bread of the Presence, illustrating to the Pharisees God's perspective, "I desire mercy, and not sacrifice."
12:23:+	after healing a blind and dumb man, the crowds say, "This is not the Son of David, is it?" The Pharisees' response: Jesus exorcises by the Prince of Demons.
12:42:	in connection with Solomon's wisdom, "something greater than Solomon is here."
15:22:+	the Canaanite woman cries on behalf of her demon-possessed daughter, "Have mercy on me, O Lord, Son of David."
20:30:*	two blind men cry: "Have mercy on me (us), Son of David."
20:31:*	two blind men cry: "Have mercy on me (us), Son of David" (transposed order).
21:9:+	at Jesus' entry into Jerusalem, the crowds cry, "Hosanna to the Son of David!"
21:15:+	after the healing of the blind and the lame, the children in the Jerusalem temple cry, "Hosanna to the Son of David!"
22:41–46:#	the so-called "Son of David" question.

In this list the name of David's physical son "Solomon" has several connotations in the gospel. He is David's actual descendant and heir (1:6-7), he is remembered for the beauty of his dress (6:29), and he is cited for his wisdom (12:42), which by the first century CE, and in later Judean material, is associated with magic; so Solomon becomes a magician called "Son of David."[10] The Matthean writer notes Solomon's

---

10. Fisher, "Can This Be the Son of David?"; Lövestam, "Die Davidssohnfrage"; Berger, "Die königlichen Messiastradition"; Duling, "Solomon, Exorcism, and the Son of David"; *The Testament of Solomon*.

wisdom in a context of exorcism (Matt 12:42), an association that might hint at this magical tradition; yet, it should also be added that when he portrays Jesus as the miracle working "Son of David," he avoids explicit magical-manipulative connotations (in contrast to Mark 8:22–26).[11]

Apart from Solomon, the direct descendant of David, "Son of David" in the Gospel of Matthew has clear plurisignification: 1) ancestral (genealogical) descent and kinship (1:20 [Joseph]); 2) ancestral royal kingship (21:9); 3) ancestral (genealogical) kinship/kingship (1:1 [Jesus]; 21:9 [Jesus]; cf. 22:41–46 [implied for the Messiah]; cf. 1:6, 17 [Jesus]); 4) ancestral kinship/kingship associated with healing/exorcism as a title of honor or prominence label (9:27; 12:23; 15:22; 20:30; 20:31; 21:15 [all Jesus]); 5) Jesus' Davidic disregard for Temple purity (21:15). *Quantitatively*, the majority of references related to "Son of David" refer either to 1) royal Davidic descent (1:1, 6, 17, 20; 22:41–46) or 2) healing/exorcism (9:27; 12:23; 15:22; 20:30; 20:31; 21:15). With regard to *form*, there are two distinctive cries of greeting, both addressed to Jesus. The first cry, "Son of David, have mercy on me," occurs in connection with healing (9:27; 15:22; 20:30; 20:31). The second cry, "Hosanna to the Son of David," is found in connection with both royal and healing connotations (21:9, 15).[12] Finally, the gospel itself stresses plurisignification by raising the question about the true sense in which Jesus may be called the "Son of David" (Matt 22:41–46 [parallels Mark 12:35–37a; Luke 20:41–44]).

I shall now attempt to offer more social contextual meaning to these references. I begin with the first of the two prominent types quantitatively, the royal descent passages.

The Royal Son of David and Social Stratification

The key passage for royal descent of the Son of David is the genealogy in Matthew 1:1–17. The opening verse says that Jesus is the "Son of David" and the "Son of Abraham" (1:1). Then follows an interpretative genealogy with three sections of fourteen generations (1:17), the first

---

11. Duling, "The Therapeutic Son of David."

12. It would be desirable, but hardly practicable, to examine each of these references from various times, places, and perspectives, as well as from different ways of evaluating social status, as in Lenski's "distributive system" adjusted for the Roman Empire, on which see chap. 9.

listing ancestors from Abraham to David, the second from David to the Exile, and the third from the Exile to Jesus (fourteen generations). David is thus the dividing line between the first and second divisions; all who follow him in the second and third divisions—two-thirds of the genealogy—are his descendants, or "sons," which recalls a widespread, powerful "promise" tradition in Judean literature.[13] The second division traces his descent line through the well known kings of Judah (three omitted) in David's city, Jerusalem. To nail down the connection with the title "Son of David" in verse one, Jesus' father Joseph is addressed later as "Son of David" by the dream-vision angel (1:20).

One way to shed light on the royal descent of Jesus as the "Son of David" in the Gospel of Matthew (contrast the Gospel of Luke) is to relate kinship to the social hierarchy of the day. You will recall from the first three chapters that Gerhard and Jean Lenski, Geza Alföldy, and Gideon and Andrée Sjøberg provided us with etic, macrosocial models for various types of preindustrial and industrial societies.[14] Although the Lenskis acknowledged the importance of other developments in subsistence technology, they settled on the plow as the most important technological innovation for the shift from horticulture to agriculture, an advancement that took place in the fourth millennium BCE. The *iron-tipped* plow in the late second millennium led to further technological progress. *Economically*, there was greater division of labor, growth in business, commerce, and more migration to increasingly larger cities. *Politically*, there emerged the proprietary theory of the state, growth of the elites' administrative staffs and retainers, greater exploitation of peasants, and occasional peasant unrest. The *family* lost some of its integrating power, though it was still economically important. *Religiously*, there was a greater sense of universalism, continued religious legitimation of the state, decline in theocracy, and the growth of fatalism and resort to magic.

David Fiensy combined Lenski's and Alföldy's models of vertical stratification and "regionalized" them for Herodian Palestine.[15] In the following model I have simply added estimated percentages to Fiensy's model.[16]

13. Duling, "The Promises."
14. See esp. chap. 3.
15. Fiensy, *The Social History of Palestine*, 158.
16. Duling, *The New Testament*, 17.

Model 4.1 Social Stratification in First-Century Palestinian Society
(adapted from Fiensy, *Social History*, 158; compare Nolan and Lenski, *Human Societies* (8th ed.), 190, and Alföldy, *Social History* [Model 3.3]; see also Hanson and Oakman, *Palestine*, chap. 3; Duling, *The New Testament*, 17; statistics are calculated guesses)

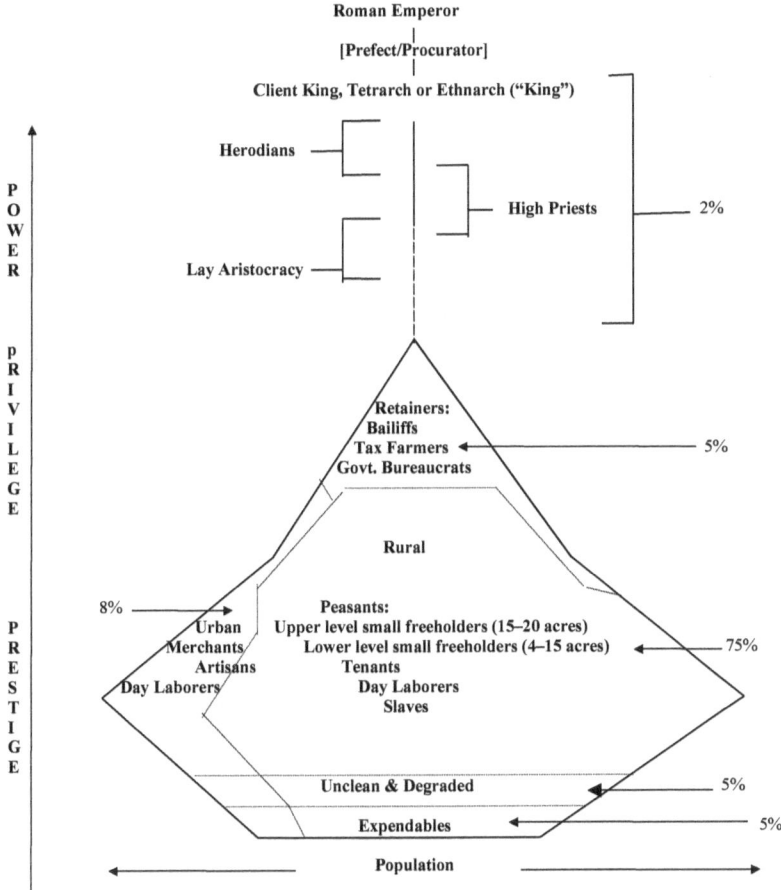

Fiensy supports his revised model with four chapters of empirical data about land tenure and peasant life from the Scriptures, Josephus, archaeology, and the rabbinic literature. I accept it as a background to Matthew's pre–70 CE *story* of Jesus, although later in this book I shall distinguish several roles of scribes.[17]

---

17. See chaps. 7, 8, and 9 in this book.

In this chapter I shall use the Fiensy revision of the Lenski model as a lens to visualize socially stratified persons and groups in the Gospel of Matthew, as in Chart 4.2.

Chart 4.2 Social Stratification of Persons and Groups in the Gospel of Matthew

1. *Highest Ruling Stratum.* Caesar (22:17, 21 [3x]); Rulers of the Gentiles (20:25); "Great Ones" (20:25; cf. 5:35).
2. *Provincial Rulers.* Prefects/Procurators. General (2:6 [Mic 5:2]; 10:18); Pilate (27:2, 11 [2x], 14, 15, 21, 27); Kings and Client Kings. General (10:18; 11:8; 17:25; 18:23; 22:2, 7, 11, 13; 25:34, 40); Herod (2:1, 2, 3, 9); Archelaus (2:22); Philip (14:4); Antipas (14:1, 9); Ancient kings (1:2–17; 12:3).
3. *Local Priestly Aristocracy.* High Priest Caiaphas (26:3, 57, 58, 62, 63, 65); chief priests; (2:4; 16:21; 20:18; 21:15, 23, 45; 26:3, 14, 47, 51, 59; 27:1, 3, 6, 12, 20, 41, 62; 28:11); priests (8:4; 12:4, 5); compare Sadducees (3:7; 16:1, 6, 11, 12; 22:23, 34).
4. *Lay Aristocracy.* Elders (15:2; 16:21; 21:23; 26:3, 47, 57; 27:1, 3, 12, 20, 41; 28:12); "landowner" (21:33); "ruler (of the synagogue)" (9:18, 23).
5. *Merchants* (10:29; 13:44, 45).
6. *Retainers.* Toll collectors (5:46, 5:47; 9:10, 11; 10:3; 11:19; 18:17; 21:31, 32); military personnel, general (3:14; 5:25); Roman centurions (8:5, 8, 13; 27:54); High Priest's guards (26:58; 28:11; 27:65, 66; 28:11); scribes (2:4; 5:20; 7:29; 8:19; 9:3; 12:38; 13:52; 15:1; 16:21; 17:10; 20:18; 21:15; 23:2, 13, 15, 23, 25, 27, 29, 34; 26:57; 27:41).
7. *Artisans* (13:55), *fishermen* (4:18–22; 13:47–50), *day laborers* (20:1, 2, 8; cf. 9:37, 38; 10:10).
8. *Peasants; Urban Poor and Destitute; overlaps with expendables and Unclean*: crowds (50 references!); the anxious (6:25–34); laborers of the harvest (9:37–38); tenant farmers (21:33); sower (13:3–8, 18–23, 24–30, 31–32, 33, 36–43).
9. *Herders* (9:36; 25:32; 26:31 [Zech 13:7]).
10. *Slaves* (*doulos*: 8:9; 10:24, 25; 13:27, 28; 18:23, 26, 27, 28, 32; 20:27; 21:34, 35, 36; 22:3, 4, 6, 8, 10; 24:45, 46, 48, 50; 25:14, 19, 21, 23 [2x], 30; 26:51; *pais*: 8:6, 8, 13; 12:18 [Isa 42:1]; 14:2; 17:18; 21:15?).
11. *Expendables and unclean (samples); overlaps with Peasants, Urban Poor and Destitute*: blind (9:27, 28; 11:5; 12:22; 15:14; 15:30; 15:31; 20:30; 21:14); lame (11:5; 15:30, 31; 18:8; 21:14); withered hand (12:9–14); deaf (11:5); dumb (9:32, 33; 12:22 [2x]; 15:30, 31); paralytics (4:24; 8:6; 9:2 [2x], 6); epileptics (4:24); demoniacs (8:28–34; 12:22, 43–45; 15:21–28); lepers (8:1–4; 10:8; 11:5); bandits (21:13 [Jer 7:11]; 26:55; 27:38, 36); thieves (6:19–20).

The vertical social strata from Lenski's macrosocial model in this list are very significant social strata for understanding the royal Son of David in Matthew's pre-70 CE story. I shall briefly discuss each of them.

For most of the first century CE Judeans in the Roman Empire were ruled locally by native kings. David Braund has made a full-scale study of such "client kings."[18] These regional rulers, usually descended from a royal line, were permitted by the Romans to rule if they preserved the peace and collected taxes, a large portion of which was shipped off to Rome. They and their households, along with the aristocratic urban elite who directly served them, that is, priestly families and lay aristocracy ("elders," "leaders"), made up a very small percentage of the population, perhaps as little as 1–2 percent. Normally the sons of these royal families were educated at Rome where they developed and maintained social and political networks. They were "clients" to their Roman "patrons," and "slaves" to their Roman "masters," but they were occasionally given the honor of being labeled "friend," "ally," and sometimes, often with reluctance, but if deemed loyal, the privileged title "king." They usually received Roman citizenship.[19] Thus, a full analysis would have to take into account other well-known kinds of social relations in antiquity: patron/client, master/slave, friend/friend, and so on.[20]

The Herodians were client kings. The Messiah "Son of David" in the gospel, who is legitimized by the Matthean author with the credentials of a native king, is a threat to them as illustrated by the actions of Herod (the Great) in the infancy story of Matthew 2.[21] Yet, Roman authorities who control them, as represented especially by the Roman Prefect Pontius Pilate, tend in this gospel to be viewed somewhat neutrally, or even positively (Matt 27:11–26).[22]

Another small percentage of the population, perhaps about 5 percent, consisted of what Lenski called "retainers," or those who served the aristocracy at somewhat lower levels: administrative and financial bureaucrats, tax collectors, household agents, judges, professional soldiers, educators, and, most important for the Gospel of Matthew, scribes (Greek *grammateus*), that is, agents who could write

18. Braund, *Rome and the Friendly King*.

19. Ibid., 9–53.

20. Ibid.; Wallace-Hadrill, *Patronage*; Elliott, "Patronage and Clientage"; Malina, "Patron and Client"; Moxnes, "Patron-Client Relations"; Bartchy, "Servant, slave," and "Slavery"; Fitzgerald, *Friendship*; cf. Boissevain, *Friends of Friends*.

21. Horsley, *Liberation*.

22. For the gospel's inconsistency on many matters, see chap. 5 below.

(Greek *gramma*, "writing").[23] Many scribes, drawn from various levels of society, served the ruling elites in record keeping, correspondence, and the like and shared in the economic surplus going to their superiors. Primarily urban dwellers, they were moderate, conventional, pious, and relatively well-off.[24] Orton's research on the ancient ideology of scribes in Judean antiquity argues that the scribe was not always a "secular" copier of manuscripts; often, he was honored for maintenance of religious beliefs, norms, and values; inspiration; exceptional insight; understanding of "parables" and "mysteries"; "righteousness"; true interpretation of the law and the prophets; communal authority; teaching; soothsaying; the creation of new "wise sayings" as a way of passing on his new insights; and the composition of hymns and apocalypses. In effect, he was believed to be a "wise sage."[25] Scribes were professionals and could be members of any party, but in the Matthean gospel, they are sometimes linked with the Pharisees and the Sadducees, Jesus' opponents; however, some scribes are valued highly in the gospel.[26] Indeed, it is likely, as we have noted above, that the author of the Matthean gospel was himself a scribe (Matt 13:51–52).[27]

Near the bottom of the social ladder was the vast majority of people, perhaps about 90 percent of the population. In this stratum were the poverty-stricken urban poor, peasants on the land, tenant farmers who tilled the soil,[28] perhaps about 75 percent of the total. There were also a few artisans, perhaps about 5 percent, who were living in cities and villages.[29] Some analyses place them below the peasants because in an advanced agrarian society, ownership of land carried with it honor, and artisans were usually those displaced from their ancestral lands.[30] It is an often debated question whether the

23. For dissatisfaction with the description "retainers" for some scribes, see chap. 9 below.

24. Lenski, *Power and Privilege*, 243–48; Carney, *Shape*, 47–82; Saldarini, *Pharisees*, 41–42, 241–76; Davies, "Social World"; Bar-Ilan, "Scribes."

25. Orton, *Understanding Scribe*, 111–18, 161–62; cf. Smith, "Wisdom and Apocalyptic"; Davies, "Social World"; for more discussion of scribes and several kinds of scribes, see chaps. 7 and 9 below.

26. Orton, ibid., 20–38, 137–64; Saldarini, *Pharisees*, 157–66.

27. Orton, ibid., 165–76; see chaps. 7 and 9 below.

28. Oakman, *Jesus and the Economic Questions*; Crossan, *Historical Jesus*.

29. Lenski, *Power and Privilege*, 279; Wolf, *Peasants*; Oakman, ibid.

30. Lensk, ibid., 278.

artisans, and thus Jesus, shared the beliefs, values, and behavior of the peasants on the land; a recent study suggests that they did.[31] Finally, there were also the expendables and unclean, perhaps another 10 percent, mostly all living at a bare subsistence level.[32] In any case, the gospels portray Jesus as carrying out his ministry primarily among these lower strata.[33]

This macrosocial model suggests the possibility of potential political and economic conflict between the rulers and the ruled, between the aristocratic elite and the peasants, between the rich and the poor, between the haves and the have-nots.[34] In Palestine, the potential conflict became actual in a series of incidents leading to full-scale war in 66–70 CE.[35]

After the Roman-Judean wars, however, significant changes occurred in Palestine with respect to the aristocratic elite. There seems to have been a decline of the power of the Herodian kings and their families.[36] To be sure, the pro-Roman Agrippa II, who had obtained the traditional right to appoint high priests and to supervise the Temple and its funds at his father's death (44 CE), had been granted control of Philip's lands, some territory in northern Lebanon (53 CE), the west coast of the Sea of Galilee (Tiberias and Taricheae), and two regions in southern Perea (54 CE). He was highly respected in Rome as the most powerful Judean monarch, was rewarded with more lands after the war (where is not known), and apparently reigned in peace until about 85/86 CE. Yet, Agrippa II's lands were largely scattered and almost exclusively Gentile—he did not regain control of Samaria, Judea, or Judean Galilee—and since he did not die until about 92/93 CE, his (Judean?) lands seem to have been taken from him.[37] We hear

31. Oakman, *Jesus and the Economic Questions*.

32. Lenski, *Power and Privilege*, 283; Esler, *Community and Gospel*, 171–79; Pilch, "Health Care System"; Stark, "Antioch."

33. For a similar analysis of the Gospel of Mark, see Rohrbaugh, "Social Location."

34. Lenski, ibid., 274, 279; Theissen, *Sociology*; Esler, *Community and Gospel*, 171–79; Horsley, *Sociology*; Stark, "Antioch"; Vledder in chap. 3; cf. Milibrand, "Class Analysis."

35 Horsley, *Jesus and the Spiral of Violence*; Duling, *The New Testament*, 19–24.

36. Jones, *Herods*, 217–61; Schürer, Vermes, and Millar, *History*, 1:471–83.

37. Schürer, Vermes, and Millar, ibid., 481; White, "Crisis Management," 213–14; cf. Jos. *Ant.* 17.2.2 (§28). See chap. 2 above.

very little about Agrippa II after 70 CE, and since he had no children, it seems that his kingdom was incorporated into the province of Syria at his death.

Even more significant was the decline in power of the priestly aristocracy after 70 CE. It is true that some loyalists among the priestly aristocracy were given, or allowed to retain, land. For example, Josephus, who claimed priestly descent (Jos. *Life* 1.1), was given land by Titus after the war (Jos. *Life* 76.422). Similarly, the priest Eleazar ben Harsom was remembered to have been land rich (*b. Yoma* 35b), presumably because of his loyalty to Rome.[38] Nonetheless, the Holy City had been destroyed and the Holy Temple, which was not only the center of religious life but the "national treasury" and the "national archives," was gone forever. The half-shekel tax that had gone to support the Temple and its priesthood now went to Rome (cf. Matt 17:24-27). Finally, the ranking of the scribal retainers who served this power elite shifted down considerably, and this shift was important for Matthew, who came from scribal circles.

In short, at the time the gospel was written, the political power of the client kings, the high priestly elite, and their retainers, including their bureaucratic scribes, would have lost much of their influence. From this perspective, it is perhaps no accident that explicit opposition to the "power elite" in the gospel especially stresses the Herodians rather than the Romans.[39]

Returning to the gospel, in some contexts Matthew's Jesus favors fictive kinship over actual kinship.[40] The prospective would-be follower of Jesus who wishes first to bury his real father honorably is told: "leave the (spiritually?) dead to bury their (real?) dead" (Matt 8:22 [Q 9:60]). The real family is the fictive family, that is, the true "brother" and "sister" and "mother" are those who, as "the son" says, "do the will of my father who is in heaven" (Matt 12:50 [Mark 3:35: "will of God"]; cf. Matt 3:17; 17:5; 16:16b-19). In the case of "father," metaphorical kinship overrides fictive kinship within the new family: call no *man* your "father" on earth. However, the same judgment does not pertain to the

---

38. Cf. Fiensy, *Social History*, 37.

39. For emphasis on the Romans, see Carter, *Matthew and Empire*; Riches and Sim, eds., *Gospel of Matthew*.

40. I distinguish primarily between "real" and "fictive" kinship; for "metaphorical," a more literary category, see above, p. 93.

fictive "brother": "you are all *brothers*" (23:9, 8b). The true "father" is the father in heaven, who is also the King above the king, the "Great King" (Matt 5:35),[41] and his household is the fictive royal household (cp. 1 Pet 2:5, 9).[42] In *this* kingdom and this household, conventional social stratification, not to mention purity, will be significantly reversed (Matt 5:19; 18:1–5). Such, at least, is the ideology.[43]

Yet, Matthew does not abandon actual kinship and at times there seems to be ranking in the kingdom. The Pharisees are called "hypocrites" when they value their tradition over written Torah commands that they should honor their parents (Matt 15:2, 10–20). Matthew adds Jesus' missing father and removes the apparent slur on Mary by calling Jesus "son of *the carpenter* (artisan)" (Matt 13:55 [Mark 6:3 "the son of Mary"]). Thus, while fictive kinship defines the *new* family—"brothers" who are "righteous" (Matt 5:17–20), "have faith" (Matt 6:30; 8:26; 14:31; 16:8; 17:20; cf. 8:10; 9:21, 28, 29; 15:28), "bear fruit" (Matt 7:17, 20), and the like—the main "son" of this fictive family descends from real parents, Joseph and Mary (Matt 1:18–19).

In short, Jesus' "actual" kinship, symbolic as it may be, does not disappear. For further illustration, I turn to the familiar infancy narrative.

Jesus as Legitimate Messianic King of David's Line (Matt 1:1–25)

The legitimation of Jesus as someone special is established through his dual paternity, each paternity introduced by the same term, *genesis*, or "origin" (Matt 1:1, 18). The first *genesis* ("genealogy") demonstrates his patrilineal descent from David and Abraham via Joseph; the second *genesis* ("birth") is his virginal conception implying divine paternity.[44] The plurisignification of "son of" is evident: his "divine" origin shows that he is "Son of God" (Matt 1:1, 19); his human origin shows that he is "son of Abraham," but, above all, "Son of David."

---

41. Duling, "'[Do not Swear] ....'"
42. Elliott, *Home* (1990), 186–87.
43. Elliott, "Jesus Was Not an Egalitarian"; "The Jesus Movement was not Egalitarian."
44. Schaberg, *Illegitimacy*, 20–77.

Thus, "Son of David"—descent from David and his sons, the kings of Israel—demonstrates that he has a royal lineage; it is critical for his human origins, and so "Son of David" is placed first in the introduction to the genealogy (Matt 1:1). Moreover, David and his royal descendants are the centerpiece of the genealogy itself (Matt 1:6–11). This is confirmed by the genealogy that has three divisions, each comprising fourteen generations (Matt 1:17), fourteen apparently being a *gematria* from the three-letter Hebrew orthography of David's name in the Torah, prophets, and psalms, namely, d-v-d = 4+6+4,[45] which add up to fourteen (Matt 1:17). While the presence of the women and the lack of Joseph's biological/genealogical connections to Jesus in the genealogy may hint at what used to be called "illegitimacy,"[46] Joseph is nonetheless addressed by God's messenger as "Son of David" (Matt 1:20), and he names the child (Matt 1:21, 25), thus accepting him as his own. Jesus has the human prerequisites to be the native messianic king. He is "Son of David."

Genealogical and symbolic legitimation, yes! Yet, this human king is not like the client kings of Rome. From the perspective of the macrosocial model above, they are part of the ruling strata. *This* messianic king, however, is a threat to the ruling strata (Matt 2; 14:3–12)![47]

The macrosocial perspective outlined above, while implying real and fictive kinship, is explicitly political and economic. It helps to understand Jesus as the "Son of David" in the Gospel of Matthew, especially his royal descent and its implications as a threat to Herodian power. But in the Matthean gospel it is the Pharisees who are Jesus' main opponents, and once again the "Son of David" comes into play. I now take up this dimension of plurisignificance and look at the "Son of David" from the perspective of social-scientific models of groups.

Groups and the Matthew Group

Drawing on Mediterranean anthropologist Jeremy Boissevain, Bruce Malina distinguishes two general types of groups, corporations and

---

45. Freedman, "Spelling."
46. Schaberg, *Illegitimacy*.
47. See Horsley, *Liberation*; more recently, Carter, *Matthew and Empire*; Riches and Sim, *Gospel of Matthew*.

Matthew's Plurisignificant "Son of David"

coalitions. The corporate group "might be defined as a collection of people forming a corporate body with a permanent existence, recruited on recognized principles, with common interests and rules or norms giving the rights and duties of the members in relation to each other and to these common interests."[48] In a corporate group individuals have a high level of security and protection; they derive power, privilege, and prestige from those with honor ascribed to them by birth or other honorable persons ("ascribed honor").[49]

Those who are ruled by the ruling classes, that is, the vast majority of people who are poor and destitute, do not have the same security and protection. At the microsocial level, they are members of other kinds of groups. At this level, Nolan and Lenski make a microsocial distinction between "primary groups" and "secondary groups."[50] If we revise their analysis on the basis of Boissevain and Malina's view of groups, the result might look like Model 4.2.

Model 4.2 Primary and Secondary Groups

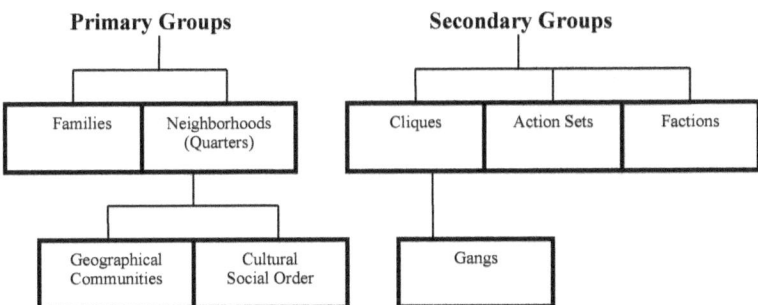

In primary groups, families are based on kinship relations (physical descent) and neighborhoods or quarters are based on shared values and rituals rooted in the cultural and social order, for example, births, circumcisions, weddings, and funerals. In such neighborhoods, social closeness is more significant than residential proximity, though

48. Malina, "Patron and Client," 20.

49. Ibid., 19–31; *Christian Origins*, 13–67; "A Conflict Approach," 14; cf. Boissevain, *Friends of Friends*, 203; see p. 113 below.

50. Nolan and Lenski, *Human Societies*, 45. For more "group theory," see chaps. 6 and 7; for a history of small group theory in the social sciences and its significance for the New Testament, see Duling, "Small Groups."

the two may overlap.⁵¹ Yet, neighborhoods are also rooted in larger "geographical communities" based on spatial proximity at various levels of abstraction, that is, regions, cities, towns, and villages.⁵² The cultural and social order is based on matters such as race or ethnic origin, which can overlap with geography.

The "secondary groups" in Model 4.2 above correspond to Boissevain's and Malina's second type, "coalitions." A coalition is defined as "a collection of people within some larger, encapsulating structure [such as a kingdom or empire] consisting of distinct parties in temporary alliances for some limited purpose."⁵³ As secondary groups coalitions include subtypes termed cliques, gangs, action sets, and factions. People in cliques are not recruited, but are unintentionally assembled; they are generally without goals and leaders, but "hang out" together because of affection, common interests, and common identity. "Gangs" are somewhat larger cliques in which one person emerges as the central person or group leader who makes decisions for the group; their activities usually take place out of doors. "Action sets" are pragmatic and instrumental groups that, in contrast to cliques and gangs, come together to coordinate their activities to achieve specific pragmatic or instrumental goals; central persons or leaders emerge only as, or after, they meet.

The fourth kind of coalition is a "faction," defined as follows: "[a] *faction* is a coalition of persons (followers) recruited personally, according to structurally diverse principles by or on behalf of a person in conflict with another person(s) with whom they (coalition members) were formerly united over honor and/or control of resources and/or 'truth.'⁵⁴ When coalitions have as their purpose to change the social structure, in other analyses (particularly conflict analysis) they are politically motivated and called "social movements,"⁵⁵ or "conflict

---

51. Eickelman, *Middle East*, 107.

52. See chap. 3 above, Chart 3.1, for Ritzer's macroscopic to microscopic continuum of levels of abstraction, from higher (world systems) to lower (individuals). "Groups" are below "organizations" (corporations).

53. Malina, "Patron and Client," 20; "A Conflict Approach," 15; cf. Boissevain, *Friends of Friends*, 171.

54. Malina, "Patron and Client," 24.

55. Lenski and Lenski, *Human Societies*, 45–46; Wilson, *Magic*, 18–30; Saldarini, *Pharisees*; Elliott, *Home*; for Wilson's typology of sects, see chap. 1, Chart 1.1.

groups."⁵⁶ All such groups legitimize themselves, as well as roles and persons within them, and do so interacting with "elite corporations," other groups, and persons.

The historical Jesus group with its emphasis on recruitment of new members has led Malina to term it a "person-centered faction."⁵⁷ The Sadducees were almost equivalent to the priestly aristocracy; thus, it is better to think of them as a well-organized, hierarchical group. From the lens of this model they can be considered a "corporation." The Pharisees and the Matthean Christ-believers, the two groups of most concern here, are more difficult to locate among the model's groups. Historically, the Pharisees seem to have emerged as a social movement or conflict group. They were intent on applying Temple purity—and thus the norms, values, and behavior of the priestly Sadducees—to everyday life, especially in the home and at the table.⁵⁸ From the perspective of the Lenski-Alföldy-Fiensy macrosocial model, they might be considered retainers of the ruling classes. Although they held views different than those of the Sadducees, as the historical conflict with them shows, and the Pharisee Zaddok was a member of what Josephus terms the "Fourth Philosophy," a resistance group that opposed taxes imposed by Rome, the Pharisees had become a permanent group that developed a Torah piety that stressed rules or norms giving the rights and duties of members in relation to each other, as opposed to outsiders. Thus, they can be considered a type of incipient corporation, namely, a sacred in-group.

What, then, of the Matthew group? From the lens of this model, the author of the gospel portrays the rival Pharisees as a group with the "wrong" beliefs, goals, and values, and as those who label their central persons inappropriately; in contrast, he promotes followers of the Jesus group as a faction, a non-hierarchical network structure, a kind of "leaderless group" (Matt 23:8–12 ["leaderless groups" are not leaderless]).⁵⁹ Despite this faction *ideology*, however, there appear to

56. Dahrendorf, *Class and Class Conflict*, 180.

57. Malina, "Patron and Client," 20–27; "A Conflict Approach," 15–16. For the Jesus Movement as faction, see also Elliott, "Phases"; Seland, "Jesus as Faction Leader." For factions *within* the Matthean community, see chap. 6.

58. So Saldarini, *Pharisees*, 42; cf. Neusner, "The Idea of Purity"; "Formation."

59. On "leaderless groups," see Fisher, *Small Group Decision Making*; Herbst, *Alternatives to Hierarchies*; see pp. 171–73 below. For Matthew, see Garland, *The Intention of Matthew 23*; Krentz, "Community and Character"; Viviano, "Social

be in the Matthew group undefined central persons with scribe-related labels and functions: "apostles" (10:2); "prophets" (5:10–12; 10:40–42; 11:9; 13:57; 21:11, 23–27; 23:29–36; the formula quotations); "teachers" (5:19; 28:20); "scribes" (13:52; 23:34); "righteous men" (10:41–42); "wise men" (Matt 23:34).[60] When considering these labels, the ascription of honor to Peter (lower status) by Jesus (higher status) is suggestive (16:17–19).[61] Thus, like the Pharisees, the Matthew group is not *simply* a faction, but moving toward a corporation. A major theme of the Matthean story, then, is conflict between two groups in process of becoming corporations. I shall explore these themes further in chapters 6, 7, and 9.

The Merciful, Compassionate, Therapeutic "Son of David"

The author of the Gospel of Matthew has a special interest in the Son of David's merciful and compassionate healing.[62] Jesus heals every illness and infirmity (4:23; 9:35; cf. 10:1, 8a; 11:5 and 15:29–31 [Isa 25:5–6; 29:18–19; LXX 61:1]) and all persons (12:15b). He exorcizes simply with a word, and he heals all who are sick. His healing fulfills Isaiah 53:4 (Hebrew): "He took our infirmities and bore our diseases" (8:17). Jesus says, "Something greater than Solomon is here" (12:42), suggesting Solomon the Magician.[63] Yet, Matthew portrays the healer without Solomonic-style magical manipulation (Matt 15:29–31 [Mark 7:31–37]; Mark 8:22–26 is omitted; reduction of exorcisms).[64] Four of the five instances of the verb "to have compassion" (*splangchnidsomai*) and five of the eight instances of the verb "I have mercy" (*eleeō*) occur in connection with healing, and in almost every case the plurisignificant titles "Lord" and/or "Son of David" appear as part of the semantic field. This is summarized in Chart 4.3.

World." For more on the historical Jesus' Galilean network, see Duling, "The Jesus Movement" (Parts I and II) and "Recruitment."

   60. See chap. 6.

   61. Duling, "Binding and Loosing"; see below.

   62. For redactional details, see Duling, "The Therapeutic Son of David," which influenced Le Donne, *The Historiographical Jesus*, chap. 6; see also Loader, "Son of David"; Pilch, "The Health Care System in Matthew."

   63. Duling, "Solomon, Exorcism, and the Son of David."

   64. Fisher, "Can This Be the Son of David?"; Duling, "The Therapeutic Son of David."

Chart 4.3 Son of David, Compassion, Mercy, and Healing

20:30:		"*Have mercy* on us,		Son of David!"		
20:31:	"Lord,	*have mercy* on us,		Son of David!"	20:34:	*compassion*
9:27:		"*Have mercy* on me,		Son of David!"	9:36:	*compassion*
15:22:		"*Have mercy* on me,	O Lord,	Son of David!"	15:32:	*compassion*
17:15:	"Lord,	*have mercy* on my son			17:20:	*(much) faith*
12:23:		"Can this be the		Son of David?"		
14:14:		"...healed their sick..."			14:14:	*compassion*
Compare:						
15:25:	"Lord,	help me."				
18:26:	"Lord,	have patience with me."			18:27	*compassion*
18:33:	("Lord")	have mercy			18:33:	*mercy*
Compare again:						
5:7:	"Blessed are	*the merciful*	for they shall receive (from God)			*mercy*

Jesus' healing is clearly related to God's and Jesus' mercy (*eleos*) in the gospel. Support from sacred texts is added by the Matthean author twice, both from Hosea 6:6: "I desire mercy (*eleos*), and not sacrifice" (Matt 9:13; 12:7). The first instance, which is another example of challenge/response (see below, Model 4.3), occurs after the call of Matthew the toll collector, when Jesus is banqueting with "tax collectors and sinners" (other retainers and the impure). The *Pharisees*—precisely the group that attempts to carry out Temple purity in everyday life (also in Matthew's day)[65]—respond with disbelief. Jesus retorts: "Go and learn what this means, 'I desire mercy (*eleos*), and not sacrifice' (Hosea 6:6). I came not to call the righteous, but [unclean] sinners" (9:13). It is precisely the rival Pharisees who do *not* have the God-required mercy (Matt 23:23), who seek to destroy Jesus when he has compassion on the "lost sheep" (12:11–12, 14; cf.

---

65. Neusner, *Early Rabbinic Judaism*, 44.

10:5-6; 15:24; 18:10-14; cf. CD 13:9-10), and who label him as an evil exorcist (9:34; 12:22-24).[66]

The second instance of quoting Hosea 6:6 falls at the end of the only passage that relates a story about David. It stresses David's disobedience of the laws about Temple purity in order to meet human need for food (Matt 12:1-8). The merciful and compassionate "Son of David," kin and heir of the greatest of all native kings, David, the one who disobeyed the laws of Temple purity for human need, stands in direct conflict with the Temple rulers and their Pharisaic retainers who implement that purity in daily life. When the Temple is gone in the post–70 era, they have become a rival group. In the process King David's ancestral son and heir makes his "home" with the peasants, expendables, and unclean.[67] "I desire mercy, and not sacrifice" (Hos 6:6).

The Therapeutic Messiah/Son of David in the Jerusalem Temple

In the Matthean story Jesus enters the Holy Temple on the same day that he enters the Holy City (contrast Mark 11:12, 15-19). At both locations he is addressed with the cry, "Hosanna to the Son of David!" (cf. *Did.* 10:6: "God of David."). The first cry comes from the festival "crowds" (Matt 21:9) who in the Matthean world include urban poor and festival peasants. The passage reflects the literal wording of the Zechariah prophecy about the lowly "Coming One"/Davidic king Messiah who enters the city (21:5 [Zech 9:9]; cf. 21:2, 3, 7). The scene recalls the imprisoned Baptist's question about whether Jesus is "the Coming One" (Matt 11:3), which is answered by a healing summary in Jesus' words taken from Matthew's favorite prophetic book, Isaiah, and which refers to healing "the blind" and "the lame" (Matt 11:5; see LXX Isa 61:1; 35:5-6; 39:18). Similar associations are later made in the story of the Canaanite woman story: the woman cries, "Son of David, have mercy on me" (Matt 15:22, 30-31) and the story concludes with a healing summary that includes "the blind" and "the lame."[68]

---

66. Malina and Neyrey, *Calling Jesus Names*; for Malina and Neyrey on labeling theory, see chap. 2.

67. Elliott, "Temple versus Household."

68. See Love, *Jesus and Marginal Women*, 146-65.

Matthew's Plurisignificant "Son of David" 111

After Jesus enters Jerusalem he goes into the Holy Temple (Matt 21:12) and, after overturning the table of the moneychangers, he heals "the blind" and "the lame" (21:14).[69] The enigmatic "children" (true disciples? cf. Matt 18:1–9)[70] then cry, "Hosanna to the Son of David!" as the entering Passover pilgrims had done. The scene reaches a climax in the Temple—the institutional heart of politics, economics, and religion—with a challenge/response.[71] The King Messiah/"Son of David" heals those who are impure in the center of purity, the Jerusalem Temple, and the ruling religious elite and their retainers, the chief priests and the scribes, object. The King's patronage and benefactions are directed to those who have need of his mercy and compassion, despite purity rules and the center of purity. As such, he is also fictively the Son of the Great King, the representative of God.[72]

This scene has what is called a challenge-and-response ("challenge and riposte") sequence (see below, Model 4.3): action + "Son of David" cry; chief priests' and scribes' complaint; and Jesus' scriptural response, a defense about "perfect praise" (LXX Ps 8:2). Jesus wins the debate. This pattern can be explored further by analyzing Jesus' debates with opponents in the Temple. They culminate in the "Son of David Question."

Challenge and Response in the Temple: "In what sense is he Son of David?"

Thus far in the Matthean story, the Son of David has been presented as plurisignificant, that is, with a variety of meanings that can be illuminated by a variety of social-scientific models: King Solomon, the son who wears beautiful clothes and is known to work his magic; Joseph, Jesus' father, who is called "Son of David," and Mary who is a virgin giving birth to God's son; Jesus' genealogy showing that he is descended from the great King David; Jesus' birth as a political threat to the

---

69. According to Lev 21:16–20 (cf. 2 Sam 5:8) children are unclean and should not be in the Temple! The Mishna says that the blind and lame were among those who were not required to sacrifice at the Temple (*m. Hagiga* 1:1).

70. In 5 Ezra they are disciples; see Stanton, "5 Ezra."

71. Elliott, "Temple versus Household," 231 (Fig. 8–1), 234 (Fig. 8–2).

72. Malina, "Patron and Client"; Moxnes, "Patron-Client Relations."

Herodian client kings; Jesus as a healer who is addressed with the cry, "Son of David, have mercy on me (us)," and who responds with compassionate and merciful healing; and Jesus as glorified with "Hosanna to the Son of David" by pilgrims as he enters the Holy City and by children when he heals the blind and lame in the Holy Temple. Thus, despite his royal pedigree, Jesus Son of David appears as a preacher and a folk healer who, like David, was willing to go against purity laws on behalf of his disciples.[73] Thus, the Gospel of Matthew takes up the question of the sense (Greek *pōs*) in which the Messiah is the Son of David, an interchange that can be illumined by the social-scientific model "challenge and riposte" mentioned above.

First, a little background about "challenge and response." As discussed in the first three chapters, Mediterranean society is an advanced agrarian or peasant society in which "honor" and "shame" are core values. Such societies can also be termed "honor/shame societies." What is honor? A definition is appropriate. "Honor might be described as socially proper attitudes and behavior in the area where the three lines of power, sexual status, and religion intersect."[74] In other words, the power exerted by males over females in one's primary group, the family, and in other social arrangements, is central to the honor code, and in a patriarchal society that relationship is supported by religious tradition. Honor is the claim to worth, but more: the social acknowledgement of worth within one's primary groups and beyond. To hold and maintain one's honor is paramount; to lose it is shame. Paradoxically, to have the proper degree of shame in certain social situations is honorable.

Honor/shame societies have been described as "agonistic," from the Greek term *agōn*, "contest, combat." In such societies social relationships outside the immediate family or close friends often become competitions or contests for honor. Above all it is critical to defend family honor. In advanced agrarian, or peasant, or honor/shame societies, honor can be obtained in two ways, *ascribed or acquired*.

First, honor can be *ascribed*. This happens either through the accident of birth, that is, being born to honorable parents and de-

---

73. On folk healing in Matthew, see Pilch, "The Health Care System"; "Reading Matthew Anthropologically."

74. Malina, *The New Testament World*, (1981 ed.), 27; Neyrey, *Honor and Shame*; see chap. 2.

scended from honorable ancestors, or by grant from some powerful, honorable person. Native kings, such as Herod "the Great," have descent honor by means of a royal genealogy.[75] Honor can be ascribed also by a grant from a superior to an inferior, as when a Herodian ruler is granted the title of "king" from the Roman Emperor, his patron.[76] In Matthew's Gospel, Jesus' honor is *ascribed*, too. It is ascribed by both his human and divine *genesis*, as Son of David and Son of God, as just discussed. God also names him his "son" in the language of Psalm 2:7 in the Baptism/Temptation sequence (Matt 3:17; 4:3, 6) and the transfiguration story (17:5). The fisherman Simon has honor *ascribed* to him by Jesus who renames him *Petros*/"Rock," for Jesus' community will be built upon a *petra*, "rock" (Matt 16:17-19).

Second, honor can also be *acquired* (or forfeited), that is, achieved (or lost) by some ability. In "agonistic societies," this is often done so by contests and competitions, physical (the medieval joust) or verbal, normally between equals. When a person is challenged (positively or negatively) by some word or deed of another person, when he and the public perceive it as a challenge, and when with a surprising or witty response/riposte he wins, he gains honor. If he loses, he loses honor. Bruce Malina develops a model for challenge/response honor contests, Model 4.3 (see below).[77]

As Model 4.3 shows, challenge/response in an agrarian, agonistic, honor/shame society has the following structure: challenge by the challenger, often in the form of a question or trick question, or by a challenging act, about the claims or implied claims of the one challenged; perception of the challenge by the one challenged and the public; response of the one challenged; and the evaluation of the interchange by the public.[78] This is an etic, homomorphic micromodel that will help to illumine the debates between Jesus and his opponents.

---

75. Hanson, "Kinship"; Hanson and Oakman, *Palestine* (2nd ed.), chap. 2.
76. For detail, see Duling, "'[Do not Swear] . . . .'"
77. Malina, *The New Testament World* (1981), 31.
78. Malina, *The New Testament World* (1981), 29-33.

Model 4.3 Challenge and Response in an Agonistic Honor/Shame Society

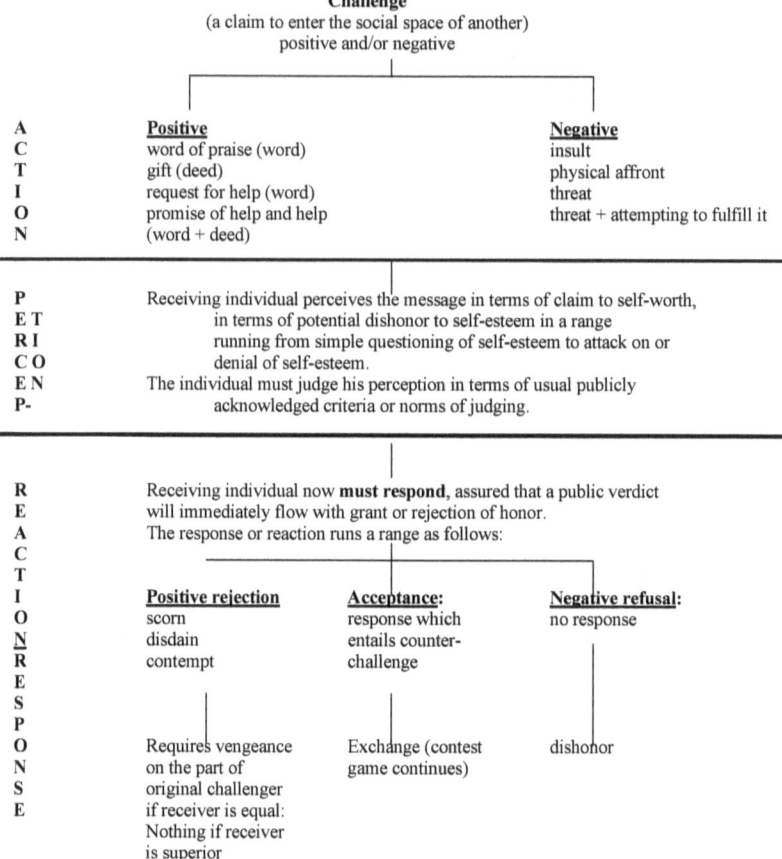

The debates between Jesus and his opponents in the Jerusalem Temple (Matt 21:15–22:46 [Mark 12:13–37a]) fit the agonistic challenge/response pattern, although the crowd or its response is not explicit (21:46; 22:1, 33, 46; 23:1). In this contest, the Pharisees are highlighted as the main opposition group (21:45; cf. 21:23 [Mark 11:27]; 22:15, 34–35 [Mark 12:28], 41). Jesus' honor is publicly challenged. He wins all these debates; his successful responses imply public honor. The final challenge, however, comes from the challenged one himself, Jesus, that is, in the "Son of David Question." The whole sequence is a challenge/riposte sequence that may echo a characteristic rabbinic form.[79] The exchange is illustrated by the bold type in Chart 4.4.

79. Daube, *The New Testament and Rabbinic Judaism*, 158–69; Malina and Neyrey, *Calling Jesus Names*, 72–81.

Chart 4.4 Challenge and Response in the Temple

Matthew	Source	Opponent(s)	Challenge	Response
21:23–27	Mk 11:27–33	chief priests and elders	By what authority are you doing these things?	Was the baptism of John from heaven or men?
21:28-32	———			What do you think? A man had two sons
21:33–41	Mk 12:1–10			Hear another parable: vineyard
21:42–44	Mk 12:11–12	chief priests, scribes try to arrest Jesus		Have you never heard in the Scriptures? Rejected stone and Kingdom given to nation producing fruits
22:1–10	Q 14:16–24			Marriage feast (others invited)
22:11–14				Wedding Garment
22:15–22	Mk 12:12: chief priests, elders ("they")	Pharisees consult how to trap Jesus in his talk; their disciples and Herodians	Is it lawful to pay taxes to Caesar?	Render to Caesar the things that are Caesar's, and to God the things that are God's
22:23–33	Mk 12:18–27	Sadducees	Which of seven deceased husbands will be his wife?	You know neither the Scriptures nor the power of God. Astonishment.
22:34–40	Mk 12:28–34	lawyer of Pharisees	Which is the great commandment?	Love God; love neighbor
22:41–46	Mk 12:35–37	Jesus	Whose son is the Messiah? David calls him Lord. How can he be his son?	*Pharisees*: David's. No one was able to answer him a word; nor from that day did any one dare to ask him any more questions.

How is Jesus' "Son of David" argument made? In Matthew's Narrative Source there are three challenges by opponents and Jesus' three responses (Mark 12:13–34). Then Jesus himself takes the initiative and raises the trick question: "How can the scribes say that the Messiah is the Son of David?" Jesus continues by observing that when King David prophesied "in the spirit," he said, "the Lord (God) said to my Lord (the Messiah) . . ." (Ps 110:1a). David called the Messiah "my Lord," and since a father never calls his son "my Lord," how (*pothen*) can the Messiah be David's son? The argument is very casuistic.

The author of the Gospel of Matthew makes small, but very significant, redactional changes that reinforce Jesus' acquired honor in the challenge/riposte. First, Jesus' respondents, unspecified by Mark, are specified as *Pharisees*, the group most opposed by Matthew. Second, he shifts to direct discourse, intensifying the challenge/response drama: *Jesus* asks: "What do you think of the Messiah? *Whose* son is he?" The Pharisees respond: "David's," implying that the Messiah is legitimated by birth and descent from David. Again Jesus challenges in direct discourse: "How is it then that David, inspired by the Spirit, calls him 'Lord'?" and quotes the prophetic Psalm 110:1. Here Matthew first changes *legō*, "I call," to *kaleō*, "I call," "I name," his term for "prominence labeling" (Matt 1:21–25).[80] For Matthew, "Lord" has plurisignification: it is an address of honor and an address to a deity in worship.[81] Third, Matthew reformulates the challenge by changing *pothen*, "how," to *pōs*, which can mean, "*in what sense,*" that is, "in what sense is he his son?" The subtlety of the reformulation implies a balanced couplet:

> (If the Messiah is David's son),
>   in what sense does David . . . call him "my lord" . . .
> If . . . David calls him "my lord,"
>   in what sense can he be his (David's) son?

Just as "lord" has plurisignification, so has "Son of David." This is no out-and-out rejection of the "Son of David" honor title; it poses the question: "*in what sense?*" (*pōs*; cf. *Barn.* 12:10).

Fourth, Matthew now dramatically intensifies Jesus' victory in this challenge/response: he relocates the conclusion from the previous Great Commandment debate in Mark (Mark 12:28–34) to this

---

80. Malina and Neyrey, *Calling Jesus Names*, 96–97.
81. Matt 8:25; 17:4; Bornkamm, "End Expectation," 41–43.

last scene: "And from that day on no one dared to ask him any questions" (Matt 22:46). Jesus wins the debate. His response meets the challenge successfully. The net effect of this scribal argument is that in the very center of Judean purity, the Jerusalem Temple, Jesus is publicly honored and the Pharisaic group is publicly shamed. The implication for Matthew as scribe in contrast to the Yavneh scribes in the post-70 period is the author's own implied victory in the contest. The question remains open: *in what sense* is the King/Messiah/Lord the "Son of David"?

Plurisignification plays a vital role in Matthew. Among the designations of Jesus in the Gospel of Matthew are "Messiah" (1:1, 16, 17, 18; 2:4; 11:2; 16:16, 20; 22:42; 23:10; 24:5, 23; 26:63, 68; 27:17, 22, 25; 27:15); "King" (21:5 [Zech 9:9]); "King of the Judeans" (27:11, 29, 37); "King of Israel" (27:42). These are all royal designations used for the ruling aristocracy. He is also called "Son of David." This can be a royal designation (1:1), and as such Jesus competes with the ruling aristocracy. However, it is not usually a royal title, but one of the other nuances, most especially merciful and compassionate healing, predominates (9:27; 12:23; 15:22; 20:30, 31; 21:9, 15; 22:42, 43, 45). Does Matthew hint at the real significance of Jesus as "Son of David"?

Conclusion

In this chapter I have interpreted the "Son of David" in the Gospel of Matthew through the lenses of three models: an etic, macrosocial model for social stratification in an advanced agrarian society; an etic, microsocial model for groups and their interaction and conflict; and an etic, microsocial model for challenge/response in an honor/shame society. The models help interpret the text in at least five ways.

First, insight about the "Son of David" in the Gospel of Matthew can be gained from understanding social stratification in an advanced agrarian society. For the wise scribe who composed the gospel, "Son of David" is sometimes a designation that demands ascription of high honor to Jesus. It legitimizes Jesus through his descent from King David and his royal descendants, the native Davidic kings of Israel (Matt 1:1–25). This claim is a clear instance of Jesus' legitimation as Messiah by both birth and ancestral tradition, thus that Jesus meets the conditions for great power, privilege, and prestige. He has the credentials to be a king. Indeed, in an ironic way he is the king of Israel, and as king he is also Messiah and Son of God. Thus, Jesus has honor ascribed to him both by virtue of his actual human kinship from native kings and by the Great King, God himself, as God's son (e.g., Matt 3:17; 4:4, 6; 16:16; 17:5). As such, Matthew's "Son of David" can be contrasted with the Herodian client kings (Matt 2; cf. 14:3–12) who extracted burdensome taxes from the people. Such is the plan of God (Matt 21:28–22:14).

Second, like David, but unlike the Sadducees and Pharisees, Jesus need not maintain Temple purity; indeed, as the great healer/exorcist, the great patron or benefactor of the peasants, the impure, and the expendables, he heals not only in Galilee, but in the very center of Judean political, economic, and religious life, the seat of religious purity, the Jerusalem Temple. The response of the "children" signifies that he has honor in contrast to the Temple establishment, the high priestly aristocracy and their scribal retainers (21:1–17).

Third, microsocial analysis of groups and group conflict suggests that the merciful, compassionate, therapeutic "Son of David" stands against the hypocritical Pharisee group, which preserves the legacy of Temple purity in daily life (Matt 9:27; 12:23; 15:22; 20:30; 20:31; 21:9, 15; cf. 12:1–8).

Fourth, Matthew shows how the Jesus who has been ascribed honor by his descent also has *acquired* honor. By viewing the debates through the lens of a challenge/response model, it is possible to see more clearly how Jesus gains this honor by dishonoring his opponents, especially the Pharisees. He does so by defeating them in scribal debate, raising the mystifying question *"in what sense* is Jesus the Son of David?" (Matt 22:41–46). Clearly its plurisignificance lends significance to the question and perhaps even masks an answer.

Fifth, all this has implications for the scribal author of the Gospel of Matthew and the communities among whom he writes. In the post–70 period the Matthean group stands against the Pharisee group. Jesus' defeat of the Pharisees in the challenge/response setting mirrors Matthew's own attempt to stand against the Yavneh Pharisees who, with the decline of the Herodians and priestly aristocracy, have grown in importance.

In short, Matthew's "Son of David" has all of the birth and lineage prerequisites for extensive power, privilege, and prestige, for ascribed honor from the rich and powerful ruling classes. However, the main source of the Son of David's honor is different: Jesus does not extract from the poor, crying, and needy what little they have to give; he offers them his great benefactions, his compassionate and merciful power of healing and health. Moreover, by showing how Jesus wins honor from the Pharisees and receives Hosannas from the "children" in the Jerusalem Temple, Matthew, a scribe and disciple trained for the Kingdom, gives new significance to the "Son of David," and thus implicitly makes a claim of honor for himself against the Pharisees of his own day.

CHAPTER 5

Matthew and Marginality[1]

THERE IS AN INCREASING tendency in New Testament study to refer to Jesus, Jesus movements, gospel characters, and Christian movements as "marginal."[2] This tendency has also found its way into study of the Gospel of Matthew. Janice Capel Anderson has forcefully argued that the woman with the hemorrhage (Matt 9:20-22) and the Canaanite woman (Matt 15:21-28) are not marginal only because they come from socially marginal groups, that is, the ritually unclean and Gentiles, but also because they are women: they are "doubly marginal."[3] From the perspective of redaction criticism, John R. Donahue contends that the allegorical parable of the Sheep and the Goats in Matthew 25 is the hermeneutical key to the gospel and in that parable, "the criterion of judgment [for the least of my brothers and sisters] will be works of charity and mercy shown toward the

---

1. A version of this chapter was discussed at the EGLBS in April, 1993, then published in *SBL 1993 Seminar Papers*, 642-71, and discussed at the Matthew Section of the SBL in Washington, D.C., November, 1993. It was republished as Duling, "Matthew and Marginality," *HTS* 51:1-30. For some of its influence, see Arlandson, *Women*; Vledder, *Conflict, passim*; Carter, *Households and Discipleship*; "Matthew and the Margins"; *Matthew and the Margins*, 18, 43-49; Wainwright, *Towards a Feminist Critical Reading*; Hertig, "The Galilee Theme"; "Geographical Marginality." Surveys of Matthew research have highlighted the paper; see Anderson, "Life on the Mississippi," 173, 174; "Response to Donald Senior's 'Directions in Matthean Studies'"; Senior, "Gospel of Matthew in Current Study"; "Matthean Scholarship"; "Between Two Worlds." In 1999 the Matthew Section of the Society of Biblical Literature at Boston devoted its session to marginality, and this study was cited as foundational.

2. E.g., Schüssler Fiorenza, *In Memory of Her*; Meier, *A Marginal Jew*; Kloppenborg, "Blessing and Marginality"; Karris, *Jesus and the Marginalized*.

3. Anderson, "Matthew: Gender and Reading."

marginal, the poor, and the suffering of the world."[4] Recent social historians have viewed the Matthean community as sectarian,[5] and if one were to argue that sects are marginal groups, the conclusion would be that the Matthean community as a whole is marginal.[6] Finally, Bruce Malina and Jerome Neyrey's work on deviance and labeling in the Matthean gospel might be seen from the perspective of marginality.[7]

In this chapter, I have two aims. First, I explore the conceptuality of marginality among certain social scientists. Second, I try to show from this perspective in what sense the author of Matthew is concerned about marginal people and in what sense he might be considered a marginal figure himself.[8] First, then, some social-scientific discussion about marginality.

Marginality Theory

"Marginal Man"

In 1928 Robert E. Park, leader of the Park School of sociology of the University of Chicago, first used marginality as a distinct theoretical concept to describe ethnic immigrants to the United States in relation to the dominant Anglo-Saxon majority.[9] Park referred to "Marginal Man," which he conceived as a person who is condemned to live in two different, antagonistic cultural worlds, but does not fully belong to either. Such persons are not fully acculturated. The "marginal man" or "marginal woman" can also be the child of marriages from two different cultural representatives.

In 1937 Everett V. Stonequist elaborated Park's insight in a fascinating and influential social psychological work titled *The Marginal*

---

4. Donahue, "Parable of the Sheep and the Goats"; *Gospel in Parable*, 125.

5. Overman, *Matthew's Gospel*; Balch, ed., *Social History*, passim; Saldarini, *Matthew's Christian-Jewish Community*.

6. For a discussion of the sect model and Bryan Wilson's sect typology, see chap. 1 above.

7. Malina and Neyrey, *Calling Jesus Names*; see chap. 2 for a summary.

8. See chaps. 6, 7, and 8 below for expansion of this theme.

9. Park, "Human Migration"; "Personality"; cf. Schermerhorn, "Marginal Man," 406–7.

Man.[10] For Stonequist, "[T]he marginal personality is most clearly portrayed in those individuals who are unwittingly initiated into two or more historic traditions, languages, political loyalties, moral codes, or religions."[11] Stonequist organized his study around two types of marginals: racial mixtures (e.g., Eurasians of India; "Cape Colored" of South Africa; "Mulattoes" of the United States) and cultural mixtures, which were further subdivided into migrant foreigners (Europeanized Africans; Westernized Orientals), second generation American immigrants, American Negroes, and Jews emancipated from the ghetto. Stonequist also mentioned the *parvenu*, the upwardly mobile marginal, often satirized (e.g., the ancient Trimalchio) or praised (e.g., the modern Horatio Alger), and the opposite, the *déclassé*, or downwardly mobile marginal. Noted as well were the migrants from the farm to the city and women who find themselves in a new social role previously occupied only by men.[12]

In subsequent studies American sociologists discussed marginality in connection with high crime rate, family dysfunction, and emotional distress among immigrants. They eventually turned to other types of social contact, mostly subcultures within a larger culture. There was continued study of movements up and down various gauges of the social ladder, ethnic subcultures in relation to the dominant culture, and urbanization and detribalization in Africa—in short, anything that produced "status incongruence."[13]

In line with such developments, a computer search of the word "marginality" today will turn up hundreds of titles that range from studies of the poor, particularly in Latin America, and migrant workers in Germany, to French avant-garde literary figures, the handicapped, and women in higher education. For my purposes, it will be important to explore two more theoretical areas, or what I shall call involuntary marginality and voluntary marginality.

---

10. Stonequist, *Marginal Man*.
11. Ibid., 3.
12. Ibid., 5–6.
13. Schermerhorn, "Marginal Man," 407. For the concepts of "status dissonance," "status discrepancy," or "status incongruence" as contrasted with "status crystallization" or "status congruence," see chap. 1, n. 72 above and chap. 9 below.

Involuntary Marginality

Gino Germani has written a useful work on theoretical sociology titled simply *Marginality* (1980).[14] He states that at the descriptive level, one can observe certain phenomena typical of urban ecological environments: segregated shantytowns, squatter settlements, poor working conditions, low standard of living, and the exclusion of such groups from the decision-making process that affects their lives. Germani thinks that similar phenomena can exist in rural areas. These phenomena represent subcultures, sometimes ethnic populations, with differing norms, values, and attitudes than those held by the majority culture; such persons are dominated by economic, political, and cultural elites. They are not in "the center" (usually modern and developed), but are on "the periphery" (usually archaic and underdeveloped). When they exist side by side in a single political entity, such as a national state, these phenomena point to a kind of internal colonialism, a society within a society. Germani argues that such groups and persons are roughly equivalent to those who live in poverty and that they have some level of social participation, however minimal; therefore, they do not represent a totally separate class unrelated to the rest of the social structure, as some analysts have said.

At the explanatory level, Germani offers five basic, interrelated causal factors for these phenomena: economic and social (especially unemployment); political (limitation of participation on the basis of class, race, sex, ethnicity); demographic (overpopulation); cultural (domination of one cultural group by another; [neo]colonialism; rural-urban contrasts); and psychosocial (powerlessness; helplessness; status inferiority; inadequate early socialization). After considering the origins of the concept of marginality, and arguing for some similarity between developed and developing countries (despite the ubiquity of the phenomenon in developing countries), Germani observes certain correlations with social stratification. While there is some validity in correlating "marginals" with the bottom of the social hierarchy, it is also possible to think of marginals at each level of the social hierarchy in terms of a participant/nonparticipant continuum. On this basis, Germani arrives at a generalized definition of marginality: "we may define marginality as the lack of participation [exercise

14. Germani, *Marginality*.

of roles] of individuals and groups in those spheres in which, according to determined criteria, they might be expected to participate."[15]

The "lack of participation" in this definition means the inability of persons to conform to expected social roles with respect to sex, age, occupation, civil life, and social life in relation to levels of status in the social system. These statuses are based on social norms, values, and expectations rooted in law and legitimated by custom. In other words, the marginal person no longer participates in what Germani calls "the normative scheme," that is, the set of values and norms that define the categories (status); the legitimate, expected, or tolerated areas of participation; and the assignment mechanisms of individuals to each category.[16]

Lack of participation often occurs because of a new and competing "normative scheme."[17] For marginal persons there are two related elements. First, the usual "objective resources," both material and non-material—education, jobs, purchasing power, housing—are not available. Second, the "personal conditions" needed to exercise their social roles are not present. These elements refer to psychological features on the emotional, volitive, and intellectual level as well as cognitive patrimony: attitudes, propensities, motivations, behavior patterns, or more generally, type of personality, intellectual capacity, and general and technical knowledge.[18] I refer to this type of marginality with the shorthand expression "involuntary marginality."

The above analysis leads Germani to a methodological approach for studying marginality: "in whatever analysis, the interpretation of the data and situations, the empirical research and the diagnosis of marginality must be made explicit with regards to the normative scheme, and marginality criteria and the explanatory system utilized."[19]

Much of Germani's analysis focuses on "modernization" in relation to the third world, that is, Enlightenment conceptions of political freedom, economic development, secure employment, and

15. Ibid., 49.

16. Ibid., 50.

17. Competing "normative schemes" is like competing "plausibility structures" from the perspective of sociology of knowledge; cf. Berger and Luckman, *Social Construction*, 154–63.

18. Germani, *Marginality*, 51.

19. Ibid., 54.

Matthew and Marginality 125

industrialization. This orientation is too Western and modern for direct application to Greco-Roman antiquity. Yet, Germani's general analysis is abstract enough to engage almost any social system. Thus, in analyzing Matthew and marginality, one ought to develop the "normative scheme" in the social context of the Gospel of Matthew, and to indicate, if possible, how and to what extent the author of Matthew and/or his group are marginal with respect to marginality criteria.

Voluntary Marginality

The anthropologist Victor Turner takes quite a different approach to marginality.[20] It is part of his influential analysis of ritual. Building on van Gennep's classic analysis of rites of passage,[21] Turner sees a common three-phase ritual pattern:[22]

separation → liminality → reaggregation

The first phase, "separation," removes individuals or groups from their accepted statuses or roles in a social system marked by law, custom, convention, and ceremonial—the center—and locates them to the margins, usually secluded physically. In the transitional phase, which Turner calls the "liminal" phase (Latin *limen*: "threshold"), individuals or groups are in limbo. They are "neither here nor there"; they are "betwixt and between."[23] In the third phase, the initiate reenters the social system as a neophyte, often with higher status. Turner characterizes the second liminal or marginal phase by the term *communitas*, a status-less, role-less phrase marked by spontaneity, concreteness, intense comradeship, and egalitarianism. Those in this phase are often considered sexless and anonymous, sometimes symboled by nakedness.

Turner also views this model in terms of structure/anti-structure. "For me, communitas emerges where social structure is not."[24] Structure refers to a "differentiated, and often hierarchical system of politico-legal-economic positions with many types of evaluation, sep-

---

20. Turner, *Ritual Process*; *Dramas, Fields, and Metaphors*.
21. Van Gennep, *Rites of Passage*.
22. Turner, *Ritual Process*, 94–95.
23. Ibid., 95.
24. Ibid., 126.

arating men in terms of 'more' or 'less.'"²⁵ In structure, there are fixed "relationships between statuses, roles, and offices."²⁶ Contrariwise, anti-structure is "spontaneous, immediate, concrete"; "individuals are not segmentalized into roles and statuses but [existentially] confront one another...."²⁷

I stated previously that the specifics of Germani's analysis are too modern for Greco-Roman society. Likewise, the specifics of Turner's analysis are drawn too much from small-scale tribal societies, notably the Ndembu, for direct application to Greco-Roman society. Yet, as Germani generalizes, so does Turner:

> The time has now come to make a careful review of a hypothesis that seeks to account for the attributes of such seemingly diverse phenomena as neophytes in the liminal phase of ritual, subjugated autochthonous, small nations, court jesters, holy mendicants, good Samaritans, millenarian movements, "dharma bums," matrilineal systems and monastic orders. Surely an ill-assorted bunch of social phenomena! Yet all have this common characteristic: they are persons or principles that (1) fall in the interstices of social structure, (2) are on its margins, or (3) occupy its lowest rungs.²⁸

Turner goes further and develops another general principle: "the spontaneity and immediacy of communitas ... can seldom be maintained for very long. Communitas itself soon develops a structure..."²⁹ From this insight Turner distinguishes three kinds of communitas:

> (1) *existential* or *spontaneous* communitas—approximately what the "hippies today" [*sic*!] would call "a happening," and William Blake might have called "the winged moment as it flies," or, later, "mutual forgiveness of each vice"; (2) *normative* communitas, where, under the influence of time, the need to mobilize and organize resources, and the necessity for social control among the members of the group in pursuance of these goals, the existential communitas is organized into a perduring social system; and (3) *ideological* communitas,

---

25. Ibid., 96.
26. Ibid., 131.
27. Ibid., 127, 132.
28. Ibid., 125.
29. Ibid., 132.

which is a label one can apply to a variety of utopian models of societies based on existential communitas.[30]

Whereas spontaneous communitas stands apart from social structures, normative communitas represents an emergent microsocial group *within* a macrosocial system.[31] Finally, ideological communitas presents communitas as *desired vision*, or what is known in Christian history as the *ecclesiola in ecclesia*, "the little church within the church." As examples, Turner analyzes the early Franciscans of medieval Europe and the *Sahajys* of fifteenth- and sixteenth-century India.

For Turner normative communitas is on the way to structure, and ideological communitas is voluntary "outsiderhood."[32] The latter is not *socially imposed* marginality, but *voluntarily chosen* marginality.[33] That he is not developing the concept of involuntary marginality is clear from his statement about poverty:

> Liminal poverty must not be confused with real poverty, although the liminally poor may become actually poor. But liminal poverty, whether it is a process or a state, is both an expression and instrumentality of communitas. Communitas is what people really seek by voluntary poverty.... The principle is simple: cease to have and you are; if you "are" in the relationship of communitas to others who "are," then you love one another.[34]

Marginality Summary

The concept of "marginality" in the social science literature examined above has three dimensions:

a) *the "Marginal Man"*: individuals and groups who, because of birth, migration, conquest, and the like are "doomed" to live in two different, antagonistic cultures without fully belonging to either (Park;

---

30. Ibid., 132.

31. One hears echoes of Max Weber's "charisma" and "routinization" (Weber, *Economy and Society*); indeed, Turner, ibid., 133, mentions Weber in this context..

32. Turner, *Dramas*, 133.

33. Turner, ibid. 133, admits that he is not thinking of Park's and Stonequist's "Marginal Man."

34. Ibid., 266.

Stonequist); this social-psychological type is closely related to the second dimension.

b) *involuntary marginality*: individuals and groups who for reasons of race, ethnicity, sex, "underdevelopment," and the like are not able to participate in normative social statuses, roles, and offices and their obligations and duties. Most fail to share in both material and nonmaterial resources available to other members at the center of society, and thus who experience themselves as personally alienated (Germani).

c) *voluntary marginality*: individuals and groups who consciously and by choice live outside the normative statuses, roles, and offices of society because they reject hierarchical social structures, although there will be attempts to perpetuate this spontaneity by social control or in conventicles within the normative social system. Though freely chosen, they will eventually share in some of the same conditions as involuntary marginals (Turner).

The two terms I have chosen, "involuntary" and "voluntary," need to be used with caution. It is important not to transfer the modern, enlightened democratic ideology of "voluntary associations" and "freedom of assembly" to Greco-Roman antiquity and thus the Christ Movements.[35] Yet, within certain social restrictions Greco-Roman society had its own sort of voluntary associations: *collegia*, clubs, trade guilds, burial societies, as well as schools, mystery cults.[36] Moreover, within Israel there existed a variety of religious groups and parties. Thus, after a further comment about method, I shall also attempt to indicate how one might interpret the Gospel of Matthew through these three types of marginality.

Texts and Contexts

How is the book of Matthew related to social realities? How does one move from text to social context? This is not the place to develop either a social-historical or social-scientific hermeneutic.[37] Yet, I would

---

35. For discussion of various kinds of voluntary associations, see chaps. 6 and 7 below.

36. Danker, "Associations, Clubs, Thiasoi."

37. See van Staden, *Compassion*. Some scholars resist moving from text to context, see chap. 8 below.

say that there is a dialectical relationship between text and social context: economically/socially/politically located ideology generates literature, but literature also challenges economically/socially/politically located ideology.[38]

I still try to discover how the narrative world is related to authorial intention and how text is related to social-historical context. One possible metaphor is that Matthew's narrative is not a steamy bathroom mirror that, when wiped with a towel, allows you to see yourself better; rather, it is a foggy window that *can* be a mirror, but is nonetheless a *window*. By wiping away the fog at the appropriate places, one can see through the text to the author's social-historical context. The keys are the appropriate models and the appropriate places.

Matthew and Marginality

Normative Scheme A: A Macrosocial Model, the Advanced Agrarian Society

As noted above, according to Germani the first task is to define "the normative scheme," that is, the values and norms that define status; the legitimate, expected, or tolerated areas of participation; and the assignment mechanisms of individuals to each category.[39] What is the center from which various persons and groups can be seen to be marginal? What are the missing objective and personal dimensions? This determination is not a simple task because there are competing "normative schemes" and correspondingly different marginalities in Greco-Roman and Judean antiquity and the New Testament.

As a point of departure for gaining access to one part of the normative scheme, recall again George Ritzer's macroscopic-microscopic

---

38. From the perspective of Marxist literary criticism, literature as art is part of an ideological consciousness related to a superstructure that is determined by the economic base or infrastructure, but literature is not the mere passive, unconscious reflection of economics. The relation is not simply productive forces → social relations → ideology → text, an interpretation called "vulgar Marxism." Rather, art can also challenge the ideology of which it is a part, and thus confront the social, political, and economic order that undergirds it. Art is an expression of ideology, but it also distances itself from ideology. See Eagleton, *Marxism*; McLellan, *Ideology*; Larrain, *Concept of Ideology*.

39. Germani, *Marginality*, 50.

continuum of social levels.[40] One of the highest macrosocial levels in Ritzer's scale, "societies," can be understood for the writings of the New Testament period through the Lenskis' model of an advanced agrarian society, used by a number of scholars[41] including myself.[42] Its main features correspond to what Ramsay MacMullen has called "verticality" in Roman society.[43] I have also noted that David Fiensy, drawing on G. Alföldy's work and data from archaeology and ancient writers, adjusted the Lenski model for Palestine,[44] and that I added a few speculative percentages from various authors.[45]

In this model the primary bases of social stratification—power, privilege, and prestige—are primarily economic and political. Kinship and religion are implied, but they are less conspicuous. There are a very few at the top of the vertical social structure. The vast majority are at the bottom. There is no real "middle class." Indeed, one should think of a "status hierarchy" rather than "social classes" based on economics.[46] The lower part of the model is divided into urban and rural sections, with rural peasants dominating. The upper strata are virtually all urban.[47] Retainers (mainly bureaucrats), merchants, artisans, fishermen, day laborers, and many expendables belong in or near the towns and cities, while the upper level small freeholders (15–50 acres), lower level small freeholders (4–15 acres), tenant farmers, some day laborers, and most slaves belong in the rural districts. The expendables have now been subdivided into "unclean and degraded" and "expendables." The model implies accepted institutional authority. Clearly it is in Victor Turner's terms a "structure,"[48] in this case a hierarchical structure. In Germani's terms it is a "normative scheme."

40. Ritzer, *Contemporary Sociological Theory*, 309; see chap. 3, Chart 3.1.

41. Discussions in chaps. 1–3 above, esp. chap. 3, nn. 42, 43 for literature.

42. See esp. chaps. 4 and 6.

43. MacMullen, *Roman Social Relations*; Meeks, *First Urban* Christians, 51–73.

44. Fiensy, *Social History*, 158.

45. See p. 97, Model 4.1 above for the revised model; Lenski, *Power and Privilege*, 243–48; Saldarini, *Pharisees*, 40–45; Fiensy, *Social History*, 155–70, passim; also, Duling, *The New Testament*, 17.

46. Explicit descriptions of "class" in antiquity are rare and limited to Rome; see Meeks, *The First Urban Christians*, 53–55; Rohrbaugh, "Social Location of Thought," 103–19.

47. Rohrbaugh, ibid.; Oakman, *Jesus and the Economic Questions*.

48. For Turner's views, see above.

Matthew and Marginality 131

There are further modifications of the above macrosocial model that need to be made, all of which have to do with decisions about Matthew and marginality. First, the reconstructed model roughly corresponds to certain dimensions of Palestine at the time of Jesus. It does not correspond quite as well to the usual time for the composition of the Gospel of Matthew itself, ca. 80–90 CE. Thus, the Herodians should be removed and the priests have much declined in political power. Second, some client rulers may have experienced "psychological" marginality simply because they were Roman colonials ("relative deprivation");[49] nonetheless, in what follows I shall exclude the upper strata, including Idumeans and Judeans (Caesar; rulers of the Gentiles; prefects/procurators; ancestral native kings; Herodian client kings; the High Priest Caiaphas; chief priests; elders). Third, for the same reasons, it is probably also best from the perspective of *this* model to exclude the retainers of the upper strata (toll collectors; Roman centurions; High Priest's guards; most priests; most scribes). Fourth, this model operates best for certain forms of economic and political oppression, especially the "colonial" context of the Eastern Empire, and for rural-urban contrasts, demography (population shifts), and perhaps psychosocial marginality (powerlessness; helplessness; status inferiority). Fifth, other important status criteria (based on other models) need to be considered, especially in relation to Palestine, for example, units further down Ritzer's continuum, notably kin groups, regional and ethnic groups (Idumeans; Samaritans; Gentiles in general), religious parties (Essenes), and gender within patriarchal contexts. As an example, toll collectors and scribes would not be considered marginal from the perspective of the above macrosocial model because they were retainers of the ruling classes; yet, toll collectors, while economically and somewhat politically advantaged, were universally despised by *native* peoples in the Roman Empire, and scribes were sometimes considered marginal if they belonged to a marginal group, e.g., the Essenes.[50] Sixth, it is not always easy to distinguish between "unclean and degraded" and "expendable" in the Judean context. Prostitutes, those with skin diseases,

---

49. Eleazar, son of Ananias the High Priest and governor of the Temple, was instrumental in the revolt against Rome (*B.J.* 2.17.2 [#409]). See Aberle, "A Note," 209–14; Gager, *Kingdom and Community*, 27–28.

50. Donahue, "Tax Collector"; Lewis, *Life in Egypt*, 156–84.

and demoniacs, for example, might fall into both categories. Finally, one might make a case that in a limited good society, especially in the colonial context like Palestine, all peasants—about three-quarters of the population—are marginal. Given that this is a peasant society, I have elected to omit those nearer to the top.

With these qualifications, I suggest that from the above macrosocial perspective the lower social strata would have been seen as "involuntary marginals." Here is a sample inventory of these strata implied in Matthew's Gospel:[51]

Outline 5.1 Lower Social Strata in the Gospel of Matthew

1. Forced laborers (implied): 5:37.
2. Day laborers (*ergatēs*): 20:1, 2, 8; perhaps 9:37, 38; 10:10.
3. Some slaves:
    a. "Slave/servant" (*doulos*): 8:9; 10:24, 25; 13:27, 28; 18:23, 26, 27, 28, 32; 20:27; 21:34, 35, 36; 22:3, 4, 6, 8, 10; 24:45, 46, 48, 50; 25:14, 19, 21, 23 [twice], 30; 26:51.
    b. "Slave/son" (*pais*): 8:6, 8, 13; 12:18 [Isa 42:1]; 14:2; 17:18; 21:15?
3. Some peasants, urban poor, and destitute:
    a. "Crowd(s)" (*ochlos*): 50 references!
    b. "Tenant farmers" (*georgēs*): 21:33.
    c. "Poor" (*ptōchos*): 5:3; 11:5; 19:21; 26:9, 11.
    d. Receivers of alms (implied by *eleēmosunē*, "alms" in 6:1–6; 19:21).
4. Unclean and degraded (dishonored):
    a. Eunuchs (*eunouchos*): 19:12 (three times).
    b. Ritually unclean: (Jesus and) certain disciples: 15:2.
    c. Lepers (*lepros*): 8:2; 10:8; 11:5; 26:6.
    d. Women believed to be dishonored (*pornē*; *porneia*): 5:32; 15:19; 19:9; cf. 1:19.
    e. Woman with hemorrhage: 9:20–22.
    f. Women outside their usual home "space" (who follow Jesus) e.g., 27:55–56.
    g. Those with "every disease and every infirmity": 4:23 and 9:35; with "various diseases and pains": 4:24; "all who were sick": 8:16; "their sick": 14:14; "sick": 14:35.
    h. Blind (*typhlos*): 9:27, 28 (two blind men); 11:5; 12:22 (and dumb); 15:14 (four times); 15:30; 15:31; 20:30 (two blind men); 21:14.
    i. Lame (*chōlos*): 11:5; 15:30–31; 18:8; 21:14.
    j. Deaf (*kōphos*): 11:5.
    k. Dumb (*kōphos*): 9:32, 33; 12:22 [twice]; 15:30, 31.
    l. Maimed (*kullos*): 15:30, 31.
    m. Paralytics (*paralytikos*): 4:24; 8:6; 9:2 [twice], 6.
    n. Demoniacs (*daimonizomenos*): 4:24; 8:16; 8:28–34; 15:21–28.
    o. Epileptics (*selēniazomenos*): 4:24.

51. For a fuller, but slightly different arrangement, see p. 98 above; for various kinds of scribes, see chap. 9.

5. Expendables:
   a. Bandits (*lēstēs*): 21:13 [Jer 7:11]; 26:55 (contrasted w. Jesus); 27:38, 36 (mock Jesus on cross).
   b. Prostitutes (*pornē*): 21:31, 32.

A few more remarks are in order. Matthew's "crowds" are undifferentiated. Nonetheless, the writer implies that they contained women and those with all manner of debilitating disease and sickness.[52] Perhaps they also contained bandits, eunuchs, slaves, tenant farmers, and other artisans and fishermen. Matthew writes that Jesus had compassion on "the crowds" who are "like sheep without a shepherd" (9:36).[53] The above strata can be seen to represent the "lost sheep of the house of Israel" to whom Jesus and the disciples direct their activities (Matt 10:6; 15:24). They do not participate in normative social statuses, roles, and offices, and they fail to share in both material and nonmaterial resources. It might be argued that peasants and village artisans who have lost their ancestral lands,[54] and fishermen whose activities were heavily taxed,[55] should be included. Jesus and some of his disciples are from this group. Herders (*poimēn*) fall within another social structure, but they would also be marginal, although in the gospel the term "shepherds" is used positively as metaphor (9:36; 25:32 [sheep/goats]; 26:31, "strike the shepherd" [Zech 13:7]). In this context, I would exclude them.[56] Nonetheless, whatever decisions are made about center and margin, it is clear that the percentage of involuntary marginals would have been quite high, even omitting some peasants.

52. Duling, "Therapeutic Son of David."

53. See Levine's view, pp. 40-41 above, and see also chap. 4 above.

54. For this reason, some analysts place village artisans, despite some economic success, below peasants.

55. Hanson, "Galilean Fishing Economy."

56. In this model peasants represent the majority; for the debate about whether one can speak of marginality in traditionally structured societies where those of lower social status see themselves as elites see them, for example, in caste systems, see Germani, *Marginality*, 52: "In such a society the very concept of marginality does not emerge as a social perception scheme." Such a traditionally structured society corresponds with the Marxist concept of "hegemony," on which see Gramsci, *Selections*; for a critique of hegemony, see Scott, *Weapons of the Weak*, 46-47; see chap. 3, "Everyday Peasant Resistance."

It is impossible here to discuss all these groups and persons in the First Gospel. Let us take an example, "the poor." The term *ptōchoi*, which in the synoptics in general refers to the destitute,[57] is used clearly as an actual social condition in four verses (11:5; 19:21; 26:9, 11), to which one must contrast "poor in spirit" (*hoi ptōchoi tō pneumati*) in 5:3. In Matthew 26:9, which simplifies Mark 14:5, the disciples are angered at the woman's "waste" of an alabaster flask of "very expensive perfume" (v. 7): "For this perfume might have been sold for much (*pollou* [money]) and given to the poor (*ptōchois*)" (v. 9). Jesus' defends the woman's "good work" (v. 10: *ergon . . . kalon*) to him: "The poor (*tous ptōchous*) you always have with you, but me you do not always have" (26:11). In this passage, the perpetual presence (and pervasiveness) of the poor is assumed (*pantote*, "always"). Yet, the act of one marginal—probably a "promiscuous" woman who encounters Jesus at table[58]—appears to override social concern for other marginals, in this case, the poor.

One might conclude from these comments that the "preferential option for the poor" in Matthew is qualified by the woman's symbolic act preparing Jesus for burial (Matt 26:12-13). There is probably some validity to this perception: for Matthew ideology—Christology and eschatology—is paramount. Furthermore, the impression is related to Matthew's apparent tendency to think in terms of the city and wealth, and to his addition of "in spirit" to "the poor" in 5:3.[59] One can conclude that the portrayal of the disciples' irritation is understandable in the light of what has gone before with regard to the young man (Matt 19:16-22; see Mark 10:17-22; Luke 18:18-23). Jesus has told him, "If you want to be perfect (*teleios*), go, sell your

---

57. Schottroff and Stegemann, *Jesus and the Hope of the Poor*, 16. In general, see Sobrino, *True Church*; Stegemann, *Gospel and the Poor*; Stegemann and Schottroff, eds., *God of the Lowly*; Malina, "Interpreting the Bible with Anthropology"; Hanks, "Poor, Poverty (New Testament)."

58. Corley, *Private Women*, 89-93, 178, concludes that Matthew was the most androcentric of the gospels, but placed women, including "sinners," at Jesus' meals. See also Anderson, "Matthew: Gender and Reading," 3-27; Love, "The Place of Women"; more recently, Klinghardt, *Gemeinschaftsmahl und Mahlgemeinschaft*; Smith, *From Symposium to Eucharist*.

59. Kingsbury, "The Verb *Akolouthein*"; Crosby, *House of Disciples*, 39-43. Crosby argues that Matthew does not "canonize" poverty, but neither does he "spiritualize" it (154-55).

possessions (*ta huparchonta*) and give to the poor (*ptōchois*), and you will have treasure (*thēsauron*) in heaven, and come follow me" (19:21). Apparently "the poor" would have had much to gain, for the young man has "many possessions" (v. 22: *ktēmata polla*). Here, of course, are Matthew's familiar discipleship/following terms, and with them at least the question of *voluntary* poverty is articulated: The true disciple is *commanded* not to store up treasures on earth, but in heaven (6:19–21).[60]

Another passage is John's question to Jesus and Jesus' answer, reworked from Q (Q 7:18-23; Matt 11:2-5).[61] Jesus' miracle working in Matthew 11:5 is full of allusions to Isaiah (Isa 26:19; 29:18; 35:5-6; 42:7, 18; 61:1),[62] and "the poor have good news preached to them" alludes to the famous Jubilee passage in Isaiah 61:1 (1QH 18:14; Luke 4:18 [*ptōchois*]). That Isaiah is Matthew's favorite scriptural text[63] suggests that he is quite aware of these scriptural allusions. While the verb *euangelizomai* occurs only once in Matthew, its cognate *euangelion* calls forth the key Matthean summaries about Jesus' speaking and healing (4:23; 9:35) and, indeed, the central proclamation of the Kingdom of Heaven.[64] There is no theme more central than this theme in the gospel. Thus, Matthew's view on *actual* poverty is somewhat mixed. It will have to be compared to his ideal of voluntary marginality.

---

60. What is implied might have been the redistribution of wealth in a limited good society, so Malina, "Interpreting the Bible with Anthropology," 155–56.

61. It is generally accepted that *ta erga tou Christou*, "the deeds of the Christ," in Matt 11:2 refers back to Jesus' miracles in Matt 8-9; evidence in Duling, "The Therapeutic Son of David," 392–410. Davies and Allison, *Matthew*, vol. 2, 240 argue that it also refers to Matthew 5-7 because of 11:5-6, "the poor have good news preached to them" in relation to 4:23-26. In the light of 5:16 ("*see your kala erga*") and 11:20 (*hai pleistai dynameis*), this conclusion seems to stretch the meaning of *ta erga* in Matthew 11:5.

62. Matthew adds "lepers," apparently in accord with Matt 8:1-4.

63. See more recently Beaton, *Isaiah's Christ*.

64. Duling, "Therapeutic Son of David"; "Kingdom of God, Kingdom of Heaven," 57–58.

Normative Schemes B, C, D: Three Microsocial Models

Another way to understand marginality is to move further down Ritzer's macroscopic/microscopic continuum to groups (level 4).[65] Groups are also important for involuntary marginality, but they are especially significant for voluntary marginality. In Turner's terms, voluntary individuals and groups are those who spontaneously but consciously choose to live outside the normative statuses, roles, and offices of society because they reject hierarchical social structures ("spontaneous communitas"). Nonetheless, says Turner, there will be gradual attempts to perpetuate this spontaneity by social control within the group ("normative communitas") or in conventicles within the normative social system ("ideological communitas").

Ever since Weber's contrast between charisma and routinization, social theorists have persistently contrasted structured institutions with non-structured groups. Victor Turner's contrast between structure and anti-structure and his view that anti-structure tends toward structure is only one example. Bruce Malina, building on the work of the Mediterranean network anthropologist Jeremy Boissevain, contrasts "corporations" as hierarchical structures with "coalitions" as non-hierarchical structures.[66] Drawing further on the work of Ph. G. Herbst,[67] Malina has also attempted to contrast hierarchical organizations with non-hierarchical groups on the basis of "task allocation," a version of the division of labor.

---

65. Ritzer, *Contemporary Sociological Theory*, 309; see chap. 3 above, Chart 3.1.

66. Boissevain, *Friends of Friends*, 170–205; Malina, *Christians Origins*, 13–67; "Patron and Client," 19–31; "A Conflict Approach," 14. For more on corporations and coalitions, see chaps. 4 and 6.

67. Herbst, *Alternatives to Hierarchies*, 18–19, 29–40.

Model 5.1 Task Allocation Models: Hierarchical vs. Non-hierarchical Groups
(according to Herbst, *Alternatives to Hierarchies*, 18–19, and Malina, *Christian Origins*, 66–67)

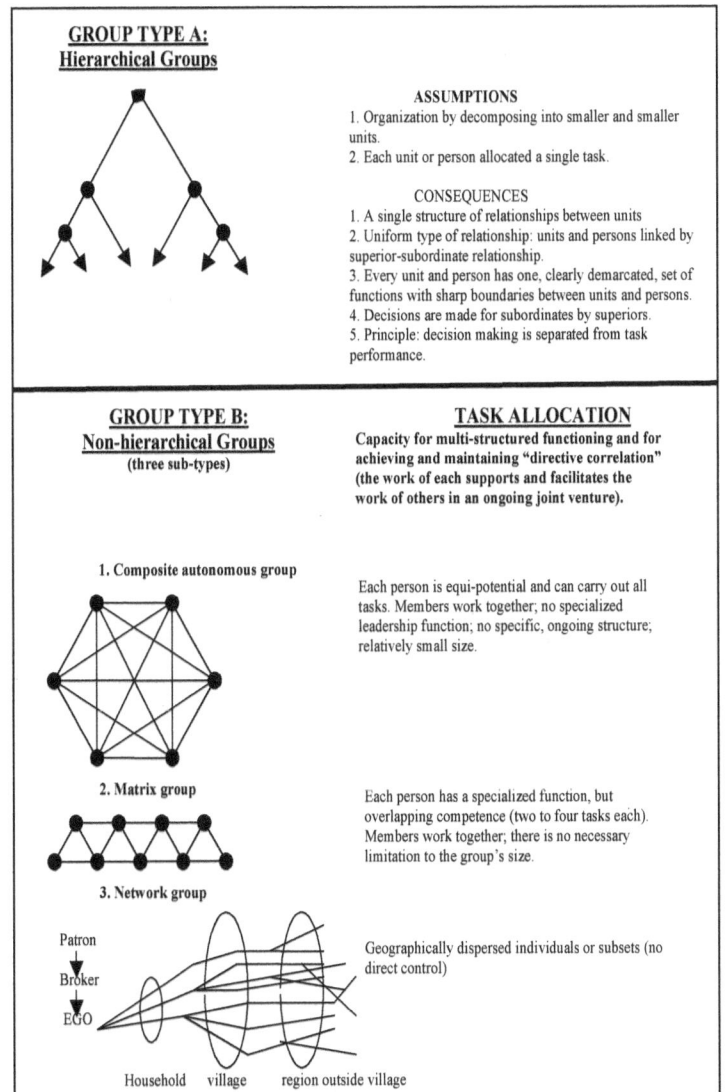

Except for the last (network group), these models are drawn from modern industrial relations. Yet, with respect to structure, there is a rough correspondence between Groups 1, 2, and 3 in reverse order and Victor Turner's three types of non-hierarchical groups:

Chart 5.1 Groups (Turner Compared with Herbst)

TURNER	HERBST
ideological communitas	
normative communitas	
	matrix group
spontaneous communitas	composite autonomous group
	network group

(with a vertical upward arrow on the left side spanning the Turner column)

These non-hierarchical groups can be viewed as illustrations of "voluntary marginality," though in the case of Herbst's composite autonomous and matrix groups there is some "industrial engineering." As the vertical arrow indicates, there is at the group level a gradual tendency toward hierarchy, as Turner realized. Time, size, the need for social control, and increasing division of labor (task allocation) lead toward normative communitas and eventually hierarchy.

Matthew and Marginality from Microsocial Perspectives: Voluntary Marginality

Where does the Gospel of Matthew belong with respect to voluntary marginality? In this regard, the First Gospel reveals a mixed social context. There are clear indications of spontaneous sub-groups of the network type from the days of the historical Jesus. The best example is the mission charge in Matthew 10, especially 10:9–15. This passage, which has echoes in *Didachē* 11, 12, and 16:3, represents an ideology similar to, though not exactly like, that of the itinerant Cynic philosophers.[68] The command to take "no gold" and "no bag" for food (cf. 1 Cor 9:4, 14, 17–18; *Didachē* 11.6), no change of tunic, and no sandals (a sign of wealth) are indications of *voluntary* poverty. If the "no bag" is a contrast to itinerant Cynic preachers who carried a bag that symbolized their self-sufficiency, the stress may be less on actual begging than on eating common meals together with others.[69] In

68. E.g., Downing, *Christ and the Cynics*, 47–48; Theissen, *Sociology*, 14–15; Theissen and Merz, *Historical Jesus*, 216 ("contrast"); Crossan, *Historical Jesus*, 72–88, 421–22; Betz, "Jesus and the Cynics"; Schottroff and Stegemann, *God of the Lowly*, 160–67; Horsley, *Sociology*, 46–47.

69. Crossan, *Historical Jesus*, 261–64, calls this phenomenon as unbrokered, open egalitarian commensality and supports it with Scott, "Protest and Profanation," 225–26; see also Crossan, *The Birth of Christianity*, 299–300. See below chap. 6 and pp. 149–53, n. 38.

Matthew and Marginality

this regard, the itinerant apostles, wise men, prophets, and scribes of Matthew's Gospel are commanded to carry on the Jesus tradition of a non-hierarchical faction. "Therefore I send you prophets *and wise men and scribes*, some of whom you will kill *and crucify, and some you will scourge in your synagogues* and persecute *from town to town*...." (Matt 23:34; italics = Matthean additions). The danger, as in the *Didachē*, is the influence of *false* prophets (*Didachē* 11; Matt 7:15-23). Yet, one would have to modify the network model slightly since the itinerants themselves clearly have some status and authority.[70]

This is not the only non-hierarchical model in the Gospel of Matthew. I turn now to an "appropriate passage" that points to a slightly different model, one that may suggest a more settled community, namely, Matthew 23:7b-10.

[The Pharisees love...] to be called Rabbi by the people.
8) But (as for) you (pl.),
do not be called *Rabbi*,
for one is your *teacher*,   but (pl.) you are all brothers.
9) And *father* do not call yourselves (pl.)   on earth,
for one is your (pl.) father,   the heavenly.
10) Neither be called (pl.) *tutors*,
for your (pl.) tutor is one,   the Christ.

Benedict Viviano represents common opinion when he says that this passage contains "a critique of synagogue offices and titles that are merging in and around the rabbinic academy of Jamnia/Yavneh at this time...."[71] The rejected titles of honor are "Rabbi," known from Rabbinic references to teachers prior to 135 CE[72] and from inscriptions[73] but used elsewhere in Matthew only by the traitor Judas (Matt 26:25, 49); "father," also known from rabbinic and inscriptional references;[74] and *kathēgētēs*, which Bruce Winter has shown to mean "private tutor" in Greek,[75] though it might represent the Hebrew *mōreh*, as in *mōreh hazzedek*, the "*Teacher* of Righteousness" (4QpPs^{a}37 [= 4Q171]

---

70. See further, Theissen, *Sociology*.
71. Viviano, "Social World," 10.
72. Lapin, "Rabbi."
73. Cohen, "Epigraphical Rabbis."
74. Viviano, "Social World," 20; Hengel, "Synagogeninschrift"; Hachlili, "Synagogue," 260.
75. Winter, "Messiah as the Tutor."

3:15–16; 1QpHab 2:8; CD 1:9–11).⁷⁶ Viviano notes four "run-ons" which I have placed at the right in the above quotation from Matthew 23. I would add that since the heavenly/earthly contrast and the Christ are Matthean redactional emphases, so probably is the designation for members of Matthew's group, "brothers." This is the language of "fictive-" or "pseudo-kinship."⁷⁷ Although crowds are mentioned, clearly the intended recipients are "disciples"—in other words, the Matthean brotherhood (23:1)—and this points to the recipients of the gospel as a "brotherhood" (cf. also 5:21–26; 7:1–15; 12:46–50; 18:15–22). This "brotherhood" has a *limited* "egalitarian" ideology. Pharisaic titles of status in relation to the central activity of teachers and those taught are rejected by the author of Matthew for the "brotherhood."⁷⁸

The ideology of this passage represents a version of Turner's non-hierarchical group, an ideological communitas. It also represents Boissevain's and Malina's "faction" and Herbst's "composite autonomous group." Each person can carry out all tasks; each person is equipotential; members work together; there is no specialized leadership function, and no specific, ongoing structure. One could develop this contrast of structure and antistructure much further.

It should be emphasized again that Matthew's "network" and "composite autonomous" orientations represent an *ideological* communitas. However, as Turner was aware, there are pressures toward hierarchy. Thus, despite this Matthean ideology, there appear to be in the Matthew group those who are more equal than others.⁷⁹ In the first place, there are undefined central persons with labels and functions:

1. "Apostles" (10:2)
2. "Prophets" (5:10–12; 11:9; 10:40–42; 13:57; 21:11, 23–27; 23:29–36; all of the formula quotations, including Pss 78:2 and 110:1, are from "prophets")
3. "Teachers" (5:19; 28:20)
4. "Scribes" (13:52; 23:34)
5. "Righteous men" (10:41–42)
6. "Wise men" (23:34).

76. Viviano, "Social World," 11.
77. Pitt-Rivers, "Pseudo-Kinship."
78. See chap. 8 below.
79. See chap. 6 below for more detail.

Moreover, the renaming of Peter (lower status) by Jesus (higher status), an example of ascribed honor, implies a transfer of authority (16:17–19).[80] Thus, like its rivals, the Pharisees, the Matthew group is not simply a non-hierarchical communitas, but is on its way toward becoming a hierarchical structure (normative communitas). I have elsewhere attempted to represent this movement as a so-called leaderless group.[81]

In short, from the perspective of groups, there are several types of voluntary marginality represented in the Matthean gospel. One example of what Turner calls spontaneous marginality would be ideology of a sub-group of the network type from the days of the historical Jesus (e.g., 10:5–15, 40–42; 23:34). Another would be the ideology of "leaderless group," or "faction" (Boissevain; Malina), or at least the group without titles of honor (23:8–10). This would be Boissevain's and Malina's "faction" and Herbst's "composite autonomous group." Nonetheless, in my view there is also a clear tendency toward structure, or what Turner calls "normative communitas."

From this perspective, we can return to the example of "the poor." The macrosocial model of an agrarian society offers a lens through which to view statements about those who are involuntarily marginally poor in the First Gospel. Microsocial groups offer a lens through which to see the ideal of voluntary poverty. The mission statements that fit the network model are commands to perpetuate the ideal of voluntary poverty (e.g., 10:5–15, 40–42; 23:34). A similar ideology occurs in the story of the rich young man: he cannot "follow" because he cannot give up his "many possessions" (19:16–22). Many other examples could be cited, not least of which is the passage that Donahue claims is the hermeneutical key to the gospel, the parable of the Sheep and the Goats (25:31–46). On the one hand, the language reflects the ideal of voluntary poverty; on the other, the ideal reflects actual poverty: "Truly I say to you, as you did it to one of the least of these my brothers (and sisters), you did it to me" (25:40, 45). At the same time, those critics who sense a step back from the ideal perceive the move toward "normative communitas": "For the poor you always have with you, but me you do not always have" (26:11). Indeed, perhaps here we

---

80. Duling, "Binding and Loosing," 21.

81. Duling, "Response to E. Krentz"; Fisher and Ellis, *Small Group Decision Making*, show that there are no "leaderless groups." See pp. 171–73 below.

have the clue to Matthew's "Blessed are the poor *in spirit*, for theirs is the kingdom of heaven" (Matt 5:3).

The Author of Matthew as "Marginal Man"

If we once again define a "Marginal Man" as an individual who, because of birth, migration, conquest, and the like is "doomed" to live in two different, antagonistic cultures without fully belonging to either, how does the Matthean author look? I shall outline a proposal.

1. The author of the gospel is a scribe (13:52). There has been an explosion of study on writing and writers in antiquity[82] and many of them have to do with the Gospel of Matthew.[83] Current estimates of those who could write in antiquity are quite low. From the perspective of macrosocial stratification, the author of Matthew ranks at least as a retainer of the elite strata. Moreover, he has much honor from the perspective of scribalism in traditional Israel. Yet, he is concerned about those from the lower strata and represents a tradition infused with involuntary marginality, and so stands between two cultures.

2. The scribe's opponents are Pharisees, a rival faction within Israel. Yet, for the gospel writer, Pharisaism is becoming a "normative structure," that is, the center; again, he is between two cultures.

3. The Matthean author "brings out of his treasure (storeroom) what is new and what is old" (13:52), a dominant theme in the gospel concerned especially with the Torah and its interpretation (e.g., 5:17–48). He stands between the old and the new. His "synagogue Greek" is derived in part from the Septuagint; yet, he uses sources from the Christ Movement: Mark and Q. He improves Markan syntax, yet his language is semitizing.[84]

4. The emphasis on genealogy, Jesus' unusual genesis, and the star legend suggest that Matthew knew conventional forms of the

---

82. E.g., Lemaire, "Writing and Writing Materials."

83. E.g., Saldarini, *Pharisees*; Orton, *The Understanding Scribe*; Wire, "Gender Roles"; Yaghjian, "Matthew's Scribe?" See Arnal, *Jesus*; Horsley, *Scribes*; Kloppenborg, *Formation*; *Tenants*. See chap. 9.

84. Luz, *Matthew 1–7*, 49–76.

encomium of the *Progymnasmata*,[85] as the modified *bios* form suggests. Yet, his use of the formula quotations and his stress on interpreting and making a hedge around the Torah (5:17–6:48) point to Pharisaic scribalism. Matthew seems to stand on the boundary between Greek and Judean education.

5. Matthew's Gospel still has concern for the "lost sheep of the house of Israel" (10:6; 15: 24) but ultimately the mission is to all peoples (28:16–20).

6. Is the author of Matthew a "Jewish Christian" or a "Christian Jew"?[86] Would he have understood this question?

Conclusion

A concept that appeared with increasing frequency in the early 1990s was "marginality." There was no careful social-scientific analysis of the concept in the biblical research field. This chapter, based on an article at that time, analyzes three social-scientific theories: 1) Robert Park's and Everett V. Stonequist's "Marginal Man," that is, a person who is forced to live between two competing cultures without fully belonging to either; 2) "involuntary marginals," that is, those who are mainly at the bottom of the social hierarchy, but, according to Gino Germani, include those who at *any* social level do not participate in their expected social roles; and 3) "voluntary marginals," that is, those who, according to Victor Turner, are members of a "liminal" group that *chooses* to separate itself from normative statuses, roles, and offices, who choose ideological *communitas*. Exegesis of Matthean terms shows the pervasiveness of involuntary marginals who are equivalent to those at the bottom of Lenski's hierarchy, namely, retainers, artisans, peasants, expendable persons, and the unclean. Such an analysis also points to the ideological ambiguity of the writer, a literate scribe who voluntarily chooses to affiliate with a Jesus messianic group. This scribe was between elite and non-elite, between literate scribes and illiterate peasants, between men and women, between emergent and growing normative Pharisaism and his Jesus group, between Semitic

---

85. Neyrey, "Encomium."
86. Overman, *Matthew's Gospel*; Balch, ed., *Social History*.

and Greek languages, between Judean and Greco-Roman culture, and in general between what is "the old" and "the new" (Matt 13:52). In other words, he was a "Marginal Man," but in this case there was choice in the matter, that is, he had an ideology of "voluntary marginality."[87]

---

87. For expansion on these themes, see chaps. 7 and 9 below.

CHAPTER 6

"Egalitarian" Ideology, Leadership, and Factional Conflict within the Matthean Group[1]

CONFLICT IS A MAJOR characteristic of the Gospel of Matthew. Literary critics have argued that its plot turns on progressively intensified conflict, especially between Jesus and the Judean leaders.[2] Historical and redaction critics have long held that this plot reflects a post-70 CE conflict between the Pharisees attempting to assert their dominance over late first-century Israel and the Matthean group. The major debate has been whether or not this conflict implies a complete break between the so-called "Jewish synagogue" and the "Matthean church."[3]

Social historians and social-scientific critics have reinterpreted aspects of Matthean conflict. Arming himself with conflict theory, social historian Richard Horsley has suggested that the Matthean infancy narrative reflects a conflict between the ruling elite and the Palestinian peasantry, the "haves" and the "have-nots."[4] Graham Stanton

1. An early version of this chapter was delivered at the Synoptic Gospels Section of the SBL at San Francisco, November, 1992. Its projected publication in Germany did not materialize, but it was later published in 1997 in *BTB* 27: 124–37. Since it was written earlier than chap. 7, although published later, I have put it before that chapter. I have inserted into it a discussion of small groups that was originally in the earliest version of chap. 7; otherwise, it contains only minor variations from the original.

2. Kingsbury, "The Developing Conflict"; *Matthew as Story*, 17–24, 115–27; Anderson, *Matthew's Narrative Web*, 97–126; Powell, "Characterization," 171–77.

3. E.g., Stanton, "Origin and Purpose," 1910–21; *A Gospel*, 113–14; Hagner, "Sitz im Leben," 45–53.

4. Horsley, *Liberation*, 39–60. Horsley's key theorist was Ralf Dahrendorf, on

has also used conflict theory to interpret the separation of synagogue and church.[5] Anthony Saldarini, Andrew Overman, Alan Segal, and Michael White have reformulated the view that the gospel betrays an "inner-Jewish" conflict, specifically a sectarian conflict between Pharisees and ancient "Jewish Believers-in-Jesus."[6] Leland White has examined the Sermon on the Mount as an honor/shame code in conflict with that of the Pharisees.[7] Bruce Malina and Jerome Neyrey have analyzed Matthean conflict from the perspective of deviance and labeling theory;[8] Saldarini has also taken up this approach.[9] I have looked at conflict through Matthean stratification ("haves" versus "have-nots") and marginality (core and periphery), and so has Evert Jan-Vledder.[10]

However one resolves the problem of conflict with outsiders, there are also implicit and explicit conflicts *within* the Matthean group itself: "false prophet" accusations (Matt 7:15–20); true and false disciples (8:18–22); implied status ranking among the disciples (10:2–4); a parable about weeds among the wheat (13:24–30; cf. 13:36–43); evildoers in the Son of Man's kingdom (13:41); the central role of Peter (23 references) as compared with the other disciples, especially the transference of teaching authority to Peter (16:13–20); instructions about disciplining "sinners" (18:15–20); the status conflict between the sons of Zebedee (and their mother) and the other ten disciples (20:20–28); warnings against the use of titles of honor within the group (23:8–10); and Judas' betrayal (26:14; 26:25; 26:47; 27:3). These tensions and conflicts have not gone unobserved by critics past and present.[11]

---

whom see the sketch in Vledder's study of Matthew 8–9 in chap. 2; see further, chap. 2, n. 67 below.

5. Stanton, *Gospel*, 85–107.

6. Overman, *Matthew's Gospel*; Segal, "Matthew's Jewish Voice"; Saldarini, *Pharisees*; "Gospel of Matthew"; *Matthew's Christian-Jewish Community*; White, "Crisis Management"; for earlier representatives, see Stanton, ibid., 118–24.

7. White, "Group and Grid."

8. Malina and Neyrey, *Calling Jesus Names*.

9. Saldarini, *Matthew's Christian-Jewish Community*, 112–16.

10. See chaps. 4 and 5 above; Vledder, *Conflict*.

11. E.g., Hummel, *Auseinandersetzung*; Davies, *Setting*, 316–66; Garland, *Intention*; Viviano, "Social World."

Much less has been written about this internal conflict in Matthew from the perspective of social-scientific criticism. A few examples have been noted by Bruce Malina who argues that conflicting norms and values within a group do not necessarily suggest "cognitive dissonance,"[12] but rather a culturally acceptable "sociological ambivalence."[13] Andrew Overman and Anthony Saldarini have made some valuable observations with respect to the specific question of order within the Matthean group.[14] I have discussed the transference of authority to Peter in Weberian terms[15] and more recently group formation and scribal leadership in the Matthean group.[16] Graham Stanton has also taken up "internal affairs."[17] For the most part, however, historians using the social sciences have not devoted as much attention to internal conflicts in the gospel.

My thesis in this chapter is that in the Matthean group there is a tension between a *limited "egalitarian" leadership ideology* and a *developing social reality that is moving toward a hierarchical "corporate" structure*. In chapter 3, I cited Ritzer's macroscopic-microscopic continuum of social levels from "higher" to "lower" levels of abstraction as a way to conceive the level of analysis for any social-scientific study.[18] This chapter concentrates on level 4, "groups"; it is a microsocial level of analysis. In this case the models are developed at the end of the chapter. I laid some groundwork in the discussion of hierarchical groups and non-hierarchical organizations in chapter 5.

Two Assumptions

First, texts and contexts. In any analysis it is important to attempt to discover how a writer's "narrative world" is related to "authorial intention" and "actual audience," and how text is related to historical,

12. Gager, *Kingdom and Community*; see chap. 2 above.
13. Argued by Malina, "Normative Dissonance."
14. Overman, *Matthew's Gospel*, 101-6; *Church and Community*, 236-61; Saldarini, *Matthew's Christian-Jewish Community*, 102-7.
15. Duling, "Insights from Sociology for New Testament Christology," 360-64; "'Binding and Loosing,'" 21.
16. See chaps. 5, 7, and 9.
17. Stanton, "Revisiting Matthew's Communities," 18-23.
18. See chap. 3 above; see Ritzer, *Contemporary Sociological Theory*, 309.

social, and cultural context.[19] My metaphor for texts and contexts is that Matthew's narrative story is a foggy or steamy window that can function as a mirror, but can also function as a transparent window. By wiping away the fog or steam at the appropriate places, it is possible to see something of the author's social-historical context.[20] My metaphor should not be given the label "allegory," which in modern scholarship is often judged negatively, that is implying that secret, symbolic meanings and prior knowledge are necessary for understanding—in other words, "inauthentic language."[21] Rather, the metaphor refers to reading literary texts in one way that social-scientific critics have in common with redaction critics, social-historical interpreters, Marxist literary critics, and new historicists: texts do not arise in a vacuum but are in various ways "transparent" for the historical and social contexts in which they were written.[22]

Second, recent social-historical research. I accept the majority historical-critical opinion that the author of the First Gospel remolded and developed the sources Mark, "Q," and Special M. I also agree with recent social-historical research that the gospel was written by what are usually called an anonymous "Jewish Christian" or "Christian Jew"— highly problematic language for the first century CE[23]—a male marginal scribe who probably lived in an urban environment in the Roman East. He was reasonably well-off and wrote about 80–90 CE, the period in which the Pharisees were seeking to assert their dominance over other groups in Judaism. He perceived himself and the group in and for which he wrote to be in conflict with the dominant Pharisee group about Torah interpretation and Jesus' significance.[24]

19. E.g., Van Staden, *Compassion,* 74–103; Malina and Neyrey, *Calling Jesus Names,* 135–43; see Stanton, "Communities of Matthew," 380, 389 n. 2; above, pp. 46–47, 54–55.

20. See chap. 5 above.

21. See Stanton, "Revisiting Matthew's Communities," 12 n. 11; the critique of allegory as inauthentic language and as completely alien to the teaching of Jesus goes back to Jülicher, *Die Gleichnisreden Jesu,* 1, 203–322.

22. Eagleton, *Marxism*; Veeser, *The New Historicism*; Saldarini, *Matthew's Christian-Jewish Community,* 85; Anderson, "Life on the Mississippi," 173.

23. Pilch, "Jews and Christians"; Hanson and Oakman, *Palestine in the Time of Jesus,* 2nd ed., 11; more recently, Esler, *Conflict and Identity in Romans,* 67–68; Elliott, "Jesus the Israelite."

24. Overman, *Matthew's Gospel*; Saldarini, *Matthew's Christian-Jewish Community*; see chaps. 6 and 9.

Terms and Concepts

The terms "group," "ideology," "egalitarian," "leadership," and "conflict" in the title of this chapter are much debated terms that need to be discussed.

Group. By "group" I mean: "a more or less cohesive collection of individuals who relate to each other personally [e.g., "face-to-face"] and at intervals in more or less patterned ways [more than chance] because they share certain beliefs, values, affections, motives, norms, and roles and have a common goal."[25] "Group" rather than "community" is the better term in this context because the latter term, while conveying a certain intimacy ("sense of community"), has been used for whole collectivities and at a higher level of abstraction than is here intended.[26]

Ideology. By "ideology" I do not mean either the Enlightenment's utopian-minded "science of ideas," on the one hand, or Marx's "false consciousness," that is, false mental representations of socio-economic roles and relations that perpetuate keeping the lower classes in their place, on the other.[27] To be sure, social reality contributes to the formation of ideology, but ideology is not a simple and direct reflection of social reality ("vulgar Marxism"); rather, ideology can also affect social relations. In other words, there is an interaction, a dialectic, between them.[28] Edward Shils' definition captures this more neutral sense of ideology, namely, "explicitly formulated, value-laden ideas with affective overtones, all centering around some common theme, with its adherents forming a collectivity which believes that these ideas are distinctive, and which commits itself totally to follow them and by disciplined action to implement them."[29]

Egalitarian. The term "egalitarian" has turned up frequently in recent New Testament study, especially in descriptions of the Jesus

---

25. Duling, "Small Groups," 180.

26. Saldarini, *Matthew's Christian-Jewish Community*, 85-87; Malina, "Early Christian Groups." See the discussion of groups below.

27. Lorrain, *Concept of Ideology*; McLellan, *Ideology*; Eagleton, *Ideology*; see the hegemony discussion in chap. 3 above.

28. On ideology and art, see chap. 5 n. 38 above.

29. Shils, "Ideology"; Van Staden, *Compassion*, 87-93.

Movement,[30] but also of the Pauline groups.[31] It has occasionally surfaced to describe a social ideal in the Gospel of Matthew, as well.[32] Yet, the term should be used with caution when describing a movement or group in antiquity. Ancient society was not "egalitarian" in the modern Enlightenment, individualist, political-philosophical sense in which equality is a self-evident human right and/or social goal for everyone. To be sure, some anthropological studies of "preindustrial" political systems—decentralized bands and tribes with informal situational leadership and no formal means of political succession—are sometimes called "egalitarian."[33] A type of egalitarianism has been documented for modern peasant villages. People in a Lebanese Sunni Muslim village, in commenting on their economic status, say, "We are all equal here."[34] These studies are suggestive, but they deal with whole societies of the simpler, small-scale type. While Mediterranean society was not industrialized, it was nonetheless more complex—a stratified advanced agrarian society,[35] or what is sometimes called a peasant society.[36]

What, then, of "egalitarianism" in advanced agrarian or peasant societies? In relation to Mediterranean antiquity, J. Dominic Crossan associates Jesus Movement meal practices with peasant-village egalitarianism of the sort that eliminated male-female, poor-rich, and Gentile-"Jew" hierarchies.[37] To support Jesus Movement egalitarianism, Crossan draws on anthropologist James Scott's summary of the peasant vision of society:

> peasant culture and religion is actually an anticulture, qualifying alike both the religious and political elites that oppress it. It is, in fact, a reflexive and reactive inversion of the pattern of exploitation common to the peasantry *as such*. "The radi-

30. E.g., Schüssler Fiorenza, *In Memory of Her*; Crossan, *Historical Jesus*, 263–64.

31. Atkins, *Egalitarian Community*.

32. Krentz, "Community and Character," 572; Saldarini, "Gospel of Matthew," 52; *Matthew's Christian-Jewish Community*, 106.

33. Service, *Primitive Social Organization*; Fried, *Evolution of Political Society*; Lewellen, *Political Anthropology*.

34. E.g., Rothenberger, "Social Dynamics of Dispute Settlement," 158–59.

35. Lenski and Lenski, *Human Societies* (1987).

36. Wolf, *Peasants*; see chaps. 4, 5, and 7 in the present volume.

37. Crossan, *Historical Jesus*, 263.

cal vision to which I refer," he [Scott] continues, "is strikingly uniform despite the enormous variations in peasant cultures and the differing great traditions of which they partake . . . At the risk of overgeneralizing, it is possible to describe some common features of the reflexive symbolism. It nearly always implies a society or brotherhood in which there will be no rich and poor, in which no distinctions of rank and status (save those between believers and non-believers) will exist. Where religious institutions are experienced as justifying inequalities, the abolition of rank and status may well include the elimination of religious hierarchy in favor of communities of equal believers. Property is typically, though not always, to be held in common and shared. All unjust claims to taxes, rents, and tribute are to be nullified. The envisioned utopia may also include a self-yielding and abundant nature as well as a radically transformed human nature in which greed, envy, and hatred will disappear. While the earthly utopia is thus an anticipation of the future, it often harks back to a mythic Eden from which mankind has fallen away."[38]

Not all critics accept the notion that the Jesus Movement was egalitarian.[39] More importantly here, interpreters of the Matthean gospel are not convinced that it has an "egalitarian" perspective in the peasant sense that Crossan and others associate with the Jesus Movement.[40] Kathleen Corley has argued that in the Matthean gospel Jesus admits the presence of women in his meal practices;[41] however, she has considered the Matthean context to be fundamentally patriarchal.[42] Although the gospel clearly has Gentile features, it also makes well-known negative comments about Gentiles (e.g., 6:7, 32; 10:5; 18:17; 20:19, 25). And although it often has a pro-poor stance, it also appears to represent a more well-to-do writer who ranks "spiritual" and christological themes above concern for the poor (e.g., 5:3; 26:11). Finally, Scott's statement sees outsiders as an exception and

---

38. Crossan, *Historical Jesus*, 264; *Birth of Christianity*, 299–300. Both books cite Scott, "Protest and Profanation," 225–26. See chap. 5 n. 69 above; see chap. 3 above for a brief discussion of Scott's view of peasant resistance.

39. More recently, Elliott, "Jesus Was Not an Egalitarian."

40. E.g., Stanton, "Revisiting Matthew's Communities," 20.

41. Corley, *Private Women*, 147, 178; "Jesus' Table Practice."

42. Anderson, "Matthew: Gender and Reading," 7; "Mary's Difference," 184–86, 199; Corley, *Private Women*; "Jesus' Table Practice"; Love, "The Place of Women," 63.

his peasant egalitarianism does not mention women explicitly; not surprisingly, Corley argues that peasant women do not challenge male dominance and that it is unwise to romanticize "egalitarianism" among peasants.[43]

Again, the term "egalitarian" needs to be used with great caution. Here the term "egalitarian" refers to a *limited* equality as suggested by the above discussion. It focuses on Matthew's statements about a small-group "brotherhood" led by marginal scribes with an ideology that combats status hierarchy with respect to leaders.[44] While certain titles of honor may have been rejected on the basis of this "limited egalitarian" ideology in the Matthean group, I do not concentrate on the Matthean polemic about outsiders or the status of women in the group, despite their importance. Also, I leave open the question of the origins of this ideology, although it is already found in "Q"[45] and it is possible that it ultimately stems from the Jesus Movement.[46] My question is of a different, more restricted, sort: does the Matthean limited egalitarian ideology correspond to the Matthean social reality?

Factional. As presented in chapter 5, the Mediterranean anthropologist Jeremy Boissevain contrasts "corporations"—permanent, typically hierarchical institutions having governing rules and offices—with "coalitions." He defines a coalition as "*a temporary alliance of distinct parties for a limited purpose*"[47] and he stresses the instability and temporary nature of such coalitions. Normally they have a leader, a core group, and peripheral members. They arise in new situations and reflect changing circumstances. Either they disappear as their goals are achieved or they evolve into more permanent groups, in which case their goals change; indeed, they can become corporations.

Though there are many varieties of coalitions, Boissevain limits his analysis to four types: "cliques," "gangs," "action sets," and "factions."[48] Most important for this discussion is the faction, which he defines as follows: "a coalition of persons (followers) recruited personally [by a

43. Corley, *Private Women*, 176–77; "Jesus' Table Practice," 455–56.
44. See chap. 7 below.
45. See Corley, *Private Women*, 178–79.
46. Wire, "Gender Roles," 121.
47. Boissevain, *Friends of Friends*, 171; see Malina, "Patron and Client," 20; "A Conflict Approach," 15.
48. Boissevain, *Friends of Friends*, 176–205; see Model 5.1.

leader], according to structurally diverse principles by or on behalf of a person in conflict with another person or persons, with whom they were formerly united, over honor and/or control of resources."[49] This definition emphasizes recruitment by a leader and conflict with others. When factions exist to change the social structure, they are analogous to what other theorists have called "social movements,"[50] "reformist sects,"[51] or "conflict groups."[52] These groups and movements are usually part of larger social collectivities. From this perspective the Matthean group has become sufficiently developed—is large enough and organized enough—to have sub-groups within it, that is, factions. *"Factional" is derived from this meaning of faction.*

Leadership. There is a vast amount of social-scientific literature on leadership.[53] Most of it takes its departure from Max Weber's well-known analysis of "charismatic leadership." For Weber charisma is "a certain quality of an individual personality by virtue of which (s)he is considered extraordinary and treated as endowed with supernatural, superhuman, or exceptional powers or qualities."[54] Weber's definition is essentially a "personality trait" approach set within a theory of social action.[55] Yet, Weber recognizes that not all leaders possess charisma and that there are leaders in organized institutions. *In this study, leaders are those who have status in a group of followers.* They can have "ascribed" status or "acquired" (achieved) status.[56] Ascribed status comes from birth (kinship) or is granted to a person of lesser status by a person of higher status. Normally, it is associated with some preexisting, or externally legitimated, role or office. It is normally found in institutions. In contrast, leaders can have "acquired" or "achieved" status that comes from within a group on the basis of some important function the person serves in the group. Normally, group

---

49. Boissevain, ibid., 192; see Malina, "A Conflict Approach to Mark 7," 24.
50. Lenski and Lenski, *Human Societies*, 45–46; Morris and Mueller, *Frontiers*.
51. Wilson, *Magic*, 18–30; Saldarini, *Pharisees*, 72; Elliott, "The Jewish Messianic Movement"; see Chart 1.1.
52. Dahrendorf, "Toward a Theory of Social Conflict," 180.
53. E.g., Blasi, *Making Charisma*; Bottomore, *Elites and Society*.
54. Weber, *Economy and Society*, 241.
55. Duling, "Small Groups," 181.
56. Malina, *The New Testament World*, 3rd ed., 27–57; *Christian Origins*, 107–9; see chap. 5 above.

leaders have acquired status. In person-centered network factions, for example, there is a leader ("Ego") and followers ("alters"); the latter consists of a core of intimate followers ("friends" in an "intimate network"), a larger group of effective followers ("friends of friends" in an "effective network"), and then still larger group of extended followers hardly known to Ego and the core ("friends of friends of friends" in an "extended network"), all of which can be represented by concentric circles with Ego in the center.[57] I do not restrict the concept of leader to personality traits, but neither is it limited to "office." I shall have more to say about this "functional" leadership below.

Conflict. The term and concept "conflict" in the social sciences is much debated and there is no consensus.[58] Most definitions are intentionally vague, general, and abstract because social-science theorists attempt to cover a variety of social units at many levels of abstraction in order to arrive at greater explanatory power. In such definitions the accent naturally tends to fall on political conflict as a whole. My interest here is on internal conflict in groups in relation to authority, not political conflict with outsiders, whether competing groups or external political powers. With this understanding, I offer the general definition of the conflict theorist Ralf Dahrendorf. A conflict consists of "contests, competitions, disputes, and tensions, as well as . . . manifest clashes between social forces."[59]

Select Passages

I mentioned previously that it is possible to look through the textual "window" to see something about social context, in this chapter especially about leaders. I shall not examine every passage about internal conflict in the gospel, but only certain key passages related to the concepts just discussed.

---

57. See Duling, "Die Jesusbewegung und die Networkanalyse"; "Jesus Movement and Network Analysis"; "Jesus Movement and Social Network Analysis," Parts I and II. See chap. 5 above, Model 5.1, and Model 6.2 for the "Network group" as an example of a non-hierarchical group.

58. Fink, "Some Conceptual Difficulties."

59. Dahrendorf, *Class and Class Conflict*, 135 [italics mine].

"Egalitarian" Ideology, Leadership, and Factional Conflict

Probably the most important passage for determining Matthew's limited "egalitarian" ideology is Jesus' teaching to the disciples in Matthew 23:7b–10:

> [The Pharisees love ...] to be called Rabbi by the people.
> 8) But (as for) you (pl.),
> do not be called *Rabbi*,
> for [only] one is your *teacher*, but (pl.) you are all brothers.
> 9) And *father* do not call yourselves (pl.) on earth,
> for [only] one is your (pl.) father, the heavenly [one].
> 10) Neither be called (pl.) *tutors*,
> for your (pl.) tutor is [only] one, the Christ.

In chapter 5, I pointed out Benedict Viviano's "run-ons," terms and phrases that break the formal structure of the lines, which are laid out to the right.[60] For Viviano this passage contains "a critique of synagogue offices and titles that are merging in and around the Rabbinic Academy of Jamnia/Yavneh at this time. . ."[61] While one must be very cautious—the historical facts of Yavneh are much debated[62]—Viviano's statement is fairly representative of current scholarship.

The passage contains three important titles of honor: "Rabbi," "Father," and "Tutor."

Rabbi. The first rejected title of honor is "Rabbi," which means literally, "my great one." The title is well known from rabbinic references to teachers, especially prior to 135 CE.[63] It also occurs on Jerusalem ossuaries prior to 100 CE and there it is combined with proper names.[64] Subsequently, it is found on cemetery inscriptions from Joppa and Beth-She'arîm.[65] The title is probably an address to wealthy teachers who knew the Greek language and Greek culture. It seems to be equivalent to "sir," and could also represent Aramaic *mari*, "my lord." In Matthew "Rabbi" is used only by the traitor Judas (Matt 26:25, 49), and thus is inadequate for Jesus.

---

60. See pp. 139–41 above for a more detailed discussion of Matt 23:8–10.
61. Viviano, "Social World," 10.
62. See, e.g., Overman, *Matthew's Gospel*, 38–43.
63. Lapin, "Rabbi," 601; Garland, *Intention*, 58 n. 23.
64. Frey, *Corpus Inscriptionum Iudaicarum*, 2:249, 275–77, 277–79.
65. Cohen, "Epigraphical Rabbis"; Lapin, "Rabbi."

Father. "Father" is also known as a leader's title from rabbinic texts (e.g., *Pirke 'Aboth*) and various inscriptions,[66] as well as the New Testament (1 Cor 4:15). Viviano notes that ". . . among the Rabbis, Saul ben Batnith (c. 80–120 CE) is the first known Judean sage to bear the title *Abba*, father, just early enough to have incurred Matthew's criticism."[67] Viviano also mentions the synagogue inscription "father of the synagogue at Stobi" (Macedonia) from the late second, early third century.[68] Hillel and Shammai were called "fathers of the world" (*m. 'Ed.* 1.4)[69] and later local synagogue leaders were called "father of the synagogue" or "father of the people." In relation to "Rabbi" and "Father," Jehoshaphat addresses the scholar-teacher as "'Father, Father,' 'Rabbi, Rabbi,' 'Lord, Lord,'" (*b. Mak.* 24a; also *m. 'Aboth* 6.3)[70] to which one should compare, "Not everyone who says to me, 'Lord, Lord,' will enter the kingdom of heaven, but only the one who does the will of my Father in heaven" (Matt 7:21). "Father," of course, is reserved by Matthew primarily for the heavenly Father, or God, as in this passage.

Tutor. The last term, "tutor," is an unusual term (Greek *kathēgētēs*) and therefore difficult to track in rabbinic and inscriptional sources. Some have argued that it has behind it the Hebrew *mōreh*, as in *mōreh hazzedek*, the "Teacher of Righteousness" of the Dead Sea Scrolls (4QpPs^a 37 [= 4Q171] 3:15–16; 1QpHab 2:8; CD 1:9–11). Bruce Winter has argued that in Greek it means "private tutor."[71] Form and redaction critical analysts have often argued that the verse in which it occurs (23:10) has been added to the others.[72] This is possible, but it is even clearer that phrases in verses 8–10 are typical of Matthew. As stated above, Viviano observes four such "run-ons"[73] which I have set to the right. Since "the Christ" and the heavenly/earthly contrast are especially Matthean emphases, so probably is the designation for members of Matthew's group, "brothers." In this connection, it should

---

66. Frey, *CII*, 494, 509, 511; Kohler, "Abba, Father"; Urbach, *The Sages*, 186, 906 n. 38; Townsend, "Matthew XXIII.9."

67. Viviano, "Social World," 14.

68. Ibid., 20 n. 32; see also Hachlili, "Synagogue," 260.

69. Urbach, *Sages*, 906 n. 38.

70. Garland, *Intention*, 58 n. 92.

71. Winter, "Messiah as the Tutor," 152–57.

72. E.g., Meier, *Matthew*, 265.

73. Viviano, "Social World," 8.

be observed that the term "brother" is the catchword in the Matthean gospel that holds together the antithesis on murder and anger (5:21–26), the warning against hypocritical judging (7:1–5), Jesus' true family (12:46–50), the juridical process for settling group disputes (18:15–22, 35),[74] and the prohibition against titles of honor (23:8–10). "Brother" is also important for the "least of these my brothers" saying (25:40) and in reference to the eleven disciples (28:10).[75] J. Duncan Derrett stresses that "brother" is family language,[76] which in social-scientific terms is "fictive-" or "pseudo-kinship" language.[77] Thus, it must be related to current discussions about the family and household in antiquity.[78] A "brotherhood" is in many respects "egalitarian," but in the ancient world and family language of Matthew, not all in the family are equal. Andrew Overman is probably correct to conclude that there were in the Matthean group those who tried to assume such Pharisaic roles of leadership and their corresponding titles.[79] I suggest that Matthew's ideology is "egalitarian," but only to the limited extent noted above: Pharisaic titles of status in relation to the central activity of teachers and pupils are rejected by the Matthean author for the Matthean "brotherhood."

I shall now show that even this *"limited egalitarian"* ideology does not always correspond to the actual internal social reality as indicated by the gospel.[80] Matthew contains at least four kinds of status designations, the fourth of which can be further subdivided into four subcategories, for a total of seven.[81] These seven designations are: "apostle," "prophet," little ones," and teachers, that is, "teacher," "wise one," "scribe," and "righteous one." Several of these designations, along with "he who comes in the name of the Lord," are clustered in

74. See chap. 8 below.
75. See chap. 7 below.
76. Derrett, "Mt 23,8-10," 379–80.
77. Pitt-Rivers, "Pseudo-Kinship."
78. E.g., White, "Scaling the Strongman's 'Court'"; Crosby, *House of Disciples*; Elliott, *Home* (1991); "Temple versus Household"; Carter, *Households and Discipleship*; Osiek and Balch, *Families*; see chap. 7.
79. Overman, *Matthew's Gospel*, 122–24.
80. Ibid., 113–24; *Church and Community*, 319–24; see Saldarini, *Matthew's Christian-Jewish Community*, 106–7.
81. Krentz, "Community and Character."

the New Testament, for example, in relation to apostles and prophets (Eph 4:11); prophets and apostles (Luke 11:49; 1 Cor 11:28, 29); prophets and teachers (Acts 13:1; 1 Cor 11:28, 29). Especially striking are the Matthean clusters:

Chart 6.1 Clustered Status Designations in the New Testament

1 Cor 12:28, 29	apostles, prophets, teachers (cf. 6:5—wise man)
Rom 12:6–7	(prophecy); he who teaches . . . teaching
Eph 4:11	apostles and prophets
Matt 7:15	false prophets
Matt 10:2	apostles
Matt 10:41–42	prophet . . . prophet . . . prophet's reward; righteous man . . . righteous man . . . righteous man's reward . . . one of these little ones . . . disciple . . . his reward
Matt 13:17	many prophets, righteous men
Matt 13:52	every scribe trained ("discipled")
Matt 23:29	prophets, scribes, and righteous ones
Matt 23:34	prophets and wise ones and scribes
Matt 21:11, 9	the prophet Jesus; "he who comes in the name of the Lord"
Matt 23:37, 39	the prophets; "he who comes in the name of the Lord"
Luke 11:49	prophets and apostles
Acts 13:1	prophets and teachers

Similar clusterings are found in *Did.* 11:1–11, 12:1, 13:1–2, 15:1–2, and the *Martyrdom of Polycarp* 16:2. Each of these designations needs some discussion.

Apostle (apostolos)

In Paul, the expression "apostles of the churches" (2 Cor 8:23) refers to those who are "sent out" to preach the gospel and to establish new house-churches.[82] Its probable background lies in the Semitic *shaliach*, the envoy who is the full agent and representative of the sender (Isa 61:1; Ezra 7:14; Dan 5:24; John 13:16, 20).[83] In Matthew the *noun* "apostle" occurs only once, in 10:2. This statistic, however, is misleading because there are many passages in Matthew about envoys

---

82. 1 Cor 9:5; 12:28; Betz, "Apostle."
83. Agnew, "Origin," 96.

being "sent out" (*apostellō*: 10:5, 16; 11:10; 13:41; 14:35; 15:24; 21:1, 34, 36, 37; 22:3, 4, 16; 23:34, 37; 24:31; 27:19; *pempō*: 11:2, 10). The context of 10:2 is the mission of the Twelve, in some ways similar to, but no doubt competing with, the Cynic mission ideal.[84] Matthew's view of the itinerant can be illustrated by the traditional *shalîach*-type agent saying in 10:40 (cf. John 13:20): "He who receives you [with hospitality] receives me, and he who receives me [with hospitality] receives *him who sent me* (*ton aposteilanta me*)." A comparison of Matt 10:9–14 with 1 Cor 4:9–17 will show that, with the exception of Paul's crucial emphasis on his self-support, the mission of the apostle in Paul and the mission in Matthew are similar. Jonathan Draper has argued that the (constantly revised) *Didachē* was the "community rule" of the Matthean group;[85] if this is correct, the wandering teacher in *Did.* 11:3–6 and the wandering apostle in Matthew 10 must be seen together. In any case, the itinerant apostle is not an outmoded vestige from an earlier time, but still functions in the Matthean group.

Prophet (*prophētēs*)

The writer of Matthew honors what he considers to be true prophets. They are mentioned thirty-seven times, and about twenty are redactional.[86] Prophets persecuted "for righteousness' sake" are like the ancient prophets (Matt 5:10–12; cf. 7:12; 23:29–31). All of the Matthean special formula quotations pointing to the fulfillment of God's will derive from the prophets.[87] Bornkamm once suggested that the gospel's warning about *false* prophets who practice good works (7:15–23; cf. 24:11–12, 24) implies the presence of *true* prophets in the Matthean community.[88] The Matthean writer accepts a modified version of Mark's saying about Jesus that "a prophet is not without honor except in his own country" (Mark 6:4; Matt 13:57). Both Jesus (13:57; 21:11, 46) and John the Baptist (11:9; cf. 21:23–27) are seen as prophets, even if "prophet" may not be a *sufficient* title for Jesus

84. See chap. 5, n. 68 above for literature.
85. Draper, "Torah and Troublesome Apostles."
86. Luz, *Matthew 1–7* (1989), 67.
87. Duling, "Matthew and the Problem of Authority"; for Ps 78:2 as prophecy in Matt 13:35, see Fitzmyer, "David."
88. Bornkamm, "End-Expectation," 39 n. 1.

(21:37-38). In 10:40-42 "prophet" occurs in an itinerant context, where it comes before "righteous one" and "the little ones." Similarly, in 23:34, "prophet" is listed before "wise men" and "scribes," all itinerants, some of whom, says the evangelist, will be martyred.

"Little Ones" (mikroi)

The identity of the "little ones" in 18:6 and 18:14 is much debated. Suggestions range from children to new members of the community to a select group within the community to all members of the community. In 10:40-42 they are listed after the titles of prominence "prophet" and "wise one" and are itinerants and given the name "disciple." The early second-century texts 5 Ezra and the *Apocalypse of Peter* contain the expression "little ones" as a preferred designation for members of the Matthean group as a whole, and these documents reject "bishop" and "deacon" as titles. Presumably leaders with local authority are being denied authority in these latter texts,[89] but there is no such explicit denial in the Matthean gospel itself (the latter titles are missing in Matthew).

4. Teachers

This fourth category can be subdivided by means of four terms: "teacher" (*didaskalos*), "wise one" (*sophos*), "righteous one" (*dikaios*), and "scribe" (*grammateus*).

DIDASKALOS

Jesus is called or addressed as "teacher" by those who are hostile (Matt 9:11; 12:38; 19:16; 22:16; 22:24; 22:36). Yet, Jesus designates himself as *the didaskalos* (26:18) and the eleven disciples are commanded to go to the nations and *teach* Jesus' *teaching* (28:20). Draper argues that behind Matthew's pro-Torah statements in 5:17-20 lies the command to shun the wayward anti-Torah teacher in *Did.* 11:1-2. If he is right, the one who shall be called "least in the Kingdom of Heaven" for

---

89. Stanton, "5 Ezra"; *A Gospel*, 256-81.

"*Egalitarian*" *Ideology, Leadership, and Factional Conflict*   161

teaching people to relax "one of the least of these my commandments" (5:19) refers to the *Didachē*'s wrong-headed "apostle/teacher."[90] In the *Didachē* that wrong-headed teacher is itinerant. Can the term be local in Matthew? In Matt 10:24-25, the saying that "a disciple is not above his teacher" occurs in a context where the metaphors have to do with the *household*. Clearly, the teacher has status and there are hints at localization. Thus, a conflict between itinerant and local teachers may be implied.[91]

Sophos

The expression "wise one" occurs at 11:25 and 23:34. The former verse from Q (= Luke 10:21) contrasts "the wise and understanding" of the world with "babes" to whom "these things" are revealed. This is not a negative judgment on the truly wise, but a common Wisdom theme about the *worldly* wise[92] also found in 1 Corinthians 1-4. Perhaps Paul's desire for a *local* "wise one" at Corinth (6:5) is an analogy (1 Cor 1:18-29; 2:6-3:3; cf. 6:3; see below). In the second passage, 23:34, Matthew keeps Q's "prophets" but replaces Q's "apostles" (Q 11:49) with "wise ones" and "scribes." Here they are itinerant.

Dikaios

"Righteous one" occurs in 10:40-42 after "prophet" and before "little ones" as one who is "sent out." Itinerancy and hospitality are in view. Krentz suggests that the "righteous one" is any person who carries out the Jesus-interpreted Torah;[93] his references seem to yield this interpretation (13:43, 49; 25:37, 46; Ps Sol 10:3; 13:6, 7; Wis 2:12, 18). This suggestion also accents Matthew's righteousness theme correctly ("righteous": 17 times; "righteousness": 7 times). Yet, drawing on parallels in Daniel (12:2) and 1 Enoch (e.g., 1 Enoch 38:2-4; 39:6-7; 48:1), D. Hill argues that "righteous one" was a quasi-technical term

---

90. Draper, "Torah and Troublesome Apostles," 356-60.
91. Overman, *Matthew's Gospel*, 119-22.
92. Suggs, *Kingdom, Christology, and Law*, 86-87.
93. Krentz, "Community and Character," 571.

for those who teach,[94] and Kingsbury correlates it with the Teacher of Righteousness.[95]

Grammateus

"Scribe" is not only a title; it is a writing "profession" and there are several subtypes: 1) royal scribes and government bureaucrats who served the ruling elite directly; 2) public and private secretaries; 3) village and local scribes; 4) scribes of voluntary associations; 5) elementary level Sacred Text school teachers; and 6) learned Torah scholars.[96] The gospel writer polemicizes against the "scribes and Pharisees" (ch. 23) and omits the Markan "good scribe" (Mark 12:32–34). Yet, in 8:19, a scribe desires to *follow* Jesus, apparently sincerely.[97] In 13:52, a scribe is said to be trained ("discipled" [*mathēteutheis*]) for the kingdom," which might imply scribes who have joined the community, and most probably the evangelist himself. Among those whom Jesus *sends out* to the "scribes and the Pharisees" are scribes from the Matthean group, "some of whom you will kill and crucify, and some you will scourge in your synagogues and persecute from town to town" (23:34). Two of these three passages suggest an itinerant mission for Matthean scribes (8:19; 23:34), though the second has involuntary movement, as well (23:34); the third (13:52) might imply localization.

Four Observations

I make four observations about the previous text segments.

First, "apostle" (*apostolos*), "prophet" (*prophētēs*), and "teacher" (*didaskalos*) are found clustered in various combinations in Paul's letters, Matthew, and the *Didachē*, as well as a few other early Christian sources. While Harnack's view that these expressions refer to great

---

94. Hill, "DIKAIOI," 296–302.
95. Kingsbury, *Matthew as Story* (1988), 157.
96. For categorization of subtypes of scribes, see pp. 261–71 below.
97. See pp. 199–201 for interpretation and debate.

"charismatic" callings[98] has sometimes been seen as extreme, clearly such fixed roles were at least beginning to emerge.

Second, Matthew's "apostles," "prophets," and "teachers" are usually itinerants, as in the *Didachē* (e.g., Matt 5:38–39, 41; 6:19–34; 8:20; 9:6; 10:5–15, 17–20, 24–25, 40–44; 11:18–19; 12:8; 19:10–11; 23:34; *Did.* 11:3–8). In contrast, we hear nothing of local authorities, called "bishops" (*episcopoi*), "elders" (*presbyteroi*), and "deacons" (*diakonoi*), or "those who rule over" (*proistamenous*) people in the Matthean group.

These first two points suggest that in contrast to Matthew's limited "egalitarian" kinship ideology in Matthew 23, there are various itinerants being sent out from (and perhaps also coming to?) the Matthean group. While the network group is non-hierarchical, these itinerants appear to be leaders with some authority.

Third, Jesus' transfer of power to "bind and loose" to Peter in 16:19 most probably refers to Peter's authority to prohibit or permit teaching.[99] This transfer of authority seems to reflect a leadership succession as discussed by Max Weber.[100] It is also an example of "ascribed honor," that is, a grant by a person of higher status (see above). It normally occurs in relation to some externally legitimated role or office in stratified "corporations." To be sure, no role is discussed as a specific *office* in Matthew. Nonetheless, no matter how a scholar judges Peter's status—local or itinerant, functional or official—it does not easily correspond with the Matthean "egalitarian" ideology, even in the limited sense defined above. It conforms *minimally* to Kingsbury's notion that Peter is portrayed as "*first* among equals."[101] The case has been made that it implies more[102] and that case looks even stronger from the perspective of Weber's analysis of succession.

Fourth, how should we reconstruct a plausible social context for all the scribal activity represented by the First Gospel? Scribes can be itinerant (8:19; 23:34?). Yet, Stendahl once referred to a "school,"

---

98. Harnack, *Mission*, 319–68.

99. Duling, "'Binding and Loosing.'"

100. Ibid., 21; Duling, "Insights from Sociology," 360–64; Overman, *Matthew's Gospel*, 139–40; *Church and Community*, 246–51; see Weber, *Economy and Society*, 241–54.

101. Kingsbury, "Verb *Akolouthein*."

102. Hummel, *Die Auseinandersetzung*; Davies and Allison, *Matthew 1–7*, 647–51.

which suggests locality.¹⁰³ Anne Wire rejects the school hypothesis but has nonetheless argued for a "scribal community" within which there are "set roles."¹⁰⁴ Overman has argued that the disciples are transparent for the authority of local teachers.¹⁰⁵ Stanton claims there are overlapping ministries in the Matthean "communities," then agrees with Schweizer that there are no *specialized* ministries,¹⁰⁶ but finally says with respect to especially Matt 23:8-12 that "it would be rash to conclude . . . that Matthew's communities were egalitarian, without any structures at all."¹⁰⁷ In chapter 7 I shall argue that the Matthean group is led by marginal scribes.¹⁰⁸ Despite the emphasis on itinerants, such a context suggests some status roles for local persons, and I shall now attempt to gain some further clarity, first by an analogy from Paul, second by sociological models.

An Analogy from Paul

Paul's letters and Matthew's *bios* are different genres and not literarily comparable, which complicates the question whether the gospel has Pauline antinomians in mind at points, particularly in the "false prophet" passage in Matt 7:15-20.¹⁰⁹ Analogies compare similarities between things that are otherwise not comparable, so I suggest an analogy here. It is often argued that the baptismal formula in Galatians 3:28—"neither Jew [Judean] nor Greek, . . . neither slave nor free, . . . neither male nor female, [but] . . . one in Christ Jesus"—indicates an "egalitarian" ideology, which corresponds to the judgment that there were no externally legitimated institutional offices in Paul's churches, but only flexible, overlapping "roles" and correspondingly flexible, overlapping "functions." At the same time, there are indications that

---

103. Stendahl, *School of St. Matthew*.
104. Wire, "Gender Roles," 96-97, 102-3.
105. Overman, *Matthew's Gospel*, 132-40.
106. Cp. Schweizer, "Matthew's Church," 140.
107. Stanton, "Revisiting Matthew's Communities," 20.
108. See chap. 7 below.
109. Sim, *The Gospel of Matthew*, has made strong arguments that the gospel is anti-Pauline.

"Egalitarian" Ideology, Leadership, and Factional Conflict 165

local authority was beginning to surface.[110] Paul speaks of "those who labor (*kopiontas*) among you and are *over you* (*proistamenous*) in the Lord and *admonish* (*nouthetountas*) you" at Thessalonica (1 Thess 5:12); he speaks of a "catechist" at Galatia (Gal 6:6); though their precise connotations are debated, he mentions *episcopoi* and *diakonoi* at Philippi (Phil 1:1); he also recommends a "wise one" to help resolve controversies at Corinth (1 Cor 6:5); and he thinks of local women who have status, for example, the *diakonos* Phoebe (Rom 16:1-2), Prisca (Rom 16:3), and Euodia and Syntyche (Phil 4:2-3). It is also clear that Paul *ranked* the three "charismatic gifts" apostles, prophets, teachers (1 Cor 12.28). Atkins concludes that the Pauline evidence for local authorities is mixed;[111] Holmberg goes so far as to use the term "office," although in a somewhat limited sense.[112] When one adds to these ideas Paul's own claims to authority,[113] it is clear that in some of his communities the transition from "charismatic" roles to local offices was under way.[114]

In sum, several Matthean texts are windows through which one can observe emergent Matthean leadership. Though Matthew has a *limited* "egalitarian" ideology, even this ideology does not easily harmonize with four facts: first, the implied status occasionally granted to apostles, prophets, and teachers; second, the transfer of teaching authority to Peter; third, the scribal character of the Matthean group; and fourth, the context and implied authority of the Matthean writer himself.[115] Although an ideology of limited "egalitarianism" is present, there is also evidence of both itinerants with authority and roles that suggest local authority. Thus, there is a tension, a discontinuity between ideology and social reality. An analogy for this mixed situation can be found in the Pauline communities.

---

110. Holmberg, *Paul and Power*; Meeks, *First Urban Christians*, 134-36.
111. Atkins, *Egalitarian Community*, 123-44.
112. Holmberg, *Paul and Power*, 112-13; Meeks, *First Urban Christians*, 136.
113. Schütz, *Paul*.
114. See the extensive bibliography in Dunn, *Theology of Paul*, 565-66, and particularly Schütz, *Paul*; Holmberg, *Paul and Power*; Meeks, *First Urban Christians*, 111-39; and MacDonald, *Pauline Churches*.
115. See chap. 9 below for a discussion of "literacy power."

Social-Scientific Models for Groups[116]

There is no clear consensus among social scientists about small groups. Most discussions echo or critique the "classical" theorists. Probably the most famous is Max Weber's "charismatic community." Weber defined "charisma" as "a certain quality of an individual personality by virtue of which he is considered extraordinary and treated as endowed with supernatural, superhuman, or at least specifically exceptional powers or qualities."[117] A "charismatic community" (*Gemeinde*) consists of a charismatic leader and a circle of followers over whom the leader has authority. Bonded by emotional ties, its members live as a community with no clearly defined division of labor, no hierarchies, no offices, no formal rules, and no judicial processes. However, the attempt to preserve charismatic authority in a legitimate succession usually transforms the charismatic community into a bureaucratic institution in which members are related by "rational-legal" ties. Charisma becomes "routinized" (made routine) in hierarchies, offices, rules, and judicial processes. The "routinization" of charisma actually deflates charisma: it becomes "contact charisma," "kinship charisma," "hereditary charisma," or "charisma of office." For Weber, therefore, one ideal type—the informal charismatic community—evolves into a second ideal type, the bureaucratic institution, echoing Ferdinand Tönnies' ideal type contrast between *Gemeinschaft*, or the small, simple, intimate "community," and *Gesellschaft*, the large, complex, impersonal "society."[118] Weber held that modern, industrial society was becoming more bureaucratic and impersonal.

Weber occasionally wrote about "sect" and "church," but these terms are more associated with his friend Ernst Troeltsch.[119] For Troeltsch, the "sect" is a voluntary association, an intimate fellowship of love assembled around a prophetic figure. It seeks to be egalitarian. When status differentiation emerges, it is acquired on the basis

---

116. I have included this section omitted from the article in Esler, *Modelling Early Christianity*, 160; for further analysis, see Duling, "Small Groups."

117. Weber, *Economy and Society*, 241.

118. Tönnies, *Community and Society*; McKinney and Loomis, "Introduction."

119. Troeltsch, *Social Teaching*. Troeltsch also developed a third type, "mysticism," groups characterized by religious experience typical of Far Eastern and Gnostic thought.

of contribution to the goals of the group, not birth or appointment by some higher authority. Members commit themselves totally to the group and its strict ethical norms; they strive for perfection, usually in anticipation of the millennium. The sect is radical and revolutionary, setting itself against the state and "the world," and it attracts outcasts, especially members of the lower classes. In contrast, one is born into the "church." The "church" is conservative and traditionalist, and accepts the world. It is hierarchical and status is ascribed to special officers who are committed to the institution. It attracts the upper classes, is sanctioned by the state, and becomes an instrument of social control. For Troeltsch, the "sect" is always the disaffected child of the parent "church." Whereas Weber was willing to see both ancient Judean and early Christian groups as sects, Troeltsch did not describe the earliest Christ Movement as a "sect."

The American Charles H. Cooley, apparently independently of European theorists, also developed contrasting ideal types, namely, "primary groups" and their opposites, called by later sociologists "secondary groups."[120] Based on his observation of families, close friends in neighborhoods, quarters, and small villages, as well as play groups, Cooley defined primary groups as "those characterized by intimate face-to-face association and cooperation."[121] Members relate to each other on a more emotional, direct, personal basis, one that is informal, intimate, unspecialized, and yet relatively permanent. In primary groups the relationship is important for its own sake; members submerge their individuality into a common group identity for which the natural form of expression is "we." Cooley argued that such groups provide the context for forming an individual's basic nature, ideals, norms, and goals. The opposite type, Cooley said, is characterized by relationships that are indirect, impersonal, anonymous, distant, rational, specialized, and transient. In this type people relate to each other formally, more in terms of their roles or some goal shared in common. Examples of these (secondary) groups are those based on ethnicity, religion, a common type of work, or some specific task to be accomplished. Cooley held that primary groups are more characteristic of simpler societies and secondary groups are more characteristic

---

120. Cooley, *Social Organization*. For a slightly different view of primary and secondary groups, see pp. 105–6, and Model 4.2 below.

121. Ibid., 23.

of complex, industrial societies, and in this respect Cooley's theory resembles in certain respects Tönnies' distinction between *Gemeinschaft* and *Gesellschaft*.[122]

While different in many respects, these "ideal type" models also share certain similarities. They are very useful for social-scientific analysis of groups in general. Analysts of early Jesus and Christ-believing groups have often used the "sect"/"church" typology.[123] However, two issues have arisen. First, polar ideal types, as antithetical extremes, cannot, and do not intend to, describe the range of actual groups. Some analysts see this as a limitation. Thus, for example, J. Milton Yinger expands Troeltsch's "sect"/"church" typology into several groups on a broader continuum: Universal Church—*ekklēsia*—Denomination—Established Sect—Sect—Cult.[124] Yinger also develops a typology of sect subtypes: those that accept society, those that avoid society, and those that aggressively oppose society. It is clear that simpler polar ideal types operate at a high level of generality and, as such, should not be made to fit every actual group.

A second criticism has been directed primarily at Troeltsch, namely, "sect" and "church" are too culturally conditioned by an understanding of modern Western Christian groups and institutions to be useful for cross-cultural analyses. As mentioned in chapter 1, for some scholars the sect analysis of Bryan Wilson came to the rescue. Wilson rejected Troeltsch's "church" type, but reconceptualized the "sect" type through analysis of "primitive" and non-Western, third-world movements and then developed a typology of seven different "responses to the world," that is, seven responses to the prevailing social system.[125] Wilson's view of sects has borne fruit in recent study of ancient Judean and early Christ-believing groups.

However, not all have followed the revisionist sect model. A variant of the "too modern and too Western" criticism has been persistently held by Bruce Malina. Malina claims that the "sect" model is anachronistic when applied to the earliest Christ Groups because it assumes that religion can be a separate, discrete social entity; however, in Mediterranean antiquity religion is always embedded—inseparable

---

122. McKinney and Loomis, "Introduction," 14–15.
123. Cf. Holmberg, *Sociology*, 86–108.
124. Yinger, *Religion*.
125. Wilson, *Magic*; see chap. 1, Chart 1.1, for Wilson's seven sect subtypes.

from the family or politics.¹²⁶ Malina goes further. He agrees with Miyahara's view that Weber's "charismatic community" describes an alienated group's collective *illusion* about a leader, regardless of the leader's *actual* ability; indeed, says Malina, it corresponds to the Teutonic *Führer Princip*. For Malina, a better alternative model for the Jesus Movement is a group that follows the "reputational leader," one who indeed challenges the status quo, but on the basis of *legitimate, honorable, and traditional values*.¹²⁷ Malina's alternative model is a corporation/coalition model developed from the work of Mediterranean anthropologist Jeremy Boissevain and industrial organization theorist Ph. G. Herbst. It was described in chapter 5 and will be discussed again later in this chapter.

Finally, John H. Elliott attempts to synthesize several views of sect.¹²⁸ He thinks that Bryan Wilson's cross-cultural analysis satisfies Malina's objection that "sect" analysis is too modern and Western for early Christ Movements. He tries to move the discussion forward by seeing Malina's "faction" as a *preliminary stage* to "sect" in a developmental sequence. For Elliott, the Jesus Movement begins as a person-centered, deviant faction, still embedded in, and ideologically bound to Israel, in conflict with other factions (Herodians and Pharisees), and in protest against the abuses of "Israel," led by its Temple aristocracy. However, because of stress, instability, and social change, the faction undergoes social and ideological differentiation and dissociation from its encapsulating structure, Israel, a "parent body." Although only a small group, the sect considers itself to be the true Israel. It is a voluntary association open to all, especially the deprived and dissatisfied, and it offers them social acceptance and material support. It seeks to be egalitarian (it is not), yet is totalistic, stressing an ethic of perfection, distinctive values, beliefs, and behaviors, and special rituals of inclusion and exclusion. It is increasingly group-centered, insulating itself from the rest of the world. Nonetheless, the sect continues to share many values of the parent group and the macrosociety, and will undergo some accommodation for the changing needs of its members or the changing nature of the society.

---

126. Malina, "Conflict Approach," 15.
127. Malina, "Jesus as Charismatic Leader?" 56–57; Miyahara, "Charisma."
128. Elliott, "The Jewish Messianic Movement."

Elliott's view that a sect is responding to the macrosociety is indebted to Wilson's category "response to the world." His recent thesis that a faction evolves into a differentiated and dissociated sect is somewhat reminiscent of Weber's developmental schema, although Elliott focuses on an earlier developmental stage and does not analyze the bureaucratic institution type; similarly, his view that the Christ-believing sect is a "child" of its Judean "parent" is an insight indebted to Troeltsch, though Troeltsch refused to apply the model to early Christianity.[129]

It is difficult to correlate all these group models. If Malina judges Weber's and Troeltsch's "sect" to be anachronistic for the ancient world in general and therefore early Christ-believing groups, how do Cooley's primary and secondary groups fare in relation to Malina's model? Coalitions are not permanent and in that respect are like Cooley's secondary groups.[130] Three of Boissevain's subsets of coalitions—"cliques," "gangs," and "factions"[131]—share Cooley's key trait for *primary* groups, namely, face-to-face relationships, but of course they are not families.[132] The coalition type called "action sets" is goal-oriented and in that respect seems to fit Cooley's *secondary* groups, but the latter in many respects comes closer to corporations. Thus, while there are overlaps, these analyses do not always correspond. Why?

One reason is that they come from different disciplines—Mediterranean cultural anthropology (Boissevain), cross-cultural sociology (Wilson), and classical European sociology (Weber; Troeltsch), to which I have added classical American sociology (Cooley). Another reason is that the complexity of the larger Greco-Roman social system is being analyzed differently. For example, how and to what extent can separate, discrete, disembedded groups develop within the larger Greco-Roman society?

---

129. Blenkinsopp, "Interpretation," uses the parent-child metaphor; see chap. 1.

130. See chap. 4.

131. Boissevain, *Friends of Friends*, 176–205; Malina, "A Conflict Approach," 20–27.

132. See above, p. 167.

Four Group Models

In this chapter, I restrict myself to four small group models that help to illumine the Matthean group: 1) a leadership model; 2) a task allocation model; 3) a group/grid model; and 4) an organismic, evolutionary model. All four are etic, homomorphic models. They are neither true nor false, but heuristic ways of imagining groups.[133]

A Leadership Model

The first model derives from "leaderless group" theory. Paradoxically, "leaderless group" theory holds that there are no real leaderless groups. Aubrey Fisher, a communications specialist who writes about "leaderless groups," affirms that *all groups develop status hierarchy*.[134] In *so-called* leaderless groups, status is not "ascribed," either by birth or a grant from a superior, but "acquired" or "achieved," that is, awarded by the group, usually on the basis of behavior that has been of the most benefit for meeting group goals. The language and conceptuality of small group behavior in this theory are virtually the same as in Mediterranean anthropology. It should be added that the Fisher and Ellis model is not a Weberian personality trait model ("born to lead"), a theory that often lacks due attention to reciprocity between leaders and followers (see above); neither is it a "leadership style" approach (democratic or autocratic—there is no *laissez-faire* leadership), which does not pay sufficient attention to the situation; and, conversely, neither is it a situational approach, which seems to rely too heavily on social context alone. It is a *"functions" approach*, and the functions are oriented toward goal achievement and group maintenance, that is, toward task functions and socio-emotive functions.[135] Here is the Fisher/Ellis leadership model:

---

133. See further Duling, "Small Groups."
134. Fisher and Ellis, *Small Group Decision Making*, 242–44.
135. See further Duling, "Small Groups."

Model 6.1 Leader Emergence
(Aubrey Fisher in Fisher and Ellis, *Small Group Decision Making*, 243)

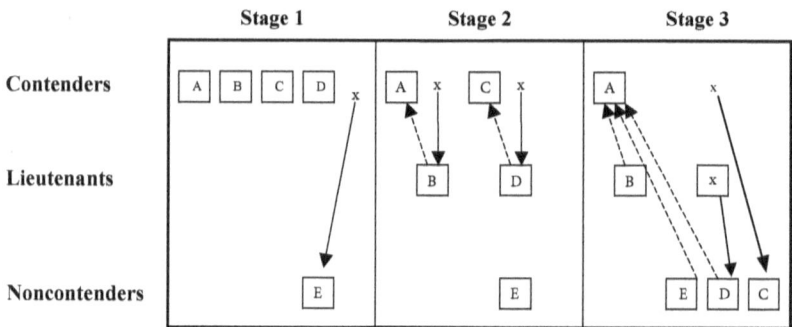

This model is a three-stage developmental model for the emergence of leaders over a period of time. During Stage One, usually brief, some members (= E) are eliminated from leadership, either because they are uninformed, excessively rigid, or in some other way do not contribute to the goals or maintenance of the group. During Stage Two, two or more contenders (= A, C) emerge by attracting lieutenants who have dropped out of leadership contention and support them (= B, D). During this stage, which is relatively longer, some potential leaders are eliminated and factions develop around the competing members (=A, C). During Stage Three, one member emerges as leader (= A) as a result of the demise of the competition (= C), and the leader may be joined by the other coalitions (= B, D, and perhaps E). Variations in the model are that Stage Two may be dropped altogether, in which case a single leader emerges very quickly. Also, a leader may be deposed, in which case the cycle would begin at Stage Two; Stage Three may not appear, in which case there would be shared leadership, although this is rare.

I suggest that Matthew's Gospel represents Stage Two anticipating Stage Three. There seem to be competing leaders within the "brotherhood," thus suggesting the emergence of factions. In the gospel the tension between itinerant and emergent local leadership is but one example. There is at least "acquired leadership." However, the scene about Peter (16:17–19) suggests "ascribed leadership," authority granted by a superior to a subordinate. This passage suggests not only "succession," but authority which moves the group toward Stage Three.[136] Additionally, literate scribal activity (including the Matthean writer's!)[137] and control of inner-group disputes (Matt 18:15-20)[138] suggest status differentiation.

A Task Allocation Model

As implied by the discussion of corporations and coalitions above, social theories since Weber and Troeltsch have persistently contrasted structured institutions with non-structured groups.[139] As discussed in chapter 5, the Mediterranean network anthropologist Jeremy Boissevain contrasts the structured *corporation* with the unstructured *coalition*, and then develops several subclassifications of coalitions, one of which is the faction.[140] For Boissevain the "corporation" has governing rules and a variety of offices, which tends to be stable and permanent and has an increasing division of labor (one person—one task).[141] The "coalition" is defined as "a collection of people within some larger, encapsulating structure [such as a kingdom or empire] consisting of distinct parties in temporary alliances for some limited purpose."[142] It lacks stability and is impermanent, has core members and peripheral members, arises in new situations, and reflects changing circumstances. When its purposes are achieved, it either disappears or evolves into a corporation. Its division of labor is less variable, thus non-hierarchical. There are three subtypes. Similar models have been developed by Ph. G. Herbst.[143] Herbst contrasts

---

136. In the third century CE Roman bishops appealed to this ascribed leadership passage to defend apostolic succession.

137. See chap. 9 below.

138. See chap. 8 below.

139. Duling, "Insights from Sociology."

140. Malina, *Christians Origins*, 19–31, 13–67; "A Conflict Approach"; "Patron and Client," 14; cf. Boissevain, *Friends of Friends*, 203.

141. Herbst, *Alternatives to Hierarchies*, 18–19, 29–40; cf. Malina, *Christian Origins*, 66–67; see chap. 5 above.

142. Malina, "Patron and Client," 15; "Conflict Approach," 20; cf. Boissevain, *Friends of Friends*, 171.

143. Herbst, *Alternatives to Hierarchies*, 29–40.

hierarchical organizations (=corporations) with two non-hierarchical groups (=coalitions) on the basis of *task allocation*,[144] that is, the "matrix group" in which one person can carry out several tasks and the "composite autonomous group" in which one person can carry out all tasks. Both Boissevain and Herbst have influenced Malina's analysis of groups, and Malina has added a third subtype, namely, "network group" in which there is a network of geographically dispersed groups and individuals and where direct control is absent.[145]

Matthew 23:8–10, the rejection of titles, seems to have an ideology of a non-hierarchical group of the composite autonomous type (B1) if one discounts modern individualism and sees this passage as a limited "egalitarian" ideology. The references to itinerant apostles, prophets, and teachers discussed above would seem to suggest an alternative non-hierarchical model, that is, Malina's network group (B3). While Malina suggests no direct control, the itinerants, though outsiders, would seem to have had *some* measure of status and authority. They are, after all, agents of a sender. Yet, this model does not seem to correspond to still another dimension, scribal leadership, or to Peter's special ascribed status. If one assumes that Matthew writes in some local place, some hint at a status hierarchy appears to be present; Matthew's text thus betrays the movement toward hierarchical organization. In Overman's terms, there is a "developing hierarchy within the Matthean community."[146]

---

144. Ibid., 16–40.
145. Malina, "Patron and Client," 67, 154; see chap. 5, Model 5.1.
146. Overman, *Matthew's Gospel*, 123.

"Egalitarian" Ideology, Leadership, and Factional Conflict

Model 6.2 Task Allocation Models (= Model 5.1)
(from Herbst, *Alternatives to Hierarchies*, and Malina, *Christian Origins*, 66–67)

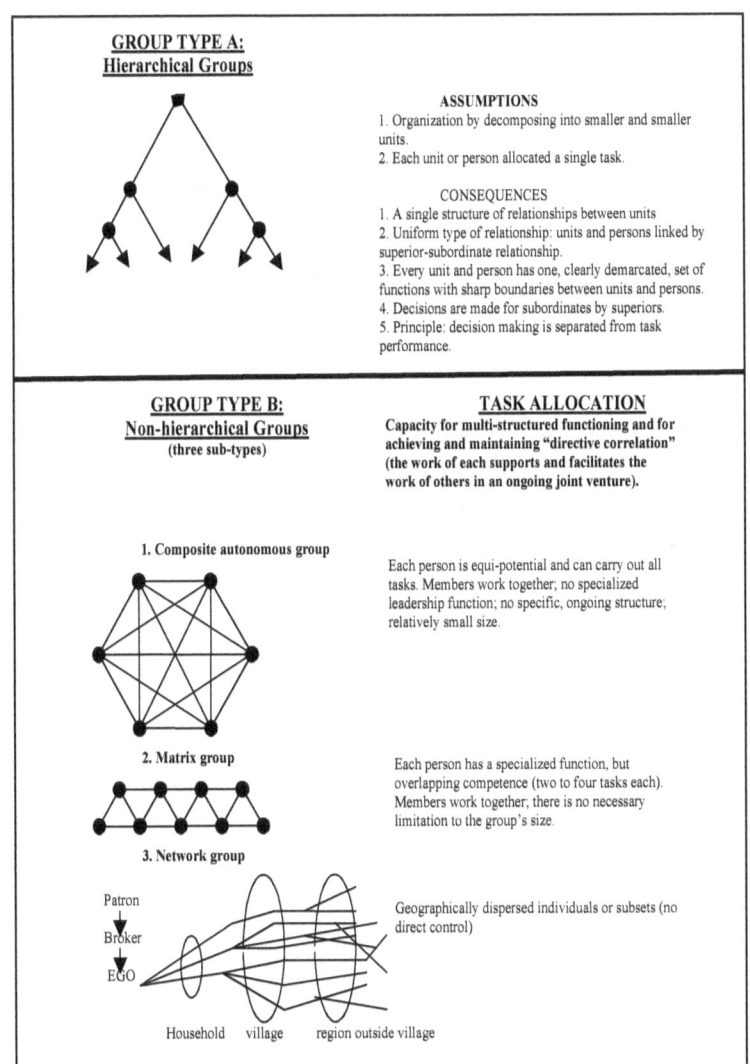

A Group/Grid Model

Malina has attempted to develop Mary Douglas' group/grid model for organizing social groups.[147] The model contains quadrants and is

147. Malina, *Christian Origins*, 28–97.

more complicated; it is necessary to pay close attention to definitions and concepts. "Group" is either strong or weak. In a *strong group* there are strong pressures to conform to the group's beliefs, norms, and behaviors. In a *weak group* the pressures to conform are weak. On the horizontal axis strong group is to the right, weak group is on the left. "Grid" refers to the extent to which one's experiences match established norms, beliefs, and practices in the larger social order. Grid is either high or low. *High grid* means a high degree of conformity to such norms, beliefs, and practices; *low grid* means a low degree of conformity. On a vertical axis high grid means more conformity, low grid means less conformity, suggesting deviance.[148] Malina sets Herbst's task group models and Boissevain's network coalition model within Mary Douglas' group/grid model,[149] as follows:

Model 6.3 A Grid/Group Model
(from Douglas, *Natural Symbols*, Boissevain, *Friends of Friends*, and Herbst, *Alternatives*, adapted by Malina, *Christian Origins*, 66–67)

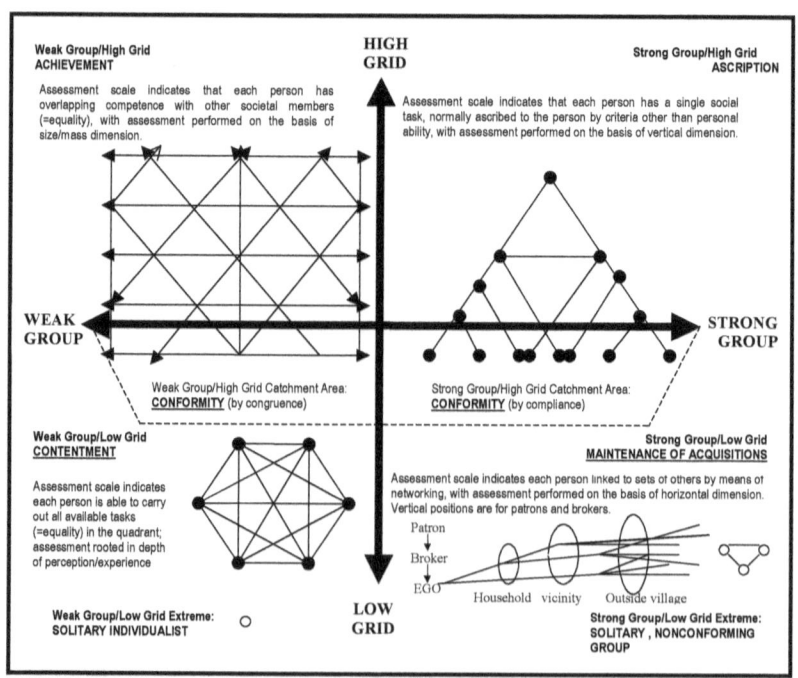

148. See chaps. 4, 6, and 8 in this book.
149. Douglas, *Natural Symbols*.

"Egalitarian" Ideology, Leadership, and Factional Conflict   177

Holding the variety of groups in mind is not easy, but it is possible to simplify. For Malina, the key point is that all the New Testament writers but the Fourth Evangelist fall into the lower right quadrant, that is, they are *strong group*, that is, have *tight boundaries*, but are *weak grid*, that is they are *deviant with respect to the values of the larger society*. In other words, they conform to the network group pattern. Leland White's analysis of the Sermon on the Mount follows Malina in placing the Matthean gospel in this quadrant.[150]

The data as interpreted above suggests that the community of Matthew fits this quadrant location, but the question is just *where* within that quadrant the Matthean group would appear, that is, *how* deviant is the Matthean group, or in what sense it is marginal? In so far as the actual reality is that Matthew's group is scribally led, contains various factions and emergent leaders, and hints at a developing status hierarchy symbolized by the status of Peter (not to mention the author), it is necessary to move the Matthean group *up the vertical axis* somewhat toward the horizontal line that demarcates a hierarchical institution, that is, *toward the high grid quadrant*. As noted in other models, assimilation is occurring. Interestingly, Atkins' study of the Pauline churches places them in a similar location.[151]

An Organismic (Evolutionary) Model

Groups are born, grow, develop, decline, and die, that is, evolve through stages, or go through a life cycle. In an attempt to arrive at a general model of group evolution, Bruce Tuckman's classic article synthesized fifty studies and isolated four stages of a typical group's development.[152] In a revised version with Jensen he later added a fifth stage illustrating the dissolution of the group.[153] This classic model can be stated: 1) *forming* (acquainting, seeking leaders); 2) *storming* (conflicts, criticizing leaders); 3) *norming* (conflict resolution, cohesion, roles, rules); 4) *performing* (productivity, problem solving); and

---

150. White, "Group and Grid," 61–90.
151. Atkins, *Egalitarian Community*, 144.
152. Tuckman, "Developmental Sequence."
153. Tuckman and Jensen, "Stages of Small-Group Development Revisited." See Malina, "Early Christian Groups," 103–6; Duling, "Small Groups," 185.

5) *adjourning*. Insofar as the Matthean group has internal conflict, it is still in the *storming* phase of development; however, its attention to Torah norms and implied roles and Petrine passages suggest a considerable development toward *norming*, and its mission activity preserves a type of *performing*.

Conclusion

I have suggested that Matt 23:8–10 represents a limited "egalitarian" ideology that approximates the ideal of Herbst's composite autonomous group. However, this "limited egalitarianism," which attempts to bond the group by rejecting Pharisaic titles of status, is in tension with the actual social reality represented in the gospel as a whole. There would appear to be itinerant leaders in the Matthean group; these represent a modified network faction and a performing stage of development. The transference of authority to Peter, an example of ascribed honor, hints at even more fixed and developed status roles. Scribal leadership and interpretation of the Torah also suggests a norming stage of development. In other words, this "leaderless group," like all "leaderless groups," shows clear signs of factional conflict and emergent leadership. Matthew's texts suggest some movement away from various coalitions *toward* an institutional hierarchy, a corporation. Although the author of Matthew instructs his group by means of a limited "egalitarian" ideology perhaps inherited from Q and perhaps the Jesus tradition, which is a counterpoint to outsider Pharisaic models of group leadership, this ideology would not easily bond the group for any extended period of time. It was inevitable that Matthew's "egalitarian" ideology was in tension with the social necessity of organizing and developing leadership roles, and that as the group continued to evolve, a new ideology was developed to conform to it.

CHAPTER 7

The Matthean Brotherhood and Marginal Scribal Leadership[1]

> "The cult-association is primarily a family. Its head is called 'pater'... The members of these sodalities are brothers..."
>
> —A. D. Nock, 1924

RESEARCH ON THE GOSPEL of Matthew in the last half century is rich with studies about the Matthean "church."[2] Within the last few years social-historical and social-scientific critics have also begun to analyze the Matthean group. Studies include the Matthean "honor code,"[3] insider and outsider labeling,[4] economics and household themes,[5] the Matthean community as a form of sectarian Judaism,[6] intra-group conflicts and the geographical location of the community,[7]

---

1. The first version of this chapter was presented at the St. Andrews Conference on New Testament Interpretation and the Social Sciences in 1994; it was published in Philip Esler, ed., *Modelling Early Christianity*, 159–82. This version contains only minor changes.

2. Stanton "Origin and Purpose"; Meier, "Matthew, Gospel of," 625.

3. White, "Grid and Group."

4. Malina and Neyrey, *Calling Jesus Names*.

5. Crosby, *House of Disciples*; Love, "The Household"; *Jesus and Marginal Women*, chap. 1.

6. Overman, *Matthew's Gospel*; Saldarini, *Matthew's Christian-Jewish Community*.

7. Viviano, "Social World"; Balch, ed., *Social History*; Theissen, *Gospels*; Saldarini, *Matthew's Christian-Jewish Community*.

gender issues,[8] marginality,[9] ideology,[10] and a variety of other social concerns.[11]

Theoretical Orientation

In this chapter I shall again use as a larger framework Gerhard Lenski's and Jonathan Turner's view that the Roman Empire is an advanced agrarian society, which for Kautsky is a commercialized aristocratic empire (chapter 3). The advanced agrarian society perspective paralleled by Alföldy's vertical arrangement of Roman orders and regionalized for Palestine by David Fiensy has been used as a macrosocial context (chapters 3–6). What has *not* been emphasized so far is Lenski's and Turner's view that in such societies small "fictive" kin groups emerge as substitute primary groups or surrogate kin groups when the bonds of real kin groups are in decline.[12] Their view suggests that social-scientific small-group theory as discussed in chapter 6 will be helpful. There I defined "group" and presented several social-scientific models of groups: the "charismatic community," the "sect," the "faction," the "leaderless group," and groups defined by "task allocation," that is, hierarchical groups versus non-hierarchical groups (composite, matrix, and networking groups, the group/grid model).

I am particularly interested in combining these macro- and micro-orientations with scholarly discussions of voluntary associations in the ancient Mediterranean world. From a social-scientific perspective, "voluntary associations" are in part surrogate family groups.[13] Such a view is not totally inconsistent with Elliott's attempt to maintain the "sect" category; indeed, it is related to other scholars who analyze Judaism and early Christianity in terms of a "sect,"[14] some of whom

---

8. Anderson, "Matthew: Gender and Reading"; Corley, "Jesus' Table Practice"; Love, "Household"; "The Place of Women"; *Jesus and Marginal Women*.

9. See chap. 5 above.

10. See chap. 6 above.

11. Stanton, "The Communities of Matthew"; *A Gospel*; see chap. 4.

12. Lenski, *Power and Privilege*; Lenski and Lenski, *Human Societies*, 164–208; Turner, *Societal Stratification*.

13. This perspective has been given support recently by Harland, "Familial Dimensions"; *Dynamics of Identity*.

14. E.g., Saldarini, *Matthew's Christian-Jewish Community*.

use the parent/child analogy indebted to Weber and Troeltsch.[15] However, as I proposed in the last chapter, the Matthean group has moved not only beyond the "Jesus faction" as Malina describes it, but is also beginning to move beyond the "sect" as Elliott describes it. The Matthean group has factions *within* it[16] and, although it preserves certain forms of "sectarian" ideology and practice, it reflects a level of assimilation, formal organization, development of norms, and style of leadership which suggest that its organization is beginning to be, in Weberian terms, "routinized," that is, it might be called an "incipient institution" or an "incipient corporation."[17]

This perspective needs to be tested with other variables in the gospel. Here I focus on three features: "brotherhood" language, internal disciplinary processes, and scribal leadership. The level of analysis is primarily microsocial and, while conflict between the Matthean group and other groups plays its role, I focus on the Matthean group itself. While this judgment is a matter of degree of formation based on a broader typological continuum than polar ideal types, and may also contain elements of a "Western" organizational criterion that would be rejected by Bryan Wilson, I shall attempt to undergird this characterization by an analysis at a lower level of abstraction, the Matthew group in relation to small "brotherhood" groups, the voluntary associations in Mediterranean society, as well as emergent leadership roles within the Matthean group, particularly "the scribe."

Voluntary Associations in Mediterranean Antiquity

Following in part the views of Gerhard Lenski, Jonathan Turner states that in advanced agrarian societies increasing vertical stratification is accompanied by some weakening of the extended family and the multiplication of small groups.[18] Turner states: "Kinship, while still important, becomes less dominant as the organization axis of the society as alternate structures proliferate and expand . . . Voluntary

---

15. E.g., Blenkinsopp, "Interpretation," 1–4; Overman, *Matthew's Gospel and Formative Judaism*, 8–9; Stanton, *A Gospel*, 85–107; Kampen, "Communal Discipline."
16. See chap. 6 above.
17. See chaps. 5 and 8.
18. Turner, *Societal Stratification*, 63–64; also Saldarini, *Pharisees*, 60.

associations increase as a highly differentiated population seeks friends and contacts in a variety of economic, political, religious, and social associations."[19] The point should not be overstated: actual families and households are still one of the indispensable social units for understanding Mediterranean society.[20] Still, the tendency for voluntary associations to appear is present. Anthropologists and sociologists have observed that voluntary associations help rural people who migrate to urban areas to preserve their ethnic heritage and cultural traditions and to adapt to a new, rapidly changing cultural context. Such associations are sometimes called "fictional kinship groups."[21]

As has been stated in previous chapters, Lenski's primary example of an advanced agrarian society is the Roman Empire.[22] It is not surprising that scholars of Greco-Roman antiquity have analyzed groups in ancient agrarian societies.[23] Typical were the so-called voluntary associations (Greek *koinoniai*; Latin *collegia*),[24] evidence for which comes primarily from inscriptions and documentary papyri.[25] These associations were different from such associations in modern, free societies in the West.[26] Most were small, often about twenty to thirty members, and mainly local. There were different subtypes: ethnic groups originally modeled on the *polis* (*koina; politeiai*); older boy's and young men's "athletic clubs" (*ephebeia; neoi*) linked to the

19. Turner, ibid., 86–87.

20. Banks, *Paul's Idea of Community*; White, "Scaling the Strongman's 'Court'"; Crosby, *House of Disciples*; Elliott, *Home* (1990); Malina, *New Testament World*, 3rd ed., 134–60.

21. Little, "The Role of Voluntary Associations," 594; see Kerri, "Studying Voluntary Associations"; Eisenstadt, "Sociological Aspects"; Geertz, "Rotating Credit Association"; Kerr, "Voluntary Associations"; Caulkins, "Voluntary Associations."

22. Lenski and Lenski, *Human Societies*, 176, 178, 179, 182, 188, 189, 191.

23. Dill, *Roman Society*, 255; Forbes, *Neoi*, 2–3; Heichelheim, "Part II: Roman Syria," 208; Rostovtzeff, *Economic and Social History*, 1048–51, 1057–66; MacMullen, *Roman Social Relations*, 17–20, 71–85; Judge, *Social Pattern*; Wilken, "Collegia, Philosophical Schools, and Theology," 280; Meeks, *First Urban Christians*, 31, 77, 205 n. 139; Kraabel, "Unity and Diversity," 52–53.

24. For an exploration of voluntary associations, see chap. 8 below.

25. Waltzing, *Étude historique*; Ziebarth, *Das griechische Vereinswesen*; Kornemann, "Koinon; Collegium"; Broughton, "Part IV: Roman Asia," 841–46; Rostovtzeff, *Social and Economic History*, 1057–66; Danker, *Benefactor*, 501; recently, Harland, "Familial Dimensions"; *Dynamics of Identity*.

26. Robertson, *Voluntary Associations*.

gymnasium; "industrial" guilds and associations of traders;[27] trade guilds; professional associations; theater guilds of actors, dancers, and artists; burial societies; and philosophical schools. The aim of most associations was, broadly speaking, "social." Normally they were supported by patrons, some of whom endowed shrines to preserve their memories in annual birthday rites. Although association members could come from various social strata, there was a natural tendency for them to mirror the larger society's ranking system. Yet, members could sometimes achieve some semblance of higher social status otherwise denied them in society at large. "Freedmen," for example, "saw in the association the only means to escape their isolation and weakness, to acquire some little consideration and even a little influence, finally to create for themselves in the society, in the city, an honorable place."[28]

The associations offered members "a sense of identity and comradeship, a social unit larger than the family and smaller than the state where they could meet together with friends, eat and drink, worship, play, and share common experiences."[29] When associations disturbed public order or were suspected of being politically motivated social movements, however, the Roman authorities labeled these *sodalitates hataeriae* and from time to time sought to dissolve them,[30] or at least control them by forbidding new groups to form, requiring official membership registration, and limiting the frequency of their meetings. Yet, in most cases, associations were legally tolerated and even sanctioned.

In varying degrees, the associations were "religious." However, some were specifically "cult associations" (*thiasoi*), formed to venerate some deity. Rostovtzeff wrote that native cult associations had long been known in the East and that such groups were progenitors of the Greek *thiasoi* known from inscriptions at Palmyra and Dura. In this part of the Mediterranean world Greeks often joined the native professional and religious associations found in the cities. Thus, the associations became hellenized and contained persons from different

27. Listed in Broughton, ibid., 841–44.
28. Jean Waltzing (1895) quoted in Wilken, "Collegia," 281.
29. Wilken, ibid., 281; see Dill, *Roman Society*, 267.
30. Johnson et al., *Ancient Roman Statutes*, 82; see esp. Suetonius *Julius Caesar* 42:3; *Augustus* 32:1.

ethnic backgrounds, although they were of similar social strata in their respective collectivities.[31]

Again, the voluntary associations can be conceived as "fictive kinship groups," that is, "brotherhoods." A. D. Nock put it this way: "the cult-association is primarily a family. Its head is called 'pater'... The members of these sodalities are brothers... The cult-association, then, is a family and feels itself such. Its great importance in history is that it provided an opportunity for the evolution of new religious ideas."[32] This description could describe many early Christ-believing groups,[33] and in my opinion certainly does describe the Matthean group—except that the writer rejected the term "father" as a leadership title.[34]

Before returning to Matthew, a comment must be made about Judean associations. Judean professional guilds were common in Palestine and elsewhere.[35] In the Diaspora, Judeans formed ethnic associations.[36] Some of them evolved out of the Judean military settlement (*katoikia*). The name for the "coming together" of a Judean cult association in the Diaspora was *synagōgē*,[37] "synagogue," or *proseuchē*, "house of prayer," although the latter term could be used for a place of worship.[38] Evidence from four of the six major Diaspora synagogues—Priene (Asia Minor), Delos (Aegean Islands), Dura (Syria), and probably Stobi (Macedonia)—shows that Judean associations met first in converted houses, and were thus "house-synagogues" (Hebrew *bet keneset*, "meeting-house"); only subsequently was money raised to convert them into buildings for community use.[39] The Dura example is especially important, for it demonstrates the conversion of a house

---

31. Rostovtzeff, *Social and Economic History* 2, 1064-65.

32. Nock, "Historical Importance," 105.

33. Meeks, *The First Urban Christians*, saw them as one of four basic models for Pauline communities.

34. On Matt 23:8-10, see chap. 6.

35. Applebaum, "Organization," 464-66; Cohen, *From the Maccabees to the Mishnah*, 119-20; Jeremias, *Jerusalem*, 18-21.

36. Leon, *The Jews*; Applebaum, "Organization"; Kraabel, "Social Systems"; "Unity and Diversity"; Cohen, *From the Maccabees to the Mishnah*.

37. Danker, *Benefactor*, 81; Kraabel, "Unity and Diversity."

38. Leon, *The Jews*, 139; Gutman, "Synagogue Origins," 3.

39. Kraabel, "Unity and Diversity," 81.

into a house-synagogue in Syria at the end of the first century CE, the period in which the Gospel of Matthew was written.[40] It corresponds to recent views that "house-synagogues" were only beginning to be transformed into actual community buildings in late first and early second-century Palestine.[41]

In Alexandria there was an officially recognized *politeuma*, or political body of foreigners, in effect an umbrella corporation of smaller associations headed by a central council of elders and priests (*gerousia*) and an *ethnarch*;[42] in Rome the smaller associations seem to have been more independent.[43] As with most ancient voluntary associations, Judean associations held regular meetings, passed resolutions, honored members and non-members, sent delegations to authorities, collected state taxes, worshipped, and studied.[44]

Finally, some Palestinian Judean factions were associations. Based on Josephus rather than the later Rabbinic literature, Anthony Saldarini claimed that "the Pharisees . . . were a literate, corporate, voluntary association which constantly sought influence with the governing class. As such they belonged to the retainer class, a group of people above the peasants and other lower classes but dependent on the governing class and ruler for the place in society . . . The Pharisees' association probably functioned as a social movement organization seeking to change society."[45] Many scholars would view the Essenes as another "literary, corporate, voluntary association," not a "reformist sect" like the Pharisees, but an "introversionist sect."[46] In addition, a variety of social-movement groups might be considered voluntary associations.[47]

Having looked briefly at some actual groups, the voluntary associations, in the ancient Mediterranean world, I now move to an even

40. Thompson, "Dura-Europos," 242.
41. Meyers and Strange, *Archaeology*, 140–41; Kee, "Transformation"; Cohen, *From the Maccabees to the Mishnah*, 114.
42. Applebaum, "The Organization," 475.
43. Leon, *The Jews*, 170, 181.
44. Applebaum, "The Organization," 488.
45. Saldarini, *Pharisees*, 281 = "Pharisees," 301–302.
46. Wilson, *Magic*, 23–24; Esler, "Introverted Sectarianism."
47. Theissen, *Sociology*; Horsley and Hanson, *Bandits*; Perrin and Duling, *The New Testament* (1994), 55–58.

lower level of abstraction, the Matthean group. I begin with brotherhood language.

The Matthean Brotherhood Association

Among the gospel writers Matthew alone uses the term *ekklēsia*, usually translated "church" (Matt 16:18: 18:17 [2x]); thus, it has become the usual term to designate the Matthean "community." Given the LXX rendering of Hebrew "assembly" (*qāhāl*) as both *synagōgē* and *ekklēsia* and the relation of these two terms to the "house-synagogue" and "house-church," it is a natural description for the Matthean group. Nonetheless, for this study I focus on the term "brotherhood" (*adelphotēs*) for three reasons. First, the *ekklēsia* translated by English "church" has become overloaded with centuries of Christian content. Second, while *ekklēsia* can be correlated with Matthew's extensive household and family/kinship language,[48] "brotherhood" is a fictive kinship term that comes closer to capturing the overtones of surrogate family language in Greco-Roman associations,[49] including Judean associations such as the Essenes (*B.J.* 2.8.3; 1QS 6:1; CD 9:2)[50] and, if they existed this early, the Pharisaic *Haburōth*, or fellowship groups.[51] Third, although the term "brotherhood" is not found in Matthew—it is attested in 1 Peter 2:17 in a "household code" context (2:11–3:12; cf. 5:19)—"brother" occurs very frequently, about twice as often as in Mark and Luke (Mark 20x; Luke 24x; Matthew 39x).[52] Sometimes it refers to actual kin or is "plurisignificant,"[53] but, whereas the Gospel of Mark has only one fictive kin passage (Mark 3:31–35 = Matt 12:46–50 = Luke 8:19–21), the Gospel of Matthew has seven passages (5:21–26; 7:1–5; 12:46–50; 18:15–22, 35; 23:8–10; 25:40; 28:10). This usage points to a "fictive kinship association"[54] and suggests that the group

48. Crosby, *House of Disciples*; Love, "The Household"; "The Place of Women."

49. Von Soden, "*Adelphos*, etc.," 144; Nock, "Historical Importance"; recently, Harland, "Familial Dimensions."

50. Gnilka, "Die Kirche des Matthäus."

51. Neusner, "The Fellowship (*Haburah*)"; Urbach, *The Sages*, 584–85; Douglas, "Matthew 18:15–17"; Wilkins, "Brother, Brotherhood," 783.

52. See Luz, *Matthew 1–7*, 54.

53. See chap. 4 above.

54. Jeremias, *Parables of Jesus*, 109 n. 82; Davies and Allison, *Matthew*, 1:512–13; see Pitt-Rivers, "Pseudo-Kinship."

in and for which the author of the First Gospel writes considered itself a "brotherhood."⁵⁵ Thus, one description of Matthew's *ekklēsia* is an *adelphotēs*, "brotherhood" (cf. 1 Pet 2:17; 5:9).

I shall now discuss the seven passages in relation to groups in Mediterranean antiquity.

Matthew 12:(46–)50: "Whoever does the will of my Father in heaven is my brother and sister and mother"

Outside the canonical texts, there are various versions of the full anecdote (*Gosp. Thom.* 99; *Gosp. Eb.* 5 [Epiph. *Ad.Haer.* 30.14.5], dependent on Matthew) and its climactic conclusion (2 Clem 9:11). The Matthean author follows his Markan source so closely that he creates anachronisms: he says that Jesus is standing "outside" (12:46b: *exō*), although he omits Mark's setting in "a house" (Mark 3:19b) and he follows Mark in adding "sister" (12:50 [Mark 3:35]; contrast 2 Clem 9:11: "my brothers"), as he also does in the Nazareth scene (13:55–56 [Mark 6:3]); cf. *Gosp. Eb.* 5), although the Matthean context demands only "mother" and "brothers" (Mark 3:31, 32 [S, B, etc.]). Thus, he makes only minor changes: Jesus speaks to the people (12:46a; cf. 12:15, 23), the anonymous individual reports to Jesus (12:47a), and Jesus says "my father in heaven" (see 6:9 and Luke 11:2).

More important is the Matthean placement of the passage in a strategic location. In Matthew 11–12 the people increasingly lack understanding and the Pharisees increasingly oppose Jesus. Q material about "this evil and adulterous generation" is inserted just before the true kinship passage (12:39). Immediately after the passage, Jesus explains with parables and allegories (Matthew 13). Then, Matthew 14–17, increasingly diverging from sources, portrays Jesus as turning more and more to his core group. Thus, this passage in Matthew 12 is pivotal: Jesus' true kin are those who, in contrast to Pharisaic-led "Israel," do the will of "my Father," namely, Jesus' true brothers.

---

55. Gnilka, "Die Kirche des Matthäus," 51; Trilling, *Das Wahre Israel*, 212; Overman, *Matthew's Gospel*, 95; Davies and Allison, *Critical and Exegetical Commentary* 1, 512–13.

Matthew 23:8-10: Ranking Forbidden: "You are all brothers"

You will recall from chapter 6 that in Matthew 23:8-10, a passage that occurs only in this gospel, the author forbids three titles for teachers: "Rabbi," "Father," and "Tutor." Four added phrases break the flow of the passage:[56] "on earth," "the heavenly," "the Christ," and "you are all brothers." The first three appear to be clearly Matthean (heaven/earth contrasts [Mark 7x; Luke 12x; Matt 16x, +7x redactional]);[57] it is therefore highly likely that the statement "you are all brothers" is also Matthean, as other "brother" passages seem to confirm. The point of the passage is that the Matthean group should not use titles of honor for teachers because Christ is the only Rabbi, God in heaven is the only Father, and Christ is the only Tutor: *"you are all brothers."* When such strong prohibitions occur, it is probable that the group either desires to practice what is forbidden, or is carrying out such practices.

It is now commonly held that this passage rejects synagogue titles of honor/status and corresponding "offices" emerging at Pharisee-led Jamnia in the late first century.[58] While this view is undoubtedly correct, the titles need to be seen in the light of a broader range of Judean cult associations. Diaspora synagogues were often formally organized as corporations and had a variety of officers with titles: *archisynagōgos* ("ruler of the synagogue"), *archōn* ("ruler"), *prostatis* ("helper," "patroness," "protector"), and *presbyteros* ("elder").[59] Cohen suggests that the local *archisynagōgos* can be translated "head of the association."[60]

Let us consider again the titles in Matthew 23.[61] "Rabbi" is found on Jerusalem ossuaries before 100 CE (*CII* 2.249, 275-77, 277-79), on later Palestinian cemetery inscriptions (Cohen 1981; Lapin 601), and in the Talmud for Pharisaic/Rabbinic teachers before 125 CE. Matthew elsewhere demotes this title by attributing its use to the traitor Judas (Matt 26:25, 49).

---

56. Viviano, "Social World," 8; see pp. 139-41, 155-58 above.

57. Luz, *Matthew 1-7*, 70.

58. Schürer et al., *History*, 325-27; Derrett, "Mt 23,8-10," 378-84; Viviano, "Social World," 10; Saldarini, "Delegitimation," 670-71.

59. Ziebarth, *Das griechische Vereinswesen*, *passim*; Setzer, "Rulers of the Synagogue," 841; Leon, *Jews*, 186-88; Meeks, *First Urban Christians*, 31.

60. Cohen, *From the Maccabees to the Mishnah*, 116.

61. See chap. 6. See Cohen, "Epigraphical Rabbis"; Lapin, "Rabbi"; Garland, *Intention*, 58 n. 23.

"Father," "Father of the Synagogue," and "Mother of the Synagogue" seem to have been titles for honored members of the Judean associations at Rome.[62] Additionally, "Father" occurs as an honorary title on synagogue inscriptions[63] and for authoritative teachers in the wisdom literature,[64] including Hillel and Shammai, and Saul ben Batnîth (ca. 80-120 CE).[65] It was said that King Jehoshaphat addressed the scholar/teacher as "Father, Father," "Rabbi, Rabbi," "Lord, Lord" (b. Mak. 24a; m. 'Aboth. 6.3;[66] compare Matt 7:21: "Lord, Lord"). "That pupils are related to their teachers as sons to fathers is a simile or parallel quite familiar in the Semitic (indeed the Asian) world."[67] "Father" is reserved by Matthew, of course, primarily for the heavenly father, as in this passage.[68]

Finally, the unusual Greek term *kathēgētēs*, or "private tutor,"[69] could be "used of founders and heads of philosophical schools."[70] Speculation exists that it might also represent Hebrew *mōreh*, "teacher," as in *mōreh hazzedek*, the "Teacher of Righteousness" (4QpPs[a] 37 [= 4Q171] 3:15-16; 1QpHab 2:8; CD 1:9-11), the founder of the Essenes, who, again, use "brothers" for their association (B.J. 2.8.3; 1QS 6:1; CD 9:2).[71]

In summary, Matthew disparages honorary titles that were in use in associations; again, it is possible that some Christ-believers in the Matthean group preferred such titles, or were using them. For Matthew they should not be used, "for you are all brothers." Yet, as observed in chapter 6, there is evidence that authoritative teachers did exist in the Matthean group. I shall say more about this apparent contradiction later.

---

62. Leon, *Jews*, 188-89.

63. Nock, "Historical Importance," 105; Leon, *Jews*, 188-89; Frey, *CII* I:494, 509, 511; Townsend, "Matthew XXIII.9"; Hengel, "Die Synagogeninschrift"; Hachlili, "Synagogue," 260; Viviano, "Social World," 20 n. 32.

64. Lemaire, "Writing and Writing Materials," 311.

65. Kohler, "Abba, Father"; Urbach, *Sages*, 186, 906 n. 38.

66. Garland, *The Intention of Matthew 23*, 58 n. 92.

67. Derrett, "Mt 23,8-10," 373.

68. Syreeni, "Between Heaven and Earth."

69. Winter, "Messiah as the Tutor."

70. Saldarini, "Delegitimation of Leaders," 670.

71. Gnilka, "Die Kirche des Matthäus."

Matthew 18:15-21, 35: Guidelines for Conflict Resolution in the Brotherhood

Matthew 18, the fourth of Matthew's five great discourses, is a tapestry of brotherhood rules. They are woven together from Mark, Q, Special M and Matthew's own additions.[72] While the whole chapter is important for my theme, and I shall analyze it in more detail in chapter 8, here I discuss only Matt 18:15-35, a section held together by the catchword "brother."

Matthew 18:15-20 contains a subunit, vv. 15-17, that reflects a legal process for conflict resolution within the Matthean group.[73]

v. 15a: if your brother	sins against you	convince him of his fault
v. 15: if he	listens to you	you have gained your brother
v. 16: if he does not	listen [to you]	take two or three witnesses
v. 17a: if he refuses to	listen to them	tell it to the *ekklēsia*
v. 17b: if he refuses to	listen to the *ekklēsia*	shun him ("tax collector/ Gentile")

Matthew 18:15 is based on Q 17:3, but the Matthean revision[74] more clearly echoes Leviticus 19:15-18,[75] especially verse 17: "You shall not hate your brother in your heart; you shall surely reproach your neighbor, and you shall bear no sin because of him" (see also 18:21; cf. 5:22). It should not be forgotten that Leviticus 19:15-18 is not only the source of Jesus' famous second commandment, "love your neighbor as yourself" (Lev 19:18; Matt 22:39 [Mark 12:31]), but contains the group regulation that hatred should not simmer inside ("in your heart") lest lying and deceit result. *One should argue one's case with the offending brother/neighbor.* The norm of reproaching one's neighbor from Leviticus became a major wisdom theme (Prov 26:24-25; 10:18; 25:9-10), and it was central for regulating group behavior among Judeans.[76]

---

72. Bornkamm, "Authority to 'Bind' and 'Loose,'" 37-40; Brooks, *Matthew's Community*, 99-107; Davies and Allison, *Matthew*, 1:750-53.

73. For a detailed analysis, see chap. 8 below.

74. Luz, *Matthew 1-7*, 65. Matthew has *kerdainō* (Mark 1x; Luke 1x; Matt 6x) and *paralambanō* (Mark 6x; Luke 7x; Matt 16x).

75. Bornkamm, "End-Expectation," 40.

76. Ben Sira 19:13-17; *T.Gad* 4:1-3; 1QS 6:1; see also CD 9:2-9; *Sifra* on Leviticus.

In Matthew group norms and judicial processes are combined. Matthew adds verses 16–17 to Q: should private reconciliation fail, taking along one or two others gives a total of "two or three witnesses." This rule echoes the Torah regulation to protect against perjury (Deut 19:15; compare vv. 19–20); a parallel occurs in the Talmud (*y. Yoma* 45c). The regulations sound similar to the rules of the *Iobakchoi*,[77] a voluntary association.

Matthew's final step, to report to the *ekklēsia*, does not explicitly mention a council of elders or other leaders, such as bishops. However, in responding to Frank Beare's view that none is present, W. D. Davies and Dale Allison write: "This is an argument from silence . . . Could one not just as easily assert that the presence of leaders is taken for granted?"[78] Perhaps Matthew is attempting to view the process in accord with the "limited egalitarian" ideology in 23:8–10; in any case *there are clearly leaders in the Matthean group.*[79] Finally, Matthew says that if the final step fails, the person is to be treated "as a Gentile and a tax collector" (Matt 5:46–57; 15:26; contrast 11:19 and 8:10 [Q]), presumably "shunned" (1 Cor 5:1–5; 2 Thess 3:6–15; 2 John 10).[80]

The authority to "bind and loose" ("Truly I say to you . . .") in verse 18, previously given to Peter alone in Matthew 16:17, is now given to a group.[81] In this context, the most convincing interpretation of *deō* ("bind") and *luō* ("loose"), used here in the plural (contrast Matthew 16), is the rabbinic sense of excommunication from (*'asar*) the group, perhaps because of sin (so John 20:23), and readmittance to (*shera*) the group (*b. Mo'ed* 16a).[82] In typical Matthean language, the human decision "on earth" will be honored by God "in heaven." *The issue is discipline in the brotherhood.* With regard to the above question about leaders within the assembled *ekklēsia*, Bornkamm comments

---

Kugel, "On Hidden Hatred and Open Reproach"; Schiffman, *Sectarian Law*, 89–109; Davies and Allison, *Matthew*, 1:786–87.

77. Douglas, "Matthew 18:15–17," 13–15.

78. Davies and Allison, *Matthew*, 2:786; cp. Brown and Meier, *Antioch and Rome*, 68–70.

79. See chap. 6 above.

80. So Harrington, *The Gospel of Matthew*, 269.

81. Thompson, *Matthew's Advice*, 193–94.

82. Dalman, *Die Worte Jesu*, 174–78; Billerbeck, *Kommentar*, 738–39; Duling, "Binding and Loosing," 9.

that in Judaism the terms *deō* ("bind") and *luō* ("loose") "describe the office which is conferred on the scribes..."[83]

Another subunit (vv. 19-20) inserted by Matthew (v. 19: "Again, I say to you") nails down the point, again in typical Matthean language, probably prayer language ("ask": 7:7-11; "in my name": 7:22; 10:22; "Father in heaven": Mark 1x; Luke 0x; Matt 12x[84]); yet, "two or three" could be witnesses/judges, that is, judicial,[85] and analogous to rabbinic scholars who gather to study Torah with the Dwelling Presence of God, or Spirit (*shekînah*) in their midst (*m. Aboth* 3:2).

Another unit (18:21-22) stresses unending reconciliation with one's "brother" (7 x 70 or 77) taken from Q 17:4 (Gen 4:24). The *Sifra* on Leviticus 19:17 has the theme of reproaching one's brother, and stresses it by doubling its "even four or five times," a rabbinic technique that means "it is to be repeated as often as necessary."[86] For the Matthean writer, the theme is further illustrated by the parable of the Unforgiving Servant (18:23-35), concluding with the necessity of forgiving "your brother" "from your heart" (18:35; *T. Gad* 6:7). Thus, one is again reminded of the Judean sayings prohibiting anger, as well as the next passage to be considered, Matthew 5:21-26.

In short, Matthew 18 incorporates a legal process for conflict resolution, a brotherhood discipline very reminiscent of other groups in Mediterranean antiquity, especially Judean cult associations such as the Essenes.

Matthew 5:21-26: "Do not be angry with your brother"

This text segment, the first of the six "antitheses" in the Sermon on the Mount, is similar to the just-discussed conflict resolution passage in Matthew 18:15-17, but it does not have the three-step legal process. In this passage the Torah command against murder (Exod 20:13; Deut 5:17) is heightened by condemning anger against one's "brother."[87]

---

83. Bornkamm, "The Authority to 'Bind' and 'Loose,'" 40.
84. Luz, *Matthew 1-7*, 65.
85. Harrington, *The Gospel of Matthew*, 269.
86. Kugel, "On Hidden Hatred and Open Reproach," 56.
87. Bultmann, *History*, 133-35; Guelich, "The Antitheses," 445.

The last two verses (5:25-26) from Q (Q 12:57-59[88]) may go back to Jesus[89] and there may be other Jesus traditions behind the anti-anger statements (esp. v. 22a[90]). However, it seems that verses 21-24 in their present form have been formulated by the Matthean writer. First, verse 21b restates the Torah prohibition against murder by summarizing Mosaic legislation about capital offenses (v. 21b: Exod 20:13; Deut 5:17; Exod 21:12 = Lev 24:17; Num 35:12; Deut 17:8-13), and in so doing it becomes formally like the verses that follow. Second, the initial thesis/antithesis (5:21-22a) is a Matthean form repeated in 5:33, modified in the other four antitheses, and analogous to Rabbinic teaching forms.[91] Third, Matthew 5:23-24 is packed with Matthean vocabulary (v. 23: *krisis, oun, prospherō, ekei, mimnēskomai*; v. 24: *aphes* [aorist imperative], *ekei, emprosthen, hypagō* [imperative?] *tote, elthōn* + verb[92]). Fourth, 5:22, formally like verse 21b, appears to contain expansions based on the Matthean tendency to form triads, and it contains parallel insults in Aramaic (`raka*) and Greek (*mōre*) (cp. 5:18).[93] Fifth, 5:24 is close to Matthew 6:2, 5, 16, but it has echoes in Mark 11:25 and *Didachē* 14:2, each of which refers to "any one"; thus, it is likely that Matthew changed "any one" to "brother" (cp. Matt 23:18-19). *In short, a plausible theory is that Matthew has created the first antithesis "on murder" from at least one Jesus tradition (5:25-27), probably more (vv. 22a, 24b), against anger. He stresses reconciliation with one's brother.*

What does "brother" mean in Matthew 5:21-26? In the first place, the context suggests that it is not gender inclusive, including "sister." The following teachings about not looking lustfully "at a woman (*gynaika*)" (5:28) and not divorcing one's wife (*gynaika*) (5:31) are clearly from a male perspective. Second, some commentators have argued that pre-Matthean traditions here require "fellow Israelite." From this perspective the "altar" (*thysiastērion*, 5:23, 24) would be the Jerusalem altar, and the *synhedrion* (v. 22) would refer to the pre-70 Jerusalem

---

88. Kloppenborg, "Blessing and Marginality," 146.

89. Funk and Hoover et al., *The Five Gospels*, 141-42.

90. Brooks, *Matthew's Community*, 30-33.

91. Smith, *Tannaitic Parallels*, 27-50; Daube, *The New Testament*, 55-60; Suggs, *Wisdom*, 111-15; Duling, "Against Oaths," 99-100.

92. Luz, *Matthew 1-7*, 281 n 9.

93. Davies and Allison, *Matthew*, 1:491.

Sanhedrin, thus giving progressively intensive forms of punishment (village tribunal → Jerusalem Sanhedrin → Gehenna fire). However, the argument that the Matthean writer formulated the passage suggests another interpretation. His love of triads and millennial themes can have led to the anachronistic *thysiastērion*. An analogy is that Mishnaic pronouncements about the Temple continued to be made after the Temple had been destroyed.[94] Correspondingly, the Matthean *synhedrion* would have referred not to the Jerusalem high court, but to a *local court*, as it does in Matthew 10:17, thus suggesting the process for conflict resolution just discussed (Mark 13:9).[95]

In any case, the passage presents *four communal rules for the brotherhood* (5:22–26) in contrast to "whoever kills shall be liable to judgment" (5:21b). I lay out the verses as follows:

1. every one who	is angry to his *brother*	shall be liable to the judgment
2. whoever says *raka*	to his *brother*	shall be liable to the sanhedrin
3. whoever	says, 'You fool!'	shall be liable to the gehenna fire
4. If you . . .	remember your *brother*	leave . . . go . . . be reconciled with your *brother*

Formally, these rules look like the much-discussed *lex talionis*-type "sentences of holy law,"[96] examples of which can be found elsewhere in Matthew (e.g., Matt 5:19; 6:14–15). With regard to content, the first rule opposes anger towards a brother (v. 22a). It echoes the influential legal text for Judean groups noted in connection with Matthew 18:15–17, namely, Leviticus 19:17 ("You shall not hate your brother in your heart . . ."). Again, there are parallels with the Leviticus "reproach" traditions of Judean associations, especially represented in the Dead Sea Scrolls. 1QS 5:25 builds on this Leviticus text when it states: "Let no man address his [brother] with anger, or ill-temper, or obduracy, or with envy prompted by the spirit of wickedness" (cf.

---

94. Harrington, *The Gospel of Matthew*, 87.

95. Luz, *Matthew 1–7*, 282 n. 17; Davies and Allison, *Matthew*, 1:511; see Matt 18:15–20; Mantel, "Sanhedrin," 784.

96. Käsemann, "Sentences of Holy Law," 67. *Lex talionis*, "law of the claw," that is, "an eye for an eye and a tooth for a tooth," proporational retaliation as legal deterence (e.g., Exod 21:24; Lev 24:20; Deut 19:21; Matt 5:38).

CD 9:6–8).⁹⁷ Matthew's second and third rules (vv. 22b, 22c) oppose insulting one's brother. The fourth rule (vv. 23–24) stresses reconciliation towards one's brother before sacrifice. Then comes the Q saying that one should make friends with one's accuser (vv. 25–26). In this context, this rule can also be applied to one's brother.

In short, "brother" language occurs in the Matthean context where it seems to be transparent for a brotherhood association and its rules are designed to help resolve conflicts. The rules themselves are similar to by-laws in Greco-Roman associations and to rules of behavior in Judean associations, notably the Essenes.

Matthew 7:1–5: "Do not judge your brother hypocritically"

This passage has two parts: a communal rule against judging and its elaboration (vv. 1–2), and the famous "speck and log" aphorism (vv. 3–5). The first part is a "Mark-Q overlap" (vv. 1, 2b = Q 6:37a, 38c–42; cf. Jas 4:12; v. 2b also = Mark 4:24b; see 1 Clem 13:2; Pol *Phil* 2:3b) that contains another "sentence of holy law";⁹⁸ its lesson derives from ancient and familiar marketplace weighing practices: "By the measure you measure it will be measured to you." Matthew may have deleted some sayings from Q (Q 7:37b–38; Crossan 1983: 182), but he has intercalated his own "sentence of holy law" in 7:2a as a balance.

The *lex talionis*-type communal rule reminiscent of the "sentences of holy law" is illustrated in the second part by the "speck and log" aphorism (Q 6:41–42; Matt 7:3–5) also found in the Talmud (*b. ʿArak* 16b) and the *Gospel of Thomas* 26. However, the Q version contains the hypocrisy charge, also a favorite of Matthew (Mark 1x; Luke 3x; Matthew 14x, ca. 9 redactional).⁹⁹ As in Matthew 18, "brothers" (vv. 3, 5) must engage in *merciful* judging; otherwise, they judge like outsiders, that is, *hypocritically*,¹⁰⁰ and might as well be the Pharisees. The irony, of course, is that the Matthean Jesus and the Matthean

---

97. Vermes, *The Dead Sea Scrolls*, 68; Kugel, "On Hidden Hatred and Open Reproach," 52–54.

98. See Davies and Allison, *Matthew*, 1:670, for many Judean parallels; also Luke 6:38.

99. Luz, *Matthew 1–7* (1989), 70.

100. See chap. 4 above.

author are constantly making judgments. Again, these "brotherhood" sayings are group norms of the "higher righteousness" honor code, the true meaning of the Law and the prophets (7:12, 17).[101]

Matthew 25:40: Caring for "the least of these my brothers"

John R. Donahue calls the "parable" of the Sheep and the Goats (Matt 25:31–46) the hermeneutical key to the Matthean gospel.[102] Interpretations of the key verse, "Truly, I say to you, as you did it to one of the least of these my brothers, you did it to me" (25:40) have been varied.[103] Three possibilities are common: (1) it refers to charity toward *anyone* who is hungry, thirsty, a stranger, poor, sick, or imprisoned; (2) it refers to charity toward *Matthean brothers* of the same description; (3) it refers to hospitality toward *emissaries from among the brothers*, that is apostles, prophets, sages, righteous ones, or scribes (10:40–42; 23:34) of the same description. Given that the context for the parable is discipleship in the group (25:1–30) and Matthew's emphasis on brothers in these passages, the first interpretation alone is unlikely. Of the latter alternatives, there is a tendency in recent study to accept the third, emissaries among the brothers,[104] but without totally excluding the passage's social implications for anyone who is poor and needy, or the first.[105]

Matthew 28:10: "My Brothers" as the "Eleven Disciples"

Psalm 22 is one of the most important psalms for the passion story (Matt 27:27 [Mark 15:34], 29, 35 [Mark 15:24], 39 [Mark 15:29], 43, 46 [Mark 15:34]), and it is not impossible that Matthew 28:10 alludes to verse 22, "I will tell of your name to *my brothers*, in the midst of the *congregation* (LXX: *ekklēsia*) I will praise you," cited elsewhere in early Christianity in reference to the vindication of the resurrected Jesus

---

101. White, "Grid and Group."
102. Donahue, "Parable of the Sheep and Goats," 3; *Gospel in Parable*, 125.
103. Gray, *Least of My Brothers*.
104. Cope, "Matthew XXV.31–46."
105. Donahue, "Parable of the Sheep and Goats"; *Gospel in Parable*, 120–25.

The Matthean Brotherhood and Marginal Scribal Leadership 197

(John 20:17; Heb 2:12; Justin *Dial.* 106; *Barn.* 6:16).[106] In any case, the resurrected Jesus' words to the women at the tomb parallel the angel's earlier commands to them after the terrifying earthquake:

Chart 7.1 Matthew 28:5, 7+8 and Matthew 28:10+16

Matt 28:5, 7+8 (angel speaks to women)	Matt 28:10+16 (Jesus speaks to women)
"Do not be afraid . . . go…tell *his disciples* . . . going to Galilee there you will see him." . . . ran to tell his disciples . . .	"Do not be afraid; go and tell *my brothers* to go to Galilee, and there they will see me." . . . eleven disciples . . .

These passages reinforce the Matthean view that "brothers" are disciples. In this case the reference is narrowed to the eleven representative disciples who receive Jesus' commission to baptize and teach his commandments.

In conclusion, six of the above seven text segments stress group norms for the "brotherhood": Jesus' true brothers (12:46–50); ranking forbidden because "you are all brothers" (23:8–10); the legal process for settling disputes in the group (18:15–22); warnings against anger among the brothers (5:21–26); warnings against hypocritical judging of brothers (7:1–15); and the necessity for hospitality toward emissaries of the brotherhood (25:40). The seventh passage refers to the eleven representative disciples as "my brothers." Since the sixth, emissary passage includes scribes, I would like to specify them further.

Scribes in the Gospel of Matthew

According to the best textual evidence, the Gospel of Matthew contains twenty-two references to "scribe(s)," ten from Mark, twelve in Matthew alone.[107] The special Matthean uses show that the writer has a serious interest in scribes, but what sort of interest? Common opinions are that the Matthean view of the scribes is at

---

106. Lindars, *New Testament Apologetic*, 93; Schweizer, *The Good News*, 523.
107. For a detailed outline of the Matthean references to "scribe," see chap. 9.

best unclear,[108] at worst confused.[109] In ten polemical contexts, only one from Mark (15:1 [Mark 7:1]), Matthew links scribes with opponent Pharisees (5:20; 12:38; 23:2, 13, 15, 23, 25, 27, 29) whom he elsewhere links with Sadducees (3:7; 16:1, 6, 11, 12[110]), a historically unlikely combination. Thus, goes the argument, Matthew blurs the historical distinctions between these three groups to portray the opponents of Jesus as a "united front."

With regard to scribes this conclusion has often been challenged by scholars, including Saldarini,[111] Orton,[112] and Overman.[113] For these three scholars, the Matthean contexts are determinative. Both Saldarini and Orton argue that deletions or replacements of "scribes" with "chief priests and elders" in Jerusalem settings (21:23 [Mark 11:27]; 26:3 [Mark 14:1]; 26:47 [Mark 14:43]; 27:1 [Mark 15:1]) and replacing scribes with Pharisees in conflict stories about purity (9:11 [Mark 2:16]; 15:12, cp. 15:1) are quite plausible historically.[114] Orton adds that the linking of scribes with other opponent groups than the Pharisees, mostly from Mark—"High Priests" (20:18 [Mark 10:33]; 21:15 [cf. Mark 11:18]; "elders" (26:57 [Mark 14:53 (+ High Priests)]); both "elders" and "High Priests" (16:21 [Mark 8:31]); 27:41 [Mark 15:31]; exception Matt 2:4)—means that *"the scribes per se never stand alone as opponents of Jesus. They are tainted by the company they keep. This looks like a tempering of the criticism of the scribes in Mark . . ."*[115] Indeed, Matthew's six deletions of Mark's "scribe(s)" (21:23 [Mark 11:27]; 26:47 [Mark 14:43]; 27:1 [15:1]; 15:1 [Mark 7:5; cf. 7:1 = Matt 15:1]; 17:14 [Mark 9:14]; 22:40 [Mark 12:32]) and his five replacements of scribes with Pharisees (9:11 [Mark 2:16 "scribes of the Pharisees"]; 9:34 and 12:24 [Mark 3:22]; Matt 22:41 [Mark 12:35]; 22:34 [Mark 12:28]) are clarifications related to Matthew's anti-Pharisaic polemic (Matt 9:11, 34; 12:24, 38; 15:12; 21:45; 16:11;

---

108. E.g., Walker, *Die Heilsgeschichte*; Van Tilborg, *Jewish Leaders*.
109. E.g., Cook, *Mark's Treatment*, 58–67.
110. Meier, *The Vision of Matthew*, 19.
111. Saldarini, *Pharisees*.
112. Orton, *The Understanding Scribe*.
113. Overman, *Matthew's Gospel and Formative Judaism*.
114. Saldarini, *Pharisees*, 160–61; Orton, *The Understanding Scribe*, 26.
115. Orton, ibid., 28.

21:45; 22:15, 34–35; 27:62). For example, Matthew omits Mark's praise of the scribe "not far from the Kingdom of God" (Mark 12:32–34) because he has just transformed him into a lawyer of the Pharisees (Matt 22:34 [Mark 12:28]). For Orton, it is the *Pharisaic* scribes whom Matthew opposes.[116]

To be sure, a positive view of scribes is not always present in the gospel: in three cases Matthew follows Mark in stressing Jesus' teaching authority in *contrast* to scribes (7:29 [Mark 1:22]; 9:3 [Mark 2:6]; 17:10 [Mark 9:11]).[117] Yet, in one of these cases Matthew replaces "the scribes" (Mark 1:22) with "*their* scribes" (Matt 7:29[118]), referring to outsiders controlled by the Pharisees (cp. "*their* synagogues," 4:23; 9:35; 10:17; 12:9; 13:54; "*your* synagogues," 23:34; "*their* cities," 11:1; cf. 12:38).[119] On the other side, Matthew allows that "the scribes and Pharisees sit on Moses' seat" and one should "practice and observe whatever they tell you . . ." (23:2–3a).[120] Also, the scribes' view that Elijah must come first is accepted (17:10 [Mark 9:11]). On the basis of "their scribes" (7:28) versus "sent" scribes (23:34), as well as scribal activity in the gospel itself and the scribe trained ("discipled") for the kingdom of heaven (13:52), Overman concludes that "the office and function of the scribe were developing in Matthew's setting. There were good scribes and bad."[121]

Finally, three references confirm the argument that some scribes in Matthew are viewed positively: 8:19, 13:52, and 23:34.

Matthew 8:19

In 8:19–22 Matthew has made insertions into Q as follows:

---

116. Ibid., 27.
117. Saldarini, *Pharisees*, 159.
118. Overman, *Matthew's Gospel*, 115.
119. Kilpatrick, *The Origins of the Gospel*, 286; Stanton, *A Gospel for a New People*, 119–20, 128.
120. See Hummel, *Die Auseinandersetzung*, 31; Garland, *The Intention of Matthew 23*, 20–22, 46–55.
121. Overman, *Matthew's Gospel and Formative Judaism*, 117.

Chart 7.2 Matthew 8:18–22 and Luke 9:57–60

Matthew 8:18–22 (Geographical setting: Galilee)	Luke 9:57–60 (Geographical setting: Samaria)
19) And *a (heis) scribe* came up and said to him, "Teacher, I will follow you wherever you go . . ." 21) *Another (heteros) of his disciples* said, "Lord, let me first go and bury my father." 23) And when he got into the boat, *his disciples* followed him . . . [Stilling of the storm, vv. 23–27]	57) . . . *someone* said to him, "I will follow you wherever you go . . ." 59) *To another* he said, "Follow me." But he said, "Lord, let me first go and bury my father." 61) Yet *another* said, "I will *follow* you, Lord; but first let me say farewell to those at my home."

A debated question is this: do the Matthean insertions, "a scribe" (8:19) and its parallel expression "another of his disciples" (8:21) imply that the writer considers "a scribe" to be a disciple? While some recent scholars have answered "no,"[122] others have answered "yes."[123] Saldarini, Orton, and Gundry have joined the ranks of the latter group. Saldarini stresses that the scribe's wish looks sincere.[124] Orton emphasizes that Matthew's changes from Q's indefinite "someone" (Q 9:57: *tis*) to definite "a (literally, *one*) scribe" (Matt 8:19: *heis grammateus*) and from Q's "another" (Q 9:59) to "another *of the disciples*" (Matt 8:21) clearly show that the scribe is a disciple.[125] Robert Gundry's finely tuned analysis suggests that the sequence implies two scribes, the *first* good, the *second* bad.[126] Building on four minor arguments of Kiilunen against Kingsbury,[127] Gundry adds: (1) Matthew *always* uses "another" (*heteros*) to compare *two of the same kind* (9x); (2) "one" (*heis*) in Matthew is always emphatic (11x), and thus "one" (v. 19) contrasts with "another" (v. 21); (3) in Matthew "one" can depend on its substantive (8x), which here must mean not

---

122. E.g., Kingsbury, "The Verb *Akolouthein*," 59–60; *Matthew as Story*; Luz *Matthew 1–7*, 23; Davies and Allison, *Matthew*, 2:41, 53–54; Kiilunen, "Der nachfolgewillige Schriftgelehrte"; Stanton, "The Communities of Matthew," 383; *A Gospel for a New People*, 127.

123. Substantial list in Kingsbury, "The Verb *Akolouthein*," 59, n. 20.

124. Saldarini, *Pharisees*, 159.

125. Orton, *The Understanding Scribe*, 36–37.

126. Gundry, "On True and False Disciple in Matthew 8.18–22."

127. Kiilunen, "Der nachfolgewillige Schriftgelehrte."

"one, a scribe," but "one scribe"; (4) "another of his disciples" points to the previously mentioned scribe because when Matthew adds a possessive genitive to a noun already mentioned, he does not reclassify the noun; (5) there are other Matthean contexts where one who is already a disciple "follows" Jesus (5x); (6) Matthew's sequence "one scribe" (v. 10), "another of his disciples" (v. 21), and "his disciples" (v. 23) shows that the scribe is among the disciples. Gundry's final argument (7) is that Matthew has probably omitted a Q saying, the scribe who wants to follow (= Luke 9:61),[128] and thereby he creates a contrasting pair in which the first scribe/disciple is true, not the second scribe/disciple. Gundry offers four grounds for this argument: those who request a *delay* to "follow" Jesus in Matthew are false disciples (9x); family obligations in Matthew are secondary to "following" Jesus (4:22; 10:35, 37; 19:29); Matthew pairs good/bad frequently; and false disciples in Matthew can also address Jesus as "Lord." In short, this passage does not portray a scribe negatively, quite the reverse: it supports the view that there are "good scribes" among Jesus' followers/disciples.

Matthew 23:34

In this verse Matthew has taken over "prophets" (*prophētai*) from Q 11:49 but has replaced "apostles" (only 1x, Matt 10:2) with "sages" and "scribes." How are these groups perceived? Matthew is elsewhere very positive toward prophets (37x, 20 perhaps redactional),[129] although he has warnings about *false* prophets (7:15-23; cf. 24:11-12, 24).[130] "Sages" (*sophoi*) occurs negatively in 11:25 (= Q 10:21), but there they are sages *of the world*, probably Pharisaic sages (12:2, 14, 24, 38).[131] In contrast, the above prophets, sages, and scribes are "sent out" (*apostellō*: 17x; *pempō*: 2x), that is, apparently they are itinerant emissaries (cp. 10:40-42).[132] Again, scribes are viewed positively.

128. Cf. Kloppenborg, "Blessing and Marginality," 64.

129. Luz, *Matthew 1-7*, 67.

130. Bornkamm, "End-Expectation," 39 n. 1; Schweizer, "Observance of the Law"; Hill, "False Prophets and Charismatics"; Overman, "Observance of the Law," 118.

131. Suggs, *Wisdom*, 84-87.

132. Hill, "DIKAIOI"; Schweizer, "Observance of the Law"; "The 'Matthaean' Church"; cf. Stanton, "5 Ezra"; Duling, "Matthew and the Problem of Authority"; "BTB Readers' Guide: Millennialism."

Matthew 13:52

Most critics agree that Matthew has composed 13:51–53 as a conclusion to the third of five major discourses he constructs for Jesus in the gospel.[133] Verse 51 is Matthew's editorial transition; in contrast to obtuse disciples in Mark, in Matthew disciples "understand" (13:13 [Isa 6:9], 19, 23, 51), specifically all "these things," or Jesus' just-told "parables of the kingdom" (13:34; cf. 13:56).[134] Word statistics overwhelmingly support Matthean composition of verse 52.[135] Orton's suggestion is very plausible:[136] Matthew created verse 52 from Q sayings about the teacher/disciple relationship (Matt 6:40) and the good man who produces good fruit out of the treasure of his heart (Matt 6:45). Formally,

Everyone fully trained will be like his teacher.
Every scribe discipled is like a householder.

Finally, verse 53 is commonly recognized as one of Matthew's five discourse-ending formulae (7:28; 11:1; 13:53; 19:1; 26:1).[137]

How does "the scribe" fare in this passage? The scribe is "trained," a transitive passive meaning literally "instructed as a disciple."[138] He is discipled for the "kingdom of heaven," Jesus' most central teaching in Matthew (Mark 0x; Luke 0x; Matt 32x),[139] a teaching that ultimately disciples also will teach (28:19; cf. 27:57 [replacing "looking for the kingdom of God," Mark 15:43]). The "householder" or "ruler of the house" brings forth all of the household imagery in Matthew.[140] Bringing out of his storehouse what is new and what is old is Matthew's view of Jesus' interpretation of the law.

---

133. Davies and Allison, *Critical and Exegetical Commentary on the Gospel*, Vol. 2, 444.

134. Ibid., 399 n. 100.

135. Listed in Orton, *The Understanding Scribe*, 230–31.

136. Ibid., 171–74.

137. Bacon, "The 'Five Books'"; *Studies in Matthew*.

138. Kingsbury, *Parables*, 126–27; Gundry, *Matthew*, 291; Luz, "The Disciples," 109; Orton, *The Understanding Scribe*, 231 n. 9.

139. Luz, *Matthew 1–7*, 56; Duling, "Matthew (Disciple)," 57–58.

140. Crosby, *House of Disciples*; Love, "The Household."

Insofar as Jesus' followers are "transparent" for followers in Matthew's day,[141] the positive instances of scribes points to scribes in the Matthean brotherhood. Matthew 13:52 determines the certain existence of scribes/disciples in the Matthean group.[142] Indeed, it is now commonly held that the verse may refer to the creative scribal activity of the gospel's author himself. Thus, a "scribe discipled for the Kingdom" is both a "self-portrait of the evangelist"[143] and a portrait of the scribes who were leaders in the Matthean brotherhood.

The Social Status of Scribes in Judean Antiquity

The goal of advanced Greek education was *paideia*, or "culture." It was the quality of highest value, the "religion of culture."[144] A place where one could learn *paideia* was in the philosophical school, the *ephēbeia*. Philosophical schools were not exactly voluntary associations. Yet, voluntary associations often supported the *ephēbeia*, and, indeed, they shared many features in common with cult associations.[145] After pointing to some common features and common terminology (*secta*, *synodos*, *thiasos*) between the associations and philosophical schools, Robert Wilken concludes: "My point is not that philosophical schools and associations were the same, nor even that one could have been mistaken for the other. My contention is that there were some similarities and that these similarities help us to understand, on the one hand, the social dimensions of philosophy at this time, and, on the other hand, the religious and ethical dimensions of associations."[146]

The question about the status of Judean scribes is in part a question about the importance of education and schools in general. Advanced education in antiquity was the privilege of urban elites.

---

141. Luz, "The Disciples."

142. Hoh, "Der christliche *grammateus*"; Bacon, *Studies*, chap. 10; Kilpatrick, *Origins*, 111; Stendahl, *School*, 30, 34 n. 4; Hummel, *Die Auseinandersetzung*, 17–18, 26–28; Trilling, *Das Wahre Israel*, 146; Strecker, *Der Weg der Gerechtigkeit*, 30, 37, 192; Kingsbury, *Matthew: Structure*, 166 n. 149; Overman, *Matthew's Gospel*, 116; Orton, *The Understanding Scribe*, *passim*.

143. Harrington, *The Gospel of Matthew*, 208.

144. Moreau, *A History of Education*, 137–46; Nock, *Conversion*, 167.

145. Culpepper, *The Johannine School*, 259.

146. Wilken, "Collegia," 280.

Despite the absence of statistics, and problems such as degrees of literacy, the distinction between reading and writing literacy, the difference between full literacy and "craftsman's literacy," and the variety of conditions from place to place, "the likely overall [full] illiteracy level of the Roman Empire under the principate is almost certain to have been above 90%."[147] Although the subject is much debated, most recent modern scholars say that the literacy level of Judeans mirrored the low literacy level of the population in general, that is, not more than 10 percent.[148] Thus, despite Rabbinic traditions to the contrary, it is unlikely that universal compulsory education for Judean children existed at this time.[149]

Judgment about schools for the upper social strata of Judeans is another matter.[150] Scribal schools for kings and priests probably existed in Jerusalem in the preexilic period, but the term "school" is explicitly mentioned for the first time in Ben Sira 51:23 (ca. 180 BCE). "Draw near to me, you who are uneducated, and lodge in the 'house of instruction' [Hebrew: *bet-midrash*; Greek *oikia paideias*]." This verse probably refers to a scribal school in Ben Sira's house. Although representative of Judean nationalism, Ben Sira's writings betray an important shift for advanced education, namely, the influence of Hellenistic *paideia* on Judean wisdom.[151] A few short years later, in 175 BCE, Jason's "Hellenistic reform," supported by the Jerusalem priestly aristocracy, included a gymnasium and *ephēbeion* (2 Macc 4:9).[152] Yet, Ben Sira also betrays a growing independence from the priestly aristocracy. First Maccabees 7:12 mentions a *synagōgē grammateiōn*, probably an "association of lay scribes." There also developed chains of tradition associated with great teachers and demands that teachers should teach without payment. Hengel writes in this regard that "the comparison

---

147. Harris, *Ancient Literacy*, 22.

148. See Ackroyd and Evans, *Cambridge History*, 37; Bar-Ilan, "Part Two: Scribes," 22; contrast Millard, "An Assessment."

149. So Cohen, *From the Maccabees to the Mishnah*, 120.

150. Hengel, *Judaism and Hellenism* 1, 58–106, esp. 78–83; Townsend, "Ancient Education," 139–63; "Education (Greco-Roman)," 312–17; Cohen, *From the Maccabees to the Mishnah*, 120–23; Fishbane, *Biblical Interpretation*; "From Scribalism to Rabbinism"; Elder, *Transformations*, 138–49; Lemaire, "The Sage"; "Writing and Writing Materials."

151. Hengel, *Judaism and Hellenism* 1, 79, 132.

152. Tcherikover, *Hellenistic Civilization*, 161.

The Matthean Brotherhood and Marginal Scribal Leadership   205

between the Jewish sects and the Greek philosophical schools in Josephus is not completely unjustified. Even the master-pupil relationship in the Rabbinate, bound up with the principle of tradition, has its model less in the Old Testament . . . than in Greece. The *didaskalos* [teacher] corresponded to the *rab* [teacher] and the *talmîd* [disciple] to the *mathētēs* [disciple]."[153] There were also, no doubt, more conservative scribal "schools," and they may well have been in the majority. One thinks also of certain Judean associations as schools, for example, the Essenes.

What then of the social status of these scribes? Shaye Cohen observes that modern scholars have used two different, contrasting grids of ranking for Palestine, one "economic," the other "religious,"[154] and he ranks the scribes in the religious grid. However, Saldarini, using the Lenski advanced agrarian society model, thinks of most scribes as agents or "retainers" of the Jerusalem aristocracy.[155] Certainly both religious and socio-economic dimensions are crucial. As educated and literate, scribes tended to come from the elite classes[156] and thus to serve the political establishment. The "retainer" ranking fits. Yet, scribes among Judeans had a special prestige or honor captured in their specifically "religious" functions over long periods of Judean history.[157]

Both social and religious status can be found in the texts themselves. As noted above, Ben Sira seems to have had a scribal school in his house. He was of priestly stock, but was essentially a lay scribe.[158] He sums up the ideal scribe (Sir 10:5; 38:24: *grammateus*) in two back-to-back poems, 38:24-34 and 39:1-11, the latter building on the former, which appears to be dependent on the Egyptian "Satire on the Trades."[159] In these poems, the scribes study Torah, the law of covenants, and the wisdom of the ancients. They penetrate prophecies, the subtleties of parables, and the hidden meanings of proverbs.

153. Hengel, *Judaism and Hellenism* 1, 81.
154. Cohen, "Political and Social History," 48-49; see pp. 261-71 for several kinds of scribes.
155. Saldarini, *Pharisees*, 274.
156. Bar-Ilan, "Part Two: Scribes," 21-22.
157. Lemaire, "The Sage."
158. Gammie, "The Sage in Sirach," 364-68.
159. Orton, *The Understanding Scribe*, 66-67; Skehan and DiLella, *Wisdom*, 445-53; Saldarini, *Pharisees*, 254-59; Gammie, ibid.

They offer thanksgiving to God and pray for forgiveness of their sins. They pour forth their own wisdom, showing learning. They meditate on the Lord's mysteries and are filled with the spirit of understanding. This is the religious dimension. However, the religious dimension is an "ideal of life which is determined by social role."[160] The poems can be summarized by contrasting the social rank of scribes with the other social groups in the passage as follows:

Chart 7.3 Scribes Contrasted with Peasants and Artisans in Ben Sira

Scribes	Peasants and Artisans
have leisure = opportunity for Wisdom are found among and appear before *rulers* serve among *the great* travel in foreign lands (learn good and evil) preserve sayings of the famous sit in judge's seat understand and make court decisions expound discipline and judgment are sought out for the people's council are eminent in the public assembly have names praised by community and nations	work night and day: *peasants*: plow furrows, goad oxen, talk about cattle, careful about heifers' fodder *artisans/master artisans*: labor with their hands into the night to finish their work well. *Examples*: signet engraver making exact images the smith at the anvil: quality work the potter: quantity and quality work

The italicized references can be ranked socially:

"the great"

rulers

scribes

master artisans

artisans

peasants

This social ranking matches perfectly the stratification model of Gerhard Lenski and David Fiensy for an advanced agrarian society, and it is interlocked with the religious dimension. The scribes are in

---

160. Nickelsburg and Stone, *Faith and Piety*, 94.

the "middle strata"; again, they would be "retainers" of the elite classes as well as religious authorities.

Here I can stress two further points. First, Ben Sira's scribal ideal sums up what has gone before and is determinative for what comes after, including scribalism in the Dead Sea Scrolls. After carefully examining the scribal ideal in intertestamental literature, David Orton concludes:

> Typically in [the intertestamental] literature the concept of the scribe involves: (1) social eminence and religious authority of the scribe—as in *Ben Sira* and the OT; (2) occupation with hidden meanings, of scripture, visions, prophecies and "parables"—as in *Ben Sira*; (3) a concomitant emphasis on "understanding," especially divinely inspired insight, and on "interpretation"—as in *Ben Sira* and the levitical scribalism of the OT; (4) function as a mediator of revealed insights, a writing teacher of contemporary and future generations, whose concern is to cause others to understand—like *Ben Sira*; (5) a "prophetic" or quasi-prophetic charisma and vocation—like some of the OT scribes (and their representation in the targums) and once again *Ben Sira*.[161]

Orton adds: "We shall find this general concept of the scribe to be very significant for a full understanding of Matthew's own concept of the scribe, as also of his Gospel."[162]

Not only does Ben Sira indicate the social ranking and give the religious ideology of the scribe for Judean society in general; it is likely that Matthew and some in his group know and have studied Ben Sira. Krister Stendahl writes of the section where Ben Sira's "house of instruction" is mentioned: "Now the context in Matthew is strongly influenced by Ecclus. [Sir] 51:23ff., where Wisdom (as an hypostasis) is speaking and where the true teaching of the school [of St. Matthew] will give the disciples the *anapausis* ("rest"). *This type of literature seems to have been studied in the school of Matthew and related to Jesus, equating Him with Wisdom . . .*"[163]

---

161. Orton, *The Understanding Scribe*, 120, italics mine.
162. Ibid., 120.
163. Stendahl, *School*, 142 (italics mine); see Suggs, *Wisdom*, 100.

Marginal Scribal Leadership in the Matthean Brotherhood

The Matthean *ekklēsia* can be described as a fictive kinship group or fictive brotherhood association. In terms of titles its ideology is that only God should be called "Father," only Christ should be called "Teacher"/"Tutor" and "Rabbi," and all others are "brothers." This is household imagery. It overlaps another household image, namely, the servants/slaves who serve their master. In Matthew, the master/slave relationship overlaps both the Christ/brothers relationship and the teacher/disciple relationship (10:24). It is possible to infer that among "brothers"/"disciples"/"slaves," all titles of honor are discouraged (23:8-10).

Yet, despite this "limited egalitarian" ideology typical of some coalitions and sects, the Matthean brotherhood has moved beyond a "coalition" of the "faction" type. If one prefers a sectarian model, it is also moving beyond the "sect," especially if one thinks of a "reformist sect."[164] One reason—there are others—is that it has several specific leadership roles. Thus, in Matthew 23:34, we find "prophets," "sages," and "scribes" linked. In 10:40-42 "prophet" is listed with "righteous one" and "little ones." If apostle is added to the list (10:2)—only the verb *apostellō* is common in Matthew—there are at least six terms for functional leaders within the Matthean brotherhood.[165]

1. "prophet" (*prophētēs* 37x, 20 redactional[166])
2. "scribe" (*grammateus* 22x, ca. 16x redactional[167])
3. "righteous (one)" (*dikaios* 17x, 7x redactional[168])
4. "teacher" (*didaskalos* 12x, 4x redactional[169])
5. "sage" (*sophos* 2x)
6. "apostle" (*apostolos* 1x [10:2], but *apostellō* 17x; *pempō* 2x)

In this list, "scribe" is the second most common Matthean leadership designation. In the Matthean brotherhood good scribes are honored,

---

164. Wilson, *Magic*; see Wilson's sect typology, chap. 1, Chart 1.1.
165. Krentz, "Community and Character"; see chap. 6.
166. Luz, *Matthew 1-7*, 67.
167. Ibid., 56.
168. Ibid., 57.
169. Ibid., 57.

and indeed the author of the gospel is most likely a scribe (13:52). He is educated, literate, and sees the secrets of Scripture in a sophisticated fashion. He is steeped in apocalyptic/millennial themes typical of scribes.[170] He is probably located where most scribes are normally located, namely, in an urban setting.[171] He embodies the ideal of the "understanding scribe" found especially in Ben Sira.[172]

Can one say more about the scribes of Matthew's group? Antoinette Wire has tried to illumine "scribal communities" in agrarian societies by developing a model based on anthropological studies of Chinese scribal clans in the Qing Dynasty (1644–1911) and comparing them to the Essenes, Pharisees, and Matthean Christians.[173] As noted in chapter 2, she claims of such scribes that, "(1) they reinterpret in writing a revered literary tradition (2) in such a way as to teach concrete ritual and ethical behavior (3) which can assure the proper fulfillment of set roles within a community of identification (4) sanctioned by adequate rewards and punishments (5) in order to reassert right order in a situation where it is perceived to be under some threat."[174] Her respondent, Pheme Perkins, is correct to suggest that for Matthew the model does not fit at one important point: scribal literacy in China was used to gain access to imperial power.[175] Also, Wire's model, as she seems to be aware, struggles a little in relation to point three, assuring the proper fulfillment of "set roles" in what she calls a "hierarchically ordered world."[176] Certainly, Matthew's *ideology* discourages "set roles" and the "roles" mentioned are not clearly defined. Nonetheless, I think that Wire is on the right track in her judgment that Matthew and his reading audience represent a classically educated, self-sufficient scribal group that dominates a mixed community.[177] I would like to take her judgment a little further.

---

170. Smith, "A Pearl of Great Price"; Davies, "The Social World"; Crossan, *The Historical Jesus*, 158; Duling, "BTB Readers' Guide: Millennialism."
171. Kingsbury, "The Verb *Akolouthein*"; "Conclusion," 264.
172. Orton, *The Understanding Scribe*.
173. Wire, "Gender Roles," 87–121; see chap. 2.
174. Ibid.; see pp. 44–45.
175. Perkins, "Gender Analysis," 123.
176. Wire, "Gender Roles," 92.
177. Ibid., 114, 118.

I suggest that Matthew's scribes be termed "marginal scribes."[178] This statement needs clarification because in many analyses the term "marginal" has become identified almost exclusively with the poor and dispossessed, or in antiquity, with peasants, the degraded, the expendable, in certain contexts the "unclean," and occasionally women. This view of marginality correctly stresses those at or near the bottom of the (macro)social hierarchy. Yet, as noted above in chapter 5, the classic analyses of marginality—those that gave it its sociological currency—had a broader view.[179] Both Park[180] and Stonequist,[181] who is indebted to Park, stressed a subtle dimension related to ethnicity and culture that should not be forgotten. Here is E. V. Stonequist's view: "[T]he marginal personality is most clearly portrayed in those individuals who are unwittingly initiated *into two or more historic traditions, languages, political loyalties, moral codes, or religions.*"[182] More recently, Gino Germani's theoretical work on marginality makes a similar point. While "marginals" can be and often are equated with the lower strata of any normative scheme of social ranking, one may also consider marginals at *each level* of the social hierarchy: "we may define marginality as the lack of participation of individuals and groups in those spheres in which, according to determined criteria, *they might be expected to participate.*"[183] Such persons are unable to conform to expected social roles with respect to sex, age, civil life, occupation, and social life, at *whatever level of the social strata they may be*. Such lack of participation may occur because of some new and competing "normative scheme," so that, again, a person may be on the margin *between two (or more) competing normative schemes*.

From this perspective, a classically educated, self-sufficient scribal group that dominates a mixed community that itself is perceived as "marginal" by the larger society, but especially the rival Pharisees within Judaism, is and experiences itself to be, despite implied claims to the contrary, "marginal." This conclusion would help explain the

---

178. See chap. 4.
179. See chap. 9.
180. Park, "Human Migration"; "Personality and Cultural Conflict."
181. Stonequist, *The Marginal Man*.
182. Ibid., 3.
183. Germani, *Marginality*.

Matthean writer's ideological apologetic stance vis-à-vis the Pharisees, *their* scribes, and *their* titles of honor, while at the same time praise the scribal role and its authority within the brotherhood. From this larger perspective on marginality, the Matthean brotherhood is led by scribes who, although having a measure of status in general, are "marginal." They understand, bring out of their treasure what is new and what is old (13:52), and teach others (5:19; 28:20).

I shall have more to say about this view in chapters 8 and 9.

CHAPTER 8

Matthew 18:15–17: Conflict, Confrontation, and Conflict Resolution in a "Fictive Kin" Association[1]

IN THE PREVIOUS CHAPTER, I explored the social-scientific thesis that the Matthean group was a fictive kinship group in the ancient Mediterranean world, specifically a voluntary association, or brotherhood, led by marginal scribes.[2] In this chapter I would like to develop this thesis in greater detail. I suggest that the community (or communities) represented by the Dead Sea Scrolls can be compared to a voluntary association, that the Scrolls provide a "close comparison" for the Matthew group as another voluntary association, and that this hypothesis will shed light on a key text briefly noted in the last chapter, Matt 18:15–17. I shall also relate this thesis to the well-known themes of "frank speech" in ancient Greco-Roman texts and "reproof" in Judean texts.

Matthew 18:15–17: Literary Context and Sources

The immediate literary context of Matthew 18:15–17 is the fourth of the five discourses that the Matthean writer attributed to Jesus, Matthew 18:1–35. Davies and Allison split this fourth discourse into

---

1. This chapter was first published in the *SBL 1998 Seminar Papers*, 253–95; it was revised and published in 1999 for *Biblical Theology Bulletin* 29/1: 4–22. I removed the initial comments about postmodernism in this version and placed them as Appendix 1 to chapter 1, and made a few minor modifications, including some reorganization.

2. See chap. 7; Kloppenborg and Wilson, *Voluntary Associations*; Kloppenborg and McLean, *Collegia*; recently, Harland, *Dynamics of Identity*.

approximately two halves (I: 18:1–14; II: 18:15–35), each containing three subsections (I: 18:1–5, 6–9, 10–14; II: 18:15–20, 21–22, 23–35), for a total of six units. Each of the six contains a key term (or terms) and a corresponding theme (or themes). The key term of subsections 4 and 5 (vv. 15–20 and 21–22) is "brother,"[3] a gospel term explored in the last chapter.[4] The overall theme is conflict, which is well known and much explored in Matthew studies,[5] but here I shall be interested in the means of resolving it among the members of a fictive kin family ("brotherhood"), which in the Matthean text is called the *ekklēsia*.[6]

Here are the first two subsections of Part II (or sections 4 and 5) of the fourth speech.

Chart 8.1 Matthew 18:15–22 and Its Lukan Parallels

Matthew 18:15–20 and 21–22[a]	Luke 17:3 and 17:4
18:15: If *your brother* sins against you, go and reprove him, between you and him alone. If he listens to you, you have gained your brother.	17:3: "Take heed to yourselves: if your brother sins, rebuke him, and if he repents, forgive him;
18:16: But if he does not listen [to you], take one or two others along with you, that every word may be confirmed by two or three witnesses.	
18:17: If he refuses to listen to them tell it to the *ekklēsia*; and if he refuses to listen even to the *ekklēsia*, let him be to you as a Gentile and a tax collector.	
18:18: "Truly, I say to you, whatever you [plural] bind on earth shall be bound in heaven, and whatever you [plural] loose on earth shall be loosed in heaven.	
18:19: "Again I say to you, if two of you agree on earth about anything they ask, it will be done by my Father in heaven.	
18:20: "For where two or three are gathered in my name, there am I in the midst of them."	

3. E.g., Davies and Allison, *Critical and Exegetical Commentary*, Vol. 2, 750–51; cp. Harrington, *Matthew*, 270.

4. See chap. 7 in this book.

5. Literature in Duling, "Matthew 18:15–17," 258 n. 10; see also the beginning of chap. 6.

6. Duling, "The Matthean Brotherhood"; chap. 7 in this book.

18:21: Then Peter came up and said to him, "Lord, how often shall *my brother* sin against me, and I forgive him? As many as seven times?" 18:22: Jesus said to him, "I do not say to you seven times, but seventy times seven."	17:4: and if he sins against you seven times in the day, and turns to you seven times, and says, 'I repent,' you must forgive him."

a. Mainly the RSV translation.

The literary sources for Matthew's construction of Jesus' fourth discourse in Matthew 18 have been much debated. The fourth and fifth subsections in the chart, with its catchword "brother" (vss. 15, 21), are part of the debate, as the following scholarly options about Matthew 18:15–22 indicate.[7]

Option 1: Neither Matthew nor Luke derived anything from Q.

Option 2: Matthew took his version from "Special M."

However, most critics think that since Matthew 18:6, 15 and 21–22 have the exact same sequence as Luke 17:1+2 and 3+4, both Matthew and Luke drew on Q. Therefore, there are three Q-related options:

Option 3: Catchpole argued that except for the Scripture reference (Deut 19:15—two or three witnesses necessary) in 18:16b, Matthew took over verses 15–17 and 21 from Q,[8] and Luke omitted what is in Matthew 18:16–17.

Option 4: Matthew took over 18:15–17 from a *secondary version* of Q while Luke retained an earlier version. In its favor are three un-Matthean words in verse 15.[9]

Option 5: Matthew inserted verses 16–20 into Q, or more precisely, he inserted verses 16–17, 18 (cf. Matt 16:19) and 19–20 between 18:15 (= Q 17:3) and 18:21–22 (= Q 17:4).[10]

---

7. Catchpole, "Reproof and Reconciliation"; Kloppenborg, *Q Parallels*, 184.

8. Catchpole, ibid.

9. "Between" (*metaxu*, only in 23:35, from Q); "alone" (*monos*, apparently from sources—4:4 = Luke 4:4; 4:10 = Luke 4:8; 14:23 = Mark 4:46–7; 17:8 = Mark 9:8); and the verb for "reprove" (*elenchon*, a Matthean *hapax*). See Davies and Allison, *Critical and Exegetical Commentary*, Vol. 2, 783.

10. E.g., Thompson, *Matthew's Advice*; Gundry, *Matthew*; Harrington, *Matthew*.

I take this last, fifth option to be most likely: the Matthean writer inserted Matthew 18:16-20 (16-17, 18, 19-20) between 18:15 and 18:21-22. The reasons for taking this option, I hope, will become clear in the forthcoming analysis. One way toward a solution is to view the Matthean changes in relation to fictive kin associations in general and voluntary associations in particular, as I did in the last chapter. First, a further word about fictive kin associations.

Voluntary Associations as "Fictive Kin Groups" in Mediterranean Antiquity

The thesis that the Matthean group was a fictive kinship group, specifically a voluntary association or brotherhood, gains credibility by taking up discussion of voluntary associations as "fictive kin groups" in general.

First, consider some recent anthropological analysis. The expression "voluntary association" was accepted into anthropology as a way to describe groups that are not based on natural kinship, but on criteria such as age, sex, work, ethnic origin, or ideology. The anthropologist Caulkins writes: "Voluntary associations or sodalities tend to have all or most of the following characteristics: explicit purposes or goals; members who are socialized into a proper mode of behavior; identity is conferred on members and they are distinguished from nonmembers; members are given social support; an aim to secure benefits for members or some client group; sponsorship or the carrying out of ritual or ceremonial activities; collective recognition by others in the society; and some influence on people and activities outside the association."[11] Anthropologists of the contemporary Middle East and Africa have shown that such sodalities help rural peoples who migrate to urban areas preserve their ethnic heritage and cultural traditions as they adapt to a new, rapidly changing cultural context.[12] In other words, the weakening of natural kinship and other group ties leads displaced urban migrants to join voluntary associations for various kinds of support and networking.

---

11. Caulkins, "Voluntary Associations," 1352.

12. Eisenstadt, "Sociological Aspects"; Little, "The Role of Voluntary Associations"; Geertz, "The Rotating Credit Association"; Kerri, "Studying Voluntary Associations"; Kerr, "Voluntary Associations in West Africa."

The modern Middle Eastern and African parallels with Mediterranean antiquity are apparent. In chapter 7 I noted that that in advanced agrarian societies small substitute primary groups—"fictive" or surrogate kin groups—appear when the bonds of real (natural) kin groups are in decline.[13] Similarly, the decline of the *polis* and the growth of cities in the Hellenistic and Roman periods was paralleled by the proliferation of voluntary associations.[14] Such associations were usually small, some as little as twenty to thirty members, a few as many as 300–400, and one as many as 1200.[15] Ascough argues that the common generalization that the associations were local is in some respects an oversimplification since translocal networks, however casual, were common.[16]

While it is difficult to arrive at a clear taxonomy of voluntary associations,[17] several types can be distinguished: older boy's and young men's "athletic clubs" (*ephebeia*; *neoi*) connected to the *gymnasium*; ethnic groups modeled on the *polis* (*koina*; *politeiai*); trade guilds and associations;[18] professional associations; theater guilds of actors, dancers, and artists; philosophical schools; and "cult associations." John Kloppenborg doubts whether "burial societies" were a distinctive type, although most associations who had members from the lower social strata would have helped bury their members.[19] These associations offered resources related to education, ethnicity, work, burial, and the arts, and all of them appear to have had some religious function. Yet, their primary aim was generally "social." As such, they offered people "... a sense of identity and comradeship, a social unit larger than the family and smaller than the state where they could meet together with friends, eat and drink, worship, play, and share common experiences."[20]

13. Based on Lenski, *Power and Privilege*; Lenski and Lenski, *Human Societies*, 164–208; Turner, *Societal Stratification*.

14. Klinghardt, "Manual of Discipline," 257 n. 25.

15. Kloppenborg, "Collegia and Thiasoi," 30 n. 4; Ascough, "Matthew and Community Formation," n. 18.

16. Ascough, ibid., 223; cp. Wilson, "Voluntary Associations," 3; Kloppenborg, "Collegia and Thiasoi," 3.

17. Kloppenborg, "Collegia and Thiasoi," 18.

18. Broughton, "Part IV: Roman Asia," 841–44.

19. Kloppenborg, "Collegia and Thiasoi," 18.

20. Wilken, "Collegia," 281; see Dill, *Roman Society*, 267; Kloppenborg, "Collegia and Thiasoi," 18.

Most, although not all, people in voluntary associations were urban poor, slaves, and freedmen. Lower status members of these fictive kin groups could sometimes achieve some semblance of social status and honor otherwise denied them.[21] At the same time, voluntary associations tended to become hierarchical and thus mirror social stratification in the macrosociety.

Most ancient associations were legally tolerated and even sanctioned. However, they also were sometimes suspected of being political and occasionally disturbed public order. When that occurred, they were labeled *hetaeriae* by the Roman authorities. Indeed, from time to time the Romans tried to dissolve them, to forbid the formation of new groups, to require members to officially register, and to put limits on how many times they could meet.[22] It is thus not quite accurate to contrast voluntary associations and "sects" on the basis that the latter, in contrast to the former, had reforming political interests, as does Walker-Ramisch.[23] From the other side, not all "sects" were political. This judgment is reinforced by Bryan Wilson's familiar typology.[24]

Although all associations had a religious dimension, some were specifically "cult associations" (*thiasoi*) established to venerate some deity. Malina argues that religion (as well as economics and education) in Mediterranean antiquity did not exist as a separate, differentiated, and distinctive social institution, but that it could have existed in surrogate or fictive polities or fictive kinship arrangements.[25] Voluntary associations are just such fictive kin associations.

Native cult associations had long been prevalent in the Roman East (Semitic *mazzah* and *gev*). These groups were progenitors of the Greek *thiasoi* known from inscriptions at Palmyra and Dura. Professional guilds were also prevalent in Palestine.[26] In this part of the Mediterranean world Greeks often joined native professional and

---

21. Jean Waltzing [1895] in Wilken, ibid., 281; Kloppenborg, ibid., 23.

22. Johnson et al., *Ancient Roman Statutes*, 82; Cotter, "The Collegia and Roman Law"; see, e.g., Suetonius *Julius Caesar* 42:3; *Augustus* 32:1.

23. Walker-Ramisch, "Graeco-Roman Voluntary Associations," 136, 142; see chap. 9.

24. Wilson, "An analysis of Sect Development"; *Magic*; see Chart 1.1 in chap. 1.

25. Malina, "'Religion' in the World of Paul," 86.

26. Applebaum, "Organization," 464-66; Cohen, *From the Maccabees to the Mishnah*, 119-20.

religious associations in the cities, and thus the associations became Hellenized and contained persons from different ethnic backgrounds, though they were usually of similar social strata in their respective collectivities.[27] In the Diaspora, Torah observers tended to form "ethnic" associations.[28] Some seem to have evolved from military settlements (*katoikia*), and some of these were also cult associations, for example, the "synagogue" (*synagōgē*) or "house of prayer" (*proseuchē*).[29] Although hotly debated, there is scholarly opinion that synagogues in Palestine were also voluntary associations.[30] Similarly, Palestinian groups can also be seen as associations, for example, the Pharisees[31] and, as the following discussion shows, the Qumranites.

In thinking about the voluntary associations as fictive kin groups, one must, of course, keep in mind the centrality of the ancient family. Although there is not space to develop real family relations here[32]—Crosby and Carter have explored many of the essential themes for the Gospel of Matthew[33]—it should not be forgotten, first, that kinship and politics were the two most dominant social domains of antiquity, and, second, that the family was hierarchical and patriarchal. This will be important to keep in mind for exploring the associations, and in this chapter the Dead Sea Scrolls community (or communities) can be seen as an association (or associations) parallel to Matthew 18:15–17. To take this position, it is first necessary to look at a debate about the Dead Sea Scrolls and the Qumran Community in relation to voluntary associations, one that has direct implications for the thesis that the Matthean community can be correlated with a voluntary association as well as a sect.

27. Rostovtzeff, *Social and Economic Histoy* 2, 1064–65.

28. Leon, *Jews*; Applebaum, "Organization," 464; Gutman, "Synagogue Origins"; Kraabel, "Social Systems"; "Unity and Diversity"; Cohen, *From the Maccabees to the Mishnah*.

29. Danker, *Benefactor*, 81; Kraabel, "Unity and Diversity"; Richardson, "Early Synagogues as Collegia"; Ascough, "Matthew and Community Formation," n. 27.

30. Richardson, ibid.

31. Saldarini, *Pharisees*, 281.

32. Cohen, *Jewish Family*; Malina, *New Testament World*; Pilch, "'Beat His Ribs'"; Carter, *Households and Discipleship*, 95–113; Hanson, "Kinship"; Osiek and Balch, *Families*; Moxnes, *Constructing Early Christian Families*; Hanson and Oakman, *Palestine*, 19–62.

33. Crosby, *House of Disciples*; Carter, *Households and Discipleship*.

Moshe Weinfeld's Common Traits of Guilds and Associations: A Methodological Debate about the Dead Sea Scrolls and "Sects"

Specialists in current study of the Dead Sea Scrolls and voluntary associations ask (a) whether it is still possible to analyze the scrolls as a collection, (b) whether it is possible to derive from them social organization data about a group (or groups), and if so, (c) whether such a group can be favorably compared to Mediterranean voluntary associations. The debate is important for both method in general and for the texts in particular. A key issue—again—is "level of abstraction" and the old historians-versus-social sciences debate.[34]

The first scholar to offer a comprehensive study comparing and contrasting organizational features of the Dead Sea Scrolls and ancient voluntary associations was Moshe Weinfeld, who notes earlier scholars such as H. Bardtke and C. Schneider.[35] Weinfeld said that his "sole concern" was "the formal structure of the religious sect."[36] Taking the Dead Sea Scrolls (e.g., 1QS and CD) as representative of the Essenes, Weinfeld analyzed their vocabulary to show that specialized terms—terms not found in any other Second Temple–period literature—were *intended* to correspond to those known from Hellenistic voluntary associations. Then he compared and contrasted the Qumran Community (*yachad*) and voluntary associations on procedures of admission, norms for discipline at meetings, general ethical teachings, and other community rules and penalties. Weinfeld concluded that *the organizational structure and penal code of the Qumran yachad and the Greco-Roman guilds and associations were nearly identical*.

For all the striking terminological and structural similarities between the *yachad* and the voluntary associations, Weinfeld stressed three crucial differences: 1) the *yachad* had no association-type regulations about sacrifices, oblations, or assemblies in temples because, he argued, it had separated itself from the Jerusalem Temple; 2) the *yachad* had no association-like burial and funeral rites because its members lived together communally in the same place; and 3) the

---

34. See chaps. 1 and 2 above.

35. Weinfeld, *Organization Pattern*; see Bardtke, "Der gegenwätige Stand"; Schneider, "Zur Problematik."

36. Weinfeld, ibid., 7.

yachad had no membership fees and pecuniary fines, so typical of the associations. Weinfeld concluded that the reason for these differences was that the *yachad* was a "Jewish sect" with its own sectarian ideology and nature, and a religious "sect" is not exactly an "association."

Sandra Walker-Ramisch objects to Weinfeld's views. She argues that scholars who have taken the Dead Sea Scrolls as evidence for a single group and its practices have usually accepted the early, widespread view that the "Qumran Community" was a "monastic" group identified with "the Essenes."[37] She protests on several grounds. First, any attempt to correlate literature with archeology is questionable. Second, citing Green,[38] the presence of a document in a group says nothing about who produced it or how the group thought about it. Third, any putative synthesis about the group's social life is in the final analysis a Weberian "ideal type" and ideal types have no historical reality; indeed, all ancient texts are selective and unable to yield a Geertzian "thick description."[39] Fourth, Moshe Weinfeld's comparison of the "Qumran Community" (the *yachad*) with ancient voluntary associations[40] follows the dubious procedure of accepting both the "Qumran Community" and "Christianity" as harmonizing constructs.

Walker-Ramisch's alternative is to compare only *one* Qumran text, the Damascus Document, with the voluntary associations. Her comparison yields a negative conclusion. Her main argument is that the Damascus Document is a "sectarian" text. The community it represents demands exclusivity and is opposed to the accepted socio-political order. It does not fit the pattern of voluntary associations, which in her view are both inclusive and generally acceptable to the socio-political order.

Walker-Ramisch holds a classic historical position and many scholars would second a number of her points.[41] Chaim Milikowsky

---

37. Walker-Ramisch, "Graeco-Roman Voluntary Associations." This is the well-known "Essene-Qumran hypothesis," which was put forward by such luminaries as Roland de Vaux, John Strugnell, and Frank Cross; see VanderKam, *The Dead Sea Scrolls Today*. For criticisms, see, e.g., Norman Golb, *Who Wrote the Dead Sea Scrolls?*

38. Green, "Reading the Writing of Rabbinism," 195.

39. Geertz, "Thick Description."

40. Weinfeld, "The Organization Pattern"; see Weinfeld's views below.

41. E.g., the discussions in Collins et al., *Methods of Investigation*; VanderKam, *Dead Sea Scrolls Today*.

makes a similar critique of the harmonizing tendencies of Lawrence Schiffman.[42] Yet, Walker-Ramisch's view is not without its problems. First, her attempt to compare one document to voluntary associations also harmonizes the disparate associations. Second, from a social-scientific perspective, it is permissible to analyze at any chosen level of abstraction.[43] Indeed, the editor of the volume in which her contribution appears warns that "the emphasis on differences rather than similarities and the decision to exclude one local example from the general category [of voluntary associations] is arbitrary... What belongs or does not belong in a category depends to some degree on how broadly it [the category] is defined."[44] Third, the view that the scrolls represent a single group is still supported by many scholars.[45] On the other hand, and fourth, Matthias Klinghardt argues that it is not necessary to think of the scrolls as a whole or even any single document among them as representing *only* a single group at a single point in time—even the Essenes—to argue that scroll organizational patterns have a number of elements in common with those of the Mediterranean associations.[46] It is worth considering in more detail Klinghardt's view of Weinfeld's thesis.

Matthias Klinghardt argues that Weinfeld proved his case, but did not draw the necessary conclusion: not only the external form and organizational structure but the *groups themselves are alike*.[47] For Klinghardt, a broader study of *all the associations*, not just Weinfeld's *selection* from Ptolemaic Egypt, Greece, and Rome, will result in removing Weinfeld's three crucial differences, and thus also in removing his distinction between "sect" and "association." With a broader association database it can be shown, first, that many associations— probably the majority—did *not* practice sacrifice; second, that though many associations had burial regulations, some (especially those of

---

42. Milikowsky, "Law at Qumran"; Schiffman, *Sectarian Law*.

43. See chap. 3 above for a discussion of levels of abstraction in Ritzer's macroscopic/microscopic continuum.

44. Wilson, "Voluntary Associations," 8.

45. E.g., Newsom, "'Sectually Explicit' Literature," 171, 185; VanderKam, *Dead Sea Scrolls Today*, 71-98.

46. Klinghardt, "Manual of Discipline."

47. Klinghardt, "Manual of Discipline," 253.

the higher social strata) did *not* stress them; and, third, some associations did not charge regular fees, while the view that 1QS requires all members to hold property in common, rather than charging fees and fines, is doubtful, especially in light of financial liability for damages (1QS 7:6-8). In contrast to Walker-Ramisch, Klinghardt thinks that Weinfeld *understated his case.*

> [I]f one takes into account the abundant epigraphical evidence for Hellenistic associations in general (of which the statutes form only a very small part) it is evident that the description of the communal life in 1QS perfectly fits into the general structure of those associations. Clearly, the group to which the *serekh* of 1QS applied was organized exactly like an association. That means that the so-called "sect" was a private association in a legal sense. The accuracy with which the statutes, the *serekh*, are formulated does not allow any doubt that its members understood themselves to be anything other than members of an association, not of a cenobitic sect (if this social form can be determined at all). The often claimed religious uniqueness of the so-called Qumran sect, that would distinguish its compatibility with associations, must therefore be understood differently: the particularly Israelite theological (and social!) concepts, such as covenant, purity, holiness, *etc.* were, under the altered circumstances of the Hellenistic culture, realized in the categories of religious associations and thus achieved innovative social concretion in a new political and social setting.[48]

Walker-Ramisch uses a single document (CD) to draw her contrast between the sect and voluntary associations, but Klinghardt uses a single document (1QS) to demonstrate many common features between them; moreover, whereas Walker-Ramisch argued against Weinfeld that the scrolls do not necessarily represent a single sect, for Klinghardt 1QS may have represented several similar groups. In noting this issue, Klinghardt writes: "I have no problems with the idea that 1QS applies to several groups which, of course, would have assembled in different places . . . The variety of meetings and meeting places mentioned in 1QS can, therefore, be explained in two ways: The statutes of 1QS could either belong to different groups (which means different meeting places), or they could apply to only one

48. Ibid., 256-57

group that assembled in different places and at different occasions."[49] Furthermore, the claim of the group to represent all of Israel is not unparalleled in the voluntary associations; indeed, a parallel claim is typical of Dionysiac "cult associations."

Summarizing, the approach taken in this chapter is similar to that of Walker-Ramisch and Klinghardt in comparing *one document*, in this case the Gospel of Matthew, to the voluntary associations. However, it agrees with Klinghardt against Walker-Ramisch that Weinfeld has made his point. At a certain level of abstraction it is possible to draw positive comparisons, as well as contrasts, between the various Greco-Roman associations, *including* the group(s) represented by the Dead Sea Scrolls, and the various Christ-believing groups represented by the various early Christ-believers' texts. Indeed, it is possible with Klinghardt to see what is usually called a "sect" (in the language of Weinfeld and others) as a type of "association," not only organizationally, but with respect to the group itself. Thus, the rest of this chapter attempts to draw positive comparisons between various kinds of groups in the circum-Mediterranean and the Gospel of Matthew. I shall take the position that the kind of group (or groups) represented by the Dead Sea Scrolls, as well as that (those?)[50] represented by the Matthean writer, *can* be seen as associations. At a certain level of abstraction, the associations, including that (those) represented in the scrolls, provide comparative data to understand the organization of the Matthean group in terms of fictive kinship. Richard Ascough agreed with my suggestion, citing for support the work of both Anthony Saldarini and Michael Crosby.[51] He wrote: "Duling is not only interesting but also compelling. However, his thesis that the Matthean community can be understood as a voluntary association can be strengthened when one takes account of a broader database of material from the associations."[52]

---

49. Ibid., 268.

50. See Stanton, "Communities of Matthew"; *A Gospel*; "Revisiting Matthew's Communities."

51. Saldarini, *Matthew's Christian-Jewish Community*; Crosby, *House of Disciples*.

52. Ascough, "Matthew and Community Formation," 2–3.

Matthew 18:15: Conflict, Personal Confrontation, Honor, and Conflict Resolution

The essential question is, does Matthew 18:15–17 contain a judicial process, or at least a quasi-judicial process, analogous to those characteristic of ancient fictive kin voluntary associations? Recall again the view taken here: the Matthean writer inserted verses 16–17, 18 (cf. Matt 16:19), and 19–20 into Q, that is, between 18:15 (= Q 17:3) and 18:21–22 (= Q 17:4). I take up first Matthew 18:15 from Q (Bold = common underlying Greek in Matthew and Luke; underlined = different Greek *form* in Matthew and Luke; brackets = "little or no probability of an origin in Q" [Kloppenborg][53]; *italics* = special to Matthew).

Matthew 18:15	Luke 17:3
	["Take heed to yourselves;]
But **if your brother sins** *against you* **go and reprove him**, *between you and him alone.* **If he** *listens to you,* **you have gained your brother.**	**if your brother sins**, **rebuke him**, and if he repents, forgive him;

Luke 17:3 contains a general statement about *any* sin. Galatians 6:1 may be a parallel, although it seems to skip individual response and moves to an immediate *group* response: "Brothers, if a person is overtaken *in any trespass*, you (pl.) who are spiritual should restore him in a spirit of gentleness, looking to yourself, lest you too be tempted." Presuming that Luke 17:3 better represents Q, the First Evangelist adds the following: "against you," "between you and him alone," and "your . . . to you . . . your" in the singular. The major Uncial manuscripts, Sinaiticus and Vaticanus, do not have "against you [*eis se*, singular]." Earlier editions of the Nestle Greek text omitted these words, but the Nestle-Aland text places them in brackets as difficult to determine. One possibility is that "against you" was omitted from Matthew, either accidently, or intentionally, to apply the saying to sin in general, as in Luke. Another option is that "against you" was added by a later copyist, perhaps suggested by v. 21 [*eis eme*].[54] However, internal textual

---

53. Kloppenborg, *Q Parallels*, xvi.
54. Metzger, *A Textual Commentary*, 36.

evidence—the personal nature of the Matthean context as a whole—suggests that the Matthean writer himself added "against you" to Q. Gundry holds this view and thinks that Matthew also added "between you and him alone," "alone" being a Mattheanism.[55] It should be noted that Luke 17:4 is *also* personal. If Matthew made the additions, the change has a *very strong stress on an initial personal confrontation*. The addition of "listens" has the connotation of "obeys" and might be translated "heeds."[56] If so, when it is used again in verse 17 it ". . . means, as it does uniformly in the LXX, 'hear without heeding.'"[57] In other words, the meaning would be that if he does not refuse to listen, "you have gained your brother."

"To sin" in the Matthean context refers to an offense or insult against one's "brother" (18:21). No particular personal offense is mentioned. We know, of course, about some kinds of public offenses in the Greco-Roman voluntary associations. Examples include singing, applauding, creating a disturbance, acting disorderly, fist-fighting, and brawling at meetings. In the Dead Sea Scrolls, primarily the Community Rule, at communal meetings there are many offenses mentioned: not asking permission to speak, interrupting someone else's speech, not speaking according to hierarchical rank, defending a position against the group norm, falling asleep, spitting, answering with stubbornness or anger, and scoffing at another member.[58] However, there are private offenses such as lying, insulting, deceiving, not caring, slandering, going naked, gesticulating with the left hand, and the like.[59] Most of the references to offenses against one's "brother" in Matthew outside Matthew 18 seem to be similar, though less graphic, for example, insults (5:22), having something against one's brother (5:23), and judging others unjustly (7:3, 4, 5).[60]

In Matthew the offended brother attempts to work out the offense with the offending brother privately. The offended brother first confronts the offending brother. Why? By implication the motive—only in

---

55. Gundry, *Matthew*, 367, the evidence being Matthew's 9x to Luke's 0.
56. Davies and Allison, *Matthew*, 2:783.
57. Ibid., 2:785.
58. Weinfeld, *Organization Pattern*, 55–57.
59. Vermes, *Dead Sea Scrolls*, 70–71.
60. See chap. 7 for further discussion of the Matthean brotherhood.

Matthew—is "to gain" or "win over" the brother who is the supposed perpetrator. Not only is *kerdainō*, "I win over," a Mattheanism;[61] the redaction of Q is suggested by the context as a whole: the offending brother needs to be forgiven and joyfully retrieved like the "lost sheep" in 18:12-13.[62] Perhaps even more important is the apparent change of terms for confrontation: from "rebuke" (QLuke 17:3: *epitimēson*) to "reprove" (Matt 18:15: *elenchon*). This change is especially striking when one looks at "reproof" in Torah-minded groups and at "frank speech" in the Graeco-Roman philosophical schools, both of which are in the Matthean author's cultural environment.

"Reproof" and "Frank Speech" Etiquette in Mediterranean Society

Among Judeans there is an extensive "reproof" tradition that contains a norm for conflict resolution. Some sense of this tradition will reinforce the point about the First Evangelist's changes. Here I am especially indebted to the work of James Kugel.[63]

Leviticus 19:15–17 is the sacred source text. It stresses *private reproof as the honorable way to resolve conflict in a group*:

> 15) "You shall not render an unjust judgment; you shall not be partial to the poor or defer to the great; with justice you shall judge your neighbor. You shall not go around as a slanderer among your people, and you shall not profit by [stand by, ignore] the blood of your brother: I am the LORD. 17) *You shall not hate in your heart your brother, but you* surely reprove *your neighbor, lest you bear a grudge* (LXX: "sin") *against him*. 18) You shall not take vengeance or bear any grudge against the sons of your own people, but you shall love your neighbor as yourself: I am the LORD. (NRSV, slightly modified)

Initially, it should be noted that the act of reproving *can* be part of God's final judgment of outsiders, especially in millennial messianic passages (e.g., 1 Enoch 1:9; 4 Ezra 12:33–38);[64] however, the more common tradition is human reproof of other humans. Also, in the LXX,

---

61. Matt 5x; Mark 1x; Luke 1x.
62. Thompson, *Matthew's Advice*, 187; Davies and Allison, *Matthew*, 2:784.
63. Kugel, "On Hidden Behavior and Open Reproach."
64. Buechler, "*Elenchō*," 474–75.

the Greek *elenchō*, "I reprove," can translate a variety of Hebrew terms that mean "to rebuke," "to shame," even "to punish," "to condemn," "to convict," "to test," "to examine."[65] However, it commonly translates the Hebrew *yākah*, "he reproves," and indeed may be contrasted with the term usually translated "I rebuke" (Greek *epitimaō*), which is sharper and negative, as the gospel exorcism stories clearly show.[66]

With regard to the main "reproof" tradition, the statements in Lev 19:15–18 are part of regulations about ritual and moral holiness (Leviticus 19) in the "Holiness Code" (Leviticus 17–26). They forbid a) judging one's neighbor on the basis of social status, b) slander, c) profiting by the death of one's brother, d) continuing to hate one's brother, and e) grudge bearing. If there is any unity in these seemingly diverse categories, it may be, as Kugel says, in the view that *relationships cannot be enforced simply by legal fiat but depend on one's internal disposition, or "purity of heart."*[67] It is important to see that behind "You shall *surely reprove*" in Leviticus 19:17 is an emphatic doubling in Hebrew (*hōkhēach tōkhîach*) which generates comments in the Rabbinic traditions. The LXX Greek translators tried to imitate it (*elegmō elencheis*).[68] Of this emphasis, Kugel says, "All modern commentators . . . see the verse as expressing a single, basic injunction: do not let hatred simmer inside you—if your fellow has done something to incite your hatred, reproach him openly and avoid, thereby, being led into sin."[69] Thus, the command to gently confront a "brother" or "neighbor" is meant to foster an internal disposition designed to honorably avoid destructive interpersonal conflict in a group. It is part of group conflict resolution.

What group is in view? Some Hebrew terms associated with reproof (ʿ*am*: "people," "kinsperson"; *ach*: "brother," "relative," "kinsman") suggest the clan, thus kinship. Other Hebrew terms associated with reproof (ʿ*amîth*: "associate," "fellow," "relation," "comrade," "neighbor"; *ra*ʿ: "neighbor," "friend," "companion"; "fellow"; "comrade") might point to the village or town. Sometimes the two different social categories occur in the same passage, suggesting the

65. Ibid., 473.
66. Kee, "Terminology of Mark's Exorcism Stories."
67. Kugel, "On Hidden Behavior and Open Reproach," 44–45.
68. Ibid., 55 n. 34.
69. Ibid., 45.

possibility that there was a historical shift from a nomadic clan context to a pastoral/agricultural village context, and, further, to leadership by priestly families and the High Priest, that is, a hierocracy centered in the Jerusalem Temple.[70] The late Levitical writer might have deliberately alternated the Hebrew terms/contexts.[71] The LXX translators then translated Hebrew ʿam ("people"; "kinsperson") by Greek *ethnos* ("people"; "tribe"; "nation") or *laos* ("people"), and Hebrew *ach* ("brother") by Greek *adelphos* ("brother"). However, to make matters more confusing (for us) they also translated *both* Hebrew terms by the *same* term, *plēsion* ("neighbor"). Stated simply, Hebrew "brother" is translated sometimes as "brother," sometimes as "neighbor." It would appear that this crossover makes it easier at a still later time to apply these terms and commands to *fictive* kin groups.

In the early second century BCE, Ben Sira continues the Levitical reproof practice of Lev 19:17 (Sir 28:7), but it is now related to teaching and training as a part of the Hellenistic cultural value of *paideia*, that is, proper "education for culture."[72] The teacher reproves and trains and teaches his students, and turns them back, as a shepherd his flock. He has compassion on those who accept his discipline (*paideian*) and who are eager for his judgments (Sir 18:13b-14). In the Gospel of Matthew similar themes are the shepherd/sheep (7:15; 9:36; 10:6, 16; 12:11, 12; 15:24; 18:12; 25:32, 33; 26:31), compassion (9:36; 14:14; 15:32), and judgment (especially 5:21, 22; 7:2). In Ben Sira to *avoid* compassionate confrontation (reproof) is "sin" (21:6; 32:17), yet even the wise can be seduced into avoiding it by gifts (20:29). The *right time* for reproof is crucial (20:1): for example, one should never reprove at a banquet (31:31)! Again, one hears the key theme: "How much better it is to reprove (*elenchai*) than to stay angry! And the one who confesses his fault will be kept from loss" (20:2).

The clearest, most complete statement is in Ben Sira 19:

> 13 *Reprove* a friend, perhaps he did not do it;
> but if he did anything, so that he may do it no more.
> 14 *Reprove* a neighbor, perhaps he did not say it;
> but if he said it, so that he may not say it again.

70. Levine, "Discharging Responsibility," 319–320.

71. Kugel, "On Hidden Behavior and Open Reproach," 45.

72. Moreau, *A History of Education*; Hengel, *Judaism and Hellenism*, Vol. 1, 79, 132. See above, pp. 203–4.

> 15 *Reprove* a friend, for often it is slander;
> so do not believe everything you hear.
> 16 A person may make a slip without intending it.
> Who has never sinned with his tongue?
> 17 *Reprove* your neighbor before you threaten him;
> and let the law of the Most High take its course.

There are parallels elsewhere in Ben Sira between "friend" and "brother" (Sir 7:12, 18) and between "brothers" and "neighbors," including "friendship" (Sir 25:1; 6:17). Reproving friends is not only a means to correct offenses, but a process for helping to discover slander where no offense was actually committed (cf. Jas 3:1-12). It is important to recall again that Ben Sira's book may have actually been known to the First Evangelist.[73]

The Dead Sea Scrolls take up the "reproof" tradition and develop it into a more formal judicial process, and the scrolls *might* have been known to the First Evangelist.[74] John Kampen has argued that the Matthean writer knew not only the ideology of the scrolls, but perhaps some of its specific documents.[75] I shall delay this point until later since it can be discussed more profitably in connection with Matt 18:16-17.

It is not possible to prove that the First Evangelist knew the *Testaments of the Twelve Patriarchs*. Nonetheless, the testimony of the *Testaments* is important for illustrating Torah-minded groups in the period of the First Evangelist and the Dead Sea Scrolls.[76] The *Testament of Gad* 4:1-3 continues to stress the values of avoiding hatred, slander, and public dishonor in court. Correspondingly, avoiding reproof dishonors God's command to love one's neighbor (Lev 19:18) and, indeed, God himself. The *Testament of Gad* also elaborates Levitical themes with a stress on the honor of not allowing hatred to simmer, and one does so by pursuing private reproof (compare also Prov 26:24):[77]

---

73. Stendahl, *School*, 142.
74. Ibid.
75. Kampen, "A Reexamination"; "Communal Discipline," 9.
76. Nickelsburg, *Jewish Literature*, 233-34.
77. Kugel, "On Hidden Behavior and Open Reproach," 52.

> 1) "Now my children, each of you *love his brother* [Lev 19:18]. Drive hatred out of *your hearts* [Lev 19:17]. Love one another in deed and word and inward thoughts. 2) For when I stood before my father I would speak peaceably about Joseph, but when I went out, the spirit of hatred darkened my mind and aroused my soul to kill him. 3) *Love one another from the heart* [Lev 19:17, 18], therefore, and if anyone sins against you, *speak to him in peace* [Lev 19:17]. Expel the venom of hatred, and do not harbor deceit in your heart. If anyone confesses and repents, forgive him. 4) If anyone denies his guilt, do not be contentious with him, otherwise he may start cursing, and you would be sinning doubly [Lev 19:18]. 5) In a dispute do not let an outsider hear your secrets, since out of hatred for you he may become your enemy, and commit a great sin against you. He may talk to you frequently but treacherously, or be much concerned with you, but for an evil end, having absorbed from you the venom. 6) Even if he denies it and acts disgracefully out of a sense of guilt, be quiet and do not become upset. For he who denies will repent, and avoid offending you again; indeed he will honor you, will respect you and be at peace. 7) Even if he is devoid of shame and persists in his wickedness, *forgive him from the heart* [19:17] and leave vengeance to God." (*T. Gad* 6:1–6)

In 4 Ezra, also datable to the period of the First Evangelist,[78] Ezra is to reprove his people like a father/master of the household, which includes "comforting the lowly" and instruction to those that are wise. Ezra's response suggests that reproof is also a warning (v. 19; compare 14:13–22).

The theme of unending reproof is also found among the rabbis.[79] A *Sifra* on Lev 19:17 says that one should avoid shaming the offender in public. Here the emphatic doubling in Hebrew (*hōkhēach tōkhîach*) in verse 17 is interpreted as "even four or five times ... [and] further," that is, *repeatedly*. The same point is made in Babylonian tractate *Baba Mezia* 31a: "One of the Rabbis said to Raba: *hōkhēach tōkhîach*—perhaps *hōkhēach* means 'one time' and *tōkhîach* means 'twice.' He said: *hōkhēach* means even a hundred times." The similarity with the Matthean forgiving "not . . . seven times, but seventy times seven" (18:21–22) is striking. The opposition position, however, is found in

---

78. Nickelsburg, *Jewish Literature*, 287; Esler, "God's Honor and Rome's Triumph."
79. Kugel, "On Hidden Behavior and Open Reproach," 55.

Targum Pseudo-Jonathan on Lev 19:17. While to let hate simmer and "speak smooth words" (flattery?) is hypocrisy, the one who ultimately reproves should not take responsibility for any public shame.[80]

Turning from Israelite to Greco-Roman texts, among the philosophers *elenchō* very often means "I shame."[81] For Plato, the philosopher "reproves" when he refutes a proposition (*Soph.* 241d; 529a; *Gorg.* 570c; *Theaet.* 171d; *Phae.* 273c). Aristotle, in a treatise on correcting sophistical reproof, uses it for negative demonstration (the other side of epideictic rhetoric). The one who reproves should be free from the same fault; otherwise the reproved person is not properly shamed (*Rhet.* 1384b). Closer to the Torah-based groups are the Stoics. Zeno is said to have written two treatises called "Reproof" (Diog. L. 7.4) and Epictetus considered it a duty to accept reproof, however difficult (e.g., *Diss.* 2.14, 20; 1.26,17). Indeed, with roots in Cynicism, *elenchō* and its cognates became technical terms in the healing of souls.[82]

An instructive parallel is the philosophical virtue of *parrēsia*, usually translated "frank speech." *Parrēsia* can be private, but also has public, political connotations, namely, words spoken boldly and openly by free, male citizens of the *polis*; thus, resident aliens, foreigners, slaves, and women could not practice it.[83] For the Cynic philosopher Epictetus, *parrēsia* is divinely appointed. For Lucian it improves others and promotes friendship. In his essay *Peri Parrēsias*, the Epicurean philosopher Philodemus says that the wise man should use *parrēsia* to correct disciples and advance moral development among friends. Some, especially the young or those with little knowledge of themselves, resist it. Nonetheless, "frank speech" is absolutely necessary for the development of virtue, Philodemus stresses. One must point out to friends and students their "sin" in order to remove it. Benjamin Fiore notes a number of parenetic terms for the practice of "frank speech" or "frank criticism" in Philodemus' essay and

---

80. Ibid., 56–57; cf. Kampen, "Communal Discipline," 2–3.
81. Buechler, "*Elenchō*," 473 n. 2; 475.
82. Buechler, "*Elenchō*," 475.
83. Neyrey, *Paul in Other Words*, 67; see, e.g., Acts 2:29, 29, 31; 28:31.

among them are *elenchō* and its cognates.[84] Philo, too, is aware of the relationship between friendship and frank speech.[85]

"Frank speech" and "reproof" are honorable ways to solve personal disputes in a group setting by direct personal confrontation. It is important to remember that the Matthean writer, a Torah-minded scribe writing in some eastern Greco-Roman city for a Torah-based group or groups, has a striking number of allusions and references to the book of Leviticus, particularly Leviticus 19, some of which are clearly added from Mark and Q:

a) 5:21-26 (Lev 19:14, 16-17); 5:23-24 (Lev 19:21-22); 5:33-37 (Lev 19:11-12) [Matt adds]; 5:38-42 (Lev 19:17, 17-18a); 5:43 (Lev 19:18) [Matt adds]; 5:44 (Lev 19:34) [Q]; 5:48 (Lev 19:2) [Q]; and

b) 18:15 (Lev 19:17) [Q]; 19:18 (Lev 22:39) [Matt adds]; 19:19 (Lev 19:18) [Matt adds]; 20:8 (Lev 19:13) [M?]; 22:29 (Lev 19:34).

J. Duncan Derrett offers a list of twenty-three items alluding to or quoting Leviticus 18-24 in the Sermon on the Mount![86] In Matthew 5, the higher righteousness tends to transcend the Levitical commands; yet, in Matthew 18-20, love of neighbor (see below) and brotherly reproof from Leviticus 19 are viewed as group norms.[87] It should be noted that Matt 7:1-5 also hints at Lev 19:15-18. As mentioned above, the Matthean author probably also knows Ben Sira and writes in the same general period as the redaction of the *Testaments of the Twelve Patriarchs* and 4 Ezra. That the Matthean author knows about Greco-Roman philosophical reproof and frank speech as honorable ways to solve personal disputes in a group cannot be shown clearly, but it is very likely. Q, the author's source, already offers the general norm of "rebuke" and its personalized practice (Q 17:3, 4). Paul and the Pauline School seem to know about it, as well (Gal 6:1; see further below). The First Evangelist goes further. His modification of Q 17:3 in Matt 18:15 alludes to Lev 19:17. That he shares the practice of reproof with his authorial audience should not be doubted. It is

---

84. Fiore, "Pastoral Epistles"; cf. Konstan, "Friendship, Frankness, and Flattery."
85. Sterling, "Bond of Humanity," 207.
86. Derrett, "Christ and Reproof," 277.
87. Carter, *Households and Discipleship*.

also suggested by the probable social contexts for Q and the Gospel of Matthew: Q fits village life where natural kinship would be a more viable context; the Gospel of Matthew fits an urban environment, the context for fictive kin voluntary associations.

In short, Matt 18:15 revises Q 17:3 in relation to private, personal "reproof" as known from the Torah (Lev 19:17), Judean tradition, and his own authorial audience. Most probably it reflects widespread practices in Torah-minded groups, philosophical groups, and voluntary associations. What then of the next two verses? Does Matt 18:16–17 imply a formal judicial process?

Matthew 18:16–17 and Conflict Resolution: Development of a Formal Judiciary Process?

Matthew 18:16–17a reads:
16) But if he does not listen take one or two others along with you, that "every word may be confirmed by the evidence of two or three witnesses" (Deut 19:15)
17a) If he refuses to listen to them
tell it to the *ekklēsia* . . .

This segment has no parallel in Luke 17. With respect to language, "take" in 18:16 is typically Matthean (Matthew 16x; Mark 6x; Luke 7x) and so is *ekklēsia* in 18:17 (Matthew 3x; Mark 0x; Luke 0x). Again, the verses are Matthew's addition to Q (see above) and clearly imply some sort of process. As with Matthew 18:15, the attempt will be to understand that authorial audience from within a broader cultural context.

Four of the common features isolated by Weinfeld (and implied by Klinghardt) are of great interest for an interpretation of Matt 18:15–17: reproof of members, exclusion from the Purity, temporary expulsion, and final expulsion. In Weinfeld's view reproof and exclusion from the Purity are found in the Dead Sea Scrolls, the New Testament, and the Pharisaic/Rabbinic literature; temporary expulsion is found only in the Dead Sea Scrolls; final expulsion is attested in the Egyptian Demotic texts, the Dead Sea Scrolls, and the Greco-Roman associations. I shall suggest a slightly modified stance. Focusing on the association called the *Iobakchoi* and the Torah-based reproof texts and their groups, especially in the Dead Sea Scrolls, *it is likely that a more formalized procedure that included expulsion originally existed in the Matthew group but that the Matthean author muted it in light of the earlier reproof traditions and his ideology of unlimited mercy*.[88]

Lines 33–165 of an inscription recording the *Iobakchoi*'s minutes of a meeting convened to revise its by-laws (ca. 150 CE) offer a glimpse of its disciplinary procedure.[89] Beginning in line 74 the document states that the "sin" may be quarreling, uncivil behavior, taking someone's place (of honor at a meeting?), (verbal) insults, or demeaning another in the group. I summarize these processes.

In the case of a "sin" against the offended:

- There is no private, personal reproof.
- The offended party and two witnesses present the case (to whom? The Priest or Vice-Priest? or the assembled *Iobakchoi*?).
- The witnesses hear the party testify under oath.
- The pecuniary punishment for the guilty party is twenty-five light *drachmai*.
- The guilty party is excluded until the fine is paid.

In the more physical case of one who claims to have been struck first in a fistfight at the meeting:

- There is no private, personal reproof.
- A written complaint is filed with the Priest or Vice-Priest.
- The Priest or Vice-Priest convenes a meeting of the *Iobakchoi*.
- A decision is rendered, whether for the plaintiff or the defendant.
- The offender is excluded for a time specified at the meeting.
- The offender is fined a fine not to exceed twenty-five light *drachmai*.[90]

---

88. Cp. Duling, "Binding and Loosing."

89. See especially Danker, *Benefactor*, 156–66; Weinfeld, *The Organization Pattern*; Douglas, "Matthew 18:15–17."

90. It can be added that lines 123–26 rank the officers as follows: "Priest, Vice-Priest, Arch-Bakchos, Treasurer, the Rustic Performer, those who play the roles of

In the case of an offense or "sin," if the sergeant-at-arms does not intervene he must share in the guilt; if he does not act to see that the brawlers are ejected, he is also given a fine not to exceed twenty-five drachmai. Lines 137–45 state: "The sergeant-at-arms . . . shall place the official wand of our God next to anyone who is guilty of inappropriate or disruptive behavior. Anyone who has this wand deposited near his person shall, upon the decision of the priest or the arch-Bakchos, depart from the banqueting hall. Should he refuse to accept the eviction, the Horses appointed by the priests shall eject him and he shall be liable for the fine applicable to brawlers." [91] As Weinfeld observed, there is no practice of private reproof mentioned. Either there was no such practice or it was omitted because the inscription deals with discipline at public assemblies, not conflict resolution in the case of private disputes. Nonetheless, in the case of milder incidents there are testimonies made before *three witnesses*—to whom is not quite clear—or in the case of physical fighting, a written complaint is issued to an officer followed by defenses and a judgment of the whole assembly. In this instance the association hierarchy clearly has a role in conflict resolution. It is noteworthy that in the case of brawls the sergeant-at-arms is held responsible and that the fine is stiffer—double—for those who do not show up for the hearing. Exclusion is apparently temporary until the fine is paid, but, of course, it could be permanent if the fine is not paid.

In short, although the context is public assembly—one is reminded of conflicts in 1 Corinthians[92]—there is some correlation with Matt 18:16–17a.

Most important for conflict resolution in the *ekklēsia* in Matt 18:16–17a is the "reproof" tradition as it is developed in the Dead Sea Scrolls, briefly noted above. Here I shall explore it in more detail.

Dionysos, Kore, Palaimon, Aphrodite, and Proteurythmos. All members are, however, to be eligible for the roles of the deities." The sergeant-at-arms is either chosen by lot or appointed by the Priest.

91. Danker, *Benefactor*, 159. The "Horses" are apparently "bouncers." Also, those who refuse to attend a meeting convened to decide such issues are fined fifty light *drachmai* payable to the association. They are excluded by the Treasurer until the fine is paid.

92. Pfitzner, "Purified Community—Purified Sinner."

Personal reproof in the presence of witnesses in the Dead Sea Scrolls is more than an honorable practice for conflict resolution; it is a *legal requirement*. It must be carried out prior to a judicial decision that involves punishment. Some specialists claim that it is part of the association's "penal code." 1QS 5:24–6:1 says: "(Members ought) ... to reprove (25) each his neighbor in tru[th] and humility and in lovingkindness to a man: Let him not speak to hi[m] in anger or in complaint (26) or stub[bornly or in jealousy] caused by an evil disposition. Let him not hate him in [...] his heart but on that very day let him reprove him, lest he (27) bear sin because of him. And also, let no one bring a charge against his neighbor before the assembly [lit. "the Many"] which is not with reproof before witnesses."[93] In a context of ranking group members for promotion, this passage interprets the reproof passage in Lev 19:17 in relation to the spirit of "lovingkindness" (ḥesed) in Mic 6:8:[94] "He has showed you, O man, what is good; and what does the LORD require of you, but to do justice, and to love kindness, and to walk humbly with your God?" The principle, immediate reproof of one's brother "on that day," is repeated in CD 7:2–3: "to reprove (lēhōkhēach) each man his brother according to the commandment [Lev 19:17: hōkhēach tōkhîach] and not to bear a grudge from one day to the next." The time limitation in both passages is most likely before sunset on the same day. Schiffman compares the time limitation to "from day to day" in CD 9:6 and "that very day" in 1QS 5:26, and to Tannaitic and Karaite law about time limitations for annulling the wife's vow, which requires that it be done before sunset (cf. Num 30:15). Compare also the statement in Eph 4:25b–26a: "... let every one speak the truth with his neighbor, for we are members one of another. Be angry but *do not sin* [Deut 24:15]; *do not let the sun go down on your anger*..." The New Testament book of Hebrews might refer to the same principle: "Exhort one another every day, as long as it is called 'today,' so that none of you may be hardened by the deceitfulness of sin" [Heb 3:13].) The stress on a "brother" in 1QS implies *insiders* (compare 1QS 9:16–17).[95] In 1QS 5:24–25 the first sentence ("each his neighbor") seems to suggest an initial private,

---

93. Trans. mainly Schiffman, "Sectarian Law," 93, 94; *in his heart* and *bear sin* are renderings in accordance with Kugel's interpretations.

94. Schiffman, *Sectarian Law*, 94, 105–6 n. 57.

95. Forkman, *Limits*, 48.

personal reproof, as in Matthew. However, the last sentence clouds the issue ("before witnesses"). Perhaps the passage is evidence for a development in the process. Early passages in 1QS imply that the whole group made judgments about discipline; later passages (after 6:12), CD 10:1–10 and 4Q 159, seem to give the collegium of 12 and 3 this authority. Göran Forkman says: "The simplest way of solving these difficulties is to assume that the latter half of the scroll [1QS] reflects later conditions within the sect... The sect which the Manual of Discipline describes has obviously gone through a certain development in the field of consolidation and institutionalization, through which the power of judgment was concentrated in the priests. The text of the Manual seems to have grown alongside this development."[96] In any case, reproof stresses the usual element of internal disposition, but it is a required prerequisite to avoid accusation before "the Many."

Linguistically similar to 1QS 5:24–6:1 is the key reproof text, CD 9:2–8:

> (2) As to that which He said, "You shall not take revenge and you shall not bear a grudge against your kinsfolk (Lev 19:18a)," every man from among those who have entered the (3) Covenant who shall bring a charge against his neighbor which is not with reproof ($b^e hōkhēach$) before witnesses, (4) or brings it (the charge) when he is angry (with him) or relates it to his (the accused's) elders to make them despise him, is taking vengeance and bearing a grudge. (5) Is it not written that only "He (God) takes vengeance on His adversaries and bears a grudge against His enemies (Nah 1:2)?" (6) (But) if he kept silent about him from day to day, and accused him of a capital offense (only) when he was angry with him, (7) his (the accused's) guilt is upon him (the accuser), since he did not fulfill the commandment of God who said to him, "You shall surely (8) reprove ($hōkhēach\ tōkhîach$) your neighbor, lest you bear a grudge because of him (Lev 19:17)."[97]

Leviticus 19:17–18 is now part of a *formal judicial procedure* that has several emphases. First, the offended party must reprove the offender—again!—to avoid grudge bearing, and thus self-incrimination. Second, one must not procrastinate about confrontation—again!—

---

96. Ibid., 51.

97. Translation mainly Schiffman, *Sectarian Law*, 89, reformatted; numbered; I have added Hebrew transliterations.

"from day to day." Third, the main motive is—again!—to avoid accusing one's brother in the heat of anger. Nahum 1:2 is cited to show that only God has the right of anger, revenge, and grudge bearing (cf. Deut 32:35), a point also made in the Fragment and Neofiti Targums on Deut 32:35. Recall that Paul paraphrases Deut 32:35 in Rom 12:19: "Vengeance is mine, I will repay, says the Lord."[98] Fourth—now there is a major difference—the reproving in this first step is *clearly in the presence of witnesses, not privately*. The precise number of witnesses is not stated, but the "two or three" of Deut 19:15-21 is very likely (see CD 9:16b-22 below).[99] Fifth—this is very new—the accuser must not attempt to dishonor a member *before his superiors, the elders,* which may be parallel to bringing the case before the "the Many" in 1QS.[100]

A third, related reproof text, CD 9:16b-22, which for space reasons I shall omit here, deals with "reproof" by a single witness to a "neighbor's" offense—not personally to the witness himself—three times *seriatim, each* of which must be recorded by "the Examiner" or "Overseer." The number of required witnesses for punishment in capital offenses is at least three, but the testimony of two witnesses involving a punishment of separation from pure food is less clear, since either one or separate offenses is possible. Deuteronomy 19:15 might suggest either two or three.[101]

Despite a few variations (related to group development?), these texts show that reproof is a required preliminary step in a judicial process, that in some cases there must be (two or three) witnesses, and that should reproof fail, appearance before a larger judicial group is involved. That initial reproof must be in the presence of witnesses is a new theme when compared to the earlier stress on direct personal confrontation. The reason for this allowance may be because there is no clear indication that a reputed "victim" must be the one who reproves, or even that the offense involves an offended *person*. It could result from violation of some rule. This appears to mean that initial private, personal reproof is especially important where there is a "victim," that is, where there is one offended who is in more danger of

---

98. Schiffman, "Reproof," 90.
99. So Forkman, *Limits*, 49.
100. So Kugel, "On Hidden Behavior and Open Reproach," 54.
101. Schiffman, "Reproof," 74–75; Milikowsky, "Law at Qumran," 243.

letting the offense simmer "in his heart." In such cases, whoever the reporter of the offense is, he should not bypass the offender and go directly to the group, as is also the case in Matt 18:15–17. Moreover, one must reprove on the same day, otherwise he will be guilty of "sin." In some cases, the offense is to be recorded by the Overseer. Failure to conform results minimally in demotion in status, and beyond that, total expulsion from the group.[102]

In the Dead Sea Scrolls, the *natural* groups of Leviticus and the other earlier groups that passed on the Levitical practice have been replaced by a *voluntary* group. "Your people" as a natural village or ethnic collectivity has become "the Covenant"; the "sons of your people" have become members who "enter" a group under strict regulations. All this signals a low grid, but strong group with sharp boundaries and hierarchical organization.[103] In short, reproving group members is an honorable way to help maintain group purity and group cohesion.

It may be added that similar processes are carried on among the rabbis. With respect to Deut 19:15, "Samuel said: Whoever sins against his brother, he must say *to him*, I have sinned against you. If he hears, it is well; if not let him *bring others*, and let him appease him before them" (*y. Yoma* 45c).[104] There is also a parallel function between formal judicial reproof and the rabbinic "warning" (*hatra'ah*) which says that there can be no conviction unless the defendant has been previously warned about the illegality of the offense. However, in this case only *one* offense is required, and no record keeping is necessary.[105]

In Matt 18:16 the First Evangelist uses the text for witnesses that was commonly used in Torah-minded groups, Deut 19:15 (two or three witnesses). This Deuteronomy passage was also known and cited in Pauline and Johannine groups (2 Cor 13:1; 1 Tim 5:19; John 8:17).[106] However, the most detailed and closest parallels to Matthew 18:16–17a are practices in the Dead Sea Scrolls developed above. That the author shared this "witness" with others in his culture is highly

---

102. Forkman, *Limits*, 63.
103. Ibid., 50. See pp. 173–75.
104. Davies and Allison, *Matthew*, 2:784.
105. Schiffman, "Qumran Law," 73–74; *Sectarian Law*, 97–98.
106. Van Vliet, *No Single Testimony*.

likely. His emphasis may be further indicated by other uses of two and three in the gospel. The author explicitly highlights two sets of brothers/disciples (4:18, 21; 10:2; 17:1; 20:24). He makes the healing of a blind man into two blind men (20:30), and does so twice (9:27). He specifically mentions that there were two false witnesses at Jesus' trial (26:60; see Mark 14:57). There are also two instead of three female witnesses to the empty tomb (28:1; see Mark 16:1) and again to the resurrection (28:9). The First Evangelist transforms Mark's accusations against Peter by a maid and bystanders into a series of three: a maid, a second maid, and bystanders, and in each case there is a denial and a cock crow (26:69-75; compare Mark 14:66-72). Thus, the First Evangelist is especially aware of the evidence of two or three witnesses.

What is the *ekklēsia* in Matt 18:17a? First, the term *ekklēsia* in 18:17 (and 16:19) always poses a special problem.[107] In classical, Hellenistic, and Roman settings, the *ekklēsia* denoted the public assembly of free male citizens to conduct the affairs of the *polis*.[108] However, in Roman Syria, villages and towns were often governed by a *local council* with the same name. In the LXX, *ekklēsia* sometimes translated the "Assembly (Hebrew *Qāhal*) of Yahweh," but also rendered terms for its decision making bodies (e.g., Ezra 10; Nehemiah 13). The language of the *polis* was also transferred to voluntary associations and their ruling bodies, for example, the council of ruling elders in the Dead Sea Scrolls. In Matthew 16:19 "my [Jesus'] *ekklēsia*" could have referred to the whole association. In Matt 18:17 it could have meant a council of elders.[109] Probably the brother who insults another brother and fails to respond to the reproof is liable to the association council (Matt 5:22). Given the Dead Sea Scrolls' development of priestly authority in relation to the rules of evidence and similar roles of officers among the *Iobakchoi*, and given that that there is no evidence that a serious offense is in view, let alone a capital case, a council is certainly not out of the question.

Lastly, the First Evangelist's conclusion in 18:17b, "And if he refuses to listen to the *ekklēsia* let him be to you as an *ethnikos* and a toll collector," is not easy to interpret.[110] It is well known that the

---

107. Duling, "Binding and Loosing."
108. Douglas, "Matthew 18:15-17," 3 n. 8.
109. Davies and Allison, *Matthew*, 2:786-87.
110. See chap. 10 below.

Gospel of Matthew contains positive passages about *ethnē/ethnikoi*. The gospel places Jesus' message and activity mainly in "Galilee of the Peoples/Nations/Gentiles" (4:15: *Galilaia tōn ethnōn* [Isa 8:23 in Hebrew]; 4:23) and Jesus attracts people from Syria, Galilee, the Decapolis, Judea, and beyond the Jordan (4:24–25). John the Baptizer implies non-Judeans when he says that "God can raise up children to Abraham from these stones" (3:9). Jesus is offered the kingdoms of the world (4:1–11). Matthew is positive toward certain *ethnikoi*, for example, women of Jesus' genealogy (1:3, 5, 6) or those who respond favorably to Jesus—magi (2:1–12), a centurion (8:5–13), a Canaanite woman (15:21–28). The Servant should proclaim justice to the *ethnē* who have hope in him (12:18, 21), disciples are to witness to them (10:18), the gospel will be preached to them (24:14), and Jesus' final commission includes making disciples of them. (28:19). The kingdom will be given to an *ethnos* producing the fruits of it (21:43).[111]

Yet, the author also says that disciples should not go into "the way of the *ethnē*" and "enter no city of the Samaritans" (10:5). Saldarini notes that for Matthew, "the rulers of the nations [*ethnōn*] lord it over their subjects (20:25), their kings burn Judean cities (22:7), and nations war with one another (24:6–7 [*ethnos epi ethnos*]."[112]

How should one interpret Matthew's "Let him be to you as an *ethnikos* and a toll collector" in 18:17b? One strategy is to observe the closest parallel to the combination "toll collectors and *ethnikoi*," namely, Matt 5:43–48. Elsewhere in the gospel the author says that "loving *your neighbor* as yourself" (Lev 19:18)—the context of the all-important reproof passage—is a commandment that must be kept (19:19); indeed, it is the second Great Commandment (22:39). However, in Matthew 5, the sense of the combined "tax collectors and *ethnikoi*" is negative, at least in a relative or comparative sense. As a contrast those who hear the Sermon on the Mount (5:1: disciples; 7:28: crowds) are told that loving *only* your neighbors and saluting *only* your brothers, generally considered normative behavior in the culture, is nothing beyond the cultural norm, merely "loving *those who love you*."[113] That is inadequate. The hearers must go further: "love your

---

111. Ibid. See pp. 300–327 below.
112. Saldarini, *Matthew's Christian-Jewish Community*, 77.
113. For parallels, see Betz, *Sermon on the Mount*, 318.

enemies and pray for those who persecute you" (5:44). Something greater is required of Jesus' true neighbors and brothers: "perfection"! One may perhaps gain a little further insight by comparing this treatment of "toll collectors and *ethnikoi*" with Matt 11:19. John the Baptizer does not follow conventional norms ("eating and drinking") and "they" say, "he has a demon" (11:18). Jesus eats and drinks and "they" say, "Behold, a glutton and a drunkard, a friend of toll collectors and sinners" (11:19). Here, the expression "a glutton and a drunkard" appears to be a slogan describing the stubborn and rebellious son who, according to the ancients, should be stoned (Deut 21:20).[114] "A friend of toll collectors and sinners" may be a similar slogan (compare 21:32). Such expressions suggest the *impurity of outsiders*. Could "*ho ethnikos kai ho telōnēs*" also be such an expression?

If so, the statement "Let him be to you as an *ethnikos* and a toll collector" in 18:17b in contrast to Weinfeld could mean *permanent* expulsion. However, opinions varied and changed in Judean literature. The following Tosefta uses the term "tax collector" and its context suggests that among the Pharisees there was a development from permanent expulsion in the first century to temporary expulsion:[115] "At first they used to say: if an associate becomes a tax-collector, he is deprived of his status as associate. Later they altered this and said: As long as he is a tax-collector, he is not considered reliable; once he has withdrawn from being a tax-collector, he is reliable" (*t. Demai* 3.4 [49]; compare *b. Bek.* 31a; *y. Demai* 2.3, 23a).

Clearly, the failure to heed discipline in the Dead Sea Scrolls and *Iabakchoi* by-laws results in various penalties, the ultimate penalty being expulsion from the association.[116] It is equally clear that while Paul and the Paulinist, and perhaps Hebrews as well, preserved the tradition of reproof (Gal 6:1; Eph 4:25b–26; see Heb 3:13), Paul himself lamented that there was no "wise man" to handle internal affairs and seemed to expect expulsion of unrepentant sinners (1 Corinthians 5–6). Matthew seems to have held the same view. Yet, the practice could, over time, have been muted in line with what the Tosefta says.

---

114. Compare Gundry, *Matthew*, 213; Neyrey, "Loss of Wealth," 150.
115. Forkman, *Limits*, 90.
116. Forkman, ibid.; Danker, *Benefactor*.

Conclusion

The process as *now recorded* in Matt 18:15-17 is not as explicitly developed as it is in the voluntary associations such as the *Iabakchoi* and especially the Dead Sea Scrolls. Thus, Schiffman thinks that "this process of reproof was not part of the legal system in the rest of Palestine. Rather, reproof as a forensic procedure was developed uniquely by the [Qumran] sect."[117] Yet, I have argued by implication that just such a process may lie buried in this text. Matthew 18:15-20 contains eight conditional sentences.[118] Such constructions are typical of casuistic law,[119] and thus a set of legal norms and/or practices. Moreover, the three-step legal process in Matthew 18:15-17 receives divine ratification by the Matthean "binding and loosing" (18:18-20; cf. 16:17-19; compare 1 Cor 5:1-5).[120] Given other hints of organization in the Matthean association, there is a possibility that the First Evangelist's process masks a group juridical process, that is, that it is only the tip of the iceberg.

Is this the end of the matter? Hardly. The three-step process is set within a literary context of unbounded merciful love and forgiveness as the basis for reconciliation between "brothers." The process suggests that there are limits to offenses within the group; there are strong group boundaries, insiders and outsiders. Yet, the context seems determined by the traditions of *unbounded* reproof as a means of "gaining" one's "brother," as though there are no limits—at least within the group. As Davies and Allison state:

> Reproving one's brother is always a most delicate matter, and one must undertake the sad task in a spirit of love and humility. One can make the case that the three paragraphs before vv. 15-20 and the two that follow serve as buffers of a sort; that is, they emphasize the qualities which are required if one is going to be so bold as to carry out the directions of 18:15-20 . . . [The writer] surrounds the material on fraternal correction with material promoting a spirit of generosity, humility, and

---

117. Schiffman, *Sectarian Law*, 96.
118. *Eán* + subjunctive; see e.g., Thompson, *Matthew's Advice*, 176.
119. Duling, "Torah Orientation," 174.
120. Duling, "Binding and Loosing."

forgiveness. In short, the way in which Matthew encircles vv. 15–20 is proof of his deep pastoral concern.[121]

If the above discussion holds, this context is an expression of the author's attempt to check the potential assimilation of process of conflict resolution toward cultural norms and practices that are more explicitly judicial—traditions he shares with certain members of his authorial audience—by attention to the original motivation of the Torah in the light of what he understands to be the meaning and message of Jesus.[122]

---

121. Davies and Allison, *Matthew*, 2:751.
122. See chap. 6 above.

CHAPTER 9

Matthew as Marginal Scribe in an Advanced Agrarian Society[1]

"MATTHEW AND MARGINALITY" (CHAPTER 5 above) was conceived in 1993 at a time when the concept "marginality" was increasingly being used in biblical study, but without much theoretical understanding.[2] Such theoretical investigation was much needed. With Gerhard Lenski's macrosocial model of an advanced agrarian society and models of small groups in mind,[3] I explored three senses of marginality found in the social sciences and named them: 1) involuntary marginality, 2) voluntary marginality; and 3) the "Marginal Man."[4] My proposal was that the Gospel of Matthew was written by a scribe who freely associated with a Jesus messianic group ("voluntary marginality") that in Lenski's terms included retainers, artisans, peasants, expendable persons, and the unclean ("involuntary marginality"), and that even though his association was voluntary, this scribe was

1. First developed in Duling, "Marginality Revisited," Context Group, Portland, OR (March 16, 2000). The original conception in chap. 5 was refined with special attention to Billson, "No Owner Soil"; Berry, "Psychology of Acculturation"; and Lee, *Marginality*. Versions were then presented at the 2000 SSCNT section of the SBL, the 2001 international meeting of the Context Group at the University of Pretoria, South Africa, and by invitation at the Matthew group of the *SNTS* in Montreal, 2001. It was published in *HTS* 58/2 (2002) 520–75. In this chapter, I have done some reorganization, added a clarifying model from Weisberger, "Marginality," and made a few other minor revisions.

2. See chap. 5 above, n. 1.

3. Lenski, *Power and Privilege*; Lenski and Lenski, *Human Societies*; chap. 2 above. For small group theory and New Testament study, see Duling, "Small Groups."

4. Involuntary: Germani, *Marginality*; voluntary: Turner, *The Ritual Process*; Marginal Man: Park, "Human Migration"; "Personality and Cultural Conflict"; Stonequist, *The Marginal Man*, developed from Park's views. See chap. 5 above.

nonetheless an "in between" figure, a person of "status incongruity," and in that respect similar to that of a "Marginal Man" under stress. His "in betweenness" can help to explain a number of conflicting and unresolved tensions in the gospel: the elite and the lower strata, literate scribes and illiterate peasants, men and women, an increasingly normative Pharisaism and his Jesus group, Semitic and Greek languages, Judean and Greco-Roman culture, and in general between what is "the old" and "the new" (Matt 13:52).

In a subsequent study, "The Matthean Brotherhood and Marginal Scribal Leadership" (chapter 7 above), I suggested that this "marginal scribe" provided leadership for a "voluntary association" perceived as a "marginal" group by the larger society, particularly the rival Pharisees.

In this chapter, I return to the suggestion that the Matthean author is a marginal scribe in a marginal group in an advanced agrarian society. I want first to further refine *the concept* of social ranking in the ancient Mediterranean world; second, the marginality *concept*; third, the *role of scribes* in the ancient Mediterranean world, especially Judean antiquity; and then the sense in which the Matthean writer is marginal and representative of a marginal community in an advanced agrarian society.

Social Ranking in an Advanced Agrarian Society

Lenski's macromodel of an advanced agrarian society presented in chapter 3 and modified for the ancient Palestinian context in chapter 4 is at a high level of abstraction and therefore has great explanatory power. Prominent social theorist Jonathan Turner states that the single most important influence on him was Lenski, and finds Lenski's synthesis to be especially attractive. However, he also thinks that Lenski's macromodel sometimes obscures other ranking variables that should be considered.[5] Lenski himself addresses this problem when he acknowledges that people actually rank themselves in a variety of ways. He calls these variables "class systems" and includes among them smaller "status groups" (Weber's *Stände*), that is, groups that develop distinctive subcultures and are usually hereditary. In short, people rank others and themselves in a number of ways, for

---

5. Turner, *Societal Stratification*, ii, 49, 54–55, 81, 84, 158–59.

example, kinship, gender, occupation, race, ethnicity, and religion.[6] All these together he terms *"the distributive system."*

To illustrate his distributive system Lenski imagines a fictional Latin American society and ranks people in it according to four "class systems": politics, wealth, occupation, and ethnicity.[7] He theorizes, moreover, that there are differences *within* these "class systems." These differences are based on factors such as range of vertical stratification in each ("span"), pattern of distribution ("shape"), degree of mobility, and degree of institutionalization (ideologically based custom or law). Moreover, each "class system" can be assigned a different "weight" of importance.

Although Lenski's fictional Latin American distributive system is modern, it is derived from a hierarchically ranked agrarian society and thus has potential for understanding ancient agrarian societies. I suggest some revision and elaboration. I follow Malina's view that politics and kinship are the two most important social domains in the ancient Mediterranean world,[8] and, recognizing the importance of gender domains in antiquity, I also give politics, kinship, and gender more "weight." Also, I expand Lenski's four variables to seven and I remove "shape" and "span." Finally, because the sociological term "class" is rooted in Marxist theory about the means of production in modern industrial societies and is thus not preferred by some scholars of antiquity,[9] I replace Lenski's "class system" with the simple expression "ranking variable." This revised fictional distributive system is presented in Chart 9.1.

6. Lenski, *Power and Privilege*, 77, 78, thinks that class can include "caste" and "estate." See above, p. 71.

7. Ibid., 80–82. See below, p. 261, Chart 9.3, for Cohen's economic and religious grids.

8. Malina, *Christian Origins*, 86; "Interpreting the Bible with Anthropology," 152–53; *New Testament World*, 82–83, 134–60; Hanson and Oakman, *Palestine in the Time of Jesus*, devote one chapter to each of these four institutions: kinship (chap. 2), politics (chap. 3), economics (chap. 4) and religion (chap. 5).

9. Most analysts of the ancient Mediterranean prefer the term "status" to "class" because "class" has Marxist overtones related to modern industrial economies that do not fit ancient agrarian economics; indeed, there was no large middle class in antiquity. See Finley, *Ancient Economy*, 49; Meeks, *First Urban Christians*, 53–54; Alföldy, *Social History*, 99; MacMullen, *Roman Social Relations*, 89, 94. Turner prefers not to use "class," but does so because it is prevalent in the sociological literature (*Societal Stratification*, 146). Rohrbaugh thinks that Lenski's "power class" is acceptable terminology for antiquity *if* one defines it in terms of an elite that controls the economic surplus (Rohrbaugh, "Methodological Considerations," 534, 537, 542). See chap. 4 above, n. 46.

Chart 9.1 A Fictional Distributive System for the Roman Empire (modified from Lenski, p. 80; w = weight of importance from 2–10)

The Political Ranking Variable (W = 10)	The Property Ranking Variable (W = 5)	The Occupational Ranking Variable (W = 2)	The Ethnic Ranking Variable (W = 3)	The Educational Ranking Variable (W = 2)	The Religious Ranking Variable (W = 5)	The Gender Ranking Variable (W = 10)	The Family Ranking Variable (W = 10)
The elite	The wealthy	Large landowners	Romans	Educated	Emperor	Males	Fathers
The bureaucracy	The moderately wealthy	• Independent farmers • Officials • Merchants	Greeks	Scribes & Moderately Educated	High Priests		Mothers
The apolitical class	The poor	artisans peasants	barbarians Judeans: Judeans Proper Galileans Idumeans Samaritans	Artisans' Literacy	Priests Scholars Laity		Sons
				Illiterate & uneducated	"pagans"	females	Daughters
Suspected enemies of the regime	The impoverished	Beggars, Prostitutes, Unemployed, etc.	Other ethnic groups				Other Kin

Study of this chart suggests that a person's status ranking in various categories is *usually* coordinate with political and economic power ranking in Lenski's simpler macromodel—*but not always*. While there is *some* correlation between various ranking systems, there can also be competition among them. There are also temporal and local variations and ethnocentric rankings which move the ranking toward emic criteria. Weights can change in specific contexts. Ranking of Greeks and Romans within a Judean version of the ethnic/religious class system would look quite different from ranking in the more general distribution system. When ranking is relatively high in one status system and relatively low in another—for example, low status birth versus high level of education—"status dissonance," says Lenski, can result.[10]

Later in this chapter it will be instructive to ask about the status of scribes, first from the perspective of more specific ways of ranking in a distributive system (adjusted for Mediterranean antiquity), and then historically, by documenting some different kinds of scribes at that time that are known from ancient literature. The scribes in Matthew can then be compared and contrasted. First, however, I return to marginality theory.

Vertical Social Ranking and Marginality

Lenski's macrosocial model of an advanced agrarian society and the reformulated distribution system chart above are examples of what Ramsay MacMullen described as "verticality."[11] It includes T. F. Carney's ancient "pyramids of power."[12] This is vertical social ranking from "high" to "low" (or vice versa), "upper" to "lower" (or vice versa). Marginality as a concept initially shifts this vertical ranking to a horizontal flat surface, that is, a center with concentric circles at various "distances" from the center, like a stone thrown into a lake.[13] Yet,

10. For the concepts of "status dissonance," "status discrepancy," or "status incongruence" as contrasted with "status crystallization" or "status congruence," see Lenski, "Status Crystallization"; and Barnett, "Introduction," 177–81; also chap. 1 above and n. 72.

11. MacMullen, *Roman Social Relations*, 94; cf. 51–73.

12. Carney, *Shape of the Past*.

13. This concentric circle model is typical of networking theory; see Duling, "The Jesus Movement and Network Analysis" and "Die Jesusbewegung und die

concentric circles can be imagined vertically, like a target, and thus the two models overlap. The following simple model illustrates the point.

Model 9.1 The Overlap between Vertical and Marginal Ranking

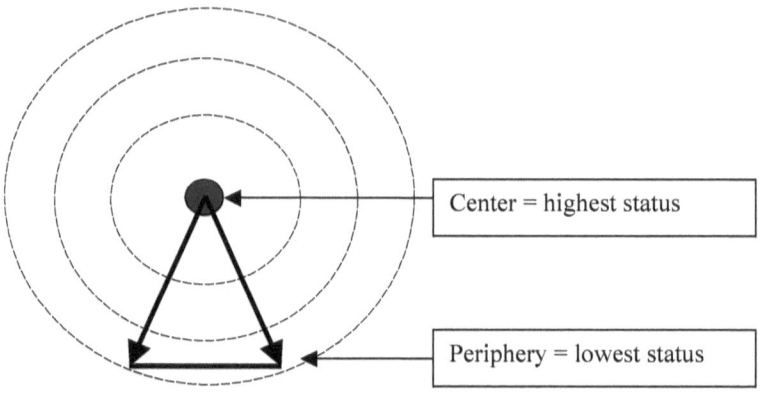

Lenski's social stratification pyramid is primarily political and socio-economic, as has often been noted, but it can be made more complex with other variables, as suggested above by the fictional distribution system. Similarly, there are a number of variables in marginality related to politics, economics, ethnicity, gender, and the like. Again, a special example is that "status inconsistency" or "status incongruence" produced by different, competing rankings in the stratification system, as Gerhard Lenski knew, can produce social stress and dislocation. As I shall indicate, "status incongruence" is somewhat analogous to the "in betweenness" or "double consciousness" of marginal persons.[14] Finally, there are also variables in the *types* of marginality, as noted in chapter 5.

Some Recent Directions in Marginality Theory

Having noted some correlations between vertical social ranking and status dissonance on the one hand and marginality and "in betweenness" in a conceptual way, I would like to refine the marginality theory

---

Networkanalyse," where I combine it with Theissen's analysis of the Jesus Movement and three concentric circle spaces. See chap. 2 above for a small group analysis that uses Boissevain, *Friends of Friends*, and my images.

14. Starr, "Marginality"; "Status Inconsistency."

Matthew as Marginal Scribe in an Advanced Agrarian Society

in "Matthew and Marginality" (chapter 5). I shall do so by using the analyses of four marginality theorists: 1) sociologist J. M. Billson; 2) cross-cultural psychologist J. W. Berry;[15] 3) sociologist Adam Weisberger; and 4) multicultural theologian Jung Young Lee. I shall eventually attempt to see if these concepts and models contribute to a better understanding of Matthew as a marginal scribe.

J. M. Billson's Marginality Categories

Billson surveyed the marginality concept from Park's "Human Migration and the Marginal Man" to her own writing (1928–1988).[16] The categories I developed in chapter 5, which the reader may consult for greater detail, can be aligned with her comparable categories, adding one of my own, as in the following chart.

Chart 9.2 Duling and Billson Marginality Categories Compared

Duling (chap. 5)	Billson (plus Duling)
"Involuntary marginality"	"structural marginality" and/or "social role marginality"
"Marginal Man"	"cultural marginality"
"voluntary marginality"	"ideological marginality" (Duling)

A brief clarification of the four categories at the right is in order.

STRUCTURAL MARGINALITY

Billson's language, "structural marginality" represents sociological conceptuality better than "involuntary marginality," a description that I created from Gino Germani's sociological analysis of marginality theory based on Latin America.[17] Germani meant *primarily* those who are unable to share political, social, and economic power, that

---

15. Berry, "Psychology of Acculturation"; cf. Berry and Dasen, "Culture and Cognition."

16. Billson, "No Owner Soil." For a summary of this update based on Billson, see also Love, *Jesus and Marginal Women*.

17. Germani, *Marginality*.

is, the poverty-stricken and oppressed, who have no access to goods and services, and who follow deviant norms, values, and attitudes. They are sometimes an ethnic minority. They are *not* totally separate from the rest of society, however. Rather, because of economic, social, political, demographic, cultural, and psychosocial factors, they form "a society within a society," a sort of "internal colonialism."

Billson calls them "structurally marginal," referring to their location *primarily* at or near the bottom of the social hierarchical structure. However, Germani allowed that *any* persons at *any* social level *can* be structurally marginal if they are excluded from participating in their *expected social roles* (see below). Thus, Germani ended up defining marginality as ". . . the lack of participation of individuals and groups in those spheres in which, according to determined criteria, they might be expected to participate."[18]

Social Role Marginality

"*Social Role Marginality*," which is included in Germani's abstract definition of marginality ("expected social roles"), is a separate type of marginality in Billson's typology. She defines it as "the product of failure to belong to a [desired] positive reference group."[19] This definition reflects its source, Robert Merton's examination of marginality in relation to "reference group theory."[20] Modern examples of social role marginality are women and minority persons who want to enter professions or positions previously denied them. In Mediterranean antiquity, there is much less potential for upward social mobility, but there are exceptions—military advancement, for example—and in relation to scribes, there are some documented possibilities: masters sending their slaves to be educated as scribes, talented lower level scribes being rewarded with a scribal position of higher status, and women as scribes (see further below).

---

18. Germani, *Marginality*, 49.
19. Billson, "No Owner Soil," 184.
20. Merton, *Social Theory and Social Structure*.

Cultural Marginality

"*Cultural Marginality*" is Billson's more inclusive social-scientific language for Park's social-psychological category "Marginal Man."[21] Park had mainly immigrants to the United States in mind when he described the "Marginal Man" as one who is "condemned" to live "in between" two different, antagonistic cultural worlds (the "old world," the "new world") without fully belonging to either, as one who is therefore "caught" between two competing cultures. The psychological dimension is that the "Marginal Man" experiences "acceptance or rejection, belonging or isolation, in-group or out-group," "ambiguities of status and role," and finally "isolation, identity confusion, and alienation." Everett V. Stonequist enlarged Park's concept, defining the "Marginal Man" as "unwittingly initiated into *two or more* historic traditions, languages, political loyalties, moral codes, or religions, one of which is more dominant."[22] Cultural marginals do not fully assimilate; they are said to be "in between," to have "status incongruence"[23] and psychological uncertainty.[24] A Venn diagram can illustrate the "in between" nature of cultural marginals:

---

21. Park, "Personality"; "Migration"; "Billson, "No Owner Soil," 184; see also Antonovsky, "Toward a Refinement," 56. Park drew many insights from Simmel's classic, "The Stranger"; see the section on Weisberger below.

22. Stonequist, *The Marginal Man*, 3.

23. Schimmerhorn, "Marginal Man," 407.

24. In *Race and Culture*, Park extended the concept to include races that never fully assimilate. It is equivalent to "status dissonance," "status discrepancy," "status inconsistency" in the studies of Gerhard Lenski, Gerd Theissen, and Wayne Meeks (see chap. 1 above, n. 72).

Model 9.2 A Venn Diagram of Culturally Marginal Persons and Groups

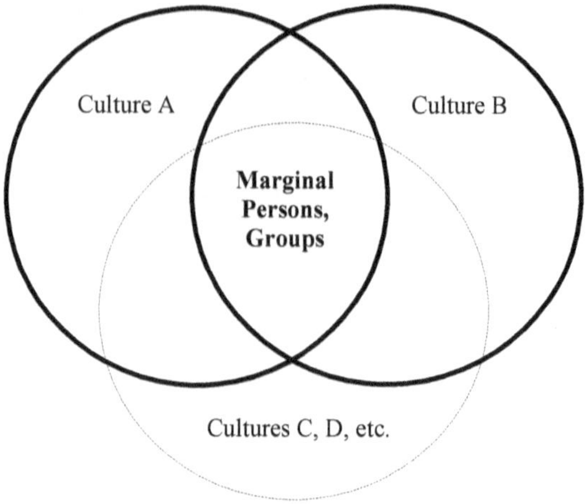

(Venn diagram: two overlapping circles labeled "Culture A" and "Culture B", with a dashed circle labeled "Cultures C, D, etc." overlapping both. The central intersection is labeled "Marginal Persons, Groups".)

Since there is a conflict of cultures, Billson prefers to replace "Marginal Man" with more inclusive, non-gendered language, "*cultural marginality.*" For more on cultural marginality/the "Marginal Man," see Adam Weisberger's contribution below.

Ideological Marginality

"*Ideological Marginality*" is not one of Billson's categories,[25] but is my expression in more social-scientific language for what I called "voluntary marginality." It comes from the anthropological field and, namely, anthropologist Victor Turner's concept of *ideological communitas*.[26] Turner is rightly known for his analysis of ritual, and in this case, puberty rites. He says that those who enter "manhood" in small-scale societies such as the Ndembu in Zambia are separated from the everyday normative social system, are initiated there (usually in the bush), and then are reintroduced to tribal society as neophytes with new, often higher, statuses. Turner calls this time of separation "marginal" or "liminal" (Latin *limen*: "threshold"). During this temporary period, initiates experience equality and intense comradeship, or *communitas*. They are said to be "betwixt and between," "neither here nor there,"[27]

---

25. Billson, "No Owner Soil," 197, does mention voluntary homelessness.
26. Turner, *Ritual Process*; *Dramas, Fields, and Metaphors*; see chap. 4 above.
27. Turner, *Ritual Process*, 95.

status-less, role-less, spontaneous, sexless (sometimes symbolized by nakedness), and anonymous. This marginality lacks formal structure; it is an "anti-structure."[28] It is not the puberty rite, but—this is the main point here—Turner's observation that such *communitas* can be a *chosen* utopian vision for society. Thus, unlike structural, cultural, or social marginality, it becomes *voluntary* "outsiderhood"[29] or *ideological communitas*.[30] One of Turner's examples is the well-known ideal in church history called the *ecclesiola in ecclesia* (the "little church within the church"), that is, a group that seeks to reform the institution from within. Turner wrote that "*communitas* is what people really *seek* by *voluntary* poverty,"[31] one of the three monastic ideals. *Ideological marginals* freely choose to follow a "higher" lifestyle outside the conventional statuses, roles, and offices of everyday society.[32]

John Berry's Cross-Cultural Psychological Analysis of Marginality (1990; 1997)[33]

Light on the experience of Billson's "cultural marginal" (Park's "Marginal Man") comes from cross-cultural psychologist John W. Berry, who, like Park, is especially interested in migrants, but also refugees and indigenous peoples. He focuses his work on the acculturation or non-acculturation (psychological, sociocultural, and economic adaptation or non-adaptation) of such individuals and groups ("the acculturating group") in relation to a dominant or "host" culture. Marginality in his acculturation research is only one of four options for "non-dominant" individuals and groups who *want or do not want to assimilate to the dominant group.*[34] I have reconfigured Berry's question-answer data-gathering model into quadrants that will illustrate these possibilities.[35]

28. Ibid., 126.
29. Ibid., 133.
30. Ibid., 132.
31. Ibid., 266 (italics mine).
32. Ibid., 133; see chap. 5 above, Chart 5.1.
33. This section was an appendix to the original article and has been slightly modified.
34. Berry, "Psychology of Acculturation," 201; "Lead Article," 7.
35. Ibid., 218.

Model 9.3 Marginality and Four Degrees of Acculturation (Berry)

	IT IS A VALUE TO MAINTAIN CULTURAL IDENTITY AND CHARACTERISTICS		
IT IS A VALUE TO MAINTAIN RELATIONSHIPS WITH OTHER GROUPS/THE LARGER SOCIETY	INTEGRATION	SEPARATION	IT IS *NOT* A VALUE TO MAINTAIN RELATIONSHIPS WITH OTHER GROUPS/THE LARGER SOCIETY
	ASSIMILATION	MARGINALIZATION	
	IT IS *NOT* A VALUE TO MAINTAIN CULTURAL IDENTITY AND CHARACTERISTICS		

"Integration" and "separation," Berry says, are more collective; "assimilation" is more individual. *Marginalization can be either.* Cultural marginals do not value maintaining strong relationships with other groups in the "larger society" (in cases of immigration, the "host" culture), and yet they are willing to some extent to abandon their cultural identity and characteristics so that they are not totally separate or segregated. With echoes of Park and Stonequist, says Berry, the cultural marginal is "trapped between his two possible identity groups, neither accepting nor being accepted by them ..."

Berry graphs his four acculturation strategies *over time*. The following figure illustrates the idea that cultural marginality is, in contrast to the other strategies (assimilation, integration, and isolation), as one might expect from being "trapped" between two groups—analogous to being "caught between"—characterized by *continuing conflict and increased tension*.[36]

---

36. Malina, "Normative Dissonance," suggests that a degree of sociological ambivalence is culturally acceptable.

Matthew as Marginal Scribe in an Advanced Agrarian Society

Model 9.4 Degree of Cultural and Psychological Change as a Function of Phases and Varieties of Accumulation (Berry)

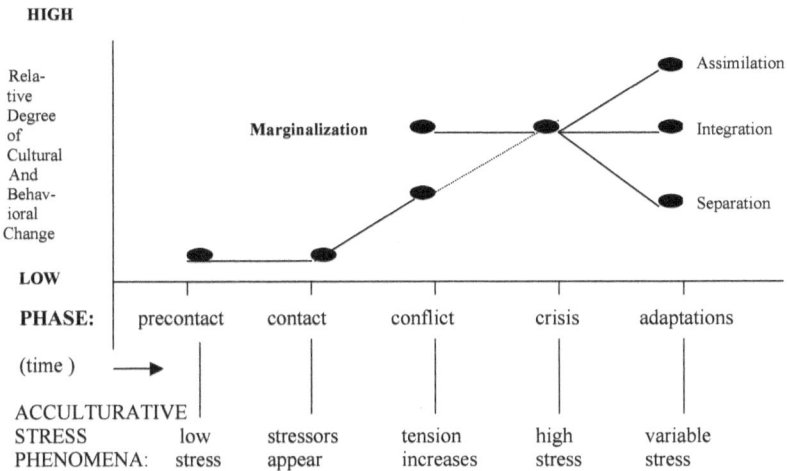

"In betweenness" and its tensions originally suggested by Park are confirmed by acculturation stress research in cross-cultural psychology.

The acculturation strategies of migrants and refugees cannot be shown to be directly relevant to marginality in relation to the writer of the Gospel of Matthew or his community. One may only speculate whether, whatever his authority and status, the writer was a recent migrant to the place of composition, such as Antioch, some other place in Galilee or Syria, or beyond the Jordan (e.g., Pella). In any case, it is plausible, if not probable that if, as Michael White argued, the gospel was written in a time of social stress, and that such a stress is exhibited in internally inconsistent social roles, norms, attitudes, and behaviors throughout the gospel,[37] the conditions for cultural marginality are present. In short, the analysis of cultural marginality is suggestive for understanding such inconsistencies and the possibility that the writer himself is a cultural marginal (Marginal Man).

---

37. White, "Crisis Management"; see chap. 2 above (nn. 38, 39).

Adam Weisberger's "Marginality and Its Directions" (1992)

Adam Weisberger builds on Park's famous 1928 essay and attempts to reconstruct a more complex general theory of marginality,[38] one that stresses the Marginal Man's "*double* ambivalence" and offers four "ideal type" directions, options, or responses that marginals may take.[39] Weisberger notes that at the University of Berlin, Park heard the lectures of Georg Simmel, whose classical essay "The Stranger" (1908), highlighted the one who "comes today and stays tomorrow," who is "close to us" yet "far from us," who is "no owner of soil,"[40] who is more objective, and who, like Simmel himself (a Jew in German society), cannot fully assimilate. In other words, he stands "between": between creativity and "spiritual distress." This ambivalence is echoed in Park's "Marginal Man." However, for Weisberger, Park did not exploit the Marginal Man's ambivalence enough.

> The marginal person is not only unable to sever ties with his or her own culture and to merge into the new one, *but also is unable to return to the native culture or shrug off the influence of the new one.* Park understands the former relationship, but misses the latter. His image of being betwixt and between is unidirectional, whereas the marginal person is caught in a cross-current, located within a *structure of double ambivalence*. This person is ambivalent toward his or her own culture, wants to return but cannot, wants to leave but cannot do that either; and is ambivalent toward the new culture, wants to assimilate but cannot, and wants to reject it but cannot.[41]

Weisberger offers his own structural model of four ideal type response strategies. These can be represented: 1) poise (remaining in a state of ambivalence); 2) return (to the native culture after culture contact); 3) transcendence (creating a "third way" that surpasses the native and host cultures); 4) assimilation (absorption into the host culture). Weisberger suggests that these "directions of marginality" can be represented in graphic terms as follows.

---

38. Weisberger, "Marginality." Weisberger is now a lawyer in Boston.

39. Weisberger, "Marginality," applies it to German Jewry during the Second Reich; cf. Park, "Migration." (1928).

40. The title of Billson's essay.

41. Weisberger, "Marginality," 429.

Model 9.5 Four "Directions" of Marginality (Weisberger)

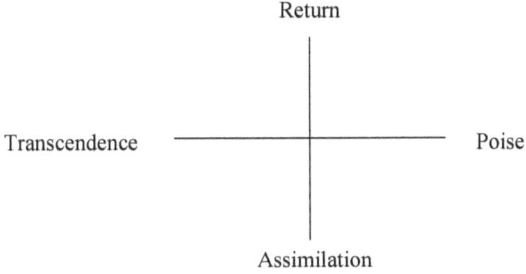

In this model, Weisberger's "directions of marginalization" are not exactly coordinate with Berry's strategies and degrees of cultural change since for Berry only one of the four responses is labeled "marginalization," while for Weissberger, all four are directions of marginalization. Yet, "Assimilation" corresponds to Berry's "Assimilation" and "Return" is analogous to "Separation." "Poise," or remaining in a state of abivalence, is like the traditional cultural marginality (Marginal Man), and thus is closest to Berry's "Marginalization." The language and conceptuality "double ambivalence" strengthens the notion of being caught "in between" cultures.

Jung Young Lee's Defense of Cultural Marginal Psychology

Jung Young Lee levels a critique at traditional social-scientific marginality theorists who tend to describe the "in between," stressful ambivalence of "Marginal Man" in less than complementary psychological terms, for example, "identity confusion." Berry states although "acculturative stress" ("culture shock") can occasionally lead to psychological and social illness, earlier theories claiming that marginality *inevitably* leads to this result are no longer valid.[42] In this regard, Jung Young Lee's analysis of marginality is willing to accept the stressful "in betweenness" of cultural marginality,[43] but also challenges theories of psychological "maladjustment," "cultural schizophrenia,"

---

42. Berry, "Lead Article," 12–13.
43. Lee, *Marginality*, 48, 58. I owe knowledge of this book to Warren Carter.

"excessive self-consciousness," and "extreme race consciousness."[44] Lee envisions the "in between" experience as also *"in both,"* that is, sharing both cultures without either being blended,[45] and *"in beyond"* (at least in a pluralistic society, being a "new marginal person" embodying a holistic state of being): "To transcend or to live in-beyond does not mean to be free of the two different worlds in which persons exist, but to live in both of them without being bound by either of them. The new marginal person is a liberated person, a person who is truly free . . ."[46]

In short, although the experiences of migrants and refugees cannot from our sources be related to the context of the Matthean gospel and its author with any certainty, acculturation studies are helpful for better understanding the ambiguities of cultural marginality in relation to social conflict and social stress—if such analyses are not perpetually reduced to theories of psychological maladjustment. It is precisely conflict and social stress that are found in the analyses of the Matthean writer and his gospel.

I shall return to these theories and models again after taking up the second area of refinement I want to address, the ranking of ancient scribes.

---

44. Ibid., 62–63. See also Carter, *Matthew and the Margins*, 43–45. Billson is aware of the weakness of "maladjustment" theories about marginal persons. She qualifies: "The term 'maladjustment' is used here for convenience and lack of a more neutral term which would still embrace multiple *potential* problems associated with marginality. It is recognized that marginality may in fact produce innovation, creativity, or other positive consequences for individual and/or society . . . Nonetheless, the sense in which marginality has been utilized historically (and is used here) implies that the person who experiences a marginal role will be faced with special problems of 'adjustment' which others in non-marginal roles will not have to face" ("No Owner Soil," 190 n. 4).

45. Lee, *Marginality*, 62.

46. Ibid., 63. I add that in light of the gene pool the notion of "race" is scientifically untenable. It is rooted in nineteenth-century theories of evolution related to Euro-Americans' ethnocentric views of their cultural superiority (Birx, "Human Variation, Adaptation, and Ecology"). That does not deny the social, economic, political, and psychological reality of "race." For my similar attempt to de-psychologize psychological stress theories, see Duling, "Recruitment to the Jesus Movement."

Ranking Scribes in Mediterranean Society

Shaye Cohen once observed that influential scholars of the social world of ancient Israelite religion have ranked persons by using two very different, contrasting ranking "grids," one "economic," the other "religious."[47] Here are outlines of these two grids:

Chart 9.3 Economic and Religious Grids for Ranking Ancient Judeans (Cohen)

Economic	Religious
I. The Rich	I. "Jews"
A. The city rich	A. The Religious Establishment
B. The country rich	1. High priests, priests, and Levites
(owners of large estates)	2. The patriarch and his court
II. The "Middle Class"	3. *Scribes*, elders, rabbis, sages, members of
A. Artisans, merchants,	the Sanhedrin
etc. (city)	B. The Sects and "Unofficial" Authority
B. Owners of moderate	Figures
Estates (country)	1. Hasidim, Pharisees, Sadducees,
III. The "Lower Class"	Boethusians, Essenes, Qumran sect,
A. The city poor	"Fourth Philosophy," Judeo-Christians,
B. The country poor	Samaritans (?), *Haberim* (?), rabbis (?)
1. Peasant farmers	C. Other "Jews"
2. Landless peasants	1. The ʾam hāʾaretz and other "nonsectarian"
IV. "Non-Persons"	Jews
A. Women and children	2. "Hellenistic Jews"
B. Slaves	3. Proselytes
	II. Non-"Jews"
	A. The Romans and the Roman army
	B. "Greeks," hellenized pagans, not-so-
	hellenized pagans
	C. Samaritans (?)

Cohen did not put scribes in his economic grid. They are in his "religious" grid, and rather high: they are part of "the religious establishment." This judgment is based on the view that scribes were Torah scholars, a matter of some debate, as we shall see. In contrast, in Gerhard Lenski's macrosociological model of an advanced agrarian society (chapter 3)[48]—Greco-Roman society is Lenski's key

---

47. Cohen, "The Political and Social History," 47; see also Kampen, "Discussion of Fiensy," 207–208. For more of Cohen's views, see chap. 7 above.

48. Lenski, *Power and Privilege*, 284. Lenski holds that theory and modeling must be based on empirical data ("Rethinking Macrosociological Theory," 166).

example[49]—scribes belong in the "retainer class."[50] This stratum involves professional soldiers, government bureaucrats, household servants, and petty officials, including tax collectors.[51] Not only do scribes serve the elite in the Lenski model; they function as social brokers who communicate between the rulers and the ruled. For example, they collect a portion of the economic surplus as taxes and at the same time deflect resentment of the lower social strata toward those who wield elite power, privilege, and prestige. As their reward they receive a slightly greater share in the economic surplus and a higher status than the masses. Lenski estimates that retainers would have made up about 5 percent of the population. New Testament scholars have often accepted this view of scribes.[52] Yet, David Fiensy's adjusted Lenski model for Herodian Palestine deliberately *omitted* scribes because he did not consider them to be a "class."[53]

If one takes the Lenski distribution system, or the ranking variables, into consideration, it is obvious that in the occupational class system scribes are "officials." In the educational class system they are among the literate elite, although not at the very top. In the family class system, there can be scribal families. In the gender class system, scribes are almost always male.[54] Finally, in various ethnic and religious class systems, scribes can be ranked much higher.

In what follows I accept Lenski's ranking for scribes in the macromodel but I want to add the educational, occupational, and religious ranking systems from the revised distribution system. First, however, it is crucial to say more about scribes in Mediterranean society, particularly Judean scribes.

49. Lenski, *Human Societies* (1988), 166, 167, 169, 170, 173, 175, 176, 177, 180. See also Lenski, *Power and Privilege*, 198.

50. Lenski, *Power and Privilege*, 243–48; see the discussions by Saldarini, *Pharisees*.

51. Because of this variety, status ranking *within* any "class" is difficult. Members of the military and literates receive some status enhancement and corresponding wealth, though wages are mostly modest. They also compete with each other and continually seek to maximize their rights and privileges; such ambitions threaten the ruling classes only in the case of the military. Despite the difficulties I shall clarify by distinguishing several kinds of scribes.

52. For lists of scholars, see chap. 3 above, nn. 41 and 42; for a more general discussion, see chap. 2 above.

53. Fiensy, *Land Is Mine*, 158. For his view, see chap. 4 above.

54. See, however, Haines-Eitzen, "'Girls Trained in Beautiful Writing,'" n. 130.

Ranking of Scribes in Mediterranean Antiquity from Emic Information

In the Lenski model, scribes are a single category, always and everywhere the same. That is an oversimplification, as noted above with respect to the fictive distribution system. Moreover, it is necessary to look more carefully at emic, historical information. Drawing especially on Saldarini, Schams, Richards, and Kloppenborg, it is possible to describe at least *six kinds of scribes* mentioned in the ancient literature.

Royal Scribes and Government Bureaucrats Who Served the Ruling Elite Directly

In Mesopotamia royal schools for scribes probably existed already in third millennium BCE.[55] In ancient Egypt, professional scribes were educated in schools to copy, recite, and memorize documents. They served in the royal court as political and financial administrators and record keepers, sometimes reaching the highest levels of government.[56] Egyptian "royal scribes" can be documented down into the Ptolemaic period.[57] The Greeks developed a similar role, the *Basilikos Grammateus*. The Romans had "imperial secretaries" promoted to equestrian status.[58] Some scholars argue that a comparable picture of government scribes can be drawn for preexilic Israel if Temple functions are stressed.[59]

Public and Private Secretaries

For the larger Greco-Roman world in the Hellenistic period the *grammateus* is, according to Richards,

---

55. Baker, "Scribes as Transmitters of Tradition," 66–67.
56. Richards, *The Secretary*, 15.
57. Ibid., 15–16 and n. 7.
58. Ibid., 16–18; on the Romans, 15–20.
59. Saldarini, *Pharisees*, 243–44; "Scribes"; Fishbane, "From Scribalism to Rabbinism," 25–27; Viviano, "Methodology," 55; Heaton, *School Tradition*; Davies, "Were There Schools in Ancient Israel?" Perhaps scribal schools for kings and priests existed in Jerusalem prior to the Exile.

a person employed to write out correspondence for another, whether as a professional or only as an amateur, whether with or without financial compensation, whether maintained full-time by one individual or used only for one assignment, and whether used throughout the entire letter writing process or only for preparing the final draft. This definition includes everyone from the public secretaries usually hired in the agora, to the private secretaries usually retained by wealthy persons, to the friend who writes out a letter for another. His skills could range from a minimal competency with the language and/or the mechanics of writing to the highest proficiency at rapidly producing an accurate, proper, and charming letter.

Greek writers use the same term, *grammateus*, to describe several positions. A *grammateus* could mean a secretary, public [that is, hired in the *agora*] or private [that is, usually employed by the wealthy], or a government official. The Latin language is more specialized: *scriba* denotes a public or official secretary, *librarius*, a private secretary as does the rarer term *amanuensis*, and *notarius*, a shorthand writer.[60]

Josephus' references to *grammateus* reflect this rather broad Greco-Roman "secular" orientation,[61] which was current in the Judean Diaspora.[62]

Village and Local Scribes

In the Egyptian administrative system there were local scribes (*topogrammateus*) and village scribes (*komogrammateus*) who reported to the "royal scribes." They sometimes cultivated land, but their main functions were administration of the land and processing petitions; they were mainly record keepers and brokers between with higher of-

---

60. Richards, *Secretary*, 10–11. Richards's n. 59 adds: "In the LXX and the New Testament a third possibility exists: an expert in religious (Jewish and Christian) law." That is the second type in this list. For scribes' standing and sitting postures for writing, see Parássoglou, "DECIA XEIR KAI GONU."

61. Josephus generally uses the "secular" meaning. When he refers to two teachers of the Torah, Judas and Matthias, he uses the term *sophistai* (Jos. *Ant.* 17.149). See Snyder, *Teachers and Texts*, 184–85.

62. In the *Letter of Aristeas* learned sages are not called "scribes" and the designation of Eleazar, the Jerusalem priestly leader, as "scribe" in Palestinian 2 Maccabees 6:18 has vanished in the Diaspora's 4 Maccabees 5:4.

ficials and subordinates (see Menches, Appendix 3 below).[63] Josephus mentions village scribes (Jos. *B.J.* 1.24.3 [§479]).[64] The papyri also show that educated slaves could be secretaries (*POxy.* 3273).[65] Recent studies have suggested that it was *village* scribes who copied and transmitted Jesus Movement documents such as Q[66] and Mark.[67]

Scribes of Voluntary Associations

There were record-keeping scribes in voluntary associations.[68] Judean inscriptions from synagogues at Rome suggest that some of these scribes, although capable of reading and writing, were *not* highly educated.[69] To these four types of scribes, one may add two special types of scribes often noted in discussions of ancient Israel.

Scribes Who Teach Elementary Education

In the Rabbinic literature the term *sopherim* could sometimes refer to educators at an elementary level in contrast to learned Torah scholars.[70]

---

63. Goodman, "Texts, Scribes, and Power," 59; Richards, *Secretary*, 15; Kloppenborg, *The Formation of Q*, 171–245, 342–45; "Literary Convention," 81–86; Arnal, "The Rhetoric of Marginality," 482–92; "Gendered Couplets in Q"; for the earlier period, see Millard, "Assessment," 303. Much information has been retrieved from the wastepaper "archive" of a successor of the Greek Menches, village scribe of Kerkeosiris, Egypt, who reported to the *Basilikos Grammateus* and whose patron, Dorion, at distant Alexandria, defended him. See Verhoogt, *Menches, Komogrammateus of Kerkeosiris* , esp. 67–68, 70, 88–89; for a model of his network and status, see Appendix 3 in this chapter.

64. Saldarini, "Scribes," 1014; Horsley, *Sociology*, 203; Kloppenborg, "The Formation of Q Revisited," 212–13.

65. Richards, *Secretary*, 38 n. 105 quotes *P.Oxy* 724, in which Panechotes (Panares), the ex-cosmetes of Oxyrhynchus, sends his slave boy Chaerammon to Apollonius, "a writer of shorthand," to teach him to write fluently and read faultlessly like Apollonius' son.

66. Kloppenborg, "Literary Convention," 83–85; Arnal, *Jesus and the Village Scribes*, 151–55; 170–72.

67. Beavis, *Mark's Audience*, 39–42, 50–67, 167–70.

68. See chap. 6 above; Ascough, "Matthew and Community Formation."

69. Saldarini, "Scribes," 1016b, derived from Leon, *Jews*. Judean scribes were keepers of records and contracts and were not highly educated.

70. So Daube, *New Testament and Rabbinic Judaism*, 205–23. Daube argues that "as one having authority, and not as the scribes" (Mark 1:22) and "a new teaching with

Learned Torah Scholars

In Second-Temple Israel, Ezra was described as a "priest and scribe of the law of the God of Heaven" (Ezra 7:12; cf. 7:14, 21 [see 7:6]).[71] He was, thus, a learned Torah scholar (Ezra 7:6; 8:5, 10; Neh 8) and a powerful Judean political leader (Ezra 7:20, 25).[72] About 180 BCE the sage Ben Sira sketched the "ideal scribe" as a man of leisure, an international traveler, ambassador, community leader, and expert in all areas of knowledge—thus, a sage and Torah scholar. In the Maccabean period, a guild of *lay* scribes (*synagōgē grammateōn*) apart from the priests seems to have arisen (1 Macc 7:11). In the first century BCE 1 Enoch refers to the "scribe of righteousness" (1 En. 12:3-4; 15:1) and in the late first century CE the apocalyptic visionary Baruch is also depicted as a scribe (2 Bar. 2:1; 9:1—10:4). Finally, in the later rabbinic literature, the "words of the scribes" were still authoritative.[73]

As might be expected, these multiple roles and functions of scribes have produced a scholarly debate about how to rank Judean scribes. This debate focuses primarily on whether they were professional writers—copyists, secretaries, and recorders, in or out of government—or Torah scholars with higher status. The distinction corresponds to Cohen's contrast between "economic scribes" and "religious scribes."[74] It is the latter, the Torah scholar role, that has dominated the attention of modern Jewish and Christian scholars.[75] David Orton's synthetic view fits this generalization. He holds that scribes study Torah, the law of covenants, and the wisdom of the ancients; they penetrate prophecies, the subtleties of parables, and the hidden meanings of proverbs; they offer thanksgiving to God and pray for forgiveness of their sins; they pour forth their own wisdom, showing

---

authority" (Mark 1:27) make the distinction between ordinary teachers (*sōpherim*) and ordained learned scholars (*reshuth*).

71. See North, "Ezra (Person)."
72. Contrast, however, Ezra 10:5 and Neh 8:13; 10:1. Scholars debate the point.
73. Saldarini, "Scribes," 1015; Hengel, *Judaism and Hellenism* 1, 79, 132-60.
74. See above, n. 24. For Cohen, see pp. 261-63 and Chart 9.3.
75. E.g., Christian scholars such as Schürer, Billerbeck, Schlatter, Jeremias, and Hengel. Jewish scholars include Urbach, Bar-Ilan, and Neusner. But see the view of Schams, *Jewish Scribes*, below.

learning; they meditate on the Lord's mysteries and are filled with the spirit of understanding.[76]

Not all agree. Christine Schams has developed a case against this received view.[77] She notes that Elias Bickerman considered the Torah scholar view of scribes to be a "phantom category" indebted to Luther's translation of *grammateus*, "scribe," by *Schriftgelehrte*, "text (Torah) scholar."[78] E. P. Sanders added that *grammateus* as "Torah scholar" is a complex scholarly myth with little or no evidence.[79] Pursuing this point of view, Schams argues, first, that the Torah scholar view is a redactional idealization of Second Temple writers without much historical reality, and, second, that New Testament and especially rabbinic views have been inappropriately read back into the earlier Judean and Christ-believing texts.

In my view, two points need to be kept in mind. First, redactional idealizations, like any literary products, not only distort, but also mirror, historical/social realities.[80] Second, as historical Jesus scholars well know, redacted idealizations can have a profound effect on later views whether they were originally historical or not. Thus, even if the Torah scholar role was an idealization, it may well have had its historical significance and effects. In my view it should remain among the normative role options for scribes in Second Temple Israel and the early Christ communities. Jonathan Z. Smith states, "The scribes were an elite class of learned, literate men, an intellectual aristocracy which played an invaluable role in the administration of their people in *both religious and political affairs* . . ."[81]

Ben Sira's "Ideal Scribe"

The preceding judgments imply that the description of Ben Sira's idealized scribe about 180 BCE, even if exaggerated, should be taken

---

76. Orton, *Understanding Scribe*, 120.
77. Schams, *Jewish Scribes*.
78. Bickerman, *The Jews in the Greek Age*.
79. Sanders, *Judaism*.
80. E.g., Eagleton, *Literary Theory*.
81. Smith, "Wisdom and Apocalyptic," 168.

seriously.[82] Ben Sira, who may have had a scribal school in his house (Sir 51:23: Hebrew: *bet-midrāš*; Greek: *oikia paideias*),[83] sums up the ideal scribe in two poems, both thought to reflect the Egyptian "Satire on the Trades" (Sir 38:24-34 and 39:1-11).[84] In chapter 7 I summarized Ben Sira's contrast between scribes and other social groups and ranked them hierarchically.[85] The social ranking of groups in Ben Sira generally fits the ranking of the Lenski macromodel for an advanced agrarian society, that is, scribes are retainers of the elite and social brokers. In the educational and professional class systems they rank relatively high. These might fit Cohen's "economic" model (see above). However, they *also* appear to be sages/Torah scholars and have even more prestige in Lenski's religious ranking system, or Cohen's "religious" model. Education, professional, and religious roles are fused. As Nickelsburg and Stone put it, Ben Sira's ideal is an "ideal of life which is *determined by social role*."[86]

The high ranking of some Judean scribes can be reinforced by taking into consideration the importance of "literacy power" in antiquity, which deserves brief consideration.

Literacy, Power, and Scribes

The term "scribe" in Hebrew (*sōfer*) from the root *sāfar*, "he writes," refers to a written message, then a writing, and finally one who could write.[87] The term *grammateus* in Greek means one who "knows letters," that is, can (read and) write. William Harris' view of ancient literacy, often authoritatively cited in this connection, is that probably no more than 10 percent of the population of the Greco-Roman

---

82. Rivkin, "Scribes," 139, once argued that it was precisely Ben Sira who changed the meaning of *sōpher/grammateus* to Torah scholar: "The *sōfer* of Ben Sira's day was an intellectual, not a scribe; a scholar, not a copyist; a sage, not a secretary." His image looks like Orton's, the image that Schams contests.

83. Hengel, *Judaism and Hellenism* 1, 79, 132; however, Schiffman, *The Halachah at Qumran*, 55, does not think it likely that the expression *ben midrash* was technical as early as Ben Sira, ca. 180 BCE.

84. See chap. 7 above, n. 159.

85. See chap. 7 above, Chart 7.3.

86. Nickelsburg and Stone, *Faith and Piety*, 94.

87. Saldarini, "Scribes," 1012.

world could *read and write*.⁸⁸ This estimate includes what Lucretia Yaghjian calls "scribaliteracy," a more advanced literate education, but also "craftsmen's literacy," that is, a fairly low level of reading and writing necessary for trade or business.⁸⁹

An intriguing historical question is: was the literacy level of Judeans *higher* than other ancient Mediterranean peoples? This is a question about the extent and level of education in ancient Israel. A. R. Millard once argued on the basis of epigraphic and seal evidence that Judean literacy was very widespread and Demsky agreed;⁹⁰ Bar-Ilan, P. R. Ackroyd and C. F. Evans, and Shaye Cohen, however, hold the opposite opinion.⁹¹ Cohen thinks that compulsory education for Judean children was *not* likely.⁹² Although this issue is debated, Millard has softened his position somewhat⁹³ and it seems likely that the literacy level of ancient Judeans and Christ believers including all forms of literacy probably did not exceed that of the wider population, that is, about 10 percent.⁹⁴

Another factor is oral communication, which was still important in the Mediterranean world.⁹⁵ Some could read without the ability to

88. "The likely overall *illiteracy* level of the Roman Empire under the principate is almost certain to have been above 90%" (Harris, *Ancient Literacy*, 22 [italics mine]).

89. Yaghjian, "Ancient Reading," also discusses "oculiterate reading," the ability to decode a written text, whether one could write or not; "*aura*literacy," or correct *hearing*; and "*orali*teracy," or *oral memorization and recitation*. For my view of the latter, see Duling, "Memory."

90. Millard, "The Practice of Writing," 108, said that "writing was theoretically within the competence of any ancient Israelite . . . and . . . was, in fact, quite widely practiced." Aaron Demsky in Millard, "An Assessment of the Evidence," adds: "Already by the late Second commonwealth period, elementary education had been organized along communal lines and children were studying in the *Beth Sepher*—the House of the Book" ("An Assessment of the Evidence," 352).

91. Bar-Ilan, "Part Two: Scribes and Books," 22; Ackroyd and Evans, *Cambridge History of the Bible*, 1:37; Cohen, *From the Maccabees to the Mishnah*, 120.

92. Cohen, ibid., 120.

93. Millard, "An Assessment of the Evidence," 306, 307, considers that his earlier 1972 statement (see n. 90 above) was perhaps "too optimistic", but nonetheless says, "We conclude that few ancient Israelites were out of reach of the written word . . ."

94. See above, nn. 72, 73. Millard admits that *most* reading and writing was carried out by professional scribes ("Literacy [Israel]," 339).

95. Papias of Hieropolis (ca. 150 CE) is cited by Eusebius to have said: "For I did not suppose that the things from the books would aid me so much as the things from the living and continuing voice" (Eusebius, *Church History* 3.5). See Kelber, *Oral and Written Gospel* and n. 73 above.

write; still others possessed "craftsman's literacy," enough writing ability to engage in everyday trade. The level of literary sophistication in the Gospel of Matthew surely requires us to focus on "scribaliteracy" at a relatively high level. Indeed, the Matthean scribe comes very close to the role and status of Torah scholar—at least in the groups for which he writes. In terms of the hypothetical distribution system above, his status would have been very high in professional, educational, and religious categories—higher than retainer status in the macrosociety, and certainly so for the Matthean group(s).

Ranking in the Lenski macromodel is based on a consideration of power, privilege, and prestige, generally in the political and economic sense, and thus scribes are ranked as "retainers," that is, political and economic office holders, or bureaucrats. The point just made about the higher rank of scribes in Israel is nonetheless reinforced by a consideration of what some scholars have called "literacy power." In the Introduction to *Literacy and Power in the Ancient World*, A. K. Bowman and G. Woolf offer the following five summary points about the essays in their collection.[96]

1. Power is related to literacy in predominantly two ways:
   - "power over texts" means that "an elite or restricted group determines both the status of particular kinds of texts and also which people or bodies may use them to legitimize their behavior."[97]
   - "power exercised through texts," which means that texts legitimize deeds and spoken words through their (re)interpretation.

2. Texts unite communities as well as establish and entrench relations of dominance. Indeed, "[g]radations of literacy created and corresponded to gradations in power."[98]

---

96. Bowman and Woolf, *Literacy and Power*, 2–3, say that many social anthropologists and historians are cautious about overstating the case for the power of literacy; they now tend to focus on local case studies, not generalizing grand theory.

97. Ibid., 6. This power includes restrictions on writing, reading, access, and possession, and sometimes stress education in a sacred language. "The most common justification for such manipulation is *religio*" (p. 12). Their example is *florilegia*. An analogy in Matthew would be the formula quotations.

98. Ibid., 13.

3. "In the administrative context of the Greek world and the Roman East, the title and position of *grammateus* often did not simply describe a function but *a position with some status and power.*"[99]

4. In Judean and Jesus Movement contexts the Greek and Semitic languages, like Latin and Greek in the empire, preserved and spread an elite culture that marked social boundaries and reinforced "political and cultural coherence, or group identity."[100]

5. Finally, in Judean and Jesus Movement groups, "the very act of writing a sacred text could bestow status and power on the scribe."[101] Such groups were "textual communities" in which a "sacral graphocentrism" was at work.

In short, scribes were "scribaliterate" and possessed literacy power, indeed Torah-scholar power, in Jesus Movement and Judean "textual communities." As Goodman puts it, "[p]erhaps the two roles of scribes, as writers and interpreters, were mutually reinforcing."[102] To what extent, then, can the scribe be termed "marginal"?

Scribes in the Gospel of Matthew and Its Social Context

A case for the view that the author of the First Gospel was a marginal scribe himself can begin with refining how he understood scribes, an issue of disagreement in Matthean studies. The best, earliest manuscripts of the Gospel of Matthew contain twenty-two references to the Greek term *grammateus*, "scribe."[103] For convenience, I categorize and distribute them with respect to sources and links to other groups.[104]

---

99. Ibid., 10 (italics mine).
100. Ibid., 12.
101. Ibid., 12. For a critique of this view, see Schams, *Jewish Scribes*, 58.
102. Goodman, "Texts, Scribes, and Power," 108.
103. Matt 23:14, omitted by Aleph, B, and others, is usually judged to be an interpolation based on Mark 12:38a, 40 ("Beware of the scribes . . . who devour widows' houses and for a pretense make long prayers. They will receive the greater condemnation") or its parallel, Luke 20:46a, 47. The verse is now placed in the Nestle-Aland apparatus.
104. See an earlier statement in chap. 5 above.

Outline 9.1 Twenty-Two References to *Grammateus* Categorized

A. Parallels with Mark	10x		
1. Direct parallels		9x	7:29 (Mark 1:22); 9:3 (Mark 2:6); 15:1a (Mark 7:1); 16:21 (Mark 8:31); 17:10 (Mark 9:11); 20:18 (Mark 10:33); 21:15 (Mark 11:18); 26:57 (Mark 14:53); 27:41 (Mark 15:31)
2. Indirect parallel?		1x	23:2 (Mark 12:38?)
B. Deletions from Mark	7x		
1. The term itself		4x	9:11 (Mark 2:16); 21:23 (Mark 11:27); 26:47 (Mark 14:43); 27:1 (Mark 15:1)
2. Term in deleted clauses		3x	15:1b (Mark 7:5); 17:14 (Mark 9:14); 22:40 (Mark 12:32)
C. Substitutions of Mark	4x/5x		
1. Replaced by "Pharisees"		3x/4x	9:34/12:24 (Mark 3:22: "scribes"); 22:41 (Mark 12:35: "scribes"); 22:34 ("lawyer of the Pharisees"; Mark 12:28 "one of the scribes")
2. Replaced by "elders of the people"		1x	26:3 (Mark 14:1); cp. 26:47; 27:1
D. No parallels	12x		
1. In a Q context		9x	8:19 (Q 9:57); 12:38 (Q 11:16); 23:13, 15, 23, 25, 27, 29, 34 (Q 11:39b-44, 46-52).
2. In another context		3x	2:4; 5:20; 13:52
E. No links to other groups	5x		
1. Markan parallels		3x	
A. Scribes = opponents			2x: Matt 9:3 (Mark 2:6); 7:29 (changes "the scribes" in Mark 1:22 to "*their* scribes")
B. Scribes neutral			1x: Matt 17:10 (Mark 9:11).
2. No Markan parallels		2x	Matt 8:19; 13:52.
F. Links to other groups			
Markan parallels:	6x		
1. "Pharisees and scribes"		1x	15:1 (Mark 7:1)
2. "High Priests and scribes"		2x	20:18 (Mark 10:33); 21:15 (cf. Mark 11:18)
3. "scribes and elders"		1x	26:57 (Mark 14:53 [+ High Priests])
4. "elders, High Priests, and scribes"		1x	16:21 (Mark 8:31)
5. "High Priests, scribes, and elders"		1x	27:41 (Mark 15:31)
G. Links to other groups:			
no Markan parallels	10x		
1. "High Priests and scribes"		1x	2:4
2. "scribes and Pharisees"		9x	5:20; 12:38; 23:2, 13, 15, 23,25,27,29

This list illustrates several levels of complexity that need to be summarized. With regard to sources, almost half of the twenty-two Matthean references to "scribe" (10x) are from Mark (A), which in turn represent almost half of the Markan references (21x; A + B, C). Note that slightly more than half of Matthew's references (12x) are found *only in Matthew* (D), and that most of them (9x) are distributed into *Q contexts* (D1). With respect to other groups, in five instances the Matthean scribes stand alone (E). In two of them, both from Mark (E1A), scribes are clearly opponents. Indeed, *most Matthean references to scribes (16x) yoke them with opponents of Jesus*

Matthew as Marginal Scribe in an Advanced Agrarian Society 273

(F, G). Scholars usually agree that the Matthean author has created the majority of these "opponent links" (esp. G2); that most of those are with the Pharisees (G2), the usual Matthean opponents; and that this result corresponds with the fact that Pharisees are Matthew's usual opponents, also when he makes a substitution (C). The Matthean author omits the so-called "good scribe" passage from Mark, that is, the scribe "who is not far from the Kingdom" (Mark 12:32–34).

As noted in chapter 7, this complicated, mixed data has produced a scholarly debate. Some scholars conclude that the Matthean author simply was not clear,[105] or was even confused about these groups;[106] still others say that he intentionally distorted Jesus' opponents to show that they formed a "united front."[107] David Orton is representative of a fourth option held by a number of scholars, including Saldarini and Overman, that some scribes in the gospel are viewed positively. His point is this: "*the scribes* per se *never stand alone as opponents of Jesus. They are tainted by the company they keep.*"[108] The company refers especially to the Pharisees.[109]

I accept this positive view of some scribes in Matthew.[110] There are four reasons.

1. Some of Matthew's created links about scribes—with Pharisees in polemical contexts and elders in Jerusalem—are in a general way historically plausible.[111]

---

105. Walker, *Die Heilsgeschichte*; Van Tilborg, *Jewish Leaders*.

106. Cook, *Mark's Treatment*, 58–67.

107. Meier, *The Vision of Matthew*, 19, thinks that Matthew's linking of Pharisees and Sadducees (Matt 3:7; 16:1, 6, 11, 12) is "unhistorical."

108. Orton, *The Understanding Scribe*, 28.

109. Saldarini, "Political and Social Roles"; Overman, *Matthew's Gospel and Formative Judaism*; Orton, *The Understanding Scribe*; Saldarini, *Pharisees*, 267 n. 67 notes other scholars. Matthew's deletions and his replacements of scribes with Pharisees (see C and G in text above) are related to his relentless anti-Pharisaic polemic (e.g., 9:11, 34; 12:24, 38; 15:12; 16:11; 21:45; 22:15, 34–35; 27:62).

110. See chap. 7 above.

111. Deletions of "scribes" with "chief priests and elders" in Jerusalem settings (21:23 [Mark 11:27]; 26:3 [Mark 14:1] 26:47 [Mark 14:43]; 27:1 [Mark 15:1]) and replacing scribes with Pharisees or narrowing to the Pharisees (15:12; see 15:1) in conflict stories about purity (9:11 [Mark 2:16]) are historically plausible. See Saldarini, *Pharisees*, 160–61; Orton, *Understanding Scribe*, 26.

2. An apparent exception is that Matthew omits Mark's "good scribe," but that omission can be explained, that is, he has just transformed him into a Pharisaic lawyer who tests Jesus (Matt 22:34-35 [Mark 12:28]).

3. Two of five cases where scribes stand alone and are sometimes said to be polemical can be interpreted differently. One case refers to "*their* scribes" (Matt 7:29)—in context scribes of the Pharisees[112]— and the other qualifies the reference with the expression "*some of* the scribes" (Matt 9:12 [Mark 2:6]).

4. Most importantly, there are five scribe passages that are arguably positive. I place them in what I considered to be an ascending order of importance:

   a. Matthew accepts the *scribal* view in Mark that Elijah is the forerunner of the Messiah (Matt 17:10 [Mark 9:11]);[113]

   b. Only Matthew's Jesus says that the scribes and Pharisees sit on Moses' seat and the crowds and disciples should practice and observe what they teach (Matt 23:2.);[114]

   c. Matthew alone inserts "a scribe" into the Q sayings about the difficulty of "following" Jesus (cp. Q Luke 9:57-60),[115] and I agree with those who argue that this saying implies that the follower is a disciple;[116]

---

112. See "*their* synagogues," 4:23; 9:35; 10:17; 12:9; 13:54; "*your* synagogues," 23:34; "*their* cities," 11:1; cf. 12:38 (Kilpatrick, *Origins*, 286; Stanton, "The Communities of Matthew," 119-20, 128; Overman, *Matthew's Gospel and Formative Judaism*, 115).

113. Matthew interprets him to be John the Baptist.

114. There is negativity here, but it is related to the link with the Pharisees, and despite their reputed hypocrisy, their teaching is said to be correct. Matthew is sometimes inconsistent; Hummel, *Auseinandersetzung*, 31; Garland, *The Intention of Matthew 23*, 20-22, 46-55.

115. Cp. Q Luke 9:57-60.

116. For the negative view of scribes, see Kingsbury, "The Verb *Akolouthein*," 59-60; Luz, *Das Evangelium*, 23; Davies and Allison, *Critical and Exegetical Commentary*, Vol. 2, 41, 53-54; Kiilunen, "Der nachfolgewillige Schriftgelehrte"; Stanton, "The Communities of Matthew," 383; *A Gospel*, 127; and Carter, *Households and Discipleship*, 52; *Matthew: Storyteller, Interpreter, Evangelist*, 66. For the positive view of scribes, see Saldarini, *Pharisees*, 159; Orton, *Understanding Scribe*, 36-37; Gundry, "On True and False Disciples." For the arguments of the latter, see chap. 7 above. On the "foxes have holes . . ." saying (v. 20), see *GTh* 86 and Kloppenborg, *Formation of Q*, 65.

d. Matthew changes Q's itinerant "prophets and apostles" sent out by Jesus to "prophets, sages, *and scribes*."[117]

e. Finally, Matthew composed the formulaic conclusion to the third speech, which speaks of a scribe "trained ('instructed as a disciple')[118] for the kingdom of heaven" (Matt 13:52). Daniel Harrington's comment that this description is a "self-portrait of the evangelist" is a very widespread, one might say almost universal, view.[119] I agree.

Thus, a plausible interpretation of the complex data is that while *most* instances of the term "scribe(s)" in the Gospel of Matthew are negative because of their association with Jesus' opponents, *some are positive* and, indeed, *it is very probable that the author of the gospel himself was a scribe*. This conclusion permits refining the sense in which Matthew was a marginal scribe in an advanced agrarian society.

The Author of Matthew as a "Marginal Scribe"

Using Billson's social-scientific categories, it is possible to refine the sense in which the scribe who wrote the Gospel of Matthew might have been "marginal." Lenski's macromodel is useful, but it needs to be qualified by specific variables in the distribution system. The role of the scribe as "retainer" is one possibility, but educational, occupational, and religious rankings also need to be considered. It must also be tested with historical information about the varieties of ancient scribes, as I attempted to do earlier in this chapter (see Ranking of Scribes in Mediterranean Antiquity).

Structural Marginality. In structural marginality, center/marginal and vertical upper/lower status models overlap. Though by definition

---

117. Q 11:49; Matt 23:34. "Prophets" occur 37 times, 20 of which are perhaps redactional, and are generally viewed with favor in the gospel (Luz, *Matthew 1–7*, 67). The negative instances are Matthean warnings about *false* prophets (7:15–23; cf. 24:11–12, 24); see Hill, "False Prophets and Charismatics"; Overman, *Matthew's Gospel and Formative Judaism*, 118. "Sages" (*sophoi*) occurs negatively in Matt 11:25 (= Q 10:21), but they are sages *of the world*, probably Pharisaic (12:2, 14, 24, 38); see Suggs, *Wisdom*, 84–87; Overman, *Matthew's Gospel and Formative Judaism*, 117.

118. See Kingsbury, *Parables*, 126–27; Gundry, "On True and False Disciples," 281; Luz, *Das Evangelium*, 109.

119. Harrington, *The Gospel of Matthew*, 208.

marginality can occur at any level of the social hierarchy, *most* marginal persons are at or near the lower end of the vertical social hierarchy. In the Lenski macromodel they are the expendables, but include lower peasants and artisans. For Kautsky, their marginality would have been greater because of their loss of land and extraction of taxes under a new redistribution economy.[120]

However, if we broaden the analysis to include a "distribution system," those who are marginal *structurally* (as contrasted with social role, cultural, and ideological marginality) would include suspected enemies of the state (the political ranking system); the impoverished (the property ranking system); beggars, prostitutes, and unemployed (the occupational ranking system); those not of one's ethnic group (the ethnic ranking system); the illiterate and uneducated, without "literary power" (the educational ranking system); "pagans" (the ethnic and religious ranking systems); women (the gender ranking system); and potentially those outside of one's kin group (the family ranking system). The Matthean story includes examples of such marginal persons: forced laborers, day laborers, some slaves, tenant farmers, poor, those in need of alms, eunuchs, ritually unclean, lepers, a woman with a hemorrhage, women who follow Jesus, the diseased and infirm, the blind, the lame, the deaf, the dumb, the deformed, paralytics, demoniacs, epileptics, bandits, and prostitutes.[121]

From the perspective of the Lenski macromodel combined with marginality theory, a scribe would *not* have been structurally marginal; he was a "retainer" of the elite. He was literate and would have had a somewhat higher social status and literacy power. Descriptions of Judean scribes, even if idealized, suggest an even higher status. Though there is a spectrum, many could have been educated Torah scholars who played a significant role in political and religious affairs. Ben Sira's ideal scribe certainly contributed to and reinforced this role perception, for scribes seem to have been ranked just below rulers. Again, from the macromodel perspective, scribes were not structurally marginal.

---

120. Kautsky, *Politics of Aristocratic Empires*; Hanson and Oakman, *Palestine*, 197 ("extractive economy"), 202 ("redistribution").

121. See chap. 5 above, Chart 5.1; also Vledder, *Conflict*; Rohrbaugh, "The Social Location of the Marcan Audience."

If we add in distribution system variables, a similar picture emerges. In the political ranking system the Judean scribe would have been part of the bureaucracy, in the property class system he was moderately wealthy, and in the occupational system he was an administrative official. With respect to gender, scribes were normally male, though according to Eusebius there were "girls trained in beautiful writing."[122] With respect to kinship, there may have been scribal families.[123]

A problem arises, however, when the *fuller range of scribes* within the *occupational* class system is considered, for it is necessary to add in village scribes and other, somewhat lesser educated scribes, for example, scribes in voluntary associations. Some of these scribes were of relatively lower status. Should we see them as structurally marginal? In Lenski's macromodel they are certainly not among the elite. However, neither are they at the lower levels. In microcontexts— small villages, voluntary associations, and the like—they would have a certain amount of power and status in view of the general low level of illiteracy at large. Only in terms of Germani's broader definition— not being permitted to fulfill one's expected role—might one conclude that such scribes were structurally marginal, but that judgment would have pertained to scribes who had had a higher social status, even Torah scholars. In other words, an ancient scribe *could* have been structurally marginal vis-à-vis the macrosociety *if* he had been excluded from his expected role as retainer by someone with higher scribal status or some elite patron. From a microsocial perspective, however, such scribes were not marginals. Given levels of literacy in antiquity, even scribes of *relatively* low status in the macrosociety would have had relatively high status in villages or voluntary associations. What becomes more significant, then, are *"we-they" judgments of one group by another*. That is precisely what we have in relation to the Pharisees and the Matthean group.

---

122. Haines-Eitzen, "'Girls Trained in Beautiful Writing,'" 629–46. Eusebius writes: "As [Origen] dictated there were ready at hand more than seven shorthand writers (*tachygraphoi*), who relieved each other at fixed times, and as many copyists (*bibliographoi*), as well as girls trained for beautiful writing; for all of these Ambrose supplied without stint the necessary means" (Eusebius, *HE* 6.23, trans. LCC, modified by Haines-Eitzen).

123. Verhoogt, *Menches, Komogrammateus of Kerkeosiris*, 53.

If the author of Q was written by a village scribe,[124] the Matthean writer certainly exemplified a still higher level of education and, indeed, in the traditional Judean religious context, approximated the role of the Torah scholar. This is indicated at least by his level of writing, his striking interpretations of the Torah in relation to matters of Judean concern, his probable multilingualism, and his perceived Pharisaic opponents: "their scribes" and "their synagogues." It might be reinforced by his attention to details of wealth and the probability that he was urban. While this description of the Matthean scribe is common in Matthean studies, it also says that from the perspective of the macrosociety the author of Matthew was not marginal in the most usual, or structurally marginal, sense of that term. It is still possible, of course, that he was marginal in the definitional sense that he was not fulfilling a role *expected* of him. However, that is conjectural. Most important, in a "textual community" in which a growing "sacral graphocentrism"[125] was at work—even if the vast majority could not read and the gospel functioned as a guide for community leaders—it suggests that he had literacy power over texts and through texts.[126]

Social Role Marginality and Ideological Marginality. Germani's more inclusive definitional view of structural marginality, which includes those who are not able to carry out their expected social roles at any level of the hierarchy, is similar to Billson's separate category, "social role marginality." Had the Matthean writer been denied his social role as a scribe in society at large? It is possible. It is tantalizing to suggest that if he had, he would have regained prestige in his social role as a leader of a marginal group that did not conform to the beliefs, norms, and behaviors of either the macrosociety or, at a lower level of abstraction, those of a powerful and emergent group, the Pharisees. In such a case, his "literacy power" (as discussed above) would have been transferred, even enhanced. Thus, ironically, being part of a group voluntarily, a group considered by those in the center to be marginal—"ideological marginality"—could easily have led to status

---

124. Kloppenborg, *Excavating Q*, 196–97; Arnal, *Jesus and the Village Scribes*, 150–55, 168–72.

125. Bowman and Woolf, *Literacy and Power*, 13, in reference to the authority of texts and the expert readers who interpret them as a mutually reinforcing enterprise.

126. See the section "Literacy, Power, and Scribes" above.

enhancement. In other words, social role marginality in the macrosociety would have been offset by social role leadership within the Matthean group. While the author's scribal leadership in his group can be defended,[127] this tantalizing possibility remains, again, speculative.

Cultural Marginality. Analyzing the Matthean author from the perspective of cultural marginality is more promising if one avoids psychological "maladjustment" theories. The description of cultural marginality as having to exist between two or more "historic traditions, languages, political loyalties, moral codes, and religions" (see the Venn diagram above) fits the Matthean author very well.[128] The most probable cause for his cultural marginality is his *ideological* marginality, that is, his "voluntary outsiderhood" as a member of a Christ-believing group.[129] In other words, while he comes from the literate and educated strata, his ideology led him to align himself with many who were *structurally* marginal in his group, in this case those at the bottom of the social ladder. Yet, his cultural marginality did not allow him to totally assimilate with the new group (see examples below).

This sense of "in betweenness" and the conflict and tensions that accompany it pervades the gospel. I illustrate with three major areas of modern debate about the gospel and then with some well-known examples.

1. "Jewish Christianity" or "Christian Judaism"?[130] Had the Matthean group separated from Israel or not? Was it part of Israel or had it become a separatist Christ-believing group? To use the common scholarly description, was it *extra muros* ("outside the walls [of Israel]")[131] or *intra muros* (still "inside the walls [of Israel]")?[132] Scholarship on the Gospel of Matthew is filled with cautious evaluations

127. See chaps. 6 and 7 above.

128. Stonequist, *Marginal Man*, 3 (n. 108 above).

129. See chap. 7 above, which suggests that the Matthean group is a form of voluntary association; also see chap. 8 above.

130. The debate is usually formulated with the terms "Christian Judaism" and "Jewish Christianity." For my preference for "Judean" or "Israelite" (the latter is Matthean) and "Christ-believer," see chap. 1 above, n. 6.

131. Scholars who hold this view include the later Bornkamm, Stendahl, Schweizer, Hare, Trilling, Strecker, Kümmel, Luz, Stanton, and Hagner, e.g., Stanton, *A Gospel*, 142: "shortly after a painful separation from Judaism."

132. Scholars who hold this view include Kilpatrick, the early Bornkamm, Hummel, W. D. Davies (and Allison), Goulder, Overman, Saldarini, Levine, and Sim.

and qualifications, such as positing some sort of transition *beginning* to taking place or some *very recent* separation. The expressions "Christian *Judaism*" and "Jewish *Christianity*" have symbolized the fine-line issue. Donald Senior names his contribution, "Between Two Worlds: Gentile and Jewish Christians in Matthew's Gospel."[133] I suggest that such "in betweenness" would have been typical of a "culturally marginal" scribe.

2. *The Mission.* Closely related to this question, scholars have long debated whether the mission is to "the lost sheep of the house of Israel," as Jesus is recorded to have said in the mission speech,[134] or is to "all the peoples," often understood as "Gentiles," that is, those outside Israel, as the resurrected Jesus finally commands at the end of the story.[135] The difficulty of this question has led to mediating solutions such as a both/and salvation historical sequence, or a both/and Gentile mission that nonetheless is still open to Judeans, or a both/and Diaspora mission that does not exclude Gentiles. Such ambiguity would have been typical of a culturally marginal scribe.

3. *Was our scribe himself a Judean (Israelite) or a Gentile (non-Israelite)?* It is especially his focus on the Scripture and Torah matters that has led scholars to think of a Judean author.[136] But would a Judean have used Hebrew poetic parallelism so oddly (Matt 21:6) and not mention circumcision?[137] What of the apparent confusion about parties mentioned at the outset of this chapter? A number of scholars have held that the author was a Gentile.[138] I suggest that the author was a marginal Judean scribe who was "in between" in a variety of ways, thus giving rise to the difficulty of answering the question.

---

133. Near his conclusion he draws on Duling, "Matthew and Marginality" (see chap. 5 above).

134. Matt 10:6; cp. 15:24. See chap. 2 above for Levine's view.

135. Matt 28:19. On the interpretation of "all the *ethnē*" as "all the Gentiles," see Hare, "How Jewish?" and Harrington, "'Make Disciples." Contrast Jackson, "Are the 'Nations' Present?"

136. For scholars who hold this view, see above, n. 123.

137. Sim, "Christianity and Ethnicity," accepts the "Christian Judaism" perspective and thus the view that circumcision is taken for granted in the gospel; see chap. 10.

138. They include Meier, *Vision of Matthew*, 18, who lists in support Clark, Nepper-Christensen, Strecker, Trilling, Walker, van Tilborg, Pesch, and Frankemölle, though not all are quite so explicit.

Viewing these three major issues through the lens of a model of cultural marginality can bring fresh light to bear on the subject. Let us briefly consider several other possibilities.

Politics. On the one hand, there is an implied political conflict with the elite in the story of Herod and the infant Jesus, as Horsley has argued,[139] and many anti-elitist political stances lie just under the surface of the story, as Warren Carter thinks.[140] Yet, Pontius Pilate seems to get off fairly easily. Had the author of Matthew held a position in the Herodian administration at one time? Was he not "in between" with regard to his community and the larger political world?

Economics. Where did our scribe stand on the economic ladder? What was our scribe's position on wealth? On the one hand, Jesus' parable says that those who feed the hungry, give drink to the thirsty, welcome the stranger, clothe the naked, and visit the sick and imprisoned will be rewarded at the final judgment. This parable has been seen as a paradigm for the Matthean gospel as a whole (Matt 25:31–46).[141] On the other hand, the Matthean writer presents Jesus' beatitude as, "Blessed are the poor *in spirit*," not "you poor," as in Luke, and in the Matthean account of the anointing of Jesus at Bethany Jesus observes that, "you always have the poor with you" (Matt 26:11). The writer consistently speaks of large sums of money typical of the wealthy, leading contemporary scholars to link him with wealth.[142] Had he not yet *fully* identified with the lower level *structural* marginals about whom he writes?

Gender. Had our scribe moved beyond the patriarchalism of his culture? On the one hand, the faith of the Canaanite woman—also a Gentile—is so great that Jesus heals her daughter (Matt 15:21–28)[143] and the woman at Bethany will be remembered for her symbolic act (26:6–13). Yet, the male Jesus and his male disciples control the story and it is men who have the lusty eye (5:27).[144] Again, while

---

139. Horsley, *Sociology*.

140. Carter, *Households and Discipleship*; *Matthew and the Margins*.

141. See Donahue, "Parable of the Sheep and the Goats."

142. Kingsbury, "Verb *Akolouthein*," who also notes the many references to cities.

143. See Anderson, "Matthew: Gender and Reading," 10–17.

144. See Love, *Jesus and Marginal Women*, chap. 5, for further study in relation to marginality as discussed here.

patriarchalism remains in place, there are tensions typical of a culturally marginal perspective.

This is only a sampling of "in between" situations in the Gospel of Matthew. One might add "between languages,"[145] "between Torah intensification and Torah abandonment"(Matt 5:17–20 and with the antitheses in Matt 5:21–48),[146] "between fasting appropriately and not fasting at all,"[147] and the like. Each in its own way illustrates the "in betweenness" of the cultural marginal.

The Matthean scribe was culturally marginal. He was clearly "in between." This seems clear in the "in betweenness" of his own leadership role. On the one hand, he perpetuated a form of the radical Jesus Movement tradition, perhaps best represented by Q; and Q was itself written, plausibly, by Galilean scribes. On the otherhand, he was what Lucretia Yaghjian called *scribaliterate*;[148] indeed, he inserted "have you not *read* . . . ?" into four challenge-riposte settings, which hints at his own view of what A. K. Bowman and G. Woolf called the power of literacy.[149] In these terms, he expressed his power *over* sacred texts by his choices of quotations and *how* they are to be read. He expressed his power *through* the sacred texts by his frequent references to promise and fulfillment. He expressed such power also by his redaction of the Jesus sources and traditions. Yet, he was ideologically and socially marginal, and he associated with and gave hope to the structurally marginal in the narrower sense. That is one main reason why his narrative can be considered "good news."

---

145. The problem is whether his scriptural citations, which represent Hebrew, Aramaic, Greek, and Syriac, represent language versions or simply a text tradition still in flux.

146. My view is found in Duling, "[Do not Swear] . . ."

147. Jesus' disciples are said not to have fasted, but the narrative says that Jesus himself did (Matt 4:2) and that the wedding guests would fast after the bridegroom is taken away (9:14–17); indeed, it offers instructions on *how* to fast (Matt 6:16–18).

148. Yaghjian, "Ancient Reading," 209.

149. Bowman and Woolf, *Literacy and Power*. The references to reading are spoken to Pharisees (about David and the priests, Matt 12:3, 5); to high priests and (their) scribes (out of the mouth of babes, 19:4); to Pharisees, chief priests, and elders of the people (rejected cornerstone, 21:42); to Sadducees (I am the God of Abraham, Isaac, and Jacob, 22:31).

Implications for the Matthean Social Context

What about the "authorial audience," which, to follow Warren Carter, needs to be correlated with the Matthean scribe's first readers or hearers?[150] Many scholars, particularly redaction critics, have held that each evangelist wrote his gospel for a specific community and that that community could to a reasonable extent be described. Richard Bauckham has objected that this view has been assumed, but not argued. His alternative proposition is that the gospels were, like Paul's letters, for *all* the churches of the Jesus Movement.[151] Graham Stanton's suggestion is that the First Gospel may have circulated as a "foundation document" in a "cluster" of Christ-believing communities. For Stanton, those communities were probably in Syria and the gospel story offered what he termed "legitimizing answers" for a "new people."[152] Even if one does not accept Stanton's *extra muros* view, his regional hypothesis seems to me more likely. This more limited view fits some things that we know about regionalism, for example, clusters of towns and villages and networking among them via emissaries.[153]

Combining Stanton's and Elaine Wainwright's suggestion, that we take more seriously 90-95 percent of the population, that is, the *structurally* marginal ones mentioned in the gospel,[154] we might think of local scribal recipients of gospels *reading* them aloud to Christ-believing groups in a particular region, groups consisting mainly of structurally marginal persons in the usual sense (Paul's majority in 1 Cor 1:26). Indeed, "Let *the reader* understand" (a statement already in Mark 13:14) might have been an "aside" (if it was not a gloss) not simply to a private reader, but to a public house-church reader who would need to explain the code language to his

---

150. For my view on authorial readers and real readers, see chap. 8 above.

151. Bauckham, *Gospel for all Christians*. For critique, see Sim, "Gospels for All Christians?"

152. Stanton, "Revisiting Matthew's Communities," 17, who clearly has Matt 21:43 in mind: "Therefore I tell you, the kingdom of God will be taken away from you and given to a people [*ethnei*] producing the fruits of it," on which see below.

153. Duling, "Jesus Movement and Network Analysis."

154. Wainwright, "Only to the Lost Sheep." For a list of Lenski-type social strata in the Gospel of Matthew, see chap. 4 above, and for a list of "involuntary" or structural marginals, see chap. 5 above.

assembled listeners (Matt 24:15).[155] In the Matthean gospel this could be correlated with the many admonitions about right hearing and understanding.[156] If the author was a culturally marginal scribe, as I have argued in this chapter, there is an analogy in the network of scribes known from ancient Egypt (see Menches' network, Appendix 3). If we consider the Matthean scribe to be a Torah scholar with some authority (and power) in his network, he may well have written a gospel story that others, perhaps village scribes, would have read to their listeners. The Matthean author, in writing to his churches, might be analogous to the *Basilikos Grammateus* (although not a status this high) who writes to *topogrammateis* or *komogrammateis* in the towns and villages of his region (see Appendix 3).[157]

Again, I have suggested that the Matthean scribe was "culturally marginal." Evidence can be found in a number of ambiguities and inconsistencies scattered throughout his gospel. However, this cultural marginality may have been a result of his freely chosen ideological marginality, which identified him, although incompletely, with the structurally marginal.[158] In other words, his "in betweenness" in those communities where his story was read and heard may have grown out of his voluntary association with the have-nots and those who do not participate in the roles expected of them. In short, his marginality, especially his cultural marginality, is consistent with and enhances what it means to be a scribe "instructed for the Kingdom bringing out of his storehouse what is old and what is new."

---

155. *Ho anaginōskōn noeitō*.

156. Hearing: Matt 11:15; 13:9, 13:13, 14, 15, 16, 17, 18, 19, 20, 22, 23, 26, 43; 15:8, 10; 21:16, 33, 45; 22:22, 33; 15:8, 10; 21:16, 33, 45; 22:22, 23; understanding: 11:25; 13:13, 14, 15, 19, 23; 15:10; 15:16; 24:15. See Wainwright, "Only to the Lost Sheep."

157. The Menches archives mention "brother officials" (see Appendix 3 in this Chapter); in chap. 7 I argued that the Matthean *ekklēsia* is something like a brotherhood. In the sense just described, one would have to think of a cluster of churches/brotherhoods.

158. For my view of ideology and society, see chap. 5 above.

Appendix 1

Caste, Class, and Structural Marginality

To speak of marginality it is necessary to have some conception of the center. In Germani's work that center is the "normative scheme." A complication is that Germani's analysis highlights "modernization" and modern consciousness. A further complication is that to a certain extent the very notion of marginality came about historically because of the industrial revolution and modern conceptions about political freedom, economic development, and secure employment. Thus, one must be cautious in applying such concepts to ancient society. I have assumed that they are useable at a rather high level of abstraction.

Germani says that there are instances where the normative scheme is so internalized that there is no consciousness of marginality. This is a version of the "dominant ideology hypothesis," or what Karl Marx called "false consciousness" and the Marxist Antonio Gramsci called "hegemony."[159] In such cases a stratified social system is seen as part of the

> natural or divine order, usually rationalized in religious or equivalent terms. This is the case of a caste society . . . : slaves see themselves as their masters see them. In such a society the very concept of marginality does not emerge as a social perception scheme. In effect, this occurs only when participation becomes problematic or conflicting because there exists more than one normative scheme (or it has become internally incoherent), and/or necessary resources do not exist, or are not accessible, and/or members of one or more categories do not possess required personal conditions.[160]

Mediterranean society was not a rigid caste society; yet, it was highly stratified and one might make the argument that in some ways it was more like a caste society than a modern society. How acute could the consciousness of marginality have been? Certainly, the existence of political and familial, as well as economic, social, and religious reform movements (factions, parties, sects, voluntary associations, philosophical movements, and so forth) suggests that

---

159. For a discussion of everyday peasant resistance and Gramsci, see chap. 2.
160. Germani, *Marginality*, 52.

a structurally marginal consciousness was possible. To help reflect about such questions, consider Table 9-1 as a model. Here Germani crisscrosses three possible degrees of participation in the "normative structure" with four possible kinds of consciousness of marginality.

Table 9.1 Marginal Status and Marginality Consciousness (Germani, *Marginality*, 66–67)

Degree of participation in terms of power, and/or prestige, and/or wealth, and/or education, etc.

Consciousness of one's own and/or alien marginality	Highly favored sectors (elites)	Middle or low participating sectors (partial marginality)	Marginal sectors (generalized marginality)
No consciousness Of Marginality	**A** Established conservative elites (strictly defending the status quo)	**B** Middle and/or popular sectors, established, conservative or apathetic (defending the status quo)	**C** Marginal sectors, Apathetic, and/or submissive in religious and/or traditional terms
Consciousness of only one's own Marginality	**D** Partially displaced elites (intra-elite conflicts; "palace rebellions")	**E** Partially available and/or mobilizabile mass (reformist movements)	**F** Marginal people totally or partially available and mobilizable with propensity to change, migrate, "develop the community" (socio-political movements)
Consciousness of one's own and alien marginality	**G** Elites partially displaced (reformist or revolutionary propensity in alliance with other sectors, exercising leadership)	**H** Available or mobilizable mass (reformist or revolutionary propensity, in alliance with other sectors)	**I** (Slightly probable)
Consciousness of only alien marginality	**J** Established elites (reformist tendencies; change within the established order)	**K** Established middle and popular sectors (reformist tendencies)	**L** (Improbable or impossible)

One might correlate the three degrees of participation (across the top) with various levels of vertical stratification in the macromodel and distribution system. Consciousness of marginality might be correlated with various types of groups and movements within that society. The author of Matthew might be put in the G quadrant and most structurally marginal persons in the C and F quadrants.

Appendix 2

Model 9.6 Menches' Network: Lines of Correspondence between Menches, the Village Scribe, and His Superiors and Subordinates (Verhoogt, 71)

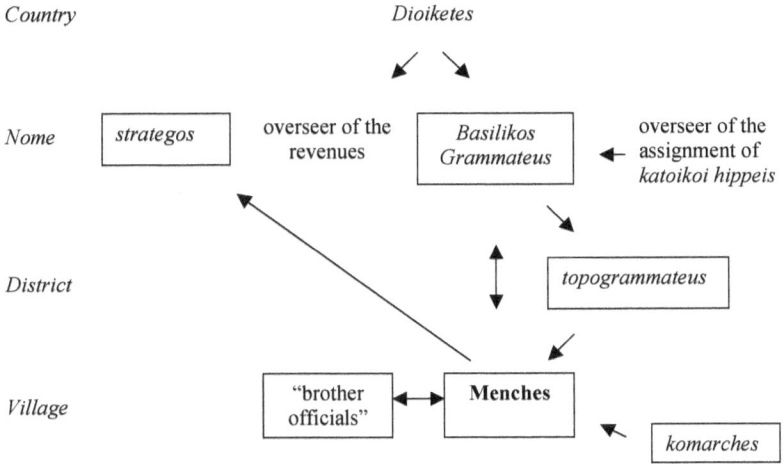

CHAPTER 10

Ethnicity, Ethnocentrism, and the Matthean *Ethnos*[1]

"ETHNIC CLEANSING" IS ONE of the tragedies of modern times. Not surprisingly, modern scholars have increasingly analyzed ethnicity and ethnic conflict.[2] Experts in the field of religion have been quick to see it as a significant area of research,[3] and specialists in biblical interpretation have begun to explore its importance for antiquity and the Bible.[4] Two scholars, David Sim and John Riches, have addressed the topic in relation to the Gospel of Matthew.[5] In this chapter I shall summarize their views, offer a brief overview of modern ethnicity theory, and develop a simple model for interpreting ethnicity. After exploring how the model is linguistically and conceptually useful for interpreting ancient groups, I shall attempt to show how such modeling can offer insights into ethnicity in Matthew, and in particular how priestly voluntary associations called *ethnē* might be of help in inter-

---

1. This chapter was discussed at the Context Group (2003) and in revised form as an invited paper at the Socio-Rhetorical Section of the *SNTS* in Bonn, Germany (August, 2003). It was later published in *BTB* 35/4 (2005) 125–43 where it was dedicated to my Afro-Amerasian son, who came to us at age two and a half from Viet Nam in 1974. For influence, see Cromhout, *Jesus and Identity*, chap. 2; *Walking in Their Sandals*.

2. Scott, "A Resynthesis"; Jenkins, "Rethinking Ethnicity: Identity"; "Ethnicity Etcetera"; "Rethinking Ethnicity: Arguments"; Sollors, "Christianity and Ethnicity"; Hutchinson and Smith, *Ethnicity*; Yang, *Ethnic Studies*.

3. Buell, "Ethnicity and Religion."

4. Brett, *Ethnicity and the Bible*; Denzey, "The Limits of Ethnic Categories"; Esler, "Ethnicity"; Duling, "'Whatever Gain I Had . . .'"; "2 Corinthians 11:22"; "Ethnicity and Paul's Letter"; Matlock, "Jews by Nature."

5. Sim, "Christianity and Ethnicity"; Riches, *Conflicting Mythologies*, chaps. 7, 8.

preting a verse that often puzzles Matthew scholars, the fruit-bearing *ethnos* of Matt 21:43.

Previous Study of Ethnicity in Matthew: Sim and Riches

David Sim's excellent article can be summarized in three points:[6]

1. To be considered ethnically "Jewish"[7] in the first century, a person had to have been born "Jewish" or have become a full proselyte, which, within the framework of what E. P. Sanders called "covenantal nomism"[8] and its privileges, meant strict Torah observance according to the norms of one's sect. For males this included the requirement of circumcision. By this legal standard uncircumcised male "God-fearers" were not considered to be fully "Jewish." With rare exceptions—Josephus and Philo mention instances in which proselytes to Judaism were not circumcised—circumcision was thought to be the primary ritual boundary marker for Jewish (male) ethnic identity.

2. Diaspora "Jewish" and Pauline communities did not require strict Torah observance for Gentile proselytes. Thus, circumcision was not an absolute requirement in these groups. In both Pauline letters and Acts, Paul's opponents are called "the circumcision party" (Gal 2:12; Acts 11:12; cf. Titus 1:10). Paul attacks such persons as "mutilators of the flesh" (Phil 2:3) and this group (or one like it) is behind the conflict at Antioch about whether one should eat with Gentiles (Gal 2:9). In contrast, the writer of Matthew required a stricter Torah observance, at least until the *parousia* (Matt 5:18; 28:20). The Matthean debates are not about keeping the Torah as such, but rather the correct *interpretation* of the Torah (Matt 5:17–20). Thus, says Sim, the Matthean writer, in contrast to Paul, considered his group to be ethnically "Jewish."

---

6. Sim, ibid.

7. In this section describing Sim's view, I use his preferred term, "Jewish," rather than the terms preferred in this book, "Judean" or the Matthean writer's preference, "Israelite." See chap. 1, n. 6.

8. Sanders, *Paul and Palestinian Judaism*; *Judaism*, 190–240.

3. Yet, the writer of Matthew never mentions circumcision—baptism is the only explicit entry rite to the community (28:19)—but, Sim deduces, the Matthean "Christian-Jewish" group *must* have required circumcision for male Gentile proselytes because of the writer's approach to the Torah. Sim proposes that the reason for the writer's silence is that the Matthean church's mission included non-believing "Jews" (10:6) as well as Gentiles. This dual emphasis is the best meaning of the gospel's being preached to "*all* the *ethnē*" in the final scene (29:19). Thus, circumcision was not at issue between Matthew and his Pharisaic opponents. "[C]ircumcision for male Gentiles is simply taken for granted,"[9] just as it is, argues Sim, in passages about admitting proselytes to the Qumran sect (1QS 6:13–23).[10]

John Riches has a very different slant on ethnicity in the Gospel of Matthew. His goal is to illumine the Matthean community's "sense of identity" by stressing two ethnic markers, kinship and place.[11] This different approach yields a different result. Consider each marker.

With respect to *kinship*, the Matthean writer, building on Mark, holds that true discipleship is not based on family, but on following the itinerant, homeless Jesus.[12] Descent in the gospel matters only in one instance, the genealogy of Jesus himself, where Matthew seems to stress putative "Jewish" descent from Abraham and David (Matt 1:1–17).[13] However, says Riches, this genealogy actually flaunts Jesus' *Gentile* ancestry because it originates with the prototypical wanderer Abraham, a Gentile (e.g., Deut 26:5), and the four women who are mentioned in the genealogy have Gentile background. Ironically, claims Riches, Jesus' apparent "Jewish" roots imply universalism.[14] So much for kinship!

Similarly, Riches asserts, Matthew "remakes" *place*. Here Riches agrees with W. D. Davies: in Matthew "theology is de-territorialised

---

9. Sim, "Christianity and Ethnicity," 193.

10. As far as I can see, however, this passage is not about admitting Gentile proselytes, but those in "Israel" (6:13).

11. Riches, *Conflicting Mythologies*, chaps. 7 and 8.

12. Davies and Allison, *Matthew*; Davies, *Gospel and the Land*.

13. Riches, *Conflicting Mythologies*, 291.

14. Ibid., 231.

Ethnicity, Ethnocentrism, and the Matthean Ethnos   291

and attachment to Land and Temple replaced by attachment to the person of Jesus."[15] For example, whereas Deutero-Isaiah's vision of the "way of the Lord" takes remnant Israel from the desert to Mount Zion in Israel (e.g., Isa 40:3), the Matthean writer replaces "Mount Zion with a mountain in Galilee."[16] As in Mark, *being with Jesus* is place enough (Matt 8:20–22; Riches later argues that Matthew goes beyond Isaiah's Zion tradition).[17] Again, Moses and the new Exodus/ promised land motifs are universalized. Thus, place-oriented formula quotations in the infancy (Matt 2:6 [Bethlehem], 2:15 [Egypt], 2:23 [Nazareth]) anticipate the place-oriented formula quotation "Galilee of the Gentiles" as the special "place" where Jesus offers salvation to those who "sit in darkness"(4:14–16). Finally, this passage anticipates the final, universal mission to "all Gentiles" (*ethnē*, 28:19).

A few of Riches' examples will illustrate. The crowd responds to Jesus' victory over Satan with the words, "never was anything like this seen *in Israel*" (9:33). The Gentile centurion has faith unlike anything ever seen "*in Israel*" (Matt 8:10) and represents those who come "from east and from west" to receive salvation. A *Canaanite* woman of "great faith" is healed (15:21–28). In the weeds parable, the seed falls *everywhere* and the *whole world* is to be judged (13:24–30, 36–43). *Israel's election is called into question* "by the crowd's rejection of its Messiah" (27:15). The messianic banquet is *wherever Jesus is present with his disciples* (18:20; cf. 1:23; 28:20). "God rejects Israel's leaders: the kingdom has been taken away from them and given 'to a nation [*ethnei*] producing the fruits of it' (21:43)."[18] In short, evil is so pervasive that an *ethnos* based on descent, ancestral customs, or land always falls short. There is both continuity and discontinuity with historical Israel; ethnic boundaries grow to include outsiders. "Matthew metaphoricises ethnicity."[19]

Although I admire Sim's analytical prowess in taking the thesis of Matthew's "Christian Judaism" to its logical conclusion, my own view of the gospel's tensions and ambiguities about Israelites and

---

15. Ibid., 254; Davies, *Gospel and the Land*, 366–76.
16. Riches, *Conflicting Mythologies*, 254.
17. Ibid.
18. Ibid., 252.
19. Ibid., 318–19.

non-Israelites has more in common with the position of Riches.[20] However, in what follows, I broaden Riches' view of ethnicity. I also make rather different arguments about *ethnos* in the Matthean gospel itself. Finally, I develop Matthean ethnicity based on the study of voluntary associations and marginality: the Matthean group stands *between* Israel and non-Israel.[21]

As a beginning, it is necessary to say a few brief words about ethnicity theory.

Contemporary Ethnicity Theory

The now familiar term "ethnicity" appears not to have been coined until 1941 as an alternative to "race."[22] It first appeared in the *Oxford English Dictionary* in 1953 and did not actually become a major social-scientific *concept* until the 1960s. In this early period two major approaches to ethnicity appeared, and their influence continues to the present.

The first approach, derived chiefly from Edward Shils and Clifford Geertz,[23] is now called *Primordialism*. Its representatives say that ethnic groups are held together by "natural affections." These are bonds so compelling, so passionate, so "coercive," and so overpowering, that they are fixed, *a priori*, involuntary, ineffable, even considered "sacred." These bonds are deeply rooted in family, territory, language, custom, and religion. They are the major foundation for group norms, values, and behavior. They are "primordial," hence the term "Primordialism."

Within the Primordialist camp there are two major alternatives. *Socio-biological* Primordialists stress what is "natural," that is, they hold that humans, who are fundamentally self-interested, seek to maximize their individual "fitness" by kin selection within their own kin group.[24] In contrast, *Cultural* Primordialists, who are in the majority, follow in the footsteps of Shils and Geertz and argue that these bonds, although considered "natural," are actually culturally generated.

20. See chap. 9 above.
21. Duling, ibid.; chap. 7; Senior, "Between Two Worlds."
22. Warner and Lunt, "Ethnicity (1942)," in Sollors, *Theories of Ethnicity*, 13–14.
23. Shils, "Primordial, Personal, Sacred and Civil Ties"; Geertz, *The Integrative Revolution*.
24. Van den Berghe, *Ethnic Phenomenon*.

The major alternative to Primordialism is *Constructionism*. This perspective is associated with Frederik Barth[25] who in the 1960s leveled a critique at traditional Cultural Primordialists' tendency to think that the cultural markers of ethnic identity are more or less "objective." For Barth the "cultural stuff"—place of origin, dress, food practices, and the like—is important for marking social boundaries, but not as important as the act of social boundary marking itself. From this perspective ethnic identity is not inherent, fixed, or natural; rather, it is fluid, freely chosen, and thus can be seen to be continually reconstructed. Barth shifts the theoretical emphasis from ethnic features to *how* and *why* ethnic groups construct and maintain their group boundaries. The subtitle of his work reflects this emphasis: "the social organization of cultural difference." Barth's position is formalist,[26] abstract, ahistorical, and "subjectivist." In a self-evaluation in 1994, he considered himself to have anticipated postmodernism, which has notable de-objectifying emphases.[27]

Three other, related approaches may be noted. The approach of *Instrumentalism* takes Constructionism further by arguing that a group's conscious construction of its ethnicity is rational and self-interested, that is, ethnic identity is constructed by the group to further its political-economic agenda. A *Social Psychological* approach argues that cultural and economic advantages of a particular ethnic group lead it to develop kinship myths based on collective honor and to stereotype outsider groups ethnocentrically.[28] Finally, *Ethno-symbolists* analyze the way that an ethnic group's nostalgia about its perceived past—cosmogonic myths, election myths, memories of a golden age, symbols—shapes its ability to endure, yet change and adapt.

There have been attempts to critique, integrate, and synthesize these various approaches.[29] Generally, most ethnicity theorists agree with Barth that ethnic group members ascribe their ethnicity to themselves and change their self-identity periodically. Thus, Constructionism has become the dominant theoretical perspective. Yet,

25. Barth, *Ethnic Groups and Boundaries*, 13–14.
26. "Formalism" in this case refers to the tendency to focus on form rather than content, as in the form of art or literature.
27. Barth, "Enduring and Emerging Issues."
28. Horowitz, *Ethnic Groups in Conflict*.
29. Scott, "Resynthesis"; Yang, *Ethnic Studies*, 47–56.

there is still great interest in the "cultural stuff," that is, the cultural differences, of ethnicity. Also, there is still wide disagreement about whether self-constructed ethnicity is irrational and ineffable, as Primordialism suggests, or rational and self-interested, as the offshoot of Constructionism, Instrumentalism, holds. In what follows, I attempt to construct a model based on an expansion of the "cultural stuff" first laid out by the early Primordialists, but I agree with the Barthian Constructionists that over time its cultural characteristics are subject to self-definition and change by the group itself.

A Socio-Cultural Model of Ethnicity

As mentioned above, Shils and Geertz highlight five cultural features of ethnicity: family, territory, language, custom, and religion. Richard Alonzo Schermerhorn's ethno-symbolic refinement, which analyzes "the *ethnie*" (an ethnic community), replaces "family" with "kinship patterns," and "territory" with "physical contiguity"; he also adds three new features, "tribal affiliation," "nationality," and "phenotypical" features.[30] John Hutchinson and Anthony Smith expand Schermerhorn's eight cultural features with three more: 1) a common proper name that identifies and expresses the "essence" of the ethnic group; 2) myths of common ancestry (often fictive) that often include great heroes and heroines; and 3) shared historical memories, which can also be fictive.[31] These eleven cultural features highly influence, but are also shaped by, the *ethnie's* values, norms, and behavior.

In what follows, I have attempted to construct a model that incorporates these eleven features, but I have reduced them to nine by combining family, tribe, and nation, placing them at the same level in concentric circles. The model is a socio-cultural umbrella—I have shaped it like an umbrella—that highlights the "cultural stuff" of the earlier theorists, but its broken lines and temporal arrow attempt to

---

30. Schermerhorn, "Marginal Man," 12 (quoted in Hutchinson and Smith, *Ethnicity*, 12). Phenotypical features refer to observable traits such as genetic characteristics, physiology, typical behavior, and the like. They result from the genes, the environment, and the interaction between them.

31. Hutchinson and Smith, *Ethnicity*, 6.

allow for Barth's widely held perspective that the critical point is the way the "cultural stuff" is socially organized.³²

Model 10.1 A Socio-Cultural Model of Ethnicity (Duling)

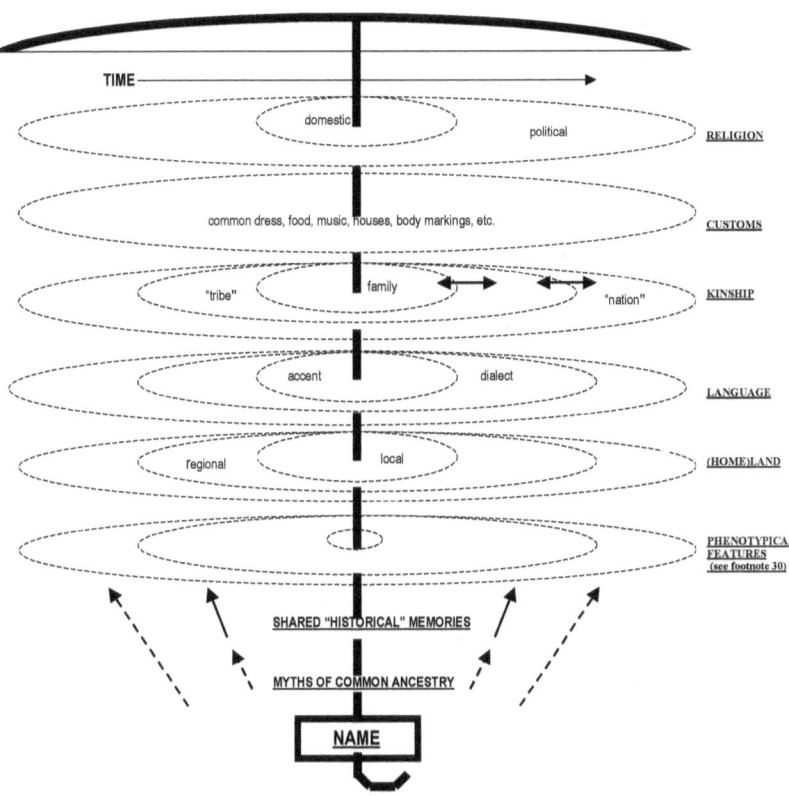

Not every analysis of ethnicity stresses every one of these cultural features. Furthermore, the Constructionist critique of Cultural Primordialism's "objectivism" raises the important question whether *any* feature is *so constitutive* that there is no "ethnicity" without it.³³ While there is no definitive answer to this question, even Constructionists usually admit that kinship relations and myths of common ancestry are virtually universal and that some reference to

---

32. I have constructed a more temporal model in Duling, "Ethnicity and Paul's Letter to the Romans"; see further, Cromhout, *Walking in Their Sandals*.

33. Buell, "Ethnicity and Religion," 243–44.

a homeland, that is, territory or land, is not far behind. Given that generalization, Riches' focus on kinship and place in Matthew (sketched above) is quite apt.

Finally, Constructionists claim that groups construct their ethnic boundaries primarily in two ways: a) in relation to like-minded, like-practiced peers, a "we" *aggregative* self-definition, and b) in relation to *others*, a "we-they" *oppositional* self-definition.[34] The latter is usually ethnocentric.

Ethnicity and Antiquity

The above model of ethnicity, which highlights key representative socio-cultural features, is an outside observer's model that is used to organize the available data. It is general and abstract; it therefore runs the risk of oversimplifying distinctive local ethnographic and historical information. It is, in short, a homomorphic, etic model. While it is in danger of being academically ethnocentric,[35] it should be remembered that models that omit detail in this way should not be seen as true or false, but rather heuristic. They accentuate in order to illuminate. They invite criticism and modification—even alternative reconstruction. In the meantime, discussions of "ethnicity" can look for just such salient features in ancient writers' comments about themselves and others. Here are four examples of such comments.

The first example comes from Herodotus:

> For there are many great reasons why we should not ... [desert to the Persians], even if we so desired; first and foremost, the burning and destruction of the adornments and temples of our gods, whom we are constrained to avenge to the utmost rather than make pacts with the perpetrator of these things, and next the *kinship of all Greeks in blood* and *speech*, and *the shrines of gods and the sacrifices that we have in common*, and the likeness of *our way of life*, to all of which it would not befit the Athenians to be false. (Hdt. 8.144.2, italics mine [LCL (Godley)])

---

34. Hall, *Ethnic Identity*, 47.
35. Denzey, "Limits of Ethnic Categories," 489–93.

Herodotus emphasizes several characteristic features of our ethnicity model: 1) common blood (name, biological family, kinship patterns, and perhaps phenotypical features and myths of common ancestry); 2) common language; 3) common religion (temples and religious practices, with shared historical memories implied); 4) common customs (customs, dress, food, music, houses, body markings, and the like). Hall calls Herodotus' comment an *"oppositional* self-definition."[36] Shaye Cohen would accept Herodotus' view as Constructionist when he calls it "transitional."[37] Yet, "cultural stuff" is important.

A second example comes from the ancient geographer Strabo: "For the *ethnos* of the Armenians and that of the Syrians and Arabians betray a close affinity, not only in their *language*, but in their *mode of life* and in their *bodily build*, and particularly *wherever they live as close neighbors*" (*Geogr.* 1.2.34 [italics mine]). The emphasis in Strabo is on language, customs, phenotypical features, and land or territory.

It is instructive to compare these statements with two comments in the biblical "table of nations": "He also said, 'Blessed by the LORD my God be Shem; and let Canaan be his slave'" (Gen 9:26). "These are the sons of Shem, by their families (LXX *phylais*), their languages (*glōssas*), their lands (*chōrais*), and their nations (*ethnesin*)" (Gen 10:31). In these biblical examples language, family, territory, and the religion of Shem (a mythical ancestor of the Israelites) are being contrasted with those of Ham (a mythical ancestor of the Canaanites).

There is obviously much overlap between modern and ancient views of ethnicity, although one needs to tread carefully. I would like to test this similarity, first by examining the term *ethnos* in the Matthean author and his world.

Ethnos in Antiquity

The ancient Greek word *ethnos* originally had a broader semantic range than the modern term "ethnicity" suggests. In early Greek writings the singular *ethnos* could refer to almost *any* kind of group or grouping—and of almost *any* size: flocks of birds, swarms of flies or bees, bands of warriors and young men, and groups of the dead

36. Hall, *Ethnic Identity*, 45–51.
37. Cohen, *Beginnings of Jewishness*, 132.

(Sophocles *Phil.* 1147; *Ant.* 344).³⁸ It could also refer to the gender categories men and women (Pindar, *Olympian Odes* 1.66; *Pythican Odes* 4.252)³⁹ or the inhabitants of a small village, a city, several cities, or a whole region.⁴⁰ In some of these cases "group" would be a quite legitimate translation, although in others "people" or "nation" (but not a modern nation-state) seems more accurate. Herodotus allowed that people in different geographical regions could be of the same *ethnos* if they had migrated to those regions. Finally, *ethnos* could also refer to a guild or trade association.⁴¹ In a personal communication to me John Kloppenborg quotes in this regard S. R. Llewelyn: "... Plato refers to various types of trade or social groupings as *ethnē*, i.e., doctors, shipbuilders, citizens, soldiers, bandits, thieves and any other association (*allo ti ethnos*)" (*Gorg.* 455b and *Resp.* 351c).⁴² Kloppenborg adds other references.⁴³ Clearly, an *ethnos* was not only an *ethnie* or ethnic group in the modern theoretical sense of ethnicity, but could have other connotations.

This broad semantic range persisted into the Hellenistic period. However, by this time the Greeks increasingly referred to *other* peoples with the term *ethnos*—in Athens, for example, a voluntary association of Thracians was called an *ethnos*⁴⁴—but the Athenians preferred to call themselves *genos*, a term that suggests common ancestry, as in the expression *genos Hellēnōn*, "a family of Hellenes." The Romans made the same distinction in Latin: others were a *natio* but they were a *populus*. In Greek the *plural* form *ta ethnē* was more frequently used for other peoples; indeed, it usually had the ring of ethnocentric stereotyping, although it was not as oppositional as the term *barbaroi*, that is, those who are believed to speak incoherently.⁴⁵

---

38. Saldarini, *Matthew's Christian-Jewish Community*, 68–83; Hall, *Ethnic Identity*, 34.

39. Hall, ibid., 35.

40. Ibid., 34.

41. Saldarini, *Matthew's Christian-Jewish Community*, 59.

42. Llewelyn, *New Documents*, 39.

43. Petrie III 59.B.4; OGIS 90.A.17 [196 BCE]; CPR XV 32.v.8 [II/III CE]; *Poxy* XLIX 3470.16 [131 CE].

44. IG 22 1283 [260/61 BCE].

45. Geary, "Barbarians and Ethnicity"; cf. Denzey, "Limits of Ethnic Categories," 494–95.

With respect to ancient Israelites in particular, J. G. Muthuraj has reexamined the terms *ethnos* and *ethnē* in the LXX, 1 Maccabees, Philo, Josephus, and the early historiographical literature.[46] He argues that the dominant meanings of Hebrew *goy* and *goyîm* and Greek *ethnos* and *ethnē* are simply "people(s)" or "nation(s)" of the world, that is, the terms have a positive or neutral sense. When "otherness" is in view, he claims, Israelite writers sought prefixes with *allo-*, "other," "different," such as *allotrios* ("non-Israelite"), *allophylos* ("foreigner"), *allotria ethnē* ("foreign nations"). These prefixed terms lead Muthuraj to conclude that when *ethnos/ethnē* is rendered by "Gentile(s)," "pagan(s)," or "heathen(s)," ethnocentric English translation biased by modern Jewish or Christian monotheists is at work. Muthuraj's argument offers an important insight, especially since *ethnos* in the Maccabean and Philonic literature can at times represent the Israelites themselves (1 Macc 8:23; 10:25; 11:30; 12:3; 13:36; 14:28; 15:1–2; 2 Macc 11:27; *Decal.* 96). Nonetheless, it is also clear that *goyim* in the Hebrew Bible and *ethnē* in the LXX are often oppositional terms for outsiders. This is especially the case in the Maccabean literature, which is similar to the increased delimitation of meaning in Greek and Latin literature. For example, the author of 1 Maccabees says that those who practiced epispasm (reversed their circumcision by an operation) "abandoned the holy covenant" and "joined with the *ethnē* and sold themselves to do evil" (1 Macc 1:15). 2 Maccabees refers to "blasphemous and barbarous *ethnē*" (2 Macc 10:4 [*blasphēmois kai barbarois ethnesin*]; cp. 2:21 [*ta barbara plēthē*]). The adjective *ethnikos* and the adverb *ethnikōs* often carry similar nuances. It is true that a few ancient intellectuals offered etymologies trying to show that Israelites and Spartans were from the *same ethnos* (descended from Abraham) and that Israelite writers—Eupolemus, Artapanus, Aristobulus, and even Josephus—attributed Hellenistic culture to the Israelites.[47] However, while these usages affirmed Greek culture, they in fact asserted the superiority of the Israelites. The conclusion is that Muthuraj's generalization is somewhat overdrawn; *context* will determine whether *ethnos* is neutral (e.g., Gen 17:6, 16; Tob 3:5) or oppositional (Zech 12:9; cf. Zech 14:16; Tob 3:4), whether it can or should be translated as "people" or "Gentile," "pagan," or "heathen."

46. Muthuraj, "Meaning of *ethnos* and *ethnē*."
47. Gruen, "Jewish Perspectives on Greek Culture," 91 n. 81.

In summary, in early ancient Greco-Roman literature, *ethnos* and *ethnē* had a wide variety of meanings. The singular originally referred to any group of any size. However, in the Hellenistic period, the Greeks' use of singular *ethnos* and both Greek and Israelite use of plural *ta ethnē* could at times take on a negative valence. Context rules, but ethnocentric usage of the term *ethnos* is growing.

Ethnos in Matthew

How does the writer of Matthew use the terms *ethnos* and its plural, *ethnē*? The fifteen instances of *ethnos/ethnē* and three instances of the adjective *ethnikos* in the gospel also have a wide semantic range.[48] I suggest the following categories:

1. Indefinite singular *ethnos* used in a general, apparently neutral, way ("*ethnos* will rise against *ethnos*"), taken from Mark (Matt 24:7 [Mark 13:8]).

2. Indefinite plural *ethnē*, probably used as an oppositional stereotype: disciples/missionaries should not go out among the *ethnē* or enter any town of the Samaritans (Matt 10:5).

3. Indefinite plural *ethnē* used oppositionally as an ethnocentric stereotype: *ethnē* materialistically seek food, drink, and clothing (you must not); rulers of the *ethnē* lord it over them (you must not) (Matt 6:31–32 [Q 5:29–30]).

4. A more definite plural expression ("all the *ethnē*") used as specific opponents of Jesus and the disciples: Jesus will be delivered to the *ethnē*, who will mock, scourge, and crucify him (Matt 20:19 [Mark 10:33]); Jesus' followers will be hated by "all the *ethnē*" (Matt 24:9); followers will "be dragged before rulers and kings "for my sake," to bear witness before them and the *ethnē* (Matt 10:18 [cf. Mark 13:10]).

5. Indefinite *ethnikoi* in the plural used oppositionally: the *ethnikoi* salute only their own brothers like the toll collectors who love each other (Matt 5:46 [Q 6:32], 5:47 [Q 6:33]), and they heap up empty phrases when they pray (Matt 6:7). When unrepentant Matthean members are banned from the community, they should

---

48. Saldarini, *Matthew's Christian-Jewish Community*, 78–81.

be treated "like *ethnikoi* and toll collectors" (Matt 18:17; cf. 5:46 just noted).

These five categories suggest that especially the plurals (*ta*) *ethnē* and *ethnikoi* are negative, oppositional terms in Matthew and that they parallel a growing hostile oppositional usage in late antiquity. However, several other, different instances of *ethnē* in Matthew preserve the persistent neutral or more positive sense.

6. *Ethnē* used neutrally, perhaps positively, in two formula quotations. The formula quotation about "Galilee of the *ethnē*" (Matt 4:15 [Isa 8:23–9:1 LXX]), which follows other formula quotations about place,[49] hints at Jesus' inclusiveness, and another formula quotation says that Jesus proclaims justice to the *ethnē* who place their hope in him (Matt 12:18 [Isa 42:1 LXX]; 12:21). These verses point forward to the mission to the *ethnē* at the conclusion of the gospel (Matt 28:19).

7. "All the *ethnē*" used neutrally or positively. In contrast to category 4, the Matthean version of the little apocalypse has Jesus command that the gospel be preached throughout "the whole world" as a testimony to all the *ethnē* (Matt 24:14). This comment seems to point forward to the gospel's concluding statement, "Go therefore and make disciples of all the *ethnē*, baptizing them in the name of the Father and of the Son and of the Holy Spirit" (Matt 28:19). The usual interpretation is that it means outsiders—"nations," meaning "Gentiles"—and the usual debate concerns whether it is meant to include or exclude Israelites. However one answers that question, certainly the final thrust of the gospel is the inclusion of non-Israelite *ethnē* (contrast Matt 10:6).[50]

8. The *ethnos* that produces fruit (Matt 21:43). This last text is quite distinctive. I shall consider it more carefully after taking up some other aspects of ethnicity.

The above references suggest that there is an outsider/insider ambiguity or tension about the *ethnē* in Matthew, which is not surprising

---

49. See Riches' discussion of "de-territorialisation" above.

50. For the view that Matt 28:19 refers to Diaspora Judeans, however, see Jackson, "Are the 'Nations' Present in Matthew?"

considering other Matthean tensions typical of cultural marginality.[51] The more positive references to outsiders can be illustrated by other terms and themes in the gospel, some noted by Riches. One example is the four uses of *hekatontarkoi*, "centurions." Three are found in the centurion's servant from Q (Matt 8:5 [Q 7:1]; 8:8 [Q 7:6]; 8:13), which says that "not even *in Israel* have I found such faith" (Matt 8:10 = Q 7:9). A fourth reference is the centurion's confession of Jesus as Son of God in the crucifixion story taken from Mark (Mark 15:39 = Matt 27:54). A second example is the story of the Canaanite woman in which, again, an outsider (and woman!) becomes the model for faith, and Jesus is finally willing to cross ethnic boundaries (Canaanite "dogs" are accepted like lost Israelite "children").[52] Third, Pilate claims that he is innocent of the blood of Jesus in contrast to "the people" (*ho laos*) who say, "His blood be on us and on our children" (Matt 27:25). Finally, one should recall Simon the Cananaean and the cross-bearer Simon of Cyrene (Matt 10:4; 27:32), outsiders who become insiders in the narrative.

In short, while plural *ethnē* is often used oppositionally to create and reinforce self-identity among Israelites and members of the Matthean group, the Matthean writer also has representatives of the *ethnē* who are valued positively, and on occasion they provide models of true behavior and confession. Context rules, and there are powerful examples of ethnic inclusiveness in the gospel.

Exploring Features of the Ethnicity Model

Nicola Denzey goes so far as to say, "One could argue that to speak of 'Jewish ethnicity' or 'Christian ethnicity' in antiquity is dangerously anachronistic, since both context and content of the term *ethnos* in the first century before the Common Era and the three centuries that followed remained rather different than what modern social theorists mean by ethnicity in the contemporary context."[53] Although it is true that the ancient term *ethnos* has a broader semantic range than the

---

51. See chaps. 5, 7, and 9 above.

52. Cf. articles in Levine and Blickenstaff, *A Feminist Companion*; Love, "Place of Women."

53. Denzey, "The Limits of Ethnic Categories," 495.

modern terms *ethnie*, ethnic group, ethnicity, and the like, there is also much overlap. One must attempt to clarify likenesses and differences in the larger semantic field and analyze the context. Here I sketch what Barth called the "stuff" of ethnicity (noted above) and comment on the gospel in relation to it. There is much material, so I shall be selective.[54]

Name

Various groups refer to themselves and others ethnically by names. Herodotus speaks of Ionians, Dorians, Herakleeidai, and Akhaians *among* the Greeks, that is, with *aggregative* self-definitions ("we"). However, Herodotus' descriptions of Persians, Egyptians, Skythians, and Libyans as *barbaroi* betray an *oppositional* self-definition ("we" versus "they").[55] One finds the same phenomenon in ancient Israel. Deuteronomy refers oppositionally to driving out seven impure "nations" (Hebrew *goyim*; LXX *ethnē*) from the land (Deut 7:1-4). As noted previously, in the Maccabean literature the Israelites themselves can be called an *ethnos*, but *ethnē* in the plural can describe those who are to be put out of the "country" (*ek tēs choras*), to be replaced by "Judaean men" (*andras Ioudaious*) to preserve ethnic purity (1 Macc 14:35-40).

The writer of the Gospel of Matthew prefers to use geographical origins (homeland!) to identify outsiders (e.g., Matt 4:24-25). Concrete examples are "a Canaanite woman from that region" [Tyre and Sidon] (Matt 15:21-28 [Mark has "a Greek, Syrophoenician by birth" (Mark 7:26)]), and "a man of Cyrene, Simon by name" (Matt 27:32). He prefers "Israel" (Matt 2:6; 2:20; 2:21; 8:10; 9:33; 10:23; 15:31; 19:28; 27:9; 27:42) or "House of Israel" (Matt 10:6, 15:24) for insiders. Nine of his twelve references, which refer mainly to land, belief, and descent, are most likely redactional and reflect the author's view ("Israel" [9:30]; Israel as God's people in a formula quotation [2:6 (2 Sam 2:5)]; "God of Israel" [15:31]; "sons of Israel" [27:9]; "house of Israel" [10:6; 15:24]; "land of Israel" [2:20, 21]; "towns of Israel" [10:23]); three of the twelve come from his sources (the title "King

---

54. For more detail, see Duling, "'Whatever Gain I Had . . .'"
55. Hall, *Ethnic Identity*, 47.

of Israel" [27:42 (Mark 15:3)] and two references to "Israel" from Q [8:10 (Q 7:9) and 19:28 (Q 22:30)], both political/territorial). In short, the customary ethnic usage in Matthew is "Israel" and "Israelite" with respect to land, belief, and mythical descent.

The term *Ioudaios* has generated much analysis and controversy.[56] It was originally used as an outsider's description of an Israelite, often in a neutral, descriptive sense (Hec. Ab.; *Geogr.* 16.2,2.).[57] However, some Israelites began to use *Ioudaioi* for themselves in expressions such as "the *ethnos of the Ioudaiōn*," or simply "the *Ioudaioi*" (1 Macc 8:23, 25, 27: *[to] ethnos tōn Ioudaiōn*; 8:29: *tōn Ioudaiōn*).[58] Not surprisingly, Diaspora literature picked up what was originally outsider usage, as well. Hanson and Oakman list five nuances of *Ioudaios* in the period under consideration, depending on context: 1) the inhabitants of Judea (geographical); 2) all the inhabitants of Palestine (more broadly geographical); 3) all those in the Mediterranean and Middle East with "ethnic" connections to Judea; 4) those who professed allegiance to the state religion of Judea, including converts (political); 5) elites of Judea in contrast to peasants (social).[59] Shaye Cohen's nuances overlap, but only in part.[60] He lists: 1) an "Israelite" by birth and/or geography, broadly defined (including Galileans, Idumeans, and the like); 2) *Ioudaios* as a citizen or ally of the Israelite state (political); and 3) "Jew" as one who follows certain practices (religion or culture). Cohen's willingness to continue using the term "Jew" for a religious category derives from his judgment that in the second half of the second century BCE male non-Israelites could become proselytes by circumcision without any "ethnic (birth)-geographical" association. His main example is Izates of Adiabene (*Ant.* 20.2.3-5 [17-53]), who thought he could not become a *Ioudaios* without being circumcised. Cohen thinks that there is no apparent connection in the account with "geographic/ethnic" meaning. He then argues that

---

56. Von Rad, Kuhn, and Gutbrod, "*Ioudaios*," 360-61; Kraemer, "On the Meaning of the Term 'Jew'"; Harvey, *The True Israel*; Hanson and Oakman, *Palestine*; Cohen, *The Beginning of Jewishness*, 70; Esler, "Ethnicity, Ethnic Conflict"; Elliott, "Jesus the Israelite"; Pilch, "Jews and Christians: Anachronisms."

57. Cohen, ibid., 71 n. 5; Denzey, "The Limits of Ethnic Categories," 496.

58. Von Rad, Kuhn, and Gutbrod, "*Ioudaios*," 360-61.

59. Hanson and Oakman, *Palestine*, 2nd ed., 162.

60. Cohen, *The Beginnings of Jewishness*, 70.

this "ethnic" (religious/cultural) sense remained when the geographical sense waned in the Diaspora. However, it could be argued that in the Izates of Adiabene example, the homeland/geographical nuance did not totally disappear. When Izates's mother saw how satisfied and happy Izates was with his new Israelite identity, she made a pilgrimage to Jerusalem to worship in the Temple (*Ant.* 20.2.3–5 [17–53]).

In the Gospel of Matthew, four of five uses of *Ioudaios*, three from Mark, are in the expression "King of the *Ioudaiōn*" used by outsiders (Matt 2:2 [the *magoi*, used in a political sense]; 27:11 [Mark 15:2]; 27:29 [Mark 15:18]; 27:37 [the *titulus* on the cross, Mark 15:26]). In contrast, Matthew's Israelites used the formulation "King of the Israelites" (Matt 27:42).[61] This usage suggests that the evangelist was aware of the fact that this description continued to be in use by outsiders. However, a fifth usage, namely, his literary aside directly to his reader(s)/hearer(s), that the story of the theft of Jesus' body "has been spread among the *Ioudaioi* to this day" (Matt 28:15), is in a different category. Some scholars have argued that this verse shows that the author was *not* a *Ioudaios*, but this argument seems to have lost favor. If not held, the reference is to Israelites. Either way, the reference is ethnic.

Myths of Common Ancestry

When Herodotus writes about Ionians, Dorians, Herakleeidai, Akhaians he also mentions myths of origins in relation to genealogies of the eponymous ancestors Helen, Doros, Aiolos, Ion, and Akhaios.[62] Recall that wealthy Greeks could enhance their status by paying temple priests to create ancestral genealogies for them.[63] Among the Israelites biblical genealogies with fictive ancestors were common; indeed, the very names "Israelite" and *Ioudaios* derive from Jacob/Israel and Judah, eponymous ancestors. "Sons of Abraham" also recalls the ancestor. Some ancient Israelite writers claimed that both Israelites and Spartans were descended from Abraham.[64]

---

61. This point has been stressed recently by Elliott, "Jesus the Israelite."
62. Hall, *Ethnic Identity*, 43.
63. Ibid., 41; cf. Hood, "The Genealogies of Jesus."
64. See p. 299 above and n. 47.

Linguistic fields that pertain to myths of common ancestry have generated such terms as *genos* ("[birth] family," "offspring," or "descendants"), *phylē* ("tribe," "people," "clan"), *patēr* ("father") in the sense of eponymous ancestor, *oikos* ("house"), and a host of agricultural/horticultural metaphors—*rhiza* ("root" or "descendant"), *anatolē* ("descendent" or "offspring," from *anatellō*, "I cause to rise," [translating Hebrew *zemach*, "shoot"]), *karpos tēs osphyos* ("fruit of the genitals"), *sperma* ("seed"), and *spora* ("what is sown," "seed," "ancestry," "parentage").[65] The genealogy of Matthew (Matt 1:1–17; *geneseōs*, "of the origin [genealogy]" in 1:1 implies *genos*) makes the status claim that Jesus was descended from Abraham and especially King David through royal ancestors. Non-Israelite associations of Abraham are also present. One ancient Israelite tradition says that Abraham was from the "land of Aram," a Syrian ancestral homeland (Deut 26:5).[66] Another tradition says that Abraham and his clan were from "Ur of the Chaldeans," a Mesopotamian ancestral homeland (Gen 11:28, 31). In either case, the "father" of the Israelites turns out to be an "outsider," as Riches said, and it is he who will become the "father of a multitude of *ethnōn*" (Gen 17:4–5 LXX). Once again, however, there is a tension drawn from the Q-based Baptist saying, ". . . do not presume to say to yourselves, 'We have Abraham as our father; for I tell you, God is able from these stones to raise up children to Abraham" (Matt 3:9); baptism as a form of initiation supersedes Abrahamic descent.

To be sure, the *genos* of Jesus remains important in relation to that other great ancestor, King David (Matt 1:1; 1:17; 1:20), and to his place of birth, Bethlehem (Matt 2:1). While the gospel retains this means of ethnic identity, the metaphorical sense of "Son of David" in the healing stories ultimately transcends *genos* (Matt 9:27 [Mark 10:46]; 12:23; 15:22; 20:30 [Mark 10:46]; 21:9, 15). David is also the author of psalm-prophecies about the Messiah (Matt 22:41–46 [Mark 12:35–37]), and the "key of David" (Isa 22:22) suggests the keys of the Kingdom (16:19). As Riches observes, counter-themes subvert both kinship and place among Jesus' followers.[67] Indeed, it is possible for

---

65. See further Duling, "'Whatever Gain I Had . . .'"
66. Millard, "Arameans," 345–50.
67. Riches, *Conflicting Mythologies*.

the author to raise the question in what sense the Messiah is to be the Son of David (Matt 22:42).[68]

Shared "Historical" Memories

Greco-Roman examples are Homer's *Iliad* and Greek and Roman histories. Israelite examples are patriarchal stories, the Deuteronomic history, the Court History of David, and Josephus' *Antiquities* and *Wars*. Authors of the Jesus Movement remembered many of the same stories. Quotations and allusions to sacred texts and biblical "history" in Matthew are too extensive to detail here, but key examples are descent into Egypt (Matt 2:13–14), Passover (Matt 2:15; 26:2, 17–29 [Mark 14:1, 12–25]), Exodus (Matt 2:13 [Hos 11:1]), desert temptation (Matt 4:1–11 [Deut 8:3; 6:13, 16; Exod 19:1–6]), Moses themes (Matt 2:15, 16; 5:17–20; 4:8; 4:1–11; 5:1; 8:1; 8:4; 8–9; 14:23; 15:29; 17:1, 2, 9; 19:7; 22:2–3; 22:24; 28:16; and the five-book structure),[69] Joseph themes (Gen 37:5–11; cf. Matt 1), Elijah themes (Matt 3:4; 4:17 [Mark 1:15]; 3:2; 11:5, 7–19; 12:40; 17:9–13), David themes and psalms (see above), Solomonic magic (1 Kgs 19:2, 5–8), and Isaianic allusions and quotations (e.g., Matt 4:14–16 [Isa 61:1]). In all of this, the Gospel of Matthew, more than the other canonical gospels, lives and breathes the shared historical memories of the Israelites and Jesus Movement people.

Kinship

Key social domains or social institutions in Mediterranean antiquity were kinship, politics, economics, and religion. Kinship and politics were the most important.[70] Kinship, or family, is a major indicator of social status and includes patrilineal descent lines (except for magical texts—matrilineal descent lines are more certain!), patrilocalism,

---

68. For discussion, see pp. 111–17 above.

69. Allison, *New Moses*.

70. Malina, "Interpreting the Bible with Anthropology," 152–53; *The New Testament World* (2001), 82–83, chap. 5; Hanson and Oakman, *Palestine*, devote a chapter to each of the four institutions: kinship (chap. 2), politics (chap. 3), economics (chap. 4) and religion (chap. 5).

defense strategies of marriage, and identity by male generation. These themes, of course, were an expression of pervasive male dominance, or patriarchy. With respect to the semantic field in the Gospel of Matthew, there is a superabundance of terms relating to kinship and family.[71] Recall also that the ancients often used kinship terms in referring to members of fictive kinship groups such as voluntary associations.[72] Examples are *patēr* ("father") as an association or synagogue leader and *adelphoi* ("brothers") for group members.[73]

In the Gospel of Matthew, Mary (human mother), Joseph (human father of Davidic descent), and Jesus' siblings are important for Jesus' human *genos* (Matt 1:1, 16; 13:53–58 [Mark 6:1–6a]). Jesus honors his human parents (Matt 15:4). Nonetheless, Jesus also has a more-than-human *genos* (Matt 1:18). God is his more-than-human father and his fictive family is more significant than his human family—if its members do the will of its more-than-human father (Matt 12:46–50 [Mark 3:31–35]). The most dramatic illustration is that the necessity of burying one's father is made secondary to following Jesus (Matt 8:22 [Q 9:59–60]; cf. Tob 4:3–4). Finally, although the Matthean gospel has a softer version of the hard saying in QLuke that disciples should "hate" family members (Q 14:26; cf. *Gosp. Thom.* 55; 101), it still emphasizes that a true disciple should not love family "more than me" (Matt 10:37), a version that conflicts with the importance of honoring one's family: the ambiguity or tension in Q persists in Matthew.

Phenotypical Features

Phenotypical features in antiquity were often associated with family, land, and especially climate.[74] Such features evoked outsiders' descriptions, which were typically ethnocentric. For example, it was believed that Ethiopians were dark and had curly beards and hair because the sun had scorched them, but Europeans were white and had frosty skin and straight, yellow hair because of their northern climate (*NH* 2:80.189). Big people were thought to come from rugged, mountainous regions; tall people from highlands; and dark-skinned people from

71. Duling, "'Whatever Gain I Had . . .'"; Louw and Nida, *Greek-English Lexicon*.
72. Duling, "Matthew 18:15–17."
73. See chap. 7 above.
74. Malina and Neyrey, *Portraits of Paul*, chap. 1.

lowlands (*Aer.* 24:1–4 [Loeb]). Corinthians and Leucadians were said to be small-limbed with small eyes and a small face (*Physio.* 808a, 30–33e). Yet, Cohen maintains that "not a single ancient author comments on the distinctive size, looks, or coiffure of the Jews [as Jews]," although there are notations about their beards.[75]

There are no *ethnos/genos*-related phonotypical features in Matthew.

(Home)land

Spatial proximity, territory, and geography ("land" or "homeland") are terms that can be used to refer to one of the three most important identity markers, the other two being kinship and mythical ancestry.[76] Indeed, common place of origin is often connected with *genos*, one's origins by common descent and parentage.

Among the Greeks, religious practices were sometimes associated with regions.[77] In Israel the covenant promise included the land (Gen 15:18–21). The semantic field for place (*topos*) takes on great significance for both individual and collective identity.

Land and place associations related to ethnic collectivities are also very common in the Gospel of Matthew.[78] The writer mentions "part" or "district" (*ta merē*) three times, one each in relation to Galilee (Matt 2:22), Tyre and Sidon (Matt 15:21), and Caesarea Philippi (Matt 16:13). Galilee occurs by itself twelve times (Matt 3:13; 4:12; 4:23, 25; 17:22; 19:1; 21:11; 26:32; 27:55; 28:7; 28:10, 16) and the Sea of Galilee three times (Matt 4:18; 15:29; 28:16). The gospel also has references to "land (*gē*) of" Judah (Matt 2:6), Israel (Matt 2:20, 21), Zebulun (Matt 4:15), Naphtali (Matt 4:15), and Sodom and Gomorrah (Matt 10:15; 11:24). It mentions the "region (*ta horia*) of Judea beyond the Jordan," the wilderness of Judea, and simply Judea (Matt 19:1; 3:1; 2:1, 5, 22; 3:5; 14:16). One of the most illustrative statements is the Matthean summary in 4:23–25: "And he went about all *Galilee* . . . 24) So his fame spread throughout all *Syria*, . . . 25)

75. Cohen, *Beginnings of Jewishness*, 28.

76. Malina and Neyrey, *Portraits of Paul*, chap. 1.

77. Hall, *Ethnic Identity*, 45.

78. Duling, "Matthew as a Marginal Scribe"; "Jesus Movement and Network Analysis."

And great crowds followed him from *Galilee* and the *Decapolis* and *Jerusalem* and *Judea* and from *beyond the Jordan*." A key reference pertaining to Jesus, as Riches noted, is the reference to his homeland, "Galilee of the *ethnōn*" (Matt 4:15). Yet, in apparent tension with it is 10:5: "Go nowhere among the Gentiles (*hodon ethnōn*), and enter no town of the Samaritans." Egypt is also mentioned (Matt 2:13, 14, 15, 19). To these we may add persons identified by place, such as Simon the Cananaean, the Canaanite woman, and Simon of Cyrene (Matt 10:4; 15:22; 27:32).

It is common to identify persons ethnically by their (home)land in the gospel, but it is also true that the gospel contains much topographical symbolism, for example, the mountain, especially in relation to Moses.[79] This localization moves beyond literal place. There are possible hints in the story that the Gospel of Matthew was written "beyond the Jordan," that is, east or northeast of the Jordan (Matt 19:1; 4:15);[80] however, Antioch and Galilee/southern Syria are most often preferred by scholars. It is consistent with Riches' point about metaphorization: the most important "place" is with Jesus.

Common Language

The Herodotus quotation above illustrates language as a major ethnic marker. Indeed, languages in antiquity preserved and spread an elite culture that marked social boundaries and reinforced "political and cultural coherence, or group identity."[81] The Greek term *barbaros* seems to have referred originally to the babbling of non-Greeks (*Ar. Av.* 199–200, Pl. *Menex.* 242a, Pl. *Ep.* 8 353e).[82] Egyptians called those who did not speak Egyptian "other-tongued," and Persians thought that those who have the same language should not engage in war with each other.[83] Cohen argues that there was no special "Jewish Greek";

---

79. E.g., Allison, *New Moses*, passim.

80. See Slingerland, "Transjordanian Origin"; Theissen, *Gospels in Context*, 249–52.

81. Bowman and Wolff, *Literacy and Power*, 12.

82. Hall, *Inventing the Barbarian*, 172; Harrison, "Herodotus' Conception"; see Hall, *Ethnic Identity*, 45.

83. Harrison, ibid.

Israelites spoke Greek like everyone else.[84] However, Mark Hamilton claims that "the use of Hebrew in the post-exilic books of the Bible was itself a conscious act of establishing ethnic identity and boundaries. The use of Hebrew allowed one to assert one's Jewishness simply by speaking."[85] On the Greek language side, Diaspora synagogue Israelites spoke an in-group Greek colored by their Greek "Bible," the Septuagint, as did ancient Christ believers.[86]

The clearest reference to language as an ethnic marker in Matthew is the well-known challenge to Peter: "Certainly you are also one of them, for your *lalia* betrays you" (Matt 26:73). The term *lalia* in this verse means literally "form of speaking"; it is usually translated "accent," but can also refer to "dialect."[87] Either way, the comment refers to regional specificity. Special Israelite customs were also distinctive, as the following section indicates.

Customs

The Greek terms *to ethos, to ēthos, tē synētheia,* and *ta nomima* can refer to "custom" or "habit," that is, traditionally accepted, socially sanctioned patterns of behavior. The root meaning of *ta nomima* implies conformity with law (*nomos*), and thus it also means "statutes," "ordinances," "dues."[88] A good example of conformity to customs is that a sixth-century BCE Greek poet, Anakreon, remarks that Dorians were known by their dress,[89] and Thucydides mentions that the inhabitants of Gela in Sicily adopted Dorian customs (Pindar, *Pythian Odes* 1.62–65). On the Judean side, an illustration of religious "customs" comes from 1 Maccabees 1: "And the king sent letters by messengers to Jerusalem and the cities of Judah; he directed them to follow customs strange to the land (*nomimōn allotriōn tēs gēs*), . . ." whereupon a number of cultic practices and items are mentioned (1 Macc 1:44). Cohen argues that outsiders normally would

---

84. Cohen, *Beginnings of Jewishness*, 34–35.
85. Hamilton, "Who Was a Jew?"
86. Malherbe, *Social Aspects*, 35–41.
87. Liddell-Scott-Jones-McKenzie, *Greek-English Lexicon* (1966), 1026.
88. Ibid., 1179b.
89. Hall, *Ethnic Identity*, 38.

not have identified Israelites by any customs, for example, special Israelite names, occupations, or distinctive dress, but he admits that the rabbis themselves considered tasseled fringes (*tzitzit*) and phylacteries (*tefillin*) specific to Israelites.[90] Yet, traditionally accepted Israelite *nomima* were usually considered to be religious (1 Macc 1: circumcision; Sabbath) in contrast to non-Israelite *nomima*, and thus in most respects they were oppositional.

Ordinary Israelite customs in the Gospel of Matthew are mentioned in passing. They include formal meal etiquette (advance invitations, Matt 22:3; seats of honor, Matt 23:6); customary fasts (Matt 6:16–18); male dress, including fringes on the male's outer garment (*tzitzit*) and phylacteries (*tefillin*) for prayer (Matt 9:20–22; 23:5; 11:8; 3:11; fringes: Num 15:37–41; Deut 22:12; *Aristeas* 157–158; Jos *Ant*. 4.213; phylacteries: *Aristeas* 157–158; in the rabbinic imagination, fringes and phylacteries were Israelite ethnic markers);[91] sandals (Matt 3:11; 10:10); tearing one's clothes in times of distress (Matt 26:65 [cp. 2 Kgs 18.37–19.3; Acts 14.14]); repentance in sackcloth and ashes (Matt 11:21); marriage customs (Matt 1:18–25; 11:17a [see Jer 9.17–22]; 25:1–13); divorce certificates (Matt 19:7 [Mark 10:4]); and funeral customs (Matt 8:21 [Q 9:57]; Matt 11:17b; 27:59; 23:27). Many of these customs reinforce traditional Israelite patriarchy, as well as communal solidarity.

Yet, there are clear challenges to law and custom in Matthew. Neither the dress (Matt 3:4) nor the diet (Matt 3:4) of the Baptizer is customary, although expected of certain prophets. Jesus leaves his village and does not follow his father's trade (Matt 13:55). He associates with women in public and eats and drinks with the expendables and the unclean. He is charged with being a "glutton and a drunkard, a friend of tax collectors and sinners" (Matt 11:18–19 [Q 7:34]), an expression that in Deuteronomy 21:20 refers to the stubborn and rebellious son. He is said to recommend for his followers a lifestyle that includes no wealth, no change of clothes, and no sandals (Matt 10:9). There is some inconsistency about fasting: Jesus fasts, but his disciples do not (but would in the future), and when fasting, one should fast privately, not publicly (Matt 4:1–11; 6:16–18; 9:14–17 [Mark 2:18–22]). Honoring one's parents is important (Matt 19:19), but, as noted above,

---

90. Cohen, *Beginnings of Jewishness*, 30–34.
91. Ibid., 34.

Ethnicity, Ethnocentrism, and the Matthean Ethnos   313

one should not love them "more than" Jesus (Matt 10:37, softening Q 14:26). Following him apparently absolves one from burying one's father (Matt 8:21). Jesus' true family is not biological, but consists of those who do the Father's will (Matt 12:46–50 [Mark 3:31–36]). Jesus teaches that except in cases of *porneia*, divorcing a woman leads her to commit adultery; indeed, a divorced man's remarriage is an act of adultery, and so is his marriage to a divorced woman (whether he has been married or not) (Matt 5:32; 19:9). Such teachings are customary for Christ believers; they overlap with religious law, the next category.

Common Religion and Religious Practices

Herodotus claimed that one feature of Greek self-identity is religion (Herodotus, *Hist.* 8.144.2). The primary emphasis in Greek religion, according to Jenifer Neils, was ritual, that is, festivals, religious processions, oracles, athletic contests, gifts, and sacrifices.[92] While ritual was central to Israelite culture, a more important norm after the sixth-century BCE Babylonian Exile was the sacred text and its interpretation by specialists. Here I must limit myself to law, especially the Sabbath, food, and circumcision, which are critical issues for Israelite ethnic identity.

With respect to law, David Sim focuses on E. P. Sanders's "covenantal nomism," which stressed salvation as God's special gift to his covenant people, rooted in three emphases: the promises of land and descendants to ancestor Abraham, deliverance of Israel by God's gracious acts, and obedience to God's commandments. The sign of covenantal election was male circumcision.[93] For Sanders covenantal nomism was normative in Palestine and very widespread in the Diaspora, although secondary in writers such as Philo.[94] John Collins offers a somewhat different perspective. Collins emphasizes that in Diaspora literature Torah laws that were offensive to non-Israelites were usually avoided. Even in Palestinian literature alternatives to covenantal nomism existed, for example, the seer's revelatory vision and wisdom. Collins says, "Despite the undeniably central role of the

---

92. Neils, *Goddess and Polis*.
93. Sanders, *Paul and Palestinian Judaism*; see above, sec. 1.
94. Ibid., 426, 235–36.

covenant law in the Jewish tradition, not all strands of Judaism had their primary focus on the law, and even those that did understood it in various ways."[95] For Collins there was no universal means by which Israelites identified themselves (at least at the ideological level).[96] Given Sim's dependence on Sanders, Collins' shift in emphasis is a significant counterweight. A major point with respect to the gospel is that law is both intensified and yet reinterpreted by Matthew's Jesus, as of the antitheses of the Sermon on the Mount (Matt 5:21–48) show,[97] but here I must focus on three of Collins' law-based examples relevant for ethnic identity: Sabbath, dietary regulations, and circumcision.

The Romans recognized that Israelites would not do business on the Sabbath (Ovid, *Remedia Amoris* 217–20; Frontinus, *Strategemata* 2.1.17;[98] for the Sabbath, see Gen 2:1–3; Exod 20:11: 31:17). Indeed, Seneca and Tacitus said that Judeans were lazy for not working on the Sabbath (Seneca, *On Superstitions*, cited by Augustine, *City of God* 6, 11; Tacitus, *Histories* 5.4.3), and Josephus wrote that Plutarch and Agatharchides ridiculed them for refusing to engage in war on the Sabbath (Plutarch, *On Superstitions* 8; Jos. *Ap.* 1.210). In contrast, Josephus claimed that non-Israelites were attracted to Israelite religious observances, including the Sabbath rest, fasting, and food regulations (Jos. *Ap.* 2.282 [39]); he himself vacillated on the issue of waging war on the Sabbath (opposed it: Jos. *Ap.* 2.21–27; *Ant.* 16:27–30; defended it: Jos. *Ap.* 2.282). While there are extensive rabbinic debates about what kinds of work are forbidden on the Sabbath,[99] the tendency in Diaspora writings was to avoid mentioning the Sabbath laws (*Sib. Or.* 161; *T12Patr*).[100] Moreover, although Philo stressed observance, he universalized it by allegorizing it (Philo, *Op. Mund.* 89–128).

The Matthean writer also has a "loose constructionist" view. Nine of ten Sabbath references are clustered in back-to-back stories (Matt 12:1–8 [Mark 2:23–28] and 9–14 [Mark 3:1–6]; cf. also Matt 28:1 [Mark 16:1]). Five references in this context are from Mark (Matt 12:1 [Mark 2:23]; Matt 12:2 [Mark 2:24]; Matt 12:8 [Mark

---

95. Collins, *Between Athens and Jerusalem*, 15.
96. Cp. Hamilton, "Who Was a Jew?" for the Achaemenid Period.
97. Duling, "'Do not Swear . . .'"
98. Yang, *Jesus and the Sabbath*.
99. Ibid., 91–95.
100. Collins, *Between Athens and Jerusalem*, 147, 153.

2:28]; Matt 12:10 [Mark 3:2]; Matt 12:12 [Mark 3:4]); the Matthean writer adds four (Matt 12:5 [2x]; 12:11; 12:24) in which Jesus challenges the Pharisees' "strict constructionist" views. In the first story, Jesus defends the disciples' unlawful act of plucking grain on the Sabbath by drawing on David's precedent of unlawful eating the bread of the Presence (1 Sam 21:1–7), "for the Son of Man is lord of the Sabbath" (Matt 12:8 [Mark 2:28]). He adds that temple priests were permitted to break the Sabbath law (Matt 12:5; see Num 28:9–10) and in any case mercy is more important than temple sacrifice (Matt 9:13; 12:7 [Hos 6:6]), implying it is also more important than strict Sabbath observance. In the second story, Jesus heals the man with the withered hand on the Sabbath. It is crucial to remember that while there is no Torah prohibition against healing on the Sabbath, and at least some rabbis allowed for helping an animal get itself out of the pit (such as with a ramp) or feeding it while it is still in the pit to keep it alive (*m. Yoma* 8.6; *Mek.* on Exod 22:2),[101] stricter rabbinic views forbade *healing* or *lifting* an animal from the pit on the Sabbath (*M. Besa* 3.4).[102] Such strict views can be found also in the Dead Sea Scrolls (CD 11.13–14; cf. Jos. *Wars* 2:8, 9). The Matthean writer does not abrogate the Sabbath (12:7–8 [contrast Mark 2:27]), but he goes against the strict interpretation of Sabbath observance when he adds to Mark Jesus' words that it is permitted to *lift* a sheep out of the pit on the Sabbath (Matt 12:11–12 [Mark 3:1–6). Jesus is thus portrayed as a "loose constructionist" on Sabbath interpretations, and thus with respect to rabbinic interpreters he is closer to the House of Hillel than to the House of Shammai.[103]

The key dietary prohibitions are found in Leviticus 11, and the author of 1 Maccabees says that pious Israelites "resolved in their hearts not to eat unclean food" (1 Macc 1:62). I have already noted Josephus' opinion that some non-Israelites adopted Israelite food practices (Jos. *Ap.* 2.282 [39]). Collins, however, says that dietary laws were deemphasized in the Hellenistic Israelite literature.[104] Similarly, the Matthean writer accepts and highlights the Markan anti-Pharisaic view that "not what goes into the mouth defiles a man, but what comes

---

101. Davies and Allison, *Matthew*, 2:318.
102. Schiffman, *Reclaiming the Dead Sea Scrolls*, 278.
103. Ibid., 315.
104. Collins, *Between Athens and Jerusalem*, 143.

out of the mouth, this defiles a man" (Matt 15:11 RSV [Mark 7:15]). There is certainly a precedent for the priority of "religion of the heart" in Israel (Ps 18:26; 24:4; 1QS 3:6-9; 5:13-14; Jos. *Ant.* 18.117), but there is also strong evidence that stricter Israelites did not eat with non-Israelites (e.g., Dan 1:8-16; Tob 1:10-11; Judith 12:2; Dan 1:8-16; 1 Macc 1:62; 2 Macc 6:18; Gal 2:11-14). The writer of Matthew again represents a loose, not a strict, construction of dietary prohibitions.

The third practice, circumcision, is, as previously indicated, the most debated of these three Israelite religio-ethnic practices. Genesis 17:11 contains the Torah command: "You shall be circumcised in the flesh of your foreskins, and it shall be a sign of the covenant between me and you." Ezekiel adds that the house of Israel breaks the covenant when it allows foreigners (LXX *allogenēs*) who are "uncircumcised in heart and flesh" to profane the temple by entering it (Ezek 44:6-9). 1 Maccabees claims that Israelites (i.e., males) distinguish themselves from Greeks chiefly by circumcision; indeed, Israelites who wanted to look more Greek-like practiced epispasm.[105] It is argued by some scholars that Philo thought circumcision to be a necessary requirement for Judeans (Philo, *Migr. Abr.* 91). While some Roman writers were aware that other groups practiced circumcision (Herodotus, *Hist.* 2.104.1-3; Diodorus Siculus, *Bibl. Hist.* 1.28.3; Origen, *Contra* 1.22),[106] they associated the practice chiefly with the Israelites (Horace, *Satires* 1.9.69-70; Persius, *Satires* 5.184; Petronius, frag. No. 37; Martial, *Epigrams* 7.30.5; Celsus, *De Medicina* 7.25.1; Suetonius, *Domitian* 12.2; Tacitus, *Histories* 5.5.1-2; Juvenal, *Satires* 14.96-106).[107] Cohen asserts that no evidence exists for assuming that native Israelites ever dispensed with the eighth-day circumcision requirement.[108] Clearly, the evidence for the circumcision requirement is strong; hence, if circumcision is in view, there is a good case for Sim's emphasis on "covenantal nomism" based on the work of E. P. Sanders, noted at the beginning of this chapter.

Yet, even here there is some cause for pause. Cohen believes that circumcision was everywhere practiced, but adds that because

105. Hall, "Epispasm," 71-86.

106. Lieu, "Circumcision," 360 n. 8.

107. Collins, "Symbol of Otherness," 163; *Between Athens and Jerusalem*, 6; Cohen, *Beginnings of Jewishness*, 40-41.

108. Cohen, *Beginnings of Jewishness*, 30, 158, 169, 215.

it excludes half the population (women) and other Eastern peoples were known to have practiced it,[109] it could not have been a boundary marker for Israelite self-identity in the East, as is usually thought. He adds that there is no evidence that any Israelite male actually checked another Israelite male to see whether he was circumcised (a modesty factor) and concludes generally that "Jews and Gentiles in antiquity were corporeally, visually, linguistically, and socially indistinguishable."[110]

A few texts need to be cited that at least make this conclusion open to question. 1 Maccabees says that Mattathias and his friends "forcibly circumcised all the uncircumcised boys that they found within the borders of Israel" (1 Macc 2:45). The author of Jubilees attacks those who failed to circumcise their sons, clearly implying that some did not (*Jub.* 15:25-34). With respect to Diaspora literature, circumcision is not mentioned in the *Letter of Aristeas* or *Pseudo Phocylides*. In a much debated passage, Philo mentions pure allegorists who had either abandoned circumcision or defended the practice, but he did so without condemning those who did not as being unfaithful Israelites (Philo, *Migr. Abr.* 89-94). John Barclay reacts negatively to Daniel Boyarin's view that there was a homology between the ideas of Philo and Paul, and that Philo, like Paul, universalizes circumcision.[111] Sim, of course, is aware of Philo's liberal position. In any case, Collins concludes, "In view of Philo's comments on the allegorists, we must allow that there were some ethnic Jews who abandoned circumcision without repudiating Judaism, however much other Jews may have 'blamed' them."[112] Since Harry A. Wolfson's work, some scholars have argued that Philo himself might have leaned in this direction, although other scholars contest Wolfson's view.[113]

Crucial to the circumcision question is whether male *proselytes* were always and everywhere circumcised in order to become full proselytes. Evidence suggests that in some areas they were. The book of Judith says that the proselyte Anchior underwent circumcision (Jdt

---

109. Ibid., 39-56.
110. Ibid., 37.
111. Barclay, "Paul and Philo on Circumcision"; cf. Boyarin, *Radical Jew*.
112. Collins, "A Symbol of Otherness," 173.
113. Wolfson, *Philo*; see Borgen, *Philo, John and Paul*.

14:10). Josephus wrote that circumcision was forced on conquered non-Israelite males in Maccabean Palestine, that males who married into the Herodian family were circumcised, and that the Roman general Metilius converted and was circumcised (Jos. *Ant.* 13.9.1 [257–258]; 16.7.6 [225]; *War* 1.17.10). In the conversion of Izates, king of Adiabene, the Galilean Eleazar convinced the king that circumcision was a necessary requirement and he finally submitted (Jos. *Ant.* 20.2–4). The Jerusalem Talmud normally views circumcision of proselytes as a requirement.[114] Tacitus wrote that those who "crossed over" were required to be circumcised (Tacitus, *Histories* 5.5.2; cf. Juvenal, *Satires* 14.96–105).[115] Thus, some scholars have justifiably argued that to become a full proselyte one had to be circumcised.[116]

Again, however, there is some question about its universality. As with Sabbath and dietary regulations, the subject of circumcision of proselytes was avoided in Israelite Diaspora literature.[117] The Sibylline Oracles stress that conversion entails worshipping the one true God in the Jerusalem Temple, but does not mention circumcision. In the Izates story, the *Israelite* merchant Ananias who initially advised the royal family told the king that circumcision was not necessary to worship the God of Israel (Jos. *Ant.* 20.2–4). To be sure, Philo defended circumcision in the flesh (Philo, *Spec. Leg.* 1:1–11). Barclay claims that Philo never abandoned literal circumcision. He gives six reasons: 1) it prevents infection; 2) it prevents collection of dirt; 3) a circumcised heart (Jer 9:25) requires circumcised flesh; 4) it aids in delivering sperm; 5) it checks sensuous pleasures; and 6) it helps guard against the conceit that humans generate under their own power.[118] However, in one passage, Philo virtually allegorized it away when he wrote that the proselyte is "one who circumcises not his uncircumcision but his desires and sensual pleasures and the other passions of the soul. For in Egypt the Hebrew nation was not circumcised" (Philo, *Quaest in Ex.* 2.2). Collins compares Philo's view to Rabbi Joshua's view in the Babylonian Talmud, namely, that baptism, not circumcision, was the

114. Cohen, *Beginnings of Jewishness*, 219 n. 46.

115. Ibid., 157.

116. Nolland, "Uncircumcized Proselytes?"; Barclay, "Paul and Philo on Circumcision"; Cohen, ibid., 152, 219–21; "Judaism with Circumcision," 397.

117. Collins, "A Symbol of Otherness," passim.

118. Barclay, "Paul and Philo on Circumcision," 538–39.

prerequisite for conversion (*b. Yeb.* 46a). R. Eliezer and the rest of the sages disagreed. In the Jerusalem Talmud, R. Joshua was said to hold both views! For Cohen the Jerusalem Talmud represents the best view. For Collins, Philo's and R. Joshua's views in the Babylonian Talmud are "theoretical and do not prove the actual existence of uncircumcised proselytes, but they have at least potential significance nonetheless."[119] There are other scholars who speculate about the existence of uncircumcised proselytes.[120] Despite his open position, Cohen remains unconvinced.[121] However, it seems inconsistent to say that proselyte circumcision was necessary and at the same time claim that it was not a self-identifying social/religious boundary marker. Philo knew that others practiced it, but still identified his people with it; some Greek and Roman writers also knew that others practiced it, but identified Israelites with it.

In short, circumcision was no doubt one self-identifying religio-ethnic practice—even if other peoples practiced it and Israelite males did not check each other. It was the norm and can be considered part of the religious practice of Israelites; however, there seem to have been exceptions to the norm.

Was one of them the writer of Matthew? This gospel, so full of debates about interpretation of the law, does not mention any of the common expressions related to either eighth-day or proselyte circumcision or the failure to practice it, for example, *hoi anomoi* ("those who do not follow the Law [Torah]"), *hē akrobystia* ("the foreskin [people]"), "those called circumcision (*peritomēs*) of the flesh" (cf. Gal 2:7–9), *akrobystos* ("an uncircumcised man"), *sebomenoi ton theon* ("God fearers"), *prosēlytēs* ("proselytes"), and *prosēlyta* ("full converts to the house of Israel"). Thus, any arguments about circumcision in relation to the Matthean group are ultimately conjectural and based on logic and inference, especially a scholar's overall perspective on the gospel. If a scholar defends the Palestinian provenance, "Christian Judaism," and the norms of covenantal nomism, circumcision is more likely to be defended as taken for granted. Matthew's initial statement about Jesus not coming to destroy the Torah, but to fulfill it (Matt 5:17–20)

---

119. Collins, "Symbol of Otherness," 174.

120. E.g., Wolfson, *Philo*, 2:369–71; McEleney, "Conversion, Circumcision, and Law"; Borgen, *Philo, John and Paul*, 61–71, 217–24; Lieu, "Circumcision," 363.

121. Cohen, *Beginnings of Jewishness*, 152 n. 41.

becomes the usual norm for everything else; anyone banned from the community should be treated like a *ethnikos* and a *telōnēs*, "toll collector" (Matt 18:17). Only Torah *interpretation* is at stake. It thus becomes necessary to explain the Matthean silence in the mission statement, which stresses baptism, and the best explanation seems to be that there are Israelites in the Matthean community. This is Sim's view.

However, the reverse logic is possible. If the gospel was written outside the homeland, say in Antioch; if Diaspora writers avoided Israelite practices that would be offensive to Hellenists; if covenantal nomism was not always and everywhere so normative; and if, as indicated above, the Matthean writer is a loose constructionist on issues such as Sabbath and diet, there is at least room for reasonable doubt also about circumcision. Matthew could have omitted reference to circumcision because of the *ethnē* in his community, not because it consisted of *Ioudaioi* and was taken for granted. Perhaps the Matthean community had different requirements for Israelites and male Gentile converts.[122] Matthew focused on the weightier *ethical* matters of the Torah, not the lighter cultic and ritual requirements. Some Israelite communities were known to have waived the requirement in favor of baptism.[123] From this perspective the possibility that circumcision was not practiced must remain.

Sim has offered a very strong case, indeed, but in the main I have taken a position closer to that of Riches. I have presented a broader perspective on ethnicity in antiquity and attempted to relate it to a broader view of the Gospel of Matthew. In both cases there are some ambiguities, and this is especially the case with the gospel. Since a general perspective on the gospel is a major factor in interpreting the particulars, it is necessary that I briefly present my own perspective.

Marginality

As illuminated by the types of marginality discussed in chapter 9, the author of Matthew has great concern for *structurally* marginal persons—mainly, but not exclusively, those at or near the bottom of the social ladder—represented especially in Jesus' stories about the

---

122. Davies and Allison, *Matthew*, 1:492–93.
123. Saldarini, *Matthew's Christian-Jewish Community*, 156–60.

outcast. The possibility also exists that the Matthean author himself was a "*social role* marginal," that is, had been a (Pharisaic?) scribe who was denied the social status he expected, but regained his social status as a leader by affiliating with a structurally marginal group in conflict with an opponent group, the Pharisees. This view is speculative, but the expectation was typical of those who joined voluntary associations. The author of Matthew did affiliate—probably voluntarily—with a marginal group. I have assumed that he was also *ideologically* marginal, that is, that he freely made this choice on the basis of specific ideas and interests. Despite his ideological stance, I have also argued, paradoxically, that the author was a *culturally* marginal scribe (a "Marginal Man") in a *culturally* marginal community populated with many *structurally* marginal persons. He was between two or more "historic traditions, languages, political loyalties, moral codes, and religions." It is hardly any wonder that scholars have debated the identity of the author on a spectrum from "Gentile Christian" to "Christian Jew." If the writer of Matthew was culturally marginal, he was negotiating the "in betweenness" of culturally marginal clusters of communities.[124] He himself was a revisionist scribe "instructed for the Kingdom [and] bringing out of his storehouse what is old and what is new" (Matt 13:52). It is this perspective on the gospel that is consistent with the author's view of ethnicity.

With these more specific views of marginality in mind, it is time to take up in more detail that special use of *ethnos* in the Gospel of Matthew previously noted, but reserved for later comment.

The Matthean *Ethnos* (Matthew 21:43)

Matthew 21:43 has a very distinctive use of the term *ethnos*, one that is not found in the other canonical gospels or elsewhere in the Matthean gospel. It states: "Therefore I tell you [plural], the kingdom of God will be taken away from you [plural] and given to an *ethnos* producing the fruits of it." The meaning of "fruits" as deeds in Matthew is well established, as for example, "you will know them by their fruits" (Matt 7:16, 20, referring to false prophets), repentance and bearing fruit (3:8), good and bad trees (5:17–19), and the like (e.g., 7:17–20;

---

124. Stanton, "Revisiting Matthew's Communities."

12:33; 13:22–23). In Matthew 21, the tenants of the vineyard will give the lord of the vineyard "the fruits in their seasons at harvest time" (21:41). This *ethnos* will accomplish good deeds.

More difficult to interpret are the opponents to whom the *ethnos* saying is addressed (the "you," plural) and the *ethnos* reference itself. The problem of the opponents must take into consideration the larger Matthean contextual sequence: the "rejected stone" prophecy from Ps 118:22–23 (Matt 21:42), followed by the fruit-producing *ethnos* saying (21:43), and then the stone's power to destroy (21:44, if it was not inserted into the text).[125] The first item in the sequence, the "rejected stone" (v. 42), is taken from the Markan source (Mark 12:10). However, the second, the *ethnos* saying (v. 43), and the third, the stone's power to destroy (v. 44), have been inserted by the writer of Matthew into the Markan context. Moreover, the second, the *ethnos* verse, begins with "Therefore," suggesting that it is intended to interpret the first, the "rejected stone," and that surely points back further to the rejected, murdered son in the previous Wicked Tenants allegory (Matt 31:33-41) taken from Mark 12:1-12. This allegory is in turn related to the still earlier Two Sons allegory (Matt 21:28–32) and ultimately the initial question about the source of Jesus' authority (Matt 21:23–27). Thus, the plural "you" in "Therefore I tell *you*" introducing the *ethnos* saying appears to refer back to opponents in that initial question (21:23), that is, "chief priests and the elders of the people" in the Temple (Mark 11:27: chief priests, *and scribes,* and elders).[126] This group seems to be implied also by the "you" (plural) that introduces the Two Sons (Matt 21:28), and by the repetition of "you" plural in the Two Sons interpretation that tax collectors and prostitutes will enter into the kingdom before "you" (Matt 21:31). One would therefore think that the "you" that is being replaced by the fruit-bearing *ethnos* has been clearly identified back in 21:23: "the chief priests and *elders of the people.*" However, as often happens in Matthew, the "you" plural

---

125. The 3rd edition of the Aland, Black, Martini, Metzger, and Wikgren text of the United Bible Societies puts v. 44 in brackets as a debatable "C" reading. Metzger, *A Textual Commentary*, 47, says that those who reject it see it as an interpolation from Luke 20:18. Those who accept it note the different Lukan wording, a better location for insertion at Matt 21:42, an eye-error omission skipping from *autēs* (v. 43) to *auton* (v. 44), and the antiquity of the text.

126. For a discussion of Matthew's omissions of scribes in Mark, see chap. 9 above.

Ethnicity, Ethnocentrism, and the Matthean Ethnos 323

may refer not to the opponents *previously* identified in the context, but those who are identified *after* this section in Matt 21:45, namely, the "chief priests *and Pharisees*," "who realized he was speaking about *them*." In other words, Matthew replaces his previous reference to *elders* of the people (21:23) at the beginning of the section with his favorite opponents, the *Pharisees*, at the end (21:45). The section concludes with the Marriage Feast allegory, probably redacted from Q (Matt 22:1-14//Luke 14:16-24//GTh 64), to which the Matthean writer adds the Wedding Garment allegory (Matt 22:11-14).

These contextual complications have led to a variety of interpretations. Some interpreters have focused on the whole unit in the light of the Matthean tendency to allegorize. In this view the Kingdom of God would be taken from Israel and its leaders (tenants) because of their rejection and execution of, first, John the Baptizer, and then Jesus, the rejected stone. It would then be given to the Gentile church (uninvited guests) after the destruction of Jerusalem ("miserable death"/"destruction of murderers"/burning of the city), because Israel deserved punishment for her sin of rejection/murder. The Kingdom would therefore taken from "you" (Israelites and their leaders) and given to a fruit-producing *ethnos*. This common salvation-historical interpretation depends heavily on the Wedding Banquet allegorically interpreted parable, that is, God punished Israel by destroying Jerusalem (Matt 22:7) because she persecuted her own prophets (first set of servants), as well as the apostles (second set of servants), and she rejected and killed God's son, Jesus. Thus, God has now offered salvation to the church. The main alternative is that the "you" plural refers to Israel and her leaders, but the *ethnos* as church is (in more recent exegesis) neither "Jewish" nor "Gentile," but a "third race." Both Graham N. Stanton and W. D. Davies and Dale Allison have defended a version of this "third race" option, namely, there was a break between the synagogue and the church and the *ethnos* is a new "nation," the Christian church, made up of both Judean and Gentile believers.[127] My view that the author and his community are "in between" can be coordinated with this "third race" view, but only if the "break" is a fine-line fracture.

---

127. Stanton, *Gospel for a New People*, 11-12, 151-52, and passim; "Revisiting Matthew's Communities," 9-23; Davies and Allison, *Matthew*, 1:23.

However, several recent scholars have argued that the conflict is not between "Jews" and "Christians," whether "Jews" or Gentiles, but between "Jews" who believe in Jesus and "Jews" who do not. Anthony Saldarini, who is representative of this interpretation, had a special interest in this new *ethnos* verse:

> ... the author of Matthew almost certainly refers to his own group as the *ethnos* which produced the fruit of the kingdom. Even if he did mean all the Christian communities in the Roman Empire, and even if we imagine them as much more institutionalized than they seem to have been in the late first century, this *ethnos* would not match the definition of a nation or even that of a coherent ethnic group. Matthew, then, uses the term *ethnos* of his own group in a restricted sense. The ordinary meaning of *ethnos* that fits Matthew's usage is that of a *voluntary organization or small social group. The Matthean ethnos is a small subgroup, whose exact make-up is not specified.*[128]

Saldarini is willing to call this small group a voluntary organization or a sect.[129] However, in reference to the allegory of the vineyard, he clarifies what this interpretation means. "Thus the *ethnos* bearing (literally "making") fruit (21:43) is a new group of tenants (that is, true leaders *of Israel*) who will give the owner his share of the fruits at the appropriate time (21:41)."[130] Here the term refers to a Matthean group as the true leaders of Israel. Yet, he also merges his leaders group with their followers. "The *ethnos* is a *group of leaders, with their devoted followers*, that can lead Israel well."[131] Obviously, this is not an *ethnie* in the usual sense of the ethnicity model in this chapter; it is built on the meaning of the term *ethnos* as any sort of (small) group, and a very particular one: leaders and their followers.

Sim appears to follow Saldarini on this *ethnos* verse, as his footnotes show, but not quite all the way. Yes, the old tenants are clearly the "Jewish" leaders who have the Kingdom taken away from them, but the new tenants are "either the *Matthean community alone* or *Christian Judaism in general.*"[132] Concerned (like Saldarini) to show

---

128. Saldarini, *Matthew's Christian-Jewish Community*, 60 (italics mine).
129. Ibid., 90–123.
130. Ibid., 60.
131. Ibid., 61.
132. Sim, *Gospel of Matthew*, 149.

Ethnicity, Ethnocentrism, and the Matthean Ethnos   325

that "Christian Judaism" was still "Judaism," he does not distinguish leaders and their followers in the way that Saldarini does; rather, "Matthew's Christian Jewish *group* claimed (albeit unsuccessfully) a leadership role *within* the Jewish community and *within* the Jewish religion."[133]

Riches, who calls this *ethnos* a "fictive nation" consisting of "sons of God," also goes part way with Saldarini, but his interpretation is very unlike Sim's.

> Much of . . . [Saldarini's position] . . . seems to me to be right; I cannot believe that the meaning here is that the church is to be seen as a new ethnic grouping similar to, but wholly distinct from, Israel. But some qualifications do also need to be made. I do not think the self-understanding of the Matthean community is that of 'a small sub-group' or of a voluntary organisation or small social group. On the contrary, they see themselves as part of the "many who will come to set at table with Abraham, Isaac, and Jacob" (8:11), as those commissioned by the Son of Man, to whom *all* authority has been given, to go and make disciples of all nations (28:19), and this pressing of the metaphor of the vineyard must, sooner or later, lead to its extension. Precisely because of the corporate sense of *ethnos*, one cannot detach the nature of the leadership from the nature of the people they lead. Israel led by the followers of Jesus will be a different kind of grouping from that led by the Jewish leaders opposed to Jesus and Matthew's community.[134]

Riches' main concern to "extend the metaphor" to a larger, more inclusive community brings with it a critique of Saldarini's small group sociological focus, that is, a few leaders and their followers. It leads in the direction of a different kind of, more inclusive, Israel, and it tends to collapse the group's leadership into the group.

I have come down more on the side of Riches than Sim in this chapter, and I agree with Riches' focus on greater inclusiveness. However, here I part company, since, as previous chapters show, I would have to agree with Saldarini's focus on "sect," voluntary association, and small group and with his initial attempt to focus on it as leaders and followers. If the *ethnos* in this passage refers to a small group of leaders and followers, as Saldarini says, it is opposed to another group

133. Ibid., italics mine.
134. Riches, *Conflicting Mythologies*, 221–22 n. 84

of leaders, the *priestly ethnos*, to which the author of Matthew adds his favorite antagonists, *the Pharisees*, in the following passage.

I base this suggestion especially on discussions in chapter 9 and a special interpretation of *ethnos*. The community of Matthew can be interpreted in terms of a voluntary association, which is also a fictive kin group.[135] Moshe Weinfeld viewed the Qumran Community as a voluntary association.[136] Weinfeld's conclusion was that with three exceptions—the absence of regulations about Temple sacrifices, funeral and burial rites, and membership fees and fines—the organizational structure and penal code of the Qumran Community and the Greco-Roman guilds and associations (Ptolemaic Egypt, Greece, and Rome) were nearly identical. Weinfeld himself was unwilling to call the community an "association"; he preferred the term "sect" because of its ideology and the three exceptions just mentioned. However, Klinghardt extended Weinfeld's analysis and concluded that there was no reason not to call the Qumran "sect"—even if represented by a single scroll—an "association": the distinction should be removed. "The sect was a private association in a legal sense . . . [T]he particularly Israelite theological (and social!) concepts, such as covenant, purity, holiness, etc., were under the altered circumstances of the Hellenistic culture, realized in the categories of religious associations and thus achieved innovative social concretion in a new political and social setting."[137] Four of the eight common features isolated by Weinfeld are precisely those of greatest interest in Matt 18:15-17: reproof of members, exclusion from the community, temporary expulsion, and final expulsion.[138]

Saldarini realized that *ethnos* could refer to guilds and trade associations and Kloppenborg with some reservations has offered confirmatory evidence.[139] On the one hand, Kloppenborg thinks that Saldarini's reference to F. Poland's evidence[140] is not accurate since

---

135. Duling, ibid., 520-75; "Matthew 18:15-17" and chap. 8 in this book; also Duling, "Jesus Movement and Network Analysis"; cf. Ascough, "Matthew and Community Formation."

136. Weinfeld, *Organization and Pattern*.

137. Klinghardt, "Manual of Discipline," 256-57.

138. See chap. 8.

139. Saldarini, *Pharisees*, 42, 59, 69, 72, 74; Kloppenborg, "Personal E-Mail Communication."

140. Poland, *Geschichte*.

Ethnicity, Ethnocentrism, and the Matthean Ethnos 327

Poland does not say that *ethnos* was an important designation for an association; also, Saldarini's use of information from Liddell-Scott-Jones-McKenzie[141] does not provide a good example of an *ethnos* as a voluntary association since in those references the term probably refers to a worker who "takes on the role of the guard of the people and the workshops."[142] On the other hand, Kloppenborg provides his own evidence for an *ethnos* as a voluntary association. Saldarini also considered not only Pharisees, but priests, in terms of *ethnos* as a voluntary association,[143] and Kloppenborg points to more texts that show that the term *ethnos* was used specifically in relation to priestly associations (*hiera ethnē*[144] and *hieroethnoi*, "priestly associations").[145]

Is it possible that the special use of the term *ethnos* for priestly associations triggered the Matthean special use here? If so, he considered the leaders of his group to be a special *ethnos* in opposition to the priestly leaders as an *ethnos*, with whom he has also linked his main opponents, the Pharisees.

Summary and Conclusion

It is generally accepted that groups construct their boundaries and attempt to maintain them; yet, they use some common cultural features to do so. The term *ethnos* in ancient Greek has a wider semantic range than what modern scholars usually mean by an ethnic group or an *ethnie*. Nonetheless, discussions of ethnicity can help develop a model that will highlight key socio-cultural features of the group under analysis.

The model can then be used to interpret ethnicity in antiquity and the Gospel of Matthew. At times in the gospel the boundaries of the old ethnicity are being maintained, but at other times they are not. This observation is consonant with the Matthean group as a culturally marginal group. It is "in between." The Matthean group thus stands on the boundary "between" Israel and non-Israel, which is just where the

141. Saldarini, *Matthew's Christian-Jewish Community*, 245 n. 64; the references are P. Petrie III 32r.2, v.i.3–4, ii.10–11 (III BCE).
142. Kloppenborg, *Tenants in the Vineyard*, 193.
143. Saldarini, *Pharisees*, 69.
144. Petrie III 59.B.4 [III BCE]; OGIS 90.A.17 [196 BCE].
145. *CPR* XV 32.v.8 [II/III CE] ; *POxy* XLIX 3470.16 [131 CE]; 3471.14 [131 CE]).

marginal Matthean writer himself stands. The group is therefore in the process of (re-)constructing its ethnic boundaries. From this perspective, the writer is silent about circumcision precisely because circumcision is in danger of drawing the boundaries between insiders and outsiders too sharply. There is occasional precedent for such openness in the Israelite communities, especially in the Diaspora. Finally, there is the special case of a fruit-bearing *ethnos* in Matthew 21. This *ethnos* is opposed to the priestly authorities and the Pharisees. It appears at first glance to refer to the Matthean association itself. However, since the term *ethnos* can refer to ancient priestly associations, it seems better to think of this particular *ethnos* as an alternative leadership association. If so, it pits one *ethnos* association of leaders, that of the Matthean group, against another, that of Israel at large.

CHAPTER 11

A Marginal Scribe

Putting It All Together

A SET OF DIFFERENT studies on the Gospel of Matthew written over a period of twenty years and revised is inevitably not a unity. Nevertheless, there are some common themes.

Chapter 1 explores the appearance of the social sciences as a tool of biblical criticism. This use of the social sciences is not new. There had been a long history of conflict and cooperation between historians and the forerunners of social-scientists since the Enlightenment, and in the late nineteenth and early twentieth centuries a few New Testament scholars were drawn to the social sciences. Important early influences were Weber's views of charismatic leadership, Weber and Ernst Troeltsch's ideas about sect, and Karl Marx's theories about social class. In the New Testament field Adolf Deissmann's view that New Testament Greek was the language of the masses and the Chicago School's theme that the social environment of the New Testament was critical to the interpretation of its literature were the most prominent. This sort of research peaked in the 1920s. It waned in the 1930s for a variety of reasons. Marxist ideas were increasingly judged to be the ideological foundation of the international Communist threat; the focus on this-worldly social contexts ran headlong into the dominant theology of the day, an otherworldly "Neo-Orthodox" theology; and most New Testament scholars saw the significance of church-related contexts, but concluded that the sources of the New Testament yielded little information about everyday social life.

However, after the war, as historians and social scientists at large began to talk together again and produce interdisciplinary journals, the social sciences once again became important for New Testament scholars. The tone and emphasis, however, was different. E. A. Judge's studies of Paul rejected the notion that the early church was predominantly populated by the "lower classes," which had been a Marxist influence. Pioneer Gerd Theissen argued that Jesus had a poor, homeless, itinerant lifestyle; however, it was not forced upon him by his oppressive Palestinian social circumstances, but freely chosen; moreover, his followers were judged to be mainly from the marginal middle classes. Theissen, Wayne Meeks, and other scholars explored the names of leaders and wealthy patrons who led or supported Paul's urban communities. Ronald Hock even argued that the artisan Paul loathed his "tentmaking" trade. Abraham Malherbe suggested that a perhaps "new consensus" might be emerging, one in which the social level of the early Christ believers was higher than Deissmann had imagined. As the older social analysis had been buttressed by Max Weber and Ernst Troeltsch, the newer approach found support in the work of sect theorist Bryan Wilson and "new religions" sociologist Rodney Stark, who held that an original Judean rural sect became an urban cult that, like modern cults, drew its converts from the upper social strata.

Yet, the older view did not totally disappear, nor could it. Robin Scroggs, Wolfgang Stegemann, Justin Meggitt, Todd Still, and others emphasized the importance of the widespread concern for the poor and the oppressed in the New Testament, as well as Paul's low status. Theissen and Meeks gave voice to a mediating position: while converts to the Christ Movements were drawn mainly from the lower social strata, their leaders came from a higher stratum. Much of the early work was done by these prominent social historians. Very important for this book, there also appeared a group of scholars who, like John Gager, placed somewhat greater value on social-scientific theory and modeling, namely, the social-scientific critics. Led by John Elliott, who was influenced by Wilson's sect analysis and sociological theory, and Bruce Malina, who pioneered cultural anthropological theories and models, a number of these scholars became members of the "Social Context Group" while remaining active in other biblical societies.

What of the gospels? In the latter twentieth century two dominant interpretative methods of the gospels, form criticism and redaction criticism, often theorized about "community," but the "New

Literary Criticism" was less inclined, and all three tended to ignore *everyday* social life. Yet, the winds of change were beginning to blow. The Gospel of Mark was interpreted with Marxist theory and sect analyses and, by the late 1980s, scholars of the other three gospels began to combine redaction criticism's insights about community with social-scientific models (Esler: "socio-redaction criticism"). These new explorations turned to methods and matters such as macrosocial analysis of advanced agrarian societies or peasant societies, sect analysis of new religious movements, labeling and deviance theory, the honor/shame model, ancient economics, health care systems, patron and client relations, gender analysis, ritual theory, linguistic theory, small group theory, marginality theory, and eventually social memory studies, social identity theory, ethnicity theory, and empire theory.

Chapter 2 turns from the general renewal of social-scientific interest among New Testament scholars to social-historical and social-scientific work on the Gospel of Matthew in particular, work that began to appear in the late 1980s. In 1988 Amy-Jill Levine, although not a social-scientific critic, argued that when Jesus shifted the disciples' mission from "the lost sheep of the house of Israel" (Matt 10:5–6; cf. 15:24) to all peoples (Matt 28:19), it was not an *ethnic* shift from particularism to universalism as such, but an *ethical* shift from care of marginal people in Israel (10:6) to all "marginal" people (Matt 28:19). That same year Bruce Malina and Jerome Neyrey produced the first social-scientific analysis of a gospel, namely, an interpretation of the charge that Jesus exorcized demons by Beelzeboul, the Prince of Demons (a "witchcraft accusation"), as an example of labeling theory, that is, Jesus was being labeled as a social deviant, a perspective that also proved useful for interpreting the Matthean trial narrative. The following year four papers produced for a social history conference on Matthew in Dallas, Texas (published in 1991), also emphasized social-scientific theories: revitalization movements and sect/cult theory (Rodney Stark); sect and deviance theory (Anthony Saldarini; Michael White); and agrarian macrosociological models, preindustrial city life, and a Chinese "scribal community" model (Antoinette Wire). Meanwhile, in 1990 Andrew Overman and Graham Stanton analyzed the Matthean community as a Judean sect, for Stanton *separated from* Israel, for Saldarini *within* Israel, the latter considered to be a "deviant voluntary association/sect." Warren Carter then interpreted the gospel with the help of some of my reflection on social stratification and marginality (along with Jung Young Lee's). He concluded (as did I) that the gospel writer legitimated a marginal way of life in the sense of living between two competing worlds (the "in betweenness" of the "Marginal Man"). Meanwhile, Jerome Neyrey again used an "honor and shame" model to interpret the ancient Greco-Roman rhetoric "praise and blame" and the man of honor in Matthew. Evert-Jan Vledder then interpreted details of the Matthean miracle stories against the backdrop of Ralf Dahrendorf's social conflict theory and my Lenski-based analysis of an advanced agrarian society in the Gospel of Matthew. Stuart Love showed how the Matthean writer resisted assimilating Jesus' teaching to the hierarchical social and gender norms of Mediterranean society. Chapter 2 closes with addenda defending social-scientific criticism against the critiques of ahistorical literary criticism and monochromatic views of Mediterranean anthropology attributed to the Context Group.

Chapter 3 discusses social-scientific theories and models as a way to illustrate social-scientific method and to create a bridge to subsequent chapters. These theories and models include the advanced agrarian society macrosocial model by the Lenskis; hierarchical Roman orders by Geza Alföldy; the analysis of aristocratic empires by John Kautsky; models of Roman imperial expansion by Michael Doyle and Alexander Motyl; a model of the ancient city by Gideon and Andrée Sjøberg; the study of peasant society by James C. Scott; theories of peasant rebellion studied by Stephen Dyson; the model of millennial movements; and several theories and models of small groups.

Chapters 4–10 are specific studies of the gospel that attempt to use these and other theories and models, along with redaction criticism, to interpret the Gospel of Matthew. Chapter 4 shows that all the prerequisites of the ruler—power, privilege, prestige—in Lenski's "advanced agrarian society" model are met in Matthew by his view of the birth and lineage accounts of Jesus as the Son of David. However, ultimately a Son of David's "ascribed" royal honor recedes behind a Son of David's "acquired" honor, that is, a challenge/response model helps illustrate how Jesus acquires honor by defeating his opponents, especially the Pharisees, in debate, raising the question "in what sense is Jesus the Son of David?" The plurisignificance of the title suggests that although the birth/descent honor ascribed to Jesus is important, of much greater significance is the Son of David who, unlike the Pharisees (retainers of the upper strata), sheds Temple purity demands and, more importantly, acts as a merciful, compassionate healer of the poor and lowly, climaxed by the children's acclamation in the Jerusalem Temple. Moreover, as redaction critics know, the Son of David's conflict with the Pharisees is transparent for the Matthean writer and his community's own conflicts with the Yavneh Pharisees in the post–70 CE period.

Chapter 5 takes up a concept that was becoming popular in early 1990s biblical research, namely, "marginality." Since at that time there was no social-scientific analysis of the concept in New Testament study, I brought forward three social-scientific theories: 1) Robert Park and E. V. Stonequist's "Marginal Man," that is, a person who because of circumstances (migration, for example) must live between two (or more) competing cultures (languages, political loyalties, moral codes, religions, etc.) without fully belonging to either (or any); 2) "involuntary marginality," referring to those who are at the bottom of the social hierarchy (one sense of "the margins"), but, according to marginality theorist Gino Germani, can also include individuals and groups at *any* social level who do not participate in their expected social roles; and 3) "voluntary marginality," drawn from Victor Turner's notion of "voluntary outsiderhood," or ideological *communitas*, that is, a "liminal" group that *chooses* to separate itself from normative statuses, roles, and offices in a utopian community. I suggested that analyses of Matthean terms demonstrate the pervasiveness of involuntary marginals (coordinated with Lenski's retainers, artisans, peasants, expendable persons, and the unclean) and Jesus' concern to teach and heal them. This approach also sheds light on the ideological ambiguity of the writer, that is, his "in betweenness." Even though he is a literate scribe who *freely* associated with a Jesus messianic group, and so is a "voluntary marginal," at the same time he is like a "Marginal Man" who is "caught" between two (or more) cultures—for example, Judean and Greco-Roman culture, Semitic and Greek languages, elite and non-elite, literate scribes and illiterate peasants, men and women, emergent and growing normative Pharisaism and his Jesus group. In general he is between "the old" and "the new" (Matt 13:52).

There are also tensions and ambiguities in the gospel about leadership, the subject of chapter 6. This issue can be explored in relation to social-scientific models of small groups and small group leadership, such as "factions" within the larger Matthean group(s) and whether the ideology represented in the gospel is, as often discussed in New Testament studies, "egalitarian." Matthew 23:8–10 is a key text. It prohibits the followers of Jesus, who are called "brothers," from using titles of honor for leaders ("Rabbi," "Father," "Tutor") known to have been in use among the Pharisees. Again, was this prohibition "egalitarian," which would fit a "composite autonomous group" model in which group tasks are performed equally by all group members? With vertical social stratification as the cultural norm again, as well as passages that subordinate women and Gentile outsiders, indeed even the poor, the gospel at best contains a "*limited* egalitarianism" ideology. Yet, even that is in tension with what seem to be emergent roles suggested by the terms "prophet," "scribe," "righteous (one)," "teacher," "sage," "apostle," and perhaps "little ones," as well as by the appointment of itinerant missionaries and the ascription of honor to Simon, the "Rock." These passages point to a stage of group development that, using Bruce Tuckman's model, goes beyond "forming," "storming," and "norming" to at least "performing" (but not yet "adjourning"). Another model, Aubrey Fisher and Donald Ellis's "leaderless groups," shows that there is a struggle between factions in the Matthean community and corresponding leaders are developing. In short, Matthew's text portrays movement beyond a loose-knit "coalition." It indicates a movement *toward* an institutional "corporation." Even the author's limited egalitarian ideology is in tension with evolving group factions and leaders.

Chapter 7 addresses the importance of the term "brothers" mentioned in Matt 23:8–10 for Matthean group members and raises the possibility that the Matthean community might be considered a brotherhood or "voluntary association" (or associations) that can be further illumined by a model of "fictive kinship." Among the Matthean leadership roles, "scribe" is second (twenty-two times, sixteen most likely redactional) only to "prophet" (thirty-seven times). Since scribes in the gospel are *sometimes* seen positively, it is plausible that the Matthean writer, most likely an urban scribe—educated, literate, sophisticated, and steeped in apocalyptic/millennial ideas, like

Ben Sira's "understanding scribe"—was a scribe-leader. Antoinette Wire offers insight with her suggestion that a Chinese "scribal community" that preserves a revered literary tradition, teaches ritual and ethical behavior, and tries to maintain set roles in the community, with rewards and punishments, is an analogous model for comparison. Although the gospel at times discourages set roles and frequently mentions those of low social status (involuntary marginals), I suggested (building on marginality theory in chapter 5) that Matthew's scribes were "marginal scribes," although by choice, and that they led a community that included "involuntary marginals." This conclusion helps explain the Matthean writer's ideological apologetic stance vis-à-vis the Pharisees, *their* scribes, and *their* titles of honor, yet praise the scribal role within the brotherhood.

Chapter 8 addresses the possibility that the Matthean community (*ekklēsia*) was, as Saldarini suggested, a voluntary association. Building on chapter 7 my focus shifts to leadership roles and factional disputes in the association, with a special emphasis on a passage that describes a three-step process designed to resolve disputes between "brothers." In Matt 18:15-17 1) the offended brother is to "reprove" the offending brother alone; 2) if he does not "listen," the offended brother "reproves" the offending brother in the presence of witnesses; 3) and if he still does not listen, the "offender" is treated as a Gentile and a tax collector, that is, presumably, banished. This quasi-judicial process is not an innovation. In Greco-Roman literature "reproof" is a common value and, similarly, "frank speech" is used to correct disciples, advance moral development among friends, and develop virtue. Even more important, there is a long, documentable Israelite tradition based on Lev 19:17 in which an offended brother/neighbor must "reprove" an offending brother/neighbor lest anger simmer in his heart and lead to further conflict. This tradition, found elsewhere in the New Testament, became an explicit forensic rule in the Dead Sea Scrolls, which is "close comparison" material for Matthew. Matthew 18:15-17 is less formally explicit, but it surely represents some sort of legal procedure for conflict resolution. Although the three-step process implies strong group boundaries—banning ratified by "binding and loosing" (18:18-20)—it is softened by being set within a literary context of unbounded merciful love and forgiveness ("seventy times seven"), with parallels in the rabbinic literature. In short, the author perpetuates a conflict-resolution "reproof process," but attempts to check its assimilation to normatively strict legal practice by locating it in a context of mercy and forgiveness presumably inherited from Jesus.

Chapter 9 reinforces the idea that there are scribal leaders in the Matthean community (or communities), including the writer himself, with five neutral or pro-scribe passages. However, there are different types of ancient scribes and ranking them for a particular community is not easy. The Greek term *grammateus* ("scribe") can refer to lower status village scribes such as Menches in Egypt, or scribes of voluntary associations, or simply public and private secretaries. Hebrew *sopherim* among the rabbis sometimes refers to elementary school teachers. On a Lenski political-economic power, privilege, and prestige model (a higher level of abstraction), scribes are "retainers" of the elite, which in general corresponds to the Greek term *grammateus* when it refers to royal scribes and bureaucrats. However, if one adds ranking variables such as "education," scribes are higher because of their literacy power. I follow those who claim that in Judean passages they can be honored as learned Torah scholars, such as one finds in the description of Ben Sira's "ideal scribe."

What kind of scribe wrote the Gospel of Matthew? Certainly, he was more advanced than a village scribe or a secretary. Had he ever been someone like a "royal scribe," for example, a retainer of the Herodian or some other court? Had he been a scribe among the dominant Pharisees? Possibly, but the gospel compared to Judean sources suggests that he came closest to the Torah scholar ideal and, as such, had literacy power, all the more so in his mixed community. If so, he wrote a story that others (village scribes?) would have read or recited to early listeners who were mostly illiterate involuntary marginals. His many admonitions about right hearing and understanding take on something like performance connotations, and the comment "Let *the reader* understand" taken from the Gospel of Mark fits a context of public reading, perhaps in house churches in a particular region, as Stanton suggested.

The idea was advanced in chapter 5 that the Matthean writer can be understood with concepts such as "Marginal Man," "voluntary marginality," and "involuntary marginality." In chapter 9 I attempt to refine this language/conceptuality with more social-scientific analyses:

A Marginal Scribe

"Marginal Man"	= "cultural marginality"
"involuntary marginality"	= "structural marginality" (at or near the bottom of the social hierarchy), and/or
	= "social role marginality" (does not fulfill expected social roles)
"voluntary marginality"	= "ideological marginality" (chosen alternative ideology)

Using these social-scientific concepts, I suggest that ambiguities and tensions in the gospel point to a writer who is *culturally marginal*, who perhaps also experienced *social role marginality*, but also voluntarily affiliated with a group that *ideologically* believed that Jesus was the Messiah, most of whose members were *structurally marginal*. I attempt to expand on the analysis of chapter 5 with several social-psychological analyses.

In chapter 10, I suggest that the "in betweenness" of a culturally marginal writer suggests looking more closely at the question of his ethnicity within a larger context. David Sim hypothesized that the Matthean community was still admitting "Jews," and was therefore ethnically "Jewish." John Riches, however, noted the gospel's favorable remarks about Gentiles, the lack of interest in kinship (except for Jesus' genealogy), and the negation of attachment to homeland (and temple) by attachment to Jesus (W. D. Davies: "theology is de-territorialized"). The possibility of reading the Gospel of Matthew with virtually opposite ideas about ethnicity is suggestive for the hypothesis that the writer is "in between," or culturally marginal, as discussed in earlier chapters. It also forces further reflection about ethnicity in the gospel. Fredrik Barth's "Constructionism" emphasized that the "features" of ethnic identity (language, customs, etc.) are less significant than the fact that ethnic groups continually *reconstruct* their ethnicity: ethnicity is not fixed or "primordial." However, Barth recognized the impossibility of totally dispensing with ethnic features. Thus, it is possible in my view to develop a model that includes the critical importance of Constructionism (Barth later held that it was "postmodern"), yet continue to emphasize common features. The model stresses name, myths of common ancestry, shared "historical" memories, phenotypical description, homeland, language, kinship, customs (dress, food, and the like), and religion. While the term *ethnos* in ancient Greek can mean almost any kind of group, a survey of the terms *ethnos/ethnē* show that there is an increasing tendency in Judean literature to use it negatively for outsiders and that the ancients referred to the features of the ethnicity model. Comparing them to gospel usage helps yield some indication of the Matthean writer's (and his community's) understanding of ethnicity. Gospel references to *ethnē* point to the ever-present outsider/insider ambiguity in the gospel, especially in conflicting passages about Gentiles. This is not surprising, given the writer's cultural marginality.

Finally, the much debated fruit-bearing *ethnos* in Matthew 21, which is opposed to the Pharisees and especially the priestly authorities, may refer to a group of leaders within the Matthean community, especially since the term *ethnos* can refer to ancient *priestly* associations, with whom the writer linked the Pharisees. If so, it pits one *ethnos* association of leaders against another.

In conclusion, it has sometimes been claimed that ancient documents cannot reveal the social contexts in which their writers wrote them. I have not accepted this view, but have maintained that with the aid of social-scientific theory and heuristic modeling one can at times see social realities of a writer and his community that might otherwise have been missed. Not all theories and models can be used with all passages, of course, but at the same time it is not always necessary to limit oneself to a single model. Choices must be made. Moreover, the interpretative quest here is not for absolute truth, but heuristic understanding and explanation. Of the social-scientific theories and models advanced in chapters 3–10, those that hold together these studies most are the social hierarchical models of the Roman Empire, small group theory, and marginality theory. Marginality must be correlated with small groups in an advanced agrarian society as a way of looking at the writer of the gospel as he relates to his community, its factions, its ethnicity, and its leadership. Thus, the book is titled *A Marginal Scribe*.

Permissions

THE AUTHOR AND PUBLISHER wish to express their appreciation to the following journals and publishers for their permission to republish the following articles and essays in revised form.

Chapter 3: "Empire: Theories, Methods, Models." In *The Gospel of Matthew in Its Roman Imperial Context*, edited by John Riches and David C. Sim, 49–74. London: T. & T. Clark, 2005. From Continuum International Publishing Group (T. & T. Clark).

Chapters 4: "Matthew's Plurisignificant 'Son of David' in Social Science Perspective: Kinship, Kingship, Magic, and Miracle." *Biblical Theology Bulletin* 22/3 (1992) 99–116.

Chapters 5: "Matthew and Marginality." *Hervormde Teologiese Studies* 51/1 (1995) 1–30.

Chapter 6: "Egalitarian Ideology, Leadership, and Factional Conflict within the Matthean Group." *Biblical Theology Bulletin* 27 (1997) 124–37.

Chapter 7: "The Matthean Brotherhood and Marginal Scribal Leadership." In *Modelling Early Christianity*, edited by Philip F. Esler, 159–82. London: Routledge, 1995.

Chapter 8: "Matthew 18:15–17: Conflict, Confrontation, and Conflict Resolution in a 'Fictive' Kin Association." *Biblical Theology Bulletin* 29/1 (1999) 4–22.

Chapter 9: "Matthew as a Marginal Scribe in an Advanced Agrarian Society." *Hervormde Teologiese Studies* 58/2 (2002) 520–75.

Chapter 10: "Ethnicity, Ethnocentrism, and the Matthean *Ethnos*." *Biblical Theology Bulletin* 35/4 (2005) 125–43.

Bibliography

Aberle, D. "A Note on Relative Deprivation Theory as Applied to Millenarian and Other Cult Movements." In *Millennial Dreams in Action: Studies in Revolutionary Religious Movements*, edited by Sylvia Thrupp, 537-41. New York: Schocken, 1970.

Abrams, Philip. *Historical Sociology*. Ithaca: Cornell University Press, 1983.

Ackroyd, P. R., and C. F. Evans. *The Cambridge History of the Bible*. Vol. 1. Cambridge: Cambridge University Press, 1970.

Adams, Robert M. "Review of *The Preindustrial City Past and Present*." *AA* 63 (1961) 1105-1107.

Agnew, Francis H. "The Origin of the NT Apostle-Concept: A Review of Research." *JBL* 105 (1986) 75-96.

AHR Forum (2006). No pages; paragraphs numbered. Online: www.historycooperative.org/journals/ahr/111.3/horden.html#REF2.

Albera, Dionigi. "The Mediterranean as an Anthropological Laboratory." *AFJC* 16 (1999) 215-32. Sección de Antrolopogía Social, PDF.

———. "Anthropology of the Mediterranean: Between Crisis and Renewal." *HistAnth* 17 (2006) 109-33.

Albera, Dionigi, Anton Blok, and Christian Bromberger, editors. *L'anthropologie de la Méditerranée*. Maison méditerranéenne des sciences de l'homme. Paris: Maisonneuve & Larose, 2001.

Alföldy, Geza. *Die römische Gesellschaft*. 3rd ed. Wiesbaden: Steiner, 1984.

———. *The Social History of Rome*. Translated by D. Braund and F. Pollock; Totowa, NJ: Barnes & Noble, 1985.

Allison, Dale C. *The New Moses: A Matthean Typology*. Minneapolis: Fortress, 1993.

———. *Jesus of Nazareth: Millenarian Prophet*. Minneapolis: Fortress, 1998.

Anderson, Janice Capel. "Matthew: Gender and Reading." In *The Bible and Feminist Hermeneutics*, edited by Mary Ann Tolbert, *Semeia* 28: 3-27. Chico, CA: Scholars, 1983.

———. "Mary's Difference: Gender and Patriarchy in the Birth Narratives." *JR* 67 (1987) 183-202.

———. *Matthew's Narrative Web: Over and Over, and Over Again*. JSNTSup 91. Sheffield, UK: JSOT Press, 1994.

———. "Life on the Mississippi: New Currents in Matthean Scholarship, 1983-93." *CurBS* 3 (1995) 169-218.

———. "Response to Donald Senior's 'Directions in Matthean Studies.'" Matthew Group, Society of Biblical Literature, Orlando, Florida, 1998.

Anonymous. "Aims and Scope" of *HistAnth*, 2010. No pages. Online: www.tandf.co.uk/journals/titles/02757206.asp.

Antonovsky, Aaron. "Toward a Refinement of the 'Marginal Man' Concept." *SocForces* 35 (1956) 57–62.
Applebaum, Shimon. "The Organization of the Jewish Communities in the Diaspora." In *The Jewish People in the First Century*, edited by S. Safrai and M. Stern, Vol. 1, 464–503. 2 vols. Assen, Netherlands: Van Gorcum, 1974.
Arlandson, James Malcomb. *Women, Class, and Society: Models from Luke–Acts*. Peabody, MA: Hendrickson, 1997.
Arnal, William E. "The Rhetoric of Marginality: Apocalypticism, Gnosticism, and Sayings Gospels." *HTR* 4 (1995) 471–94.
———. "Gendered Couplets in Q and Legal Formulations: From Rhetoric to Social History." *JBL* 116 (1997) 75–94.
———. *Jesus and the Village Scribes: Galilean Conflicts and the Setting of Q*. Minneapolis: Fortress, 2001.
Arnold, Charles Harvey. *Near the Edge of Battle: A Short History of the Divinity School and the "Chicago School of Theology."* Chicago: Divinity School Association. The University of Chicago, 1966.
Ascough, Richard S. "Translocal Relationships among Voluntary Associations and Early Christianity." *JECS* 5 (1997) 223–41.
———. "Matthew and Community Formation." In *The Gospel of Matthew in Current Study. Studies in Memory of William G. Thompson*, edited by David E. Aune, 96–126. Grand Rapids: Eerdmans, 2001.
Atkins, Robert A. *Egalitarian Community: Ethnography and Exegesis*. Tuscaloosa: University of Alabama Press, 1991.
Aune, David E., editor. *The Gospel of Matthew in Current Study: Studies in Memory of William G. Thompson*. Grand Rapids: Eerdmans, 2001.
Bacon, B. W. "The 'Five Books' of Matthew Against the Jews." *Exp* 15 (1918) 56–66.
———. *Studies in Matthew*. New York: Holt, 1930.
Baird, William. *History of New Testament Research*. Vol. 2, *From Jonathan Edwards to Rudolf Bultmann*. Minneapolis: Fortress, 2003.
Baker, David W. "Scribes as Transmitters of Tradition." In *Faith, Tradition, and History: Old Testament Historiography in Its Near Eastern Context*, edited by A. R. Millard, James K. Hoffmeier, and David W. Baker, 65–77. Winona Lake, IN: Eisenbrauns, 1994.
Balch, David L. "Hellenization/Acculturation in 1 Peter." In *Perspectives on First Peter*, edited by C. H. Talbert, 79–101. NABPR Special Studies Series 9. Macon, GA: Mercer University Press, 1986.
———. *Let Wives Be Submissive: The Domestic Code in 1 Peter*. SBL Monographs 26. Chico, CA: Scholars, 1981. Reprint 1988.
———, editor. *Social History of the Matthean Community: Cross Disciplinary Approaches*. Minneapolis: Fortress, 1991.
Bambach, Charles. *Heidegger's Roots: Nietzsche, National Socialism, and the Greeks*. Ithaca, NY, and London: Cornell University Press, 2003.
Bang, Peter F., Mamoru Ikeguchi, and Hartmut G. Ziche. *Ancient Economies, Modern Methodologies: Archaeology, Comparative History, Models and Institutions*. Bari, Italy: Edipuglia, 2006.
Banks, Robert. *Paul's Idea of Community: The Early House Churches in their Historical Setting*. Grand Rapids: Eerdmans, 1980.
Barclay, J. M. G. "Paul and Philo on Circumcision: Romans 2:25–29 in Social and Cultural Context." *NTS* 44 (1998) 536–56.

Bardtke, Hans. "Der gegenwätige Stand der Erforschung der in Palästina neu gefundenen hebräischen Handschriften, 44: Die Rechtsstellung der Qumran-Gemeinde." *TLZ* 86 (1961) 93–104.
Bar-Ilan, M. "Part Two: Scribes and Book in the Late Second Commonwealth and Rabbinic Period." Pp. 21–37 in *Mikra*. Edited by J. J. Mulder; Ex. edited by H. Sysling. Philadelphia: Fortress, 1988.
Barnet, John A. *Not the Righteous but Sinners: M. M. Bakhtin's Theory of Aesthetics and the Problem of Reader—Character Interaction in Matthew's Gospel*. JSNT Sup. 246. London: T. & T. Clark International, 2003.
Barnett, Bernice McNair. "Introduction: The Life, Career, and Social Thought of Gerhard Lenski—Scholar, Teacher, Mentor, Leader." *SociolTheor* 22 (2004) 163–93.
Baron, Salo Wittmayer. *A Social and Religious History of the Jews. I, To the Beginning of the Christian Era; II, Christian Era—The first Five Centuries*. 2nd ed. New York: Columbia University Press, 1952.
Bartchy, S. Scott. "Servant, slave," and "Slavery." In *ISBE* 4 (1988) 419–21, 539–46.
———. "Slavery (Greco-Roman)." In *ABD* 6 (1992) 65–73.
Barth, Frederik. *Ethnic Groups and Boundaries: The Social Organization of Cultural Difference*. Boston: Little, Brown, 1969. Reprint 1998.
———. "Enduring and Emerging Issues in the Analysis of Ethnicity." In *The Anthropology of Ethnicity: Beyond "Ethnic Groups and Boundaries,"* edited by H. Vermeulen and C. Govers, 11–32. Amsterdam: Het Spinhuis, 1994.
Barthes, Roland. *S/Z*. Translated by Richard Miller. New York: Hill & Want, 1974.
Bauckham, Richard J. *The Gospel for all Christians: Rethinking Gospel Audiences*. Edinburgh: T. & T. Clark, 1997; Grand Rapids, Michigan: Eerdmans, 1997.
Bauer, David R., and Mark Allan Powell, editors. *Treasures New and Old: Recent Contributions to Matthean Studies*. SBL Symposium Series. Atlanta: Scholars, 1996.
Baumgarten, Albert I. *The Flourishing of Jewish Sects in the Maccabean Era: An Interpretation*. JSJSup 55. Leiden: Brill, 1997.
Baur, F. C. "Die Christuspartei in der korinthischen Gemeinde, der Gegensatz des petrinischen und paulinischen Christenthums in der ältesten Kirche, der Apostle Petrus in Rom." *TZT* 4 (1831) 61–206.
Beardslee, William. *Literary Criticism of the New Testament*. Guides to Biblical Scholarship. Philadelphia: Fortress, 1970.
Beavis, Mary Ann. *Mark's Audience: The Literary and Social Setting of Mark 4.11–12*. Mahwah, NJ: Paulist, 1989.
Becker, Howard S. *Outsiders: Studies in the Sociology of Deviance*. New York: Macmillan, 1963.
Bellah, Robert N. "Durkheim and History." *ASR* 24 (1959) 447–61.
———. "Max Weber and World-Denying Love: A Look at the Historical Sociology of Religion." *JAAR* 67 (1999) 277–304.
Belo, Fernando. *A Materialist Reading of the Gospel of Mark*. Translated by Matthew J. O'Connell. Maryknoll, NY: Orbis, 1981.
Bendix, Reinhard. *Kings or People: Power and the Mandate to Rule*. Berkeley: University of California Press, 1978.
Ben-Yehuda, Nahman. *Deviance and Moral Boundaries: Witchcraft, the Occult, Deviant Sciences and Scientists*. Chicago: University of Chicago Press, 1985.
Berger, Klaus. "Die königlichen Messiastradition des Neuen Testaments." *NTS* 20 (1973) 1–44.

———. *Exegese des Neuen Testaments: Neue Wege vom Text zur Auslegung.* 3rd ed. Heidelberg: Quelle & Meyer, 1991.

———. "Wissenssoziologie und Exegese des Neuen Testaments." *Kairos* 19 (1977) 124–33.

Berger, Peter L., and Thomas Luckmann. *The Social Construction of Reality: A Treatise its the Sociology of Knowledge.* Garden City, NY: Anchor, 1966.

Berry, John W. "Psychology of Acculturation." In *Nebraska Symposium on Motivation, 1989, Volume 37: Cross Cultural Perspectives,* edited by John J. Berman, 201–34. Lincoln: University of Nebraska Press, 1990.

———. "Lead Article: Immigration, Acculturation, and Adaptation." *AppPsych* 46 (1997) 5–68.

Berry, John W., and P. R. Dasen. "Introduction: History and Method in the Cross-Cultural Study of Cognition." In *Culture and Cognition: Readings in Cross-Cultural Psychology,* edited by J. W. Berry and P. R. Dasen, 1–20. London: Methuen, 1974.

Best, T. F. "The Sociological Study of the New Testament: Promise and Peril of a New Discipline." *SJT* 36 (1983) 190–194.

Betz, Hans Dieter. "Apostle." In *ABD* 1 (1992) 309–11.

———. "Jesus and the Cynics: Survey and Analysis of a Hypothesis." *JR* 74 (1994) 453–475.

———. *The Sermon on the Mount.* Hermeneia. Minneapolis: Fortress, 1995.

Bickerman, Elias. *The Jews in the Greek Age.* Cambridge: Harvard University Press, 1988.

Billerbeck, Paul (and Hermann L. Strack). *Kommentar zum Neuen Testament aus Talmud und Midrasch I: Das Evangelium Nach Matthäus.* Munich: Beck, 1926.

Billson, J. M. "No Owner Soil: The Concept of Marginality Revisited on its Sixtieth Birthday." *IRMS* 18 (1988) 183–204.

Birx, H. James. "Human Variation, Adaptation, and Ecology." In *Human Evolution,* edited by James H. Birx, 241–48. Springfield, IL: Thomas, 1988.

Blasi, Anthony J. *Early Christianity as a Social Movement.* New York: Peter Lang, 1988.

———. *Making Charisma: The Social Construction of Paul's Public Image.* New Brunswick, NJ: Transaction, 1991.

———. "Biblical Studies." In *Encyclopedia of Religion and Society,* edited by William H. Swatos, Jr., 55–58. Walnut Creek, CA: AltaMira, 1998.

———, Jean Duhaime, and Paul-André Turcotte. *Handbook of Early Christianity: Social Science Approaches.* Walnut Creek, CA: AltaMira, 2002.

Blenkinsopp, Joseph. "Interpretation and Sectarian Tendencies: An Aspect of Second Temple History." In *Jewish and Christian Self-Definition,* edited by E. P. Sanders, 2:1–26. Philadelphia: Fortress, 1981.

Boas, Franz. *Race, Language, and Culture.* Chicago: University of Chicago Press, 1940.

Boer, Roland. "Twenty-Five Years of Marxist Biblical Criticism." *CBR* 5/3 (2007) 298–321.

———. "On Christian Communism: The Legacy of Engels, Luxemburg, and Kautsky." *Arena Journal* 31 (2008) 63–78.

Bohannan, Paul, and Mark Glazer. *High Points in Anthropology.* 2nd ed. New York: McGraw-Hill, 1988.

Boissevain, Jeremy. "The Place of Non-groups in the Social Sciences." *Man* 3 (1968) 542–56.

———. *Friends of Friends: Networks, Manipulators and Coalitions*. Pavilion Series. Oxford: Blackwell; New York: St. Martin's, 1974.
———. "Towards as Social Anthropology of the Mediterranean." *CA* 20/1 (1979) 81–93.
Booth, Wayne C. *The Rhetoric of Fiction*. Chicago: University of Chicago Press, 1961.
———. "Where is the Authorial Audience in Biblical Narrative in other Authoritative Texts?" *Narr* 4/3 (1996) 235–53.
Borgen, P. *Philo, John and Paul: New Perspectives on Judaism and Early Christianity*. BJS 131. Atlanta: Scholars, 1987.
Bornkamm, Günther. "End-Expectation and Church in Matthew." In *Tradition and Interpretation in Matthew* by G. Bornkamm, G. Barth, and H. J. Held, 15–57. Translated by P. Scott. Philadelphia: Westminster, 1963.
———. "The Stilling of the Storm in Matthew." In *Tradition and Interpretation in Matthew* by G. Bornkamm, G. Barth, and H. J. Held, 52–57. Translated by P. Scott. Philadelphia: Westminster, 1963.
———. "The Authority to 'Bind' and 'Loose' in the Church in Matthew's Gospel: The Problem of Sources in the Gospel." In *Jesus and Man's Hope*, Perspective Book 1, 37–50. Pittsburgh: Pittsburgh Theological Seminary, 1970.
Bottomore, Tom B. *Elites and Society*. 2nd ed. New York: Routledge, 1993.
Bowman, A. K., and G. Woolf, editors. *Literacy and Power in the Ancient World*. Cambridge: Cambridge University Press, 1994.
Boyarin, Daniel A. *Radical Jew: Paul and the Politics of Identity*. Berkeley: University of California Press, 1994.
Brandon, S.G.F. *Jesus and the Zealots: A Study of the Political Factor in Primitive Christianity*. New York: Scribner, 1967.
Braudel, Fernand. *The Mediterranean and the Mediterranean World in the Age of Philip II*, Vol. 1. Translated by Richard Mayne. Berkeley: University of California Press, 1996. Original French 1949.
Braund, David. *Rome and the Friendly King: The Character of Client Kinship*. New York: St. Martin's, 1984.
Brett, Mark G., editor. *Ethnicity and the Bible*. Biblical Interpretation Series 19. Leiden: Brill, 1996.
Bromberger, Christian. "Towards an Anthropology of the Mediterranean." *HistAnth* 17/2 (2006) 91–107.
Brooks, Stephenson H. *Matthew's Community: The Evidence of His Special Sayings Source*. JSNTSup 16. Sheffield, UK: JSOT Press, 1987.
Broughton, T. R. S. "Part IV: Roman Asia." In *An Economic Survey of Ancient Rome*, edited by Tenney Frank, 499–916. 4 vols. Baltimore: Johns Hopkins Press, 1938.
Brown, Peter. "Sorcery, Demons, and the Rise of Christianity from Late Antiquity into the Middle Ages." In *Witchcraft, Confessions, and Accusations*, edited by Mary Douglas, 17–45. London: Tavistock, 1970.
———. "The Rise and Function of the Holy Man in Late Antiquity." *JRS* 61 (1971) 80–101.
———. *The World of Late Antiquity: AD 150–750*. New York: Harcourt, Brace, Jovanovich, 1971.
Brown, Raymond E. *The Birth of the Messiah*. Garden City, NY: Doubleday, 1977.
———, and John P. Meier. *Antioch and Rome. New Testament Cradles of Catholic Christianity*. New York: Paulist, 1983.

Brown, Schyler. "The Matthean Community and the Gentile Mission." *NovT* 22 (1980) 193–221.
Büchler, A. *"Elenchō*, etc." In *TDNT* 2 (1963) 473–76.
Buell, D. K. "Ethnicity and Religion in Mediterranean Antiquity and Beyond." *RSR* 26 (2000) 243–49.
Bultmann, Rudolf. *History of the Synoptic Tradition*. Translated by John Marsh. New York: Harper & Row, 1963.
———. *Jesus and the Word*. Translated by L. P. Smith and E. H. Lantero. London: Collins, 1952.
Burger, Christoph. *Jesus als Davidssohn. Eine traditionsgeschichtliche Untersuchung*. Göttingen: Vandenhoeck & Ruprecht, 1970.
Burke, Peter. *Sociology and History*. Controversies in Sociology 10. London: George Allen and Unwin, 1980. See Burke, *History and Social Theory*.
———. *The French Historical Revolution: The Annales School, 1929–1989*. Cambridge: Polity Press, 1990.
———. *History and Social Theory*. 2nd edition of *Sociology and History*. Ithaca, NY: Cornell University Press, 1993. See *Sociology and History*.
Burnett, F. W. "Historiography." Pp. 106–12 in A. K. M. Adam, editor, *Handbook of Postmodern Biblical Interpretation*. St. Louis: Chalice, 2000.
Burridge, Kenelm. *New Heaven, New Earth*. New York: Schocken, 1969.
Bushnell, Thomas. Translation of *Res Gestae Divi Augusti*. No pages. Online: classics.mit.edu/Augustus/deeds.html.
Cadaux, C. J. *The Early Church and the World*. Edinburgh: T. & T. Clark, 1925.
Carmody, Timothy R. "Matt 18:15–17 in Relation to Three Texts from Qumran Literature (CD 9: 2–8, 16–22; 1QS 5: 25–6: 1)." In *To Touch the Text: Biblical and Related Studies in Honor of Joseph A. Fitzmyer, SJ*, edited by Maurya P. Horgan and Paul J. Kobelski, 141–58. New York: Crossroad, 1989.
Carney, T. F. *The Shape of the Past: Models and Antiquity*. Lawrence, KS: Coronado, 1975.
Carter, Warren. *Households and Discipleship: A Study of Matthew 19–20*. JSNTSup 103. Sheffield, UK: Sheffield University Press, 1994.
———. *Matthew: Storyteller, Interpreter, Evangelist*. Peabody, MA: Hendrickson, 1996.
———. "Matthew 4:18–22 and Matthean Discipleship: An Audience-Oriented Perspective." *CBQ* 59 (1997) 58–75.
———. "Matthew and the Margins." Paper delivered at the 1997 Catholic Biblical Association. University of Seattle. Seattle, WA, 1997.
———. *Matthew and the Margins: A Sociopolitical and Religious Reading*. Maryknoll, NY: Orbis, 2000.
———. *Matthew and Empire: Initial Explorations*. Harrisburg: Trinity Press International, 2001.
Case, Shirley Jackson. *The Evolution of Early Christianity*. Chicago: University of Chicago Press, 1914.
———. "The Historical Study of Religion." *JR* 1 (1921) 1–17.
———. *The Social Origins of Christianity*. Chicago: University of Chicago Press, 1923. Greenwood Press Reprint, 1970.
———. *Jesus: A New Biography*. Chicago: University of Chicago Press, 1927.
———. *The Social Triumph of the Christian Church*. New York: Harper & Row, 1933.
Catchpole, David. "Reproof and Reconciliation in the Q Community: A Study of the Tradition-history of Mt 18,15–17.21–22/Lk 17,3–4." *SNTSU* 8 (1983) 83–84.

Caulkins, R. Douglas. "Voluntary Associations." In *ECA*, Vol. 1, edited by David Levinson and Melvin Ember, 1351–56. New York: Holt, 1996.
Chaney, Marvin. "Systematic Study of the Israelite Monarchy." *Social-Scientific Criticism of the New Testament and Its Social World. Semeia* 35, edited by John H. Elliott, 53–76. Decatur, GA: Scholars, 1986.
Chatman, Seymore. *Story and Discourse*. Ithaca, NY: Cornell University Press, 1978.
Chilton, Bruce. "Jesus ben David: Reflections on the *Davidssohnfrage*." *JSNT* 14 (1982) 88–112.
Christ, K. "Grundfragen der römischen Sozialstruktur." In *Studien zur antiken Sozialgeschichte. Festschrift F. Vittinghoff*, edited by W. Eck, H. Galsterer, and H. Wolff, 197–228. Cologne: Bohlein, 1980.
Cohen, Shaye J. D. "Epigraphical Rabbis." *JQR* 72 (1981) 1–17.
———. "The Significance of Yavneh: Pharisees, Rabbis and the End of Jewish Sectarianism." *HUCA* 55 (1984) 27–53.
———. "The Political and Social History of the Jews in Greco-Roman Antiquity: The State of the Question." In *Early Judaism and Its Modern Interpreters*, edited by Robert A. Kraft and George W. E. Nickelsburg, 33–56. Atlanta: Scholars, 1986.
———. *From the Maccabees to the Mishnah*. Philadelphia: Westminster, 1987.
———. *The Beginnings of Jewishness: Boundaries, Varieties, Uncertainties*. Berkeley: University of California Press, 1999.
———, editor. *The Jewish Family in Antiquity*. Atlanta: Scholars, 1993.
———. "Judaism with Circumcision and 'Judaism' without 'Circumcision' in Ignatius." *HTR* 95 (2002) 395–415.
Cohn, Bernard S. "History and Anthropology: The State of Play." *CSSH* 22 (1980) 198–221. Reprinted in Cohn, *An Anthropologist among the Historians and Other Essays*. New York: Oxford University Press, 1987.
Coleman, John A. "1998 Paul Hanly Furfey Lecture: The Bible and Sociology." *SociolRelig* 60 (1999) 125–48.
Collins, John J. "A Symbol of Otherness: Circumcision and Salvation in the First Century." In *To See Ourselves as Others See Us: Christians, Jews, Others in Late Antiquity*, edited by Jacob Neusner and Ernest S. Frerichs, 163–86. Chico, CA: Scholars, 1985.
———. *Between Athens and Jerusalem: Jewish Identity in the Hellenistic Diaspora*. New York: Crossroad, 1986.
———. *The Apocalyptic Imagination*. New York: Crossroad, 1987.
———, Michael O. Wise, Norman Golb, and Dennis Pardee, editors. *Methods of Investigation of the Dead Sea Scrolls and the Khirbet Qumran Site: Present Realities and Future Prospects*. Annals of the New York Academy of Sciences 722. New York: New York Academy of Sciences, 1994.
Comte, Auguste. *Course of Positive Philosophy*. 6 Vols. Translated by Harriet Martineau. London: Bell, 1896.
Condorcet, Marie Jean Antoine Nicolas de Caritat, marquis de. *Sketch for a Historical Picture of the Progress of the Human Mind*. Translated by June Barraclough. London: Weidenfeld & Nicolson, 1955.
Cook, Michael J. *Mark's Treatment of the Jewish Leaders*. Leiden: Brill, 1978.
Cooley, Charles H. *Social Organization*. Glencoe, IL: Free Press, 1956. Reprint of 1909.
Coote, Robert B., and Keith W. Whitelam. "The Emergence of Israel: Social Formation and State Formation Following the Decline in Late Bronze Age Trade." In *Social Scientific Criticism of the Hebrew Bible and Its Social World: The Israelite*

Monarchy, *Semeia* 37, edited by Norman K. Gottwald, 107–47. Dacatur, GA: Scholars, 1986.

Cope, O. Lamar. "Matthew XXV.31–46, 'The Sheep and Goats' Reinterpreted." *NovT* 11 (1969) 32–44.

———. *Matthew: A Scribe Trained for the Kingdom of Heaven*. Washington, DC: Catholic Biblical Association of America, 1976.

Corley, Cathleen E. "Jesus' Table Practice: Dining with 'Tax Collectors and Sinners,' Including Women." In *SBL 1993 Seminar Papers*, edited by Eugene H. Lovering, 444–59. Atlanta: Scholars, 1993.

———. *Private Women: Public Meals*. Peabody, MA: Hendrickson, 1993.

Coser, Louis. *The Functions of Social Conflict*. London: Free Press of Glencoe, 1956.

Cotter, Wendy. "The Collegia and Roman Law: State Restrictions on Voluntary Associations." In *Voluntary Associations in the Graeco-Roman World*, edited by John S. Kloppenborg and Stephen G. Wilson, 74–89. London: Routledge, 1996.

Craffert, Pieter F. "Relationships Between Social-Scientific, Literary, and Rhetorical Interpretation of Texts [NT]." *BTB* 26 (1996) 45–55.

———. "An Exercise in the Critical Use of Models: The 'Goodness of Fit' of Wilson's Sect Model." In *Social Scientific Models for Interpreting the Bible: Essays by the Context Group in Honor of Bruce J. Malina*, edited by John J. Pilch, 21–46. Leiden: Brill, 2001.

Cromhout, Markus. *Jesus and Identity: Reconstructing Judean Ethnicity in Q*. Matrix: The Bible in Mediterranean Context. Eugene, OR: Cascade Books, 2007.

———. *Walking in Their Sandals: A Guide to First Century Israelite Ethnic Identity*. Eugene, OR: Cascade Books, 2010.

Crook, Zeba A. "Method and Models in New Testament Interpretation: A Critical Engagement with Louise Lawrence's Literary Ethnography." *BTB* 32 (2006) 89–97.

———. "Manufacturing Orientalism, or How the Context Group Got to Abu Ghraib." Review of Crossley, *Jesus in an Age of Terror: Scholarly Projects for a New American Century*. Society of Biblical Literature, Atlanta, 2010.

Crosby, Michael H. *House of Disciples: Church, Economics, and Justice in Matthew*. Maryknoll, NY: Orbis, 1988.

Crossan, John Dominic. *In Fragments: The Aphorisms of Jesus*. San Francisco: Harper & Row, 1983.

———. *The Historical Jesus: The Life of a Mediterranean Jewish Peasant*. San Francisco: HarperCollins, 1991.

———. *The Birth of Christianity*. San Francisco, CA: Harper, 1998.

Crossley, James G. *Jesus in an Age of Terror: Scholarly Projects for a New American Century*. London: Equinox, 2008.

Cullmann, O. "Les recéntes études sur la formation de la tradition évangelique." *RHPR* 5 (1925) 459–77, 564–79.

Culpepper, Alan R. *The Johannine School: An Evaluation of the Johannine-School Hypothesis based on an Investigation of the Nature of Ancient Schools*. Missoula, MT: Scholars, 1975.

Dahrendorf, Ralf. "Toward a Theory of Social Conflict." *JCR* 2 (1958) 170–83.

———. *Class and Class Conflict in Industrial Society*. Stanford, CA: Stanford University Press, 1959.

Dalman, Gustav. *Die Worte Jesu*. 2nd edition. Leipzig: Hinrichs, 1930.

Bibliography

Danker, Frederick W. *Benefactor: Epigraphic Study of a Graeco-Roman and New Testament Semantic Field.* St. Louis: Clayton, 1982.

———. "Associations, Clubs, *Thiasoi*." In *ABD 1* (1992) 501–3.

Daube, David. *The New Testament and Rabbinic Judaism.* New York: Arno, 1973.

Davies, G. I. "Were There Schools in Ancient Israel?" In *Wisdom in Ancient Israel: Essays in Honour of J. A. Emerton*, edited by John Day, Robert P. Gordon and H. G. M. Williamson, 199–211. Cambridge: Cambridge University Press, 1995.

Davies, Philip R. "The Social World of Apocalyptic Writings." In *The World of Ancient Israel: Sociological, Anthropological, and Political Perspectives*, 251–71. Cambridge: Cambridge University Press, 1989.

———. *Sects and Scrolls: Essays on Qumran and Related Topics.* Atlanta: Scholars, 1996.

Davies, W. D. *The Setting of the Sermon on the Mount.* Cambridge: Cambridge University Press, 1964.

———. *The Territorial Dimension of Judaism: With a Symposium and Further Reflection.* Minneapolis: Fortress, 1991.

———. *The Gospel and the Land: Early Christianity and Jewish Territorial Doctrine.* Sheffield, UK: JSOT Press, 1994.

———, and Dale C. Allison. *Critical and Exegetical Commentary on the Gospel according to Matthew.* Vol. 1. Edinburgh: T. & T. Clark, 1988.

———, and Dale C. Allison. *Critical and Exegetical Commentary on the Gospel according to Matthew.* Vol. 2. Edinburgh: T. & T. Clark, 1991.

———, and Dale C. Allison. *Critical and Exegetical Commentary on the Gospel according to Matthew.* Vol. 3. Edinburgh: T. & T. Clark, 1997.

Davis, John. *People of the Mediterranean: An Essay in Comparative Social Anthropology.* London: Routledge & Kagan Paul, 1977.

Deissmann, Adolf. *Light from the Ancient East.* Translated by L. R. M. Strachan. New York: Harper & Row, 1927.

Demsky, Aaron. "Respondent to Alan J. Millard's 'An Assessment of the Evidence for Writing in Ancient Israel.'" In *Biblical Archaeology Today: Proceedings of the International Conference on Biblical Archaeology*, 349-53. Jerusalem: Israel Exploration Society, 1984.

Denzey, Nicola. "The Limits of Ethnic Categories." In *Handbook of Early Christianity*, edited by A. J. Blasi, J. Duhaime, and P.-A. Turcotte, 489–507. Walnut Creek, CA: Altamira, 2002.

Derrett, J. Duncan. "Mt 23,8–10 a Midrash on Is 54,13 and Jer 31,33–34." *Bib* 62 (1981) 379-80.

———. "Christ and Reproof (Matthew 7:1–5 and Luke 6:37–42)." *NTS* 34 (1988) 271–81.

DeSilva, David. *Despising Shame: The Social Function of the Rhetoric of Honor and Dishonor in the Epistle to the Hebrews.* SBLDS 152; Atlanta: Scholars, 1995.

Dill, Samuel. *Roman Society from Nero to Marcus Aurelius.* New York: Meridian, 1905.

Donahue, John R. "The Parable of the Sheep and Goats: A Challenge to Christian Ethics." *TS* 47 (1986) 3–31.

———. *The Gospel in Parable.* Philadelphia: Fortress, 1988.

———. "Tax Collector." In *ABD* 6 (1992):337–38.

Douglas, Mary T. *Witchcraft Confessions and Accusations.* London: Tavistock, 1970.

———. *Natural Symbols: Explorations in Cosmology.* New York: Vintage, 1973.

———, and Edmund Perry. "Anthropology and Comparative Religion." *Theology Today* 41 (1985) 410–27.
Douglas, R. C. 1992 "Matthew 18:15–17 and the Hellenistic-Roman Polis." Unpublished paper.
Downing, F. Gerald. "Cynics and Christians." *NTS* 30 (1984) 584–92.
———. *Christ and the Cynics: Jesus and Other Radical Preachers in First-Century Judaism*. JSOT Manuals 4. Sheffield, UK: JSOT Press, 1988.
———. "'Honor' among Exegetes." *CBQ* 61 (1999) 53–73.
Downs, R. M., and D. Stea, editors. *Maps In Minds*. New York: Harper & Row, 1977.
Doyle, Michael. *Empires*. Ithaca, NY: Cornell University Press, 1987.
Draper, Jonathan. "Torah and Troublesome Apostles in the *Didachē* Community." *NovT* 33 (1991) 347–72.
Drescher, Hans-Georg. *Ernst Troeltsch: His Life and Work*. Louisville: Westminster John Knox, 1993.
Duling, Dennis C. "The Promises to David and Their Entrance into Early Christianity Nailing Down a Likely Hypothesis." *NTS* 20 (1973) 55–77.
———. "Solomon, Exorcism, and the Son of David." *HTR* 68 (1975) 235–52.
———. "The Therapeutic Son of David in Matthew's Gospel." *NTS* 24 (1978) 392–410.
———. "Behold, Something is Not Greater Than Solomon Here—or Is it?" NEH Seminar Paper, Yale University, 1979.
———. *Jesus Christ through History*. San Diego: Harcourt Brace Jovanovich, 1979.
———. "The Testament of Solomon and New Testament Demonology." Eastern Great Lakes Biblical Society, April 1980, Pittsburgh, PA (unpublished).
———. *Testament of Solomon: A New Translation and Introduction*. In *The Old Testament Pseudepigrapha*. Vol. 1: *Apocalyptic Literature and Testaments*, edited by J. H. Charlesworth, 935–87. Garden City, NY: Doubleday, 1983.
———. "Matthew and the Problem of Authority: Some Preliminary Observations." *EGLBSP* 3 (1983) 59–68. Reprinted in *Explorations: Journal for Adventurous Thought* 3 (1984) 15–24; and in *New Testament Perspectives*, edited by William P. Frost, 33–42. Dayton, OH: College Press, 1984.
———. "The Legend of Solomon the Magician in Antiquity: Problems and Perspectives [Presidential Address, EGLBS]." *EGLBSP* 4 (1984) 1–22.
———. "Insights from Sociology for New Testament Christology: A Test Case [Matthew]." In *SBL 1985 Seminar Papers*, edited by Kent H. Richards, 351–68. Atlanta: Scholars, 1985.
———. "The Eleazar Miracle and Solomon's Magical Wisdom in Flavius Josephus' *Antiquitates Judaicae* 8.42." *HTR* 78 (1985) 1–25.
———. "Sociological Reflections on the Christology of the Gospel of Matthew and Its *Sitz im Leben*." *Theologisches Seminar*, Heidelberg, Germany, 1985 (unpublished).
———. "Binding and Loosing (Matt 16–19; 18:18; John 20:23)." *Forum* 3/4 (1987) 3–31.
———. "Response to E. Krentz, 'Community and Character: Matthew's Vision of the Church.'" Unpublished paper at the SBL Matthew Section, Boston, MA, 1987.
———. "Review: J. D. Kingsbury, M*atthew as Story*." *Int* 41 (1987) 187–90.
———. "The Testament of Solomon: Retrospect and Prospect." *JSP* 2 (1988) 87–112.
———. "Recent Research on the Testament of Solomon." EGLBS (SBL/AAR/ASOR), Columbus, OH. 1989 (unpublished).
———. "Against Oaths [Matt 5:33–37]." *Forum* 6/2 (1990) 1–45.

———. "'[Do not Swear] . . . by the City of the Great King' (Matthew 5:35)." *JBL* 110 (1991) 271–89.

———. "Matthew's Infancy in Social Science Perspective." Context Group, Portland, March, 1991.

———. "Review: Richard Horsley, *Sociology and the Jesus Movement*." *BTB* 21 (1991) 123–24.

———. "Kingdom of God, Kingdom of Heaven: New Testament and Early Christian Literature." In *ABD* 4 (1992) 57–58.

———. "Kingdom of God/Heaven (OT, Early Judaism, and Hellenistic Usage)." In *ABD* 4 (1992) 49–56.

———. "Matthew (Disciple)." In *ABD* 4 (1992) 618–22.

———. "Matthew's Plurisignificant 'Son of David' in Social Science Perspective: Kinship, Kingship, Magic, and Miracle." *BTB* 22 (1992) 99–116.

———. "Solomon, Testament of." In *ABD* 6 (1992) 117–19.

———. "Torah Orientation (Law-Mindedness)." In *Biblical Social Values and Their Meaning: A Handbook*, edited by John J. Pilch and Bruce J. Malina, 171–78. Peabody, MA: Hendrickson, 1993.

———. "Matthew and Marginality." In *SBL 1993 Seminar Papers*, edited by Eugene H. Lovering, Jr., 642–71. Atlanta: Scholars, 1993.

———, and Norman Perrin. *The New Testament: An Introduction*. Fort Worth: Harcourt Brace, 1993.

———. "BTB Readers Guide: Millennialism." *BTB* 24 (1994) 132–42. See "Millennialism."

———. "Matthew and Marginality." *HTS* 51 (1995) 1–30. Revision of 1993.

———. "The Matthean Brotherhood and Marginal Scribal Leadership." In *Modelling Early Christianity*, edited by Philip F. Esler, 159–82. London: Routledge, 1995.

———. "Response to Shawn Kelley: 'Cultural Anthropology, Ideology, and the Bible.'" Eastern Great Lakes Biblical Society (SBL/AAR/ASOR), Pittsburgh, PA, 1995 (unpublished).

———. "Small Groups: Social Science Research Applied to Second Testament Study." *BTB* 25 (1995) 179–93.

———. "Millennialism." In *The Social Sciences and New Testament Interpretation (SSNTI)*, edited by Richard L. Rohrbaugh, 183–205. Peabody, MA: Hendrickson, 1996. See "BTB Readers Guide: Millennialism."

———. "Social-Science Reflections on Matthew 26:47–56." EGLBS (SBL/AAR/ASOR), Columbus, OH, 1996 (unpublished).

———. "Review: *Portraits of Paul: An Archeology of Ancient Personality* by Bruce J. Malina and Jerome H. Neyrey, Peabody, MA: Hendrickson, 1996." EGLBS, Columbus, OH, 1999 (unpublished).

———. "Egalitarian Ideology, Leadership, and Factional Conflict within the Matthean Group." *BTB* 27 (1997) 124–37.

———. "Matthew 18:15–17: Conflict, Confrontation, and Conflict Resolution in a 'Fictive' Kin Association." *BTB* 29 (1999) 4–22; revised from "Matthew 18:15–17: Conflict, Confrontation, and Conflict Resolution in a 'Fictive' Kin Association." In *SBL 1998 Seminar Papers*, edited by Kent H. Richards, 253–95. Atlanta: Scholars, 1998.

———. "The Jesus Movement and Social Network Analysis (Part I: The Spatial Network)." *BTB* 29 (1999) 156–75.

---. "Dots and Lines: the Jesus Network." Eastern Great Lakes Biblical Society, Cleveland, Ohio, 2000 (unpublished Power Point presentation).

---. "The Jesus Movement and Social Network Analysis (Part II: The Social Network)." *BTB* 10 (2000) 3–14.

---. Review of Evert-Jan Vledder, *Conflict in the Miracle Stories: A Socio-Exegetical Study of Matthew 8 and 9*. *JBL* 119 (2000) 137–39.

---. "Recruitment to the Jesus Movement in Social-Scientific Perspective." In *Social Scientific Models for Interpreting the Bible: Essays by the Context Group in Honor of Bruce J. Malina*, edited by John J. Pilch, 132–75. Leiden: Brill, 2001.

---. Review of *Reconstructing the Society of Ancient Israel* (Library of Ancient Israel) by Paula McNutt. EGLBS, Wheeling, WV, 2001 (unpublished).

---. "The Jesus Movement and Network Analysis." In *The Social Setting of Jesus and the Gospels*, edited by Bruce J. Malina, Wolfgang Stegemann, and Gerd Theissen, 301–32. Minneapolis: Fortress, 2002.

---. "Die Jesusbewegung und die Networkanalyse." In *Jesus in neuen Konteksten*, edited by Wolfgang Stegemann, Bruce J. Malina, and Gerd Theissen, 134–57. Stuttgart: Kohlhammer, 2002.

---. "Matthew as a Marginal Scribe in an Advanced Agrarian Society." *HTS* 58 (2002) 520–75.

---. "'Whatever Gain I Had . . .': Ethnicity and Paul's Self-Identification in Philippians 3:3–5." In *Fabrics of Discourse: Essays in Honor of Vernon K. Robbins*, edited by David B. Gowler, L. Gregory Bloomquist, and Duane F. Watson, 222–41. Harrisburg, PA: Trinity, 2003.

---. *The New Testament: History, Literature, and Social Context*. 4th ed. Belmont, CA: Thomson/Wadsworth, 2003. See Perrin and Duling.

---. "Ethnicity, Ethnocentrism, and the Matthean *Ethnos*." *BTB* 35 (2005) 125–43.

---. "Empire: Theories, Methods, Models." In *The Gospel of Matthew in Its Roman Imperial Context*, edited by John Riches and David C. Sim, 49–74. London: T. & T. Clark, 2005.

---. "2 Corinthians 11:22: Historical Context, Rhetoric, and Ethnic Identity." In *The New Testament and Early Christian Literature in Greco-Roman Context: Studies in Honor of David E. Aune*, edited by John Fotopoulos, 65–91. NovTSup 122. Leiden: Brill, 2006.

---. "The Gospel according to Matthew." In *The HarperCollins Study Bible: New Revised Standard Version*. Rev. ed. Edited by Harold W. Attridge, 1665–721. San Francisco: HarperSanFrancisco, 2006.

---. "Ethnicity and Paul's Letter to the Romans." In *Understanding the Social World of the New Testament*, edited by Dietmar Neufeld and Richard E. DeMaris, 68–89. London: Routledge, 2010.

---. "The Gospel of Matthew." In *The Blackwell Companion to the New Testament*, edited by David E. Aune, 296–318. Malden, MA: Wiley-Blackwell, 2010.

---. "Memory, Social Memory, Cultural Memory, Orality, and Gospel." In Festschrift for Andries Van Aarde. *HTS Teologiese Studies/Theological Studies* 67/1 3–13. Online: http://www.hts.org.za/index.php/HTS/article/view/915/1496 or http://www.hts.org.za/index.php/HTS/article/view/915/1411.

Dunn, James D. G., editor. *Jews and Christians: The Parting of the Ways. A.D. 70 to 135*. Grand Rapids: Eerdmans, 1999.

Dyson, Stephen L. "Native Revolts in the Roman Empire." *Hist* 11 (1962) 239–74.

---. "Native Revolt Patterns in the Roman Empire." In *ANRW* II.3 (1975) 138–75.

Bibliography

Eagleton, Terry. *Marxism and Literary Criticism*. Berkeley: University of California Press, 1976.

———. *Literary Theory: An Introduction*. Minneapolis: University of Minnesota Press, 1983.

———. *Ideology: An Introduction*. New York: Verso, 1991.

Edwards, Douglas, and C. Thomas McCollough. *Archaeology and the Galilee: Texts and Contexts in the Graeco-Roman and Byzantine Periods*. Southern Florida Studies in the History of Judaism 143. Atlanta: Scholars, 1997.

Edwards, Richard A. "Reading Matthew: The Gospel as Narrative." *Listening* 24 (1989) 251–61.

Ehrman, Bart. *Jesus: Apocalyptic Prophet of the New Millennium*. Oxford: Oxford University Press, 1999.

Eickelman, Dale F. *The Middle East: An Anthropological Approach*. 2nd ed. Englewood Cliffs: Prentice Hall, 1989.

Eisenstadt, S. N. "Sociological Aspects of the Economic Adaptation of Oriental Migrants in Israel: A Case Study in the Problem of Modernization." *EDCC* 4 (1956) 269–78.

———. *The Political Systems of Empires: The Rise and Fall of the Historical Bureaucratic Societies*. Glencoe, IL: Free Press, 1963.

———. "Processes of Change and Institutionalization of the Political Systems of Centralized Empires." In *Exploration in Social Change*, edited by G. Zollschan, K. and W. Hirsch, 432–51. Boston: Houghton Mifflin, 1964.

———. "Introduction." In S. N. Eisenstadt, *Decline of Empires*, 3–5. New Brunswick, NJ: Transaction, 1993.

———. *Revolution and the Transformation of Societies: A Comparative Study of Civilizations*. New York: Free Press, 1978.

Elder, Linda Bennett. "Transformations in the Judith Mythos: A Feminist Critical Analysis." PhD diss., Florida State University, 1991.

Elliott, John H. "1 Peter, Its Situation and Strategy: A Discussion with David Balch." In *Perspectives on First Peter*, edited by C. H. Talbert, 61–78. National Association of Baptist Professors of Religion Special Studies Series 9. Macon, GA: Mercer University Press, 1986.

———. "Social-Scientific Criticism of the New Testament and Its Social World: More on Method and Models." *Semeia* 35 (1986) 1–33.

———. "Temple versus Household in Luke-Acts: A Contrast in Social Institutions." In *The Social World of Luke-Acts: Models for Interpretation*, edited by Jerome H. Neyrey, 211–40. Peabody, MA: Hendrickson, 1991.

———. *What Is Social-Scientific Criticism?* Guides to Biblical Scholarship. Minneapolis: Fortress, 1993.

———. "The Jewish Messianic Movement: From Faction to Sect." In *Community and Gospel in Luke-Acts*, edited by Philip F. Esler, 75–95. Cambridge: Cambridge University Press, 1995.

———. "Patronage and Clientage." In *The Social Sciences and New Testament Interpretation*, edited by Richard L. Rohrbaugh, 144–56. Peabody, MA: Hendrickson, 1996.

———. "Phases in the Social Formation of Early Christianity: From Faction to Sect—A Social Scientific Perspective." In *Recruitment, Conquest, and Conflict: Strategies in Judaism, Early Christianity, and the Greco-Roman World*, edited by Peder Borgen, Vernon K. Robbins, and David B. Gowler, 273–313. Atlanta: Scholars, 1998.

———. "On Wooing Crocodiles for Fun and Profit: Confessions of an Intact Admirer." In *Social-Scientific Models for Interpreting the Bible: Essays by the Context Group in Honor of Bruce J. Malina*, edited by John J. Pilch, 5–20. Leiden: Brill, 2001.

———. "Jesus Was Not an Egalitarian: A Critique of an Anachronistic and Idealist Theory." *BTB* (2002) 75–91.

———. "The Jesus Movement Was Not Egalitarian but Family-Oriented." *BibInt* 11 (2003) 1–38.

———. *A Home for the Homeless: A Social-Scientific Criticism of 1 Peter, Its Situation and Strategy*. 2nd ed. 1990. Reprinted, Eugene, OR: Cascade Books, 2005.

———. "Jesus the Israelite Was Neither a 'Jew' nor a 'Christian': On Correcting Misleading Nomenclature." *JSHJ* 5 (2007) 119–55.

———. "From Social Description to Social-Scientific Criticism: The History of a Society of Biblical Literature Section 1973–2005." *BTB* 38 (2008) 26–36.

Engels, Frederik. "Bruno Bauer and Early Christianity." Original German *Sozialdemokrat*, 1882. Reprinted in Marx and Engels, *On Religion*, Progress Publishers, 1966. No pages. Online: http://www.marxists.org/archive/marx/works/1882/05/bauer.htm.

———. "On the History of Early Christianity." Original German in *Die Neue Zeit*, 1894–1895. Translated by Institute of Marxism-Leninism, 1957. No pages. Online: http://www.marxists.org/archive/marx/works/1894/early-christianity/index.htm.

Ericson, Kai T. *Wayward Puritans: A Study in the Sociology of Deviance*. New York: Wiley, 1966.

Ericson, Paul A., and Liam Donat Murphy. *A History of Anthropological Theory*. 3rd ed. Peterborough, ON: UTV (Broadview), 2008.

Esler, Philip F. *Community and Gospel in Luke-Acts: The Social and Political Motivations of Lukan Theology*. Cambridge: Cambridge University Press, 1987.

———. "Introverted Sectarianism: Qumran and the Johannine Community." In *The First Christians in Their Social Worlds: Social-Scientific Approaches to New Testament Interpretation*, edited by Philip F. Esler, 70–91. London: Routledge, 1994.

———. "Sectarianism and the Conflict at Antioch." In *The First Christians and Their Social Worlds: Social-scientific Approaches to New Testament Interpretation*, edited by Philip F. Esler, 52–69. London: Routledge, 1994.

———, editor. *Modelling Early Christianity*. London: Routledge, 1995.

———. "God's Honour and Rome's Triumph: Responses to the Fall of Jerusalem in 70 CE in Three Jewish Apocalypses." In *Modelling Early Christianity*, edited by Philip F. Esler, 239–58. London: Routledge, 1995.

———. *Conflict and Identity in Romans: The Social Setting of Paul's Letter*. Minneapolis: Fortress, 2003.

———. "Ethnicity, Ethnic Conflict, and the Ancient Mediterranean World." In *Conflict and Identity in Romans: The Social Setting of Paul's Letter*. Minneapolis: Fortress, 2003.

———. "The Context Group Project: An Autobiographical Account." In *Anthropology and Biblical Studies: Avenues of Approach*, edited by Louise J. Lawrence and Mario I. Aguilar, 46–61. Leiden: Deo, 2004.

Evans-Pritchard, E. E. *Witchcraft, Oracles and Magic among the Azande*. Oxford: Clarendon, 1937.

———. *Social Anthropology*. London: Faber & Faber, 1951.

Farmer, William R. "The Post-Sectarian Character of Matthew and Its Post-War Setting in Antioch of Syria." *PRS* 3 (1976) 235–47.
Festinger, Leon. *A Theory of Cognitive Dissonance*. Stanford, CA: Stanford University Press, 1957.
———, Henry W. Riecken, and Stanley Schachter. *When Prophecy Fails: A Social and Psychological Study of a Modern Group that Predicted the End of the World*. Minneapolis: University of Minnesota Press, 1956.
Fiensy, David A. *The Social History of Palestine in the Herodian Period: The Land Is Mine*. SBEC 20. Lewiston, NY: Mellen, 1991.
Filson, Floyd V. "The Significance of the Early House Churches." *JBL* 58 (1939) 105–12.
Fink, Clinton F. "Some Conceptual Difficulties in the Theory of Social Conflict." *JCR* 12 (1968) 412–60.
Finley, Moses I. *The World of Odysseus*. Rev. ed. Harmondsworth, UK: Viking Penguin, 1965.
———. *The Ancient Economy*. Berkeley: University of California Press, 1973.
———. *Ancient History: Evidence and Models*. London: Pimlico, 1985.
Fiore, Benjamin. "Friendship in the Exhortation of Romans 15:14–33." *EGLMBSP* 7 (1987) 95–103.
———. "The Pastoral Epistles in the Light of Philodemus' 'On Frank Criticism.'" In *Philodemus and the New Testament World*, edited by John T. Fitzgerald, Dirk Obbink, and Glenn S. Holland, 271–93. NovTSup 111. Leiden: Brill, 2004.
Fishbane, Michael. "From Scribalism to Rabbinism: Perspectives on the Emergence of Classical Judaism." In *The Garments of Torah: Essays in Biblical Hermeneutics*. Bloomington: Indiana University Press, 1985. Reprinted in *The Sage in Israel and the Ancient Near East*, edited by John G. Gammie and Leo G. Perdue, 439–56. Winona Lake, IN: Eisenbrauns, 1990.
———. *Biblical Interpretation in Ancient Israel*. Oxford: Clarendon, 1989.
Fisher, B. Aubrey, and Donald G. Ellis. *Small Group Decision Making: Communication and the Group Process*. 3rd ed. New York: McGraw-Hill, 1990.
Fisher, Loren R. "Can This Be the Son of David?" In *Jesus and the Historian: Written in Honor of Ernest Cadman Colwell*, edited by F. Thomas Trotter, 82–97. Philadelphia: Westminster, 1968.
Fitzgerald, John T., editor. *Friendship, Flattery, and Frankness of Speech: Studies on Friendship in the New Testament World*. NovTSup 82. Leiden: Brill, 1996.
Fitzmyer, J. A. "The Son of David Tradition and Matthew 22:41–46 and Parallels." *Con* 20 (1967) 75–87.
———. "David, 'Being Therefore a Prophet . . .'" *CBQ* 34 (1972) 332–39.
Foakes-Jackson, Frederick J., and Kirsopp Lake, editors. *The Beginnings of Christianity*. 5 vols. Grand Rapids: Baker, 1920–1933.
Forbes, Clarence Allen. *Neoi: A Contribution to the Study of Greek Associations*. Philological Monographs of the American Philological Association 2. Middletown, CT: American Philological Association, 1933.
Forkman, Göran. *The Limits of Religious Community: Expulsion from the Religious Community Within the Qumran Sect, within Rabbinic Judaism, and within Primitive Christianity*. Lund: Gleerup, 1972.
Foucault, Michel. "What Is an Author?" Lecture in Societé Française de Philosophie 1969. Translated by Josué Harari. In *The Essential Foucault*, edited by Paul Rabinow and Nicolas Roads, 239–53. New York: New Press, 2003.

Frank, Tenney. *An Economic Survey of Ancient Rome.* 6 vols. Baltimore: Johns Hopkins Press, 1933–1940.
Frankemölle, Hubert. *Jahwebund und Kirche Christi.* Münster: Aschendorff, 1974.
Freedman, David N. "The Spelling of the Name 'David' in the Hebrew Bible." *HAR* 7 (1983) 89–104.
French, D. "The Relationship of Anthropology to Studies in Perception and Cognition." In *Psychology: A Study of A Science*, edited by S. Koch, 6:388–428. New York: McGraw-Hill, 1962.
Frey, J. B. *Corpus Inscriptionum Iudaicarum (CII).* 2 vols. Rome and Paris. Vol. 1 republished as *Corpus of Jewish Inscriptions: Jewish Inscriptions from the Third Century B.C. to the Seventh Century A.D.* New York: Ktav, 1936.
Freyne, Sean. *Galilee, Jesus and the Gospels: Literary Approaches and Historical Investigations.* Minneapolis: Fortress, 1988.
Fried, Morton. *The Evolution of Political Society.* New York: Random House, 1967.
Frye, Northrop. *The Great Code: The Bible and Literature.* San Diego: Harcourt Brace Jovanovich, 1982.
Fuglseth, K. S. *Johannine Sectarianism in Perspective.* NovTSup 119. Leiden: Brill, 2005.
Fuller, Reginald. *The Foundations of New Testament Christology.* New York: Scribner, 1965.
Funk, Robert W., Roy W. Hoover, and the Jesus Seminar. *The Five Gospels: The Search for the Authentic Words of Jesus.* New York: Macmillan, 1993.
Gager, John. *Kingdom and Community: The Social World of Early Christianity.* Englewood Cliffs, NJ: Prentice-Hall, 1975.
———. "Social Description and Sociological Explanation in the Study of Early Christianity: A Review Essay." *RSR* 5 (1979) 174–80. Reprinted in *The Bible and Liberation: Political and Social Hermeneutics*, edited by Norman K. Gottwald, 428–40. Maryknoll, NY: Orbis, 1983.
———. "Shall We Marry Our Enemies?" *Int* 36 (1982) 56–65.
Gale, Aaron M. *Redefining Ancient Borders: The Jewish Scribal Framework of Matthew's Gospel.* London: T. & T. Clark, 2005.
Galt, Anthony H., and Larry J. Smith. *Models and the Study of Social Change.* New York: Wiley, 1976.
Galtung, Johan. "A Structural Theory of Imperialism." *JPR* 8 (1971) 81–117.
Gammie, John G. "The Sage in Sirach." In *The Sage in Israel and the Ancient Near East*, edited by John G. Gammie and Leo G. Perdue, 355–72. Winona Lake, IN: Eisenbrauns, 1990.
Garland, David E. *The Intention of Matthew 23.* NovTSup 52. Leiden: Brill, 1979.
Gasque, W. Ward. *Sir William M. Ramsay: Archaeologist and New Testament Scholar.* Baker Studies in Biblical Archaeology. Grand Rapids: Baker, 1966. Online: http://www.biblicalstudies.org.uk/pdf/ramsay/ramsay_gasque.pdf.
Geary, P. J. "Barbnarians and Ethnicity." In *Late Antiquity: A Guide to the Postclassical World*, edited by G. W. Bowersock, Peter Brown, and Oleg Grabar, 107–29. Cambridge: Harvard University Press, 1999.
Geertz, Clifford. "The Rotating Credit Association: A Middle Rung in Development." *Economic Development and Cultural Change* 10 (1962) 241–63.
———. "The Integrative Revolution." In Clifford Geertz, editor, *Old Societies and New States*, 108–13. New York: Free Press, 1963.
———. "Deep Play: Notes on the Balinese Cockfight." In *The Interpretation of Cultures* by Clifford Geertz, 412–53. San Francisco: Basic Books, 1973.

Bibliography

———. "Thick Description: Toward an Interpretive Theory of Culture." In *The Interpretation of Cultures* by Clifford Geertz, 3–30. San Francisco: Basic Books, 1973.
Gennep, Arnold van. *Rites of Passage*. Chicago: University of Chicago Press, 1960.
Germani, Gino. *Marginality*. New Brunswick, NJ: Transaction, 1980.
Gibbs, J. M. "Purpose and Pattern in Matthew's Use of the Title 'Son of David.'" *NTS* 10 (1964) 446–64.
Giddens, Anthony, and Jonathan Turner. *Social Theory Today*. Stanford, CA: Stanford University Press, 1987.
Giesen, Heinz. "Zum Problem der Exkommunikation nach dem Matthäus-Evangelium [Matt 16:19; 18:15–18]." *Studia Moralia* 8 (1970) 185–269.
Gilmore, David D. "Anthropology of the Mediterranean Area." *ARA* 11 (1982) 175–205.
———, editor. *Honor and Shame and the Unity of the Mediterranean*. Washington, DC: American Anthropological Association, 1987.
Gnilka, J. "Die Kirche des Matthäus und die Gemeinde von Qumran." *BZ* 7 (1963) 55–66.
Golb, Norman. *Who Wrote the Dead Sea Scrolls? The Search for the Secret of Qumran*. New York: Touchstone, 1995.
Good, Deirdre. "The Verb *anachoreō* in Matthew's Gospel." *NovT* 32 (1991) 1–12.
Goodman, M. D. "Texts, Scribes, and Power in Roman Judaea." In *Literacy and Power in the Ancient World*, edited by A. K. Bowman and G. Woolf, 99–108. Cambridge: Cambridge University Press, 1994.
Goody, Jack. "Introduction." In *Literacy in Traditional Societies*, edited by Jack Goody, 1–26. Cambridge: Cambridge University Press, 1968.
Gottwald, Norman K. *The Tribes of Yahweh: A Sociology of Liberation of Liberated Israel, 1250–1050 BCE*. Sheffield, UK: Sheffield Academic, 1979.
———, editor. *Semeia* 37: *Social Scientific Criticism of the Hebrew Bible and Its Social World*. Decatur, GA: Scholars, 1986.
———. "Revisiting the Tribes of Yahweh." No pages. Online: http://www.servicios-koinonia.org/relat/374e.htm.
Gramsci, Antonio. *Selections from the Prison Notebooks*. Edited and translated by Q. Hoare and G. N. Smith. London: Lawrence & Wishart, 1971.
Grant, Robert M. *Early Christianity and Society: Seven Studies*. New York: Harper & Row, 1977.
Gray, Sherman W. *The Least of My Brothers: Matthew 25:31–46. A History of Interpretation*. SBLDS 114. Atlanta: Scholars, 1989.
Green, Barbara. *Mikhail Bakhtin and Biblical Scholarship: An Introduction*. SBLSS 38. Atlanta: Society of Biblical Literature, 2000.
Green, H. B. "The Structure of St. Matthew's Gospel." In *Studia Evangelica* 4, edited by F. L. Cross, 47–59. TU 102. Berlin: Akademie, 1968.
Green, William Scott. "Reading the Writing of Rabbinism: Toward an Interpretation of Rabbinic Literature." *JAAR* 51(1983) 191–206.
Gruen, E. S. "Jewish Perspectives on Greek Culture." In *Hellenism in the Land of Israel*, edited by John J. Collins and Greg E. Sterling, 61–93. Notre Dame: Notre Dame Press, 2001.
Guelich, R. A. "The Antitheses of Matthew 5:21–48: Traditional and/or Redactional?" *NTS* 22 (1976) 444–57.
Gundry, Robert H. *Matthew: A Commentary on His Handbook for a Mixed Church under Persecution*. Grand Rapids: Eerdmans, 1982. 2nd ed., 1994.

———. "On True and False Disciples in Matthew 8.18–22." *NTS* 40 (1994) 433–41.
Gutiérrez, Gustavo. *A Theology of Liberation: History, Politics, and Salvation*. Translated and edited by Sr. Caridad Inda and John Eagleson. Maryknoll, NY: Orbis, 1973. Rev. ed., 1981.
Gutman, Joseph. "Synagogue Origins: Theories and Facts." In *Ancient Synagogues: The State of Research*, edited by Joseph Gutman, 1–6. BJS 22. Chico, CA: Scholars, 1981.
Hachlili, Rachael. "Synagogue (Diaspora Synagogues)." In *ABD* 6 (1992) 260–63.
Haenchen, Ernst. *Acts of the Apostles: A Commentary*. Translated by Bernard Noble and Gerald Shinn. Philadelphia: Westminster John Knox, 1971.
Hagner, Donald A. "The *Sitz im Leben* of the Gospel of Matthew." In *Treasures New and Old: Recent Contributions to Matthean Studies*, edited by David R. Bower and Mark Allen Powell, 27–68. SBLSS 1. Atlanta: Scholars, 1996.
Haines-Eitzen, Kim "'Girls Trained in Beautiful Writing': Female Scribes in Roman Antiquity and Early Christianity." *JECS* (1998) 629–46.
Hall, Edith. *Inventing the Barbarian: Greek Self-Definition through Tragedy*. Oxford Classical Monographs. Oxford: Oxford University Press, 1989.
Hall, Jonathan M. *Ethnic Identity in Greek Antiquity*. Cambridge: Cambridge University Press, 1997.
Hall, R. G. "Epispasm and the Dating of Ancient Jewish Writings." *JSP* 2 (1988) 1–86.
Halliday, Michael A. K. "Anti-Languages." *AA* 78 (1975) 570–584.
———. *Language as Social Semiotic: The Social Interpretation of Language and Meaning*. Baltimore: University Park Press, 1978.
Hamilton, Mark. "Who Was a Jew? Jewish Ethnicity during the Achaemenid Period." *RestQ* 37 2 (1998–2002). No pages. Online: http://www.acu.edu/sponsored/restoration_quarterly/archives/1990s/vol_37_no_2_contents/hamilton.html.
Hanks, Thomas D. "Poor, Poverty. New Testament." In *ABD* 5 (1992) 414–24.
Hanson, K. C. "How Honorable! How Shameful! A Cultural Analysis of Mathew's Makarisms and Reproaches." *Semeia* 67 (1996) 147–70.
———. "Kinship." In *The Social Sciences and New Testament Interpretation*, edited by Richard L. Rohrbaugh, 62–79. Peabody, MA: Hendrickson, 1996.
———. "The Galilean Fishing Economy and the Jesus Tradition." *BTB* 27 (1997) 99–111.
Hanson, K. C., and Douglas E. Oakman. *Palestine in the Time of Jesus: Social Structures and Social Conflicts*. 2nd ed. Minneapolis: Fortress, 2008.
Hare, Douglas R. A. "How Jewish Is the Gospel of Matthew?" *CBQ* 62 (2000) 264–77.
Harland, Philip A. *Associations, Synagogues, and Congregations*. Minneapolis: Fortress, 2003.
———. "Familial Dimensions of Group Identity: 'Brothers' (*Adelfoi*) in Associations of the Greek East." *JBL* 124 (2005) 491–513.
———. *Dynamics of Identity in the World of the Early Christians: Associations, Judeans, and Cultural Minorities*. London: T. & T. Clark, 2009.
Harnack, Adolf von. *The Mission and Expansion of Christianity in the First Three Centuries*. 2 vols. London: Williams & Norgate, 1908.
Harrington, Daniel J. "'Make Disciples of All the Gentiles' (Mt 28:19)." *CBQ* 37 (1975) 359–69.
———. "Sociological Concepts and the Early Church: A Decade of Research." *TS* 41 (1980) 181–90.
———. *The Gospel of Matthew*. SP 1. Collegeville, MN: Liturgical, 1991.

Harris, David Russell, editor. *The Archaeology of V. Gordon Childe: Contemporary Perspectives.* Chicago: University of Chicago Press, 1994.
Harris, Marvin. "History and Significance of the Emic/Etic Distinction." *ARA* 5 (1976) 329–50.
Harris, William V. *Ancient Literacy.* Cambridge: Harvard University Press, 1989.
Harrison, T. "Herodotus' Conception of Foreign Languages." *Hyst* 2 (1998). No pages. Online: http://www.dur.ac.uk/Classics/histos/1998/harrison.html.
Harste, J., C. Burke, and V. Woodward. "Children's Language and World: Initial Encounters with Print." In *Reader Meets Author: Bridging the Gap a Psycholinguistic and Sociolinguistic Perspective,* edited by J. Langer and M. Smith-Burke, 105–31. Newark, NJ: International Reading Association, 1982.
Harvey, G. A. P. *The True Israel: Uses of the Names Jew, Hebrew and Israel in Ancient Jewish and Early Christian Literature.* Arbeiten zur Geschichte des antiken Judentums und des Urchristentums. Leiden: Brill, 1996.
Headland, Thomas N., Kenneth L. Pike, and Marvin Harris. *Emics and Etics: The Insider/Outsider Debate.* Frontiers in Anthropology 7. New York: Sage, 1990.
Heaton, E. W. *The School Tradition of the Old Testament.* Bampton Lectures 1994. Oxford: Oxford University Press, 1994.
Heichelheim, F. M. "Part II: Roman Syria." In *An Economic Survey of Ancient Rome,* edited by Tenney Frank, 121–257. 4 vols. Baltimore: Johns Hopkins University Press, 1938.
Hellholm, David. "The Problem of Apocalyptic Genre and the Apocalypse of John." *Semeia* 36 (1986) 13–64.
―――, editor. *Apocalypticism in the Mediterranean World and the Near East.* Tübingen: Mohr/Siebeck, 1983.
Hengel, Martin. "Die Synagogeninschrift von Stobi." *ZNW* 57 (1966) 145–83.
―――. *Judaism and Hellenism.* 2 vols. Translated by John Bowden. Philadelphia: Fortress, 1974.
―――. *The Charismatic Leader and His Followers.* Translated by James Greig. New York: Crossroad, 1981.
Herbst, Ph. G. *Alternatives to Hierarchies.* Leiden: Nijhoff, 1976.
Hertig, Paul. "The Galilee Theme in Matthew: Transforming Mission through Marginality." *Miss* 25 (1997) 155–63.
―――. "Geographical Marginality in the Matthean Journeys of Jesus." In *SBL 1999 Seminar Papers,* edited by Kent H. Richards, 472–89. Atlanta: Scholars, 1999.
―――. *Matthew's Narrative Use of Galilee in the Multicultural and Missiological Journeys of Jesus.* Mellen Biblical Series 46. Lewiston, NY: Mellen, 1999.
Herzfeld, Michael. "Honour and Shame: Problems in the Comparative Analysis of Moral Systems." *Man* 15 (1980) 339–51.
―――. "Of Horns and History: The Mediterraneanist Dilemma Again." *AE* 12 (1985) 778–80.
―――. "'As in Your Own House': Hospitality, Ethnography, and the Stereotype of Mediterranean Society." In *Honor and Shame and the Unity of the Mediterr*anean, edited by David D. Gilmore, 75–89. Washington, DC: American Anthropological Association, 1987.
―――. "Excuses for Everything, from Epistemology to Eating." In *Rethinking the Mediterranean,* edited by William V. Harris, 45–53. Oxford: Oxford University Press, 2005.

Herzog, William R., II. *Parables as Subversive Speech: Jesus as Pedagogue of the Oppressed.* Louisville: Westminster John Knox, 1994.

———. *Jesus, Justice, and the Reign of God: A Ministry of Liberation.* Louisville: Westminster John Knox, 1999.

Hill, David. "DIKAIOI as a Quasi-Technical Term." *NTS* 11 (1965) 296–302.

———. "False Prophets and Charismatics: Structure and Interpretation in Mt. 7:15–23." *Biblica* 57 (1976) 327–48.

Hochschild, Ralph. *Sozialgeschichtliche Exegese: Entwicklung, Geschichte und Methodik einer neutestamentlichen Forschungsrichtung.* NTOA 42. Göttingen: Vandenhoeck & Ruprecht, 1999.

Hock, Ronald F. "Paul's Tentmaking and the Problem of his Social Class." *JBL* 97 (1978) 555–64.

———. *The Social Context of Paul's Ministry: Tentmaking and Apostleship.* Philadelphia: Fortress, 1980.

Hoh, J. "Der christliche *grammateus* (GK) (Mt 13,52)." *BZ* 17 (1926) 265–69.

Hollenbach, Paul W. "Recent Historical Jesus Studies and the Social Sciences." In *SBL 1983 Seminar Papers*, edited by Kent H. Richards, 60–78. Chico, CA: Scholars, 1983.

Holmberg, Bengt. *Paul and Power: The Structure of Authority in the Primitive Church as Reflected in the Pauline Epistles.* Lund: Gleerup, 1978.

———. *Sociology and the New Testament: An Appraisal.* Minneapolis: Fortress, 1990.

Hood, R. T. "The Genealogies of Jesus." In *Early Christian Origins: Studies in Honor of H. R. Willoughby*, edited by A. Wikgren, 1–15. Chicago: Quadrangle, 1961.

Horden, Peregrine, and Nicholas Purcell. *The Corrupting Sea: A Study of Mediterranean History.* Oxford: Blackwell, 2000.

———. "Four Years of Corruption: A Response to Critics." In *Rethinking the Mediterranean*, edited by W. V. Harris, 348–75. Oxford: Oxford University Press, 2005.

———. "The Mediterranean and 'the New Thalassology.'" *AHR* 3/3 AHR Forum (2006). No pages. Online: http://www.historycooperative.org/journals/ahr/111.3/horden.html#REF2.

Horowitz, D. *Ethnic Groups in Conflict.* Berkeley: University of California Press, 1985.

Horrell, David G. *The Social Ethos of the Corinthian Correspondence. Interests and Ideology from 1 Corinthians to I Clement.* SNTW. London: T. & T. Clark, 1996.

———. "The Origins and Revival of Interest in the Social World of Early Christianity." In *Handbook of Early Christianity*, edited by A. J. Blasi et al., 3–28. Walnut Creek, CA: AltaMira, 2002.

———. "Between Conformity and Resistance: Beyond the Balch-Elliott Debate towards a Postcolonial Reading of 1 Peter." In *Reading First Peter with New Eyes: Methodological Reassessments of the Letter of First Peter*, edited by R. L. Webb and B. Bauman-Martin, 111–43. LNTS 364. London: T. & T. Clark, 2007.

Horsley, Richard A. "Questions about Redactional Strata and the Social Relations Reflected in Q." In *SBL 1989 Seminar Papers*, edited by David J. Lull, 186–203. Atlanta: Scholars, 1989.

———. *The Liberation of Christmas: The Infancy Narratives in Social Context.* 1989. Reprint, Eugene, OR: Cascade Books, 2006.

———. *Sociology and the Jesus Movement.* New York: Crossroad, 1989.

———. *Jesus and the Spiral of Violence: Popular Jewish Resistance in Roman Palestine.* Minneapolis: Fortress, 1993.

———. *Galilee: History, Politics, People.* Valley Forge, PA: Trinity, 1995.

Bibliography

———. *Archaeology, History, and Society in Galilee: The Social Context of Jesus and the Rabbis.* Valley Forge, PA: Trinity, 1996.
———. *Paul and Empire: Religion and Power in Roman Imperial Society.* Harrisburg, PA: Trinity, 1997.
———. *Jesus and Empire: The Kingdom of God and the New World Disorder.* Minneapolis: Fortress, 2003.
———. *Religion and Empire: People, Power, and the Life of the Spirit.* Minneapolis: Fortress, 2003.
———. "Foreword." In *Christian Origins*, edited by Richard Horsley, 1-20. A People's History of Christianity 1. Minneapolis: Fortress, 2005.
———. *Scribes, Visionaries, and the Politics of Second Temple Judea.* Louisville: Westminster John Knox, 2007.
———, and John S. Hanson. *Bandits, Prophets, and Messiahs: Popular Movements at the Time of Jesus.* Minneapolis: Winston, 1985.
Hummel, Reinhart. *Die Auseinandersetzung zwischen Kirche und Judentum im Matthäusevangelium.* Munich: Kaiser, 1963.
Hutchinson, John, and Anthony D. Smith. *Ethnicity.* Oxford Reader. Oxford: Oxford University Press, 1996.
Hynes, William J. *Shirley Jackson Case and the Chicago School: The Socio-Historical Method.* Chico, CA: Scholars, 1981.
Iggers, Georg G. *Historiography in the Twentieth Century: From Scientific Objectivity to the Postmodern Challenge.* Hanover, NH: Wesleyan University Press, 1997.
Iordachi, Constantin. "Social History: Schools, Methods and Case Studies." A University Course at Central European University, 2007.
Isenberg, Sheldon R. "Millenarism in Greco-Roman Palestine." *Relig* 4 (1974) 26-46.
Iser, Wolfgang. *The Act of Reading.* Baltimore: Johns Hopkins University Press, 1978.
Jackson, Bernard S. "Damascus Document IX, 16-23 and Parallels." *RevQ* 9 (1978) 445-50.
Jackson, Glenna S. "Are the 'Nations' Present in Matthew?" *HTS* 56 (2000) 935-48.
Jarvie, I. C. *The Revolution in Anthropology.* London: Routledge & Kegan Paul, 1964.
Jefford, Clayton N. "The Milieu of Matthew, the *Didachē*, and Ignatius of Antioch: Agreements and Differences." In *Matthew and the Didachē: Two Documents from the Same Milieu?*, edited by Huub van de Sandt, 35-48. Minneapolis: Fortress, 2005.
Jenkins, Richard. "Rethinking Ethnicity: Identity, Categorization and Power." *ERS* 17 (1994) 197-223.
———. "Ethnicity Etcetera: Social Anthropological Points of View." *ERS* 19 (1996) 807-22.
———. *Rethinking Ethnicity: Arguments and Explorations.* London: Sage, 1997.
Jeremias, Joachim. *The Parables of Jesus.* Translated by S. H. Hooke. Rev. ed. New York: Scribner, 1963.
———. *Jerusalem at the Time of Jesus. An Investigation into Economic and Social Conditions during the New Testament Period.* Translated by F. H. and C. H. Cave. Philadelphia: Fortress, 1969.
Jewett, Robert. *The Thessalonian Correspondence: Pauline Rhetoric and Millenarian Piety.* Philadelphia: Fortress, 1986.
Johnson, Allan Chester, Paul Robinson Coleman-Norton, and Frank Card Bourne. *Ancient Roman Statutes.* Vol. 2. Austin: University of Texas Press, 1961.

Johnson, Christopher. *Claude Levi-Strauss: The Formative Years*. Cambridge: Cambridge University Press, 2003.
Johnson, M. D. *The Purpose of the Biblical Genealogies with Special Reference to the Setting of the Genealogies of Jesus*. Cambridge: Cambridge University Press, 1969. Reprint, Eugene, OR: Wipf & Stock, 2002.
Jokiranta, Jutta. "Learning from Sectarian Responses: Windows on Qumran Sects and Emerging Christian Sects." In *Echoes from the Caves: Qumran and the New Testament*, edited by Florentino García Martínez, 177–209. STDJ 85. Leiden: Brill, 2009.
Jones, A. H. M. *The Herods of Judaea*. Oxford: Clarendon, 1967.
Judge, E. A. "The Early Christians as a Scholastic Community." *JRH* 1 (1960) 4–15; 125–37.
———. *The Social Pattern of the Christian Groups in the First Century*. London: Tyndale, 1960. Reprinted in Scholer, *Social Distinctives of the Christians in the First Century: Pivital Essays by E. A. Judge*, 1–56. Peabody, MA: Hendrickson, 2008.
———. "The Social Identity of the First Christians: A Question of Method in Religious History." *JRH* 11/2 (1980) 201–17. Reprinted in Scholer, *Social Distinctives of the Christians in the First Century: Pivital Essays by E. A. Judge*, 1–56. Peabody, MA: Hendrickson, 2008.
Julian, C. "Fabri." In *Dictionnaire des antiquités grecques et romaines d'après les textes et les monuments*. 4 vols. (1877–1919), Vol. 2, edited by C. Daremberg and E. Saglio, 947–59. Paris: Hochette, 1896.
Jülicher, Adolf. *Die Gleichnisreden Jesus*. 2 vols. Tübingen: Mohr/Siebeck, 1899.
Kampen, John. "A Reexamination of the Relationship between Matthew 5:21–48 and the Dead Sea Scrolls." In *SBL 1990 Seminar Papers*, edited by David J. Lull, 34–59. Atlanta: Scholars, 1990.
———. "Communal Discipline in the Social World of the Matthean Community." *Dead Sea Discoveries* 1 (1994) 338–63.
———. "Discussion of David A. Fiensy, *The Social History of Palestine in the Herodian Period: the Land is Mine* [1991]." *EGLMBSP* 14 (1994) 205–10.
Kaplan, Stephen, and Rachael Kaplan. *Cognition and Environment*. New York: Praeger, 1982.
Karris, Robert J. *Jesus and the Marginalized in John's Gospel*. Collegeville, MN: Liturgical, 1990.
Käsemann, Ernst. "Sentences of Holy Law in the New Testament." In *New Testament Questions of Today*, 66–81. Translated by W. J. Montague. Philadelphia: Fortress, 1969.
Kautsky, John H. *Karl Kautsky and the Social Science of Classical Marxism*. International Studies in Sociology and Social Anthropology. Leiden: Brill, 1989.
———. *The Politics of Aristocratic Empires*. Chapel Hill: University of North Carolina Press, 1982.
Kautsky, Karl. *The Foundations of Christianity*. Translated by Henry F. Mins. London: Allen & Unwin. 1953.
Kee, Howard Clark. "Terminology of Mark's Exorcism Stories." *NTS* 14 (1968) 232–46.
———. *Community of the New Age: Studies in Mark's Gospel*. Philadelphia: Westminster, 1977.
———. "The Transformation of the Synagogue after 70 C.E.: Its Import for Early Christianity." *NTS* 36 (1990) 1–24.

Bibliography 363

Kelber, Werner. *The Oral and Written Gospel.* New Introduction. Bloomington: Indiana University Press, 1997.

Kerr, Graham B. "Voluntary Associations in West Africa: 'Hidden' Agents of Social Change." In *The Social Sciences and African Development Planning,* edited by Phillips Stevens, Jr., 87-100. Waltham, MA: Crossroads, 1978.

Kerri, J. N. "Studying Voluntary Associations as Adaptive Mechanisms: A Review of Anthropological Perspectives." *CA* 17 (1976) 23-47.

Kheng, Cheah Boon. *Social Banditry and Rural Crime in Kedah, 1910-1929.* Oxford: Oxford University Press, 1988.

Kiilunen, J. "Der nachfolgewillige Schriftgelehrte: Matthäus 8.19-20 im Verständnis des Evangelisten." *NTS* 37 (1991) 268-79.

Kilpatrick, G. D. *The Origins of the Gospel according to St. Matthew.* Oxford: Clarendon, 1950.

Kingsbury, Jack Dean. *The Parables of Matthew in Matthew 13.* St. Louis: Concordia, 1969.

———. "The Title 'Son of David' in Matthew's Gospel." *JBL* 95 (1976) 591-602.

———. "The Verb *Akolouthein* ('to follow') as an Index of Matthew's View of His Community." *JBL* 97 (1978) 56-73.

———. "The Developing Conflict between Jesus and the Jewish Leaders in Matthew's Gospel: A Literary-Critical Study." *CBQ* 49 (1987) 57-73.

———. *Matthew as Story.* 2nd ed. Philadelphia: Fortress, 1988.

———. *Matthew: Structure, Christology, Kingdom.* Rev. ed. Philadelphia: Fortress, 1988.

———. "Conclusion: Analysis of a Conversation." In *Social History of the Matthean Community: Cross-Disciplinary Approaches,* edited by David L. Balch, 259-69. Minneapolis: Fortress, 1991.

Klinghardt, Matthias. "The Manual of Discipline in the Light of Statutes of Hellenistic Associations." In *Methods of Investigation of the Dead Sea Scrolls and the Khirbet Qumran Site: Present Realities and Future Prospects.* Annals of the New York Academy of Sciences 722, edited by John J. Collins, Michael O. Wise, Norman Golb, and Dennis Pardee, 251-70. New York: New York Academy of Sciences, 1994.

———. *Gemeinschaftsmahl und Mahlgemeinschaft. Soziologie und Liturgie frühchristlicher Mahlfeiern.* TANZ 13. Tübingen: Franke, 1996.

Kloppenborg, John S. "Blessing and Marginality: The 'Persecution Beatitude' in Q [6: 22ab, 23ab], Thomas, and Early Christianity." *Forum* 2/3 (1986) 36-56.

———. *The Formation of Q: Trajectories in Ancient Wisdom Collections.* Philadelphia: Fortress, 1987.

———. *Q Parallels: Synopsis, Critical Notes, & Concordance.* Sonoma, CA: Polebridge, 1988.

———. "The Formation of Q Revisited: A Response to Richard Horsley." In *SBL 1989 Seminar Papers,* edited by David J. Lull, 204-15. Atlanta: Scholars, 1989.

———. "Literary Convention, Self-Evidence, and the Social History of the Q People." *Semeia* 55 (1991) 77-102.

———. "Collegia and Thiasoi." In *Voluntary Associations in the Graeco-Roman World,* edited by John S. Kloppenborg and Stephen G. Wilson, 16-30. London: Routledge, 1996.

———. "Personal E-Mail Communication about Voluntary Associations and *ethnē*." 2003.

———. "Response to Dennis Duling's 'Matthew and Marginality Reconsidered.'" Delivered at the Context Group annual meeting, March 2003. Unpublished.

———. *The Tenants in the Vineyard.* WUNT 195. Tübingen: Mohr/Siebeck, 2006.

———, and Stephen G. Wilson, editors. *Voluntary Associations in the Graeco-Roman World.* London: Routledge, 1996.

Knight, Douglas A. "Political Rights and Powers in Monarchic Israel." *Semeia* 66 (1994) 93–117.

Kohler, K. "Abba, Father: Title of Spiritual Leader and Saint." *JQR* 13 (1901) 567–80.

Konstan, David. "Friendship, Frankness, and Flattery [in Classical Literature and the New Testament]." In *Friendship, Flattery, and Frankness of Speech: Studies on Friendship in the New Testament World*, edited by John T. Fitzgerald, 7–19. NovTSup. 82. Leiden: Brill, 1996.

Kornemann, Ernst. "Koinon; Collegium." In *PW* 4.1 (1900) 380–479; Sup. 4, 915ff.; Sup. 5, 453ff.

Kottaridis, Dimitris. "Empires: A Comparative Study in a World Context" (bibliography). No pages. Online: http://www.worldhistorycenter.org/whc/gradstudy/bibliograd/themes/KottaridisD.htm.

Kraabel, A. Thomas. "Social Systems of Six Diaspora Synagogues." In *Ancient Synagogues: The State of Research*, edited by Joseph Gutman, 79–91, BJS 22. Chico, CA: Scholars, 1981.

———. "Unity and Diversity Among Diaspora Synagogues." In *The Synagogue in Late Antiquity*, edited by Lee I. Levine, 49–60. Philadelphia: American Schools of Oriental Research, 1987.

Kraemer, Ross Shepard. "On the Meaning of the Term 'Jew' in Graeco-Roman Inscriptions." *HTR* 82 (1989) 35–43.

Kreissig, H. "Zur sozialen Zusammensetzung der frühchristlichen Gemeinden im ersten Jahrhundert u. Z." *Eirene* 6 (1967) 91–100.

Krentz, Edgar. "Community and Character: Matthew's Vision of the Church." In *SBL 1987 Seminar Papers*, edited by Kent H. Richards, 565–73. Atlanta: Scholars, 1987.

Kroll, W. "*Iobakchoi.*" In *PW* 9 (1916) 1828–32.

Kugel, James L. "On Hidden Hatred and Open Reproach: Early Exegesis of Leviticus 19:17." *HTR* 80 (1987) 43–61.

Kümmel, Werner Georg. *The New Testament: A History of the Interpretation of Its Problems.* Translated by S. McLean Gilmour and Howard C. Kee. Nashville: Abingdon, 1972.

La Barre, Weston. "Materials for a History of Studies of Crisis Cults: A Bibliographic Essay." *CA* 12 (1971) 3–44.

Laney, J. Carl. "The Biblical Practice of Church Discipline." *BSac* 143 (1986) 353–64.

Lapin, H. "Rabbi." In *ABD* 5 (1992) 600–601.

Larrain, Jorge A. *The Concept of Ideology.* Brookfield, VT: Gregg Revivals, 1992.

Lawrence, Louise Joy. "'For truly I tell you, they have received their reward' (Matt 6:2): Investigating Honor Precedence and Honor Virtue." *CBQ* 64 (2002) 687–702.

———. *An Ethnography of the Gospel of Matthew.* WUNT 2/165. Tübingen: Mohr/Siebeck, 2003.

Leany, A. R. C. *The Rule of Qumran and Its Meaning.* Philadelphia: Westminster, 1966.

Le Donne, Anthony. *The Historiographical Jesus: Memory, Typology, and the Son of David.* Waco, TX: Baylor University Press, 2009.

Lee, Jung Young. *Marginality: The Key to Multicultural Theology.* Minneapolis: Fortress, 1995.

Lemaire, André. "The Sage in School and Temple." In *The Sage in Israel and the Ancient Near East*, edited by John G. Gammie and Leo G. Purdue, 165–81. Winona Lake, IN: Eisenbrauns, 1990.
———. "Writing and Writing Materials." In *ABD* 6 (1992) 999–1008.
Lendesta, G. *The American "Empire."* Oslo: Norwegian University Press, 1990.
Lenski, Gerhard. "Status Crystallization: A Non-Vertical Dimension of Social Status." *ASR* 19 (1956) 405–13.
———. *Power and Privilege: A Theory of Social Stratification*. New York: McGraw-Hill, 1966; Chapel Hill: University of North Carolina Press, 1984.
———. "Marxist Experiments in Destratification: An Appraisal." *SocForces* 57 (1978) 364–83.
———. "Rethinking Macrosociological Theory." *ASR* 53 (1988) 163–71.
———. "Societal Taxonomies: Mapping the Social Universe." *ARS* 20 (1994) 1–26.
———, and Jean Lenski. *Human Societies: An Introduction to Macrosociology*. 5th ed. New York: McGraw-Hill, 1987. See Nolan 2004 for the 9th ed.
Leon, Harry J. *The Jews of Ancient Rome*. Philadelphia: Jewish Publication Society of America, 1960.
Levine, Amy-Jill. *The Social and Ethnic Dimensions of Matthean Salvation History: Go Nowhere Among the Gentiles (Matt 10: 5b)*. SBEC 14. Lewiston, NY: Mellen, 1988.
———. "Discharging Responsibility: Matthean Jesus, Biblical Law, and the Hemorrhaging Woman." In *Treasures New and Old: Recent Contributions to Matthean Studies*, edited by David R. Bauer and Mark Allan Powell, 379–97. Atlanta: Scholars, 1996. Reprinted in *A Feminist Companion to Matthew*, edited by Amy-Jill Levine, with Marianne Blickenstaff, 70–87. Sheffield, UK: Sheffield Academic, 2001.
———. "Leviticus, Book of." In *ABD* 4 (1992):311–21.
———. "Matthew." In *The Women's Bible Commentary*, edited by Carol A. Newsom and Sharon H. Ringe, 252–62. Louisville: Westminster John Knox, 1992.
———, editor, with M. Blickenstaff. *A Feminist Companion to Matthew*. Sheffield, UK: Sheffield Academic, 2001.
Lewellen, Ted C. *Political Anthropology: An Introduction*. South Hadley, MA: Bergin & Garvey, 1983.
Lewis, Naphtali. *Life in Egypt under Roman Rule*. Oxford: Clarendon, 1983.
Lichtheim, George. *Imperialism*. New York: Praeger, 1971.
Liddell, Henry George, Robert Scott, Henry Stuart Jones, and Roderick McKenzie. *A Greek-English Lexicon*. 9th ed. Oxford: Clarendon, 1996.
Lieu, Judith M. "Circumcision, Women, and Salvation." *NTS* 40 (1994) 358–70.
Lindars, Barnabas. *New Testament Apologetic*. Philadelphia: Fortress, 1961.
Linton, Ralph. "Nativistic Movements." *AA* 45 (1943) 230–40. Reprinted in W. A. Lessa and E. Z. Vogt, *Reader in Comparative Religion: An Anthropological Approach*, 499–506. 4th ed. San Francisco: HarperCollins, 1979.
Lipset, Seymour M. "History and Sociology: Some Methodological Considerations." In *Sociology and History: Methods*, edited by Seymore M. Lipset and Richard Hofstadter, 20–58. New York: Basic Books, 1968. Reprinted in *Revolution and Counterrevolution: Change and Persistence in Social Structures*, revised edition by Seymour M. Lipset, 3–34. New York: Basic Books.
Little, Daniel. "Local Politics and Class Conflict: Theories of Peasant Rebellion in Nineteenth-Century China." New England Historical Association, 1987, and

The Bellagio Conference on Peasant Culture and Consciousness, January, 1990. Online: www-personal.umd.umich.edu/~delittle/BELLAGI2.PDF.

Little, Kenneth. "The Role of Voluntary Associations in West African Urbanization." *AA* 59 (1957) 579–96.

Llewelyn, S. R., editor. *New Documents Illustrating Early Christianity*. Vol. 9. Grand Rapids: Eerdmans, 2002.

Loader, W. R. G. "Son of David, Blindness, Possession, and Duality in Matthew's Gospel." *CBQ* 44 (1982) 570–85.

Lofland, John. "'Becoming a World-Saver' Revisited." *American Behavior Scientist* 20 (1977) 805–18. Reprinted in *Conversion Careers: In and Out of the New Religions*, edited by James T. Richardson, 10–23. Beverly Hills: Sage, 1978.

Lofland, John, and Rodney Stark. "Becoming a World Saver: A Theory of Conversion to a Deviant Perspective." *ASR* 30 (1965) 862–75.

Lohmeyer, Ernst. *Soziale Fragen im Urchristentum*. 1921. Reprinted, Darmstadt: Wissenschaftliche Buchgesellschaft, 1973.

Lorrain, Jorge A. *The Concept of Ideology*. 2nd ed. Brookfield, VT: Gregg Revivals, 1992.

Louw, J., and Eugene A. Nida. "Greek-English Lexicon of the New Testament Based on Semantic Domains." *BibleWorks* 6.

Love, Stuart L. "Gender Roles in Certain Second Testament Passages: A Macrosociological View." *BTB* 17 (1987) 50–59.

———. "The Household: A Major Social Component for Gender Analysis in the Gospel of Matthew." *BTB* 23 (1993) 21–31.

———. "The Place of Women in Public Settings in Matthew's Gospel: A Sociological Inquiry." *BTB* 24 (1994) 52–65.

———. "Jesus Heals the Hemorrhaging Women." In *The Social Setting of Jesus and the Gospels*, edited by Wolfgang Stegemann et al., 83–91. Minneapolis: Fortress, 2002.

———. *Jesus and Marginal Women: The Gospel of Matthew in Social-Scientific Perspective*. Matrix 5. Eugene, OR: Cascade Books, 2009.

Lövestam, E. "Die Davidssohnfrage." *SEÅ* 27 (1963) 72–82.

Luomanen, Petri. "The Sociology of Sectarianism in Matthew: Modeling the Genesis of Early Jewish and Christian Communities." In *Fair Play: Diversity and Conflicts in Early Christianity. Essays in Honor of Heikki Räisänen*, edited by Ismo Dunderberg, Kari Syreeni, and Christopher Tuckett, 107–30. NovTSup 103. Leiden: Brill, 2002.

———. "The Potential of Stark and Bainbridge's General Theory of Religion in the Study of Early Christianity." *FJT* 6 (2004) 531–44.

Luxemburg, Rosa. *Socialism and the Churches*. Polish Social Democratic Party, 1905. No pages. Online: www.marxists.org/archive/luxemburg/1905/misc/socialism-churches.htm.

Luz, Ulrich. "The Disciples in the Gospel according to Matthew." In *The Interpretation of Matthew*, edited by Graham Stanton, 98–128. Issues in Religion and Theology 3. Philadelphia: Fortress, 1983.

———. *Matthew 1–7: A Commentary*. Translated by Wilhelm C. Linss. Continental Commetaries. Minneapolis: Augsburg, 1989. Translated by James E. Crouch. Hermeneia. Minneapolis: Fortress, 2007.

———. *Matthew 8–20*. Translated by James E. Crouch. Hermeneia. Minneapolis: Fortress, 2001.

———. *Matthew 21–28*. Translated by James E. Crouch. Hermeneia. Minneapolis: Fortress, 2005.
MacDonald, Margaret Y. *The Pauline Churches: A Socio-historical Study of Institutionalization in the Pauline and Deutero-Pauline Writings*. SNTSMS 60. Cambridge: Cambridge University Press, 1988.
Mack, Burton L. *A Myth of Innocence: Mark and Christian Origins*. Minneapolis: Fortress, 1988.
MacMullen, Ramsay. *Roman Social Relations: 50 B.C. to A.D. 284*. New Haven: Yale University Press, 1974.
———. *The Second Church: Popular Christianity AD 200–400*. Writings from the Greco-Roman World Supplements Series. Atlanta: Society of Biblical Literature, 2009.
Makkreel, Rudolf A. *Dilthey: Philosopher of the Human Studies*. Princeton: Princeton University Press, 1993.
Malherbe, Abraham J. *Social Aspects of Early Christianity*. 2nd ed. Philadelphia: Fortress, 1983.
Malina, Bruce J. *Christian Origins and Cultural Anthropology: Practical Models for Biblical Interpretation*. Atlanta: John Knox, 1986.
———. "A Conflict Approach to Mark 7." *Forum* 4/3 (1988) 3–30.
———. "Conflict in Luke-Acts: Labelling and Deviance Theory." In *The Social World of Luke-Acts: Models for Interpretation*, edited by Jerome H. Neyrey, 97–122. Peabody, MA: Hendrickson, 1991.
———. "Early Christian Groups: Using Small Group Formation Theory to Explain Christian Organizations." In *Modelling Early Christianity: Social-scientific Studies of the New Testament in its Context*, edited by Philip F. Esler, 96–113, London: Routledge, 1995.
———. "Honor and Shame in Luke-Acts: Pivotal Values of the Mediterranean World." In *The Social World of Luke-Acts: Models for Interpretation*, edited by Jerome H. Neyrey, 25–65. Peabody, MA: Hendrickson, 1991.
———. "Interpretation: Reading, Abduction, Metaphor." In *The Bible and the Politics of Exegesis: Essays in Honor of Norman K. Gottwald on His Sixty-Fifth Birthday*, edited by David Jobling, 253–66. Cleveland: Pilgrim, 1991.
———. "Interpreting the Bible with Anthropology: The Case of the Poor and the Rich." *Listening* 21 (1986) 148–59.
———. "Jesus as a Charismatic Leader?" *BTB* 14 (1984) 55–62.
———. *The Palestinian Manna Tradition: The Manna Tradition in the Palestinian Targums and Its Relationship to the New Testament Writings*. Arbeiten zur Geschichte des späteren Judentums und des Urchristentums 7. Leiden: Brill, 1968.
———. *The New Testament World: Insights from Cultural Anthropology*. 3rd ed. Louisville: Westminster John Knox, 2001.
———. "The Social Sciences and Biblical Interpretation." *Int* 37 (1982) 229–42.
———. "Normative Dissonance and Christian Origins." In *Social–Scientific Criticism of the New Testament and Its Social World*. Semeia 35, edited by John H. Elliott, 35–59. Decatur, GA: Scholars, 1986.
———. "'Religion' in the World of Paul." *BTB* 6 (1986) 92–101.
———. "Patron and Client: The Analogy behind Synoptic Theology." *Forum* 4/1 (1988) 2–32.

———. "Reading Theory Perspective: Reading Luke-Acts." In *The Social World of Luke-Acts: Models for Interpretation*, edited by Jerome H. Neyrey, 3–23. Peabody, MA: Hendrickson, 1991.

———. "Mediterranean Cultural Anthropology and the New Testament." In *La Bíblia i el Mediterrani. Las Biblia y el Mediterráneo. La Bible et la Méditerranée. Las Bibbia e il Mediterraneo: Actes del Congrés de Barcelona 18–22 de setembre de 1995*. Vol. 1, edited by Augustí Borrell, Alfonso de la Fuente and Armand Puig, 151–78. Abadia de Montserrat: Associació Bíblica de Catalunya, 1997.

———. *Social Science Commentary on the Gospel of John*. Minneapolis: Fortress, 1998.

———. "Review of Evert-Jan Vledder, *Conflict in the Miracle Stories: A Socio-Exegetical Study of Matthew 8 and 9*." *BTB* 29 (1999) 45–46.

Malina, Bruce J., and Jerome H. Neyrey. *Calling Jesus Names: The Social Value of Labels in Matthew*. Sonoma, CA: Polebridge, 1988.

———. "First-Century Personality: Dyadic, Not Individualistic." In *The Social World of Luke-Acts: Models for Interpretation*, edited by Jerome H. Neyrey, 67–96. Peabody, MA: Hendrickson, 1991.

———. *Portraits of Paul: An Archeology of Ancient Personality*. Peabody, MA: Hendrickson, 1996.

Malina, Bruce J., and Richard L. Rohrbaugh. *Social-Science Commentary on the Synoptic Gospels*. Minneapolis: Fortress, 1992. 2nd edition, 2003.

Mallard, A. R. "An Assessment of the Evidence of Writing in Ancient Israel." *BAT* 1984 (1985), 301-12.

Manning, J. G., and Ian Morris. *The Ancient Economy: Evidence and Models*. Minneapolis: Fortress, 2007.

Mantel, H. "Sanhedrin." *IDBSup*, edited by Keith Crim, 784–86. Nashville: Abingdon, 1976.

Marshall, Gordon. "Historical Sociology." *A Dictionary of Sociology*. Oxford: Oxford University Press, 1998. No pages. Online: http://www.wiley.com/bw/journal.asp?ref=0952-1909.

Marx, Karl. "Preface." *A Contribution to the Critique of Political Economy*. Translated by S. W. Ryanzanskaya; edited by M. Dobb. London: Lawrence & Whishart, 1971. Original German, 1859.

———, and Friedrich Engels. *Die heilige Familie, oder Kritik der kritischen Kritik. Gegen Bruno Bauer & Consorten*. Frankfurt: Literarische Anstart (J. Rütten), 1845. No pages. Online: http://www.marxists.org/archive/marx/works/1845/holy-family/index.htm.

Mathew, Parackel K. "Authority and Discipline (Matt 16:17–19; 18:15–18) and the Exercise of Authority and Discipline in the Matthean Community." *CommViat* 28/3–4 (1985) 119–125.

Mathews, Shailer. *Jesus on Social Institutions*. Reprint, edited by Kenneth Cauthen. Lives of Jesus Series. Philadelphia: Fortress, 1971.

Matlock, R. Barry. "'Jews by Nature': Paul, Ethnicity and Galatians." In *Far From Minimal: Celebrating the Work and Influence of Philip R. Davies*, edited by Duncan Burns and John W. Rogerson. The Library of Bible/Old Testament Studies 484. London: T. & T. Clark. Forthcoming in 2011. Online: http://tandtclark.typepad.com/Davies_FS_Files/Davies_FS_Matlock.pdf.

McCracken, David. "Character in the Boundary: Bakhtin's Interdividuality in Biblical Narratives." *Semeia* 63 (1993) 29–42.

McEleney, N. J. "Conversion, Circumcision, and Law." *NTS* 20 (1974) 328–33.

McIver, Robert Kerry. *The Problem of Synoptic Relationships in the Development and Testing of a Methodology for the Reconstruction of the Matthean Community.* Diss. Andrews University. UMI Dissertation Information Service 1416, 1988.
McKinney, John C., and Charles P. Loomis. "Introduction." In Ferdinand Tönnies, *Community and Society.* Translated and edited by Charles P. Loomis, 1–29. East Lansing: The Michigan State University Press, 1957.
McKnight, Edgar V. *Postmodern Use of the Bible: The Emergence of Reader-Oriented Criticism.* Nashville: Abingdon, 1988.
McLellan, David. *Ideology.* Milton Keynes, UK: Open University Press, 1986.
McNutt, Paula. *Reconstructing the Society of Ancient Israel.* Library of Ancient Israel. Louisville: Westminster John Knox, 1999.
McVann, Mark. "Rituals of Status Transformation in Luke-Acts: The Case of Jesus the Prophet." In *The Social World of Luke-Acts: Models for Interpretation*, edited by Jerome H. Neyrey, 333–60. Peabody, MA: Hendrickson, 1991.
Meeks, Wayne A. "The Man from Heaven in Johannine Sectarianism." *JBL* 91 (1972) 44–72.
———. "'Since Then You Would Need to Go out of the World': Group Boundaries in Pauline Christianity." In *Critical History and Biblical Faith: New Testament Perspectives*, edited by T. J. Ryan, 4–29. Villanova, PA: College Theology Society, 1979.
———. *The First Urban Christians: The Social World of the Apostle Paul.* New Haven, CN, and London: Yale University Press, 1983.
———. *The Moral World of the First Christians.* Philadelphia: Westminster, 1986.
———, and Robert Wilken, editors. *Jews and Christians in Antioch in the First Four Centuries of the Common Era.* Missoula, MT: Scholars, 1978.
Meggitt, Justin J. *Paul, Poverty, and Survival.* Studies of the New Testament and Its World. Edinburgh: T. & T. Clark, 1998.
Meier, John P. *Law and History in Matthew's Gospel.* Analecta Biblica 71. Rome: Biblical Institute, 1976.
———. *The Vision of Matthew: Christ, Church, and Morality in the First Gospel.* New York: Crossroad, 1991. Original edition 1979.
———. *Matthew.* Wilmington, DE: Michael Glazier, 1980.
———. "Antioch." In *Antioch and Rome: New Testament Cradles of Catholic Christianity by* Raymond E. Brown and John P. Meier. New York: Paulist, 1983, 12–27.
———. *A Marginal Jew: Rethinking the Historical Jesus.* 4 vols. New York: Doubleday. Vol. 1, 1991 (The Roots of the Problem and Person); Vol. 2, 1994 (Mentor, Message, and Miracles); Vol. 3, 2001 (Companions and Competitors); Vol. 4, 2009 (Law and Love).
———. "Matthew, Gospel of." In *ABD* 4 (1992) 622–41.
Merton, Robert. *Social Theory and Social Structure.* New York: Free Press, 1957.
Metzger, Bruce M. *A Textual Commentary on the Greek New Testament.* 2nd ed. Stuttgart: United Bible Societies, 2002.
Meyers, Eric M., and James F. Strange. *Archaeology, the Rabbis, and Early Christianity.* Nashville: Abingdon, 1981.
Milibrand, Ralph. "Class Analysis." In *Social Theory Today*, edited by Anthony Giddens and Jonathan Turner, 325–46. Stanford: Stanford University Press, 1987.
Milikowsky, Chaim. "Law at Qumran: A Critical Reaction to Lawrence H. Schiffman, Sectarian Law in the Dead Sea Scrolls: Courts, Testimony and the Penal Code." *RevQ* 12 (1985–1986) 243–44.

Millar, Furgas. *The Roman Empire and Its Neighbours*. 2nd ed.; London: Duckworth, 1981.
Millard, A. R. "The Practice of Writing in Ancient Israel." *BA* 35 (1972) 98–111.
———. "An Assessment of the Evidence for Writing in Ancient Israel (and Responses)." In *Biblical Archaeology Today*. Proceedings of the International Congress on Biblical Archaeology, 301–70. Jerusalem: Israel Exploration Society and American Schools of Oriental Research, 1985.
———. "Arameans." In *ABD* 1 (1992) 345–350.
———. "Literacy (Israel)." In *ABD* 4 (1992) 337–40.
Mills, Theodore M. *The Sociology of Small Groups*. Englewood Cliffs, NJ: Prentice-Hall, 1967.
Minear, Paul S. "Church, Idea of." *IDB* 1 (1962) 607–17.
Miyahara, Kojiro. "Charisma: From Weber to Contemporary Sociology." *Sociological Inquiry* 53 (1983) 368–388.
Mommsen, Wolfgang J. *The Political and Social Theory of Max Weber: Collected Essays*. Chicago: University of Chicago Press, 1989.
Montesquieu, Charles-Louis de Secondat, baron de La Brède et de. *The Spirit of the Laws*. Translated by A. M. Cohler, B. C. Miller, and H. Stone. Cambridge Tests in the History of Political Thought. Cambridge: Cambridge University Press, 1989. Original French 1748.
Moore, Barrington, Jr. *Social Origins of Dictatorship and Democracy: Lord and Peasant in the Making of the Modern World*. Boston: Beacon Press, 1966.
Moore, Stephen D. *Poststructuralism and the New Testament: Derrida and Foucault at the Foot of the Cross*. Minneapolis: Fortress, 1994.
Moreau, H. I. *A History of Education in Antiquity*. Translated by George Lamb. New York: Sheed & Ward, 1956.
Moreland, Richard L., and John M. Levine. "Group Dynamics Over Time: Development and Socialization in Small Groups." In *The Psychology of Time: New Perspectives*, edited by Joseph E. McGrath, 151–81. London: Sage, 1986.
Morris, Aldon, and Carol McClurg Mueller, editors. *Frontiers in Social Movement Theory*. New Haven: Yale University Press, 1992.
Motyl, Alexander J. *Imperial Ends: The Decay, Collapse, and Revival of Empires*. New York: Columbia University Press, 2001.
Moxnes, Halvor. *The Economy of the Kingdom: Social Conflict and Economic Relations in Luke's Gospel*. 1988. Reprint, Eugene, OR: Wipf & Stock, 2004.
———. "Patron-Client Relations and the New Community in Luke-Acts." In *The Social World of Luke-Acts: Models for Interpretation*, edited by Jerome H. Neyrey, 241–68. Peabody, MA: Hendrickson, 1991.
———, editor. *Constructing Early Christian Families: Family as Social Reality and Metaphor*. London: Routledge, 1997.
Muthuraj, J. G. "The Meaning of *ethnos* and *ethnē* and Its Significance to the Study of the New Testament." *BTF* 29/10 (1997) 3–36.
Myers, Ched. *Binding the Strong Man: A Political Reading of Mark's Story of Jesus*. Maryknoll, NY: Orbis, 1988; reissued 2008.
Naquin, Susan. *Millenarian Rebellion in China: The Eight Trigrams Uprising of 1813*. New Haven: Yale University Press, 1976.
Neils, Jenifer. *Goddess and Polis: The Panathenaic Festival in Ancient Athens*. Princeton: Princeton University Press, 1992.

Neusner, Jacob. "The Fellowship (*Haburah*) in the Second Jewish Commonwealth." *HTR* 53 (1960) 125–42.

———. *Development of a Legend: Studies in the Traditions concerning Yohanan ben Zakkai*. Leiden: Brill, 1970.

———. "'By the Testimony of Two Witnesses' in the Damascus Document IX, 17–22 and in Pharisaic-Rabbinic Law." *RevQ* (1973) 197–217.

———. *Early Rabbinic Judaism: Historical Studies in Religion, Literature, and Art*. Leiden: Brill, 1975.

———. "Damascus Document IX,17–22 and Irrelevant Parallels." *RevQ* 9 (1978) 441–44.

———. "The Formation of Rabbinic Judaism: Yavneh from A.D. 70–100." In *ANRW* II.19.2: 3–42.

Newsom, Carol A. "'Sectually Explicit' Literature from Qumran." In *The Hebrew Bible and Its Interpreters*, edited by W. H. Propp, B. Halpern, and D. N. Freedman, 167–87. Winona Lake, IN: Eisenbrauns, 1990.

Neyrey, Jerome H. "Unclean, Common, Polluted, and Taboo." *Forum* 4/4 (1988) 72–82.

———. *Paul in Other Words: A Cultural Reading of His Letters*. Louisville: Westminster John Knox, 1990.

———. "Ceremonies in Luke-Acts: The Case of Meals and Table-Fellowship." In *The Social World of Luke-Acts: Models for Interpretation*, edited by Jerome H. Neyrey, 361–87. Peabody, MA: Hendrickson, 1991.

———, editor. *The Social World of Luke-Acts: Models for Interpretation*. Peabody, MA: Hendrickson, 1991.

———. "The Symbolic Universe of Luke-Acts: 'They Turn the World Upside Down.'" In *The Social World of Luke-Acts: Models for Interpretation*, edited by Jerome H. Neyrey, 271–304. Peabody, MA: Hendrickson, 1991.

———. "Josephus' *Vita* and the Encomium: A Native Model of Personality." *JSJ* 25 (1994) 177–206.

———. "Loss of Wealth, Loss of Family and Loss of Honor: A Cultural Interpretation of the Original Four Makarisms." In *Modelling Early Christianity: Social-Scientific Studies of the New Testament in Its Context*, edited by Philip F. Esler, 139–58. London: Routledge, 1995.

———. "Ancestors." In *The Collegeville Pastoral Dictionary of Biblical Theology*, edited by Carroll Stuhlmuller, 22–24. Collegeville, MN: Liturgical, 1996.

———. "Family." In *The Collegeville Pastoral Dictionary of Biblical Theology*, edited by Carroll Stuhlmuller, 308–311. Collegeville, MN: Liturgical, 1996.

———. "Father." In *The Collegeville Pastoral Dictionary of Biblical Theology*, edited by Carroll Stuhlmuller, 315–19. Collegeville, MN: Liturgical, 1996.

———. *Honor and Shame in the Gospel of Matthew*. Louisville: Westminster John Knox, 1998.

———. "Deception, Ambiguity, and Revelation: Matthew's Judgmental Scenes in Social-Science Perspective." In *When Judaism and Christianity Began*, edited by Alan Avery-Peck, Daniel Harrington, and Jacob Neusner, 199–230. Leiden: Brill, 2004.

Nickelsburg, George W. E. *Jewish Literature between the Bible and the Mishnah*. Philadelphia: Fortress, 1981.

———, and Michael Stone. *Faith and Piety in Early Judaism: Texts and Documents*. Philadelphia: Fortress, 1983.

Niebuhr, H. Richard. *The Social Sources of Denominationalism*. 1929. Reprint Kessinger, 2004.

Nielsen, Kai. *Equality and Liberty: A Defense of Radical Egalitarianism*. Totowa, NJ: Roman & Allanheld, 1985.

Nock, A. D. "The Historical Importance of Cult Associations." *CR* 38 (1924) 105–9.

———. *Conversion*. New York: Oxford University Press, 1933.

———. "The Vocabulary of the New Testament." *JBL* 52 (1933) 131–139.

Nolan, Patrick, and Gerhard Lenski. *Human Societies: An Introduction to Macrosociology*. 7th ed. Boston: McGraw Hill, 1995.

———. *Human Societies: An Introduction to Macrosociology*. 8th ed. Boston: McGraw Hill, 1998.

———. *Human Societies: An Introduction to Macrosociology*. 9th ed. Boston: McGraw Hill, 2004.

Nolland, J. "Uncircumcised Proselytes?" *JSJ* 12 (1981) 173–94.

Norris, Frederick W. "Artifacts from Antioch." In *Social History of the Matthean Community: Cross Disciplinary Approaches*, edited by David L. Balch, 248–58. Minneapolis: Fortress, 1991.

North, Robert. "Ezra (Person)." In *IDB* 2 (1992) 726–28.

Oakes, Peter. *Rome in the Bible and the Early Church*. Grand Rapids: Baker Academic, 2002.

Oakman, Douglas E. *Jesus and the Economic Questions of His Day*. SBEC 8. Lewiston, NY: Mellen, 1986.

———. "The Herodian Temple and the Jesus Tradition: An Essay in Conceptual Modeling." Social Sciences and New Testament Interpretation Section, AAR/SBL National Meeting, New Orleans, LA, November 1990.

———. "The Jesus Tradition and the Herodian Temple." Unpublished paper for the Context Group, 1990.

———. "The Countryside in Luke-Acts." In *The Social World of Luke-Acts: Models for Interpretation*, edited by Jerome H. Neyrey, 151–79. Peabody, MA: Hendrickson, 1991.

———. "The Archeology of First-Century Galilee and the Social Interpretation of the Historical Jesus." In *SBL 1994 Seminar Papers*, edited by Eugene H. Lovering. Atlanta: Scholars, 1994.

———. "After Ten Years. A Draft History of the Context Group: Project on the Bible in its Socio-Cultural Context," 1996. Unpublished.

———. "Was Jesus a Peasant?" In *Jesus and the Peasants*, 164–80. Matrix 4. Eugene, OR: Cascade Books, 2008.

———. See Hanson and Oakman.

Orton, David E. *The Understanding Scribe: Matthew and the Apocalyptic Ideal*. JSNTSup 25. Sheffield, UK: JSOT Press, 1989.

Osiek, Carolyn. *What Are They Saying about the Social Setting of the New Testament?* 2nd ed. New York: Paulist, 1992.

———, and David L. Balch. *Families in the New Testament World: Households and House Churches*. Louisville: Westminster John Knox, 1997.

Overholt, Thomas. *Cultural Anthropology and the Old Testament*. Guides to Biblical Scholarship. Minneapolis: Fortress, 1996.

Overman, Andrew. *Matthew's Gospel and Formative Judaism: The Social World of the Matthean Community*. Minneapolis: Fortress, 1990.

———. *Church and Community in Crisis. New Testament in Context.* Valley Forge, PA: Trinity, 1996.
Oxford English Dictionary. 2nd ed. Oxford: Clarendon, 1969.
Pantle-Schieber, Klaus. "Anmerkungen zur Auseinandersetzung von Ekklesia und Judentum im Matthäusevangelium." *ZNW* 80 (1989) 145–62.
Parásslglou, George M. "DECIA XEIR KAI GONU: Some Thoughts on the Postures of the Ancient Greeks and Romans When Writing on Papyrus Rolls." *Scrittura e civiltà* 3 (1979) 5–21.
Park, Robert E. "Human Migration and the Marginal Man." *AJS* 33 (1928) 881–93.
———. "Personality and Cultural Conflict." *PASS* 25 (1931) 95–110.
———. *Race and Culture.* Glencoe, IL: Free Press, 1950.
Pauly, August, Georg Wissowa, Wilhelm Kroll, Kurt Witte, Karl Mittelhaus, Konrat Ziegler, editors. *Paulys Realencyclopädie der classischen Altertumswissenschaft: neue Bearbeitung.* Stuttgart: Metzler, 1894–1980.
Patte, Daniel. *What Is Structural Exegesis?* Guides to Biblical Scholarship. Philadelphia: Fortress, 1976.
———. *The Gospel according to Matthew.* Philadelphia: Fortress, 1987.
Paul, Garrett E. "Why Troeltsch? Why Today? Theology for the 21st Century." *ChrCent* (1993) 676–81.
Pedersen, Johannes. *Israel: Its Life and Culture* I–II. London: Oxford University Press, 1926.
———. *Israel: Its Life and Culture* III–IV. London: Oxford University Press, 1940.
Peristiany, J. G., editor. *Honour and Shame: The Values of Mediterranean Society.* London: Weidenfeld & Nicolson, 1965.
———, and Julian Pitt-Rivers, editors. *Honour and Grace in Anthropology.* Cambridge: Cambridge University Press, 1992.
Perkins, Pheme. "Gender Analysis: A Response to Antoinette Clark Wire." In *Social History of the Matthean Community*, edited by David L. Balch, 122–26. Minneapolis: Fortress, 1991.
Perrin, Norman. *What Is Redaction Criticism?* Guides to Biblical Scholarship. Philadelphia: Fortress, 1969.
———, and Dennis C. Duling. *The New Testament: Proclamation and Parenesis, Myth and History.* 3rd ed. Fort Worth: Harcourt Brace College Publishers, 1994.
Pesch, W. *Matthäus der Seelsorger.* SBS 2. Stuttgart: Katholisches Bibelwerk, 1966.
Petersen, Norman R. *Literary Criticism for New Testament Critics.* Guides to Biblical Scholarship. Philadelphia: Fortress, 1978.
Peterson, Dwight N. *The Origins of Mark: The Markan Community in Current Debate.* Leiden: Brill, 2000.
Pfitzner, Victor C. "Purified Community—Purified Sinner: Expulsion from the Community according to Matt 18:15–18 and 1 Cor 5:1–5." *ABR* 30 (1982) 34–55.
Pfuhl, Stephen. *Images of Deviance and Social Control: A Sociological History.* New York: McGraw-Hill, 1985.
Pike, K. L. "Emic and Etic Standpoints for the Description of Behavior." In *Language in Relation to a Unified Theory of the Structure of Human Behavior*, Part I, 8–28. Glendale, CA: Summer Institute of Linguistics.
Pilch, John J. "The Health Care System in Matthew: A Social Science Analysis." *BTB* 16 (1986) 102–6.

———. "Reading Matthew Anthropologically: Healing in Cultural Perspective." *Listening* 24 (1989) 278–89.

———. "Sickness and Healing in Luke-Acts." In *The Social World of Luke-Acts: Models for Interpretation*, edited by Jerome H. Neyrey, 181–209. Peabody, MA: Hendrickson, 1991.

———. "'Beat His Ribs While He Is Young' (Sir 30: 12): A Window on the Mediterranean World." *BTB* 23 (1993) 101–13.

———. "Illuminating the World of Jesus through Cultural Anthropology." *The Living Light* 31/1 (1994) 20–31.

———. "Jews and Christians: Anachronisms in Bible Translations." *Issues* 25 (1996) 18–25.

———. "Forgiveness." In *CDB*, edited by John J. Pilch, 59–64. Collegeville, MN: Liturgical, 1999.

———. "The Honoree: Bruce John Malina." In *Essays by the Context Group in Honor of Bruce J. Malina*, edited by John J. Pilch, 1–4. Biblical Interpretation Series 53. Leiden: Brill, 2001.

———. "Recollections: CBA Task Forces." Discussed at the Task Force on the Social Sciences and New Testament at the annual CBA meeting at Creighton University, Omaha, NE, 2009.

———. "Birth and *Vorgeschichte* of the Context Group." Personal communication, 2010.

Pina-Cabral, João de. "The Mediterranean as a Category of Regional Comparison: A Critical View." *CA* 30 (1989) 399–406.

Piper, Ronald A. "The Language of Violence and the Aphoristic Sayings in Q." In *Conflict and Invention: Literary, Rhetorical and Social Studies on the Sayings Gospel Q*, edited by John S. Kloppenborg, 53–72. Valley Forge, PA: Trinity, 1995.

Pitt-Rivers, Julian Alfred, editor. *The People of the Sierra*. New York: Criterion, 1954.

———. "Honor." In *IESS* 6 (1968):503–11.

———. *Mediterranean Countrymen: Essays in the Social Anthropology of the Mediterranean*. Paris: Mouton, 1963.

———. "Pseudo-Kinship." In *IESS* 8 (1968):408–13.

———. *The Fate of Shechem, or the Politics of Sex: Essays in the Anthropology of the Mediterranean*. Cambridge Studies in Social Anthropology 19. Cambridge: Cambridge University Press, 1977.

Plummer, A. *An Exegetical Commentary on the Gospel according to St. Matthew*. London: Stock, 1909.

Poland, F. *Geschichte des griechischen Vereinswesens*. Leipzig: Teubner, 1909.

Powell, Mark Allen. "Characterization on the Phraseological Plane in the Gospel of Matthew." In *Treasures New and Old: Contributions to Matthean Studies*, edited by David R. Bower and Mark Allen Powell, 161–77. Atlanta: Scholars, 1996.

Rabinowitz, Peter J. "Truth in Fiction: A Reexamination of Audiences." *CI* 4 (1977) 121–41.

———. *Before Reading: Narrative Conventions and the Politics of Interpretation*. Ithaca, NY: Cornell University Press, 1987.

———. "Whirl without End: Audience-Oriented Criticism." In *Contemporary Literary Theory*, edited by G. D. Atkins and L. Morrow, 81–100. Amherst: University of Massachusetts Press, 1989.

———. *Authorizing Readers: Resistance and Respect in the Teaching of Literature*. New York: Teachers College Press,1998.

Rad, Gerhard von, K. G. Kuhn, and W. Gutbrod. *"Ioudaios."* In *TNDT* 3 (1965) 360–61.
Ramsay, William Michael. *St Paul the Traveller and the Roman Citizen.* London: Hodder & Stoughton, 1895.
Ranke, Leopold von. *History of the Latin and Teutonic Peoples from 1494 to 1514.* Translated by Philip A. Ashwokth. London: Bell, 1887.
Ransom, John Crowe. *The New Criticism.* New York: New Directions, 1941.
Reed, Jonathan L. *Archaeology and the Galilean Jesus: A Re-examination of the Evidence.* Harrisburg, PA: Trinity, 2000.
Rhoads, David M., Donald M. Michie, and Joanna Dewey. *Mark As Story: An Introduction to the Narrative of a Gospel.* 2nd ed. Minneapolis: Fortress, 1999.
Richards, E. Randolph. *The Secretary in the Letters of Paul.* Tübingen: Mohr/Siebeck, 1989.
Richardson, Peter. "Early Synagogues as *Collegia* in the Diaspora and Palestine." In *Voluntary Associations in the Graeco-Roman World*, edited by John S. Kloppenborg and Stephen G. Wilson, 90–109. London: Routledge, 1996.
Riches, John K. *Conflicting Mythologies: Identity Formation in the Gospels of Mark and Matthew.* Edinburgh: T. & T. Clark, 2000.

———. "Matthew's Missionary Strategy in Colonial Perspective." In *The Gospel of Matthew in Its Roman Imperial Context*, edited by John K. Riches and David C. Sim, 128–42. London: T. & T. Clark, 2005.
Riches, John K., and David C. Sim. *The Gospel of Matthew in Its Roman Imperial Context.* London: T. & T. Clark, 2005.
Ritzer, George. *Contemporary Sociological Theory.* New York: Knopf, 1983.
Rivkin, Ellis. "Scribes, Pharisees, Lawyers, Hypocrites: A Study in Synonymity." *HUCA* 49 (1978) 135–42.
Robbins, Vernon K. "The Social Location of the Implied Author of Luke-Acts." In *The Social World of Luke-Acts: Models for Interpretation*, edited by Jerome H. Neyrey, 305–32. Peabody, MA: Hendrickson, 1991.

———. *Matthew: Storyteller, Interpreter, Evangelist. Rhetoric, Society and Ideology.* London: Routledge, 1996.
Robertson, D. B., editor. *Voluntary Associations: A Study of Groups in Free Societies: Essays in Honor of James Luther Adams.* Richmond: John Knox, 1966.
Robinson, H. Wheeler. *The Corporate Personality.* Rev. ed. Edinburgh: T. & T. Clark, 1981.
Rohner, Ronald P. "Toward a Conception of Culture for Cross-cultural Psychology." *JCCP* 15 (1984) 111–38.
Rohrbaugh, Richard L. *The Biblical Interpreter: An Agrarian Bible in an Industrial Age.* Philadelphia: Fortress, 1978.

———. "Methodological Considerations in the Debate over the Social Class Status of Early Christians." *JAAR* 52 (1984) 519–46.

———. "'Social Location of Thought' as a Heuristic Construction in New Testament Study." *JSNT* 30 (1987) 103–19.

———. "The Pre-Industrial City in Luke-Acts: Urban Social Relations." In *The Social World of Luke-Acts: Models for Interpretation*, edited by Jerome H. Neyrey, 125–49. Peabody, MA: Hendrickson, 1991.

———. "The Social Location of the Marcan Audience." *BTB* 23 (1993) 114–27.

———. "The Social Location of the Marcan Audience." *Int* 47 (1993) 380–95.

———, editor. *The Social Sciences and New Testament Interpretation.* Peabody, MA: Hendrickson, 1996.

Rostovtzeff, M. *The Social and Economic History of the Roman Empire*. Oxford: Clarendon, 1926. Reprinted, 1957.
Rothenberger, John E. "The Social Dynamics of Dispute Settlement in a Sunni Muslim Village in Lebanon." In *The Disputing Process—Law in Ten Societies*, edited by Laura Nader and Harry F. Todd, 152–80. New York: Columbia University Press, 1978.
Rowland, Christopher. "Reading the New Testament Sociologically: An Introduction." *Theol* 88 (1985) 358–64.
Runesson, Anders. "Rethinking Early Jewish-Christian Religions: Matthean Community History as Pharisaic Intragroup Conflict." *JBL* 127 (2008) 95–132.
Said, Eduard W. *Orientalism*. New York: Vintage, 1978.
———. "Afterword." In *Orientalism*. Reprinted, New York: Vintage, 1994.
Saldarini, Anthony J. *Pharisees, Scribes, and Sadducees in Palestinian Society: A Sociological Approach*. Wilmington, DE: Glazier, 1988.
———. "Political and Social Roles of the Pharisees and Scribes in Galilee." In *SBL 1988 Seminar Papers*, edited by David J. Lull, 200–209. Atlanta: Scholars, 1988.
———. "The Gospel of Matthew and Jewish-Christian Conflict." In *Social History of the Matthean Community: Cross-Disciplinary Approaches*, edited by David L. Balch, 38–61. Minneapolis: Fortress, 1991.
———. "Delegitimation of Leaders in Matthew 23." *CBQ* 54 (1992) 659–80.
———. "Pharisees." In *ABD* 5 (1992) 289–303.
———. "Scribes." In *ABD* 5 (1992) 1012–16.
———. *Matthew's Christian-Jewish Community*. Chicago: University of Chicago Press, 1994.
Sanders, E. P. *Judaism: Practice and Belief 63 BCE–66 CE*. London: SCM, 1992.
———. *Paul and Palestinian Judaism*. London: SCM, 1977.
Sant Cassia, Paul. "Review Article: Navigating an Anthropology of the Mediterranean: Recent Developments in France." *HistAnth* 14 (2003) 87–94.
Sarbin, Theodore R., and Allen, Vernon L. "Role Theory." In *HSP* I., edited by Gardner Lindzey and Elliott Aronson, 488-567. 2nd ed. Reading, PA: Addison-Wesley, 1968.
Schaberg, Jane. *The Illegitimacy of Jesus: A Feminist Theological Interpretation of the Infancy Narratives*. San Francisco: Harper & Row, 1967.
Schams, Christine. *Jewish Scribes in the Second-Temple Period*. JSOTSup 291. Sheffield, UK: Sheffield Academic, 1998.
Schermerhorn, Richard Alonzo. "Marginal Man." In *DSS*, edited by Julius Gould and William L. Kolb, 406–7. New York: Free Press, 1964.
Schiffman, Lawrence H. *The Halakhah at Qumran*. Studies in Judaism in Late Antiquity 16. Leiden: Brill, 1975.
———. "The Qumran Law of Testimony." *RevQ* 8 (1975) 603–12.
———. "Jewish Sectarianism in Second Temple Judaism." In *Great Schisms in Jewish History*, edited by R. Jospe and S. Wagner, 1–46. New York: Ktav, 1981.
———. *Sectarian Law in the Dead Sea Scrolls: Courts, Testimony, and the Penal Code*. BJS 33. Chico, CA: Scholars, 1983.
———. "Reproof as a Requisite for Punishment in the Law of the Dead Sea Scrolls." In *Jewish Law Association Studies* II, edited by B. S. Jackson, 59–74. Atlanta: Scholars, 1986.
———. *Reclaiming the Dead Sea Scrolls*. New York: Doubleday, 1994.

Schneider, C. "Zur Problematik des Hellenistischen in den Qumrantexten." In *Qumranprobleme*, edited by H. Bardtke, 299-344. Berlin: de Gruyter, 1963.
Schökel, Luis Alonso. "The Vision of Man in Sirach 16:24—17:14." In *Israelite Wisdom: Theological and Literary Essays in Honor of Samuel Terrien*, edited by John G. Gammie, 235-45. Missoula, MT: Scholars, 1978.
Scholer, David M. *Social Distinctives of the Christians in the First Century: Pivital Essays by E. A. Judge*. Peabody, MA: Hendrickson, 2008.
Schottroff, Louise. *The Parables of Jesus: A Feminist Approach*. Translated by Linda M. Mahoney. Minneapolis: Fortress, 2006.
———, and Wolfgang Stegemann. *Jesus and the Hope of the Poor*. Translated by Matthew J. O'Connell. 1986. Reprinted, Eugene, OR: Wipf & Stock, 2009.
Schottroff, Willy, and Wolfgang Stegemann. *God of the Lowly*. Matthew J. O'Connell. Maryknoll, NY: Orbis, 1984.
Schubert, Paul. "Shirley Jackson Case, Historian of Early Christianity: An Appraisal." *JR* 29 (1949) 30-46.
Schulze, Winfried. *Soziologie und Geschichtswissenschaft: Einführung in die Probleme der Kooperation beider Wissenschaften*. Munich: Fink, 1974.
Schumacher, R. *Die soziale Lage der Christen in apostolischen Zeitalter*. Paderborn: Schöningh, 1924.
Schürer, Emil, Geza Vermes, Fergus Millar, and Matthew Black. *The History of the Jewish People in the Age of Jesus Christ (175 B.C.-A.D. 135)*. 5 vols. Edinburgh: T. & T. Clark, 1973-1987.
Schüssler Fiorenza, E. *In Memory of Her: A Feminist Theological Reconstruction of Christian Origins*. New York: Crossroad, 1983.
Schütz, John. *Paul and the Anatomy of Apostolic Authority*. SNTSMS 26. London: Cambridge University Press, 1975.
———. "Steps Toward a Sociology of Primitive Christianity: A Critique of the Work of Gerd Theissen." AAR/SBL Meeting, December 27-31, 1977, San Francisco, California, 1977.
———. "Introduction." In *The Social Setting of Pauline Christianity* by Gerd Theissen, 1-23. Philadelphia: Fortress, 1982.
Schweitzer, Albert. *The Quest of the Historical Jesus*. Edited by John Bowden. Translated by W. Montgomery, J. R. Coates, Susan Cupitt, and John Bowden. Minneapolis: Fortress, 2001.
Schweizer, Eduard. "Observance of the Law and Charismatic Activity in Matthew." *NTS* 16 (1970) 213-30.
———. *Matthäus and seine Gemeinde*. Stuttgarter Bibelstudien 71. Stuttgart: Katholisches Bibelwerk, 1974.
———. "The 'Matthaean' Church." *NTS* 20 (1974) 216.
———. *The Good News according to Matthew*. Translated by D. E. Green. Atlanta: John Knox, 1975.
———. "Matthew's Church." In *The Interpretation of Matthew*, edited by Graham Stanton, 129-55. IRT 3. Philadelphia: Fortress, 1983.
Scott, G. M. Jr. "A Resynthesis of the Primordial and Circumstantial Approaches to Ethnic Group Solidarity: Towards an Explanatory Model." *ERS* 13 (1990) 147-71.
Scott, James C. *Moral Economy of the Peasant: Rebellion and Subsistence in Southeast Asia*. New Haven: Yale University Press, 1977.
———. "Protest and Profanation: Agrarian Revolt and the Little Tradition (Part 2)" *TheorSoc* 4 (1977) 211-46.

———. *Weapons of the Weak: Everyday Forms of Peasant Resistance.* New Haven: Yale University Press, 1985.

———. *Domination and the Arts of Resistance: Hidden Transcripts.* New Haven: Yale University Press, 1990.

Scroggs, Robin. "The Earliest Christian Communities as Sectarian Movement." In *Christianity, Judaism and Other Greco-Roman Cults: Studies for Morton Smith at Sixty*, edited by Jacob Neusner, 2:1–23. Studies in Judaism in Late Antiquity 12. Leiden: Brill, 1975.

———. "The Sociological Interpretation of the New Testament: The Present State of Research." *NTS* 26 (1980) 164–79.

Seeman, Christopher. "The Urbanization of Herodian Galilee as an Historical Factor Contributing to the Emergence of the Jesus Movement." MA Thesis. Graduate Theological Union, Berkeley, 1993.

Segal, Alan. "Matthew's Jewish Voice." In *Social History of the Matthean Community: Cross-Disciplinary Approaches*, edited by David L. Balch, 3–37. Minneapolis: Fortress, 1991.

Seidman, Steven. *Contested Knowledge: Social Theory Today.* 3rd ed. Oxford: Blackwell, 2003.

Seland, Terry. "Jesus as a Faction Leader: On the Exit of the Category 'Sect.'" In *Context*, edited by Peter Wilhelm Bøckman and Roald E. Kristiansen, 197–211. Trondheim: TAPIR, 1987.

Senior, Donald P. *What Are They Saying about Matthew?* Rev. ed. New York: Paulist, 1996.

———. "Matthean Scholarship: Where Are We? and Where Are We Going?" Lecture, Matthew Group SBL, 1998.

———. "Between Two Worlds: Gentile and Jewish Christians in Matthew's Gospel." *CBQ* 61 (1999) 1–23.

———. "Directions in Matthean Studies." In *The Gospel of Matthew in Current Study: Studies in Memory of William G. Thompson*, edited by David E. Aune, 5–21. Grand Rapids: Eerdmans, 2001.

Service, Elman R. *Primitive Social Organization: An Evolutionary Perspective.* New York: Random House, 1962.

Setzer, Claudia J. "Rulers of the Synagogue." In *ABD* 5 (1992):841–42.

Sharot, Stephen. *Messianism, Mysticism, and Magic: A Sociological Analysis of Jewish and Religions Movements.* Chapel Hill: University of North Carolina Press, 1982.

Shils, Edward. "Primordial, Personal, Sacred and Civil Ties." *BJSoc* 8 (1957) 130–45.

———. "Ideology." In *IESS* 7 (1968):66–76.

Shuler, Philip L. *A Genre for the Gospels: The Biographical Character of Matthew.* Philadelphia: Fortress, 1982.

Sievers, Joseph. "Where Two or Three . . . : the Rabbinic Concept of *Shekhinah* and Matthew 18:20." In *The Jewish Roots of Christian Liturgy*, edited by Eugene J. Fisher, 47–61. New York: Paulist, 1990.

Sim, David C. "Christianity and Ethnicity in the Gospel of Matthew." In *Ethnicity and the Bible*, edited by Mark G. Brett, 171–95. Biblical Interpretation Series 19. Leiden: Brill, 1996.

———. *The Gospel of Matthew and Christian Judaism: The History and Social Setting of the Matthean Community.* SNTW. Edinburgh: T. & T. Clark, 1998.

———. "The Gospels for All Christians? A Response to Richard Bauckham." *JSNT* 84 (2001) 3–27.

Simmel, Georg. "The Stranger." In *The Sociology of Georg Simmel*, 402–8. Translated by Kurt Wolff. New York: Free Press, 1950. No pages. Online: http://media .pfeiffer.edu/lridener/courses/STRANGER.HTML.
Simon, Marcel. *Jewish Sects in the Time of Jesus*. Philadelphia: Fortress, 1967.
Sjøberg, Gideon. *The Preindustrial City: Past and Present*. New York: Free Press, 1960.
———. "The Preindustrial City." *AJS* 60 (1955) 438–45; reprinted in *Urban Life: Readings in the Anthropology of the City*, edited by George Gmelch and Walter P. Zenner, 20–31. 3rd ed. Long Grove, IL: Waveland, 2001.
———, and A. Sjøberg. "The Preindustrial City: Reflections Four Decades Later." In *Urban Life: Readings in the Anthropology of the City*, edited by George Gmelch and Walter P. Zenner, 94–103. 3rd ed. Long Grove, IL: Waveland, 2001.
Skehan, Patrick W., and Alexander A. DiLella. *The Wisdom of Ben Sira*. AB 39. Garden City, NY: Doubleday, 1987.
Skinner, Quentin, editor. *The Return of Grand Theory in the Human Sciences: Althusser, the* Annales *Historians, Derrida, Foucault, Gadamer, Habermas, Kuhn, Lévi-Strauss, Rawls*. Cambridge: Cambridge University Press, 1985.
Slingerland, Dixon. "The Transjordanian Origin of St. Matthew's Gospel." *JSNT* 3 (1979) 18–28.
Smith, C. F. W. "The Mixed State of the Church in Matthew's Gospel." *JBL* 82 (1963) 149–68.
Smith, Dennis. *From Symposium to Eucharist: The Banquet in the Early Christian World*. Minneapolis: Fortress, 2003.
Smith, Jonathan Z. "A Pearl of Great Price and A Cargo of Yams: A Study in Situational Incongruity." *HR* 16 (1976) 1–19.
Smith, Jonathan Z. "The Social Description of Early Christianity." *RSR* 1 (1975) 19–25.
———. "Wisdom and Apocalyptic." In *Religious Syncretism in Antiquity: Essays in Conversation with Geo Widengren*, edited by Birger A. Pearson, 131–56. Missoula, MT: Scholars, 1975. Reprinted in Jonathan Z. Smith, *Map Is Not Territory: Studies in the History of Religions*, 67–87. Leiden: Brill, 1978; *Visionaries and Their Apocalypses*, edited by Paul D. Hanson, 101–20. IRT 4. London: SPCK, 1983.
Smith, Morton. *Tannaitic Parallels to the Gospels*. Journal of Biblical Literature Monograph Series 6. Philadelphia: Society of Biblical Literature, 1951.
Snyder, H. Gregory. *Teachers and Texts in the Ancient World: Philosophers, Jews and Christians*. Religion in the First Christian Centuries. London: Routledge, 2000.
Sobrino, Jon. *The True Church and the Poor*. Translated by Matthew J. O'Connell. 1984. Reprinted, Eugene, OR: Wipf & Stock, 2004.
———. *Jesus the Liberator: A Historical-Theological Reading of Jesus of Nazareth*. Translated by P. Burns and F. McDonagh. Maryknoll, NY: Orbis, 1993.
Soden, H. F. von "*Adelphos*, etc." In *TDNT* 1 (1964) 144–46.
Sollors, W. *Theories of Ethnicity: A Classical Reader*. Basingstoke, UK: Macmillan, 1996.
Sorokin, Pitirim K. "Foreword." In *Community and Society* (*Gemeinschaft und Gesellschaft*). Translated and edited Charles P. Loomis, ix–x. East Lansing: Michigan State University Press, 1957.
Stambaugh, John E. *The Ancient Roman City*. Baltimore: Johns Hopkins University Press, 1988.
Stambaugh, John E., and David L. Balch. *The New Testament in Its Social Environment*. LEC. Philadelphia: Westminster, 1986.
Stanton, Graham N. "5 Ezra and Matthean Christianity in the Second Century." *JTS* 28 (1977) 67–83.

———. "The Origin and Purpose of Matthew's Gospel: Matthean Scholarship from 1945 to 1980." In *ANRW* II.25.3, 1889–951. Berlin: de Gruyter, 1985.

———. *A Gospel for a New People: Studies in Matthew*. Louisville: Westminster John Knox, 1992.

———. "The Communities of Matthew." *Int* 6 (1992) 379–91.

———. "Matthew's Gospel and the Damascus document in Sociological Perspective." In *A Gospel for a New People: Studies in Matthew* by Graham N. Stanton, 85–110. Edinburgh: T. & T. Clark, 1992.

———. "Revisiting Matthew's Communities." In *SBL 1994 Seminar Papers*, edited by Eugene H. Lovering, Jr., 9–23. Atlanta: Scholars, 1994.

———. "Matthew's Christology and the Parting of the Ways." In *Jews and Christians: The Parting of the Ways, A.D. 70 to 135*, edited by James D. G. Dunn, 99–116. Grand Rapids: Eerdmans, 1999.

Stark, Rodney. "Networks of Faith: Interpersonal Bonds and Recruitment to Cults and Sects." *AJS* 85 (1980) 1376–95.

———. "The Class Basis of Early Christianity: Inferences from a Sociological Model." *SociolAn* 47 (1986) 216–25.

———. *A Theory of Religion*. Toronto Studies in Religion 2. New York: Lang, 1987.

———. "How New Religions Succeed: A Theoretical Model." In *The Future of New Religious Movements*, edited by David G. Bromley and P. Hammond, 11–29. Macon, GA: Mercer University Press, 1987.

———. "Antioch as the Social Situation for Matthew's Gospel." In *Social History of the Matthean Community: Cross-Disciplinary Approaches*, edited by David L. Balch, 189–210. Minneapolis: Fortress, 1991.

———. "Epidemics and the Rise of Christianity." *Semeia* 53 (1992) 159–75.

———. *The Rise of Christianity: A Sociologist Reconsiders History*. Princeton: Princeton University Press, 1996.

———, and William Sims Bainbridge. "Of Churches, Sects, and Cults: Preliminary Concepts for a Theory of Religious Movements." *JSSR* 18 (1979) 117–31.

Starr, Paul D. "Marginality, Role Conflict, and Status Inconsistency." *HumRelat* 30 (1977) 949–61.

———. "Status Inconsistency and Marginality in Malaysia." *SociolPers* 27 (1984) 53–83.

Steeman, Theodore M. "Church, Sect, Mysticism, Denomination: Periodical Aspects of Troeltsch' s Types." *SociolAn* 36 (1975) 181–204.

Stegemann, Wolfgang. *The Gospel and the Poor*. Translated by Dietlinde Elliott. Philadelphia: Fortress, 1984.

———. "Vagabond Radicalism in Early Christianity? A Historical and Theological Discussion of a Thesis Proposed by Gerd Theissen." In *God of the Lowly: Socio-Historical Interpretations of the Bible*, edited by Willy Schottroff and Wolfgang Stegemann, 148–68. Translated by Matthew J. O'Connell. Maryknoll, NY: Orbis Books, 1984.

———, and Ekkehard W. Stegemann. *The Jesus Movement: A Social History of Its First Century*. Translated by O. C. Dean. Minneapolis: Fortress, 1999. Original German 1995.

———, and Luise Schottroff. *God of the Lowly: Socio-Historical Interpretations of the Bible*. Translated by Matthew J. O'Connell. 1984. Reprint, Eugene, OR: Wipf & Stock, 2009.

Stendahl, Krister. *The School of St. Matthew and Its Use of the Old Testament.* Rev. ed. Philadelphia: Fortress, 1968.
Sterling, Gregory E. "The Bond of Humanity: Friendship in Philo of Alexandria." In *Greco-Roman Perspectives on Friendship,* edited by John T. Fitzgerald, 203-23. SBL Resources for Biblical Study 34. Atlanta: Scholars, 1997.
Still, Todd D. "Did Paul Loathe Manual Labor? Revisiting the Work of Ronald F. Hock on the Apostle's Tentmaking and Social Class." *JBL* 125 (2006) 781-95.
Stonequist, Everett V. *The Marginal Man.* New York: Scribner, 1937.
Strecker, Georg. *Der Weg der Gerechtigkeit: Untersuchung zur Theologie des Matthäusevangelium.* FRLANT 82. Göttingen: Vandenhoeck & Ruprecht, 1966.
Suggs, M. Jack. *Wisdom, Christology, and Law in Matthew's Gospel.* Cambridge: Harvard University Press, 1970.
Suhl, Alfred. "Der Davidssohn im Matthäus-Evangelium." *ZNW* 59 (1968) 67-81.
Suny, Ronald Grigor. "The Empire Strikes Out: Russia, the Soviet Union, and Theories of Empire." An academic paper discussed at the conference "Empires and Nations: The Soviet Union and the Non-Russian Peoples." University of Chicago, October 24-26, 1997.
Swatos, William H. "Weber or Troeltsch? Methodology, Syndrome, and the Development of Church-Sect Theory." *JSSR* 15 (1976) 129-44.
Syreeni, Kari. "Between Heaven and Earth: On the Structure of Matthew's Symbolic Universe." *JSNT* 40 (1990) 3-13.
Taagepera, Rein. "Size and Duration of Empires: Growth-Decline Curves, 600 B.C. to 600 A.D." *SSH* 3 (1979) 115-38.
Tagawa, K. "People and Community in Matthew." *NTS* 16 (1969-1970) 144-61.
Talmon, Yonina. "Pursuit of the Millennium: The Relation between Religious and Social Change." *AES* 3 (1962) 125-48. Reprinted in Barry McLaughlin, editor, *Studies in Social Movements: A Social Psychological Perspective,* 400-427. London: Free Press, 1971.
———. "Millenarian Movements." *AES* 7 (1966) 159-200.
———. "Millenarism." In *IESS* 10 (1968):349-62.
Taylor, George E. "Karl A. Wittfogel." In *IESS* 18 (1968):812.
Tcherikover, Victor. *Hellenistic Civilization and the Jews.* Translated by S. Applebaum. New York: Atheneum, 1970.
Theissen, Gerd. *Sociology of Early Palestinian Christianity.* Translated by John Bowden. Philadelphia: Fortress, 1978.
———. "Social Stratification in the Corinthian Community." In *The Social Setting of Pauline Christianity: Essays on Corinth,* 69-119. Translated by John H. Schütz. 1982. Reprint, Eugene, OR: Wipf & Stock, 2004.
———. *The Miracle Stories of the Early Christian Tradition.* Translated by Francis McDonagh. Philadelphia: Fortress, 1983.
———. "Zur Forschungsgeschichtlichen Einordnung zur soziogischen Fragestellung." In *Studien zur Soziologie des Urchristentums,* 3-34. WUNT 19.2. 2nd ed. Tübingen: Mohr/Siebeck, 1988.
———. *The Gospels in Context: Social and Political History in the Synoptic Tradition.* Translated by Linda M. Maloney. Minneapolis: Fortress, 1991.
———. "The Social Structure of Pauline Communities: Some Critical Remarks on J. J. Meggitt, *Paul, Poverty and Survival.*" *JSNT* 24 (2001) 65-84.

———. "Social Conflicts in the Corinthian Community: Further Remarks on J. J. Meggitt, *Paul, Poverty and Survival*." *JSNT* 25 (2003) 371–91.

Theissen, Gerd, and Annette Merz. *The Historical Jesus: A Comprehensive Guide*. Translated by John Bowden. Minneapolis: Fortress, 1998. German original, 1996.

Theissen, Gerd, and Dagmar Winter. *The Quest for the Plausible Jesus: The Question of Criteria*. Translated by M. Eugene Boring. Louisville: Westminster John Knox, 2002.

Thompson, E. P. *The Poverty of Theory and Other Essays*. New York: Monthly Review Press, 1978.

Thompson, Henry O. "Dura-Europos." In *ABD* 2 (1992) 241–43.

Thompson, Leonard L. *The Book of Revelation: Apocalypse and Empire*. New York: Oxford University Press, 1990.

Thompson, William G. *Matthew's Advice to a Divided Community: Mt. 17,22–18,35*. Analecta Biblica 44. Rome: Biblical Institute Press, 1970.

Tidball, Derek J. *An Introduction to the Sociology of the New Testament*. Exeter: Paternoster, 1983.

———. "On Wooing a Crocodile: An Historical Survey of the Relationship between Sociology and New Testament Studies." *VoxEv* 15 (1985) 95–110.

Tilborg, Sjef van. *The Jewish Leaders in Matthew*. Leiden: Brill, 1972.

Tilly, Charles. "Three Versions of History and Theory." *HistTh* 46 (2007) 299–307.

Tiryakian, Edward A. "Émile Durkheim." In *Émile Durkheim: Critical Assessments*, edited by Peter Hamilton, 88–138. London: Routledge, 1994.

Tobin, Thomas H. "The Legacy of William G. Thompson, S.J." In *The Gospel of Matthew in Current Study*, edited by David E. Aune, 1–4. Grand Rapids: Eerdmans, 2001.

Tocqueville, Alexis de. *Democracy in America*. Translated by Arthur Mansfield and Delba Winthrop. Library of America. Chicago: University of Chicago Press, 2000.

Tönnies, Ferdinand. "Community and Society." In *Gemeinschaft und Gesellschaft*, translated and edited by Charles P. Loomis, 237–70. East Lansing: Michigan State University Press, 1957.

Townsend, John T. "Matthew XXIII.9." *JTS* 12 (1961) 56–59.

———. "Ancient Education in the Time of the Early Roman Empire." In *The Catacombs and the Colosseum*, edited by Stephen Benko and John J. O'Rourke, 139–63. Valley Forge, PA: Judson, 1971.

———. "Education (Greco-Roman)." In *ABD* 2 (1992) 312–17.

Toynbee, Polly. "The Last Emperor." *GU* (September 13, 2002).

Trilling, Wolfgang. *Das Wahre Israel*. STANT 10. 3rd ed. Munich: Kösel, 1964.

Troeltsch, Ernst. *The Social Teaching of the Christian Churches*. Translated by Olive Wyon. 2 vols. 1931. Reprinted, Louisville: Westminster John Knox, 1992.

Trompf, Gary W., editor. *Cargo Cults and Millenarian Movements: Transoceanic Comparisons of New Religious Movements*. Berlin: Mouton de Gruyter, 1990.

Tuckman, Bruce W. "Developmental Sequence in Small Groups." *PsyBull* 63 (1965) 384–99.

———, and M. A. C. Jansen. "Stages of Small-Group Development Revisited." *GOS* 2 (1977) 419–27.

Turner, Frederick Jackson. *The Frontier in American History*. New York: Henry Holt and Co., 1920. No pages. Online: http://xroads.virginia.edu/~HYPER/TURNER/.

Turner, Jonathan. *The Structure of Sociological Theory*. 6th ed. Chicago: Dorsey, 1997.

———. *Societal Stratification: A Theoretical Analysis*. New York: Columbia University Press, 1984.
Turner, Victor. *The Ritual Process: Structure and Anti-Structure*. Chicago: Aldine, 1969.
———. *Dramas, Fields, and Metaphors: Symbolic Action in Human Society*. Ithaca, NY: Cornell University Press, 1974.
Urbach, E. E. *The Sages: Their Concepts and Beliefs*. Translated by I. Abrahams. Jerusalem: Magnes, 1979.
Van Aarde, Andries G. *Fatherless in Galilee: Jesus as Child of Gods*. Valley Forge, PA: Trinity, 2001.
Van den Berghe, P. L. *The Ethnic Phenomenon*. New York: Praeger, 1987.
Van Staden, Piet. *Compassion—The Essence of Life: A Social-Scientific Study of the Religious Symbolic Universe Reflected in the Ideology/Theology of Luke*. HTSSup 4. Pretoria: Faculty of Theology, 1991.
VanderKam, James C. *The Dead Sea Scrolls Today*. Grand Rapids: Eerdmans, 1994.
Varshney, A. *Ethnic Conflict and Rational Choice: A Theoretical Engagement*. Cambridge: Harvard University Press, 1995.
Veeser, H. Aram, editor. *The New Historicism*. London: Routledge, 1989.
Verhoogt, Arthur M. F. W. *Menches, Komogrammateus of Kerkeosiris: The Doings and Dealings of a Village Scribe in the Late Ptolemaic Period (120–110 B.C.)*. Papyrologica Lugduno-Batava 29. Leiden: Brill, 1998.
Vermes, Geza. *The Dead Sea Scrolls in English*. 3rd ed. London: Penguin, 1988.
Verner, David C. *The Household of God: The Social World of the Pastoral Epistles*. SBLDS 71. Chico, CA: Scholars, 1983.
Viviano, Benedict. "Social World and Community Leadership: The Case of Matthew 23:1–12, 34." *JSNT* 39 (1990) 145–83.
Viviano, Pauline A. "Methodology, Chronology, Scribes, and Inspiration." *BR* 25 (1990) 51–57.
Vledder, Evert-Jan. *Conflict in the Miracle Stories: A Socio-exegetical Study of Matthew 8 and 9*. JSNT 152. Sheffield, UK: Sheffield Academic, 1997.
Vliet, H. Van. *No Single Testimony: A Study on the Adoption of the Law of Deut. 19:15 Par. into the New Testament*. Utrecht: Veen, 1958.
Waetjen, Herman C. *A Reordering of Power: A Socio-Political Reading of Mark's Gospel*. Minneapolis: Fortress, 1989.
Wainwright, Elaine M. *Towards a Feminist Critical Reading of the Gospel according to Matthew*. BZNW 60. Berlin: de Gruyter, 1991.
———. *Shall We Look for Another? A Feminist Rereading of the Matthean Jesus*. Maryknoll, NY: Orbis, 1998.
———. "Only to the Lost Sheep or To All the Nations: Social Location Constructing Elites and Marginals in the Matthean Gospel." Lecture at Matthew Seminar, Society of Biblical Literature Boston, 1999.
———. "The Mary Magdalene Tradition and the Matthean Communities." In *The Mary Magdalene Tradition: Witness and Counter-Witness in Early Christian Communities*, edited by Holly E. Hearon, 121–44. Collegeville, MN: Liturgical, 2004.
Walker, Rolf. *Die Heilsgeschichte im ersten Evangelium*. Göttingen: Vandenhoeck & Ruprecht, 1967.
Walker-Ramisch, Sandra. "Graeco-Roman Voluntary Associations and the Damascus Document: A Sociological Analysis." In *Voluntary Associations in the Graeco-Roman World*, edited by John S. Kloppenborg and Stephen G. Wilson, 128–45. London: Routledge, 1996.

Wallace, A. F. C. *The Death and Rebirth of the Seneca*. New York: Random House, 1969.
———. "Revitalization Movements." *AA* 59 (1956) 264–81.
Wallace-Hadrill, Andrew, editor. *Patronage in Ancient Society*. Leicester-Nottingham Studies in Ancient History 1. Philadelphia: Fortress, 1990.
Wallerstein, Immanuel. "World-Systems Analysis." In *Social Theory Today*, edited by Anthony Giddens and Jonathan Turner, 309–24. Stanford, CA: Stanford University Press, 1987.
Wallis, Lewis. *The Sociological Study of the Bible*. Chicago: University of Chicago Press, 1912. Online: http://www.questia.com/PM.qst?a=o&d=2015187.
Waltzing, J.-P. *Étude historique sur les corporations professionelles chez les Romains* I. 4 vols. Louvain: Peeters, 1895–1900.
Warner, W. Lloyd, and Paul S. Lunt. "Ethnicity (1942)." A passage from *The Status* (1942). In *Theories of Ethnicity: A Classical Reader*, edited by W. Sollors, 13–14. Basingstoke, UK: Macmillan, 1996.
Watt, Jonathan M. *Code-Switching in Luke and Acts*. Berkeley Insights in Linguistics and Semiotics 31. New York: Lang, 1997.
Weber, Max. "Über einige Kategorien der verstehende Soziologie." In *Gesammelte Aufsätze zur Wissenschaftslehre* by Max Weber, 427–74. Tübingen: Mohr/Siebeck.
———. *The Methodology of the Social Sciences*. Translated by Edward A. Shils and Richard A. Finch. Glencoe, IL: Free Press, 1949.
———. *Economy and Society*. Edited by Guenther Roth and Claus Wittich. Translated by Ephraim Fischoff, et al. From the 4th German edition, 1956. Berkeley: University of California Press, 1968.
———. *Das Antike Judaismus. Archiv für Sozialwissenschaft und Sozialforschung*. Published as Volume 3 of *Gasammelte Aufsätze zur Religions-soziologie*. Translated by Hans H. Gerth and Don Martindale. New York: Free Press, 1967.
———. *The Protestant Ethic and the Spirit of Capitalism*. Translated by Talcott Parsons and Anthony Giddens. New York: Scribner, 1958. Original German 1904–1905.
———. *Roman Agrarian History: In Its Relation to Roman Public and Civil Law*. Translated by Richard L. Frank. Claremont, CA: Regina, 2008.
Weinfeld, Moshe. *The Organization Pattern and the Penal Code of the Qumran Sect*. NTOA 2. Göttingen: Vandenhoeck & Ruprecht, 1986.
Weisberger, Adam. "Marginality and Its Directions." *SociolForum* 7 (1992) 425–47.
Weiss, Johannes. *Der Erste Korintherbrief*. Göttingen: Vandenhoeck & Ruprect, 1910.
Wheelwright, Philip. *The Burning Fountain: A Study in the Language of Symbolism*. Bloomington: Indiana University Press, 1954.
White, Leland J. "Group and Grid in Matthew's Community: The Righteousness Honor/Shame Code in the Sermon on the Mount." *Semeia* 35 (1986) 61–90.
White, L. Michael. "Sociological Analysis of Early Christian Groups: A Social Historian's Response." *SA* 47/3 (1986) 249–66.
———. "Scaling the Strongman's 'Court' (Luke 11: 21)." *Forum* 3/3 (1987) 3–28.
———. "Shifting Sectarian Boundaries in Early Christianity." *BJRL* 70/3 (1988) 7–24.
———. "Crisis Management and Boundary Maintenance: The Social Location of the Matthean Community." In *Social History of the Matthean Community: Cross-Disciplinary Approaches*, edited by David L. Balch, 211–47. Minneapolis: Fortress, 1991.

Wilken, Robert. "Collegia, Philosophical Schools, and Theology." In *The Catacombs and the Coliseum*, edited Stephen Benko and John J. O'Rourke, 268-91. Valley Forge, PA: Judson, 1971.
Wilkins, Michael J. "Brother, Brotherhood." In *ABD* 1 (1992) 782-83.
Wilson, Bryan. "An analysis of Sect Development." In *Patterns of Sectarianism: Organisation and Ideology in Social and Religious Movements*, 22-45. London: Heinemann, 1967.

———. *Magic and the Millennium: A Sociological Study of Religious Movements of Protest among Tribal and Third-World Peoples*. London: Heinemann, 1973.
Wilson, Stephen G. *Related Strangers: Jews and Christians 70-170 C.E.* Minneapolis: Fortress, 1995.

———. "Voluntary Associations: An Overview." In *Voluntary Associations in the Graeco-Roman World*, edited by John S. Kloppenborg and Stephen G. Wilson, 1-15. London: Routledge, 1996.
Winter, Bruce. "The Messiah as the Tutor: The Meaning of *kathēgētēs* in Matthew 23:10." *TynBul* 42 (1991) 152-57.
Wire, Anne. "Gender Roles in a Scribal Community." In *Social History of the Matthean Community. Cross Disciplinary Approaches*, edited by David L. Balch, 87-121. Minneapolis: Fortress, 1991.
Wittfogel, Karl. *Oriental Despotism: A Comparative Study of Total Power*. New Haven: Yale University Press, 1957.
Wolf, Eric. *Peasants*. Englewood Cliffs, NJ: Prentice-Hall, 1966.
Wolfson, Harry Austryn. *Philo*. 2 vols. Cambridge: Harvard University Press, 1984.
Wong, Yoke-Sum, and Derek Savor, editors. *Twenty Years of the Journal of Historical Sociology*: Volume 2: *Challenging the Field*. Oxford: Wiley-Blackwell, 2008.
Woolf, Greg. "Inventing Empire in Ancient Rome." In *Empires: Perspectives from Archaeology and History*, edited by S. E. Alcock, T. N. D. Altroy, K. D. Morrison, and C. M. Sinopoli, 311-22. Cambridge: Cambridge University Press, 2001.
Wuellner, Wilhelm W. "The Sociological Implications of 1 Corinthians 1:26-28 Reconsidered." *SE* 4, edited by E. W. Livingston. Berlin: Akademie, 1973.
Yaghjian, Lucretia B. "Was Matthew's Scribe a Social Science Critic? From Parables to Protocols of Reading and Writing Culture in Matthew 13." Society of Biblical Literature Annual Meeting, San Francisco, CA, November, 1992.

———. "Ancient Reading," In *The Social Sciences and New Testament Interpretation*, edited by Richard L. Rohrbaugh, 206-20. Peabody, MA: Hendrickson, 1996.
Yang, P. Q. *Ethnic Studies: Issues and Approaches*. Albany: State University of New York Press, 2000.
Yang, Y.-E. *Jesus and the Sabbath in Matthew's Gospel*. JSNTSup 139. Sheffield, UK: Sheffield Academic, 1997.
Yinger, J. Milton. *Religion, Society, and the Individual*. New York: Macmillan, 1957.
Zangwell, Israel. *The Melting Pot: A Drama in Four Acts*. New York: Macmillan, 1909. Rev. ed., 1939.
Ziebarth, Erich. *Das griechische Vereinswesen*. Wiesbaden: Sändig, 1896. Reprinted 1969.

www.ingramcontent.com/pod-product-compliance
Lightning Source LLC
Chambersburg PA
CBHW051204300426
44116CB00006B/430